"Darrell Bock has gathered together the fruits of his lifetime labors on Luke's works in a comprehensive account of his theology that combines lucidity and simplicity with much scholarly detail on controversial issues. This is a remarkable achievement that should become the first port of call for students in this central area of New Testament theology."

—*I. Howard Marshall, Professor Emeritus of New Testament, University of Aberdeen*

"Lukan theology has often been neglected today, with scholars sometimes simply recycling the inadequacies of older works like Conzelmann's. Bock's excellent exploration of Luke's theological approach and themes meets an important need in Lukan theology. A different scholar might want to give more attention to this or that theme, but Bock's approach to Luke's themes is consistently balanced and repeatedly shaped by Luke's own emphases."

—*Craig Keener, Professor of New Testament, Asbury Theological Seminary*

"With over thirty years invested in the topic, Darrell Bock *knows* Luke–Acts. He knows the literature, the issues, and what is really important. Unlike more abstract approaches, Darrell focuses on a detailed treatment of the biblical text, the narrative of Luke–Acts. He allows the major themes of Luke–Acts to control his approach, and he explains convincingly how these themes are developed and what their significance is. The result is an informative and practical guide for the church and anyone who cares about these major two New Testament books. This is a 'must have' for pastors, students, and church libraries."

—*Klyne Snodgrass, Paul W. Brandel Professor of New Testament Studies, North Park Seminary*

"No one in the evangelical world is better qualified than Darrell Bock to write a biblical theology of Luke and Acts. Having written major commentaries on both volumes and a monograph on Luke's Old Testament Christology, Bock brings to the task a wealth of knowledge and insight into Luke's theology and narrative purpose. Students of God's Word will find no better introduction to the major themes of the Lukan corpus. Highly recommended."

—*Mark L. Strauss, Professor of New Testament, Bethel Seminary, San Diego*

"This is an indispensable, comprehensive, yet readable work on the biblical world and thought behind Luke's writings. It provides a critical resource for scholars, pastors, and Bible study teachers who want to understand the theological threads woven together by Luke into the tapestry of Luke–Acts. I highly recommend it to all serious Bible students. Bock provides us all with the rich, underlying theological depth of Luke's masterworks, and I have not seen such thorough and yet clear coverage on this extremely important topic."

— *Grant Osborne, Professor of New Testament,*
Trinity Evangelical Divinity School

"This comprehensive and competent—indeed commanding—treatment of the theology of Luke's two-volume work provides readers with a concise yet detailed survey of essentially all areas of theology: the work and character of God, the work and person of Jesus Christ, the work of the Holy Spirit, salvation, Israel, Jews and Gentiles, the church, ethics, opposition and persecution, social questions, the law, the Old Testament Scriptures, and eschatology. Darrell Bock's focus on the text rather than on scholarly debates ensures that readers learn what Luke wanted his readers to comprehend: the fulfillment of God's promises in and through Jesus, Israel's Messiah and the Savior of the world."

— *Eckhard Schnabel, professor and author of* Acts *(ZECNT)*

"After several decades of reflection on the gospel of Luke and the Acts of the Apostles— reflection evidenced in his doctoral studies, numerous articles, several monographs, and no less than four stand-alone commentaries—one of the world's foremost Lukan scholars offers us here his matured scholarship on the theology of this ancient Christian corpus that comprises one fourth of the New Testament. Academics cannot fancy themselves Lukan scholars without knowing this author's name, and no one working in Lukan theology will attempt to do so without interacting with his work. Fifty years ago this could be said of Hans Conzelmann; for the next few decades of Luke–Acts studies this will be said of Darrell Bock."

— *Douglas S. Huffman, Professor and Chair of Biblical and Theological Studies,*
Talbot School of Theology, Biola University

"After a flurry of interest in the theology of Luke in the 1970s and 1980s, it has been quite a while since a detailed, reasonably comprehensive work on the major themes in Lukan thought in both his Gospel and Acts has appeared. Here, finally, is one that is up-to-date, thorough, evangelical, and, as an added bonus, largely based on the narrative sequence of Luke's material in his two volumes. Bock adds to his repertoire as the premier recent commentator on Luke and Acts separately. This book is a worthy successor to Andreas Köstenberger's inaugural volume on John in Zondervan's emerging Biblical Theology of the New Testament series."

— *Craig L. Blomberg, Distinguished Professor of New Testament, Denver Seminary*

GOD'S PROMISED PROGRAM,
REALIZED FOR ALL NATIONS

A THEOLOGY OF LUKE AND ACTS

BIBLICAL THEOLOGY OF THE NEW TESTAMENT

DARRELL L. BOCK

ANDREAS J. KÖSTENBERGER
GENERAL EDITOR

 ZONDERVAN®

ZONDERVAN

A Theology of Luke and Acts
Copyright © 2012 by Darrell L. Bock

Requests for information should be addressed to:
Zondervan, 3900 *Sparks Dr. SE, Grand Rapids, Michigan 49546*

Library of Congress Cataloging-in-Publication Data

Bock, Darrell L.
    A theology of Luke and Acts : biblical theology of the New Testament / Darrell L. Bock ; Andreas J. Köstenberger, general editor.
      p. cm.
    Includes bibliographical references and index.
    ISBN 978-0-310-27089-8 (hardcover)
    1. Bible. N.T. Luke—Theology. 2. Bible. N.T. Luke—Criticism, interpretation, etc. 3. Bible. N.T. Acts—Theology. 4. Bible. N.T. Acts—Criticism, interpretation, etc. I. Köstenberger, Andreas J., 1957- II. Title.
    BS2589.B63 2011
    226.4'06—dc23
    2011030526

Cover design: Rob Monacelli
Cover photography: The Supper at Emmaus, 1601, Caravaggio, Michelangelo Merisi da (1571-1610), National Gallery, London, UK / Planet Art
Interior design: Matthew Van Zomeren

Printed in the United States of America

18 19 20 21 22 23 24 25 26 27 28 /DCI/ 26 25 24 23 22 21 20 19 18 17 16 15 14 13 12 11 10 9 8 7 6

To Martin Hengel:

*Mentor and example on how to wed
scholarship and a love for the Lord*

CONTENTS

Contents (Detailed) 10
Series Preface 19
Author's Preface 21
Abbreviations 23

PART ONE
Introductory Matters 25

CHAPTER 1
The Often Lost Importance of Luke-Acts and the Orientation of this Study 27

CHAPTER 2
The Context of Luke-Acts: A Short Introduction 31

CHAPTER 3
**The Case for the Unity of Luke-Acts and Reading the Volumes
    as Luke-Acts and as Luke and Acts** 55

CHAPTER 4
Outline and Narrative Survey of Luke-Acts 63

PART TWO
Major Theological Themes 97

CHAPTER 5
The Plan, Activity, and Character of God: A Survey in Narrative Order 99

CHAPTER 6
The God of Promise, Fulfillment, and Salvation: Synthesis of Texts on the Plan of God . . 121

CHAPTER 7
Jesus the Messiah Who Is Lord and Bringer of the New Era: Narrative Order 149

CHAPTER 8
**Messiah, Servant, Prophet, Savior, Son of Man, and Lord:
    A Synthesis on the Person and Work of Jesus** 177

CHAPTER 9
**The Holy Spirit in Luke-Acts: Power and Enablement for the Promise
    and Witness of the New Era** 211

CHAPTER 10
The Salvation of God through Christ and the Healings That Picture It: Narrative Order . 227

CHAPTER 11
The Many Dimensions of Salvation in Luke-Acts: A Synthesis 239

CHAPTER 12
Israel in Luke-Acts 279

CHAPTER 13
The Gentiles and the Expression "the Nations" in Luke-Acts .291

CHAPTER 14
The Church and the Way in Luke-Acts 303

CHAPTER 15
Discipleship and Ethics in the New Community 311

CHAPTER 16
**How Response to Jesus Divides: The Opponents, the Crowds,
      and Rome as Observer of Events in Luke-Acts** 333

CHAPTER 17
Women, the Poor, and the Social Dimensions in Luke-Acts 343

CHAPTER 18
The Law in Luke-Acts 359

CHAPTER 19
Ecclesiology in Luke-Acts 371

CHAPTER 20
Eschatology, Judgment, and Hope for the Future in Luke-Acts. 389

CHAPTER 21
The Scriptures in Luke-Acts 407

PART THREE
Luke and the Canon 429

CHAPTER 22
Luke-Acts in the Canon. 431

CHAPTER 23
Conclusion. 447

Bibliography. 453
Scripture Index. 469
Subject Index 489
Author Index 493

CONTENTS (DETAILED)

Series Preface 19
Author's Preface 21
Abbreviations 23

PART ONE
Introductory Matters 25

CHAPTER 1
The Often Lost Importance of Luke-Acts and the Orientation of this Study 27

CHAPTER 2
The Context of Luke-Acts: A Short Introduction. 31
2.1 . . . . Authorship and Date of Acts. 32
2.1.1 . . . . Authorship of Acts 32
2.1.2 . . . . Date and Setting of Acts. 38
2.2 . . . . Provenance 41
2.3 . . . . Significance of Dating and Authorship for the Theology of Luke-Acts 42
2.4 . . . . Issues of Genre in Luke and Acts 43
2.4.1 . . . . On Luke as a Historian and His Use of Sources .43
2.4.2 . . . . The Genre of Luke's Gospel 44
2.4.3 . . . . The Genre of Acts. 46
2.4.4 . . . . On Philosophy of History and Acts 48
2.4.5 . . . . The Speeches in Acts 51
2.5 . . . . Conclusion 53

CHAPTER 3
The Case for the Unity of Luke-Acts and Reading the Volumes
   as Luke-Acts and as Luke and Acts 55
3.1 . . . . Is Luke-Acts a Unified Work? 55
3.2 . . . . Assessing Objections to Unity in Luke-Acts 57
3.3 . . . . On Reading Luke-Acts as a Unity. 60
3.4 . . . . The Choice of Categories for Our Study. 61

CHAPTER 4
Outline and Narrative Survey of Luke-Acts 63
4.1 . . . . An Outline of Luke 64
4.2 . . . . An Outline of Acts 65
4.3 . . . . A Narrative Overview of Luke-Acts. 66
4.3.1 . . . . I. Luke's Preface and the Introduction of John and Jesus
            (Luke 1:1 – 2:52) 67
4.3.1.1 . . . . A. Preface: Luke Carefully Builds on Precedent (Luke 1:1 – 4) 67
4.3.1.2 . . . . B. Infancy Narrative: Forerunner and Fulfillment (Luke 1:5 – 2:40) . . .67

4.3.1.3 . . . . C. Jesus' Revelation of His Self-Understanding (Luke 2:41–52) 68

4.3.2 . . . . II. Preparation for Ministry: Anointed by God (Luke 3:1–4:13) 68

4.3.2.1 . . . . A. John the Baptist: One Who Goes Before (Luke 3:1–20) 68

4.3.2.2 . . . . B. Jesus: One Who Comes After (Luke 3:21–4:13) 69

4.3.3 . . . . . . III. Galilean Ministry: Revelation of Jesus (Luke 4:14–9:50) 69

4.3.3.1 . . . . A. Overview of Jesus' Ministry (Luke 4:14–44) 69

4.3.3.2 . . . . B. Gathering of Disciples and Controversies (Luke 5:1–6:16) 70

4.3.3.3 . . . . C. Jesus' Teaching (Luke 6:17–49) 70

4.3.3.4 . . . . D. First Movements to Faith and Christological Questions
　　　　　　　　　(Luke 7:1–8:3) 70

4.3.3.5 . . . . E. Call to Faith, Christological Revelation, and Questions
　　　　　　　　　(Luke 8:4–9:17) 71

4.3.3.6 . . . . .F. Christological Confession and Instruction about Discipleship
　　　　　　　　　(Luke 9:18–50) 71

4.3.4 . . . . IV. Jerusalem Journey: Jewish Rejection and the New Way
　　　　　　　　　(Luke 9:51–19:44) 72

4.3.4.1 . . . . A. Blessing of Decision: Privilege, Mission, and Commitment
　　　　　　　　　(Luke 9:51–10:24) 72

4.3.4.2 . . . . B. Discipleship: Looking to One's Neighbor, Jesus, and God
　　　　　　　　　(Luke 10:25–11:13) 73

4.3.4.3 . . . . C. Controversies, Corrections, and Calls to Trust (Luke 11:14–54) . . .73

4.3.4.4 . . . . D. Discipleship: Trusting God (Luke 12:1–48) 73

4.3.4.5 . . . . E. Knowing the Nature of the Time: Israel Turns Away,
　　　　　　　　　but Blessing Still Comes (Luke 12:49–14:24) 74

4.3.4.6 . . . . .F. Discipleship in the Face of Rejection: Basic Elements
　　　　　　　　　(Luke 14:25–35) 74

4.3.4.7 . . . . G. Pursuit of Sinners: Heaven's Examples (Luke 15:1–32) 74

4.3.4.8 . . . . H. Generosity: Handling Money and Possessions (Luke 16:1–31) 75

4.3.4.9 . . . . .I. False Teaching, Forgiveness, and Service (Luke 17:1–10) 75

4.3.4.10 . . . . .J. Faithfulness in Looking for the King, the Kingdom,
　　　　　　　　　and the Kingdom's Consummation (Luke 17:11–18:8) 75

4.3.4.11 . . . . K. Humbly Entrusting All to the Father (Luke 18:9–30) 76

4.3.4.12 . . . . L. Turning to Jerusalem: Messianic Power, Personal Transformation,
　　　　　　　　　Warning of Responsibility, and Entry with Mourning
　　　　　　　　　(Luke 18:31–19:44) 76

4.3.5 . . . . V. Jerusalem: The Innocent One Slain and Raised
　　　　　　　　　(Luke 19:45–24:53) 76

4.3.5.1 . . . . A. Controversy in Jerusalem (Luke 19:45–21:4) 77

4.3.5.2 . . . . B. Jerusalem's Destruction and the End (Luke 21:5–38) 77

4.3.5.3 . . . . C. Betrayal and Farewell (Luke 22:1–38) 78

4.3.5.4 . . . . D. The Arrest, Trials, and Death of Jesus (Luke 22:39–23:56) 78

4.3.5.5 . . . . E. The Resurrection and Ascension of Jesus (Luke 24:1–53) 79

4.3.6 . . . . .I. Introduction: Jesus Ascends to the Father and Gives a Mission
　　　　　　　　　(Acts 1:1–11) 79

4.3.6.1 . . . . A. Review of Book 1 to the Ascension (Acts 1:1–5) 80

4.3.6.2 . . . . B. The Ascension and Final Testament: A Promise for the
　　　　　　　　　Disciples Now and a Promise to Return (Acts 1:6–11) 80

4.3.7 . . . . II. The Early Church in Jerusalem (Acts 1:12–6:7) 80
4.3.7.1 . . . . A. Community Life: Replacing Judas by Depending on God and
          Reconstituting the Twelve (Acts 1:12–26) 80
4.3.7.2 . . . . B. Pentecost: Christ Gives the Spirit of the New Era
          (Acts 2:1–41) 80
4.3.7.3 . . . . C. Summary: Community Life (Acts 2:42–47) 81
4.3.7.4 . . . . D. The Healing of the Lame Man and the Arrest of Peter and
          John (Acts 3:1–4:31) 81
4.3.7.5 . . . . E. Community Life and Problems (Acts 4:32–5:11) 82
4.3.7.6 . . . . F. Summary: Signs and Wonders (Acts 5:12–16) 82
4.3.7.7 . . . . G. More Persecution for Peter and John (Acts 5:17–42) 82
4.3.7.8 . . . . H. Community Life: The Appointment of the Seven to Help
          Hellenistic Widows (Acts 6:1–6) 83
4.3.7.9 . . . . I. Summary of the Jerusalem Community (Acts 6:7) 83
4.3.8 . . . . III. Persecution in Jerusalem Moves the Message to Judea and
          Samaria as a New Witness Emerges (Acts 6:8–9:31) 83
4.3.8.1 . . . . A. The Arrest, Speech, and Martyrdom of Stephen (Acts 6:8–8:1a) . . . 83
4.3.8.2 . . . . B. Saul the Persecutor and the Spread of the Word (Acts 8:1b–4) 84
4.3.8.3 . . . . C. Philip in Samaria and with a Eunuch from Ethiopia (Acts 8:5–40) . . 84
4.3.8.4 . . . . D. The Conversion and Early Reception of Saul (Acts 9:1–30) 84
4.3.8.5 . . . . E. Closing Summary (Acts 9:31) 85
4.3.9 . . . . IV. The Gospel to the Gentiles and More Persecution in Jerusalem
          (Acts 9:32–12:25) 85
4.3.9.1 . . . . A. Peter Performs Two Miracles at Lydda and Joppa
          (Acts 9:32–43) 85
4.3.9.2 . . . . B. Peter and Cornelius: The Gospel to the Gentiles
          (Acts 10:1–11:18) 85
4.3.9.3 . . . . C. The Church at Antioch: Barnabas, Saul, and Agabus
          (Acts 11:19–30) 86
4.3.9.4 . . . . D. Persecution in Jerusalem (Acts 12:1–23) 86
4.3.9.5 . . . . E. Summary (Acts 12:24–25) 87
4.3.10 . . . . V. The Mission from Antioch and the Full Incorporation of
          Gentiles (Acts 13:1–15:35) 87
4.3.10.1 . . . . A. The First Missionary Journey (Acts 13:1–14:28) 87
4.3.10.2 . . . . B. Consultation at Jerusalem (Acts 15:1–35) 88
4.3.11 . . . . . . VI. The Second and Third Missionary Journeys
          (Acts 15:36–21:16) 88
4.3.11.1 . . . . A. The Second Missionary Journey (Acts 15:36–18:23) 89
4.3.11.2 . . . . B. The Third Missionary Journey, Ending in Jerusalem
          (Acts 18:24–21:16) 90
4.3.12 . . . . . VII. The Arrest: The Message Is Defended and Reaches Rome
          (Acts 21:17–28:31) 91
4.3.12.1 . . . . A. In Jerusalem (Acts 21:17–23:35) 91
4.3.12.2 . . . . B. In Caesarea (Acts 24:1–26:32) 92
4.3.12.3 . . . . C. The Long Sea Journey to Rome (Acts 27:1–28:16) 93
4.3.12.4 . . . . D. Visitors in Rome: The Gospel Preached (Acts 28:17–31) 94
4.4 . . . . Conclusion 95

PART TWO
Major Theological Themes 97

CHAPTER 5

The Plan, Activity, and Character of God: A Survey in Narrative Order 99

5.1 . . . . The Infancy Material on God 100
5.2 . . . . God in Luke's Portrayal of the Ministry of John the Baptist 103
5.3 . . . . God in the Ministry of Jesus 104
5.4 . . . . God in Acts 108
5.5 . . . . Conclusion 119

CHAPTER 6

The God of Promise, Fulfillment, and Salvation: Synthesis of Texts on the Plan of God . . 121

6.1 . . . . God's Plan of Salvation: The God of Design and Concern 122
6.2 . . . . God's Direction of the Plan 127
6.3 . . . . Promise and Fulfillment in General 129
6.4 . . . . Hebrew Scripture Fulfillment in Particular 130
6.5 . . . . Themes Revealing the Plan's Outworking 134
6.5.1 . . . . . . "Today" Passages 135
6.5.2 . . . . . . John the Baptist 135
6.5.3 . . . . . . Jesus' Mission 136
6.5.4 . . . . . . Geographical Progression 137
6.5.5 . . . . . . "It Is Necessary" 140
6.5.6 . . . . . . The Kingdom 141
6.5.7 . . . . . . The Holy Spirit 143
6.5.8 . . . . . . The New Community's Ethic 145
6.5.9 . . . . . . God and Christ's Direct Intervention 147
6.6 . . . . Conclusion 148

CHAPTER 7

Jesus the Messiah Who Is Lord and Bringer of the New Era: Narrative Order 149

7.1 . . . . The Overture of the Infancy Narrative: Introducing the Sent One Who Is
                  Messiah-Lord 150
7.2 . . . . The Body of Luke's Gospel: Actions of Authority and Arrival of a New Era . . 159
7.3 . . . . The Portrait in Acts: The Lord Messiah in Kerygma and Action 169
7.4 . . . . Conclusion 175

CHAPTER 8

**Messiah, Servant, Prophet, Savior, Son of Man, and Lord: A Synthesis on the
Person and Work of Jesus** 177

8.1 . . . . The Person of Jesus Christ: From Messiah-Servant-Prophet to Lord 177
8.2 . . . . The Titles of Jesus in Luke-Acts 185
8.2.1 . . . . . . Savior 185
8.2.2 . . . . . . Christ 185
8.2.3 . . . . . . Son of David 187
8.2.4 . . . . . . Son of God and King 188

8.2.5 . . . . Prophet. 189
8.2.6 . . . . Son of Man. 193
8.2.7 . . . . Lord 197
8.2.8 . . . . Servant 198
8.2.9 . . . . Less Frequently Used Titles. 199
8.3 . . . . The Work of Jesus: Paving the Way for Salvation and the New Era. 201
8.3.1 . . . . Earthly Ministry 201
8.3.2 . . . . The Cross. 203
8.3.3 . . . . Resurrection-Ascension. 204
8.3.4 . . . . The Two-Stage Kingdom Reign of Jesus .205
8.4 . . . . Conclusion. 209

CHAPTER 9
The Holy Spirit in Luke-Acts: Power and Enablement for the Promise and
Witness of the New Era 211
9.1 . . . . The Spirit in Luke's Infancy Material 212
9.2 . . . . The Spirit in the Body of Luke's Gospel 213
9.3 . . . . The Spirit in the Book of Acts 219
9.4 . . . . Spirit and Power 225
9.5 . . . . Conclusion 225

CHAPTER 10
The Salvation of God through Christ and the Healings That Picture It: Narrative Order . . 227
10.1 . . . . Salvation in the Infancy Material 228
10.2 . . . . Salvation in the Body of Luke's Gospel 229
10.3 . . . . Salvation in the Book of Acts 233
10.4 . . . . Conclusion. 237

CHAPTER 11
The Many Dimensions of Salvation in Luke-Acts: A Synthesis 239
11.1 . . . . The Act of Proclaiming Good News 239
11.1.1 . . . . . . The Gospel. 239
11.1.2 . . . . . . Preaching 243
11.1.3 . . . . . . Teaching. 244
11.2 . . . . The Scope of Salvation 245
11.2.1 . . . . . . The Promise for Jews and Gentiles 245
11.2.2 . . . . . . To the Poor, Sinners, and Outcasts 247
11.3 . . . . The Authentication of the Message. 248
11.3.1 . . . . . . Three Levels of Authentication 248
11.3.2 . . . . . . The Miracles of Jesus and His Disciples .250
11.3.3 . . . . . . The Work of Salvation: The Cross and Jesus' Resurrection-Ascension. . . .253
11.4 . . . . The Objective Aspect of Salvation 256
11.4.1 . . . . . . Words for Salvation 256
11.4.2 . . . . . . Mercy and Judgment 262
11.5 . . . . The Subjective Side of Salvation 262
11.5.1 . . . . . . Repentance. 262
11.5.2 . . . . . . Turning. 265

11.5.3 . . . . . Faith 267
11.6 . . . . . . The Benefits of Salvation 268
11.6.1 . . . . . The Forgiveness of Sins 268
11.6.2 . . . . . Life 269
11.6.3 . . . . . Gift 271
11.6.4 . . . . . Peace 271
11.6.5 . . . . . Grace 271
11.6.6 . . . . . Justify 272
11.7 . . . . . . Other Points of Soteriology 273
11.7.1 . . . . . The Message of Salvation and Promise 273
11.7.2 . . . . . The Law 274
11.8 . . . . . . Conclusion 276

CHAPTER 12
Israel in Luke-Acts 279
12.1 . . . . . . Israel in the Infancy Material 280
12.2 . . . . . . Israel in the Body of Luke's Gospel 282
12.3 . . . . . . Israel in the Book of Acts 285
12.4 . . . . . . Conclusion 289

CHAPTER 13
The Gentiles and the Expression "the Nations" in Luke-Acts 291
13.1 . . . . . . Gentiles and Nations in the Gospel of Luke 292
13.2 . . . . . . Gentiles and Nations in the Book of Acts 297
13.3 . . . . . . Conclusion 300

CHAPTER 14
The Church and the Way in Luke-Acts 303
14.1 . . . . . . The Theme of the Way in the Gospel of Luke 304
14.2 . . . . . . The Church, the Way, and Christians in the Book of Acts 306
14.3 . . . . . . Conclusion 310

CHAPTER 15
Discipleship and Ethics in the New Community 311
15.1 . . . . . . The New Community and Its Activity as Followers of Jesus 312
15.1.1 . . . . . The New Community's Activities 312
15.1.2 . . . . . Functions in the New Community 313
15.1.3 . . . . . Descriptions of Community Members 315
15.2 . . . . . . Disciples in Luke-Acts 315
15.3 . . . . . . The Ethics of the New Community 323
15.3.1 . . . . . Total Commitment 323
15.3.2 . . . . . Love for God and for One's Neighbor 324
15.3.3 . . . . . Prayer 325
15.3.4 . . . . . Perseverance in Suffering 326
15.3.5 . . . . . Watchfulness, Patience, and Boldness 326
15.3.6 . . . . . Faith and Dependence 327
15.3.7 . . . . . Joy and Praise 328

15.3.8 . . . . . . Testimony and Witness. 328
15.3.9 . . . . . . Wealth and Possessions 328
15.3.10 . . . . . Hindrances to Discipleship. 330
15.3.11 . . . . . Commitment to the Lost 330
15.4 . . . . Luke and Empire 331
15.5 . . . . Conclusion. 332

CHAPTER 16

How Response to Jesus Divides: The Opponents, the Crowds, and Rome as Observer of Events in Luke-Acts

How Response to Jesus Divides: The Opponents, the Crowds, and Rome as Observer of
    Events in Luke-Acts 333
16.1 . . . . Official Jewish Reaction to Jesus. 334
16.1.1 . . . . . . Jewish Groups in Luke and Acts 334
16.1.2 . . . . . . Conclusion on Jewish Groups. 336
16.2 . . . . Crowds and the Multitudes. 336
16.2.1 . . . . . . Crowds and Multitudes in the Gospel of Luke 336
16.2.2 . . . . . . Crowds in the Book of Acts 339
16.3 . . . . The Role of Rome as Observer of Events in Acts 340
16.4 . . . . Conclusion. 342

CHAPTER 17

Women, the Poor, and the Social Dimensions in Luke-Acts

Women, the Poor, and the Social Dimensions in Luke-Acts 343
17.1 . . . . Women in the Gospel of Luke 344
17.1.1 . . . . . . Women in the Infancy Narrative. 344
17.1.2 . . . . . . Key Women in Jesus' Galilean Ministry 346
17.1.3 . . . . . . Women in the Journey to Jerusalem Section 347
17.1.4 . . . . . . Women in the Passion Week. 348
17.2 . . . . Women in the Book of Acts 349
17.2.1 . . . . . . Women in Acts 1 – 12. 350
17.2.2 . . . . . . Women in Acts 13 – 28 351
17.3 . . . . The Poor in Luke-Acts 352
17.4 . . . . Other Groupings: The Lame and the Blind 357
17.5 . . . . Conclusion: The Social Dimension in Luke-Acts 358

CHAPTER 18

The Law in Luke-Acts

The Law in Luke-Acts 359
18.1 . . . . The Law in the Gospel of Luke. 360
18.2 . . . . The Law in the Book of Acts 365
18.3 . . . . Conclusion. 369

CHAPTER 19

Ecclesiology in Luke-Acts

Ecclesiology in Luke-Acts 371
19.1 . . . . The Church: Old and New. 371
19.2 . . . . The Church Becomes Distinct 372
19.3 . . . . A New Thing: The Church as a Spirit-Indwelt Community 373
19.4 . . . . The Church and Jesus' Rule 374
19.5 . . . . The Apostles and the Church 376

19.6 . . . . . . Israel and the Church 377
19.7 . . . . . . Key Personalities in the Early Church 381
19.7.1 . . . . . Peter 381
19.7.2 . . . . . Stephen 382
19.7.3 . . . . . Philip 383
19.7.4 . . . . . Barnabas 383
19.7.5 . . . . . James 384
19.7.6 . . . . . Paul 384
19.8 . . . . . . Structure, Activity, and Worship in the Church 387
19.9 . . . . . . Conclusion 388

CHAPTER 20
Eschatology, Judgment, and Hope for the Future in Luke-Acts 389
20.1 . . . . The Basic Structure of Luke's Eschatology: The Kingdom Comes in
Fulfillment 389
20.1.1 . . . . . . A Two-Part Structure to the Era of Fulfillment: Already-Not Yet 389
20.1.2 . . . . . . The Timing of the Consummation 394
20.2 . . . . Eschatology and Accountability: Motivation to Faithfulness 395
20.3 . . . . The Messianic Visit and the Battle with Satan 398
20.4 . . . . The Tension between Imminence and Delay 399
20.5 . . . . The Fall of Jerusalem and the End: Typology of the End 400
20.6 . . . . . . Hope 403
20.7 . . . . . . Personal Eschatology 404
20.8 . . . . . . Conclusion 404

CHAPTER 21
The Scriptures in Luke-Acts 407
21.1 . . . . Hermeneutical Axioms Defined 409
21.2 . . . . Axiom 1: God's Design and a New Era of Realization 409
21.3 . . . . Axiom 2: Christ at the Center 411
21.4 . . . . Axiom 3: Scripture as an Interpreter of Divine Event and Current Critical
Discussion: A Defense of Promise-Fulfillment in Luke-Acts 412
21.5 . . . . Five Central Scriptural Themes in Luke-Acts Named 414
21.5.1 . . . . . . Covenant and Promise 414
21.5.2 . . . . . . Christology 417
21.5.3 . . . . . . Community Mission, Community Guidance, and Ethical Direction 420
21.5.4 . . . . . . Commission to the Gentiles 422
21.5.5 . . . . . . Challenge with Warning to Israel 423
21.6 . . . . Conclusion 426

PART THREE
Luke and the Canon 429

CHAPTER 22
Luke-Acts in the Canon 431
22.1 . . . . The Reception of Luke and Acts into the Canon 432

22.2 . . . . Luke's Contribution to the Canon 433
22.2.1 . . . . . . Contributions Tied to God, Jesus, and the Spirit 433
22.2.2 . . . . . . Contributions Tied to the Activity of the Church 437
22.3 . . . . Luke's Parallels with Other Parts of the New Testament 439
22.3.1 . . . . . . Parallels with the Synoptics 439
22.3.2 . . . . . . Parallels with John's Gospel 440
22.3.3 . . . . . . Parallels with Paul 441
22.3.4 . . . . . . Parallels with Key Catholic Epistles 443
22.3.5 . . . . . . Parallels with Revelation, 2 Peter, and Jude 443
22.4 . . . . One Final Issue: How Normative Is Luke-Acts? 444
22.5 . . . . Conclusion 445

CHAPTER 23

Conclusion 447

23.1 . . . . Six Key Theses about Luke's Theology 448
23.1.1 . . . . . . Divine Direction, Salvation-History, Continuity of Promise, and Mission . . 448
23.1.2 . . . . . . Israel's Story Includes the Nations and Is Not Anti-Semitic 448
23.1.3 . . . . . . The Spirit as the Sign of the New Era 449
23.1.4 . . . . . . Salvation and Identity Tied to Jesus' Work 449
23.1.5 . . . . . . A New Era and Structure in a Trinitarian Story 450
23.1.6 . . . . . . Realized Promise in Prophecy and Pattern 450
23.2 . . . . Conclusion: The Mighty God Who Saves and Reconciles 450

Bibliography 453
Scripture Index 469
Subject Index 489
Author Index 493

Series Preface

The Biblical Theology of the New Testament series consists of eight distinct volumes covering the entire New Testament. Each volume is devoted to an in-depth exploration of a given New Testament writing, or group of writings, within the context of the theology of the New Testament, and ultimately of the entire Bible. While each corpus requires an approach that is suitable for the writing(s) studied, all volumes include:

(1) a survey of recent scholarship and of the state of research
(2) a treatment of the relevant introductory issues
(3) a thematic commentary following the narrative flow of the document(s)
(4) a treatment of important individual themes
(5) discussions of the relationship between a particular writing and the rest of the New Testament and the Bible

While Biblical Theology is a relatively new academic discipline and one that has often been hindered by questionable presuppositions, doubtful methodology, and/or flawed execution, the field is one of the most promising avenues of biblical and theological research today. In essence, Biblical Theology engages in the study of the biblical texts while giving careful consideration to the historical setting in which a given piece of writing originated. It seeks to locate and relate the contributions of the respective biblical documents along the lines of the continuum of God's salvation-historical program centered in the coming and salvific work of Christ. It also endeavors to ground the theological exploration of a given document in a close reading of the respective text(s), whether narrative, discourse, or some other type of literature.

By providing in-depth studies of the diverse, yet complementary perspectives of the New Testament writings, the Biblical Theology of the New Testament series aims to make a significant contribution to the study of the major interrelated themes of Scripture in a holistic, context-sensitive, and spiritually nurturing manner. Each volume is written by a scholar who has written a major commentary or monograph on the corpus covered. The generous page allotment allows for an in-depth investigation. While coming from diverse academic backgrounds and institutional affiliations, the contributors share a commitment to an evangelical faith and a respect for the authority of Scripture. They also have in common a conviction that the canon of Scripture is ultimately unified, not contradictory.

In addition to contributing to the study of individual New Testament writings and to the study of the New Testament and ultimately of Scripture as a whole, the series also seeks to make a methodological contribution, showing how Biblical Theology ought to be conducted. In each case, the way in which the volume is conceived reflects careful consideration of the nature of a given piece or body of writings.

The complex interrelationships between the three so-called "Synoptic Gospels"; the two-volume nature of Luke-Acts; the relationship between John's gospel, letters, and the book of Revelation; the thirteen letters making up the Pauline corpus; and the theologies of Peter, James, and Jude, as well as Hebrews, each present unique challenges and opportunities.

In the end, it is hoped that the volumes will pay tribute to the multifaceted nature of divine revelation contained in Scripture. As G. B. Caird put it:

> The question we must ask is not whether these books all say the same thing, but whether they all bear witness to the same Jesus and through him to the many splendoured wisdom of the one God. . . . We shall neither attempt to press all our witnesses into a single mould nor captiously complain that one seems at some points deficient in comparison with another. What we shall do is rejoice that God has seen fit to establish His gospel at the mouth of so many independent witnesses. The music of the New Testament choir is not written to be sung in unison.[1]

In this spirit, the contributors offer their work as a humble aid to a greater appreciation of the magnificent scriptural symphony of God.

Andreas J. Köstenberger, series editor
Wake Forest, NC

---

1. G. B. Caird, *New Testament Theology*, compl. and ed. L. D. Hurst (Oxford: Clarendon, 1995), 24.

AUTHOR'S PREFACE

The kind invitation from Andreas Köstenberger to write a biblical theology on Luke-Acts allows me to close the loop on two volumes I have enjoyed studying for over thirty years. He was kind to trust this task to me, and I appreciate his work and vote of confidence as well as his solid advice along the way. He has done his job well.

My doctoral dissertation at the University of Aberdeen studies the use of the Old Testament for Christology in Luke-Acts. I also have written commentaries at various levels for Luke and a commentary on Acts. In a way every decade has brought a fresh Luke-Acts effort. I never have grown tired of going over the richness of these two volumes and finding new things that reflect the depth of their teaching. This effort was no exception. It has allowed me to put together in one place many things I have said before in many distinct volumes. My hope is that this study will benefit others and give them a glimpse of why I see these volumes as so important for the theology of the church.

The work reflected here has had the benefit of many conversations in many contexts as well as during years of teaching these books in many classes at both Dallas Theological Seminary and Talbot Theological Seminary. Students and their questions often lead into rich learning for the professor. That has been the case for me. There is no way to dedicate a volume to such a corporate mass of people. So I simply express my thanks to my students over thirty years of teaching. You have made teaching a joy and the learning experience that education is supposed to be.

My thanks also go to the administration of Dallas Theological Seminary for granting a sabbatical that allowed me to complete this work. Also my appreciation goes to the Humboldt Stiftung of Germany, which also supported a part of the time that was devoted to this work. To my host, the University of Tübingen in Germany, and to my faculty host, Hermann Lichtenberger, goes a note of gratitude for making a year's stay in Tübingen possible and enriching. To the fine team at Zondervan, my thanks for making more sense out of what I have tried to say.

My dedication of this volume goes to someone who influenced me greatly and made possible that Tübingen would become a second home for Sally and me, as we have spent a total four sabbaticals here. Martin Hengel passed away a few years ago, but his voice and encouragement still live with me as an example of a mentor who said pursuing and articulating the truth of the Christian faith is a great calling. I recall many conversations with him about theology and the state of the church. They were graciously held in his home that overlooks the Neckar River. His desire that one not step back from careful study and challenging ideas that are often in vogue in certain academic contexts has remained with me. So I dedicate this study to him.

My wife, Sally, also deserves thanks for being willing to leave the safety of a home culture and to experience life in another context and language so I could cloister up and write. Her love and patience are a gift from God.

Darrell L. Bock
Tübingen, Deutschland
May 16, 2011

ABBREVIATIONS

Abbreviations for books of the Bible, pseudepigrapha, rabbinic works, papyri, classical works, and the like are readily available in sources such as the *SBL Manual of Style* and are not included here.

AB	Anchor Bible
ABD	*Anchor Bible Dictionary*
ABRL	Anchor Bible Reference Library
AnBib	Analecta biblica
ANTC	Abingdon New Testament Commentaries
BAGD	W. Bauer, W. F. Arndt, F. W. Gingrich (2nd ed.; and F. W. Danker), *Greek-English Lexicon of the New Testament*
BBR	*Bulletin of Biblical Research*
BDF	F. Blass, A. Debrunner, and R. W. Funk, *A Greek Grammar of the New Testament*
BDAG	W. Bauer, F. W. Danker (ed., 3rd ed.), *Greek-English Lexicon of the New Testament*
BECNT	Baker Exegetical Commentary on the New Testament
BETL	Bibliotheca ephemeridum theologicarum lovaniensium
Bib	*Biblica*
BibSac	*Bibliotheca sacra*
BR	*Biblical Research*
BZNW	Beiheft zur Zeitschrift für die neutestamentliche Wissenschaft
CBQ	*Catholic Biblical Quarterly*
CurTM	*Currents in Theology and Mission*
Eccl. Hist.	*Ecclesiastical History*
EDNT	H. Balz and G. Schneider (eds.), *Exegetical Dictionary of the New Testament*
EKKNT	Evangelisch-katholischer Kommentar zum Neuen Testament
GNS	Good News Studies
HCSB	Holman Christian Standard Bible
HTKNT	Herders theologischer Kommentar zum Neuen Testament
HTR	*Harvard Theological Review*
ICC	International Critical Commentary
IVPNTC	IVP New Testament Commentary
JETS	*Journal of the Evangelical Theological Society*
JPTSup	Journal for Pentecostal Theology Supplement
JSNT	*Journal for the Study of the New Testament*
JSNTSup	Journal for the Study of the New Testament Supplement
JSOTSup	Journal for the Study of the Old Testament Supplement

KJV	King James Version
LXX	Septuagint
NAC	New American Commentary
NCBC	New Century Bible Commentary
NEB	New English Bible
NET	New English Translation
NICNT	New International Commentary on the New Testament
NIGTC	New International Greek Testament Commentary
NIV	New International Version
NLT	New Living Translation
NovTSup	Novum Testamentum Supplement
NRSV	New Revised Standard Version
NTD	Das Neue Testament Deutsch
NTL	New Testament Library
NTS	*New Testament Studies*
REB	Rheims English Bible
RB	*Revue biblique*
RevExp	*Review and Expositor*
RSV	Revised Standard Version
SacPag	Sacra Pagina
SBLDS	SBL Dissertation Series
SBLMS	SBL Monograph Series
SBT	Studies in Biblical Theology
SNTSMS	Society for New Testament Studies Monograph Series
SNTSU	Studien zum Neuen Testament und seiner Umwelt
Str-B	H. Strack and P. Billerbeck, *Kommentar zum Neuen Testament aus Talmud und Midrasch*
SwJT	*Southwestern Journal of Theology*
TDNT	G. Kittel and G. Friedrich (eds.), *Theological Dictionary of the New Testament*
TEV	Today's English Version
THKNT	Theologischer Handkommentar zum Neuen Testament
TNTC	Tyndale New Testament Commentaries
TUGAL	Texte und Untersuchungen zur Geschichte der altchristlichen Literatur
TynBul	*Tyndale Bulletin*
WBC	Word Biblical Commentary
WMANT	Wissenschaftliche Monographien zum Alten und Neuen Testament
WUNT	Wissenschaftliche Untersuchungen zum Neuen Testament
WW	*Word & World*

Part One

INTRODUCTORY MATTERS

Chapter 1

The Often Lost Importance of Luke-Acts and the Orientation of This Study

BIBLIOGRAPHY

Barrett, C. K. *Luke the Historian in Recent Study.* London: Epworth, 1961.
Bovon, F. *Luke the Theologian.* 2nd ed. Waco TX: Baylor University Press, 2006.
Idem. "Studies in Luke-Acts: Retrospect and Prospect." *HTR* 85 (1992): 175–96.
Fitzmyer, J. A. *Luke the Theologian: Aspects of His Teaching.* New York: Paulist,
1989. **Gasque, W.** *A History of the Criticism of the Acts of the Apostles.* Tübingen:
Mohr/Siebeck, 1975. **Gregory, A. F.** *The Reception of Luke and Acts in the Period
before Irenaeus: Looking for Luke in the Second Century.* WUNT. Tübingen: Mohr/
Siebeck, 2003. **Hengel, Martin.** *Acts and the History of Earliest Christianity.* Lon-
don: SCM, 1979. **Johnson, L. T.** "Luke-Acts, Book of." *ABD,* 4:404–20. **Kurz,
W. S.** *Reading Luke-Acts: Dynamics of Biblical Narrative.* Louisville: Westminster
John Knox, 1993. **Marshall, I. Howard.** *Luke: Historian and Theologian.* 3rd ed.
Exeter: Paternoster, 1993. **Mills, W. E., and A. J. Mattill.** *A Bibliography of the
Periodical Literature on the Acts of the Apostles (1962–1984).* Leiden: Brill, 1986.
Rowe, C. Kavin. "History, Hermeneutics and the Unity of Luke-Acts." *JSNT* 28
(2005): 131–57. Idem. "Literary Unity and Reception History: Reading Luke-Acts
as Luke and Acts." *JSNT* 29 (2007): 449–57. **Talbert, C. H.** "Shifting Sands: The
Recent Study of the Gospel of Luke." Pp. 197–213 in *Interpreting the Gospels.* Ed.
J. L. Mays. Philadelphia: Fortress, 1981.

The biblical material from Luke-Acts is probably the largest and most neglected portion of the NT. Of the 7,947 verses in the NT, Luke-Acts comprises 2,157 verses, or 27.1 percent. By comparison, the Pauline letters have 2,032 verses and the Johannine writings have 1,407.[1] In addition, only Luke-Acts tells the story of Jesus Christ from his birth through the beginning of the church into the ministry of Paul. This linkage is important, for it gives perspective to the sequence of these

---

1. Kurt and Barbara Aland, *The Text of the New Testament* (trans. Erroll R. Rhoads; Grand Rapids: Eerdmans, 1987), 29. Although a rough way to make a comparison, the next longest gospel, Matthew, occupies 87 pages in the Nestle-Aland text, while Mark takes up 60 and John 73 pages. Luke comprises 96 pages. Acts is 88 pages long. That makes for a total of 184 pages for the Lucan material. Paul's letters comprise 153 pages of text.

events. Many Christians consider Matthew and Acts together, because canonically Matthew is the first gospel and Acts includes the history of the apostolic church. But the canonical link is Luke-Acts, not Matthew-Acts, since Luke authored both volumes. So thinking biblically, it is important to keep Luke and Acts together and tell the story of Acts with an eye on Luke.

So what causes the neglect of these two volumes, especially as a unit?

First, the gospel gets absorbed in discussions about Jesus and the other gospels. Luke has always had third place among the Synoptics. In the early church, Matthew was seen as the lead gospel, having apostolic roots and being seen as the first gospel to be written. In the last two centuries, Mark has taken this central role. Now seen as most likely the first gospel to be written, this gospel now becomes a key point of focus in the study of Jesus. Its outline is the lens through which discussion of Jesus, especially the historical Jesus, is often conducted. John has always had a prime position as the "spiritual" gospel, a description that goes back to Clement of Alexandria in the second century.[2] So Luke got lost in the shuffle.

Second, Acts got separated from Luke as the canon distinguished between gospels and the history of the early church. This severed the two volumes, and people read the works as separate pieces. This has caused readers to lose the links between the two volumes and the theological story that both volumes together tell. The gospel of Luke was related to the other gospels, while Acts was left to itself on a genre island telling the story of the early church. The continuity between Jesus and the launching of the early community was lost in the shuffle.

Our goal in this look at Luke-Acts is to reconnect the volumes to each other and to tell Luke's theological story in which one cannot see Jesus without understanding the story of the community that he was responsible for launching. The key actor in this theology is God himself. It is his plan that Jesus carries out. It is his promise, long revealed and now actualized, that Jesus brings. The link that exists between God and Jesus, the one sent to bring the promise, is at the hub of the theology. Luke portrays the plan of God as worked out in fulfillment of the divine promise. The inauguration of this fulfillment came through Jesus and through the church, which consists of both Jew and Gentile. The completion of this fulfillment will come when Jesus returns (Acts 3:18–26). These books stress the continuity of God's promise, and they present this progress in a pastoral way that instructs and comforts.

Beyond this, the Spirit that Jesus himself brings is also a key part of the story, especially in the activity of the preaching and mission of the new community. So there is the outline of trinitarian activity in the two works. The enablement of the Spirit as the gift of the new era's presence is also a central theme. We will try to trace this story and its theology keeping an eye on the narrative rather than extracting themes ripped out from their context.

---

2. As reported by Eusebius, *Eccl. Hist.* 6.14.7, who attributes this to Clement of Alexandria (AD 150–211) in his work *Hypotyposes.* Eusebius says this about Clement and John's gospel, "But, last of all, John, perceiving that the external facts had been made plain in the Gospel, being urged by his friends, and inspired by the Spirit, composed a spiritual Gospel. This is the account of Clement."

Luke wrote to Theophilus to give him assurance about the things he had been taught (Luke 1:4).[3] A major supposition of that assurance is the recognition that God was at work in the recent events, events that were in fulfillment of God's promises (vv. 1–2). Two aspects of that claimed fulfillment, however, would be troubling: a dead Savior and a persecuted community of God that included Gentiles, when Israel held the hope of the promise. Since the church was undergoing persecution, as Acts so vividly portrays, Theophilus, or anyone like him, might have wondered if that persecution was God's judgment on the church for being too racially broad with his salvation. Was God really at work in the church, and was Jesus really at the center of the plan? How did the promise become so broad and how could a dead Savior bring it to pass? These are core questions of community identity that Luke-Acts explains.

Luke-Acts assured Theophilus that persecution of the church was not a sign of judgment. Instead, the persecution had been predicted and was a means by which the message could go out to even more people across the world. The work details how Jesus is at the center of God's plan, a plan that anticipated not only his death, but also more significantly his resurrection-ascension[4] to God's right hand, where he offers the benefits of salvation as Lord to any who come to him. Paul as the apostle to the Gentiles pictured the outworking of the broad mission of the promise. His role, like that of others in the church, was not undertaken on his own initiative, but was the direct result of the work of God. Thus God and his activity are at the center of Luke-Acts.

So we introduce Luke-Acts by discussing some key introductory issues and the question of its unity to start. Then we will proceed to present the theology in steps, looking at the major topics Luke treats. Often we will first survey the theme in narrative order and then synthesize the results in a separate chapter. Occasionally within the overview or the synthesis, we stop and take a closer look at specific verses and the exegetical issues tied to the theme at that point.

The overarching purpose of Luke covers important ground. Luke-Acts seeks to show that the coming of Jesus, Christ, and Son of God launched the long-promised new movement of God. The community that has come from his ministry, the suffering these believers experienced, and the inclusion of Gentiles are part of God's program promised in Scripture. In the ancient world, unlike the modern, it is not that which is new that is seen as valuable but that which is old. Thus Luke explains that this seemingly new movement is actually rooted in old promises and in a design that God promised and now has executed through Jesus, the sent promised one of God. The community tied to him suffers, not out of judgment but by design, for before exaltation there is suffering.

---

3. Darrell L. Bock, *Luke 1:1–9:50* (BECNT 3a; Grand Rapids: Baker, 1994), 15–16, discusses this theme in terms of the purpose of Luke's gospel.

4. The expression "resurrection-ascension" reflects the fact that

Luke regards these events as fundamentally one event, even though they were separate. Acts 2:20–36 shows how closely Luke linked these two events.

The controversial inclusion of Gentiles was not the rebellious act of renegade theologians but the product of direct intervention by God. The ministry of Paul, as the example of this mission and outreach to all, is not a failure but has taken the word about Jesus to the hub of the world, to Rome, as Paul faithfully follows the call of God even in the midst of persecution. This is how the community is to function in a world that often rejects the message of Jesus and persecutes those who believe it. The power of God's word and message is best displayed when those who are rejected faithfully and ethically live in a manner that reflects Christ's own rejection and faithfulness.

Power is best seen in dependent strength. Such strength measures effectiveness, not by the world's standards of the use of power, but by faithful dependence on carrying out the call and mission of God with the character God seeks to form in his people. This ability and strength comes from the Spirit whom Jesus provides as a result of God's vindication of Jesus in his resurrection. So Luke-Acts tells the story of God working through Jesus in the provision of new era of promise and Spirit-enablement so that the people of God can be the people of God in the midst of a hostile world. It is a message that still fits the church today. It is why Luke-Acts occupies such a large portion of the NT and why the church cannot neglect its message.

Chapter 2

THE CONTEXT OF LUKE-ACTS: A SHORT INTRODUCTION

BIBLIOGRAPHY

For this listing I highlight the key commentaries that also have introductory discussions. **Barrett, C. K.** *A Critical and Exegetical Commentary on the Acts of the Apostles I: Preliminary Introduction and Commentary on Acts I–XIV.* ICC. Edinburgh: T&T Clark, 1994. Idem. *A Critical and Exegetical Commentary on the Acts of the Apostles II: Introduction and Commentary on Acts XV–XXVIII.* ICC. Edinburgh: T&T Clark, 1998. **Bock, Darrell L.** *Acts.* BECNT 5. Grand Rapids: Baker, 2007. Idem. *Luke 1:1–9:50.* BECNT 3a. Grand Rapids: Baker, 1994. Idem. *Luke 9:51–24:53.* BECNT 3b. Grand Rapids: Baker, 1996. **Bruce, F. F.** *The Acts of the Apostles: Greek Text with Introduction and Commentary.* 3rd ed. Grand Rapids: Eerdmans, 1990. **Cadbury, H. J.** *The Making of Luke-Acts.* New York: Macmillan, 1927. **Fitzmyer, J. A.** *The Acts of the Apostles.* Anchor Bible. Garden City: Doubleday, 1998. Idem. *The Gospel of Luke I–IX: Introduction, Translation and Notes.* Anchor Bible. Garden City: Doubleday, 1982. **Green, Joel.** *The Gospel of Luke.* NICNT. Grand Rapids: Eerdmans, 1997. **Haenchen, E.** *Acts of the Apostles: A Commentary.* London: Blackwell, 1987. **Hemer, C.** *The Book of Acts in the Setting of Hellenistic History.* WUNT. Tübingen: Mohr-Siebeck, 1989. **Hengel, Martin.** *Acts and the History of Earliest Christianity.* London: SCM, 1979. **Jervell, J.** *Die Apostelgeschichte.* Göttingen: Vandenhoeck & Ruprecht, 1998. **Johnson, Luke Timothy.** *The Gospel of Luke.* SacPag. Collegeville, MN: Liturgical, 1991. Idem. *The Acts of the Apostles.* SacPag. Collegeville, MN: Liturgical, 1992. **Marguerat, D.** *The First Christian Historian: Writing the "Acts of the Apostles."* SNTSMS. Cambridge: Cambridge University Press, 2002. **Marshall, I. H.** *The Acts of the Apostles: An Introduction and Commentary.* TNTC. Grand Rapids: Eerdmans, 1980. Idem. *The Gospel of Luke.* NIGTC. Grand Rapids: Eerdmans, 1978. **Nolland, John.** *Luke 1:1–24:53.* WBC. 3 vols. Dallas: Word, 1989–1993. **Polhill, John.** *Acts.* NAC. Nashville: Broadman, 1992. **Witherington, Ben.** *The Acts of the Apostles: A Socio-Rhetorical Commentary.* Grand Rapids: Eerdmans, 1997.

I have already presented extensive introductions to Luke-Acts elsewhere.[1] The goal here is to present the key information that locates Luke-Acts historically, so that one can appreciate the context of the theology of the two volumes.

---

1. Bock, *Luke 1:1–9:50*, 1–44, as well as in my commentary on *Acts* (BECNT 5; Grand Rapids: Baker, 2007), 1–46. I am assuming the unity of authorship of the two volumes for this chapter. The issue of the unity of these two volumes will be the topic of the next

2.1 AUTHORSHIP AND DATE OF LUKE-ACTS[2]

Four issues are key in making a judgment about the authorship and date of Luke-Acts: (1) what one makes of the consistent early church testimony from the first four centuries that Luke is the author; (2) the nature of the "we" sections in Acts; (3) the relationship of Luke to the other gospels in terms of sequence; and (4) how one takes the ending of Acts, specifically whether it is a key to the date of Acts or represents an open literary ending that cannot help us date the book. Internal features only give hints about the answers to these questions.

The internal features concentrate on two points. First, the author was not an eyewitness to most of the events in his two volumes, especially those tied to the ministry of Jesus (Luke 1:1–2). Rather, he has relied on his study of traditions, which came from "eyewitnesses and servants of the word" (Luke 1:2–4). Second, the author apparently presents himself as a companion of Paul in those parts of Acts known as the "we" sections (Acts 16:10–17; 20:5–15; 21:1–18; 27:1–28:16). This feature, though debated with respect to its historical reliability and its role in pointing to authorship, could limit options concerning the author's identity. If the "we" sections represent a consistent self-reference, then other scenes that name companions of Paul eliminate options for the author. The best way to consider these potential candidates is to look at the external evidence about the companions of Paul and the authorship of Luke-Acts, our first key issue.

2.1.1 Authorship of Acts

Despite the wide selection of potential candidates available as companions of Paul, the tradition of the church gives attention to only one name as the author of these volumes — Luke. This tradition was firmly fixed in the early church by AD 200 and remained so without any hint of contrary opinion. The earliest manuscript of Luke's gospel that we have is the Bodmer papyri XIV from about c. AD 200, which has a title pointing to Luke as author at its conclusion. This text is more widely known as $\mathfrak{p}^{75}$. A title calling the second volume the Acts of the Apostles appears at the end of the transcribing of the book in $\mathfrak{p}^{74}$, but no author is named there. Luke is named as the author of Acts in later manuscripts of 33 (9th cent.), 189 (14th cent.), 1891 (10th cent.) and 2344 (11th cent.). The absence of any dispute about the claim of authorship across several early centuries is a strong reason to take the tradition seriously. Allusions to the gospel may appear as early as *1 Clement* 13.2 (a summary of parts of the Sermon on the Plain of Luke 6); 48.4 (perhaps the Christian gate alludes to

---

chapter. In sum, the case can be outlined as follows. Internal evidence involves first of all seeing the two volumes as one account in two parts with Acts being tied to Luke (H. J. Cadbury, *The Making of Luke-Acts* [New York: Macmillan, 1927]). Though a few critics challenge this idea (Mikeal Parsons and Richard Pervo, *Rethinking the Unity of Luke-Acts* [Minneapolis: Fortress, 1993]), the interlocking of the books with the ascension in Luke 24 and Acts 1, as well

as the prologues, points to a single work by a single author. Some stylistic variation exists between the books, but this is in part due to shifts in subject matter from being focused on an individual in Luke to discussing the mission of a community in Acts and the distinct origins of the traditions the author has used. Parallels between Jesus, Peter, and Paul also point to a unity of design.

2. I discuss the reception of Luke into the canon in chapter 22.

the image of the narrow gate in Luke 13; ca. AD 95–96); *2 Clement* 13.4 (love your enemies according to the Lucan Sermon on the Plain; ca. AD 100). In addition, a use of Jesus' teaching, as reflected in Luke 10:7, appears in 1 Timothy 5:18.

Numerous texts comment on authorship. Justin Martyr (ca. 160) in *Dial.* 103.19 speaks of Luke writing an "apostolic memoir" of Jesus, by alluding to language only in Luke and tying it to this expression. This association is vague and lacks specificity, but this changes with later references. The Muratorian Canon (ca. 170–180) attributes the gospel to Luke, a doctor, who is Paul's companion. Irenaeus (ca. 175–195) in *Haer.* 3.1.1 and 3.14.1 attributes the gospel to Luke, a follower of Paul, and notes how the "we" sections suggest the connection. It should be noted that Irenaeus probably exaggerates how close Luke was to Paul in describing him as a constant or inseparable companion (*Haer.* 3.14.1). Acts suggests Luke was with Paul here and there. The so-called Anti-Marcionite Prologue to Luke (ca. 175) describes Luke as a native of Antioch in Syria (Acts 11:19–30; 13:1–3; 15:30–35). It says he lived to be eighty-four years old, was a doctor, was unmarried, wrote in Achaia, and died in Boeotia. Tertullian (early 3rd cent.) in *Against Marcion* 4.2.2 and 4.5.3 calls the gospel a digest of Paul's gospel (he speaks of Luke as an apostolic man; authorship is also noted in 4.3; 4.5, where Tertullian notes that Marcion only uses Luke; 4.7; 4.8). The Monarchian Prologue (date disputed: either 3rd or 4th cent.) gives Luke's age at death as seventy-four. Origen (*De Principiis* 2.6) names Luke as the author in discussing infancy material. Finally, Eusebius (early 4th cent.) in *Ecclesiastical History* 3.4.2 mentions Luke as a companion to Paul, native of Antioch, and author of these volumes.

The remarks about Acts are similar. Irenaeus speaks of Luke as the author in *Haer.* 3.13.3. Tertullian in *On Fasting* 10 speaks of the Acts as a "commentary by Luke" as he discusses Peter's fasting in Acts. Added to this is Clement of Alexandria (*Stromata* 5.12.82.4: "Luke in the Acts of the Apostles"). These authors write in the late second and early third centuries. The Muratorian Canon names Luke in line 2 ("The third book of the Gospel is that according to Luke") and lines 34–39 ("[34] Moreover, the acts of all the apostles [35] were written in one book. For 'most excellent Theophilus' Luke compiled [36] the individual events that took place in his presence — [37] as he plainly shows by omitting the martyrdom of Peter [38] as well as the departure of Paul from the city [of Rome] [39] when he journeyed to Spain.").[3] So our materials point to authorship being consistently tied to Luke starting by the end of the second century.

This is where the significance of the "we sections" enters into the discussion. This material could be the most important potential internal clue to authorship of the volumes.[4] These sections appear in 16:10–17 (Arrival in Philippi and Conversion

---

3. This work is dated to around AD 170 as it refers to the episcopate of St. Pius I of Rome as recent. He died in AD 157. On this text, see Bruce Metzger, *The Canon of the New Testament* (Oxford: Clarendon, 1987), 191–201.

4. This is a much-debated part of Luke's work in Acts. Key discussions include: Hans Conzelmann, *Acts of the Apostles* (Hermeneia; trans. James Limburg, A. Thomas Krabel, and Donald H.

Juel; Philadelphia: Fortress, 1987), xxxiv–xl, 215, 221; J. Wehnert, *Die Wir-Passagen der Apostelgeschichte: Ein lucanisches Stilmittel aus jüdischer Tradition* (Göttingen: Vandenhoeck & Ruprecht, 1989); Claus J. Thornton, *Der Zeuge des Zeugen: Lukas als Historiker der Paulusreisen* (WUNT; Tübingen: Mohr-Siebeck, 1991); Vernon K. Robbins, "The We-Passages in Acts and Ancient Sea Voyages," *BR* 20 (1975): 5–18; idem, "By Land and by Sea: The We-Passages

of Lydia); 20:5–15 (From Troas to Miletus); 21:1–18 (From Miletus to Jerusalem); and 27:1–28:16 (From Caesarea to Rome). Their appearance appears to be at random parts of Acts,[5] but this is not entirely the case. Each text involves a sea trip, although in the case of Philippi it is a mere mention in two verses and more detail is given to the conversion of Lydia than to sea travel.

Nevertheless, the claim these are merely rhetorical descriptions and merely created for effect[6] is undercut by the fact that the presence of the "we" figure is limited to these voyage scenes and does not extend to other key scenes where the insertion of an "eyewitness" could have added persuasive force if rhetoric alone were the concern. If one were creating presence for credibility or mere rhetorical reasons, one would not limit such references to just these moments, despite scholarly claims to the contrary. It is not compelling that these first-hand "fantasy" settings appear and are randomly connected to events that are often less central to the major Acts story line, appearing only in moments of travel. So either the "we sections" are someone's journal of these travels or they belong to the author. At the least, they point to some type of firsthand source for these scenes, even if they do not belong to the author of Acts. As such, they suggest a genre more in line with history than romance, an issue to be treated shortly. The traditional position is to attribute the "we sections" to the author and to argue they point to a companion of Paul as the writer of the volumes.[7] The "we" of Acts ties to the "us" of Luke 1:1–2.

Ancient practice supports this understanding. Fitzmyer notes the lack of any literary precedent for a travel narrative that is a literary creation.[8] He also challenges the idea that such conventions exist for sea voyages. Rather, as Fitzmyer argues, these notes indicate when the writer of Acts was present at some of the events being portrayed, part of the valued "eyewitness motif" in Greek historiography. Colin Hemer has challenged the important work of Vernon Robbins, who argues for a "sea voyage genre" in the "we" style and in the way Robbins has cited some scenes out of context to make his case.[9] Hengel agrees that the volume of Acts needs to be taken

---

and Ancient Sea Voyages," in *Perspectives on Luke-Acts* (ed. C. H. Talbert; Perspectives in Religious Studies, Special Studies Series 5; Macon, GA: Mercer Univ. Press/Edinburgh: T&T Clark, 1978), 215–42; Claire K. Rothschild, *Luke-Acts and the Rhetoric of History* (WUNT; Tübingen: Mohr-Siebeck, 2004), 264–67. Rothschild speaks of the historiographic rhetoric of fantasy here that leads one away from argument to faith and tries to argue that the randomness of the references does not matter.

5. Joseph A. Fitzmyer, *The Acts of the Apostles* (AB 31; Garden City: Doubleday, 1998), 1–26.

6. Philip Vielhauer, "The Paulinism of the Acts of the Apostles," in L. E. Keck and J. L. Martyn, eds., *Studies in Luke-Acts: Essays Presented in Honor of Paul Schubert* (London: SPCK, 1966), 33–34, 47–48.

7. So Robert Jewett, *A Chronology of Paul's Life* (Philadelphia: Fortress, 1979), 12–17.

8. Fitzmyer, *Acts*, 100–102. Raymond Brown objects in his introduction that Robbins makes too much out of a scene in Philippi

where the "voyage" is only noted and covers two verses (*An Introduction to the New Testament* [New York: Doubleday, 1997], 322–23).

9. Colin Hemer, *The Book of Acts in the Setting of Hellenistic History* (Winona Lake, IN: Eisenbrauns, 1989), 317–19. At one point Hemer concludes, "His examples are not necessarily representative, nor are they always taken correctly in context, nor are they subject to control, nor do they prove the conclusions he draws from them. These criticisms are especially applicable to the instances he offers as the most precise parallels with Acts." Hemer deals with three texts in detail that Robbins notes as key for Acts: *Voyage of Hanno the Carthaginian* 1–3, a fragmentary papyrus known as *Episodes from the Third Syrian War*, and the *Antiochene Acts of Ignatius*. He notes in the first text that the editor has made prefacatory remarks and that the unit is not a literary unity as Robbins implies. In the second text, Hemer notes that Robbins' "we" (sea) and "they" (land) distinction does not work for the scene and undercuts his point. The third text does work as Robbins suggests, but gives evidence of being late and a composite text itself, so it lacks the unity to make

"seriously as a source."[10] Such remarks apply to the "we source" as well if its roots are in real experiences. This certainly was the early interpretation of this element of Luke, as Irenaeus testifies in *Haer.* 3.14.1.

The Pauline letters name some of the potential candidates who traveled with Paul: Mark, Aristarchus, Demas, and Luke (Phlm 24; Col 4:14). To this list, one could add figures such as Timothy, Titus, Silas, Epaphras, and Barnabas. However, the combination of those named in Acts by the author, whoever he is (and thus distinct from himself), and this external evidence points to Luke as the companion of Paul who wrote these volumes.

It is often suggested that the name "Luke" was chosen as a means of giving apostolic credibility to a work whose real author was unknown.[11] This argument is not as persuasive as it might initially seem. Luke's career is hardly distinctive in our early sources. He is named in passing in two texts (Col 4:14; Phlm 24). If one were to select a Pauline companion out of the hat to give prominence to a work, there are other better, more significant candidates. So it looks more likely that Luke became associated with the book, and consistently so, because the tradition knew him to be the author of this work. One would hardly guess Luke to be the "fill in" luminary.

For example, Titus is not named in Acts, and his credentials are as extensive as Luke's resume is. Epaphras (Col 1:7; 4:12; Phlm 23) qualifies in this regard as well, as does Rufus of Romans 16:13, Sosipater of Romans 16:21, or Stephanus of 1 Corinthians 16:15–17. The point is that Luke was not the only or even the most obvious choice for a tradition to latch onto, if a name was merely to be selected for creating an associate close to Paul and not named in Acts. In fact, one could ask why the association with Paul is a requirement for the "fill in," since Peter gets as much attention in Acts as Paul does. Why not fill in with a Petrine associate or someone who knew them both? All of this points to a quality in the tradition and to the likelihood the author was known, even though the books are anonymous.

What we can know about Luke can be divided between what the NT sources tell us or imply and what comes from outside of these early sources. That Luke was a physician, was tied to Paul, was not an eyewitness of Jesus, and wrote his gospel with concern for Gentiles are facts the NT makes clear. That Luke was from Syria, proclaimed Paul's gospel, was unmarried, was childless, and died at an old age are ideas that are not in the NT. Though the differences about Luke's age at death tell

---

the point Robbins takes from it. Later Hemer adds, "Nothing said here disposes of the fact that voyage-narratives are often couched in the 'we-form,' but this is a natural tendency dictated by the situation. Such accounts are indeed often in the first person, because they recall personal experience, and plural because they recall communal experience. That tendency is as true of colloquial English as of literary Greek (or Latin), but it is no proof of the existence of a literary style appropriate to what was not personal experience. If the narrative is fiction anyhow (as in Lucian, Achilles, Tacitus, or Heliodorus) the 'we' still functions naturally within the dramatic dimension of the fiction. Indeed, the examples discussed by Robbins are drawn

from widely differing genres (in a more usual sense of that word), and the notion that an exclusively defined Gattung can be isolated by simple or composite verbal or syntactical criteria across a wide variety of prose and poetry of different types and languages is inherently suspect. Robbins' paradigm does not work, and cannot be used to draw larger conclusions about the narrative of Acts 27–28."

10. Martin Hengel, *Acts and the History of Earliest Christianity* (London: SCM, 1979), 66–68.

11. Ernst Haenchen, *Acts of the Apostles: A Commentary* (London: Blackwell, 1987), 14.

us that not everything in these traditions is indisputably true, their unity regarding authorship makes almost certain the identification of Luke as the gospel's author. The tradition's testimony also makes Luke's connection to Paul likely.

Three other objections to Lucan authorship are important to note. The first argues that the theology of Paul is too distinct from Luke's portrayal of Paul to point to a Pauline companion.[12] This is said to touch on issues of natural law, Jewish law, Christology, and eschatology. Consequently, some pit Acts 17 and its openness to seeing God in creation against Romans 1. They discuss Luke's lack of discussion of the cross in salvation with Paul's emphasis on it. Luke is said to have an adoptionistic Christology where Jesus becomes Son of God. They note how little Luke speaks about the end times in contrast to Paul.

Responses to such objections about Luke or about the author of these volumes knowing Paul exist.[13] Romans 1 actually says the creation testifies to God, but that those who are polytheists do not appreciate to whom it points: the one God. The differing settings of the chapters are also important. Acts 17 is reaching out to ask pagan people to consider Paul's God. Romans 1 treats the rejection of him in an internal letter to Christians. Luke does note the cross and issues of substitution briefly in two texts (Luke 22:18–20; Acts 20:28). The Luke 22 passage is disputed in terms of textual criticism about its mention of the cross, but the disputed portion including a reference is more likely a part of the original text than its omission.[14]

Luke's Christology is not adoptionistic.[15] Jesus appears as Son from the very start of Luke (Luke 1:30–35). What Luke indicates is that the resurrection displayed Jesus as Son in a way that was not as transparent before that event. This is not unlike what Paul says in Romans 1:2–4, where the resurrection marks out Jesus as Son. Paul can use this language despite his high Christology, as 1 Corinthians 8:4–6 makes clear. Luke is similar. Luke has an end-time theology as the Acts 3 speech shows (esp. vv. 18–22). Luke 17:20–37 and 21:5–36 also display an eschatological concern in Luke. The issue of the view of the law is more complex, but the key is to see what Paul himself says, namely, that he is a Jew to the Jews and a Greek to the Greeks (1 Cor 9:19–23).[16]

---

12. So Vielhauer in "Paulinism" in *Studies in Luke-Acts*, 33–50.

13. E. Earle Ellis, *The Gospel of Luke* (NCBC; Grand Rapids: Eerdmans, 1974), 45–47; Fitzmyer, *Acts*, 145–47. In chapter 22 below, I show how much Luke overlaps with themes in the canon, including with Pauline emphases.

14. The textual issue turns on whether Luke originally had the "long" text of 22:17–20 yielding the sequence cup-bread-cup ($\mathfrak{p}^{75}$, ℵ, A, B, C, L, T, W, Δ, Θ, Ψ, family 1, family 13, Byz, Lect, some Itala, Vulgate, some Syriac, some Coptic; NRSV, RSV second edition 1971. , NASB, NIV) or the "short" text of 22:17–19a yielding the sequence cup-bread (D, some Itala; RSV first edition 1946. , NEB, REB). (Four other variants are dependent on these two major options.) The long text should, however, be accepted on the basis of its exceptional attestation and because it is the more difficult reading, introducing as it does a second cup that lacks parallels in any of the other Last Supper accounts. Heinz Schürmann ("Der Abend-

mahlsbericht Lk 22,19b–20 als ursprüngliche Textüberlieferung," *Bib* 32 [1951]. : 364–92, 522–41) traces indications of 22:19b–20 in Luke's original text: (1) the start of 22:21 assumes 22:20; (2) the covenant reference in 22:29 ("assigned a kingdom") assumes the new covenant reference of the long text; (3) the cup of 22:42 looks back to the "poured out" cup of 22:20; and (4) the unique vocabulary argues against the long text being formed from existing Synoptic tradition. All of these observations means that the long text should be accepted as original.

15. C. F. D. Moule, "The Christology of Acts," in *Studies in Luke-Acts*, 159–86; Simon Gathercole, *The Pre-Existent Son: Recovering the Christologies of Matthew, Mark, and Luke* (Grand Rapids: Eerdmans, 2006), 239.

16. I treat this last issue in detail in chapter 18 below, "The Law in Luke-Acts."

The second challenge is that the portraits of Luke and Paul differ in other key areas as well. The claim is that Paul argues strongly in his letters that he is an apostle, while Luke does not name him as such.[17] Acts 14:4 and 14 do name Paul as an apostle along with Barnabas, and the actions he performs that parallel what Peter was able to do put Paul in a similar light without using the title regularly. Another distinct set of emphases is said to be that Luke presents Paul as a miracle worker and great orator, unlike Paul's self-description. However, Paul is a miracle worker according to his own material (Rom 15:18–19; 2 Cor 4:7; 12:9, 12; 1 Thess 1:5). His own letters also refer to his rhetorical skills. Haenchen's description of Luke's portrayal is exaggerated insofar as Paul does fail at times as a speaker to persuade his audience. A few examples suffice: the Athenians are not moved; Festus thinks Paul is mad; and Euthycus is put to sleep. Paul's hesitancy about his own gifts in places reflects his humility.

Finally, there is the claim in this contrast between Paul in Acts and the Paul of the letters that the reasons why Paul is persecuted are not the same. In Acts, it is because he affirms the resurrection, while in Paul it is because he rejects the Law (see Galatians). However, this ignores the cause of Paul's arrest in Acts 21 and also reflects a reductionism where only one key reason from each work is highlighted. It should also be said that part of these differences of emphasis may be the difference between self-description and the impact one made on others. These differences of emphasis give depth to the portrait of a person. So Paul focuses on *how* Jesus saves, namely, through justification by faith in his letters, but Luke focuses on *who* does the saving in his book and in his treatment of Paul. Nevertheless, Luke can allude to such a concept as he does in the Pisidian Antioch speech of Acts 13 (vv. 32–39).

One final challenge involves the lack of citation of Paul's letters in Acts. Bruce argues that Acts is written too close to the time of these letters for them to have been used and that the issues of mission that Acts treats are distinct from specific issues of the letters.[18] Two issues that do overlap are those tied to circumcision and Paul's relationship to the community in Jerusalem. These accounts also can be reconciled, especially if one sees Acts 15 taking place after Galatians 2 by tying Galatians 2 to Acts 11:30.[19]

---

17. Haenchen, *Acts*, 112–16.

18. F. F. Bruce, *The Acts of the Apostles: Greek Text with Introduction and Commentary* (3rd ed.; Grand Rapids: Eerdmans, 1990), 52–59.

19. Ben Witherington, *The Acts of the Apostles: A Socio-Rhetorical Commentary* (Grand Rapids: Eerdmans, 1997), 88–97. See my *Acts*, 444–45, for more details. Eckhard Schnabel, *Early Christian Mission* (2 vols.; Downers Grove, IL: InterVarsity Press/London: Apollos, 2004), 988–89, makes the following points in supporting the Acts 11 visit equaling Galatians 2: (1) Galatians 2:1 speaks of Paul's second visit to Jerusalem, which equals Acts 11; (2) the visit was the result of a revelation, which connects to the revelation to Agabus about the famine in Acts 11:27–28; (3) both texts mention material needs in Judea; (4) contrary to the claims of some scholars, the Gentile mission is noted in the visit at Acts 11:19–26; (5) the absence of any mention of Peter is a difficulty but solved by noting that the leadership in Jerusalem had already changed by this time and the famine relief was brought to these "elders" of the church. Schnabel goes on to suggest that the leaders discussed some issues here related to Gentile mission, but circumcision, a key topic of Acts 15, was not one of them. Another study by H. Zeigan, *Aposteltreffen in Jerusalem: Eine forschungsgeschichtliche Studie zu Galater 2,1–10 und den möglichen lukanischen Parallelen* (Arbeiten zur Bibel und ihrer Geschichte 18; Leipzig: Evangelische Verlagsanstalt, 2005), 463–84, also goes this way, with three of his four reasons largely parallel to Schnabel. He also notes that it is a (1) second visit (2) with a similar context and (3) a collection as a key part. The new feature Zeigan adds is the harmony that resulted from the event, at least for the short term.

2.1.2 Date and Setting of Acts

The date of Luke's gospel is tied to two factors, Luke's relationship to the other Synoptic gospels and the date of Acts, especially as it relates to events at the end of Acts and whether those final events set the end date for the book. The last event in Acts comes from Paul's imprisonment in Rome in the early 60s. The debate is whether that event is basically the date for Acts or whether Acts ends here because the gospel gets to Rome, the theological goal of the book. Many place Acts in the 60s for this reason and then date the gospel of Luke slightly earlier. This is a possible date. The later in the 60s Acts is placed (some place it even later in the 70s or 80s, while a few move the work into the second century), the later comes the date for Luke, which is dated slightly earlier than Acts as the first volume in the sequence.

Tied to this decision is whether Luke used the other Synoptic Gospels. The most common view is that Luke did use Mark, though whether he used Matthew is debated and is seen as less than likely given the differences between those two gospels (e.g., as in the infancy material and the Sermon on the Mount).[20] Now Mark is variously dated from the mid-50s to around AD 70. Mark assumes the church is suffering persecution or anticipates that possibility, making a date in the 60s plausible as such a date fits the time of the persecution by Nero. The question, then, becomes how long after Mark Luke would have been written. With these key factors in place, let us take a closer look at the argument for the gospel's date.

Internal evidence and remarks from the church fathers help us set some limits for dating. For example, the earliest possible date would be within years of the last recorded event in Acts, which takes place probably in AD 62. On the other hand, Irenaeus (*Haer.* 3.13.3; 3.15.1) contains some indisputable citations, as does Justin Martyr in *Dial.* 103.19, so that the latest possible date is around AD 160.

On a comparison of Luke with material from Marcion, Josephus, Justin Martyr, and the Pseudo-Clementines, some scholars offer a date in the early to mid-second century.[21] But the tone of Acts does not really fit the tone of other documents of this period, such as *1 Clement* (AD 95) and Ignatius (AD 117).[22] In addition, it is unlikely that such a late work would ignore Paul's letters as much as Acts does. Finally, possible allusions in *1 Clement* 5.6–7 (to Acts 26), 2.1 (Acts 20:35), and 18.1 (Acts 13:22) argue against this date. These allusions move the latest possible date from the mid-second-century limit down to the mid-90s.[23]

The most popular date is sometime after the fall of Jerusalem, usually 80–90.[24] The reasons set forth include the following: (1) Luke is said to be after Mark, which

---

20. For discussion of these issues, see Robert Stein, *The Synoptic Problem: An Introduction* (Grand Rapids: Baker, 1987).

21. John Knox, *Marcion and the New Testament: An Essay on the Early History of the Canon* (Chicago: Univ. of Chicago Press, 1942), 110, 120; J. C. O'Neill, *The Theology of Acts in Its Historical Setting* (London: SPCK, 1961), 19; J. T. Townsend, "The Date of Luke-Acts," in *Luke-Acts: New Perspectives from the Society of Biblical Literature* (ed. C. Talbert; New York: Crossroad, 1984), 47–62.

22. Ellis, *Luke,* 55.

23. The *1 Clement* 5 reference is vague and may not be to this scene, but to a later context or functions as a summary about Paul not from Acts. The other texts are better examples.

24. Joseph A. Fitzmyer, *The Gospel of Luke I–IX: Introduction, Translation and Notes* (AB; Garden City: Doubleday, 1982), 53–57; F. F. Bruce, *The Book of the Acts* (rev. ed.; NICNT; Grand Rapids: Eerdmans, 1988), 6–13.

itself is a document of the mid to late 60s; (2) the picture of Paul as a hero figure needs time to emerge; (3) the portrait of churches like Ephesus requires a period before the Domitian persecution of the mid-90s; (4) the Lucan apocalyptic discourses with their description of the siege of Jerusalem and their focus on the city presuppose the fall and require a period after AD 70; and (5) some assert that the theology is late, even "early catholic."

Three of these arguments are less than central. The suggestion that Paul needs time to emerge as a hero is not clear. His letters and Acts agree that he was a central figure in the church who generated some following and controversy. Paul's letters show that James gained respect rather quickly, so why could the same not be true for Paul? The portrait of the churches, which are not yet under heavy Roman persecution, can fit any time before Domitian (ruled 81–96) or any time outside of Nero's persecution (64; Tacitus, *Annals* 15.44). The debate about "early catholicism" in Luke-Acts continues, but it is by no means clear that Luke's theology reflects a "late" theology.[25]

Two arguments have more substance. The suggestion that Luke follows Mark is likely (even if one thinks Matthew, not Mark, is the first gospel in order). Most still date Mark's work in the 60s or later. This date is close to the last event in Acts, which takes place in the early 60s. How quickly would Mark have been in circulation and thus accessible to Luke, especially if Luke had associations with major leaders of the church?[26] The argument that time needed to pass for Mark to gain stature is similar to the argument that Paul as a hero figure needed time to develop. But Paul was a major figure almost instantly. Now if Mark had roots to Peter, respect for his work would also have been instant. Luke sought out whatever materials were in circulation (Luke 1:1). Since he mentions several such documents, "quasi-canonical" status was not a prerequisite.

The most central argument, then, is that the eschatological discourses (Luke 19:41–44; 21:20–24) assume a post-70 date. These texts detail the siege and focus on the city of Jerusalem rather than on the temple alone, as the accounts in Matthew and Mark do. Esler has undertaken the most vigorous defense of this date.[27] He argues that the details of these discourses cannot be attributed simply to "what inevitably happens in war," because some of the features, such as building a circumvallation, total destruction of the city, and the marching off of all the captives, were not inevitable results of war. In responding in this way, Esler challenges Dodd's assertion that all "war" language in the discourse is possible for Jesus before 70, because the language fits ancient military operations against Israel, as well as parallels LXX descriptions of the sacking of Solomon's temple in 586 BC.[28] Esler argues that not all attacks involved circumvallation as Luke 19:43 maintains, nor is complete destruction required as in 19:44.

---

25. I. H. Marshall, *Luke: Historian and Theologian* (Grand Rapids: Zondervan, 1970), 81–83, 212–15.

26. Bo Reicke, *The Roots of the Synoptic Gospels* (Minneapolis: Fortress, 1986), 166–89.

27. Philip Esler, *Community and Gospel in Luke-Acts: The Social and Political Motivations of Lucan Theology* (SNTSMS; Cambridge: Cambridge Univ. Press, 1987), 27–29.

28. C. H. Dodd, "The Fall of Jerusalem and the 'Abomination of Desolation,'" *Journal of Roman Studies* 37 (1947): 47–54, esp. 49.

However, the previous Roman conquest of Jerusalem in 63 BC by Pompey had led those inside the city who sought to resist to expect a siege (Josephus, *Ant.* 14.58). That did not take place because others invited Pompey into the city. Esler argues the use of the LXX is too prevalent in Luke-Acts to be made a point of here. Esler contends Luke would naturally use the LXX to portray Jesus and his speech. Finally, he argues the use of the phrase "times of the Gentiles" in Luke 21:24 looks to a time after the sack of Jerusalem. In making the critique, however, Esler misses a key point of the OT connection. The OT judgment was exercised because of *covenant unfaithfulness*. The point is not the LXX, but the theology of risk Israel had because she was in need of returning to covenant in Jesus' view. The parallel of Jerusalem's total destruction, with siege and total defeat, could be expected as a covenantal act of God. Severe unfaithfulness could be seen to portend severe judgment. The result is that Esler's argument does not stand. There is no need to appeal to Jerusalem's fall as a *fait accompli* in the perspective of these texts.

In addition, proponents of an earlier date note that there is no direct reference to the fall of Jerusalem. That the fall is alluded to here is strictly an inference. Yet those who hold that an allusion to the fall is present also frequently hold that Luke often "updates" his material and perspective. If, as is claimed, he did this elsewhere, why not here with this major salvation-historical event in the divine calendar? Why the silence instead of a direct reference?

To sum up: the prediction of Jerusalem's fall is one that Jesus was capable of making solely on the basis of his knowledge of how God acts to judge covenant unfaithfulness. John the Baptist had threatened judgment before Jesus began his ministry. Luke makes no effort to "update" remarks here; he only clarifies that in the temple's collapse, the city is not spared either. Thus, a major argument for a date in the 80s–90s does not work. Although a date in the 80s is popular and possible, it is not the most likely.

This leaves another possibility, a date somewhere in the 60s.[29] Reasons for this date include the following: (1) the picture in Acts that Rome, knowing little about the movement, is still deciding where Christianity fits; (2) failure to note the death of either James (AD 62) or Paul (ca. late 60s); (3) the silence about Jerusalem's destruction, even in settings where it could have been mentioned editorially (e.g., Acts 6–7 [the Stephen account], 21–23 [Paul's arrest in Jerusalem]); and (4) the amount of uncertainty expressed about internal Gentile-Jewish relations, especially table fellowship, which fits a setting that parallels the Pauline letters that deal with similar tensions (Romans, Galatians, 1 Corinthians 8–10, Ephesians).

This last reason is most significant and has not been developed enough in the discussion to date.[30] Acts presupposes a racially mixed community, which in turn

29. Colin Hemer, *The Book of Acts in the Setting of Hellenistic History* (WUNT; Tübingen: Mohr-Siebeck, 1989), 365–410; Ellis, *Luke,* 57; I. H. Marshall, *The Gospel of Luke* (NIGTC; Grand Rapids: Eerdmans, 1978), 35; David Moessner, *Lord of the Banquet: The Literary and Theological Significance of the Lucan Travel Narrative* (Harrisburg, PA: Trinity International, 1989), 308–15.

30. Moessner, *Lord of the Banquet,* 312–15.

suggests an earlier date, not a later one. Details about the law, table fellowship, and practices that may offend (Acts 6:1–6; 10–11; 15) also suggest an earlier time frame. That the Gentile mission still needs such vigorous and detailed defense further suggests this earlier period, since by the 80s the Gentile character of the Christian movement was a given. That believers need reassurance in the midst of intense Jewish pressure fits an early date as well.

More difficult to determine is when in the 60s Luke was written. Some argue that the ending of Acts indicates the date of completion in the early 60s. Others suggest that texts such as Luke 11:49–51 presuppose the start of the struggle with Rome and offer a date in the later 60s. That Paul's death is not mentioned in Acts may be an indication that it is the early to mid-60s rather than the last third of the 60s. Nevertheless, the time required for Luke to receive and incorporate Mark might suggest a mid- to late-60s time frame. This is because Mark is often placed in the 60s. To get a 60s date for Luke, all the Synoptic Gospels need to be placed before the destruction, since his gospel is often seen to be the third one written. In other words, to defend a date in the 60s requires a fairly tight window for the production of each of the Synoptic Gospels.

For this pre-Jerusalem-fall date it is noted that the last event Luke discusses is Paul's imprisonment in Rome. This imprisonment took place in the early 60s. The claim by those who stress this factor is that Acts was written just after this, in the early 60s.[31] This is possible, but it assumes that Luke cares about Paul's fate in Rome, when it may be that he is only concerned about the word of the gospel getting to Rome.[32] Given this uncertainty about what the ending indicates, a date somewhere later in the 60s is more likely than one in the early 60s. Luke left the end of Paul's career open-ended because that is where matters stood when he wrote,[33] although it is possible he simply left the end of the Acts story here because the gospel getting to Rome shows the entry of the word into the key city of the Gentile world. If this note of triumph is all that concerned Luke, then the end gives us no help on dating.[34]

2.2 PROVENANCE

Where one fixes the place of Luke's writing depends on the date one posits for the work. The place of writing is unknown. Possibilities include Caesarea (60s), Rome (60s or 80s), Antioch (any date), and Greece (any date). The Anti-Marcionite

---

31. Hemer, *Book of Acts*, 383–87.

32. Fitzmyer, *Acts*, 52–53; Bock, *Acts*, 676–77.

33. If this is the case, we are anywhere before Paul's martyrdom as presented in the tradition, which is usually placed in the later part of the 60s. See *1 Clement* 5:5–7; Ignatius, *Romans* 4:2; Eusebius, *Eccl. Hist.* 2.25.8; Hemer, *Book of Acts*, 402–4.

34. I am now less certain of the dating issue than I was in my earlier treatments of dating for Luke-Acts, because my recent work on Acts 28 makes me think Luke was simply interested in the word reaching Rome. Although I still regard as more likely a date for the volumes in the 60s, I think it more likely to fall in the mid- to later 60s than I did before. A post-AD 70 date for the gospel is also possible given these factors. However, if a post-AD 70 date exists, it is likely to be some years later, not right after the fall of Jerusalem, since a date right after the fall is more likely to have made more direct mention of what would have been a recent traumatic event. So the lack of mention would point to some passing of time from this key event in Judean history.

Prologues and the Monarchian Prologue place its origins in Achaia (Greece). Irenaeus (*Haer.* 3.1.14) mentions Rome. The fact is no one knows and a locale is "anyone's guess."[35] Theophilus appears to be someone of status, but he could have lived anywhere in the Roman empire.

2.3 SIGNIFICANCE OF DATING AND AUTHORSHIP FOR THE THEOLOGY OF LUKE-ACTS

Regardless of whether we place Luke-Acts in the 60s or 80s, the setting of the work is in a context where Gentile inclusion and Jewish persecution exist side by side. The community is carrying out its mission in the face of growing reaction. The new Jesus community does not yet have a clear identity as a distinct Christian group completely separate from Judaism but is moving that way. This new movement in Jewish history is working to formulate its identity in the midst of a reality where the original Jewish recipients of the promise have by and large rejected the message. This pressure and the reality of trying to form a united community among a fresh ethnic mix of people are the key elements that drive Luke-Acts. These are people whose social history has been one of antagonism and/or separation.

Core questions extend beyond Jesus and God's sending of him to bring the new era. What God had done and was doing through Jesus was the core reality of the new community and was the only glue that could make this new mix work. Only something so transcendent could be a sociological force to bring together these diverse people who severely distrusted one another because of past conflict[36] rooted in a clash of polytheism versus monotheism that had marked Jew-Gentile relationships of the past. Add to this a renewed Jewish concern for a clear identity coming out of those past conflicts leading to the highlighting of distinctive practices, and the sources of tension are clear. The pious Jewish desire to show oneself faithful to covenant and Torah in a distinctive lifestyle of worship enables one to appreciate how the inclusion of Gentiles in the people of God could be controversial.

In the era before Jesus' ministry, a distance had obtained between pious Jews and Gentiles. In this context, one can understand how bringing these people together would have been difficult, requiring careful explanation. Thus, Luke-Acts explains the roots, nature, and needs of forging a new community made up of the people of the world who had turned to the hope represented in Jesus. This new community was part of an old promise, a promise of which some parts had been forgotten or lost. Now that the promise has been recovered and reclaimed in what Jesus taught and did, Luke-Acts explains the identity and place of the new community in the world. The message is both old and new. It also is a message still needed in today's world.

---

35. So correctly, Fitzmyer, *Gospel of Luke I–IX*, 57. The wavering of the tradition on this point is unlike its constancy on authorship. It points to a lesser certainty in the tradition at this point.

36. Think Maccabean War of 167–164 BC and the Roman takeover of Jerusalem in 63 BC that ended the Jewish Hasmonean rule that had been seen at one time as the return to a golden age for Israel, a disappointment that fed a hope of a messiah as a work like *Psalms of Solomon* 17–18 shows or the hope of a coming eschatological deliverance as the community at Qumran indicates.

2.4 ISSUES OF GENRE IN LUKE AND ACTS

One other key introductory issue remains. It is the question of genre for both of these books. The different foci, one on Jesus and the other on community, mean that the genre may not be the same for each volume.

2.4.1 On Luke as a Historian and His Use of Sources

One important point emerges from a look at Luke's use of sources in his gospel: he was careful with his material. Great debate rages about how good a historian Luke was. Many see him handling his materials with great freedom for theological (Goulder, Haenchen, Dibelius) or sociological reasons (Esler).[37] Among the items under scrutiny in Luke-Acts are Luke's association of Jesus' birth with a census from Quirinius; his timing for the rebellion under Theudas; the authenticity of certain parables and sayings; the reality of the miracles; his portrait of the trials of Jesus; the details of his resurrection accounts; the faithful rendering of speeches; his portrayal of early church harmony; the uniqueness of the meeting with Cornelius; the reality of the Jerusalem council; and his portrait of Paul.

The examination of such details must be conducted on a case-by-case basis. Differing judgments will be made in such matters, not just on the basis of the complexity of the evidence, which one must remember is not without its own historical gaps, but also because of philosophical worldview issues. Nevertheless, an examination of Luke's use of his sources shows his general trustworthiness.[38] Investigations into his descriptions of settings, customs, and locales reveal the same sensitivity.[39] Luke is a first-class ancient historian, and most good ancient historians understood their task well.[40] Efforts to argue that Luke is exclusively either a theologian or a historian, with many opting to give history a lesser place, underplay the evidence in sources that show that Luke is careful with his material. He is not careless, nor is he a fabricator of events.[41]

This point, however, does not mean that Luke cannot rearrange material for emphasis, summarize events in his own language, or bring out his own emphases as

---

37. Appeals to theological rationale for such freedom, often based on studies of Acts, come from Martin Dibelius, *Studies in the Acts of the Apostles* (ed. H. Greeven; trans. M. Ling and P. Schubert; New York: Scribner/London: SCM, 1956); Ernst Haenchen, *The Acts of the Apostles: A Commentary* (trans. B. Noble, G. Shinn, H. Anderson, and R. M. Wilson; Philadelphia: Westminster/Oxford: Blackwell, 1971); M. D. Goulder, *Luke: A New Paradigm* (2 vols.; JSNTSup 20; Sheffield: JSOT, 1989); Esler, *Community and Gospel in Luke-Acts.*

38. Marshall, *Luke: Historian and Theologian*, 21–76.

39. Hengel, *Acts and the History of Earliest Christianity*, vii, 3–49; Hemer, *Book of Acts in the Setting of Hellenistic History.* Hemer's entire monograph is dedicated to showing Luke's care in details found in Acts.

40. C. W. Fornara, *The Nature of History in Ancient Greece and Rome* (Berkeley: Univ. of California Press, 1983), 142–68, on Thucydides and Polybius.

41. Arguing for a nuanced position on this question that includes a study of rhetoric is Rothschild, *Luke-Acts and the Rhetoric of History.* She notes four key rhetorical means Luke uses: patterns of recurrence, prediction (i.e., appeal to prophecy), the use of the verb *dei*, and hyperbole (or exaggeration). She rejects distinguishing history from theology in such writing, arguing they are bound together in ancient writers like DNA. Her reading of Luke sees more creativity in his work in handling events than I see. I noted her handling of the "we sayings" above and her acceptance of this as more rhetorical than substantive, a view I challenged there. However, her point about the use of rhetorical elements and the linkage of history and theology in a way that is not unconcerned about the events is correct. I prefer the more confident take of Hengel and Hemer, who also go to great lengths to indicate numerous details on such matters.

drawn from the tradition. A study of lists of Luke's sources and their arrangement reveals these traits.[42] The Lucan speeches summarize and proclaim, as well as report. They are rhetorical summaries of what almost certainly were longer addresses. This kind of historical editorial work is common in ancient materials, and we must remember that Luke, unlike many ancient historians, is in touch with sources who were involved in these events. Luke is a sensitive observer of the events he describes. He is interested in both history and theology. He writes not just about the time sequence of events and teaching, but about their topical and theological relationship as well. He writes as a theologian and pastor, but as one whose direction is marked out by the history that preceded him. To underemphasize any element in the Lucan effort, whether pastoral, theological, or historical, is to underestimate the depth of his account.[43]

2.4.2 The Genre of Luke's Gospel

What specific type of literature is a gospel? How would an ancient reader have classified it? How should a modern reader approach it? For most of the nineteenth and twentieth centuries, it was popular to argue that the gospel genre was a creation of the early church and had no precedent. Above all, a gospel could not be considered biographical. This important distinction seemed to move the gospels one step further away from being historically oriented documents.

Skeptical scholars often make the charge that the gospels were too theological or biased in their approach to be historical. This was usually based on worldview choices about God and what he may or may not be capable of, or about specific definitions of history and what it could address about claims of divine activity.[44] The problem here is that how one even approaches texts full of divine claims in terms of worldview determines how one assesses the content and reality of those claims, regardless of the data in the text. The gospels give some evidence that those who followed Jesus often were skeptical about claims at the start, yet came to believe the things Jesus did.[45] These kinds of preunderstandings are important to appreciate and address as one approaches works such as Luke and Acts.

---

42. I provide such lists in chapter 22. Examples abound. Luke has the synagogue rejection in Luke 4 in an advanced position to show the character of the Galilean ministry. He chooses to set forth eschatology in three distinct units in Luke 12, 17, and 21, rather than all at once as in Mark 13 and Matthew 24–25. He disperses kingdom parables in Luke 8 and 13, rather than all at once as in Mark 4 or Matthew 13. He pairs male and female examples in ways the other gospels do not, a discussion detailed in chapter 17 on women.

43. Bock, *Luke 1:1 – 9:50*, 13 – 14.

44. See the discussion by Robert L. Webb of historiography and three models of approach to historiography in the gospels in Darrell L. Bock and Robert L. Webb, eds., *Key Events in the Life of the Historical Jesus: A Collaborative Exploration of Context and Coherence* (WUNT 247; Tübingen: Mohr-Siebeck, 2009), 9–93. He presents three models for how historiography is done by scholars: (1) an ontological naturalistic model, where God does not act as a matter

of worldview; (2) a methodological naturalistic model, where God can and does act, but that involves the category of theology and is not something history can address; and (3) a critical theistic model, where historical judgments can be made about how God acts on the basis of probability and appeals to the hermeneutical spiral. Most humanities departments operate in the first or second models, with the second being quite popular. I prefer to make a case and work in the third model. History and divine activity are not exclusive and walled-off categories, at least for those who are open to divine activity in the world.

45. One can think of Paul or even the reports of how the women's news about the empty tomb was initially received. These doubts do not give the sense of a created story since they make your leaders look so doubting and skeptical. They meet the criterion of embarrassment in terms of historical Jesus work.

In fact, the gospels do not give evidence of being a completely unique genre. So Luke fits into this discussion, perhaps even more so since his prologue indicates awareness of Greco-Roman literary style.[46] Recent work has shown that the gospels read much like ancient Greco-Roman biographies and that the issue of bias does not preclude a discussion of historicity. The detailed work by Richard Burridge has shown how much like an ancient *bios* each one of the gospels is. Luke fits into this model well.[47]

In addition, one should be slow to argue that a perspective or advocacy within a polemical context precludes the presentation of history. First, we all bring perspectives to our work. This was true of the ancients as well. Second, one can make a case and have a point of view. In fact, one could argue the case is better made if one is careful with the events. The modern illustration is how Jews have sought to preserve the truth of the reality of the Holocaust against those who doubt its existence, in order to prevent later generations from claiming that it did not take place and to insist that one must never forget what humans are capable of in acting against each other. These Jewish accounts certainly have a perspective they are trying to preserve and defend, but it is important to the credibility of how they wish history to be remembered that they do it carefully. A similar concern for truth is present in the gospels.

When we encounter a gospel, we are reading a literary form that the ancient world recognized as biographical. To call the gospels ancient biography is not to say they are like modern biographies. The gospels lack the modern biography's tendency to psychologize the inward motivations of the figure, to describe a person's physical features, to relate the exact details of the chronological sequence of the subject's life, or to detail the personality. Ancient biography gives us the portrait of a key figure by examining key events of which he or she was a major part as well as by giving us glimpses of the hero's thinking. Such works seek to entertain and to present people as examples to emulate or not, depending on whether the example is good or bad. They tend to present a fundamental chronological outline of key periods starting either with the birth or the arrival on the public scene. Some ancient biographies engage in flashback from the hero's death, although none of the gospels does this. Deeds tend to come with some sense of order, but teachings can be grouped together with less concern for chronological details. Such biographies often concentrate on the controversies surrounding the key figure, especially the events that lead to a dramatic death, if that is part of the history. This is the kind of work we read as we turn our attention to a gospel like Luke as the author presents to us, as history, the life of Jesus. The accounts are steeped in the promises of Scripture and are presented as important, even sacred accounts.[48]

So Luke's gospel is an ancient form of *bios*, distinct from modern biography, but rooted in telling the story of its hero and presenting him as an example for all. A caveat in all of this is that the main character of the gospel is not merely Jesus, but how God is

---

46. Rothschild, *Luke-Acts and the Rhetoric of History*, 67–71.
47. Richard Burridge, *What Are the Gospels? A Comparison with Greco-Roman Biography* (2nd ed.; Grand Rapids: Eerdmans, 2004).

48. Darrell L. Bock, *Studying the Historical Jesus: A Guide to Sources and Methods* (Grand Rapids: Baker, 2002), 213–14.

working through him. In this sense, the account is not only a *bios* but also a theological biography. In point of fact, Luke is trying to persuade his audience that when he tells the story of Jesus, one is also seeing God at work through him in promise and plan.

2.4.3 The Genre of Acts

It does not take much reflection to realize that Acts is not a *bios* in the way the gospel is.[49] No one person is the focus of its story. It is more about a movement and its emergence than about a single human figure. Also important to the story of Acts are claims of divine direction and activity, where God and the risen Jesus as well as the Spirit play important roles in the movement of events.

So where does Acts fit on the genre scale? In Hellenistic writing, the genre of "acts" normally recounts the deeds of a single great individual, such as Alexander the Great (Diodorus Siculus, *Library of History* 17.15; 18.1.6) or Augustus (*Res gestae divi Augusti*); sometimes, however, it can cover a group, such as "Acts of the Early Kings" (Diodorus Siculus, *Library of History* 3.1.1).[50] Such "acts" often were designed to present the hero as a kind of divine man or at least a man sent from God. This genre normally details the hero's acts, including miracles and anecdotes. It is likely that the title "Acts of the Apostles" was intended to highlight that the characters God uses in Acts are to be seen as sent from God.

Acts, however, is less focused on individuals than it is on the selective presentation of the growth of the community and its message. The book moves from locale to locale as God directs, starting in Jerusalem and culminating in the travels of Paul to Rome. In fact, the key character in Acts is God with his activity and plan. The book is much like the later work of the *Antiquities* by Josephus in that it details the history of a people, but it lacks the ethnic nationalism of such ethnic histories, since it is about how God is bringing diverse peoples together.

The work does follow many of the basic rules of Hellenistic histories. Van Unnik identifies two key characteristics of such histories: political understanding and power of expression; he goes on to list ten rules of such writing, most of which Luke follows.[51] The title highlights the role of witnesses in the book, but the apostolic band is not the central character of Acts. Rather, God's activity stands at the core of the account.

---

49. This section and the next two are updates of my discussion of introduction in my commentary on *Acts*, 24–28, 40–42.

50. A. Wikenhauser, *Die Apostelgeschichte* (4th ed.; Regensburger Neues Testament 5; Regensburg: Pustet, 1961), 94–104; Fitzmyer, *Acts*, 47–48.

51. W. C. van Unnik, "Luke's Second Book and the Rules of Hellenistic Historiography," in *Les Actes des Apôtres: Traditions, rédaction, théologie* (ed. J. Kremer; BETL 48; Louvain: Leuven Univ. Press, 1979), 37–60. The rules are (1) a noble subject; (2) the usefulness of the subject for readers; (3) independence of mind and absence of partiality; (4) good narrative construction; (5) adequate collection of preparatory material; (6) the selection and variety of treatment of

that material; (7) correct disposition and ordering of the account; (8) lively narration; (9) moderation in topographical detail; and (10) the composition of speeches adapted to the orator and rhetorical situation. Daniel Marguerat, *The First Christian Historian: Writing the "Acts of the Apostles"* (SNTSMS; Cambridge: Cambridge Univ. Press, 2002), 14–22, holds that Luke follows eight of the ten rules. Only the choice of subject and the lack of impartiality deviate from the list. But as Marguerat is aware, it is precisely because Luke is presenting divine acts and their significance that the subject matter is noble and a perspective that is not partial is undertaken, a perspective that is more in line with Jewish historiography.

Acts narrates God's work in establishing the church through Jesus' activity. In fact, it may even be premature to speak of the church in having a completely distinct identity, since much of Acts tries to make the point that this "new" movement is really old, connected to promises made by the God of Israel long ago and serving as the legitimate expression of Jewish hope. Both Jews and Gentiles make up the church, that is, the new people and community of Jesus that Acts often simply calls "the Way." The work of Jesus and the establishment of this community of the Spirit represent the initial fulfillment of God's promises.[52]

Furthermore, only some of the Twelve are highlighted: Peter and John are prominent in this group, but other key players in Acts are not part of the Twelve. These include Stephen, Philip, Paul, and James. Paul is called apostle in only one scene in Acts (Acts 14:4, 14), and this is when he appears with Barnabas. Others wish to highlight the Holy Spirit as key, but the Spirit's work is under God's sovereign direction and the one mediating the Spirit's distribution, Jesus (Acts 2:32–36).

In sum, Acts is a sociological, historical, and theological work explaining the roots of this new community, as a sequel to Luke's story of Jesus portrayed in his gospel.[53] It is not part of the genre of "acts" in the Greco-Roman sense; it is, rather, a "historical monograph" in the ancient sense of the term.[54] This classification also rejects the idea that the appropriate genre for this material is ancient epic.[55] Acts lacks the poetic nature of such works, is concerned with the church's relationship to Israel more than to Rome, and gives evidence, where we can check Luke's work, of being in touch with historical detail rather than being as creative with such detail as the epic classification suggests.[56]

---

52. G. Schneider, *Die Apostelgeschichte*, vol. 1: *Einleitung, Kommentar zu Kap. 1,1–8,40* (HTKNT 5/1; Freiburg im Breisgau: Herder, 1980), 73; J. Roloff, *Apostelgeschichte* (2nd ed.; NTD 5; Göttingen: Vandenhoeck & Ruprecht, 1988), 2. Without specifying the book's genre, D. Marguerat, "Voyages et voyageurs dans le livre des Actes et la culture gréco-romaine," *Revue d'histoire et de philosophie religieuses* 78 (1998): 33–59, compares Acts to a colony foundation narrative, which seeks to trace the origins of a community, something Acts does in terms of God's promise and provision. He reaffirms this in his later work *The First Christian Historian*, 34, calling it apologetic historiography, "permitting Christianity both to understand and to speak itself," that is, a "narrative of beginnings."

53. S. Shauf, *Theology as History, History as Theology: Paul in Ephesus in Acts 19* (BZNW 133; Berlin: de Gruyter, 2005), 60–61, notes ten subcategories of historical genre that scholars have attributed to Acts: general history, Greco-Roman political history, apologetic history, institutional history, continuation of biblical history, pathetic history, tragic-pathetic history, rhetorical history, succession narrative, and historical monograph. The problem is that Acts can be connected to many of these subgenres at once, and so such detailed classification is probably too specific. Acts shares traits with a variety of ancient historical genres. For example, Gregory Sterling, *Historiography and Self-Definition: Josephus, Luke-Acts, and Apologetic Historiography* (NovTSup 64; Leiden: Brill, 1992), 17,

speaks of apologetic historiography, but then also describes Acts as establishing group identity, a kind of ethnic history, defined as "the story of a subgroup of people in an extended prose narrative written by a member of the group who follows the group's own traditions but Hellenizes them in an effort to establish the identity of the group within the setting of the larger world" (see pp. 17, 350). On pp. 65–66, Shauf notes that whatever the classification, when it comes to function, most scholars agree that the identity of the community is the point. This work seeks to legitimize this new community and define its roots as solid and worthy of respect (so also Marguerat, *First Christian Historian*, xi, offering Christianity "an understanding of its identity through a return to its origins").

54. Hengel, *Acts and the History of Earliest Christianity*, 13–14, 36; Sterling, *Historiography and Self-Definition*; Witherington, *Acts of the Apostles*, 2–39.

55. *Pace* Marianne P. Bonz, *The Past as Legacy: Luke-Acts and Ancient Epic* (Minneapolis: Fortress, 2000); and Richard Pervo, *Acts: A Commentary* (Hermeneia; Minneapolis: Fortress, 2008).

56. Hemer, *Book of Acts in the Setting of Hellenistic History*. Here is an update of my comments on Paul's trial scenes in my *Acts*, on 16:11–40, which make for a good example: "The issue of the historicity of Paul's encounters with Rome has been the subject of scholarly debate that mirrors the general debate on historicity, with scholars' conclusions spanning the spectrum from truthfulness to full skepticism. Here is one of four places that we can carefully

Our careful attention to such background will reveal that Luke is a historian in the ancient mold whose historiography is rooted more in Jewish models than in Greco-Roman ones (to the extent these can be contrasted, since there is some overlap). Acts is, however, not a full treatment of origins but a selective one, highlighting themes and parallels that Luke wants the reader to appreciate. That it does not fill in the gaps distinguishes it from later apocryphal "Acts" and speaks to its authenticity.[57]

Luke reveals the selective nature of his treatment as he tells his story. For example, he does not give us the origin of every community he treats, even important ones such as Antioch and Rome. As I noted in my commentary on Luke's gospel, precedents for such a story of God's work among his people are the various works about the Maccabean period (1–2 Maccabees), not to mention parallels in the history books of the Hebrew Scripture.[58] Acts, however, is a unique account of the origins of God's new community and is best understood as a part of the two volumes that Luke composed. Luke was innovative in creating this account of how God worked to bring about a new era and community.[59] Nothing indicates the sequel nature of the work more clearly than the reference to "the first account" in Acts 1:1, looking back to Luke's gospel. The linkage between the works is further reinforced by the overlapping accounts of Jesus' ascension at the end of Luke and the beginning of Acts.[60]

2.4.4 On Philosophy of History and Acts

It has become popular in our postmodern age to define history itself as a construct and a type of fictive act. Marguerat says that "historiography should not be regarded as descriptive, but rather (re)constructive."[61] By this he means that histories are interpreted incidents sequenced together by the historian. Marguerat utilizes Ricoeur's distinctions between documentary history, which looks at showing verifiable facts; explicative history, which looks at events from a social, economic, and political viewpoint; and poetic history, which is rooted in founding myths and interprets the past to give a community its sense of identity.[62] For Marguerat, the fact that God is

---

check Luke against the cultural backdrop to assess his historical reliability instead of merely theorizing about it positively or negatively. Recent assessments have generally rated Luke favorably." See A. N. Sherwin-White, *Roman Society and Roman Law in the New Testament* (Oxford: Clarendon, 1963) and the series of six volumes launched by Bruce Winter and Andrew Clarke, *The Book of Acts in Its Ancient Literary Setting*, vol. 1: *The Book of Acts in Its First Century Setting* (Grand Rapids: Eerdmans, 1993). All those volumes make this point in one way or another. H. Omerzu, *Der Prozess des Paulus: Eine exegetische und rechtshistorische Untersuchung der Apostelgeschichte* (BZNW 115; Berlin: de Gruyter, 2002), esp. 506–8, traces the background in detail related to the rights of Roman citizens and the appeal to Caesar, before working through the scenes at Philippi, Thessalonica, Corinth, and Jerusalem, and Paul's arrest and appearance before the Sanhedrin, Felix, and Festus. He concludes that the material accurately reflects these legal relationships and that

the scenes draw from sources that have a historical core going back not to official court records but to oral traditions about Paul. This suggests that Luke is a credible ancient historian who needs to be taken seriously, as also his recent treatment by classical historians shows. A. Nobbs, "What Do Ancient Historians Make of the New Testament?" *TynBul* 57 (2006): 285–90.

57. M. Hengel and A. M. Schwemer, *Paul between Damascus and Antioch: The Unknown Years* (Louisville: Westminster, 1997), 106 and 385, n. 554.

58. Bock, *Luke 1:1–9:50*, 52.

59. Roloff, *Apostelgeschichte*, 1.

60. See chapter 3 on unity of Luke-Acts.

61. Marguerat, *First Christian Historian*, 5–7.

62. Ibid., 8–13. P. Ricoeur, "Philosophies critiques de l'historie: recherché, explication, écriture," in *Philosophical Problems Today* (ed. G. Florstad; Dortrecht: Kluwer, 1994), 1:139–201.

so active in the account makes Acts "poetic history" in many of its sections, rather than reflecting the other two categories. He observes that although Acts includes all the types of history, God's activity makes key sections "poetic" in thrust.

There is a major worldview and definitional problem here as we noted already in our discussion of Luke and issues of worldviews. How does one treat Jesus' appearance to Paul—as metaphorical and poetic or as a real documentary event? If it is a documentary event, then why are other similar events in Acts moved into this poetic category? What is one to do with the myriad scenes in Acts where God is the reason events take place? Does the description "poetic" really suffice? Such a move risks becoming a worldview imposing itself on the text, positing a metaphorical catchall category to rule out—or at least secularize—God's activity as historically out of bounds in terms of explicative social history. Acts becomes isolated and assessed for its historical quality before a page is read or an event is narrated. A key call is being made before the game even begins. It is true that these texts do invoke God and his activity, which is why these texts are called poetic. But the move suggests by its very naming that somehow we may be outside the realm of historical engagement and reality. It is not clear why a text cannot be both poetic in evoking the world beyond (which is what generates the category) and historical at the same time. The above-mentioned historiographic model of a critical theistic view of history has room for such a category.

The plurality of interpretations one can give to events affects the way history is viewed. One should be careful, however, not to go too far in making this point. The recent work of Shauf goes in an exaggerated direction.[63] Shauf sidesteps the historicity question by defining historiography as "imaginative narration" simply because the historian assembles a narrative from already limited resources, which themselves are socially constructed as well as tied to what the author himself may see.[64] This type of philosophical reading of history is becoming popular in our postmodern world. It gives history and historiography a "linguistic" spin.[65] Clark's work, which is an excellent historical-philosophical overview of historiographic discussion, endorses this tendency and is skeptical about the historical accuracy of ancient works. She says of the historical critic:

> The critic's task, then, is to show how "seemingly politically innocent objects, forms of subjectivity, actions, and events" are the effects of power and authority, that is, the task to denaturalize and rehistoricize what ideology has produced. By an Althusserian symptomatic reading, the critic looks at gaps and absences in the text, reads what in effect is "illegible," and notes how the answers given by a writer do not answer the questions posed.[66]

This type of ideological deconstruction itself needs deconstructing, since it often fails to show that the author does not, in fact, answer the question raised, but does

---

63. Shauf, *Theology as History, History as Theology*, 66–84.
64. Ibid., 66–75.
65. E. A. Clark, *History, Theory, Text: Historians and the Linguis-* *tic Turn* (Cambridge, MA: Harvard Univ. Press, 2005).
66. Ibid., 176.

so on purpose. Often an ancient author gives an answer that deftly moves from the initial question to a more comprehensive but appropriate response. The reading of the deconstructionist turns out to be culturally superficial and illiterate in terms of the ancient author's point. This ancient move is missed regularly in the skepticism with which Haenchen and other skeptics read Acts. They argue that Luke fails to address either the questions or the charges the text raises. However, just as often this skeptical reading of Luke or Acts badly misreads the text, undercutting the method's claim to credibility and missing the point the ancient author is raising.

Even more, Luke does not write from a position of power and authority, since the community of the first century did not have a powerful social position in the ancient world. Luke's appeal to God makes a claim of power only because Luke is convinced God has really acted in history, but the suffering of the community and its fringe social status mean it is not really a community of power in the typical sense. At best it reflects the perspective of hybridity that is often a part of postcolonial readings of texts where the fringe community both assimilates to and is distinct from the culture as it lives in its distinctive way in reaction to and protest against the dominant culture. It seems clear that Luke's view of Paul's experience and the autobiographical claims of Paul are relevant here as well. Some concrete act within the realities of history and human experience transformed Saul into Paul, just as another concrete act of resurrection and divine vindication provided justification for proclaiming a dead Galilean teacher, crucified for claiming to be a king, as Savior and Lord.

Such a philosophical and skeptical reading of history ignores the fact that certain events are intrinsically significant or may acquire multiple significances as they are tied to or properly associated with later events, so that this significance can be drawn in a variety of ways. That certain events are significant and transforming can be seen by the effects they generated, the expectations they created, or even the impression they initially conveyed. The ministry of Jesus and the perception of resurrection was such a reverberating event. It is possible for ideology and historical data to be combined in a way that reflects an appropriate historical perspective.

For example, was D-Day merely a social construct, or was it not an inherently significant World War II event that generated initial impressions, expectations, and results? It is true that it could be viewed as a victory or as a defeat, depending on what side one was on, but no one can deny that it was a key event seen as potentially significant from its inception. One need only examine General Rommel's initial reaction to the event to realize that events can and do have an inherent quality to them, or at least an inherent potential depending on how they do play out, especially when they are key events. As a result, aspects of those events can be read symbolically or reflectively pointing rightly to an ultimate significance for that event. In other words, it is a case, not of poetry or history exclusively, but of poetry *plus* history. Nor is the mere collection of events into a sequence that notes the events' relationship and significance to other (often later) events a distortion of history, if such connections do exist or can be reasonably established or result from an eventual linkage that connects that later event to an earlier one. To see the founding of the United Nations as a product, among others, of events in World War II or even the failure of the League of Nations after World War 1 does not distort history.

Thus, although one should not deny that a historian can and does create relationships as well as is creative (insightful?) in connecting events, this does not mean that such constructs misrepresent history, even though they may be in one sense creative or discerning observations formed in the thoughts and imagination of the historian. This historian's perceptions are very much a part of what history is and how it works itself out. Historical insights can be particularly useful in showing us where history has gone or what might have driven it. One must distinguish between the idea that there is one interpretation of a given set of events (for there are surely more) and the idea that particular interpretations are useful in pointing to what was hoped for or what resulted from a set of events, at least in the eyes of a given group impacted by those events. History may and does entail more than digging up brute facts, as recent historiography loves to point out, since these facts are interpreted; but some interpretations and points of view often do mirror what the events produced, enlightening and/or revealing the events' later historical significance and role, not to mention the effect and impact of these events on people and communities.

Nor should one read Acts and rule the role of its key player (God) out of bounds before Luke starts to string together the events and their circumstances in ways that point to God's or Jesus' presence and action. It is interesting to recall, as we have already noted, that (1) classical historians respect Luke as a historian as they use him; and that (2) a careful look at the details of Acts shows that, where we can check his accuracy, Luke is a credible historian. We should not be so skeptical about Luke. One must read Acts open to such a balanced view of its historical approach — in terms of its poetry, history, and cultural setting — as well as to the option of divine activity.

2.4.5 The Speeches in Acts

The scholarly positions about the speeches in Acts mainly parallel the debate over the historicity of Acts. This is the case, in part, because fully one-third of the book consists of speech material.[67]

On one side of opinion belong those who doubt the speeches' general accuracy and see a strong Lucan hand in their composition reflecting the theology of the church of his period. The claim is that the style and parallel themes of the speeches along with the "convention" of ancient historiographic handling of such material

---

67. John Polhill, *Acts* (NAC; Nashville: Broadman, 1992), 42–47, notes that about three hundred of its about one thousand verses are speech material. Fitzmyer, *Acts*, 104–5, lists twenty-eight speeches in the book, of which eight are tied to Peter and ten to Paul. Forms include missionary speeches to Jews, evangelistic speeches to Gen- tiles, a prophetic indictment from Stephen, two speeches that teach, two defense speeches, and one defense-debate speech. Fitzmyer, *Acts*, 106, is agnostic on the ability to decide the historicity of the speeches, other than to say that Luke had the input of sources.

mean that Luke is responsible for their content with only a minimal concern to reflect what originally took place. This position was set forth by M. Dibelius and has been defended by many scholars such as E. Schweizer.[68] Wilckens reaffirms this position in a monograph on the speeches.[69] An updated version of this argument comes from Marion Soards. He argues that the speeches are a literary device, a convention of historiography, and a theological-ideological device, and that they help Acts form a unity in its argument.[70]

On the other side stand those who agree that the wording of the speeches comes from Luke but argue that Luke is summarizing tradition with a concern to report what was said.[71] In favor of this position is the fact that Luke circulated through the church communities and would have had access to such tradition and heard apostolic speeches on a regular basis. More importantly, the content of these speeches and their Christology differ enough in the titles used to indicate that some input from tradition is likely. One need only compare the heavy use of the OT in Acts 2 or 3 with the lack of such use in Acts 10, or the shift in those same chapters from Messiah, Holy One, or servant to a singular appeal to Lord or judge of the living and the dead to see the difference.[72] Polhill notes the uniqueness of Stephen's speech in the collection as well as Paul's addresses at Mars Hill and Miletus.[73] Dodd's work on the themes of apostolic preaching still has merit in making the case that the church's public teaching did consistently address certain themes in the midst of this kind of variation. The length of the speeches in Acts, most of which are short and can be read in a few minutes at most, speaks for their character as summaries. Witherington argues that the Lucan speeches are tightly fitted into their settings, suggesting their authenticity.

When it comes to the conventions of ancient historiography, the debate turns on the remarks of Thucydides in *Peloponnesian War* 1.22.1. Here the author admits that he cannot recollect the exact words, but states that his goal is to place in the speakers' mouths sentiments proper to the occasion and to give the general purport of what was actually said.[74] Thus he claims the freedom to use wording summarizing what in fact was said. Dionysius of Halicarnassus (*Letter to Pompey* 3) criticizes Thucydides for being so committed to history over entertaining.[75] Polybius (*Hist.*

68. Dibelius presented his view as early as 1926, but his classic statement is a 1944 essay published in English in 1956. See Martin Dibelius, *Studies in the Acts of the Apostles* (London: SCM, 1956), 138–85; idem, *Die Reden der Apostelgeschichte und die antike Geschichtsschreibung* (Sitzungsberichte der heidelberger Akademie der Wissenschaften, philosophisch-historische Klasse; Heidelberg: Winter, 1949).

69. U. Wilckens, *Die Missionsreden der Apostelgeschichte: Form- und traditionsgeschichtliche Untersuchungen* (3rd ed.; WMANT 5; Neukirchen-Vluyn: Neukirchener, 1974 1961.). Similar is Haenchen, *Acts of the Apostles*, 129–32, who argues that Wilckens showed that the early speeches also have Hellenistic elements in them, proving that they are not authentic. Conzelmann, *Acts of the Apostles*, xliii–xlv, maintains that the speeches are inserted into the narrative and are literary creations.

70. Marion Soards, *The Speeches in Acts: Their Content, Context, and Concerns* (Louisville: Westminster John Knox, 1994), 1–17.

71. C. H. Dodd, *The Apostolic Preaching and Its Development* (London: Hodder & Stoughton, 1936); F. F. Bruce, *The Speeches in the Acts of the Apostles* (London: Tyndale, 1942); Herman Ridderbos, *The Speeches of Peter in the Acts of the Apostles* (London: Tyndale, 1962); I. H. Marshall, *The Acts of the Apostles: An Introduction and Commentary* (TNTC 5; Grand Rapids: Eerdmans, 1980), 39–42; F. F. Bruce, *The Acts of the Apostles: Greek Text with Introduction and Commentary* (3rd ed.; Grand Rapids: Eerdmans, 1990), 34–40; Witherington, *Acts of the Apostles*, 46–49.

72. Bruce, *Acts of the Apostles*, 37–39.

73. Polhill, *Acts*, 46.

74. Bruce, *Acts of the Apostles*, 34.

75. Witherington, *Acts of the Apostles*, 48.

2.56.10 – 12) also embraces this approach to history, noting that the historian is "to instruct and convince for all time serious students by the truth of the facts and the speeches he narrates." He goes on to stress that the truth has precedence for the historian over the goal of entertaining. Fornara in a monograph on ancient historical writing affirms this technique in *some but not all* classical authors.[76] So the question becomes, "What type of ancient historical writer is Luke?"

To answer this question, we must remember that Luke has shown that he can carefully follow sources where we can test him — namely, in his use of sources in the gospels (an example in Acts is Acts 17:1 – 9). In addition, Luke lived in closer proximity to his sources than Thucydides did, giving Luke a good opportunity to know what the apostles preached. Bruce refers to Luke as a writer who is Thucydidean but with "considerable restraint."[77] Bruce argues that the speeches give us "an extraordinarily accurate picture of the undeveloped theology of the earliest Christians, and so enable us to determine the character of the most primitive presentation of the gospel."[78] Hengel says it this way:

> On the other hand, one can hardly accuse him [Luke] of simply having invented events, created scenes out of nothing and depicted them on a broad canvas, deliberately falsifying the traditions in an unrestrained way for the sake of cheap effect. He is quite simply not concerned with pious edification at the expense of truth. He is not just an "edifying writer," but a historian and theologian who needs to be taken seriously. His account always remains within the limits of what was considered reliable by ancient standards of antiquity.... True, the speeches interspersed through Acts always also serve to develop Luke's own theological ideas, but as a rule he does this by use of older traditions, and often attempts to give an appropriate characterization of individual speakers.[79]

In sum, Luke is a careful ancient historian. He writes with style and flair, often summarizing more complex events. But he is also interested in more than entertaining. He wishes to inform and persuade at the same time. What happened is as important for him as engaging the reader in his topic. Luke is selective in presenting his history and functions as an author, but he also is careful in doing so.

2.5 CONCLUSION

So we place Luke-Acts in the context of the last third of the first century. Luke works probably early in that period. He finds himself in a social context near the end of Second Temple Judaism when it is under pressure from Rome and Greco-Roman polytheism and political culture, just as is the newly emerging Jesus community.

---

76. See Fornara, *Nature of History*, 142 – 68, on Thucydides and Polybius.

77. Bruce, *Acts of the Apostles*, 39.

78. Ibid.

79. Hengel, *Acts and the History of Earliest Christianity*, 61.

This new community still argues for its connection to the God of Israel and her people and yet is dealing with the emerging reality that many Jews not only do not accept the followers of Jesus but in fact are hostile to them. Add to this the new community's encouraged inclusion of Gentiles, as well as its giving the figure of Jesus an exalted place, and one can begin to see how the range of innovation the new community had generated might be controversial and in need of explanation.

This Luke does in his two volumes by rooting the new way in God's promise and action, first through Jesus in Luke and then through Jesus and the Spirit working through his key followers in Acts. All of this serves to legitimate the new movement as sanctioned by God. That community's role in the world is to love God fully and in a way that honors him while loving their neighbor. They are tasked with issuing a call to any who would respond to enter into the realized world of divine promise and salvation found in the message that the new community proclaims. It is this theology that Luke-Acts presents as a reflection of God's work in their midst before the world. This introduction shows that this goal is the point of his writing to Theophilus and to those beyond him who engage his two significant volumes.

Chapter 3

THE CASE FOR THE UNITY OF LUKE-ACTS AND READING THE VOLUMES AS LUKE-ACTS AND AS LUKE AND ACTS

BIBLIOGRAPHY

Bockmuehl, Markus. "Why Not Let Acts Be Acts? In Conversation with C. Kavin Rowe." *JSNT* 28 (2005): 163–66. **Gregory, Andrew.** *The Reception of Luke and Acts before the Period of Irenaeus.* WUNT. Tübingen: Mohr-Siebeck, 2003. Idem**.** "The Reception of Luke and Acts and the Unity of Luke-Acts." *JSNT* 29 (2007): 459–72. **Johnson, Luke Timothy.** "Literary Criticism of Luke-Acts: Is Reception History Pertinent?" *JSNT* 28 (2005): 159–62. **Parsons, Mikeal, and Richard Pervo.** *Rethinking the Unity of Luke-Acts.* Minneapolis: Fortress, 1993. **Rowe, C. Kavin.** "History, Hermeneutics and the Unity of Luke-Acts." *JSNT* 28 (2005): 131–57. Idem. "Literary Unity and Reception History: Reading Luke-Acts as Luke and Acts." *JSNT* 29 (2007): 449–57. **Spencer, Patrick E.** "The Unity of Luke-Acts: A Four-Bolted Hermeneutical Hinge." *Currents in Biblical Research* 5 (2007): 341–66. **Verheyden, J.** "The Unity of Luke-Acts." Pp. 3–56 in *The Unity of Luke-Acts.* Ed. J. Verheyden. Leuven: Peeters, 1999.

3.1 IS LUKE-ACTS A UNIFIED WORK?

Before one can work with Luke and Acts and present their theology as a unified whole, one must make the case that these volumes were intended to be seen as a literary unit and can be read as such. This idea was lost in the logical division of the canon along the lines of gospel and early church history. It was recovered in the early twentieth century when NT scholars began to speak of Luke-Acts, using a hyphen to tie together these two NT books. Lately, however, some have renewed a challenge to treat these works as part of one story. So we must look at this debate if we intend to treat a theology of these two volumes as reflecting one message.

It is important to be clear about what is intended in saying that Luke-Acts is a unity. The idea is that Luke wrote his gospel with the goal of writing Acts later in order to tell one basic story. Was Acts an afterthought, or was it intended to be volume 2 from early on? Is Luke-Acts one essential story, a relationship between two books, or a kind of mix of the two?[1]

---

1. This question is posed in the fine survey article by J. Verheyden, "The Unity of Luke-Acts," on p. 3, in a book he edited with the same title (Leuven: Peeters, 1999).

The idea that Luke-Acts should be read as a single unit gained great momentum from the work of H. J. Cadbury, especially his volume *The Making of Luke-Acts*.[2] He argued that Acts was not an afterthought, but part of one continuous work. Key to this presentation were the prologues, especially Luke 1:1–4. The phrase about fulfillment in verse 1, along with the note about reassuring Theophilus, has in mind events in both Luke and Acts. Important here is the time spent on Gentile inclusion because Theophilus, in Cadbury's view, was not yet a Christian. Rather, he was someone with social influence who might be hostile to Christianity. Cadbury believed these two volumes were an apologetic made in defense of the new faith.

Although one may question Cadbury's understanding of Theophilus as potentially hostile and Acts as an apology in that light, the idea that the prologue looks forward to the themes of both volumes has garnered support from C. K. Barrett, who argued for some forty-one examples from within Luke's gospel that have an eye on Acts.[3] Among the important examples here are the parable of Luke 14:15–24, which looks ahead to Gentile mission, and the themes of persecution as seen in Luke 21:12–19. Texts such as these are a clue that the design of the third gospel includes preparation to continue the story.

A full narratological study of the two volumes by Robert Tannehill also sees a fundamental unity in the account of Luke-Acts.[4] Luke presents Israel's reaction to Jesus and his new community as a tragic story — not as a rejection of Israel but more as an account of regret for how she has responded to the note of hope Jesus brought. Tannehill's account keeps a careful eye on how Luke-Acts speaks to Jewish issues and concerns in the midst of telling the story of how Gentiles came to be included in the community of the new era.

Another clue in this direction is the way Luke 24 ties into Acts 1. This was studied in detail by J. Dupont.[5] Clearly there is an interlocking connection between the two volumes by the way Acts 1 ties back into Luke 24.

Still another clue appears in the parallels that exist between Jesus, Peter, and Paul in their activity. Charles Talbert has the key study on this feature of the two volumes.[6] In his view, Luke presents Peter and Paul as replicating certain miracles Jesus performed to show continuity in how God is acting through the leaders of the new community Jesus initiated.

Other clues exist as well. The way in which the Spirit is handled in Luke-Acts shows a story line running from John the Baptist in Luke 3:15–17 through the inclusion of Gentiles in Acts 15. Christology develops along lines that build from

---

2. Cadbury, *Making of Luke-Acts*.

3. C. K. Barrett, "The Third Gospel as a Preface to Acts? Some Reflections," in *The Four Gospels 1992* (ed. F. Van Segbroeck et al.; Leuven: Peeters, 1992), 1454–66.

4. Robert Tannehill, *The Narrative Unity of Luke-Acts* (2 vols.; Minneapolis: Fortress, 1986, 1990). A more recent similar look at the two volumes is from Paul Borgman, *The Way according to Luke:*

Hearing the Whole Story of Luke-Acts (Grand Rapids: Eerdmans, 2006).

5. J. Dupont, *Nouvelles études sur les Actes des Apôtres* (Paris: Cerf, 1984), 58–111, 457–511. The French 1984 volume collected in one location these essays written and published earlier in 1973 and 1979.

6. Charles Talbert, *Literary Patterns, Theological Themes, and the Genre of Luke-Acts* (SBLMS; Missoula, MT: Scholars Press, 1974).

Jesus as the Christ to seeing him as Lord. We will trace these themes in detail in our study. All of this suggests an intentional design by Luke for the two volumes.

3.2 ASSESSING OBJECTIONS TO UNITY IN LUKE-ACTS

Yet this view has been challenged. The most rigorous effort appeared in a work by Mikeal Parsons and Richard Pervo. Looking at the issues of genre, narrative, and theology, they question how much unity can be brought to the account, preferring to see "independent but interrelated works."[7] It is important to note that this challenge is one of nuance, not outright rejection. In this model, Luke brings together a diverse array of distinct sources and allows tensions between them to remain so that there is less unity in the theological presentation than the alternative suggests. The two works possess "very distinct narratives, embodying different literary devices, generic conventions, and perhaps even theological concerns."[8]

The discussion has not abated. Several essays done since then show the point. Michael Bird's study is an analysis of the impact of the study by Parsons and Pervo.[9] He begins by noting the defense of unity garnered by I. Howard Marshall, pointing to the overlapping prologues, the links of themes between the gospel and Acts, and the way in which Luke 24 prepares for Acts.[10] Joel Green highlights the idea of fulfillment in the narrative as being the key to its unity.[11] Barrett and Talbert weighed back in as a result of the new challenge, both stressing the theme of fulfillment and the way in which the books interlock on themes.[12]

Subsequent responses go in similar directions with a prominent contribution in a volume edited by David Moessner.[13] This work is full of discussion of narrative themes, and the short four-page introduction to the volume by Moessner and David Tiede sets the stage nicely for the book and the issues it addresses with the title "*Two* Books but *One* Story?" Also significant is the appeal of Loveday Alexander that the end of Acts links effectively with the beginning of Luke 1–4.[14] Insightful is how Rome overshadows the early portion of Luke in 3:1–2 and how the journey to Rome is the concern at the end of the book. Isaiah 61 is a key text in Luke 4, while Isaiah 6 is a key text in Acts 28. At the end of her study Alexander says, "Somewhat to my own surprise, this study has convinced me that a case can be made for the proposition that Luke conceived his work from the outset as a

---

7. Parsons and Pervo, *Rethinking the Unity of Luke and Acts*, 126.
8. Ibid., 18.
9. Michael Bird, "The Unity of Luke-Acts in Recent Discussion," *JSNT* 29 (2007): 425–48.
10. I. Howard Marshall, "Acts and the 'Former Treatise,'" in Winter and Clarke, eds., *The Book of Acts in Its First Century Setting*, Vol. 1: *Ancient Literary Setting*, 163–82.
11. Joel Green, *The Gospel of Luke* (NICNT; Grand Rapids: Eerdmans, 1997), 8–12.
12. C. K. Barrett, "The First New Testament," *NovT* 38 (1996):

94–104; idem, *A Critical and Exegetical Commentary on the Acts of the Apostles II: Introduction and Commentary on Acts XV–XXVIII* (ICC; Edinburgh: T&T Clark, 1998), lxviii; Charles Talbert, *Reading Acts: A Literary and Theological Commentary on Acts of the Apostles* (New York: Crossroad, 1997), 3.
13. David Moessner, ed., *Jesus and the Heritage of Israel: Luke's Narrative Claim upon Israel's Legacy* (Harrisburg, PA: Trinity International, 1999).
14. Loveday Alexander, "Reading Luke-Acts from Back to Front," in J. Verheyden, ed., *Unity of Luke-Acts*, 419–46.

two-volume set in which the gospel story would be balanced and continued with stories of the apostles."[15]

In sum, the range of narrative connections and links suggests that however Luke used his sources and however diverse they were, he sought to weave them into a singular account and a core story line.

So what are we to make of another argument against unity, namely, that the early church never treated these texts as one, nor do we have manuscript evidence showing one work?[16] Beyond this, evidence of connecting the two does not surface until Irenaeus and the Muratorian Fragment in the late second century.[17] Gregory returned to this discussion and argued later that Irenaeus and the Muratorian Fragment read Luke-Acts as elements of one literary whole, but that reading looked different than what modern scholars mean.[18]

This argument on reception history has been pushed by C. Kavin Rowe.[19] Rowe argues that Irenaeus's discussion linking the end of Luke with the start of Acts is only a link and does not speak to the full connection of both volumes. The Muratorian Fragment only notes common authorship, not that the volumes should be read together. Rowe goes on to argue that the prologue of Acts treats Luke as a self-sufficient narrative and supposes some separation in time between the volumes; the recapitulatory preface in Acts does not assume an early separation of the volumes, for they may have always been distinct; and he also notes that the works are never next to each other in any manuscript collection. The distinction Rowe makes in the 2007 article is that "there is every reason to think that the two volumes are unified structurally, thematically, and theologically—which is to say literarily in the full sense—but it does not follow that the volumes had to be, or were intended to be, issued together as one work."[20]

Luke Timothy Johnson has an alternative to the kind of argument Rowe makes above.[21] Not only does he make the point we noted above about how little evidence we have for how any NT document was read in the second century, but he goes on to argue that the process of using these works as authoritative documents being brought into relationship to a larger corpus was impacting how they were read. There is a difference between reading a text as a part of its own story and making

15. Ibid., 438.

16. So Richard Pervo, "Israel's Heritage and Claims upon the Genre(s) of Luke-Acts: The Problems of a History," in Moessner, ed., *Jesus and the Heritage of Israel*, 128. See also Andrew Gregory, *The Reception of Luke and Acts in the Period before Irenaeus* (WUNT; Tübingen: Mohr-Siebeck, 2003), 2, who calls the hyphenated link between the two volumes a "modern construct."

17. This argument needs to be viewed with some caution since we lack extensive source material that discusses authorship in detail from this early period.

18. Andrew Gregory, "The Reception of Luke and Acts and the Unity of Luke-Acts," *JSNT* 29 (2007): 459–72. A piece of evidence of this is how Irenaeus in the opening of *Against Heresies* 3 links Luke 24 with Acts 1 but also appeals to Luke 10:16, showing some

understanding of a deeper connection, as well as how Irenaeus links Acts and Luke in his discussion in 3.14. The Muratorian Fragment discusses Luke's preface in his gospel with Acts, also showing awareness of a link.

19. C. Kavin Rowe, "History, Hermeneutics and the Unity of Luke-Acts," *JSNT* 28 (2005): 131–57. Mostly supportive of Rowe's contentions is Markus Bockmuehl, "Why Not Let Acts Be Acts? In Conversation with C. Kavin Rowe," *JSNT* 28 (2005): 163–66. Rowe developed and elaborated on some points in the argument in "Literary Unity and Reception History: Reading Luke-Acts as Luke and Acts," *JSNT* 29 (2007): 449–57.

20. Rowe, "Literary Unity and Reception History," 451.

21. Luke Timothy Johnson, "Literary Criticism of Luke-Acts: Is Reception History Pertinent?" *JSNT* 28 (2005): 159–62.

it part of a larger scriptural collection. He challenges the idea that the prologue of Acts assumes a lack of connection to Luke and its story. In fact, one can point out that by saying the first volume was about what Jesus *began* to do and teach (Acts 1:1), there is an implication that Jesus *continued* to work in the second volume, especially when our Lord directs key events, such as the calling of Saul or directing him not to go to Asia. So history of the reception of these two volumes has its limits in telling us how to read Luke-Acts as a *literary* entity.

In sum, the idea of reading Luke-Acts as a unity is challenged on two fronts. One argues that sources and tensions between the volumes challenge a unified reading. The other argues that the handling of the books in the early church and the volumes being read as distinct entities in the early church are against reading it as a tight unit. The former challenge seems weakened by the amount of connection and unity one can see between the two works. The second objection depends on whether one sees the processes that led to an emerging Jesus and community distinction in the canon as the driving force of how the two works were read. But remember that this is an argument of nuance.

Rowe recognizes the literary connections between the volumes. The challenge is whether to read the result as an intentionally issued single work. There is a touch of schizophrenia here. One could ask, even if one does see two volumes (and all do), should not the literary unity we see between those volumes be appreciated and connected in ways the author's writing of those volumes points to seeing? Just because the Star Wars epic was issued in six films over time and never spliced together into one large film does not mean we should downplay the intentional linkages between the individual episodes.

Our contention is that too much is being made of this difference when all sides acknowledge the existence of a literary linkage. This is especially important because Rowe is clear in the 2007 clarifying article that "it is demonstrable that the author of the Gospel did write Acts as a sequel to Luke."[22] Rowe is also correct to note that these volumes were not read as a unit in the ancient church. The reasons for this was because the church made a clear topical break between the accounts directly about Jesus and those dealing with the subsequent new community, a break that Acts even makes in the way the two volumes were issued. Nevertheless, the continuities that Luke-Acts shows are important theological and literary elements of how those works were designed to function. Making too much of this topical break can risk losing those connections. Rowe recognizes this in suggesting reading Luke-Acts as a unity and as Luke and Acts. That may be an effective way forward. There is value in seeing those points where Luke-Acts works together to tell a story. There also is value in letting Luke be related to the story of Jesus, alongside the way other gospels tell it, as well as treating Acts on its own terms as telling the story of a fresh new era when the community is coming to see where the impact of Jesus has placed it.

---

22. Rowe, "Literary Unity and Reception History," 451.

3.3 ON READING LUKE-ACTS AS A UNITY

So we read Luke-Acts as Luke-Acts on the basis of its literary and theological unity, not on the basis of its being issued as two volumes from one author.[23] We also keep an eye on the early church's use of the two volumes as distinctly treating Jesus on the one hand and the new community in the new era of the indwelt Spirit on the other. In this way we read it as Luke and Acts. We regard the former status as a unified work as most important for doing biblical theology, but regard the later canonical division as a recognition that the church's use of the material perceived that with the coming of the Spirit, what Jesus had promised and started came with a renewed vigor that took the new community some time to sort out as Acts shows us. The wrestling in Acts with exactly how to include Gentiles showed one of the first key issues the church had to resolve.[24]

In viewing this unity in the midst of diverse application of these volumes, we contend that Luke-Acts as well as Luke and Acts is intended to set forth the program of God as delivered through Jesus. The Christ was sent to bring the kingdom and Spirit to people of all nations who embraced his message of promise and deliverance. Jesus is the promised Messiah who also was vindicated by God to show he is Lord of all. So the kingdom message can go to all.

Yet many in the world will react negatively to this message. This reaction also was anticipated, so the deliverance will come with rejection and persecution, as the prophets promised, as Jesus experienced, and as the early church followed in his steps. This rejection was not a sign that the new community was under judgment and had become too lenient in how it let people in. Rather, it also was part of God's program. Under the leading of the Spirit, the sign of the new age, this community could face up to the rejection with boldness and live in harmony with each other as it continued to take this message to the world.

Jesus, Peter, and Paul model this way of life. Jesus brought the way, and those who follow him faithfully show the way as God works and directs to bring about his plan. This new community and a new religion of Jew and Gentile together are not really new. They were born of promises God made long ago and of the vindication and direction God gave to Jesus as he ministered and was resurrected to bring forgiveness of sins to those who embraced Jesus by turning to him in faith. A new community in the midst of the world, serving it and testifying to God, was the result.

Theophilus can be reassured that this is what he has heard, not because Theophilus is a potential opponent of the church in need of an apology, but because he

---

23. For a solid look at this issue, defending the hyphen in Luke-Acts in response to Parsons, Pervo, and Rowe, see Patrick E. Spencer, "The Unity of Luke-Acts: A Four-Bolted Hermeneutical Hinge," *Currents in Biblical Research* 5 (2007): 341–66. Citing Marshall's 1999 essay, he notes five key theological themes that unify the volumes: (1) Jesus as proclaimer and proclaimed; (2) the sending of apostles and witnesses; (3) the prominence of kingdom and Messiah; (4) discipleship as the appropriate response to the gospel; and

(5) salvation offered to all (p. 354). To these we'd add the direction and program of God as the most comprehensive of themes and the movement to bring Gentiles into the community of God as the goal of that mission.

24. Interestingly, this is where Gregory lands as well in his essay "The Reception of Luke and Acts and the Unity of Luke–Acts," 466–70. He argues for both types of readings as well, as does Bockmuehl, "Why Not Let Acts Be Acts?" 165–66.

is uncertain as a Gentile if he belongs in a movement that started out Jewish and now is facing pressure all around. All that God had promised and done in Jesus through the Spirit testified that Theophilus belonged where he was. What was true of Theophilus was true of all in the new community, so the message he received was shared with the community at large and eventually came to have an important place in the canon. This is the theology of Luke-Acts and of Luke and Acts. Now we trace that theology in more detail after covering one more key set of issues.

3.4 THE CHOICE OF CATEGORIES FOR OUR STUDY

Now that we have argued for the unity of these volumes, our categories for study of Luke-Acts will emerge as a result of our narrative overview and the key themes that surface in it. Consequently, we will next review the narrative flow of these two volumes. These categories also are the product of the study of these books over the centuries, the topics Luke has raised that have drawn the attention of others, and key terms Luke uses to treat a theme. In fact, many of our themes will trace specific terms first through the narrative and then discuss the results in more synthetic treatments.

Chapter 4

OUTLINE AND NARRATIVE SURVEY OF LUKE-ACTS

BIBLIOGRAPHY

Barrett, C. K. *A Critical and Exegetical Commentary on the Acts of the Apostles I: Preliminary Introduction and Commentary on Acts I–XIV*. ICC. Edinburgh: T&T Clark, 1994. Idem. *A Critical and Exegetical Commentary on the Acts of the Apostles II: Introduction and Commentary on Acts XV–XXVIII*. ICC. Edinburgh: T&T Clark, 1998; **Bock, Darrell L.** *Acts*. BECNT 5. Grand Rapids: Baker, 2007. Idem. *Luke 1:1–9:50*. BECNT 3a. Grand Rapids: Baker, 1994. Idem. *Luke 9:51–24:53*. BECNT 3b. Grand Rapids: Baker, 1996. **Bruce, F. F.** *The Acts of the Apostles: Greek Text with Introduction and Commentary*. 3rd ed. Grand Rapids: Eerdmans, 1990. **Ellis, E. Earle.** *The Gospel of Luke*. NCBC. Grand Rapids: Eerdmans, 1974. **Fitzmyer, Joseph.** *The Acts of the Apostles*. AB. Garden City: Doubleday, 1998. Idem. *The Gospel of Luke I–IX: Introduction, Translation and Notes*. AB. Garden City: Doubleday, 1982. Idem. *The Gospel of Luke X-XXIV: Introduction, Translation and Notes*. AB. Garden City: Doubleday, 1985. **Gaventa, Beverly Roberts.** *Acts*. ANTC. Nashville: Abingdon, 2003. **Green, Joel.** *The Gospel of Luke*. NICNT. Grand Rapids: Eerdmans, 1997. **Haenchen, Ernst.** *Acts of the Apostles: A Commentary*. London: Blackwell, 1987. **Jervell, Jacob.** *Die Apostelgeschichte*. Göttingen: Vandenhoeck & Ruprecht, 1998. **Johnson, Luke Timothy.** *The Acts of the Apostles*. SacPag. Collegeville, MN: Liturgical, 1992. Idem. *The Gospel of Luke*. SacPag. Collegeville, MN: Liturgical, 1991. **Marshall, I. H.** *The Acts of the Apostles: An Introduction and Commentary*. TNTC. Grand Rapids: Eerdmans, 1980. Idem. *The Gospel of Luke*. NIGTC. Grand Rapids: Eerdmans, 1978. **Nolland, John.** *Luke 1:1–24:53*. WBC. 3 vols. Waco, TX: Word, 1989–1993. **Spencer, F. Scott.** *Journeying through Acts: A Literary-Cultural Reading*. Peabody, MA: Hendrickson, 2004. **Talbert, Charles.** *Reading Acts: A Literary and Theological Commentary on Acts of the Apostles*. New York: Crossroad, 1997. **Witherington, Ben.** *The Acts of the Apostles: A Socio-Rhetorical Commentary*. Grand Rapids: Eerdmans, 1997.

This chapter presents the outline and narrative flow of Luke-Acts. It orients the reader to the movement of the two volumes and shows the key topics and themes for more focused consideration. First I give the outline for each volume. Then I proceed to discuss the emphases in the main sections.

4.1 AN OUTLINE OF LUKE

Luke's gospel has five main sections: Infancy Material (chs. 1–2); John the Baptist and Jesus (3:1–4:13); Ministry in Galilee (4:14–9:50); Journey to Jerusalem (9:51–19:44); and Passion Week (19:45–24:53). There is some debate as to where to divide the Journey material from the Passion Week, since 19:28 begins Jesus' entry into the city. It is a transition event. However, since Jesus is outside the city lamenting it in 19:41–44, we prefer to place the break after this scene. The full outline of Luke is as follows:

I. Luke's Preface and the Introduction of John and Jesus (1:1–2:52)
   A. Preface: Luke Carefully Builds on Precedent (1:1–4)
   B. Infancy Narrative: Forerunner and Fulfillment (1:5–2:40)
   C. Jesus' Revelation of His Self-Understanding (2:41–52)
II. Preparation for Ministry: Anointed by God (3:1–4:13)
   A. John the Baptist: One Who Goes Before (3:1–20)
   B. Jesus: One Who Comes After (3:21–4:13)
III. Galilean Ministry: Revelation of Jesus (4:14–9:50)
   A. Overview of Jesus' Ministry (4:14–44)
   B. Gathering of Disciples and Controversies (5:1–6:16)
   C. Jesus' Teaching (6:17–49)
   D. First Movements to Faith and Christological Questions (7:1–8:3)
   E. Call to Faith, Christological Revelation, and Questions (8:4–9:17)
   F. Christological Confession and Instruction about Discipleship (9:18–50)
IV. Jerusalem Journey: Jewish Rejection and the New Way (9:51–19:44)
   A. Blessing of Decision: Privilege, Mission, and Commitment (9:51–10:24)
   B. Discipleship: Looking to One's Neighbor, Jesus, and God (10:25–11:13)
   C. Controversies, Corrections, and Calls to Trust (11:14–54)
   D. Discipleship: Trusting God (12:1–48)
   E. Knowing the Nature of the Time: Israel Turns Away, but Blessing Still Comes (12:49–14:24)
   F. Discipleship in the Face of Rejection: Basic Elements (14:25–35)
   G. Pursuit of Sinners: Heaven's Examples (15:1–32)
   H. Generosity: Handling Money and Possessions (16:1–31)
   I. False Teaching, Forgiveness, and Service (17:1–10)
   J. Faithfulness in Looking for the King, the Kingdom, and the Kingdom's Consummation (17:11–18:8)
   K. Humbly Entrusting All to the Father (18:9–30)
   L. Turning to Jerusalem: Messianic Power, Personal Transformation, Warning of Responsibility, and Entry with Mourning (18:31–19:44)
V. Jerusalem: The Innocent One Slain and Raised (19:45–24:53)
   A. Controversy in Jerusalem (19:45–21:4)
   B. Jerusalem's Destruction and the End (21:5–38)

    C. Betrayal and Farewell (22:1–38)

    D. The Arrest, Trials, and Death of Jesus (22:39–23:56)

    E. The Resurrection and Ascension of Jesus (24:1–53)

The two volumes link together in the telling of the ascension, which concludes Luke and also begins the book of Acts. The role of this event in Luke is significant, because it represents the divine vindication of Jesus. The ascension is unique to Luke's gospel, depicting the culmination of Jesus' period of resurrection instruction to his disciples.

4.2 AN OUTLINE OF ACTS

Acts divides into seven sections. However, there also is a major distinction between Acts 1–12 and 13–28. The earlier chapters concentrate on activity emanating from Jerusalem and involving the twelve apostles, especially Peter and John. The later chapters have Syria Antioch as their main hub and focus on the activity of Paul in three missionary journeys. The latter portion of this larger unit treats how Paul reached Rome along with the presentation of the defense of his ministry before the Roman rulers. We note this major break because we do not focus on it in the outline, which itself is structured around summaries that point to unit transitions. The full outline of Acts is as follows:

    I. Introduction: Jesus Ascends to the Father and Gives a Mission (1:1–11)

        A. Review of Book 1 to the Ascension (1:1–5)

        B. The Ascension and Final Testament: A Promise for the Disciples Now and a Promise to Return (1:6–11)

    II. The Early Church in Jerusalem (1:12–6:7)

        A. Community Life: Replacing Judas by Depending on God and Reconstituting the Twelve (1:12–26)

        B. Pentecost: Christ Gives the Spirit of the New Era (2:1–41)

        C. Summary: Community Life (2:42–47)

        D. The Healing of the Lame Man and the Arrest of Peter and John (3:1–4:31)

        E. Community Life and Problems (4:32–5:11)

        F. Summary: Signs and Wonders (5:12–16)

        G. More Persecution for Peter and John (5:17–42)

        H. Community Life: The Appointment of the Seven to Help Hellenistic Widows (6:1–6)

        I. Summary of the Jerusalem Community (6:7)

    III. Persecution in Jerusalem Moves the Message to Judea and Samaria as a New Witness Emerges (6:8–9:31)

        A. The Arrest, Speech, and Martyrdom of Stephen (6:8–8:1a)

        B. Saul the Persecutor and the Spread of the Word (8:1b–4)

C. Philip in Samaria and with a Eunuch from Ethiopia (8:5–40)
D. The Conversion and Early Reception of Saul (9:1–30)
E. Closing Summary (9:31)
IV. The Gospel to the Gentiles and More Persecution in Jerusalem (9:32–12:25)
    A. Peter Performs Two Miracles at Lydda and Joppa (9:32–43)
    B. Peter and Cornelius: The Gospel to the Gentiles (10:1–11:18)
    C. The Church at Antioch: Barnabas, Saul, and Agabus (11:19–30)
    D. Persecution in Jerusalem (12:1–23)
    E. Summary (12:24–25)
V. The Mission from Antioch and the Full Incorporation of Gentiles (13:1–15:35)
    A. The First Missionary Journey: Cyprus, Pisidian Antioch, Iconium, Lystra, Derbe, and Back (13:1–14:28)
    B. Consultation at Jerusalem (15:1–35)
VI. The Second and Third Missionary Journeys: Expansion to Greece and Consolidation amid Opposition (15:36–21:16)
    A. The Second Missionary Journey: Lystra, Derbe, Iconium, Philippi, Thessalonica, Beroea, Athens, Corinth, Ephesus (15:36–18:23)
    B. The Third Missionary Journey, Ending in Jerusalem: Ephesus, Macedonia, Greece, Troas, Miletus, Caesarea, Jerusalem (18:24–21:16)
VII. The Arrest: The Message Is Defended and Reaches Rome (21:17–28:31)
    A. In Jerusalem (21:17–23:35)
        1. James's Request (21:17–26)
        2. Defense Scene 1: Before the Sanhedrin (21:27–23:35)
    B. In Caesarea (24:1–26:32)
        1. Defense Scene 2: Before Felix (24:1–27)
        2. Defense Scene 3: Before Festus, Appeal to Caesar (25:1–12)
        3. Defense Scene 4: Before Agrippa with Festus (25:13–26:32)
    C. The Long Sea Journey to Rome (27:1–28:16)
    D. Visitors in Rome: The Gospel Preached (28:17–31)

The conclusion of the book of Acts takes the gospel into Rome. There is a geographical movement across the two volumes as we move from Jerusalem to Rome, from the center of Israel to the center of the world. This pictures the movement of God's promise into all the world.

4.3 A NARRATIVE OVERVIEW OF LUKE-ACTS

One of the features of this biblical theology is to introduce key themes in chapters that run in narrative sequence, so that the theme can seen in its literary context. The repetition of this feature of theme development allows Luke-Acts and its narrative flow to be seen from various angles and serves as a review of the major movements in the two volumes. So in this initial overview, we concentrate on the overall movement and tone of the narrative; details will appear later as each theme that is introduced in this overview is developed.

4.3.1 I. Luke's Preface and the Introduction of John and Jesus (Luke 1:1 – 2:52)

The Lucan prologue, though short, is important. It is the one place where a gospel writer tells some of how he came to produce his gospel.

4.3.1.1 A. Preface: Luke Carefully Builds on Precedent (Luke 1:1 – 4)

Luke tells us that there were written sources and oral tradition, with the oral tradition tied to those who were eyewitnesses and ministers of the word (1:2).[1] This roots what Luke does not in literary romance and fiction, but in the portrayal of real events, rooted in apostolic memory. In fact, Justin Martyr's name for the gospels in his *Dialogue with Trypho* is the "apostolic memoirs." Luke writes to reassure Theophilus about the things he had been taught. This reassurance is rooted in this testimony that Luke passes on. The theme of witness becomes important to Luke with the resurrection and continues in the book of Acts.

4.3.1.2 B. Infancy Narrative: Forerunner and Fulfillment (Luke 1:5 – 2:40)

The infancy material has a note of joy and tells the story from the perspective of Mary. It is like an overture to the entire two volumes of Luke-Acts. God's promised salvation is coming with John the Baptist pointing the way to the one to come after him, the Davidic ruler and promised Messiah. The unit is built around three hymns: *The Magnificat, The Benedictus,* and the *Nunc Dimittis.*[2] This infancy material differs from Matthew's account. Matthew shows the division that Jesus' coming introduced into Israel and tells the story from the perspective of Joseph. The slaughter of the infants and threat to the child Jesus in the early chapters signals Matthew's focus on conflict and division within Israel. Luke, looking to how the story impacts the world in a positive way, brings notes of joy that the arrival of salvation yields. Only the remarks of Simeon indicate the division that Jesus also will bring in the differing responses made to the coming of promise.

In addition, in Luke the couple travels south to Bethlehem because of the requirements of the Roman census, while in Matthew, the focus is on the visit of the Magi to Jerusalem to consult Herod about the child and then on to Bethlehem. These differences reflect literary choices about what to highlight. As a result, one

---

1. For a full discussion of these roots, see Richard Bauckham, *Jesus and the Eyewitnesses: The Gospels as Eyewitness Testimony* (Grand Rapids: Eerdmans, 2008).

2. The names of these three hymns reflect how they begin in the Latin version. Mary, Zechariah, and Simeon utter these words of praise. Each hymn is full of key theological affirmations, as we will see when we cover the themes tied to them.

should not pit the accounts against one another as if they tell two completely different stories. These gospels complement each other. They do not contradict each other.[3]

The emphasis in this early section of the gospel is on Jesus as the promised Davidic king who brings peace and light to those in darkness (1:31–35, 78–79). It also emphasizes how people live with repentance before God, bringing reconciliation of formerly estranged groups, like fathers and children, as well as the disobedient and the wise (1:16–17). Finally, it presents a clear picture of eschatological reversal where the humble are exalted and the proud are brought down (1:50–55). Most of all is the idea that God's Word will be accomplished as he performs his promise and completes his commitment to the greats of old (1:54–55, 68–75).

4.3.1.3 C. Jesus' Revelation of His Self-Understanding (Luke 2:41–52)

When Jesus declares at the end of the unit that he must be "in my Father's house," it is this task he is describing. The infancy material closes with a glimpse of Jesus' self-understanding. The use of the idea of "must" (*dei*) is frequent in Luke and points to the divine plan.

4.3.2 II. Preparation for Ministry: Anointed by God (Luke 3:1–4:13)

Here Luke introduces the ministry of John the Baptist. It shows Jesus' acceptance of John's ministry and heaven's endorsement of Jesus as King-Servant. The unit closes with Jesus showing himself to be worthy of being the second Adam, enduring and surviving temptations from Satan.

4.3.2.1 A. John the Baptist: One Who Goes Before (Luke 3:1–20)

John is the forerunner according to Isa 40:3–5.[4] Luke lengthens this citation to show the involvement of the world. John issues a warning that ancestry alone will not save as he calls Israel to repent. This involves an ethical adjustment, for Luke 3:10–14 shows that if one repents, others will be treated differently. One of the goals of Luke is to describe how God expects people to live, not only how they can experience salvation.

John then discusses Jesus. He notes how people should not think John is the Christ because John only baptizes with water. Rather, people can know that the Christ has come when the one greater than John brings the purging baptism of Spirit and fire.

---

3. For details about how these accounts work in relationship to each other, one can see my discussions of historicity in my commentary, *Luke 1:1–9:50.*

4. For a key historical study on John the Baptist, see Robert L. Webb, *John the Baptizer and Prophet: A Socio-Historical Study* (JSNTSup 62; Sheffield: Sheffield Academic Press, 1991).

4.3.2.2 B. Jesus: One Who Comes After (Luke 3:21 – 4:13)

When Jesus comes to be baptized by John, a voice from heaven declares Jesus to be the Son whom God loves, a remark fusing Ps 2 and Isa 42. This leads into Luke's version of Jesus' genealogy. He traces it back to Adam to show that salvation will reach into all the world. This stands in contrast to Matthew's genealogy, where the goal shows Jesus as the Son of David through the use of three groups of fourteen generations from Abraham. True, Luke also notes the connection to David and Abraham, but he goes beyond this. Part of Jesus' qualifications to be a representative for humanity and son of Adam/Son of God is that he successfully overcomes the temptations of Satan. Jesus' allegiance to God prevents him from betraying the one who sent him to minister. So Jesus is ready to minister, and Luke turns his attention to Jesus' work in Galilee.

4.3.3 III. Galilean Ministry: Revelation of Jesus (Luke 4:14 – 9:50)

Luke treats Jesus' ministry in Galilee as an overview of his work in both word and deed. In most cases, his actions serve to point to the time of salvation and the kingdom as they authenticate the claims of Jesus and show divine support for his mission. Controversy also comes with Jesus, as opposition rises to his claims. There also are indications that Jesus' work will extend beyond Israel whether Israel responds to him or not. Joel Green summarizes the section as indicating "how Jesus, empowered by the Spirit, understood the nature of his vocation and engaged in its performance by means of an itinerant ministry balancing proclamation and miraculous activity and occasioning a division between supporters/disciples and opponents."[5] The section often juxtaposes deed and word or word and deed, with one explaining the other regardless of the order of the sequence.

4.3.3.1 A. Overview of Jesus' Ministry (Luke 4:14 – 44)

Luke begins this section with Jesus' rejection at the synagogue in Nazareth. This scene Luke has moved up from its position in Matthew and Mark to present it as a paradigm of Jesus' ministry experience. Jesus presents himself as the fulfillment of Isa 61:1 – 2 and Isa 58:6. The crowd is contemplating this possibility until Jesus goes on to note how in the past God ministered to Gentiles only at periods when Israel was unfaithful. This implied rebuke of the nation of Israel's spiritual condition leads the crowd to reject him.

Jesus' word is followed by his deeds in Capernaum, where he shows his miraculous power and authority. God is at work through Jesus. What Jesus declared in word at the synagogue in Nazareth is present through what he does in Capernaum.

---

5. Green, *Gospel of Luke*, 197.

4.3.3.2 B. Gathering of Disciples and Controversies (Luke 5:1 – 6:16)

Jesus also gathers disciples who "will fish for people." The sense Peter has that he is a sinner unworthy of Jesus' holy presence is something Jesus responds to by teaching that such a humble understanding makes Peter someone with whom Jesus can work in ministry.

A series of controversies follows in a section where Luke mirrors Mark's gospel. There are four topics in five scenes. The healing of the paralytic shows the Son of Man's authority to forgive sins—something only God can do but that the healing also indicates what Jesus can do. Jesus' associations are controversial because he welcomes tax collectors and sinners, for he has come to heal the sick and call them to repentance. His practices are different because he brings a new era that cannot be mixed with the old. Finally, two Sabbath controversies show how Jesus seeks to serve God by beneficial ministry, demonstrating God's mercy and compassion.[6] His acts also show that Jesus has authority over the Sabbath. Jesus appoints the Twelve in a reconstitution of Israel as he calls her to renewal and hope.[7]

4.3.3.3 C. Jesus' Teaching (Luke 6:17 – 49)

Jesus' ethical call is to love one's enemy. A disciple must live in a manner different from the love that sinners display to others. Such love also reflects how the Father is merciful and cares for everyone in the world. One must treat others the way they wish to be treated and also be careful not to judge, but be aware of one's own faults.

4.3.3.4 D. First Movements to Faith and Christological Questions (Luke 7:1 – 8:3)

Jesus' healing extends to Gentiles, as he heals a centurion's slave. Jesus notes the exceptional faith of the Gentile: his humility, lack of sense of entitlement, and trust in Jesus' authority. This illustrates again how those outside Israel may be more receptive to him. Jesus' authority is underscored again when he raises back to life the son of the widow of Nain.

Jesus points to the work he does by using the eschatological promise language of Isa 53 and 42:1 – 7 when he is asked if he is the one to come.[8] Jesus says to look at what he is doing as healings occur and as the gospel is preached to the poor; that should answer the question.

Then Jesus extols the ministry of John the Baptist and yet notes how the least in the new era will be greater than him. Such is the difference that the coming of the kingdom with Jesus makes. He also notes how this generation is not happy no

---

6. On Sabbath controversies in Jesus' ministry, see Donald A. Hagner, "Jesus and the Synoptic Sabbath Controversies," in Bock and Webb, *Key Events in the Life of the Historical Jesus*, 251 – 92.

7. On the Twelve, see Scot McKnight, "Jesus and the Twelve," in

Bock and Webb, *Key Events in the Life of the Historical Jesus*, 181 – 214.

8. Joachim Jeremias, *New Testament Theology: The Proclamation of Jesus* (trans. J. Bowden; NTL; London: SCM/New York: Scribner, 1971), 103 – 5.

matter how God's power appears, for neither John's asceticism nor Jesus' open association with people meets with approval. What we are seeing in this Galilean section is that Jesus ministers with power and exhorts people to love and righteousness, but many around him still reject him because he does not fit their expectations despite the evidence he leaves behind him that God is working through him.

Among the surprises is how Jesus welcomes sinners.[9] So he praises a woman who anoints him out of gratitude for the extension of God's forgiveness to her. Jesus notes that one who senses he or she is forgiven a great debt will love deeply.

Luke is sensitive to note the supportive role of women, so he names three who contributed to Jesus' ministry, including one woman who benefited from an exorcism and another with social status as the wife of Herod's steward.[10]

4.3.3.5 E. Call to Faith, Christological Revelation, and Questions (Luke 8:4 – 9:17)

Jesus tells kingdom parables. He notes that Satan, persecution, and the cares of the world can get in the way of being receptive to the word of the kingdom. Only a receptive heart that patiently perseveres bears fruit. In addition, the kingdom is like a lamp set out for all to see and exposes all. The true family of Jesus consists of those who receive his word and welcome it with obedience.

In a sequence that repeats the theme of word, then a deed to show its truth, Jesus performs a series of miracles: calming creation, the exorcism of a legion of demons, healing from disease, and raising from the dead.[11] This A to Z exercise of power shows Jesus' comprehensive authority. The calming of the storm echoes God's power (Ps 106). The raising of Jairus's daughter pairs with the earlier raising of the widow of Nain's son, which shows God's caring for both genders, just as earlier Simeon and Anna ministered as Jesus was born. The gospel is open to all.

Ministry extends to the Twelve as Jesus sends them out in mission. Meanwhile, Herod wrestles with the question of who Jesus might be, opting as the crowds do later that he may be some kind of a prophet. Jesus provides for five thousand hungry people in a scene that pictures people at table with the Messiah.

4.3.3.6 F. Christological Confession and Instruction about Discipleship (Luke 9:18 – 50)

It is here that things begin to turn. Peter confesses Jesus as the Christ of God, in contrast to the crowds, who see only a prophet.[12] However, Jesus tells them not to

---

9. On Jesus' interaction with tax collectors and sinners, see Craig Blomberg, "The Authenticity and Significance of Jesus' Fellowship with Sinners," in Bock and Webb, *Key Events in the Life of the Historical Jesus*, 215 – 50.

10. A focus on Luke's handling of women appears in chapter 17. These women cover the range of social strata in the culture and show the scope of Jesus' reach.

11. On the role of exorcism in Jesus' ministry, see Craig Evans,

"Exorcisms and the Kingdom: Inaugurating the Kingdom of God and Defeating the Kingdom of Satan," in Bock and Webb, *Key Events in the Life of the Historical Jesus*, 151 – 79.

12. On the authenticity of this scene and a full discussion of issues tied to it such as the messianic secret, see Michael J. Wilkens, "Peter's Declaration concerning Jesus' Identity in Caesarea Philippi," in Bock and Webb, *Key Events in the Life of the Historical Jesus*, 293 – 381.

tell anyone yet. He has things to teach them about his work to come and about following him. He announces he will suffer rejection. He tells the disciples that they must be ready to walk the same path and bear a cross. Yet, he also appears to three of his disciples in glory at the transfiguration. Here the heavenly voice repeats what was said at the baptism. Jesus is the beloved Son in whom God is pleased. One more thing is noted: they must listen to him. This language from Deut 18:18–19 pictures Jesus as a leader-saving-prophet like Moses. More predictions and healings follow, and Jesus also teaches that his followers must have faith like a child.

So we see Jesus showing who he is. The disciples come to see who Jesus is while the crowds come up somewhat short in understanding while others stand opposed to Jesus. It is at this point that Luke introduces Jesus' journey to Jerusalem section, where Luke has a great deal of material unique to his gospel, especially parabolic material.

4.3.4 IV. Jerusalem Journey: Jewish Rejection and the New Way (Luke 9:51–19:44)

In this unit Jesus "resolutely set[s] out for Jerusalem" (9:51). Three issues dominate this section. First, Jesus instructs his disciples for the era to come. Their dependence on God must be full and their values need to be right. They need to appreciate that the world will not welcome them and that attachment to riches and the world can get in their way. Second, Luke records additional opportunities for the nation to respond. God continues to work through Jesus, even mirroring actions he did earlier to show the divine support for Jesus. These include what I call "mirror miracles," where what was done earlier is done yet again to give another chance for response. Yet, third, opposition to Jesus remains and grows to the point where Jesus threatens exilic-like judgment on the nation (13:34–35; 19:41–44). Rejection of the visitation of Messiah has both personal and national consequences.

4.3.4.1 A. Blessing of Decision: Privilege, Mission, and Commitment (Luke 9:51–10:24)

The tone of the section is set when Samaria also is not receptive to Jesus. This leads the disciples to want to bring down a fiery judgment, but it is not the time for that yet. So they move on, as Jesus notes to potential disciples that following him will mean no home, no giving of priority to earthly concerns, and no looking back with longing to be in the world.

More than the Twelve engage in ministry as Jesus sends out seventy-two disciples to declare the kingdom. Here Jesus notes that despite the power the disciples have been given, what is the greatest blessing is that their names are written in the book of life. But rejection also has its price. The woes on the Galilean cities teach that to miss the kingdom is to face a judgment worse than the judgment that the worst of old Gentile cities will face.

4.3.4.2 B. Discipleship: Looking to One's Neighbor, Jesus, and God (10:25–11:13)

Now comes a section on love for one's neighbor, Jesus, and God. The parable of the good Samaritan notes how one is to *be* a neighbor rather than simply to identify who a neighbor might be. In fact, neighbors can come in surprising packages, as it is a hated Samaritan who shows what being a neighbor is. Mary sits devotedly before Jesus, earning his praise. Jesus then teaches the Disciples' Prayer (often called the Lord's Prayer) as he shows them how to depend on God and turn to him in prayer for God's will and for core material and spiritual needs.

4.3.4.3 C. Controversies, Corrections, and Calls to Trust (Luke 11:14–54)

So where does Jesus' power come from? The Jewish leaders argue it is from Beelzebul, but Jesus refutes this by arguing that Satan does not work against Satan.[13] Jesus' healing work is not that of destruction. So they can know that by the finger of God Jesus does his work. His miracles are "power points" that God's divine work is behind his rescuing acts.

Several texts issuing warnings follow. The members of Jesus' family are those who follow the word of the kingdom. The sign of Jonah involves a call to repent, which the Ninevites did do, and the seeking of wisdom is illustrated in what the Queen of the South did. People should watch what they take in through their eyes, what they welcome as truth. Finally, Jesus issues a rebuke of the Pharisees and scribes that shows Luke's readers their way of spirituality is not the way to live and honor God.

4.3.4.4 D. Discipleship: Trusting God (Luke 12:1–48)

The values in discipleship become Luke's next concern. One should not fear people who can kill the body, but God, who can judge the soul. The one sin that cannot be bypassed is denying who the Spirit shows the Son of Man to be. To deny the Spirit's work in Jesus is opting out of the way of salvation and the gift of God.

Values are also a concern for Jesus. He warns a man who asks him for help with his inheritance that those who rest in riches will not be able to take them with them when God calls them. The parable of the rich fool shows how selfish and self-satisfied one can become if one seeks riches; this displeases God. Jesus calls on disciples to trust in the Father's care, for people are more important than the birds and the grass that God cares for. They are to seek the kingdom, and God will care for them.

Disciples are also to be faithful in their stewardship if they claim to be associated with Jesus. Jesus tells a parable that outlines four responses of stewards. The faithful are rewarded. Those who fail to respond in treating others well are disciplined,

---

13. For a discussion of historicity of the key saying about the kingdom's arrival, see James D. G. Dunn, "Matthew 12:28/Luke 11:20—A Word of Jesus?" in *Eschatology and the New Testament:* *Essays in Honor of George Raymond Beasley-Murray* (ed. W. H. Gloer; Peabody, MA: Hendrickson, 1988), 29–49.

depending on whether they have acted with knowledge or ignorance. However, the one who blatantly disobeys "will be held responsible" and be placed with the unfaithful, for such a person's actions indicate no respect for or faith in the master who gave him the opportunity to serve.

4.3.4.5 E. Knowing the Nature of the Time: Israel Turns Away, but Blessing Still Comes (Luke 12:49–14:24)

There are the signs of the times that one should read properly. Jesus knows that his audience can read the weather by looking to the sky; they should also be able to "interpret this present time" by seeing what God is doing. Jesus reissues a call to repent, noting that those who suffer tragedy, whether by human hands or by natural disaster, point to a death that all who do not repent face. He offers a parable of a fruitless vineyard to warn the nation of the consequences of not repenting.

Jesus then performs more Sabbath miracles to give evidence that God is at work in his words and deeds. He tells parables about how the kingdom will grow from something small to something all-encompassing. He warns that the door of blessing is narrow. The question is not whether the saved will be few, but will you be included among the saved?

Some Pharisees then warn Jesus that Herod is after him; Jesus replies that he must meet his fate in Jerusalem soon, but that Israel will be desolate until she cries out, "Blessed is he who comes in the name of the Lord." This invoking of Ps 118:26 introduces a psalm that will continue to be of importance to Jesus in describing his suffering and exaltation.

At a meal with the Jewish leaders, Jesus urges humility from them and calls them to include outsiders like the poor and needy in their gatherings. Another Sabbath healing in this context continues to mirror his authority. He tells a parable that warns that those initially invited to the banquet will be excluded if they do not come when invited. But others will surely be included, and they will come from places unexpected by those who thought they had a seat.

4.3.4.6 F. Discipleship in the Face of Rejection: Basic Elements (Luke 14:25–35)

Turning to the disciples, Jesus stresses how one must be prepared to count the cost of discipleship to finish the task. One must also make peace with the more powerful king, who pictures God, so that one should be responsive to Jesus' message.

4.3.4.7 G. Pursuit of Sinners: Heaven's Examples (Luke 15:1–32)

Jesus' commitment to the lost, like tax collectors and sinners, is pictured in the parables of the lost sheep, the lost coin, and the prodigal son. Heaven rejoices and welcomes all sinners who return, so Jesus is taking the initiative to find them. Unlike the older brother of the prodigal who complains when his lost brother is restored, we should welcome all who were lost but are now found.

4.3.4.8 H. Generosity: Handling Money and Possessions (Luke 16:1–31)

The parable of the unrighteous steward tells disciples to think ahead with discernment about their actions and priorities. They must serve the one master who counts, God. They must also be aware that no one can serve "both God and money."[14]

Jesus brings a new era. The law was preached until John, but now the kingdom has come. Yet the demand for righteousness remains, such as keeping the vow of one's marriage. Jesus then warns the people through the fate of the rich man who ignored Lazarus; when he realized his irreversible error, he asked for Lazarus to be sent from the dead to warn his brothers. Jesus' reply is they have Moses and the prophets. If they do not listen to that Word of God and its call to love God and others, then even someone coming from the dead will not convince them. The danger of wealth is that it can make us insensitive to the needs of others.

4.3.4.9 I. False Teaching, Forgiveness, and Service (Luke 17:1–10)

What we are seeing in this journey section is a mix of ethical teaching for Jesus' disciples and for others about how God wants us to live. We must respond to Jesus and his offer of the kingdom, though many continue to reject him despite fresh opportunities to respond. All of this is setting up the climactic events in Jerusalem. Community will be driven by pursuing righteousness, avoiding sin, being forgiving, and serving as a faithful servant who does his duty. Disciples are to build community, not bring it down.

4.3.4.10 J. Faithfulness in Looking for the King, the Kingdom, and the Kingdom's Consummation (17:11–18:8)

A healing of ten lepers yields explicit gratitude only from a Samaritan. Once again, those outside Israel are shown to be more responsive.

Jesus then gives the first of two major eschatological discourses in Luke.[15] He begins by noting that the kingdom of God need not be searched for with signs, for it already is in their midst. Before the consummation of the kingdom comes, the Son of Man must suffer. Yet, judgment will appear suddenly and obviously like lightning when the Son of Man returns while people are pursuing their lives, just as in the days of Noah and Lot. It will be a day of separating people, and it will be a place of death where vultures gather. So the kingdom has come and it will come. The parable of the nagging widow who asks for justice reassures that God will vindicate his own speedily in his own time. The tension of this parable is that this justice will delay enough that the Son of Man will not find faith among some when he returns.

---

14. On issues tied to money and possessions in the NT, see Craig Blomberg, *Neither Poverty or Riches: A Biblical Theology of Possessions* (Downers Grove, IL: InterVarsity Press, 2000).

15. There is an eschatological parable about stewardship in 12:35–48. The other discourse is 21:5–37.

4.3.4.11 K. Humbly Entrusting All to the Father (Luke 18:9–30)

Values return to the fore when Jesus lifts up the humility of the tax collector who prays for mercy in contrast to the Pharisee, who is positive he honors God with his service. The picture of a child with a simple trust and dependence also points to a key value. And the challenge of the rich man to sell all and follow Jesus to gain eternal life warns how when the choice is either heaven with God by following Jesus or possessions, some will choose the latter, unless God has worked in the heart. This God has done with the disciples, who are reassured about blessing because they have come to Jesus in the way he asked the rich man to do.

4.3.4.12 L. Turning to Jerusalem: Messianic Power, Personal Transformation, Warning of Responsibility, and Entry with Mourning (Luke 18:31–19:44)

Jesus continues to predict his coming suffering in Jerusalem, but the Twelve have yet to grasp how this all works together. In contrast to the rich ruler who had everything but saw nothing, a blind man cries out with real insight to the Son of David and is healed. Also exemplary is Zacchaeus, an example of a rich man who is affirmed because Jesus responds to him. Zacchaeus also seeks to right the wrongs he has done in the past, which pictures repentance and the presence of a true son of Abraham who responds with faith.

Stewardship is again the issue in the parable of the ten minas. Those who do something with what Jesus gives them show their faith and are affirmed and rewarded. The one who sees the master as harsh shows an absence of faith and ends up with nothing.

Next, Jesus enters Jerusalem, making a claim to be her king by riding a donkey, accepting praise as the coming king, and adopting language from Ps 118.[16] This results in the Jewish leaders rejecting Jesus. As a result, Jesus weeps over Jerusalem, pronouncing a judgment that describes what will happen in AD 70. That event connects back to the threat of judgment in 13:34–35. Israel has missed her time of visitation (see also 1:68–69, 78–79). Rejection is in the program of God for the one God has sent, but salvation will still come. This leads us into the Passion Week with its death, resurrection, and ascension of Jesus.

4.3.5 V. Jerusalem: The Innocent One Slain and Raised (Luke 19:45–24:53)

Luke's picture of Jesus in the last week shows one in control with authority, one resolute to do God's will and to give himself for others in a sacrificial death, and one who is innocent, put to death, and suffering righteously for being who he claimed

---

16. On the historicity of this event, see Brent Kinman, "Jesus' Role Entry into Jerusalem," in Bock and Webb, *Key Events in the Life of the Historical Jesus*, 383–427.

to be. This innocent death allows a host of Psalms about the righteous sufferer to be applied to him to picture how the called one suffers.

4.3.5.1 A. Controversy in Jerusalem (Luke 19:45–21:4)

Authority is clearly in play early in the section in a series of challenges. Jesus begins by an act in the most sacred spot in the world for Israel, the temple. His challenge forces the leadership's hand. They must act since he has walked onto their sacred ground and demonstrated, in a prophetic and messianic-like claim, that the leadership is not properly guiding the people. The temple must be a place of prayer of reflection on God and his will, not a place for robbers and a house of merchandise.[17]

This event causes the leadership to ask from where Jesus got this authority, since they did not give it to him. Jesus replies with the example of John the Baptist, asking them where the Baptist's authority came from. When they refuse to reply to what is obvious, he says he will not respond, but Jesus' point has been made: God gave the authority.

The parable of the wicked tenants shows the poor history of response in the nation, as first servants (prophets) sent by the owner of the vineyard (God) and then his one and only Son (Jesus) are rejected. Nonetheless, the stone the builders rejected will be lifted up. Jesus again appeals to Ps 118 and uses it to say he will be rejected by the nation, but will be vindicated and lifted up by God.[18]

Efforts to trap Jesus with respect to the payment of taxes to Caesar and the Sadducees' issue of the resurrection fail to trap Jesus. In a section that parallels Mark's gospel, Luke shows how Jesus has more authority and is better equipped to lead the nation than her current leaders, no matter what their religious party affiliation or political-theological concerns.

The section on controversies concludes with Jesus' raising a question about why the Messiah is called Lord in Ps 110:1. This text will become crucial at Jesus' examination by the Jewish leadership and become a central text in the NT to explain who Jesus is.

Values are affirmed one more time as Jesus points to a widow who gives next to nothing and yet gives all, in contrast to the lack of sincerity in the leadership.

4.3.5.2 B. Jerusalem's Destruction and the End (Luke 21:5–38)

This leads us into the second eschatological discourse in Luke. Here Luke uses the prediction of the temple's destruction that came in AD 70 as a type for what the end and the return of the Son of Man will be like.[19] The time period until both

---

17. Even though the money changers performed a key role required by the law, by providing spotless sacrifices and allowing the payment of the temple tax with the proper currency, there was something about the way this was done that Jesus saw as reflective of a failure to make the temple what it should be. For a discussion of this, see Klyne Snodgrass, "The Temple Incident," in Bock and Webb, *Key Events in the Life of the Historical Jesus*, 429–80.

18. Although expressed differently, the gospel of John's theme of Jesus' being lifted up despite death goes down a similar conceptual path.

19. It is the failure to see a typology here that leads some to argue either that only AD 70 is meant or that Jesus got this wrong. The defense of this typological reading awaits the discussion on eschatology in Luke.

the destruction and the end will be one of chaos and persecution. Luke highlights the near fulfillment in ways that contrast to Matthew's focus on the end. Mark's version is more open and ambiguous as to the time frame in view. But Jesus assures his listeners that the city will be destroyed and the times of the Gentiles will come, but so will the eventual vindication of the saints by the Son of Man. Believers must stand firm until the end, staying alert by being faithful.

4.3.5.3 C. Betrayal and Farewell (22:1–38)

Judas betrays Jesus, setting the stage for the final events. At a last meal, Jesus portrays the significance of his sacrifice for sin on behalf of others and shows his authority by changing liturgy tied to Passover into a picture of his coming death.[20] One of the issues Luke raises is how Jesus shows his authority in a wide array of areas, demonstrating his claims about who he is; this is one of those acts. Jesus also calls his disciples to serve by exercising leadership in a way that contrasts with the system of benefaction common in the Roman world—not by power or patronage but by serving others. He uses language from Isa 53:12 to predict Peter's denials.

4.3.5.4 D. The Arrest, Trials, and Death of Jesus (Luke 22:39–23:56)

At Gethsemane, Jesus faces his fate, having resolved to do God's will. He is arrested after a kiss from Judas. Jesus rebukes a disciple who starts to wield a sword, for he chooses to face his death. In an important scene before the Jewish rulers, Jesus affirms that not only is he the Christ, but also is one who as Son of Man will be vindicated by God and be brought by the deity to God's right hand to share in his rule and glory.[21] A combination of Ps 110:1 and Dan 7:13–14 is present. The leadership, not believing Jesus, sees him as guilty of dishonoring God and claiming to be a king whom Rome did not appoint. So they can take Jesus to Pilate and make a political charge out of Jesus' response. In effect, technically Jesus has given the testimony that sends him to the cross.

When Jesus appears before Pilate, the ruler senses Jesus has done nothing worthy of death.[22] Luke 23 declares Jesus innocent at least six times and from various sources. Yet in an act of consummate injustice, Jesus goes to the cross.

The Lucan story of the cross is filled with a microcosm of reactions to Jesus. Women weep. Leaders and a thief mock. A thief believes. Some watch. Creation testifies with darkness and a torn curtain in the temple. A soldier seeing all of this confesses Jesus to be innocent (or justified). Scripture also testifies to the fulfillment of what takes place as Jesus suffers the death of an innocent righteous one with

---

20. On the historical roots and authenticity of this event, see I. H. Marshall, "The Last Supper," in Bock and Webb, *Key Events in the Life of the Historical Jesus*, 481–588.

21. On the historicity of this key scene, see Darrell L. Bock, "Blasphemy and the Jewish Examination of Jesus," in Bock and Webb, *Key Events in the Life of the Historical Jesus*, 589–667.

22. On the background to this scene and its historical character, see Robert L. Webb, "The Roman Examination and the Crucifixion of Jesus," in Bock and Webb, *Key Events in the Life of the Historical Jesus*, 669–773.

allusions to Psalms about lament or suffering (Pss 69 and 31). The narrative asks which reaction the reader will have and shows by creation's testimony and that of the confession of the thief and soldier what that response should be. The women from Galilee see all that takes place and observe as Joseph of Arimathea buries Jesus.

4.3.5.5 E. The Resurrection and Ascension of Jesus (Luke 24:1–53)

On the third day, what Jesus proclaimed to the Jewish leadership takes place as the tomb goes empty by the power of God when Jesus is raised from the dead.[23] The women proclaim the empty tomb, but the disciples think they are suffering from grief. But Peter runs to the tomb.

Meanwhile, Jesus walks with two disciples from Emmaus who are trying to figure out all that happened, for they had hoped Jesus was the prophet to come, the Messiah and hope for Israel. Jesus reveals himself to them and opens the Scriptures for them. He does so later with the rest of the disciples. He reviews what the Law, the Prophets, and the Psalms taught: that the Messiah would suffer and be raised, and that repentance and the forgiveness of sins should be taught to all nations, starting from Jerusalem. They are witnesses of these things. This is why they can assure others these things took place.

Moreover, the disciples are to wait to be clothed with power, that is, with enablement, when the Spirit comes upon them. The mission will launch from Jerusalem, so they must headquarter here. This geographical focus on Jerusalem differs from Matthew, Mark, and John, which present scenes from Galilee. But we must remember that the disciples had come to Jerusalem for a feast intending to go back to Galilee; they had not planned a long stay. The idea that they had to return for a time to Galilee to collect what they would need in Jerusalem is not far-fetched. So this difference of emphasis should not be overplayed into a contradiction.

Luke's gospel closes with Jesus' ascension to heaven. Where Luke ends, the book of Acts will begin. The narrative has made one thing clear: God has vindicated Jesus and has taken him to share in the promised rule of the kingdom with its accompanying promise of salvation through forgiveness that comes in response to repentance and the gifting of the indwelling, enabling Spirit, who gives life. For Luke, this is what his gospel is about. Theophilus can be assured that Jesus is who he claimed to be and is what the church proclaims about him.

4.3.6 I. Introduction: Jesus Ascends to the Father and Gives a Mission (Acts 1:1–11)

Acts opens with a note to Theophilus about "the former book," the gospel of Luke. This note indicates the connection between the two volumes. In the earlier volume, Luke discussed all Jesus "began to do and to teach." Now he will continue with the work of the Lord in forming and providing for those he has saved.

---

23. For discussion of historicity of the resurrection, see Grant Osborne, "Jesus' Empty Tomb and His Appearance in Jerusalem," in Bock and Webb, *Key Events in the Life of the Historical Jesus,* 775–823.

4.3.6.1 A. Review of Book 1 to the Ascension (Acts 1:1–5)

In the forty days after his resurrection Jesus demonstrated himself to be alive in many ways and repeated the instruction to wait in Jerusalem for the coming of the Spirit, the promise of the Father (Luke 3:16; 24:49). This link between Jesus and the Spirit is important to Luke to indicate that the new era and the Messiah have come.

4.3.6.2 B. The Ascension and Final Testament: A Promise for the Disciples Now and a Promise to Return (Acts 1:6–11)

When asked if this is the time that God will restore the kingdom to Israel, Jesus replies that that is the Father's business; in the meantime the disciples will be clothed with power when the Spirit comes so they can be witnesses "in Jerusalem, in all Judea and Samaria, and to the ends of the earth." This progression, going as far as Rome, is what Acts will cover (with Jerusalem and Syria Antioch as hubs). Nothing in what is said indicates the expectation in the question about the restoration of the kingdom to Israel is wrong. It is just not the time for this right now. Jesus is then taken up in the clouds; two angels declare he will return in the same manner as he departed. Luke alone narrates this ascension and its picture of being the reverse of the return.

4.3.7 II. The Early Church in Jerusalem (Acts 1:12–6:7)

Luke treats the witness and formation of community among Jesus' followers in Jerusalem. There is witness, boldness, generosity, correction, worship, prayer, and discipline from God in the midst of some failure. But for the most part, this is a growing and vibrant community being fused together by the Spirit even in the face of persecution.

4.3.7.1 A. Community Life: Replacing Judas by Depending on God and Reconstituting the Twelve (Acts 1:12–26)

The first order of business for the new community is to replace Judas. The unity of the group is affirmed. Prayer and Scripture (Pss 69:26; 109:8) surround the choice. Even the selection is left to God with the use of the lot. The point of the disciples is to get back to the number twelve and by doing so to picture the renewed, remnant community of Israel.[24]

4.3.7.2 B. Pentecost: Christ Gives the Spirit of the New Era (Acts 2:1–41)

Acts 2 and its speech is the pivot of Luke-Acts.[25] The coming of the Spirit is made evident through speaking in tongues, as all believers are clothed with the Spirit as Joel 2:28–32 promised about "the last days." Peter explains the event in an impor-

---

24. This is not really so different in view from Paul's speaking of a remnant continuing through the period of the church in Romans 9–11.

25. For discussion, which also treat historicity, see my *Acts*, 101.

tant speech that we will examine a number of times. The speech is built around four citations of the Scripture (in order, Joel 2; Pss 16:8–11; 132:11; 110:1). Peter argues that the Spirit shows Jesus to be Lord and Christ as God has given to the promised one of the line of David the Spirit to pour out, which indicates the last days are here (esp. vv. 30–36).

When Jesus sat down at the right hand of God (Luke 22:69) to share in divine authority, he received the Spirit, which he now pours out on his own. This represents the realization of something John the Baptist had also indicated (Luke 3:16; 24:49; Acts 1:4–5). The people in the audience are to call on the Lord Jesus to be saved and to share in a baptism that pictures the forgiveness of sins that Jesus offers and the gift of life in the Spirit that he gives to those whom God has called. In a real sense salvation has become trinitarian without using that term. God had attested to Jesus in his life and had vindicated him in resurrection according to the divine plan. To opt for faith in Jesus is to avoid the prospect of judgment that is still to come.

4.3.7.3 C. Summary: Community Life (Acts 2:42–47)

The new community gathers around the apostolic teaching, fellowship, the breaking of bread, and prayer. They also voluntarily share all things in common, showing their love and commitment to each other. The community also is growing.

4.3.7.4 D. The Healing of the Lame Man and the Arrest of Peter and John (Acts 3:1–4:31)

Peter and John heal a lame man at the temple gate. Peter's explanation of this miracle is rooted in the Torah and the activity of the God of Abraham, Isaac, and Jacob.[26] It is in the name and authority of Jesus of Nazareth that this healing has taken place. Again we have the sequence of event and then explanation, as Peter explains that through the healing, God is glorifying his servant Jesus, despite his having been delivered up for death by those in the city. The Holy and Righteous One was denied and killed, as Barabbas was released.

Faith in that name of Jesus is how the lame man was restored to perfect health. Peter calls the people to repent in the hope of expecting the rest of what Jesus will do. Heaven holds him in reserve until God completes the restoration he promised in Scripture. God had promised a prophet like Moses, and he must be obeyed or else one is cut off from the community. The prophets from Samuel on declared these days, and the promise is for the Jewish audience to which Peter is speaking, as the promise to Abraham of a blessed seed declares. The Servant whom God has sent to them first of all can bless if one turns from wickedness.

This message leads to the arrest of Peter and John as the persecution Jesus had predicted begins to fall on the community. When Peter is asked by what authority

---

26. Witherington, *Acts of the Apostles*, 176, notes that this speech has two parts: a "defense" portion in vv. 12–18 and the "delibera-tive" portion presenting the application in vv. 19–26.

they do these things, he repeats his message that "by the name of Jesus Christ of Nazareth, whom you crucified but whom God raised from the dead, that this man stands before you healed" (4:10). Peter then cites Ps 118:22 and notes that the rejected stone has become the cornerstone. Salvation is in no one else. Trying to decide what to do, the Jewish leadership asks Peter to stop speaking about Jesus, a request Peter refuses because he and John as witnesses must to obey God, not humans.

4.3.7.5 E. Community Life and Problems (Acts 4:32–5:11)

Meanwhile, the community recognizes that the opposition reflects the rejection of God's anointed as described in Ps 2:1–2 and asks for boldness to witness with God acting through them in the midst of the opposition. The Spirit's presence is made evident as they pray.

The unity of the community is again described as they hold all things in common and witness boldly in fulfillment of their prayer. Among the exemplary members is Joseph Barnabas, who gives from the proceeds of a field to the apostles—a picture of someone who handles his wealth well. This point is important, given all the warnings Jesus had issued about the use of resources in Luke.

However, all is not well. Ananias and Sapphira pretend to give all the proceeds from a sale and are struck dead for lying to the Spirit. God will exercise judgment in his community.

4.3.7.6 F. Summary: Signs and Wonders (Acts 5:12–16)

Yet, for the most part, the testimony and healing through the community continue leading to respect from those around them and to growth.

4.3.7.7 G. More Persecution for Peter and John (Acts 5:17–42)

Yet the persecution continues as the apostles are arrested again. Gaventa argues that this scene intensifies the Lucan portrait of persecution in the book.[27] God's support for the apostles shows up when an angel frees them from the prison so they can continue to preach to the people. When the empty cell is discovered, the Jewish leadership collect the apostles and question them again. When they are reminded that they were commanded not to speak about Jesus, Peter again replies they will obey God, not human beings. God had raised this Jesus whom the leadership had killed. God had exalted this Jesus to his right hand as Ruler and Savior to offer repentance to Israel and forgiveness of sins. As witnesses with the Spirit of God, they are to obey what the Spirit has called them to do.

This message given by "Peter and the other apostles" enrage the council; but Gamaliel counsels that if this movement is not of God, it will die. However, if it is of God, it cannot be stopped. His advice is to leave the apostles alone. They beat

---

27. Beverly Roberts Gaventa, *Acts* (ANTC; Nashville: Abingdon, 2003), 106.

them and let them go, telling them once again to stop their preaching. However, on their release, they are back preaching again, rejoicing since they are considered worthy to suffer "disgrace for the Name."

4.3.7.8 H. Community Life: The Appointment of the Seven to Help Hellenistic Widows (Acts 6:1–6)

Within the community, another problem arises. Hebrew widows are well taken care of, but Hellenistic widows are being ignored. When this is brought to the attention of the apostles, they suggest those who have raised the problem should appoint special people to take care of this need, and they do so.

4.3.7.9 I. Summary of the Jerusalem Community (Acts 6:7)

This first main section ends with a note that "the word of God" is spreading, by which is meant the message about the kingdom, as the number of disciples grows, even including many priests. The section as a whole shows a vibrant community, following God's call to be witnesses with boldness and in the face of persecution. They testify to the unique role of Jesus and indicate how God is keeping his promises made long ago. The new movement is rooted in old promises and commitments of God. The believers also function in a giving and engaging community, given to each other and engaging each other and those in the city with their commitment to share the gospel. Mission rooted in promise is where salvation takes this new community, which also has roots that go back to the promises made to Abraham and Moses.

4.3.8 III. Persecution in Jerusalem Moves the Message to Judea and Samaria as a New Witness Emerges (Acts 6:8–9:31)

The pressure intensifies and the bulk of the community is forced out of Jerusalem into Judea and Samaria as a result of the martyrdom of Stephen. At this scene is a zealous persecutor of the church, Saul. His turnaround and embrace of the messianic faith as a result of Jesus' appearance to him will become the focus of the second half of Acts.

4.3.8.1 A. The Arrest, Speech, and Martyrdom of Stephen (Acts 6:8–8:1a)

One of those selected to help the widows also becomes a witness to Jesus. Stephen is accused of speaking blasphemy against God, Moses, the temple, and the law. In a speech of defense, which is the longest speech in Luke, Stephen uses Scripture and God's promise to argue that historically the people of Israel have always resisted God's messengers, whether Joseph, Moses, or others. The rhetorical outline is also valuable to consider: *exordium* (call to hear; v. 2a); *narratio* (preparatory discourse; vv. 2b–34); *propositio* (proposition; v. 35); *argumentatio* (argument-application;

vv. 36–50); and *peroratio* (polemical application; vv. 51–53).[28] The Jewish commitment to the temple ignores what Isa 66:1 notes, that nothing can contain God. In addition, whether one thinks of the golden calf or Israel's later history, there was a consistent turn toward unfaithfulness and idolatry. Now they have killed the Righteous One. When Stephen describes that he sees the Son of Man standing with God, the crowd stones him for blasphemy with Saul watching over it all in support.

4.3.8.2 B. Saul the Persecutor and the Spread of the Word (Acts 8:1b–4)

Saul not only observes the martyrdom of Stephen, but he begins to arrest those of the believing community. Meanwhile, this pressure of persecution sends most believers out of the city, into Judea and Samaria. As ironic as it seems, persecution actually leads to the expansion of the movement as the scattering also produces mission and witness.

4.3.8.3 C. Philip in Samaria and with a Eunuch from Ethiopia (Acts 8:5–40)

Philip, another of the seven who had helped with the widows (cf. ch. 6), brings the gospel to Samaria and to an Ethiopian eunuch on the Gaza Road. In Samaria, Peter and John testify to this expansion. In addition, there is an encounter with a well-known regional magician, Simon Magus. Although Simon Magus appears to respond, he is really interested in being able to mimic the kind of power of the Spirit that the apostles have displayed. This meeting of the spiritual forces is something Luke will continue to watch.

The witness to the eunuch, who appears to be a proselyte of some kind if not a Jew from abroad, involves discussion of Isa 53 and the innocent suffering Jesus experienced. After showing that this text was about Jesus, Philip baptizes the eunuch, a hint of more involvement to come for those who live outside of Israel.

4.3.8.4 D. The Conversion and Early Reception of Saul (Acts 9:1–30)

Meanwhile, Saul travels to Damascus in pursuit of believers there. The Lord stops that mission by appearing to him in radiant glory and asking why Saul is persecuting him. The remark shows the solidarity Jesus has with his community.[29] Saul will be getting instructions from the Lord through Ananias in Damascus. To secure the transformation of Saul, the Lord also appears in a vision to Ananias to prepare him for Saul's arrival. Everything shows that the Lord is directing events and guiding events in the life of his community.

---

28. Details on this speech and its sources and how the speech addresses the questions raised against Stephen, something some commentators view skeptically, can be found in my *Acts*, 259–61.

29. On the importance of this event in Paul's life, see Seyoon Kim, *The Origin of Paul's Gospel* (Grand Rapids: Eerdmans, 1981).

Jesus has chosen Saul to take the gospel before Gentiles, kings, and the Jews. So the Lord brings a powerful, new witness to the community, as is seen when he preaches about Jesus as the Son of God in Damascus. Efforts by the Jews in Damascus to kill Saul fail as he hears about the plot and departs. When Saul returns to Jerusalem, Barnabas takes him in hand and vouches for him before the community.

4.3.8.5 E. Closing Summary (Acts 9:31)

The church grows in Judea, Galilee, and Samaria, experiencing peace and being built up as they fear the Lord and draw on the comfort of the Spirit.

4.3.9 IV. The Gospel to the Gentiles and More Persecution in Jerusalem (Acts 9:32–12:25)

This is the final section of Acts that focuses missionary activity in Jerusalem. Peter ventures out from the city to the coast to heal and preach, and the Lord directs him to go to Gentiles in Caesarea, the home of the Roman legion in that area. Thus, this section begins the transition to the call to the nations. Yet persecution continues in Jerusalem, as James (not the Lord's brother, but the brother of John) is martyred and Peter is arrested yet again.

4.3.9.1 A. Peter Performs Two Miracles at Lydda and Joppa (Acts 9:32–43)

In miracles that mirror the types of things Jesus did in his ministry, Peter helps a paralyzed man named Aeneas walk and raises a woman named Dorcas from the dead. The first healing takes place with Peter noting that Jesus Christ performs the healing. Many in the region of Sharon come to the Lord.

4.3.9.2 B. Peter and Cornelius: The Gospel to the Gentiles (Acts 10:1–11:18)

This key section of Acts treats the expansion of the gospel to the Gentiles, which God directs and is responsible for initiating. Gaventa shows the unit's balance, resulting from eight scenes in four parts: two visions (Cornelius: 10:1–8; Peter: 10:9–16); the journey and welcome (Cornelius: 10:17–23a; 23b–29); speeches (Cornelius: 10:30–33; Peter: 10:34–43); confirmation (the Holy Spirit: 10:44–48; the community: 11:1–18).[30]

While Peter is staying with Simon the tanner in Joppa, a centurion in Caesarea has a vision that tells him to send for Peter. As his servants are on their way, Peter also has a vision, where God commands him to eat unclean food; Peter initially rejects this as something he would never do. After the third time the command comes, along with the declaration that what God has cleansed must not be called

---

30. Gaventa, *Acts*, 163.

common, Peter comes to understand that he is being called to take the gospel directly to Gentiles. No longer are associations with Gentiles to be viewed with suspicion.

The double direction of the guidance from God is parallel to the call of Saul, which points to the importance of the event and the initiative of God to expand the mission of the community. No person is common or unclean. So at Cornelius's invitation, Peter preaches about the ministry of Jesus and the gospel, concluding that God has appointed Jesus as the judge of the living and the dead, and the prophets testify to him as one who offers forgiveness of sins through his name. As Peter continues preaching, the Spirit surprisingly comes down on the Gentiles, which indicates they have responded and that God has cleansed their hearts and given them the gift of the new era. So Peter baptizes them and stays with them for a few days.

When complaints about this act arise from some who think circumcision is necessary prior to baptism, Peter reports to the Jerusalem church what took place in fulfillment of the teaching of the Lord that he would follow John's baptism of water with a baptism of the enabling Spirit: "the same gift he gave to us who believed in the Lord Jesus Christ . . .[so] who was I to think that I could stand in God's way?" (11:17). With this, the group rejoices that God has granted repentance to life to Gentiles.

4.3.9.3 C. The Church at Antioch: Barnabas, Saul, and Agabus (Acts 11:19–30)

Persecution continues to scatter the church. The gospel reaches Phoenicia, Cyprus, and Antioch in Syria. A significant church arises in Antioch as the result of preaching of men from Cyprus and Cyrene. Barnabas is sent to check out this development. He encourages the church there, and then calls for Saul as he travels through Tarsus.

The church in Antioch, in response to a prophecy from Agabus about coming famine in Judea, sends food to the church in Jerusalem through Barnabas and Saul. The solidarity of the community extends across cities and house churches. Bruce Longenecker notes that this unit is a "chain-link interlock," an ancient rhetorical device that links separate units to each other.[31] Such accounts are linked by an overlap between separate units (Lucian, *How to Write History* 55; Quintilian, *Inst* 9.4.29). The link in Acts 11 sets up the transition from Peter to Paul as the key figure of the book. Longenecker notes that this section has been seen as either temporally contemporaneous or a flashback where the events of Acts 11 come after those of Acts 12.

4.3.9.4 D. Persecution in Jerusalem (Acts 12:1–23)

Herod intensifies the persecution in Jerusalem. James (brother of John) is slain and Peter is arrested. An angel rescues Peter after the community lifts Peter up in prayer.

---

31. Bruce Longenecker, "Lukan Aversion to Humps and Hollows: The Case of Acts 11:27–12:25," *NTS* 50 (2004): 185–204.

Peter comes to the Jerusalem church, tells the story of his rescue, asks that word be passed on to James, and departs. Herod executes the sentries who had held Peter and returns to Caesarea. Later in a speech as he points to his supplying food for Tyre and Sidon, Herod, dressed in royal robes, allows the crowd to treat him like a god. What followed was the judgment of the Lord—the death of Herod. So the persecutor comes to judgment.

4.3.9.5 E. Summary (Acts 12:24–25)

The word grows. Barnabas and Saul return to Antioch having delivered the relief to Jerusalem. John Mark is with them. The church in Jerusalem is under great pressure, but the believers continue to be faithful. As the gospel expands, other communities lend mutual support.

4.3.10 V. The Mission from Antioch and the Full Incorporation of Gentiles (Acts 13:1 – 15:35)

The move to incorporate Gentiles gets into full swing with the missionary journey of Barnabas and Paul (renamed from Saul). Starting in Cyprus, they move into areas of what is modern Turkey, encountering both acceptance and opposition. Paul becomes the lead speaker. John Mark also goes along, but he heads home when the pressure becomes too great. The issue of how to include the Gentiles leads to a meeting in Jerusalem, where Gentiles are not required to follow the law, but they are advised on certain practices they should avoid.

4.3.10.1 A. The First Missionary Journey (Acts 13:1 – 14:28)

The Spirit calls Barnabas and Saul into mission leading them to Cyprus. Here there is an encounter with a Jewish false prophet, Bar-Jesus, in Paphos. Their word of judgment leads to Bar-Jesus being struck blind, but the proconsul Sergius Paulus becomes a believer. These encounters point to the power of the Spirit in the face of opposition.

In Pisidian Antioch, Paul preaches a survey history of Israel, working from the patriarchs to David before skipping a thousand years to John the Baptist and Jesus as the fulfillment of promise about a Savior. The speech fits the style of exposition in the synagogue. According to John Bowker, this is like a proem homily, with word links presenting Deut 4:25–46 (*seder*), 2 Sam 7:6–16 (*haftorah*), and 1 Sam 13:14 LXX (proem text).[32] A proem homily contains an introductory text that links the other two liturgical readings into a sermon. Jesus' death also fulfilled God's plan, but God vindicated him in resurrection in fulfillment of Ps 2:7; Isa 55:3; and Ps 16:10. Forgiveness of sins comes to those who believe, freeing them from all that the law could not accomplish.

---

32. John Bowker, "Speeches in Acts: A Study in Proem and Yelammedenu Form," *NTS* 14 (1967–68): 96–111.

The attention the message draws leads to opposition from jealous Jews, so Paul and Barnabas turn to the Gentiles as their work continues to fulfill the call of the Servant to be light to the Gentiles and to bring salvation to the ends of the earth (Isa 49:6). Many believe, but persecution forces them on to Iconium, where the same pattern of belief and persecution arises. They leave there before a plot to stone them can be carried out.

Lystra is next. Here Paul heals a crippled man, mimicking the work of Jesus' ministry and that of the apostles in Jerusalem. The crowd thinks gods are in their midst, but Paul and Barnabas make it clear that they only seek to turn the people to the living God from such vain things; they note God's general care for them through creation. Persecution again arises and they go on to Derbe, where more become disciples. Then they return to the places they have been before returning to Antioch to report how God has opened the door of faith to Gentiles.

4.3.10.2 B. Consultation at Jerusalem (Acts 15:1–35).[33]

The demand is renewed that Gentiles must be circumcised, so leaders of the church gather in Jerusalem. Paul and Barnabas report on their ministry to Gentiles as they journey to Jerusalem. Discussion leads Peter to review what happened when Cornelius came to faith. Luke repeats key events to underscore them as he does here. Peter's key point is that inclusion of Gentiles without circumcision is something God did "by giving the Holy Spirit to them, just as he did to us. He did not discriminate between us and them, for he purified their hearts by faith" (Acts 15:8–9). Peter appeals not to add a yoke to Gentiles, but to recognize that salvation is through the grace of the Lord Jesus.

After Barnabas and Paul report on how Gentiles have been brought to faith, James speaks. He cites Amos 9:11–15 and notes that what Peter shared is what the prophets teach about God's visiting the Gentiles and taking out a people for his name. So Gentiles should not be troubled by legal requirements, but they should be urged to abstain from idols, unchastity, what is strangled, and blood. A letter to this effect goes out from the council to churches in Antioch, Syria, and Cilicia. The church in Antioch joyfully receives the letter.

So the outreach to Gentiles becomes established and the church continues to be strengthened.

4.3.11 VI. The Second and Third Missionary Journeys (Acts 15:36–21:16)

Two more journeys follow for Paul. They allow the church to reach from Asia Minor into what is now Europe. Again the pattern is preaching, acceptance, opposition, and then moving on. The opposition is both from Jews and from Gentiles, depend-

33. For a defense of the historicity of this key chapter and the issues tied to it, see my *Acts*, 442–48.

ing on the location. The positive response is mostly from Gentiles. In many locales, the message has a great impact on the city, as people either change the way they live because of their faith or oppose it for the changes it brings.

4.3.11.1 A. The Second Missionary Journey (Acts 15:36–18:23)

Paul and Barnabas separate because they cannot agree on taking John Mark again. So Barnabas takes Mark to Cyprus, while Paul strikes out with Silas. They travel initially to cities of the first journey, Derbe and Lystra. At Lystra Paul adds Timothy, who has parents of mixed ethnicity, and circumcises him.[34] By doing so, Paul opts not to place an obstacle in the way of the gospel and shows some sensitivity to Jewish concerns.

At this point, Paul receives a vision preventing him from heading into Asia and lands in Philippi, in Macedonia. There Paul brings Lydia, a worshiper of God, to faith. An exorcism of a demon-possessed girl, who was a source of revenue for her owners, leads to Paul and Silas's beating and arrest. Released by an earthquake, Paul leads his jailer to faith. The magistrates decide to release Paul and Silas, but Paul notes that they have beaten Roman citizens without a proper trial. Apologizing, they release the two missionaries.

They come next to Thessalonica. Paul preaches that Jesus is the Christ in the synagogue. Some Jews come to faith, as do many Greeks and some leading women. But again opposition arises, and Jason, a believer, is beaten. Paul and Silas are charged with acting against Caesar and turning the city upside down, so they move on.

In Berea, the preaching also meets with success. But some Jews from Thessalonica come and stir up crowds in opposition. Paul is sent away, leaving Silas and Timothy there.

Paul reaches Athens and speaks at the Areopagus about the care of God in creation and the need to repent because someone has been appointed judge of the living and the dead. When Paul gets to resurrection, the confusion stops the speech. A few listeners become believers.

In Corinth, Paul meets Priscilla and Aquila. In the synagogue Paul persuades many Jews and Greeks about Jesus. Silas and Timothy join him there. Opposition again arises, so Paul turns to the Gentiles. Titius Justus, a worshiper of God, and Crispus, a synagogue leader, come to the Lord. Directed by a vision, Paul stays in Corinth for a year and a half. Jews bring a charge before Gallio, proconsul of Achaia, of Paul's persuading people to worship contrary to the law. Gallio refuses to rule on a religious matter. But the hearing leads to a riot, and a Jew named Sosthenes is beaten. This scene shows that what Christians are doing is a matter of public religious dispute, but it is not in any violation of laws that threaten Rome or require

---

34. Some (e.g., Haenchen, *Acts*, 480–82) argue that Paul would not have circumcised Timothy as Luke describes, given his hard stand on Jewish practice in Galatians, but see responses in Marshall, *Acts*, 260, and Witherington, *Acts of the Apostles*, 474–75.

Roman attention. Paul returns to Syria after cutting his hair because of a vow he had taken, which again shows some loyalty to aspects of Jewish practice.

4.3.11.2 B. The Third Missionary Journey, Ending in Jerusalem (Acts 18:24–21:16)

The third journey leads not only into more mission along the pattern of the first two journeys, but also into a prediction of Paul's being bound in Jerusalem and placed into Gentile hands. This reflects the geographic progression of the book outlined in Acts 1:8. Paul says he is willing to face whatever God has in store for him. He shows himself to be an example of a faithful witness in the face of suffering and persecution.

The section begins with Apollos preaching in Ephesus and being instructed about the Spirit by Priscilla and Aquila. Paul also instructs some disciples of John the Baptist in Ephesus about the Spirit's having come. So Paul baptizes them with the Spirit, completing their transition into the Christian faith. Paul preaches in the synagogue and in the hall of Tyrannus, speaking about the kingdom of God. Opposition also arises, but Paul stays for two years. He performs healings there, but when some Jewish exorcists, the seven sons of Sceva, try to use Jesus' name, they experience a reaction from a demon-possessed man they try to heal and are beaten by him, with the note the demon did not recognize them. This causes the city to fear and many come to faith. Believers change how they live, burning their old books of magic. The act is not so much a protest against others as a public renunciation of the believers' former practice, since these books are not seized but are voluntarily destroyed.[35]

Paul resolves to travel through Macedonia and Asia, but before he leaves a riot breaks out in Ephesus. The makers of idols, the silversmiths, react to the impact of Christianity on their trade and begin to stir up the people in defense of Artemis and the religious trade that comes with her veneration in the city. Only the urging of the town clerk that the civil law be followed stops the riot from getting worse. This scene points to the impact of changed lives on the community and the counterreaction it created among those who do not believe.

Paul then travels through Macedonia and Greece as he planned. On a visit to Troas, he raises a boy, Eutychus, who falls to his death during Paul's long speech. The following spring Paul hurries back to Jerusalem, but stops in Miletus to address the Ephesian elders before he departs. He places them in change of the community and warns them to protect the church purchased with the precious blood of God's Son. That protection requires they keep an eye out for false teaching. Paul works his way back to Jerusalem through Caesarea, having been warned several times that he will meet opposition in Jerusalem. Agabus vividly warns Paul by using Paul's

---

35. On the practice of burning books, see Jer 36:20–27; 1 Macc 1:56; Suetonius, *Augustus* 31; Livy, *Hist. Rom.* 40.29; Diogenes Laertius, *Lives* 9.52; Lucian, *Alexander the False Prophet* 47; on the expression "Ephesian writings" for such works, see Plutarch, *Sym-* *posium* 7.5.4 [= *Moralia* 706E]; Witherington, *Acts of the Apostles,* 582; and Clint Arnold, *Ephesians — Power and Magic: The Concept of Power in Ephesians in the Light of Its Historical Setting* (SNTSMS; Cambridge: Cambridge Univ. Press, 1989).

girdle and belt to bind him and predicts Paul's being handed over to Gentiles. Paul is determined to move ahead anyway. So Paul reaches Jerusalem, as Acts transitions from Paul the missionary to Paul the defender of the faith and its mission as an expression of God's promises of old to Israel.

4.3.12 VII. The Arrest: The Message Is Defended and Reaches Rome (Acts 21:17 – 28:31)

Paul goes through a series of examinations to see if he is violating Roman law; these give him the opportunity to present his message before major ruling figures in Judea and in Rome. God protects him as he speaks by the Spirit, testifies to Jesus, and witnesses to the fact that "the Way" does not violate Roman law but merely seeks to declare that God has kept his promises of salvation and resurrection hope to Israel and the nations. The book ends with Paul declaring this message to anyone who visits him while he is under house arrest in Rome. The word of the gospel has reached the hub of the Roman empire, picturing its reaching to all the world.

4.3.12.1 A. In Jerusalem (Acts 21:17 – 23:35)

Paul visits James in Jerusalem. This leader of the Jerusalem church asks Paul to underwrite a vow for other believers and to show his respect for Jewish law, even as James reasserts the commitment not to make Gentiles keep the law and reaffirms the advice of the earlier Jerusalem council.[36] This Paul does, but some in the crowd thinks he has brought a Gentile into the temple, which causes a disturbance that Roman soldiers eventually quell. The Jews who stir up the crowd accuse Paul of teaching against the people, the law, and the temple.

When the arresting tribune mistakes Paul for a troublesome Egyptian, Paul defends himself before the people. He retells how he had persecuted "the Way" until the Lord appeared to him on a trip to Damascus and called him to be a witness. As Paul retells the story, he gets to the portion where he retells the call to go to the Gentiles; this causes the crowd to erupt in reaction. As in other texts in Luke-Acts, such as Jesus' rejection at his home synagogue, it is the mention of openness to Gentiles that produces an angry response from the crowd. The reconciliation that is inherent in the message of the kingdom produces a reaction from those who do not believe. The tribune takes Paul at this point and prepares to scourge him, only to have Paul raise the issue of his Roman citizenship and rights to a defense. That stops any beating. The tribune withdraws until the Jewish leadership can bring their official charges.

The progress of Paul to Rome in the midst of his arrest is a key example in Luke of divine providence, where what seems for ill results in good. Spencer calls this sections "the Prisoner's Progress," a solid title for what Luke portrays here.[37]

---

36. This is another scene that meets with much skepticism, given Paul's writings to the Galatians and his articulated view of the law. Still its historical character can be defended as being sensitive to the dominant Jewish context in Jerusalem in light of a text such as 1 Cor 9:12, see my *Acts*, 578 – 79; see also Roloff, *Acts*, 315; and Fitzmyer, *Acts of the Apostles*, 692.

37. F. Scott Spencer, *Journeying through Acts: A Literary-Cultural Reading* (Peabody, MA: Hendrickson, 2004), 212.

Paul defends himself before the Jewish council, saying he has a clear conscience. When the high priest orders Paul to be struck for saying this, Paul insults the high priest and then pleads ignorance of his office when he is challenged that such a response to the high priest is inappropriate. Again Paul shows respect for the law here, even citing it (Exod 22:27). Paul argues he is on trial for being a faithful Pharisee and believing in the resurrection. This divides the Pharisees and Sadducees in the meeting. They quibble among themselves since Sadducees denied resurrection while the Pharisees accepted it. Some Pharisees even defend Paul at this point.[38] The tension becomes so great that the tribune halts the meeting. The Lord appears to Paul, assuring him that he will testify for the Lord in Rome.

When Paul's nephew discovers a plot in place to trap and kill Paul as he is transferred, the tribune sends Paul on to Felix, the governor in Caesarea, in a surprise night escort. With him comes a letter to the governor explaining the situation as having an "accusation [that] had to do with questions about their law, but there was no charge that deserved death or imprisonment" (23:29). This is yet another Roman ruler indicating that what Paul has been doing is no political threat to Rome but is merely a Jewish religious dispute. So the case goes before Felix, who asks the Jewish leadership to come and make their case.

4.3.12.2 B. In Caesarea (Acts 24:1–26:32)

A series of Pauline defenses follow as the Roman rulers try to determine what to do about Paul and the new faith he represents. Tertullus, a lawyer representing the Jewish leadership, accuses Paul of being a "troublemaker," an agitator among the Jews and a member of the Nazarene sect. He also wrongly accuses him of profaning the temple. Paul's defense is to simply say he was worshiping at the temple, not disputing or stirring up anything in the city. He does confess to holding to the Way, but worships the God of their ancestors, believes the Law and the Prophets, hopes in God, and holds to the resurrection. He tries to keep a clean conscience before God and live right before other people. He was arrested while simply bringing alms to the temple in a state of ritual purity. As for other activities, he needs to be accused by Jews from Asia. So Paul claims innocence of the charges, and he is guilty only of holding to hope tied to the resurrection. Witherington notes that it also is possible that Luke had access to notes of this trial.[39]

Felix is uncertain how to proceed. So he engages Paul in private discussions, where Paul testifies to him about justice, self-control, and future judgment. Felix had hoped for a bribe to allow Paul to be released, but none comes. The portrait of Roman justice is mixed. The rulers sense he is innocent but do not release him. Some rulers also seek favors as they judge. When Felix is replaced, Festus inherits responsibility for Paul. Paul's core defense is that he is simply being a faithful Jew.

---

38. This scene is defended for its core historicity by Fitzmyer, *Acts of the Apostles*, 715. See also Sherwin-White, *Roman Society and Roman Law in the New Testament*, 54.

39. Witherington, *Acts of the Apostles*, 702. See also Winter and Clarke, eds., *The Book of Acts in Its Ancient Literary Setting*, 307–9.

Festus arranges a hearing for Paul before the Jews, refusing to transfer Paul and subject him to possible ambush. In this way, the protection of Rome is suggested in the context of God's providence. Paul's defense before Festus is like that before Felix. He has not sinned against the law, the temple, or Caesar. He is innocent no matter what the social context. When Festus asks if Paul should stand trial, Paul appeals to Caesar, a right he has as a Roman citizen. As Festus shares about the case with Herod Agrippa, he notes that "they did not charge him with any of the crimes I had expected. Instead, they had some points of dispute with him about their own religion and about a dead man named Jesus who Paul claimed was alive" (25:18–19). Agrippa asks to hear Paul, and so a hearing is scheduled. The testimony of Paul is reaching the highest levels of society in Judea.

On introducing the hearing, Festus declares that "I found he had done nothing deserving of death" (25:25). He wishes to compose a letter explaining the charge to Caesar and is seeking Agrippa's help in doing so, since he is not able to articulate the charges against Paul clearly. Again the judgment is that Paul is not lawbreaker or threat to Rome.

Paul uses this occasion to retell his transformation from persecutor to follower of Jesus. He says he is on trial for hope in the promise made to their ancestors, including the resurrection from the dead. He is simply obeying the heavenly call of the risen Jesus to bear witness to the risen one. To both Jew and Gentile, his divine assignment is to open their eyes so they may turn from darkness to light and from Satan to God, to receive forgiveness of sins and a place among those set apart for the name of God. So he has been obedient and has preached that everyone should repent, turn to God, and do work worthy of repentance. So Paul was arrested because he was keeping this calling.

Yet he continues to testify to God and teach what the prophets and Moses promised about the suffering and resurrection of the Christ while proclaiming light to Jews and Gentiles. Festus suggests that Paul is crazy, but Paul denies that conclusion and appeals to Agrippa to believe what has not taken place in a corner. In the end, these rulers conclude that "this man is not doing anything that deserves death or imprisonment" (Acts 26:31). Yet Paul's appeal to Caesar means he must sent on to Rome. This is the last judgment rendered about Paul in Acts. It underscores his innocence and portrays his continuing retention in jail as unjust, yet still as a part of God's will to bring the gospel to Rome. Caesar will hear Paul. The gospel will reach the highest locales in the empire. A movement that started in a far corner of the empire in Galilee has come a long way. One final, tough journey remains in our narrative as Paul takes to the sea to be taken to Rome.

4.3.12.3 C. The Long Sea Journey to Rome (Acts 27:1–28:16)

Two themes drive the sea voyage: (1) God's protection in getting Paul to Rome; and (2) a sense of how far away Rome is from Jerusalem.[40] Heaven is active in this

---

40. On the views tied to the historicity of the sea voyage and a defense of its likelihood, see my *Acts*, 649–51.

event. An angel assures Paul that he will get to Rome. Thus what the angel declares is God's will. So Paul has faith that God will do what he says (27:23–25). Paul, even though he is a prisoner, is shown to be competent and worth trusting as he guides and advises sailors and soldiers on the trip under this divine leading. By the time the trip ends, the centurion desires to save Paul. Indeed, things turn out as Paul says, for all survive the shipwreck.

In Malta, Paul survives a viper's bite, an event full of irony because it first looked as if having survived the dangerous sea voyage, he might fall to a similar fate elsewhere. Some of the islanders think when he is bitten that it shows he is guilty. But ideas can change quickly when circumstances go in a different direction! So when Paul survives, these polytheists think he is a god. Paul heals many on the island, so that when the travelers leave, provisions are given to them. Eventually they reach Rome with Paul kept under minimum guard. He has earned the trust of the Romans. He is no threat to anyone.

4.3.12.4 D. Visitors in Rome: The Gospel Preached (Acts 28:17–31)

Paul speaks to the Jewish leaders in Rome, declaring that "I have done nothing against our people or the customs of our ancestors" (28:17). It is for the "hope of Israel" that he is bound (28:20). The leaders note they have not heard anything about Paul, but they have heard about opposition to the movement he espouses. So Paul witnesses "to them from morning to evening, explaining about the kingdom of God, and from the Law and the Prophets he tried to persuade them about Jesus" (28:23). Some believe, but others do not. The scene closes with Paul noting the rebuke of Isa 6:9, that the people are dull of hearing and understanding. So the gospel is going to the Gentiles, who will hear.

The nature of this ending is debated, as will be treated in detail later. Is this a decisive rejection of Israel, or is it like in other locales, where there is a turn to the Gentiles, but mission to the Jews goes on in the subsequent city? The hope Luke has that one day Israel will turn (Luke 13:35: "until you say"; Acts 1:4–5; 3:18–22) speaks for an open ending here and the continuation of hope for Israel.

The scene recapitulates many elements in Luke-Acts.[41] God has led the way to Rome (1:8; 19:21; 23:11; 25:10–12; 27:24). The experience with the Jews there reflects the experience with Jews in the rest of the book: much rejection. The passage contains a summary of the entire trial sequence with Paul (chs. 21–26). Paul's innocence and suffering are like those of Jesus (Luke 23). The kingdom of God as fulfilled in Jesus according to the word of Scripture is the center of the proclamation. The call to all people to hear the message echoes themes in Luke 1–2. Paul's attitude fits with Rom 1:16 and his larger treatment in Rom 9–11.

---

41. A. Weiser, *Die Apostelgeschichte Kapitel 13–28* (Ökumenischer Taschenbuchkommentar zum Neuen Testament 5/2; Gütersloh: Mohn, 1985), 677–79.

The book closes with Paul speaking about the kingdom of God and the Lord Jesus Christ openly and unhindered for two years. The gospel has reached Rome. The program of God includes Gentiles by divine design. Theophilus can know that he belongs in this movement that had Jewish roots but is intended for all by divine promise and direction.

4.4 CONCLUSION

Luke-Acts reassures Theophilus and its readers. The program of God that has reached out in mission to Gentiles with salvation is part of his long-promised program. The key moves in Jesus' coming and the mission of the new community to Gentiles result from God's direction, fingerprints, and scriptural promise. Whether it be in Jesus' praising the faith of those outside of Israel, his direct call to Paul in making him a minister to Gentiles, or God's direction of Cornelius to Peter and Peter to the Gentile centurion, God has shown not only that has the long promised new era come with the Spirit sent by Jesus, but also that this promise extends by ancient divine design to the nations.

Luke-Acts is ultimately a book about God and his activity through Jesus, in whose name much in Acts takes place. As exemplary as many figures are in these books, the real heroes in these volumes are God, Jesus, and the Spirit. The focus of the theology is on them as the Father has sent the Son to give the Spirit to God's people to enable them to carry out their collective calling. In doing so, the people are equipped for a life of mission in honoring God. The community has taken the gospel into the world and evidenced reconciliation with God. They have also reflected the efforts at reconciliation between others that grows out of the gospel. In their response of repentance and faith, they turn to God in love for his grace and in love for their neighbor. Theology and values in life are inseparably connected in Luke-Acts. At the hub stands the activity of Jesus Christ and the divine attestation to him through his ministry depicted in Luke. In Jesus' resurrection-ascension to God's right hand, God shows the kingdom hope to be alive and well.

Part Two

MAJOR THEOLOGICAL THEMES

Chapter 5

THE PLAN, ACTIVITY, AND CHARACTER OF GOD: A SURVEY IN NARRATIVE ORDER

BIBLIOGRAPHY

Bachmann, Michael. "Jerusalem and Rome in Luke-Acts." Pp. 63–83 in *Luke and Empire*. Ed. David Rhoads, David Esterline, and Jae Won Lee. Princeton Theological Monographs. Eugene, OR: Pickwick, 2011. **Forbes, Greg W.** *The God of Old: The Role of the Lucan Parables in the Purpose of Luke's Gospel*. JSNTSup. Sheffield: Sheffield Academic Press, 2000. **Franklin, E.** "The Ascension and the Eschatology of Luke-Acts." *SJT* 23 (1970): 191–200. Idem. *Christ the Lord: A Study of the Purpose and Theology of Luke-Acts*. London: SPCK, 1975. **Green, Joel.** "God as Savior in the Acts of the Apostles." Pp. 83–106 in *Witness to the Gospel: The Theology of Acts*. Ed. I. Howard Marshall and David Peterson. Grand Rapids: Eerdmans, 1998. **Jervell, Jacob.** *The Theology of the Acts of the Apostles*. Cambridge: Cambridge University Press, 1996. **Kümmel, Werner Georg.** *Promise and Fulfillment*. Trans. Dorothea M. Barton. SBT. Naperville, IL: Allenson, 1957. **Marguerat, Daniel.** *The First Christian Historian: Writing the "Acts of the Apostles."* SNTSMS. Cambridge: Cambridge University Press, 2002. **Marshall, I. H.** *Luke: Historian and Theologian*. Grand Rapids: Zondervan, 1970. **Pokorný, P.** *Theologie der lukanishen Schriften*. Göttingen: VandenHoeck and Ruprecht, 1998. **Squires, John T.** *The Plan of God in Luke-Acts*. SNTSMS. Cambridge: Cambridge University Press, 1993.

God is the major actor in Luke-Acts. It is his program that brings the kingdom of God through Jesus Christ. This emphasis emerges in Luke 1:1 where he speaks of "the things that have been fulfilled among us" (τῶν πεπληροφορημένων ἐν ἡμῖν πραγμάτων, *tōn peplērophorēmenōn en hēmin pragmatōn*), pointing to a plan that God stands behind. Although the meaning of πεπληροφορημένων is disputed, the meaning "fulfilled" is best since Luke's emphasis in his volumes is the fulfillment of God's plan (1:20, 57; 2:6, 21–22; 4:21; 9:31; 21:22, 24; 24:44–47). This passive participle suggests God's acts with its use of the "theological" passive.[1]

These fulfilled events from the past continue to color how one should see the present. The effect of Jesus' life, death, and resurrection lives on. Luke will chronicle one of the immediate effects, the rise of the church, in his second volume. In Acts,

---

1. Marshall, *Gospel of Luke*, 41.

Luke makes the point that Jesus continues to work in the world as the exalted Lord (Acts 1:1–5).[2] In our look at God in Luke-Acts, this study will first proceed in a kind of narrative order through the two volumes before summarizing the results in a distinct chapter. This pattern of analysis uses two chapters for a topic for all our major categories, moving from literary order to a logical structure.

It is interesting to consider the use of the term God in Luke-Acts, especially in the nominative. God (ὁ θεός, *ho theos*) as a nominative appears seventy-two times in these two books, only twelve of which are in Luke. So God is a subject much more often in Acts. This difference may reflect the fact that Jesus acts for God so much in Luke's gospel, though the difference is striking.[3] Nevertheless, God's presence is prominent in both volumes as the narrative survey shows.

5.1 THE INFANCY MATERIAL ON GOD

Many of the major theological themes of the two volumes surface first in the infancy material of Luke. Those chapters have been called an overture to the two volumes, and they follow key narrative techniques for orienting the reader to Luke-Acts and presenting its theology.[4] Biblical narrative uses a variety of means to present its perspective. (1) It reviews or previews events. (2) It uses Scripture to work as commentary and reveal God's purpose. (3) God's purposes emerge through the direction of commissioned agents. (4) More commentary comes through reliable characters within the account.[5] Luke especially likes to use this last means for making theological points, doing little commenting as a narrator. Unlike Matthew's infancy material, where Matthew the narrator points to fulfillment of Scripture, Luke's characters themselves note the Scripture. So the fulfilled events both are a part of the story and receive comment from within the account.

Luke's infancy material utilizes all of these techniques. (1) The account is obviously a preview of Luke's gospel. (2) OT allusions dominate Luke 1–2. (3) Two key agents are revealed and commissioned: John the Baptist and Jesus (the role of each emerges in an announcement from Gabriel the archangel and through the hymns of Mary and Zechariah). (4) Additional testimony comes from Simeon and Anna, prophets of Jewish piety. All these characters comment on God's work that moves from John the Baptist to Jesus and the kingdom program he brings.

The infancy narrative's major goal is to give an overview of God's plan by showing the relationship of Jesus to John. John is the forerunner who announces fulfillment's approach, but Jesus is the fulfillment. In every way, Jesus is superior to John. John is born out of barrenness; Jesus is born of a virgin. John is great as a prophet before the Lord; Jesus is great as the promised Davidic ruler. John paves

2. Bock, *Luke 1:1–9:50*, 57.

3. In contrast, God as object (θεόν, *theon*) appears twenty-fives times in Luke and thirty times in Acts, a much more balanced distribution.

4. Bock, *Luke 1:1–9:50*, 69.

5. These four types of narrative technique appear in Tannehill, *Narrative Unity of Luke-Acts*, 1:20–21.

the way; Jesus is the Way. But God directs the action. He is the one who sends Gabriel to make the announcements about the divine program to Zechariah (Luke 1:19: ἀπεστάλην, *apestalēn*) and Mary (1:26: ἀπεστάλη, *apestalē*). The meaning of Gabriel's name is disputed. It means "man of God," "God has shown himself strong," or "God is my hero." But the name is not an issue for Luke, nor does the action of the narrative seem to suggest any significance for it.

Gabriel's career is tied biblically to eschatological events (in Dan 8:15–16; 9:21 he is the giver of the prophecy of the seventy weeks). Jewish tradition regards him as one of the more significant angels who served next to God. In that tradition, the number of angels who stand in God's presence varies from four to seven.[6] Because Gabriel has a major function in God's work and has direct access to him, the angel's message carries credibility.

As John Squires has shown, the sending of an angel is part of the providential activity of God that runs through the two volumes.[7] At the end of the infancy account, it is the must (δεῖ, *dei*) of the Father that causes Jesus to begin to go his own way and do the things the Father has called him to do (Luke 2:49).

The hymnic praise of the section, appearing in what Mary sings (Luke 1:46–55), Zechariah prophesies (1:68–79), and Simeon declares (2:28–32), also focuses on God and his actions. Mary praises God for his attention to the humble and the eschatological reversal that will bring down the proud and exalt those who fear God. The humble is an important category for Luke, pointing to those who will turn to God and rely on him. The Greek term for "humble state" (ταπείνωσις, *tapeinōsis*) as social-status terminology also has OT parallels to describe both Israel and individuals (Gen 29:32; Deut 26:7; 1 Sam 9:16; 2 Sam 16:12; 2 Kgs 14:26; Pss 9:13 [9:14 LXX]; 25:18 [24:18 LXX]; 31:7 [30:8 LXX]). This use also has parallels in Judaism (Jdt 6:19; 2 Esdr. [= 4 Ezra] 9:45).[8] Mary is able to praise God her Savior because he has looked upon her low social state and yet in love allowed her to bear the Messiah. What God did for her is like what he does for others in the same state (Luke 1:52).

Zechariah praises God for bringing an exalted horn from David's house to deliver his people as he overviews what John the Baptist and Jesus will do. Zechariah's praise begins by focusing on God's visitation in messianic redemption. The call to praise God for a specific act is the common introduction for a praise hymn. God is to be blessed, to be honored with praise. The language of the verse is that of OT national salvation, as the God of Israel is blessed in terms that are commonly used in the OT (Gen 9:26; 1 Sam 25:32; 1 Kgs 1:48; Pss 41:13 [41:14 MT]; 72:18; 89:52 [89:53 MT]; 106:48) and Judaism (Tob 3:11; *Pss. Sol.* 2:37). It is interesting that the parallel in 1 Kings is in David's blessing of Solomon, a decidedly regal and national context. The nationalistic blessing is also seen in the Qumranic escha-

---

6. *1 Enoch* 40.9 names four angels: Michael, Raphael, Gabriel (the angel of strength), and Phanuel (alternately called Uriel); *1 Enoch* 20 names these four as well as Saraqael, Raguel, and Suruel (Gabriel is described as caring for the garden of Eden and the cherubim). See also Tob 12:15. The early chapters of *1 Enoch* 6–10 name a myriad of angels with different roles and see many of them as contributing to the moral decline of humanity.

7. John Squires, *The Plan of God in Luke-Acts* (SNTSMS; Cambridge: Cambridge Univ. Press, 1993), 27–32.

8. John Nolland, *Luke 1–9:20* (WBC 35a; Dallas: Word, 1989), 69.

tological hymns (1QM 14.4; 1QH 5.20; 10.14). Such nationalistic features argue against reading these verses as containing only "transferred Christian significance" for Luke. The people in view here are the nation of Israel, as Luke 1:71–73 shows.

Simeon can be taken home to God in death because he has seen the Lord's Christ, the one God has sent. What follows is a hymn of prophetic praise to God for the joy of seeing the Messiah in fulfillment of God's Word. Simeon's reception of Jesus is intended to picture the arrival of messianic hope for Israel. The prophet represents the nation and, beyond that, all humanity. Simeon declares that he can now rest because in seeing Jesus, he has seen God's salvation. Simeon is like the watcher who can leave an assigned post because the anticipated event has come. The interesting feature of this verse is that seeing God's salvation is linked directly to seeing Jesus, so that a strong tie exists between salvation and the one who personifies it. This connection in turn relates to the idea of Israel's consolation in Luke 2:25. Fulfillment has come in Jesus, and so Simeon can die in peace.

The idea that the person of Jesus is at the center of soteriology is a keystone of Lucan Christology. With Jesus' birth, salvation comes. The idea of seeing God's salvation has OT echoes (Ps 98:2; Isa 40:5; 52:10; Luke 3:6; conceptually 1QH 5.12). The association of joy with seeing God's salvation appears again in Luke 10:23–24. For Luke, Messiah's coming is at the center of salvation (1:69; 2:11).[9] The mood of joy dominates the rest of the passage.

The hymns in Luke 1–2 are classic praise psalms in terms of their form. God is the subject. They focus on what God's program accomplishes through sending Jesus. Nothing shows this as clearly as the praise to God that the angels give when an unnamed angel[10] announces Jesus' birth to the shepherds in the fields near Bethlehem (2:11–14). One of the key themes of the portrait of God in Luke-Acts is the note of joy and praise that should come to the Most High for what he has done.

God as God is explicitly the grammatical subject of discussion in two key infancy texts. He is the one who gives the throne of David to the "Son of the Most High" (Luke 1:32–33). He also is the one who is praised for visiting Israel with redemption in this child who is the "horn of salvation" (1:69–74). A reference to God's visitation in 1:68 (ἐπεσκέψατο, *epeskepsato*) can refer either to a gracious act (Ps 8:4 [8:5 MT]) or to judgment (Jer 44:13). Here the reference is to God's gracious visit. The expression is common in contemporary Judaism (Wis 3:7; *Pss. Sol.* 3.11; 10.4; 11.6; 15.12; *T. Levi* 4.4; *T. Asher* 7.3; CD 1.7) and is also found in the OT (Gen 50:24–25; Exod 3:16; 4:31; 13:19; 30:12; Ruth 1:6; Pss 80:14 [80:15 MT]; 106:4; Isa 23:17). The phrase is important to Luke as a description of God's coming salvation in the Messiah Jesus (Luke 1:78; 7:16; 19:44; Acts 15:14). Within the hymn, the repetition of ἐπεσκέψατο (*epeskepsato*) in 1:68 and ἐπισκέψεται (*episkepsetai*) in 1:78 makes clear that God's visitation comes in Messiah's visitation. What that visitation

---

9. Heinz Schürmann. *Das Lukasevangelium: Kommentar zu Kap. 1.1–9.50* (HTKNT 3; Freiburg: Herder, 1969), 125, n. 203.

10. Unspecified angels of God also appear in Luke 12:8; 15:10; Acts 10:3; 27:23.

means for God's people is redemption. The rest of Luke's volumes will describe what this redemption looks like.

God is the object of praise in numerous texts in the infancy material. Mary praises her Lord and Savior (Luke 1:46–47). Zechariah blesses God when his mouth is opened again after his period of being muted, so Zechariah can learn that God will do what is declared (1:64). Mary also is told that nothing is impossible with God (1:37); her hymn of praise is the response. Angels praise God in the announcement of the birth (2:13–14). Simeon blesses God for bringing the child (2:28). Anna gives thanks to God for the arrival of the special child (2:38). The nature of God's program and the attributes of his care—his justice (1:51–55), mercy (1:78), and compassion in the face of faith (1:45)—emerge relationally through the events and reflections on how God acts within his program. Luke does not have a sterile God of isolated attributes but an engaging God who impresses himself on those who interact with him in life. This relational dimension of God stands out; he interacts with those he loves. Mary's note of praise is in response to her having found grace with God (1:30). Again God initiates and the believer responds.

So in the infancy material we are introduced to a God who is active in a program to bring deliverance to those who respond to him. His heavenly agents direct the steps of these key and unique events. Those impacted by those events contemplate what God is doing in their lives and respond humbly with praise and adoration and declare what God is doing. Thus the infancy material witnesses to God and his program, much as the witnesses of Acts will do later.

5.2 GOD IN LUKE'S PORTRAYAL OF THE MINISTRY OF JOHN THE BAPTIST

In the infancy material, we see providential direction through the use of agents and the use of Scripture to reveal God's plan. Another means Luke uses to describe God's plan is by the preaching of its content to others. Interestingly, this preached word about the program of God is often called "the word of God" in Luke (Luke 1:2; 5:1; 8:11). Today we are so used to the Word of God being Scripture that this oral word about God's program is hardly thought of in considering this term. But it is the predominant use in Luke.

So in Luke 3:2, the word of God comes to John the Baptist as he begins his ministry. The choice of ῥῆμα (*rhēma*) for the term "word" rather than λόγος (*logos*) has been taken in two ways. The term ῥῆμα suggests a particular message of God rather than the entire scope of his message, as λόγος would do. In addition, ῥῆμα is particularly Lucan in that nineteen of its twenty-six Synoptic uses are in Luke (and Luke-Acts together has thirty-three of sixty-eight NT uses). On the other hand,

---

11. Schürmann, *Lukasevangelium: Kommentar zu Kap. 1.1–9.50*, 152, nn. 36–37.

Schürmann relates ῥῆμα to the specific call to begin ministry, as the verbal parallelism to Jeremiah 1:1–4 suggests.[11] This latter sense gives specificity to ῥῆμα that is plausible here. God calls John to begin the ministry that was predicted for him. God's word again comes to pass.

John, in turn, preaches about the coming salvation of God (Luke 3:6). Here is a place where Luke as a narrator ties an OT text to an event. Normally in Luke it is the characters who introduce the scriptural ties. Not only does Luke appeal to Isa 40:3 as Mark and Matthew do concerning John the Baptist, but Luke also expands the citation through Isa 40:4–5. This allows the addition of the note that "all people" will see what God is doing in the program. This global element to the program was not as emphasized in the infancy material. It was hinted at in the generic reference to "those who fear him" in 1:50 and in the reference to God's people (τῷ λαῷ αὐτοῦ, tō laō autou) in 1:77. It was most directly expressed in 2:32 by Simeon, who declared that Jesus came as light and is "for revelation to the Gentiles."

The other aspect of God's work that John develops is the sovereign control God has over the program. In Luke 3:8, John warns that descent from Abraham does not automatically qualify one for blessing because God is able to make children of Abraham out of stones. This saying is tied to a section, shared with Matthew, where John discusses the coming wrath of God, a note of accountability with reference to divine judgment that sets a context for the call to repentance and the reception for the forgiveness of sins. This picture of cleansing shows the context for the coming of the program. Israel is in need of a spiritual washing. John sets the stage for it; Jesus executes it. However, there are consequences for a failure to respond. That note of judgment highlights the presentation of John's work and sets a context for Jesus' coming and Israel's need. Such need is extended to everyone in Acts. However, the context in Acts in the message to Gentiles is not a call about being faithful in covenant to the God of Abraham, but responding to God who is the Creator of all (Acts 14:15–17; 17:24–29).

5.3 GOD IN THE MINISTRY OF JESUS

Here I will distinguish between what Luke presents Jesus as teaching about God and what Luke says about God as characters react to events. How people relate to God is central in the presentation of God in these texts.

In Luke 1:35, Jesus is Son of God in a way distinct from John, who is merely a prophet of the Most High (1:76). The title "Son of God," rooted as it is in the unique birth of Jesus, points to a special and unique relationship to God.

However, that title is complex in Luke. Interestingly in 3:38, it is Adam who is presented as "the son of God," no doubt because God directly created him. The reference also explains why the genealogy of Jesus appears in Luke 3 versus the placement of a genealogy of Jesus at the start of Matthew's gospel. This allows Luke to juxtapose the genealogy to the temptation and make the point that Jesus was faithful to God, in contrast to Adam. Later Jesus will say those who are raised are "like the angels ... God's children" (20:36). This juxtaposition of the human sense of son and special sense of a more close, transcendent relationship with God reflects Luke's effort to indicate the tight heavenly connection between Jesus and God that also can impact others' identity when they associate with him and experience God's salvation.

Jesus' focus on allegiance to God is the highlight of the temptation accounts, where Jesus is likely to be seen as an example for disciples facing tests. In two of his replies to Satan, Jesus remarks that one should worship God (Luke 4:8), not test him (4:12). This focus on being faithful to God and giving him honor is a core Lucan theme in thinking about how Luke presents one's actions before God. Setting these tests in the context of Satan's question of Jesus' need to show he is Son of God adds to the significance of the scene. Despite being Son, Jesus relies on God. Indeed as a faithful Son, he relies on God. In the former, he shows his respect for the one Jesus will call "my Father" (10:21–22, five times; 22:30). In the second, he shows himself to be a superior Adam.

As we already noted, the term "God" appears less often in Luke than in Acts. Luke 5:25–26 may help to explain why. Here as Jesus heals the paralytic under a cloud of being charged with blasphemy for forgiving sins, which only God can do. When a healing takes place, the crowd reacts by glorifying God in amazement that such "strange things" (παράδοξα, paradoxa) have occurred.[12] For Luke, to see Jesus act is to be in the presence of God's power. The same reaction from the crowd reappears in 7:16 after the raising of the son of the widow from Nain. Another indication of this connection between what God does and what Jesus does appears in 8:39. Here Jesus tells the healed demoniac to report what God has done for him, but the healed man goes out to tell what Jesus did. Although some see this as a flawed response from the former demoniac, it is better in light of the Lucan backdrop to see that the man cannot speak of what God did without telling what Jesus did for him. The two work in conjunction for Luke (see 10:21–22).

It is in the midst of all this activity through Jesus that we get Luke's most prominent use of the term God in the genitive case: in the phrase "the kingdom of God" (τὴν βασιλείαν τοῦ θεοῦ, tēn basileian tou theou). In Luke 4:43, after some display of authority and healing, Jesus declares he must proclaim God's kingdom to other cities. This is the first of thirty-two uses of this phrase in Luke's gospel (6:2; 7:28; 8:1, 10; 9:2, 11, 27, 60, 62; 10:9, 11; 11:20; 13:18, 20, 28–29; 14:15; 16:16; 17:20 [2x], 21; 18:16–17, 24–25, 29; 19:11; 21:31; 22:16, 18; 23:51). Here program and person are bound together as Jesus acts on behalf of the program and proclaims its arrival in both word and deed. In the context of the introduction to this term, we see the idea that those sinners who respond to John the Baptist (and by implication the Jesus he points to) justify God and his program through them (7:29).

---

12. Interestingly, this term παράδοξα is the same term the first-century Jewish historian Josephus uses to describe Jesus' ministry as a miracle worker in *Ant.* 18.3.3 [63–64].

The kingdom's meaning in Luke is complex. It has both a present and a future element, and at any point either emphasis or both ideas together can appear, depending on the context. The kingdom is the topic not only of Jesus' preaching but also that of his disciples. The messages of the apostles, including Paul, involve the message of the kingdom (Luke 8:1, 10; 9:2; 10:9; Acts 8:12; 28:23, 31). The carryover of this term into Acts shows a key point of continuity between Jesus' message and the apostolic preaching. Some passages emphasize the kingdom's nearness or its having come (Luke 10:9, 11; 11:20; 12:32; 16:16; 17:20–21; 23:42–43), while others look to the total manifestation of that rule in what remains for Jesus to do (13:29; 21:31).

This "already/not yet" quality to the kingdom is like many other areas in NT theology, and one should not seek to remove either side of the tension. In the "already" period comes the demonstration of Jesus' authority over evil, his ability to deal with sin, and his reign at the right hand of God (Luke 10:9; 11:20; Acts 2:30–36). In the "not yet" period will come the total demonstration of that authority on earth and the fulfillment of all the promises made to Israel, as Acts 1:10–11 and 3:19–25 suggest.

Alongside the kingdom is the word of God about it. Jesus tells a variety of parables about this word of God (cf. Luke 8:11), while he calls his true family those who keep the word of God, which again for Luke refers to the word of the kingdom (8:21; repeated in 11:28).

Two confessions tying Jesus to God appear next. In Luke 8:28, the legion of demons refer to Jesus as Son of the Most High God, while in 9:20, Peter calls him the Christ of God. This reinforces the idea that to see Jesus is to see someone who uniquely represents God and has a role in God's kingdom rule. This is why the demoniac can report on God by reporting about what Jesus has done (8:39). This is also why Jesus' work of power leaves all astonished at the majesty of God (9:43).

This theme of glorifying or praising God for actions that come through Jesus is repeated consistently in the gospel (see Luke 13:13; 17:15; 18:43; 19:37). In 13:13, the woman's response at being healed stands in contrast to the synagogue leader's protest that a day other than the Sabbath should be reserved for healing. In the remaining three texts, it is Jesus' work in healing the ten lepers and the blind man, and his ministry in general, that leads to God's being glorified. When the Samaritan leper returns to thank God, Jesus notes that only he gave glory to God among the ten (17:18). In fact, glorifying God for his work through Jesus is the final note in the gospel as Jesus' ascension leads the disciples into praise (24:53). Thus, linking God's work through Jesus should lead to praise of the God who sent him and works through him.

At this point in Luke's gospel, the focus turns to Jesus' heading to Jerusalem. Here Jesus' teaching about God becomes more prominent as Jesus teaches his disciples in light of his approaching death and departure. Jesus also calls to others to respond to the program while there is still time to do so.

So Jesus calls on a particular scribe to reflect on what the Torah reads when he is asked about what one must do to inherit eternal life. The man replies that one must love God with all one's heart, soul, strength, and mind. Jesus commends the answer, saying that response leads to life (Luke 10:27–28). The subsequent parable of the good Samaritan shows that this response means that one's neighbor, even those whom one might not regard as a neighbor, is included in the way we love God. So just as the Ten Commandments deal with relating to God and to one's fellow human beings, so Jesus' teaching says that loving God will entail responding well to others. In a similar vein, Jesus rebukes the Pharisees for neglecting justice and the love of God (11:42). He also warns them that lack of responsiveness to God will cause them to slay the prophets and apostles whom the wisdom of God is about to send to them (11:49).

A second key area of teaching related to trusting God and relating well to others touches on issues of wealth. In the parable of the rich fool Jesus warns that judgment awaits those who are not rich toward God (Luke 12:21). This text also teaches that God is sovereign over the lives of people. No amount of money can take the place of being accountable to that God (12:20). In that parable, divine sovereignty and the need to be sensitive to it emerge in the sudden manner by which God takes the rich fool's life. Later Jesus will teach that one cannot serve both God and money (16:13), as he rebukes the Pharisees as lovers of money who exalt themselves before other people—a blasphemy to God (Luke 16:15).

God's care in a positive sense in a way that should lead to trust comes next, as Jesus shares how God cares for the flowers of the field and the birds of the air (Luke 12:24, 28; so also 12:6 of the sparrows). If God cares for them, the Father will care for his children and give them the kingdom (12:30, 32). These birds are ravens, unclean creatures (Lev 11:15; Deut 14:14). In antiquity, they were among the least respected of birds.[13] But God even cares for them. In these last two texts, God is called "your Father," and in the first text, the pronoun "your" is thrown forward for emphasis (ὑμῶν δὲ ὁ πατήρ, *hymōn de ho patēr*).

Respect for God's character is another issue on which Jesus offers teaching through the parable of the Pharisee and the tax collector. In commending the humble and nonpresumptive attitude of the tax collector, Jesus contrasts the different ways they approach God (Luke 18:11, 13). The Pharisee distorts the form of a praise psalm by thanking God that he is such a wonderful person rather than praising God. By contrast, the tax collector respects God's greatness and approaches the deity with humility. Jesus reinforces this idea in the next scene when he reminds the rich ruler that only God is good (18:19). He also tells the disciples that although it is impossible for a rich man on his own to enter the kingdom and be saved, what is impossible for humans God can do. That is, God can change a person's heart (18:27).

As we come into Jerusalem for the events of Jesus' Passion Week, references to

---

13. Joseph Fitzmyer, *The Gospel of Luke X–XXIV: Introduction, Translation and Notes* (AB; Garden City: Doubleday, 1985), 978.

God mostly recede, except at crucial points. Jesus distinguishes between rendering to Caesar what is his and rendering to God what belongs to him (Luke 20:25). This parries the insincere question where those who ask Jesus tell him they know that he teaches the way of God (20:21). Jesus also notes in the resurrection controversy how the raised righteous are like angels, being "children of the resurrection" (20:36). He also appeals to the God of Abraham, Isaac, and Jacob here, noting that these patriarchs must be alive for God to mention their names to Moses at the bush, since God is God of the living (20:37–38). Here we see a God sovereign over life again, having a sphere in which honor is due, and we also see God as having power over death.

The relationship of Jesus to God again comes to the center in the examination scene before the Jewish leadership (Luke 22:63–70). When Jesus proclaims that his audience will see "the Son of Man ... seated at the right hand of the mighty God," his examiners ask if Jesus is the Son of God. The christological implications of this exchange we will consider later, but in this crucial scene note how Luke focuses on the question of Jesus' close connection to God. God will share his presence and authority. That idea is reinforced in a summary on the road to Emmaus, where Jesus is described as powerful in work and word before God (24:19).

This relationship to God is also highlighted in the crucifixion scene. Here the believing thief on the cross rebukes his unbelieving counterpart by asking, "Don't you fear God?" (Luke 23:40). Just as Mary raised the theme of responding to God with fear (1:50), so here near the end of the gospel and during Jesus' death a note is struck that to fear God is to show respect for the one who is dying as part of the call of God. The point is further driven home a few verses later when the centurion declares, while praising God, "Surely this was a righteous man."

So, in Luke's gospel, God is presented as one who has a kingdom plan and program, which are intimately tied to Jesus. Glorifying God means appreciating what he is doing through Jesus. Beyond this, God deserves love, respect, and worship. The one who fears God and keeps the divinity's word about the gospel can anticipate blessing.

5.4 GOD IN ACTS

The expression of God's activity in Acts begins in the initial scene, where Jesus is about to ascend to heaven. In 1:3, Jesus teaches about the kingdom of God as he tells his followers to await the coming of the power of the Spirit for enablement in mission. This is the first of six references to the kingdom of God in Acts (8:12; 14:22; 19:8; 28:23, 31). For Luke, the idea summarizes a key component of the gospel (Luke 9:2, 6) that already had shown signs of arriving during Jesus' ministry (11:20; 17:21). His resurrection allows the kingdom to be preached (Acts 28:23, 31). From a literary point of view, the content or themes of what is meant here show up in the early speeches of Acts 2–4. So this remark in Acts 1 serves as a thematic introduction. The expression looks back to Luke 24:44–47 as well as forward to Acts 10:42 and 17:31.

Also here Jesus tells his followers that the Father has set the time of the return by his authority (Acts 1:7). Since "the Father" is an expression most often tied to Jesus' speech, this is the only time God is called Father in Acts. The opening scene shows that it is God's program and timing that are at work in the book. The expression οὐχ ὑμῶν ἐστιν γνῶναι (*ouch hymōn estin gnōnai*, "it is not for you to know") means that this matter is of no concern to them.[14] Barrett cites *Mekilta Exodus* 16.32 (59b): "No one knows ... when the kingdom of the house of David will be put back in its place, and when the evil kingdom will be wiped out."[15] This nicely summarizes an important Jewish view of the unknown timing of restoration and hope. But Jesus says more than this. Not only do people not know the time; it should not be a matter of great concern to them. One must be ready for Jesus' return whenever God decides to bring it.

At Pentecost, when the Spirit comes on Jesus' followers, the result is that the great acts of God are declared to the audience in a variety of languages (Acts 2:11). Peter explains the event appealing to Joel 2:28–32 (3:1–5 MT, LXX). God speaks here and promises that he will pour out the Spirit on all his people one day. Peter declares this fulfilled in events tied to "the last days." It is laid out in a this-is-that (τοῦτό ἐστιν, *touto estin*) form that is similar to what one sees in *pesher*-style interpretation found at Qumran (CD 10.16). The phrase appears seven times in the NT, twice in Luke-Acts (Luke 22:19 is at the Last Supper and has parallels in Matt 26:26; Mark 14:22, 26; also in John 6:29; 1 John 4:3). So its use for connecting Scripture in the NT is rare. This idiomatic expression serves to identify and connect two things.[16] Its role in Acts 2:11 connects what is said in Scripture with the explanation of the Pentecost event (see καὶ ἔσται, *kai estai*, in v. 17, which is a midrashic link using εἰμί, *eimi*). Peter connects his citation of Joel 2:28–32 with the events of Pentecost, calling them "the last days" (Isa 2:2 uses last-day language, the only place in the LXX the phrase ἐσχάταις ἡμέραις [*eschatais hēmerais*] appears). Again, God is directing what is taking place.

Not only is the activity of the Spirit ultimately a work of God, but so is the attestation of Jesus of Nazareth, as God was acting through Jesus attesting to him by mighty works, wonders, and signs (Acts 2:22). "Attested" (ἀποδεδειγμένον, *apodedeigmenon*) refers to something that can attest or "show forth the quality of an entity."[17] The term is rare in the NT, appearing only three other times: Acts 25:7; 1 Cor 4:9; and 2 Thess 2:4. The perfect form of the participle adds an air of permanence to the attestation. This divine attestation also includes the foreknowledge and plan of God that delivered up Jesus to death (Acts 2:23). But God's involvement did not stop there, for God also raised Jesus up from the dead to his right hand (2:24, 32–33). God, the one with power over life and death, is able to overcome death's grip and bring Jesus to life.

---

14. BDF §162.7.

15. C. K. Barrett, *A Critical and Exegetical Commentary on the Acts of the Apostles I: Preliminary Introduction and Commentary on Acts I–XIV* (ICC; Edinburgh: T&T Clark, 1994), 78.

16. BDAG 740 §1a.

17. BDAG 108 §2: "approved of God among you" in KJV; "attested to you by God" in NASB, RSV; "accredited by God to you" in NIV; "demonstrated to you to be from God" in NET.

By this means of exaltation to the right hand of God, God has made known to Israel that Jesus is "both Lord and Messiah" (Acts 2:36). This description of Jesus' position suggests an intimate connection between Jesus and the Father and an equality between them. God's vindication of Jesus is more than that he lives and others will be raised. It explains who Jesus is and how God showed him to be the Lord Messiah. The title "Lord" has its full, heavenly authority because of Jesus' position. Here is the core kerygma of the church, where God is seen as fully active. The speech explains why earlier in Luke's gospel there was such an intimate link between God's activity and what was happening through Jesus. This result is where it was all headed by divine design.

The Acts 2 speech is tied together through numerous word links, known as the *gezerah shewa* technique, which is repeatedly used throughout the speech (see vv. 17, 33 [poured out]; vv. 27, 31 [Hades]; vv. 21, 36 [Lord]; vv. 26, 31 [flesh]; vv. 27, 31 [abandoned]; vv. 27, 31 [corruption]; vv. 33, 34 [right hand]; vv. 21, 40 [save(d)]).

This program requires a response as the offer of the gift of the Spirit that enables life as a result of the forgiveness Jesus offers is called a promise God sends to those he calls (Acts 2:39). The Spirit's presence, however, surely invokes the new covenant (Isa 32:15; 44:3; Ezek 11:19; 36:26–27; 37:14; Joel 2:28–29 [3:1–2 MT, LXX]).[18] This promise is especially important for this Jewish audience and is what they need in light of their plight. The term ὑμῖν (*hymin*, for you) is thrown forward in the verse for emphasis and is a good example of a dative of advantage. The promise is also for their children (*Ps. Sol.* 8.33) and for those far off (Acts 13:33). Here promise and the hope of the divine plan as laid out in Scripture are linked to the activity of the Spirit.

Many join the community at this time, and as they gather together one of their responses is to praise God (Acts 2:47). God's activity generates joy, gratitude, and praise in his people. Praise is also the result of Peter and John's healing of a lame man, as both the man and the people praise God (3:8–9). As Peter explains where that power for healing comes from, once again it is the active God of promise who steps forward. It is the God of Abraham, Isaac, and Jacob, the God of their ancestors who glorified Jesus by raising him from the dead (3:13, 15). This tie of God to the patriarchs evokes a note of promise and the God of the nation.[19]

In almost a refrain, the term "God" appears four times in Greek text of Acts 3:13 alone. It is God, God, God, God who did this. God had foretold this program of the Messiah's suffering in the prophets (3:18). With repentance, it is God who will bring the times of refreshing and send the Christ, something else the prophets foretold as God revealed his plan through them (3:19–21). It was God who promised to raise up a prophet like Moses (3:22). It was God who set up the covenant with Abraham and the fathers promising to bless all the families of the earth (3:25). A blessing from God comes to those who turn from evil and embrace the raised servant God sent

---

18. Fitzmyer, *Acts of the Apostles,* 259, 266.

19. Exod 3:6, 15–16; 4:5; 1 Kgs 18:36; 1 Chr 29:18; Acts 7:32; Eighteen Benedictions 1: "Blessed are you, O Lord our God and God of our fathers, God of Abraham, God of Isaac, and God of Jacob." On the God of covenant promise, see Acts 3:25; 5:30; 7:32; 13:17, 32; 22:14; 26:6.

to Israel first (3:26). A day later as he explains the healing again, Peter repeats the key point: the man was healed through Jesus Christ of Nazareth, whom God had raised from the dead (4:10). Because God has acted and they live within his sight, Peter must obey God rather than people when ordered to stop preaching (4:19). The entire event leads the people to praise God. Here God's program and activity are inseparably linked to what Jesus is doing through his apostles, actions that also are in accordance with the Scriptures as the prophets also speak from God. The activity of God dominates this speech as he is responsible for the events that are taking place.

In the context of persecution, the community prays to God to ask the sovereign God to give them boldness (Acts 4:24, 29). It is God who stretches out his hand to heal through them and performs signs and wonders through his holy servant, Jesus (4:20). God acts and so does Jesus, as Luke presents a God who is linked insepara-bly to the one he sent. Their prayer is immediately answered, and they speak God's word. Again, this word is the preached message of the kingdom and its gospel (6:2, 7; 8:14; 11:1; 12:24; 13:5, 7, 44, 46, 49; 16:32; 17:13; 18:11). They deliver it with boldness. In sum, this prayer is an expression of complete dependence on God, a recognition of his sovereignty, a call for God's justice and oversight in the midst of opposition, for an enablement for mission, and for the working of his power to show that God is behind the preaching of the name of Jesus in healing and signs. If we ask what Luke desires our understanding and appreciation of God to produce, here is the community picture that should result. Here is what God's church, which he has established, should be.

But as good as things are, they are not perfect. Ananias and Sapphira lie to God and the Holy Spirit and suffer death as a result (Acts 5:3–4). Here God has knowl-edge of people's hearts and manifests the right to execute his discipline as he sees fit.

Persecution surfaces again with the arrest of Peter and John. An angel of the Lord releases them from prison. When they are challenged by the Jewish leadership not to speak about Jesus, again Peter says that they are to obey God, not people (Acts 5:29). To make the point Luke uses the divine "must" (δεῖ, *dei*). To disobey God to follow human beings is not an option for the faithful. God must be obeyed when it comes to sharing the word about Jesus. Ironically, Gamaliel says as much in Acts 5:38–39, warning his fellow Jewish leaders that if this movement is of human origin, it will fail; but if it is of God, it cannot be stopped. Luke expresses this in his own way as the two options carry distinct conditional constructions. The option about human beings is a third class condition; the option about God is a first class condition. This is Luke's way of saying that the new movement is of God, something his two volumes are also indicating.

The segment on Stephen highlights the word of God. His preached message about the kingdom is something the apostles should not neglect (Acts 6:2). It is meeting with success as the word of God is growing as people are responding to it (6:7). Although Stephen is said to be blaspheming the word of God by his opponents (6:11), his later welcome by the Son of Man at the right hand of God (7:55–56) is an indication the charge is false. In fact, Stephen's speech will be an appeal to Israel to understand what the word of God has shown about Israel's past and present unfaithful behavior before God. The divinely vindicated Jesus welcomes the vindicated Stephen, who has faithfully set forth God's word.

Stephen's speech also points to God's activity and faithfulness in Israel's history. God as the subject and actor in Israel's history dominates the speech. "The God of glory" appeared to Abraham (Acts 7:2). God took him to a new place and promised him an inheritance (7:4–5). God spoke a judgment against those who would enslave his descendants and gave the covenant of circumcision (7:6–8). God was with Joseph and rescued him, giving him favor and wisdom (7:9). When God was going to fulfill the promise of land made to Abraham (7:17), Moses was born, one beautiful before God (7:20). Moses wrongly understood that his brothers would appreciate that God was going to deliver them by his hand (7:25), but they resisted Moses' help. Forty years later God appeared to Moses at the bush as the God of Abraham, Isaac, and Jacob to commission Moses to deliver the nation (7:32). God sent this one as ruler and deliverer despite the rejection of the people (7:35). God led them out of Egypt with signs and wonders (7:36). Moses promised that God would raise a prophet like him for the people (7:37). When the people made idols as Moses received the living oracles, God gave them over to worship the hosts of heaven, something they did for generations (7:42). God directed the tabernacle be made (7:44). God thrust the nations out from the land (7:45). David enjoyed God's favor, and he wanted to build a habitation for him (7:46). But the Most High does not dwell in a building made with human hands for he sits over heaven and earth (7:48–50).

Despite all of this favorable divine activity, the people's response was poor. The repeated failure of the people to respond to God Stephen calls resisting the Holy Spirit (Acts 7:51). This indicates a close correlation between God's activity and the work of the Spirit, much as we have seen between God and Jesus. When Stephen is stoned, Jesus rises from the right hand of God to receive him (7:55–56). Just as God was active in all the events tied to Jesus in the gospel and early in Acts, the same is true of God's faithful involvement in Israel's history. Yet she failed to respond. Here is a major Lucan theme about God and Israel. God has been faithful, while the nation has been unfaithful and needs what God has supplied in Jesus.

The scene with Simon Magus is about God's not being manipulated. Simon Magus is introduced as one who had a reputation of having the power of God (Acts 8:10). He pictures what religion outside of the God of Israel can offer, which is nothing in comparison to what God brings through Jesus and the Spirit. Philip comes to Samaria and preaches to the Samaritans the good news of the kingdom of God (8:12). This passage again identifies the word of God with the word of the kingdom, making explicit what has been implicit in many passages in Acts. Any doubt about the link is removed in 8:14, for Samaria responds to Philip's message of the word of God (8:14). Simon Magus seeks to pay for the power of the Holy Spirit he sees present in Peter (8:18). Peter responds by telling Simon that his heart is not right before God (8:21). So in this scene, we again encounter the message about the kingdom being called the word of God, as well as its being made clear that God's gifts are a work of his grace and sovereignty, not available to a willing monetary bidder.

Interestingly, in the story of Saul's conversion, Jesus is the main actor. He is the one who appears both to Saul and Ananias (Acts 10:17). Saul is a chosen instrument of Jesus to carry his name before the Gentiles, kings, and Israel (9:15; see 9:27). Saul will also suffer for Jesus' name (9:16). This change in the common way of making God the subject is significant. It is another way in which Luke shows how linked the program of God is with Jesus. What Acts up to here has led us to expect to be said by and about God is now said by and about Jesus. This is why Saul can preach Jesus as Son of God after his meeting with the Risen One (9:20).

As inactive as God appears to be in Acts 9, he is busy in Acts 10–11 as he directs that the message be brought to Gentiles. In fact, as in chs. 2, 3, and 7, this scene has God directing just about everything. Cornelius is a God-fearing man (10:2), whose prayers to God (10:2) are heard. So God sends an angel of the Lord to him (10:3–4, 31). Meanwhile, God appears to Peter and gives him a vision where he calls unclean food clean (10:15; also 11:9). By doing this, God shows Peter that no person is unclean (10:28), and then instructs him to go to Cornelius. Once Peter arrives as a result of the divinely coordinated meeting, Cornelius notes that all are in the presence of God waiting to hear the message Peter brings (10:33).

In response Peter notes that God has taught him that he is no respecter of persons (Acts 10:34). He then goes on to talk about Jesus and how God anointed him with Spirit and power (10:38) and raised him on the third day (10:40). Beyond that, Jesus appeared to those whom God had appointed as witnesses (10:41). God has commanded Peter to preach to the people that this Jesus is one whom God ordained to be the judge of the living and the dead (10:42); he is also the one through whom forgiveness of sins comes when one believes through his name.

Before Peter can finish, the Holy Spirit comes down on the Gentiles present in Cornelius's household. This is a divine sign of acceptance, because the Spirit is described as "poured out" (ἐκκέχυται, ekkechytai) on them (Acts 10:45). This recalls the language of God's pouring out his Spirit in 2:17, so a divine act is present. In fact, in this chapter we see God, Jesus, and the Spirit all active. The Spirit's presence leads those in the room to praise God (10:46). Peter immediately understands what has taken place and notes that nothing can prevent them from being baptized since they have received the Spirit "just as we have" (10:47).

Commenting on this event when objections are raised later, Peter retells the story in Jerusalem of what God did. Gentiles had accepted the word of God (i.e., the preached word; Acts 11:1). God had shown him that what he had cleansed is clean (11:9). God gave the Gentiles the same gift he had given to earlier Jewish believers (11:17). How could he resist God (11:17)? So those present glorify God, acknowledging his work among the Gentiles that they too have been "granted repentance that leads to life" (11:18). Here Gentile inclusion is the direct work of God, a major point in Luke-Acts. This is why God is so active in these events; these actions have come at his direction as a part of his plan to bring together Jew and Gentile into one community. If anyone complains about Gentiles being included, their gripe is with God. This is reinforced when Barnabas goes to see the grace of God that involves Gentiles coming to faith in Antioch (11:23).

When James is killed and Peter arrested, the church responds as it did to pressure in Acts 4: it prays to God (12:5). God's direction and believers' access to God means prayer reflects a community of faith and dependence. People can be accountable to God. Herod gives a speech in which some say he has the voice of a god (12:22). But Luke notes that Herod did not give glory to God (12:23). The result is an instant judgment of death, something that recalls what was said in the parable of the rich fool ("this very night your life will be demanded from you," Luke 12:20). This is a speech that Josephus also recounts, noting that the crowd attested to Herod being more than a mere mortal (*Ant.* 19.8.2 [343–50] recounts the praise and Herod's immediate painful death, signaled by the portent of an owl seated on a rope; cf. also *Ant.* 18.6.7 [200]).

Neither Luke nor Josephus gives the speech's content, only the crowd's praise that compares Herod to a god (Acts: "the voice of a god"; Josephus: "superior to mortal nature"). The term for "god" in the Greek here is in a slightly emphatic location, preceding its noun (θεοῦ φωνή, *theou phōnē*). According to both Luke and Josephus, Herod accepts the praise, which is his downfall. Luke says that Herod did not give God the glory, and Josephus notes that he did not rebuke them or reject their "impious flattery." Josephus describes Herod's death as the result of a painful stomach condition, which lasted for five days. Accepting this kind of praise is rebuked in the Tosefta (*t. Soṭah* 7.16), the Talmud (*b. Soṭah* 41b), and the OT (Ezek 28:2, 6, 9). So his demise is typical for an enemy of God (2 Macc 8:4–10 [Antiochus Epiphanes]; Josephus, *Ant.* 17.6.5 [168–79] [Herod the Great]; *b. Giṭ.* 56b [Emperor Titus]).[20]

Despite the persecution and in the face of great secular power, God's word continues to grow (Acts 12:24). The preached word of the gospel is making an impact. The mission of Barnabas and Paul that follows shows this word of God preached with impact (13:5, 8). Again, the Lord judges, as Bar-Jesus tries to stop the hearing of the word of God (13:9). Here the word of God and the message about faith are juxtaposed. When that Jewish magician/false prophet is judged by the Lord with blindness, Sergius Paulus believes (13:10–11 with v. 12).

In the following scene at a synagogue in Pisidian Antioch, Paul gives an overview of Israel's history (a history that includes Jesus) to Jews and God-fearers (Acts 13:16, 26). Once again God is portrayed as active in the nation's history. God chose their ancestors (13:17). He gave them Saul as king (13:21). He also raised up a Savior from the seed of David according to promise (13:23). God fulfilled this promise to his children by raising up Jesus from the dead (13:33). In contrast to David, who announced the promise and performed God's purpose only to die and see corruption (13:36), the one whom God raised saw no corruption (13:37).

20. Jacob Jervell, *Die Apostelgeschichte* (Göttingen: Vandenhoeck & Ruprecht, 1998), 337.

On the following Sabbath, Paul preached again. When some responded, he persuaded them to remain in the grace of God (Acts 13:43). However, to those who refused the message, Paul and Barnabas noted that "we had to speak the word of God to you [Jews] first"; but in light of that rejection, they would take the message to Gentiles (13:46). Here we see the idea of the necessity of taking the gospel to the Jews first,[21] the idea of the preached word of the faith as God's word, and the idea of taking the message to Gentiles all in one context. Separate themes are now being brought together as the story proceeds.

Gentiles are becoming more central to the story as Acts moves along. So in Lystra, Paul and Barnabas call on the crowds to "turn from these worthless things to the living God, who made the heavens and the earth and the sea and everything in them" (Acts 14:15). Here the call is to leave the polytheism of the Greco-Roman culture and all the activity that comes with it to serve the one true God. Just as in 10:40–42, the stress in dialogue with Gentiles is on the sovereign Creator God, who has authority over life and creation.

As the missionaries conclude their first journey, they travel through the places where they have been and urge the followers that through many tribulations believers come into the kingdom of God (Acts 14:22). They return to Antioch, the place when they have been commended to the grace of God (14:26); they show that God's care of them had indeed taken place as they declare to the community in Antioch all "God has done through them" (14:27). God was active in Israel's history, and now he is active in the ministry of the new community.

At the Jerusalem council the leaders meet to discuss issues tied to Gentiles. The review of the ministry of Paul and Barnabas and Peter's experience with Cornelius leads into another declaration of God's activity. For Paul and Barnabas it was "everything that God had done through them" (Acts 15:4). For Peter it was God's choosing to bring the message to Gentiles through him (15:7). In light of God's initiative and direction, Peter challenges those raising concerns about how the Gentiles were included by asking if they are "try[ing] to test God" (15:10). In fact, God has visited (ἐπεσκέψατο, epeskepsato) the Gentiles to choose a people (λαόν, laon) for his name (15:14).

These two highlighted Greek terms are important for Luke. The idea of visiting was raised in Luke 1:68, 78 (see comments above), where God visited his people (Israel) with redemption (v. 68) and the light of messianic day (v. 78). When the widow of Nain's son is raised, God is said to have visited his people (7:16). In 19:44, Jesus weeps for Jerusalem because the nation has not known the time of the visitation. So the present text points to God's special action for his "people," now explicitly said to include Gentiles, something the following citation of Scripture from Amos 9:11–12 also affirms. So James concludes that Gentiles who turn to God should not be troubled (Acts 15:19).

---

21. This idea recalls Rom 1:16–17.

God's direction shows up next when he gives Paul a vision that takes him west to Macedonia to preach the gospel and not into Asia (Acts 16:10). This is one of several indications of God's direction, using the term for a vision to describe how God did it (on visions, using ὅραμα, *horama*, see 7:31; 9:10, 12; 10:3, 17, 19; 11:5; 12:9; 16:9, 10; 18:9).[22] The use of this distinct means here might suggest that the earlier prevention by the Spirit in 16:6 came not by a vision but by some other means. The multiple instances of direction by God underscore divine involvement in the journey's itinerary. God is engaged with his witnesses.

In Philippi, Paul meets Lydia, a worshiper of God (Acts 16:14). Luke is respectful of those who do not know the gospel but are open to God. In contrast, those who mock God are rebuked, as in a slave girl with divination who follows Paul and Silas and declares them to be "servants of the Most High God" (16:17). Although the remark is true, the way in which it is presented disturbs Paul enough that he reacts and performs an exorcism.

In the next scene in Philippi, Paul and Silas are singing hymns to God in prison when an earthquake comes to free them, an event clearly seen as an act of God (Acts 16:25). In Paul's subsequent exchange with the Philippian jailer, the guard comes to faith and is said to believe in God (16:34). So beyond agents or visions, events are also in God's control.

In Berea, Paul's preaching of the word of God brings a reaction from Jews in Thessalonica, leading to persecution when many accept Paul's message as they search the Scriptures (Acts 17:13). This sets up the fullest treatment of Paul's preaching to a purely Gentile audience in Athens. The descriptions of divine activity are full in this Athenian scene as they were earlier in speeches to Jewish audiences, but the appeal now is to the generic care of God in creation versus specific events of national deliverance. Paul's speech seeks to explain the "unknown God" (17:23). The starting point here, as it was in Lystra in a shortened version of the same kind of speech, is God as Creator, the one who made the world (17:24; cf. 14:15). This one is the Lord of heaven and earth (17:24). He is not served by human hands and does not live in a shrine, but gives life to all (17:24–25). His creation also made the boundaries for humanity (17:26). The goal was that people should seek God, for he is not far from us (17:27).

In one sense, because God is Creator, all are God's children (Acts 17:28). As a result, we should not think deity is like gold, silver, stone, or any representation of him coming from our imagination (17:29). Paul is taking on idolatry and polytheism here. The Greeks shared this idea of deity as independent (Aristobulus, frg. 4; Euripides, *Heracles* 1345–46, "God ... is in need of nothing"). Wikenhauser has several citations for verses 25–27 from Jewish and Greco-Roman sources and notes that the themes Paul uses in describing God do not reflect the silent divinity of the

---

22. Visions are also often mentioned in Greek contexts. See Herodotus, *Hist.* 7.12; Philostratus, *Life Apoll.* 4.34; Pseudo-Callisthenes, *Life of Alexander of Macedon* 1.35; Weiser, *Apostelge-* *schichte Kapitel 13–28*, 412–15, notes eight examples from Greek and Jewish writers extending into the second century AD.

23. Wikenhauser, *Apostelgeschichte*, 203–5.

Stoics.[23] The ideas are rooted in Judaism, even as they touch on ideas also expressed in some circles of Greek culture. Polhill argues that "every statement Paul made was rooted in Old Testament thought" and that this is not the immanent God of philosophy but a God who works in creation.[24]

Paul then turns to the response. This kind of ignorance God overlooked in the past (Acts 17:30). Now he calls on all human beings to repent (17:30), because he has fixed a day in which he will judge the world in righteousness by a man he appointed (17:31). So the program of the singular, sovereign Creator God extends to all nations. He calls on all people to respond to him because of an authority he shares with Jesus, whom God raised from the dead as an indication of Jesus' importance (17:31). Paul never gets to the full presentation of the gospel because the resurrection leads to discussion, but Luke in this speech gives a kind of prolegomena for how to present God to someone who lacks background about the one true God. As Paul does so, God and Jesus are again inseparably linked in the program and in the declaration of shared authority.

In Corinth, we meet another worshiper of God, Titius Justus, who is the first Gentile to whom Paul turns there (Acts 18:7). Paul spends a year and six months in Corinth, teaching God's word, this kingdom message (18:11). Some raise objections that Paul teaches people to worship God contrary to the law (18:13). This is a complaint the Roman proconsul Gallio sees as none of his business. The scenes in the latter part of Acts more consistently note the persecution and contention about the kingdom message and the inclusion of Gentiles in it.

Paul seeks a ministry that is directed by God's will, so when he is asked to remain longer at Ephesus, his reply is that he will return to them if God wills (Acts 18:21). In ch. 19, Paul is back in Ephesus. Meanwhile, before he gets there, Priscilla and Aquila explain the way of God to Apollos more accurately, by noting the availability of God's Spirit (18:26).[25] When Paul returns to Ephesus, God does miracles through his hands (19:11). When charges are raised against Paul about disrespect to Artemis, one person stands up to note that Paul has not blasphemed the goddess (19:37). Paul may preach the message of God, but he does so without directly disrespecting other gods. He allows God's message itself to make his case.

From this point on in Acts, with a few exceptions, direct references to God become less frequent. This is because Luke's attention shifts to Paul's defense of his ministry, and there is less ministry activity presented. One of these exceptions is Paul's last ministry speech to the Ephesian elders, where he notes that he testified to both Jews and Greeks of repentance to God and faith in our Lord Jesus Christ (20:21). His goal has only been to accomplish the course God has given him. His call was to testify to the grace of God (20:24). He has done this in Ephesus, announcing the whole purpose of God (20:27). The elders are now to shepherd the church of God, obtained with the blood of God's own Son (20:28). Again the

---

24. Polhill, *Acts*, 373.
25. There is a text-critical problem here, but the likelihood is that the reference to God is present because of the manuscripts that read the term, including $\mathfrak{p}^{74}$, $\aleph$, and B.

program involves a link between God and the Son. At the end of this speech, Paul entrusts these leaders to God (20:32).

The meeting with James and Paul also brings up God. When Paul reports the things God has done among the Gentiles through his ministry, James and his company glorify God (Acts 20:21). Here Luke shows that the various key segments of the church are one in terms of embracing God's plan to include the Gentiles.

In his first defense, Paul describes himself as having been zealous for God in persecuting what he calls the Way (Acts 22:3). By noting his zeal for the law, Paul indicates that at one time his attitude was like that of the crowd, implying that he understands what is motivating them (zeal: Ps 69:9; 1 Macc 2:26–27, 58; Jdt 9:4). He also notes how God chose him to know God's will, see the "Righteous One" (Jesus), hear Jesus' voice, and be a witness for him (Acts 22:14). Again, God and the program tied to Jesus are closely linked.

The incident with the high priest of God shows the tension between the two sides. When Paul says he has a clear conscience before God (Acts 23:1), the high priest orders Paul to be slapped. Paul invokes God, saying, "God will strike you, you whitewashed wall" (23:3). This leads those around him to charge him with reviling God's high priest (23:4). Paul steps back when he is reminded this is the high priest, noting one should not "speak evil about the ruler of your people" (see Exod 22:28 [22:27 LXX]). Paul's remark about not knowing the high priest is either ironic, suggesting he does not deserve to lead the people, or rhetorical in suggesting that Paul acted hastily without respect to his position.[26] This scene shows the respect each side is vying for when it comes to who represents God.

Paul's defense before Felix leads him to affirm that he serves "the God of our ancestors" (Acts 24:14) and is on trial for having hope in God associated with a resurrection of the just and unjust, as well as having a clear conscience before God (24:15–16). Paul is innocent in serving God and honoring him. However, Paul also notes how he identifies with his accusers by observing that he is merely believing the promise made to their ancestors by God. A key contention of Luke is that this faith in Jesus is connected to promises of old made to Israel.

Paul's defense before Agrippa goes in a similar direction. Paul notes how he stands on the promises made to the ancestors (Acts 26:6) and that it should not be thought incredible that God raises the dead (26:8). After retelling the story of his Damascus road experience with Jesus, Paul notes that his call was to open the eyes of the people and Gentiles so they may turn from darkness to light and from Satan to God (26:18). So he went and preached to all that they should repent and turn to God (26:20). And he has been able to do this because he has the help that comes from God (26:22). Again, God's direction and support of Paul are the point. When Agrippa responds that Paul is trying to make him a Christian soon, Paul replies that he wishes before God that all who hear him might become as he is except for his chains (26:29).

---

26. For discussion of this interpretive issue, see my *Acts*, 601–2.

Another key cluster of references to God comes in the sea voyage. Here God gives direction through an angelic appearance to Paul. This angel Paul describes as associated with the God to whom Paul belongs and whom he worships (Acts 27:23), and God will deliver all who travel with him (27:24). So Paul encourages the men that his faith in God assures him it will be as he was told (27:25). God's word revealed to his chosen vessel will come to pass. Later Paul urges them to eat, so he takes the food and gives thanks to God (27:35). Here God's protection and guidance are stressed as the long dangerous journey to Rome takes place, with Paul eventually getting to Rome as was promised.

One of the last obstacles Paul faces on that journey is being bitten by a snake in Malta. When he survives it, the people think he might be a god, something Paul has to correct them about (Acts 28:6). When Paul arrives at Three Taverns near Rome, he gives thanks to God as he gains courage from seeing fellow believers there (28:15). The feel of the entire journey is that God has watched over and protected Paul. God's providence directs the events of his servants.

The final reference to God in Acts takes place as Paul announces that the salvation of God has been sent to the Gentiles, who will listen (Acts 28:28). This is a solid round off because the first references to God in Luke-Acts came to announce the program of God through John the Baptist and Jesus. The book ends affirming the Gentile mission that Luke-Acts has sought in part to affirm and defend.

5.5 CONCLUSION

In this narrative survey of the references to God, we have seen how he is the major actor in Luke-Acts. His program guides. At key points, he acts in the new community, just as he has acted throughout the centuries in Israel's history. In Jesus' ministry, the raising of Jesus, and the direction of those who follow him in the new community this role is particularly evident. God uses a wide array of means to bring the plan to fruition. He uses agents, creation, Scripture, events (both good and bad), and visions. In our next chapter we pull all of this together in a more synthetic way. Yet walking through the story of Luke-Acts for seeing what it tells us about God in sequence is revealing. It shows a God of promise and grace, who seeks out people and offers them life. All they need do is respond to the program so inseparably linked to Jesus and what Luke loves to call "the word of God."

Chapter 6

THE GOD OF PROMISE, FULFILLMENT, AND SALVATION: SYNTHESIS OF TEXTS ON THE PLAN OF GOD

BIBLIOGRAPHY

See chapter 5.

In the present chapter, we synthesize Luke's presentation of God in Luke-Acts.[1] God is directing Israel's story of promise to be a blessing to the world. The seemingly new faith is really quite old since salvation is the product of a plan and promise that have come to fulfillment in Jesus. He is bringing in the promised new era of God's kingdom rule.

God in Luke-Acts is the God of Israel (Luke 1:68; 20:37; Acts 13:17), who has extended himself to the nations.[2] He is the God of the patriarchs (Acts 3:13; 5:30; 7:32; 22:14; 24:14) — of Abraham, Isaac, and Jacob (Acts 3:13; 7:32; cf. 7:46). The connection back to the patriarchs invokes the God of promise. Israel's history pointing to Messiah is light, a revelation for the nations and glory for Israel (Luke 2:32).

Luke 2:32 is an important passage regarding this hope. Solving a grammatical problem will determine the text's meaning. Most commentators see φῶς (*phōs*, "light") and δόξαν (*doxan*, "glory") in parallel and both in apposition to "salvation" in 2:30.[3] If this view of the syntax is adopted, then the idea is that salvation is a light to Gentiles, while it is glory to Israel. In support of this view, one can argue that glory and light are paired in parallelism in the OT (Isa 60:1–3), and either term is associated with God's salvation in the OT (Isa 49:6; 51:4–5; 42:6). The tenor of Luke is regarded as supporting this view (Acts 13:47). In addition, the alternative syntax (see below) requires the addition of certain terms to clearly express its sense.

A second approach to Luke 2:32 argues that ἀποκάλυψιν (*apokalypsin*, "revelation") and δόξαν are parallel and both are in apposition to φῶς, which in turn refers back to salvation in 2:30.[4] If this view is accepted, then salvation is described as light for all people, but in particular it is revelation to the Gentiles and glory for Israel.

---

1. This chapter represents an updating of my work on the view of Luke-Acts about God presented in *A Biblical Theology of the New Testament* (ed. Roy B. Zuck and Darrell L. Bock; Chicago; Moody Press, 1994), 88–102.

2. Jacob Jervell, *The Theology of the Acts of the Apostles* (Cam-

bridge: Cambridge Univ. Press, 1996), 18–25, stresses this point.

3. Schürmann, *Lukasevangelium: Kommentar zu Kap. 1.1–9.50*, 126, n. 209; NASB, NKJV, HCSB, NLT, NRSV.

4. Fitzmyer, *Gospel of Luke I–IX*, 428; TEV, RSV, NIV, NET, *Neu Luther*.

In support, it can be argued that in Isa 60:1–3 the relationship between light and glory is one of cause and effect. Israel receives the light of salvation and thus can be called God's glory, so that the two concepts are distinct, with glory tied to Israel. In addition, 1:78–79 describes Messiah as a light that comes to the nation. Light comes; revelation and glory result. Further, in Acts 26:22–23 the light is portrayed as coming to both Jews and Gentiles. Thus, it is a fundamental characteristic of salvation that it is light for all people, not light just for a particular group. These arguments seem to favor slightly this second view, which would be translated "light, for revelation to the Gentiles and for the glory of your people Israel."

Light suggests the coming of illumination into a place of darkness (Luke 1:79). It is a frequent NT image of Jesus and his task (Acts 13:47; cf. Matt 4:16; 5:14; John 1:7; 12:35, 46; 2 Cor 4:6). In rabbinic Judaism, especially in the midrashim, the image of Messiah as light was also frequent (Str-B, 1:161–62).

Light as illumination means this light is revelation for the Gentiles. Though in this type of noun-genitive construction (ἀποκάλυψιν ἐθνῶν, lit., "revelation of Gentiles") the genitive word often gives the source of the revelation, in this context it is clear that the Gentiles are portrayed as recipients of the revelation. God's revelation dwells in a person, an idea that implies some of what John says explicitly when he calls Jesus the Word. Old Testament ideas abound. Some passages suggest that the Gentiles are passive observers of this process, while others see them participating (passive: Isa 49:6; 52:10; Ps 98:2; participating: Isa 42:6–7; esp. Zech 2:10–11 [2:14–15 MT]). Intertestamental literature also expressed this idea in both forms (passive: Bar 4:24; participating: *Pss. Sol.* 17.31). The rest of Luke's gospel and Acts reveal that Gentiles participate as equals (esp. Acts 10–11; 15; also Eph 2:11–22; 3:3–6). Jesus as light brings salvation to all humanity, illuminating them into God's way.[5]

The hope of Israel is the hope of the world (Luke 2:29; Acts 2:39; 3:25; 13:47; 28:25). Those faithful to Israel will respond to the one God has sent as Messiah and will become a part of the community of God's people that now is becoming the church (Acts 15:14–17).

6.1 GOD'S PLAN OF SALVATION: THE GOD OF DESIGN AND CONCERN

At the beginning of his two volumes, Luke emphasizes that God has made promises. The material on the birth of Jesus in Luke 1–2 makes clear that God is carrying out a plan according to his promise and that he will deliver his people. What happens to the scope of his people in the two volumes is one of the key ideas of Luke-Acts, as now more than Israel comes into view as the gospel goes out into the world.

Luke 1:14–17 describes the mission of John the Baptist as Jesus' forerunner; John

---

5. Marshall, *Gospel of Luke*, 121; Bock, *Luke 1:1–9:50*, 244–45.

is the one who comes in the spirit of Elijah to reconcile fathers and children to the way of God. John is to produce a "people prepared for the Lord" (1:17). The roots of this idea come from texts like Mal 3:1; 4:5 and Sir 48:10. A prepared people is rooted in hope coming from Isaiah, especially the idea of a preparation for the Lord in Isa 40:3 and the idea of a prepared people in 43:7. Where as Isaiah spoke of people preparing themselves for the Lord, Luke speaks of a people prepared for God. Those who respond to John and to the one following him are ready for God and his promise.

Luke 1:17 is another important text. As just noted, the idea of a prepared people comes from Isa 43:7. With its reference to the preparation of Israel for the coming of the Lord, Isa 43 serves to complement Isa 40 and refers to the elect status of the nation of Israel, a people whom God prepared. But perhaps more relevant is 2 Sam 7:24, where the context is the Davidic covenant and hope. Here the Lord speaks of an "established" people, a nation whom God has called to himself. The Samuel and Isaiah passages stress that "a prepared people" is a special people whom God has drawn to himself for his own purposes. In light of the Davidic emphasis in Luke 1:31–35, it is probable that this wording is alluded to here.[6]

So John's ministry in Luke 1:17 is heavily influenced by OT ideas. John calls out of Israel a prepared and responding group of people who are ready to follow the Lord's way of salvation. This description of a "prepared people" has a "remnant" tone to it. God prepares a responding remnant, which is called out from the nation. The call to reform and the creation of a prepared remnant people summarize the basic ministry of John the Baptist. In his Elijah-like ministry, he establishes his "great" position before the Lord and brings joy to many in Israel. From it emerges a people who are ready for God's salvation.[7]

Remarks in the hymns of Luke 1 are important to the portrait of God. Luke 1:31–35 describe Jesus as the promised Son and Messiah. He will sit on David's throne and rule over Israel. Verses 54–55 show that these events of mercy are grounded on God's promises made to Abraham. God's covenant mercy and loyal love are for his people Israel. God will support the nation. Ἀντελάβετο (*antelabeto*) means to "take hold of, to hold up, to support" (Isa 41:8–10; 42:1; Sir 2:6; Acts 20:3). So we are telling God's story for Israel on behalf of the world.

Verses 68–75 speak of the raising up of "a horn of salvation" out of the house of David as promised by the prophets. God's acts and his Scriptures reveal the program. Jesus' task is to deliver God's people from their enemies, so that they might serve him without fear in holiness and righteousness. This is what being a prepared people means—people of faith who are ready to serve God in fearful reverence. Also mentioned in this passage is God's promise to Israel's patriarchs. We are also seeing how the hymns of the infancy material present the theology of the events. Here the word supports and explains event.

Luke 2:34 states that Jesus will bring division in Israel. Thus the infancy material introduces God's plan and various elements in it. Jesus is the one who is set for

---

6. Fitzmyer, *Gospel of Luke I–IX*, 327.   7. Bock, *Luke 1:1–9:50*, 90–91.

"the falling and rising of many in Israel," and he is a sign. The first image in this verse is drawn from passages in Isaiah, where God is portrayed as setting up a stone of stumbling over which some fall (Isa 8:14–15), a precious cornerstone that will not disappoint those who trust in it (28:13–16, esp. v. 16). The use of these texts is common in the NT (Rom 9:33; 1 Pet 2:6–8; cf. Luke 20:17–18). The image of a figure of division or of a figure who causes falling and rising was also used at Qumran (1QH 2.8–10; 1QM 14.10–11).

The infancy material does not relate the parts of the plan in detail to each other; rather, it displays them as an overture in a symphony or opera might do for a piece of music. There is a melody here and another melody there. Pieces are put together as the narrative proceeds. The key theme is that God fulfills his promises in Jesus. God is a God of design and concern. He also is a God of his word, who keeps his promises. This emphasis testifies to his faithfulness.

Luke-Acts presents God explicitly and implicitly in the words of the gospel's characters. They function as witnesses to him and his acts. God guides, predicts, directs, acts, redirects, or explains his program. Witnesses appear in situations where they are free to speak and are Spirit-enabled (Luke 1:67; 2:25; Acts 2:17). Dreams, visions, and theophanies are key means by which direction comes (see below). The "plan" is said to be present in the Scriptures, usually expressed in generic terms (Luke 24:43–47), but sometimes in specific texts on a given theme (Acts 2 and the use of Joel 3:1–5; Pss 16:8–11; 132:11; 100:1, respectively). Luke uses these means to present his view of God far more often than he presents it through narrative remarks from a narrator. Often it is the act that precedes the word, as in the infancy material births. What God is doing is announced and takes place. Then the characters' responses develop what it means. In other words, the events gain their meaning and God is revealed to act.[8]

Acts reinforces this picture of a faithful God of promise. Acts 2:17–21 speaks of God's pouring out the Holy Spirit as a fulfillment of his promise about the last days. Here Joel 3:1–5 forms the basis of the explanation and the core of the speech. However, there is help from other texts to fill out the portrait of what Pentecost means. So Peter refers to texts promising resurrection (Ps 16:8–11), a seed to sit on a divinely appointed throne to rule (Ps 132:11), and the hope of vindication and a place at God's right hand (Ps 110:1). Acts 2:38–40 makes the point that forgiveness of sins and the Holy Spirit are available to those who respond to God's call. Acts 2:38 has three basic parts: (1) "repent"; (2) "be baptized, every one of you, in the name of Jesus Christ for forgiveness of your sins"; and (3) "you will receive the gift of the Holy Spirit" (like 2:33, where we have an epexegetical genitive, so the Spirit is the gift).

The person who turns toward God calls on the name of the Lord by being baptized "in the name of Jesus Christ" (Acts 2:38). This phrase reflects the language

---

8. This point is made about Acts by Marguerat, *First Christian Historian,* 85–108.

of the speech in 2:21, "call[ing] on the name of the Lord [to] be saved." So Peter's remarks in 2:38 draw on what he has already proclaimed in Acts 2. The rite is not magical but pictures what repentance is asking God to do, to give forgiveness (5:31; 10:43; 13:38; 26:18). To agree to baptism is to affirm in a public act what the heart has already done to come into relationship with God. "Baptism is a natural part of the much more important conversion" and a "self-evident expression of conversion."[9] Thus, baptism represents the cleansing that belongs to salvation. This washing signifies the forgiveness of sins that Jesus brings and the emergence into a new, clean life with fresh enablement that his work provides (Rom 6:1–11). Peter calls for each person to be baptized in order to express a personal, visible turning to God.

Other speeches add to the picture of God and his activity through Jesus. Acts 3:22–26 indicates that Jesus is the promised Prophet like Moses who must be heeded (Deut 18:15). Acts 13:22–33 portrays Jesus as the promised Savior descended from David. Here the appeal is both to the hope of Scripture and the teaching of a greater one than John the Baptist. In this text, Scripture interacts with events tied to Jesus to explain what is taking place. This is how God reveals himself. Acts 23:4–8 speaks of Paul on trial for the hope of the promise of resurrection. Acts 26:22–23 argues that the Prophets and Moses testified of Christ and his subsequent mission. In the middle of Luke-Acts stands Luke 24:44–49, with the same theme. Jesus' death and resurrection and the church's message of repentance and the forgiveness of sins to everyone reflect OT promise. So also the promise of the Spirit is the "Father's promise."

God is graciously at work to save a people for himself. The plan is full of detail: a forerunner, the Messiah, fulfillment of promises to Israel, the execution of a plan revealed in the prophets, the inclusion of the Gentiles, and division in Israel.

Enhancing the picture of God's design are those elements of "the plan" (ἡ βουλή, hē boulē)[10] that are called "foreknown" (πρόγνωσις, prognōsis; Acts 2:23), "foretold" (προκαταγγέλλω, prokatangellō; Acts 3:18; 7:52), "predestined" or "chosen" (προορίζω, προχειρίζομαι, and προχειρτονέω, proorizō, procheirizomai, and procheirtoneō),[11] "promised" (ἡ ἐπαγγελία and ἐπαγγέλλομαι, hē epangelia and epangellomai),[12] "ordained" (τάσσω, tassō),[13] or "worked out through God's choice" (ὁρίζω, horizō).[14] Included in these descriptions are Christ's crucifixion (Acts 2:23), the promise of the Spirit to those near and far off (2:39), Christ's suffering and return (3:18–20), the persecution of Jesus and the community (4:27–28), the witnesses who testify to Jesus (10:41), the Gentiles appointed to eternal life (13:48), Jesus' sovereignty over people (17:26), a judgment day and a Judge (17:31), and the appointment of Paul as a witness to the Gentiles (22:10, 14). Behind the events recorded in Luke-Acts stand the presence of the sovereign God and his compassionate acts.

---

9. Schweizer, *TDNT*, 6:413–14.

10. Of God, seven times: Luke 7:30; 23:51; Acts 2:23; 4:28; 5:38; 13:36; 20:27.

11. προορίζω: Acts 4:28; προχειρίζομαι: 3:20; 22:14; 22:16; προχειρτονέω: 10:41.

12. ἡ ἐπαγγελία: of God, eight times: Luke 24:49; Acts 1:4; 2:33; 2:39; 7:17; 13:23; 13:32; 26:6, mostly of the Spirit or Jesus; ἐπαγγέλλομαι: Acts 7:5.

13. Of God, twice: Acts 13:48: 22:10.

14. Of God, five times: Luke 22:22; Acts 2:23; 10:42; 17:26, 31.

The terms used for God besides θεός (*theos*) show this emphasis on his sovereign authority.[15] Δεσπότες (*despotēs*) looks to one who is a master and points to God's sovereign direction in the plan and through events (Isa 3:1; 10:33; Luke 2:29; Acts 4:24). The term is rare in the NT, occurring only ten times, including the two in Luke and Acts (cf. 1 Tim 6:1–2; 2 Tim 2:21; Titus 2:9; 1 Pet 2:18; 2 Pet 2:1; Jude 4; Rev 6:10). The common κύριος (*kyrios*) has its roots in the LXX name for Yahweh. This usage is especially prominent in the infancy section, appearing twenty-five times. It also overlaps with use for Jesus, as we will see when we discuss Christology. This overlap is one of the ways Luke-Acts shows the inseparability of the work of God through Jesus.[16] The overlap and ambiguity makes counting the number of uses for God by Luke difficult to establish.[17] God is also Creator in Luke-Acts, a point made most vividly in Luke 11:40 and Acts 4:24; 17:24. A final title important early on in Luke-Acts is "Most High" (ὑψστος, *hypsistos*). It appears nine times in the two books, but many are at the start (Luke 1:32, 35, 76; 2:14; 6:35; 8:28; 19:38; Acts 7:48; 16:17). There is no other transcendent figure who can compete with God.

The character of God in Luke-Acts is set forth in part through the portrayal of God within the parables of the gospel.[18] This portrayal also points to God's plan as having a universal concern, being a God of mercy who seeks repentant hearts.[19] God is approachable according to the friend at midnight (Luke 11:5–8), a theme repeated in the picture of the unjust judge (cf. the remark about how much more God will be responsive than the judge who is pressured to respond to a nagging widow who beats him "black and blue," Luke 18:1–8). In the imagery of the parable, the judge fears being "beaten down," ὑπωπιάζη (*hypōpiazē*), a term that literally means "to give someone a black eye." Used figuratively, it means to wear down emotionally or to beat down someone's reputation.[20] God is not forced to respond. His care leads him to respond, but in his time and in his will.

God takes the initiative to care for those who have strayed according to the three parables of Luke 15 on recovering the lost like tax collectors or sinners. God cares for people more than the sparrows and gives the Spirit to those who seek him (Luke 11:9–13; 12:22–31). God cares for the ungrateful (Luke 6:35; Acts 14:17). God is merciful toward Israel, as the picture of his patience with the barren fig tree shows (Luke 13:6–9), and he receives back the prodigal as a picture of his mercy in 15:11–32. The fig tree parable portrays giving Israel plenty of time to respond as well as numerous chances to embrace salvation. The repeated offers of Jesus to the nation to enter into salvation in Luke 9–19 show the same point. Humility before God leads to mercy according the picture of the penitent tax collector in 18:14.

But God is also sovereign. One must settle accounts with him or there will be

---

15. Marshall, *Luke: Historian and Theologian*, 103–4.

16. This point is one of the key observations of C. Kavin Rowe, *Early Narrative Christology: The Lord in the Gospel of Luke* (BZNW 139; Berlin: De Gruyter, 2006).

17. Κύριος appears about 104 times in Luke and 107 times in Acts, but several of these are not a reference to God. The numbers

are approximate depending on some text-critical issues.

18. This is the burden of the study of God by Greg W. Forbes, *The God of Old: The Role of the Lukan Parables in the Purpose of Luke's Gospel* (JSNTSup 198; Sheffield: Sheffield Academic Press, 2000).

19. Ibid., 250–57.

20. Stählin, *TDNT*, 9:450, n. 88; K. Weiss, *TDNT*, 8:590–91.

consequences (Luke 12:57–59; 13:1–9). The parables of the rich fool, Lazarus and the rich man, the pounds, and the dishonest manger all point to accountability before God with resources we have that make us wealthy (12:13–21; 16:19–31; 19:11–27; 16:1–13). God is an initiating and responding God. He seeks out people who approach him humbly, knowing their need for him, living with a heart heart to serving others, and having an ear to hearing and doing his will.

6.2 GOD'S DIRECTION OF THE PLAN

How does God direct his plan? He administers it through various means: revelation; divine intervention including portents, dreams, and rescues; the work of agents, both human and angelic; the necessity of the outworking of God's plan; and the work of Christ himself.[21] Revelation fundamentally involved the declared promise of the OT, a theme so pervasive that it will receive more attention later.[22] Four themes receive special attention through these means: Jesus' passion, Gentile mission, persecution and suffering, and the work of the Spirit.[23]

It is important to detail some of the key means of direction God uses and Luke appeals to in his two volumes. God revealed his plan through angelic announcements or other heavenly agents. John's mission was revealed to Zechariah by the angel Gabriel (Luke 1:11–20). Gabriel also declared Jesus' mission to Mary (1:26–38). Angels as a group announced Jesus' birth to shepherds (2:9–14) and offered praise to God. Angels proclaimed Jesus' resurrection to women (24:1–7) and the promise of Jesus' return to the disciples (Acts 1:10–11). Philip was directed by an angel of the Lord to go to a eunuch (8:26). Cornelius was instructed about Peter by "an angel of God" (10:3–7), and an angel announced that Paul would survive a shipwreck (27:23–24). At key points in the story, God intervened and provided direction, especially as the program moved to include Gentiles.

Sometimes the raised Jesus intervened directly in Acts, such as his appearance to Saul in Acts 9 (retold in 22:6–10; 26:13–18). In addition, Ananias was directed in a vision to lay hands on Saul (9:10–16). A double appearance to both parties—Saul and Ananias—shows God's direct hand in choosing Saul. Another double intervention was Cornelius's being directed to send for Peter, while Peter had a vision in which God declared that all foods are clean. This intervention stressed that Gentiles are welcomed in God's plan (10:3–7, 10–16). Stephen saw his heavenly reception as he observed the Son of Man rising to meet him (7:55–56). Paul was also directed in a vision to go to Macedonia (16:9–10), and he was later instructed to remain in Corinth (18:9–10). Through a variety of ways Paul was told about what would happen in Jerusalem and Rome in the final chapters of Acts.

---

21. This focus is a key contribution of Squires, *Plan of God in Luke-Acts*. Squires speaks of fate, the necessity of the outworking of God's plan.

22. See ch. 21, below.

23. Squires, *Plan of God in Luke-Acts*, 194, only mentions Jesus' passion and Gentile mission as key topics for special attention in God's plan, but there are more topics.

Besides revelatory detail being provided for the direction of events, divine intervention came in other ways. Some people were aided by angelic mediation, usually in deliverance from prison (Acts 5:19; 12:7–15). At other times a natural event like an earthquake provided the deliverance (16:26). Philip was relocated after ministering to the eunuch (8:39). These examples from Acts show God sovereignly directing the foundational events of the church, especially those related to her expansion into the Gentile community.

Human agents were another major vehicle God used to direct the course of events. God worked through Jewish prophets of piety like Simeon and Anna (Luke 2:25–38). He used John the Baptist (7:24–30), the disciples (9:1–6; 10:1–12), the testimony of the church (Acts 4:24–31; 5:38–39), and the activity and witness of the apostolic band (1:8). His agents included church prophets such as Agabus and the daughters of Philip (11:27–30; 21:9–10), as well as missionaries including Barnabas (13:1), Paul (13:13), Timothy (16:1–3), and Silas (16:22). In Acts, much of this ministry is Spirit-directed as 1:8 makes clear, so even the agents in their activities relied on God's provision. In fact, the Spirit enabled these servants to do what they had not been able to. Nothing shows this more dramatically than the difference between a timid and frightened Peter who denied Jesus in Luke 22 and the bold Peter of Acts 1–12.

Of course, the most significant revelation is Jesus himself. His ministry is often summarized in the predictions about the Son of Man (Luke 9:22, 44; 17:24–25; 18:31–33; 22:22), in which his betrayal, death, and resurrection are the main focus. It was God's will and plan that these events occur (Luke 22:42; Acts 2:23). Acts 2:23 is particularly clear here. Jesus' death was no surprise to God, nor was his suffering. All the texts that Luke-Acts has cited about Jesus' suffering point to the idea that God planned out or knew that Jesus would be rejected in this way (Luke 9:21–22, 44–45; 13:33; 17:25; 18:31–33; 22:37; 24:46–47). The term for "predetermined" (ὁρίζω, *horizō*) appears eight times in the NT, with six uses in Luke-Acts (Luke 22:22; Acts 2:23; 10:42; 11:29; 17:26, 31; cf. Rom 1:4; Heb 4:7). One can also add one use of προορίζω to this theme (Acts 4:28; cf. Rom 8:29–30; 1 Cor 2:7; Eph 1:5, 11). Luke's more frequent usage underscores his belief that God is very much in control of events that are tied to Jesus, including his suffering. From the divine perspective, nothing happens outside God's plan.[24]

Jesus' rejection (Acts 4:27–28) and resurrection are part of the revealed promise (13:32–37; 24:14–15; 26:22–23, which stresses the promise according to the prophets and Moses). The sequence of suffering and vindication is something key OT texts also argue for as present in the work of God. So Ps 118:22–26 speaks of the raised-rejected stone who comes in the name of the Lord, and Isa 52:13–53:12 looks at the rejected but exalted Servant.

---

24. There is sometimes a tendency to argue that God's planned sacrifice of his Son is a distasteful teaching, almost like declaring God has led Jesus into an act of suicide. However, the plan and the story do not end here, but also include a divine vindication that makes the suicide analogy a severely distorted one of what is taking place. The work of Jesus on behalf of humanity is an act of intense love and sacrifice as John 13 and Roman 5:1–11 (esp. v. 7) argue.

6.3 PROMISE AND FULFILLMENT IN GENERAL

Within God's plan, Luke set forth Christ's role as the fulfillment of promise. It also looks to the inclusion of Israel and Gentiles in the program. This perspective is evident not only in the references to fulfillment, as noted above, but also at key structural points in the two books. First, the Lucan prologue clearly speaks of fulfillment in Luke 1:1, where the author describes Jesus' activities as events "fulfilled among us" (πεπληροφορημένων ἐν ἡμῖν, *peplērophorēmenōn en hēmin*).[25]

Second, the prologue to Acts speaks of the completion of God's plan in terms of "times" and "dates," a phrase that indicates a set schedule (Acts 1:6–7). So the term "time" (χρόνῳ, *chronō*) in 1:6 is important; it suggests a specific interval of time.[26] Many Jewish texts, as well as OT hope in general, expected that in the end Israel would be restored to a place of great blessing (Isa 2:2–4; 49:6; Jer 16:15; 23:8; 31:27–34 [where the new covenant is mentioned]; Ezek 34–37; Amos 9:11–15; Sir 48:10; *Pss. Sol.* 17–18; *1 En.* 24–25; Tob 13–14; *Eighteen Benedictions* 14).

Acts 3:18–22 also appeals to this background to the program. The question about the restoration to Israel is a natural one for Jews who have embraced the messianic hope. Luke 1–2 also expressed this hope vividly (1:69–74; 2:25, 38). What was debated in Judaism was whether the centrality of Israel would be positive or negative for Gentiles. Would it come with salvation or judgment for the nations? The disciples are not even thinking in mission terms in Acts 1:6. Their question reflects a nationalistic concern for Israel's vindication and the completion of the promise. The rest of Acts shows that the result is also positive for Gentiles, as does Luke 2:32.

Acts 1:4–5 repeats the reference to the coming of "the gift my Father promised," that is, the Holy Spirit, a promise introduced in Luke 24:49 and reaching back to remarks by John the Baptist in Luke 3:16. So both prologues discuss the same theme of events fulfilled, with Acts giving us more detail.

The gift "my Father [has] promised" links the closing chapter of Luke with the opening chapter of Acts (Luke 24:49 with Acts 1:4–5). For Luke, this promise is like an unbreakable chain between the program of God and the arrival of the new era. Luke uses the promise of God about the Holy Spirit to tie the two volumes together.[27] The other event linking the two volumes is the ascension of Jesus, which allows the coming of the Spirit to take place. It is here that Luke locates the giving of life to God's people according to promise.

Preceding the reference to the promise of the Spirit's enabling power is a summary of the center of the plan as promised in Moses, the Prophets, and the Psalms (Luke 24:44–47, "the Lucan Great Commission"). In this passage, three infinitives are prominent. Christ would suffer (παθεῖν τὸν Χριστόν, *pathein ton Christon*),

---

25. The idea of these events as "fulfilled" was treated in the previous chapter.

26. Barrett, *Critical and Exegetical Commentary on the Acts of the Apostles*, 1:76.

27. This idea will be traced more fully when we discuss Luke's view of the Spirit.

on the third day he would rise from the dead (ἀναστῆναι ἐκ νεκρῶν, *anastēnai ek nekrōn*), and then forgiveness of sins would be proclaimed in his name to all the nations (κηρυχθῆναι ... μετάνοιαν εἰς ἄφεσιν ἁμαρτιῶν, *kērychthēnai ... metanoian eis aphesin hamartiōn*). Here the work of Christ, God's exaltation of him, and the message of repentance for forgiveness available to all people of every race come together. As important as the cross is to salvation, for Luke the exaltation of Jesus is even more crucial, since it not only shows that Jesus is alive but also is the basis of his investiture into authority (Acts 2:30–36) and is the key to his ability to mediate salvation through the gift of life in the Spirit.

Just as Luke 24 summarizes the plan, so Acts 1:8 outlines the progress of the early church. Here geographical advance is described. The message will go from Jerusalem to Judea and Samaria and then to the ends of the earth. Spirit-enabled and Spirit-directed, the church takes up the mission and enablement described in 24:47–49 and carries it out from generation to generation. The disciples' calling, concern, and mission are not to focus on the timing of the end, as Acts 1:6–7 notes. Rather, as 1:8 makes clear, the disciples are to receive the enablement that God will give in the Spirit. They will be Jesus' witnesses.

The Spirit's activity is tied to "power" (δύναμις, *dynamis*), which refers here to being empowered to speak boldly by testifying to the message of God's work through Jesus. Paul says something similar of the gospel in Rom 1:16–17; for him, responding to the gospel gives power to live in a way that honors God and allows one to experience fullness of life. The term "power" appears ten times in Acts, sometimes referring to miracles or other effects of power (Acts 1:8; 2:22; 3:12; 4:7; 8:10, 13; 10:38; 19:11) and other times to enablement (4:33; 6:8). The enablement is in word and act.[28]

6.4 HEBREW SCRIPTURE FULFILLMENT IN PARTICULAR[29]

We refer here to the Hebrew Scripture and not the OT to avoid an anachronism that comes into Christian discussion when thinking of Luke-Acts in its original historical context.[30] This nomenclature is a reminder that we are telling Israel's story in Luke-Acts. The old promise to her ancestors has come to fruition in Jesus.

---

28. Jervell, *Apostelgeschichte*, 115: "miraculous power in miracle and word."

29. Chapter 21 will give much more detail to this theme, including the hermeneutical issues tied to it.

30. Of course, the designation of the OT is perfectly appropriate when thinking of the Bible as canon or as a theological category, but our point is that when Luke appealed to these texts the NT did not yet exist for there to be an OT. The designation "Hebrew Scripture" reminds us that Luke's appeal is to the story of old from the God of Israel. I will alternate between referring to the Hebrew Scripture and the OT in this study to remind us of this point about first-century use. There are many discussions today about the exact contents of

these sacred texts in the first century. However, the books to which Luke appeals, such as the Torah, Psalms, Isaiah, Jeremiah, or the twelve prophets, are for the most part not among the books discussed in the conversation about the scope of the Hebrew canon in this period. The only group that may have had a limited canon were the Sadducees, who focused on the Torah. Other groups may have considered a larger array of books beyond what we know as the OT today, but for most first-century Jews the books Josephus mentions are the ones that they most widely recognized (*Ag. Ap.* 1.8. 38.). For discussion of this issue of the canon of the OT, see Lee M. McDonald and James A. Sanders, eds., *The Canon Debate* (Peabody, MA: Hendrickson, 2002), 21–266.

Luke primarily speaks of the fulfillment of four themes predicted in the Hebrew Scriptures: Christology, the message of repentance/turning and forgiveness of sins, Israelite rejection/Gentile inclusion, and justice at the end. The warnings to heed the prophets recognize that irreversible authority resides in this message about the new era that is ultimately about Jesus. The prophets are to be believed (Luke 16:31; Acts 3:22–26; 13:27, 32, 40–41; 26:27). At the center of this message from Moses, the Prophets, and the Psalms stands Christology and the mission to the nations with the message about him (see esp. Luke 24:44–47). In fact, that text is central in introducing these key themes.

So we focus on Luke 24:46–47. Luke introduces the basic content of the scriptural teaching on God's plan, summarized in the three infinitives noted above. The first is that the Christ should "suffer" (Luke 9:22; 17:25; 22:15; 24:26; Acts 1:3; 3:18; 17:3).[31] The Psalter plays a key role for the theme of the suffering of the innocent righteous. Since this suffering has already happened, the details of the events are known to the disciples and to Luke's readers. Such suffering was anticipated by God, and Luke has told the story in Luke 23 with numerous references to such texts (Pss 22; 31; 69; 118; Isa 53), although the concept of messianic suffering seems not to have been a part of first-century Jewish expectation. Even the disciples struggled to understand how it fit into God's plan. Yet in many ways it is the key to Jesus' career, for in it came the opportunity to deal with the issue of forgiveness of sins and, as Luke says in Acts 20:28, the purchase of a church with his own blood.

The second infinitive is "to rise." Luke clearly means the promise is of a quick resurrection, since the usual Jewish hope was of a resurrection on the last day. The Lucan hope is defended in Acts primarily on the basis of two texts: Pss 16:10 and 110:1. With Jesus having suffered and having been raised by God, the message can go forward. The disciples experience this element of the hope, but there is more to the plan to which they must witness.

The third infinitive in Luke 24:46–47 is "to preach," through which the future of God's plan in the mission of the church appears. In this rich term are bound up the message's elements that the disciples are to take to the world. That message is broken down in detail, so that Luke's form of the Great Commission differs from the one in Matthew 28:18–20 and in the longer ending of Mark (16:15). The theme seems to parallel Mark 13:10 and Matthew 28:19.

The instruction to preach is based on the fact that the disciples are "witnesses" (Luke 24:48). This concept will become an important theme in Acts (Acts 1:8, 22; 2:32; 3:15; 5:32; 10:39, 41; 13:31; 22:15, 20; 26:16). The verb μαρτυρέω (*martyreō*, "to witness") is also used with this sense (23:11), and it often speaks of divine witness to the disciples' testimony (14:3; 15:8). The disciples can testify to these events because they have seen them—events such as Jesus' passion, resurrection, teaching, and work. Luke's commitment to the historicity of events is clear here. Acts 1:8 reintroduces the

---

31. BAGD, 634 §3a.

concept and calls on the disciples to function as "witnesses" to the things Jesus did and taught. The eleven disciples required that a replacement for Judas be a witness, especially of the resurrection and the earliest parts of Jesus' ministry (1:22; cf. the link of tradition and eyewitnesses in Luke 1:1–2). This shows an element of familiarity and oversight that these special witnesses were to exercise over the church's message and tradition about Jesus. The speeches in Acts serve as examples of such testimony. The disciples are to proclaim the message of God's work in Jesus. Their faith is not just an ethic or a morality; it is the testimony of God's activity in history.[32]

The first element is that this message goes out *in Jesus' name*, which is a major theme in Acts (Acts 2:38; 3:6, 16; 4:7, 10, 12, 17–18, 30; 5:28, 40; 8:12, 16; 9:14–16, 21, 27–28; 10:43, 48; 15:14, 26; 16:18; 19:5, 13, 17; 21:13; 22:16; 26:9).[33] In the Hebrew Scripture, this phrase indicates Yahweh's authority—authority that has now been transferred to Jesus, the mediator of God's promise. Baptism and other blessings come through his name (2:17–21, 38–39; 4:10, 12). This important theme reveals the absolute authority of the glorified Jesus. His name has authority and power like that of God.

The goal of the message is that others might respond appropriately to Christ's activity by repenting before God. Because Jesus here roots repentance in the Hebrew Scripture, it involves "turning," as the idea expressed in Hebrew indicates, not just "agreeing" (which is what the verb μετανοέω and the noun μετάνοια can mean in Greek). For Luke, repentance is the summary term for the response to the apostolic message (Acts 2:38; 3:19; 5:31; 8:22; 11:18; 13:24; 17:30; 19:4; 20:21; 26:20). Change in thinking, or better, direction (i.e., a reorientation) is basic to the human response called for from God's message. People must change their minds about God and the way to him, especially their thinking about sin, their (in)ability to overcome sin on their own, Christ's essential role in forgiveness, and the importance of depending on him for spiritual direction. Those responding to the apostolic message of the gospel must come to God on his terms in order to experience the forgiveness that comes in the name of Jesus.

But repentance means more than changing one's mind about God. People must also change their minds about who they are and how they can approach God. Repentance involves turning to and embracing God in faith. Forgiveness of sin comes to those who stretch out a needy hand to Jesus, clinging to him alone and recognizing that without him there is no hope, just like one who comes to a doctor for help with their physical health (Luke 5:32). The Hebrew scriptural base seems to be the plea in Joel 2:28–32 [3:1–5 MT] to call on the Lord, along with the common prophetic call to repent and turn to God (Acts 2:17–21, 38–39; Rom 10:9–12). In short, those who repent cast themselves on God's mercy, grace, direction, and plan. In this way, spiritual healing comes through the glorified Mediator, the Great Physician Jesus, who came to seek and save the lost (Luke 19:10).

---

32. Bock, *Luke 9:51–24:53*, 1941–42.   33. Bietenhard, *TDNT*, 5:278.

The message of hope tells of forgiveness of sins, although Luke does not develop much "how" this forgiveness takes place, i.e., through substitution and representation (Luke 1:77; 3:3; 4:18; Acts 2:38; 5:31; 10:43; 13:38; 26:18; only Luke 22:19 and Acts 20:28 address this issue).[34] Forgiveness of sins enables one to come into relationship with God because the barriers caused by sin are removed. For Luke Jesus has simply cleared the way for this new relationship. As a result one can experience God's enabling and transforming power, especially through the work of his Spirit. In short, forgiveness of sins brings the opportunity to leave the darkness and come into God's light (Luke 1:79; Acts 26:18).[35]

This message of hope is to go to all nations (Isa 42:6; 49:6; Luke 2:32; Acts 13:47). As Acts 10:36 puts it, Jesus is Lord of all humanity, Jew and Greek (also Rom 10:12–13). This is the message of the prophets to all who believe (Acts 10:42–43; 26:22–23). The gospel message in Jesus' name knows no national or racial barriers. It is no longer a Jewish message and hope. It starts from Jerusalem (Luke 24:49; Acts 1:8) but is designed to go to the ends of the earth.

The contrast between this universal tone and the disciples' initial response is so striking and the controversy that this universalism brought to the church was so great that many did not regard this remark as authentic.[36] The disciples initially stumbled over this element in Jesus' commission, seemingly assuming that Jesus meant the message was to go to Jews in every nation. While this would be a natural Jewish reading of this remark and a logical conclusion to draw from the international Jewish audience in Acts 2, it is not what Jesus meant. Only later (Acts 10–15) do the disciples see that this limited sense was inappropriate. A major burden of Luke-Acts is to show that Jesus Messiah is Lord of all humanity, so the message of the gospel must go to every human being. Acts depicts the working out of this commission, and Acts 10 especially argues that the church took the message to all only because God made that clear.

The mission starts in Jerusalem (Acts 1:8). Jesus had gone up to Jerusalem to meet his fate (Luke 9:51–19:44, esp. 13:31–35), but now the direction reverses and the mission goes out from Jerusalem. It is time for the benefits of Jesus' death and resurrection to be proclaimed to all. Jesus has been raised to God's right hand to distribute salvation's benefits on all who repent and come to him.

The key point of Luke 24:46–47 is that everything from suffering to universal proclamation has been predicted in the Scripture. This represents a strong emphasis on the continuity of God's plan, another major point in Luke's two volumes. While the NT argues that there are distinctions in God's plan (e.g., the difference between law and grace or references to Israel and all), one must not fail to note the emphasis on continuity in Luke. These events are part of God's will from the time of Abraham. God always intended to offer salvation to all nations through Jesus.

---

34. Luke spends his energy on *who* saves, while Paul develops in detail *how* this takes place.

35. See Bultmann, *TDNT*, 6:216 n. 315.

36. H. K. Luce, *The Gospel according to S. Luke* (Cambridge Greek Testament for Schools and Colleges; Cambridge: Cambridge Univ. Press, 1933), 364.

God always intended that the Christ suffer and be raised. God always intended that the message of salvation in the name of the Christ would be a call to repent for the forgiveness of sins. These are the fundamental aspects of God's plan.[37]

This Christological fulcrum also permeates the infancy material. John the Baptist is the forerunner, as Mal 3:1; 4:5–6 promised (Luke 1:14–17; Luke 3:4–6 adds the reference to Isa 40:3–5). Jesus is the promised Davidic King, the Son of God, who will rule over Israel forever (Luke 1:31–35). God's accomplishment of this plan reflects his mercy promised to Abraham and to the patriarchs (vv. 46–55). The promise of a "raised ... horn" from the house of David is found in Jesus (vv. 68–79—an allusion to Ps 132:17, which in turn alludes to 2 Sam 7, the Davidic covenant). Psalm 132 is part of another key allusion in Acts 2:30, thereby linking the infancy declaration to the key introductory speech in Acts.

Promise also pervades the end of Acts. Christ's death and resurrection and the spread of the gospel to Gentiles were predicted by Moses and the Prophets (Acts 26:22–23). They also testified to Jesus and the kingdom (28:23). "The Way," as Christianity is called in Acts, is in accord with the Law and the Prophets (24:14).

Numerous Lucan texts also speak of Israelite rejection and Gentile inclusion. Luke 2:34 introduces the point of division and rejection within Israel. The language here is from Isa 42:6 and 49:6. Luke's quotation of Isa 40 emphasizes the theme of the appearance of salvation before "all people" (Luke 3:4–6). Current Jewish rejection was like the pattern of ancient Israel, as Stephen argues from the nation's history in Acts 7. Certain passages raise the specter of the covenant curses for unfaithfulness, stated in Deut 18 (Acts 3:22–23). Other Lucan texts recall that Israel had earlier responded with unfaithfulness (Luke 11:49–51; 13:31–35; Acts 3:23; 7:51–53; 28:25–28).

The reality of judgment at the end of time is stressed in the OT allusions in the eschatological discourses of Luke 17:20–37 and 21:5–38. The apostles also emphasize the reality of coming judgment (Acts 2:38–40; 3:23; 10:42–43; 17:26–31). The God of design and concern has carried out his plan in Christ Jesus and through him in the church. Luke also notes other points of fulfillment from the hand of God in these events. John's birth (Luke 1:20, 59–64), Christ's mission and message (4:17–21), the times of the Gentiles (21:24), the Passover meal in the future kingdom (22:16), Judas (Acts 1:16–20), and the apostles' preaching ministry (13:47) are other events that picture fulfillment. There is a program of old that is being realized in Jesus. The new faith is really part of an old promise.

6.5 THEMES REVEALING THE PLAN'S OUTWORKING

Numerous other themes feed the picture of the divine plan in Luke-Acts. They add detail and tone to the picture of God's plan.

---

37. Bock, *Luke 9:51–24:53*, 1938–41.

6.5.1 "Today" Passages

One such theme is the emphasis on fulfillment "today" (σήμερον, *sēmeron*). This expression appears at least eleven times out of Luke's twenty uses with a force that points to special acts of God in the program. The theme begins with the announcement of Jesus' birth (Luke 2:11) as a Savior born in the city of David "today." In Jesus' synagogue speech, in which the Galilean outlines his mission, he speaks of Isa 61:1–2a and 58:6 as being fulfilled "today" (Luke 4:21). As a result of the paralytic's healing and receiving the forgiveness of sins, the people say they have "seen remarkable things today" (5:26). The journey of Jesus to Jerusalem is put in terms of what must happen "today" and tomorrow (13:32–33). Jesus declares the immediacy of salvation to Zacchaeus when he tells the tax collector that salvation has come to his house "today" (Luke 19:5, 9).

A variation of this theme is Jesus' lament over Jerusalem and her failure to know what has come to her "this day," that is, on the day of Jesus' entry into Jerusalem with acclamations of kingship (Luke 19:42). To the thief on the cross, Jesus promises that "today" the lowly but repentant man will be with him in paradise (23:42–43). In Acts 4:9, Peter and John are examined "today" for a good deed done in the name of Jesus. Jesus' resurrection shows that he is Son "today" (Acts 13:33). This emphasis on "today," besides underscoring fulfillment, also highlights the immediacy and availability of that blessing. Right now God makes available such blessings and promises. Such immediacy informs the background of other elements of God's plan. Salvation is here and now.

6.5.2 John the Baptist

John the Baptist is a bridge in God's plan. As the "last of the old order," he is also the transition to the new. Luke 1:14–17 makes this role clear when John is called the one "who will go on before the Lord, in the spirit and power of Elijah" (Mal 3:1; 4:5–6 predicted that such a one would come in the end; cf. Sir 48:10). Jesus points out that John had an "Elijah-like" ministry in his preaching repentance and his call to people to turn to God (Luke 7:27). In fact, the "turning" role of the prophet from 1:17 recalls the prophetic mission expressed in 2 Chr 15:1, 4 and a prophetic message not responded to in Sir 48:15. The idea of "turning to God" is a standard OT phrase for repentance of the covenant people, a return to the God of salvation (Deut 30:2; Hos 3:5; 7:10).[38] Variations of this theme are also linked to the prophets' messages (Jer 3:7, 10, 14; 18:8; Ezek 3:19; Dan 9:13). The idea of turning is picked up in the NT to describe conversion (Acts 9:35; 2 Cor 3:16; 1 Pet 2:25).[39] In fact, repentance, as we saw above, is part of the content of the great commission in Luke (Luke 24:47).[40]

John's role is to make ready "a prepared people" (λαὸν κατεσκευασμένον, *laon kateskeuasmenon*, Luke 1:17), a phrase unique to Luke that has a rich OT

---

38. Bertram, *TDNT*, 7:727.
39. Marshall, *Gospel of Luke*, 58.
40. Bock, *Luke 1:1–9:50*, 87.

background. As noted earlier, the language recalls verses like Isa 43:7, where Israel is prepared for the Lord, and 2 Sam 7:24, which refers to a prepared people in the context of Davidic hope. Luke 1:76–77 summarizes the mission of this prophet as preparing God's way, recalling the preparation language of 1:16–17. According to 1:76–77, John will also present "the knowledge of salvation through the forgiveness of their sins." Luke 3:1–6 underscores John's role as forerunner by referring to Isa 40. John later affirms that he is not the Christ and that one greater than he is coming, who will bring the Spirit (3:15–18). This text introduces the core evidence of the presence of the new era, the Messiah mediating the Spirit to those responsive to the message (24:49; Acts 1:4–5; 2:16–39; 11:15–18; 13:23–25).

In Luke 7:19–35, John raises a concern about his ministry. In Jesus' answer, he affirms that John is related to Elijah, and he also makes a comparison between the old era and the new. Whereas John was the greatest born among women up to that point, the least in the kingdom is greater than John (7:28). In other words, the difference between the two eras is so great that the greatest of prophets, even a prophet of the eschaton, is less than any member of the new era of fulfillment! In Luke 1–2, John is a bridge figure, but in Luke 7 he is pictured as belonging to the old era only. Together, the two passages show that John was a bridge in God's plan, which with Jesus' coming leaps forward to a significantly higher plane.

6.5.3 Jesus' Mission

An examination of Christology later will detail Jesus' role in God's plan. This section is concerned only with "mission statements," in which Jesus or others describe the sent one's mission or speak about Jesus as being sent by God. These statements describe what God has called Jesus to do and what those who follow Jesus' message proclaim in his name. They represent why Jesus came and why he was raised.

Jesus says that he was sent to preach release to the captives and to offer sight to the blind and forgiveness to the oppressed (Luke 4:18–19). He was sent to release the needy from the burden of sin and its effects in the world. In this text Jesus appeals to the OT year of Jubilee. Like that event, the current period is one in which people can be graciously released from debts (Lev 25:1–12; Deut 15:2–3; Ps 82:1–2; Isa 52:7; 61:1–2). The OT background of the passage is significant, as is the history of the interpretation of Isa 61. This Servant Song-like passage describes the prophet's role in terms used of the Servant of Isaiah (esp. Isa 42:1–4; 49:1–11). The figure of Isa 61 brings a message of God's deliverance to exiles. The passage presents a picture of forgiveness and spiritual liberation, which is at the center of Jesus' message. His salvation touches both spiritual and material realities as one's way of living is transformed to embrace God's grace, compassion, forgiveness, and justice.[41]

Comparing himself to a physician sent to make the sick well, Jesus defines his divine mission as calling "sinners to repentance" (Luke 5:32). This is one of many

---

41. That justice and compassion are in view can be seen in texts of rebuke where Jesus explains his ministry and its outreach, or where he traces the failure of religious leaders to live as God called (Luke 5:17–26; 11:37–54; 15:1–31).

places where Luke emphasizes repentance. The physician imagery of 5:31–32 shows that we must recognize our need to be treated. This type of humble openness to God for healing is what Jesus will commend in the tax collector of 18:9–14. A repentant heart is open, not closed, to God. The physician calls people to see themselves honestly, as they really are. They are ready to let God work on them. This willingness to rest in God and have him enter one's life is the essence of repentance. The Pharisees' attitude prevents this type of work from being done on them. So, Jesus goes where an opportunity for response exists. Spiritual restoration and healing can be accomplished only where the acceptance of "illness" is present. These tax collectors and sinners come to the table in the clinic, and the Physician is not about to reject their response.

Jesus offers spiritual restoration to those who recognize they are spiritually sick. He was sent as the Father's representative (Luke 10:16) to seek and save the lost (19:10). Acts 3:20 speaks of the future sending of the appointed Messiah, while 3:26 emphasizes that Jesus was sent to bless those Jews who turn from their wicked ways. In Jesus' earthly ministry, the promised one, Jesus Christ, was sent to "the people of Israel" (10:36), but now he accepts from every nation all those who fear him (10:34–35). These mission texts describe a ministry of compassion and forgiveness made available through Jesus to those who seek relief from their spiritual needs so that life can be lived in a different way on this earth. The God of design and concern makes this will and plan known through Jesus.

6.5.4 Geographical Progression

The advancement of God's plan into fulfillment receives attention in the Lucan portrait of a geographical progression that pervades the two books. In Jesus' initial mission the ministry moves from Galilee to Jerusalem (Luke 4:14–15; 9:51). In fact, of the gospel writers Luke stresses more emphatically than the others that Jesus is headed for Jerusalem (Luke 9:51; 13:33; 17:11; 18:31). This progression is reviewed in Acts 10:35–39. The advance of the church is similar but goes in the opposite direction. Acts 1:8 speaks of movement from Jerusalem to Judea and Samaria and then to the ends of the earth.

This verse deserves careful attention. The disciples are not to worry about the end of the plan (Acts 1:6–7); rather, they are called to carry the message to the end of the earth. There is dispute about what "the end of the earth" (ἐσχάτου τῆς γῆς, *eschatou tēs gēs*) means.[42] The phrase has OT roots (Isa 48:20; 49:6; Jer 10:13). Does it refer here to Spain (as in *1 Clem.* 5.7) and thus cover the ancient inhabited earth,[43] or to Rome (of Pompey's roots in *Pss. Sol.* 8.15);[44] or is it ethnic in force, looking to the Gentiles? Against this last option is that Paul engages Jews in Rome as well as Gentiles. Moore has a full discussion of the issue and notes that Palestine and Ethiopia have also been suggested as options (though, I think,

---

42. Note that while translations such as the NIV and NRSV use the plural "ends," the Greek term used here is singular.

43. Witherington, *Acts of the Apostles*, 110–11.

44. See Conzelmann, *Acts of the Apostles*, 7.

less likely).[45] Pao presents a full list of options, either geographic or ethnic: Is the "end of the earth" Ethiopia, Israel, Diaspora Jews, Rome, Spain, the whole world, Gentiles, or the farthest end of the earth?[46]

Acts does show an interest in Rome (Acts 19:21; 23:11; ch. 28). From a literary standpoint within Acts, the reference to Rome after a long providential sea journey in Acts 27 means that the message has now reached the hub of the Gentile world, from which it can proceed everywhere.[47] Thus the difference between interpreting "end of the earth" as specifying Rome or as looking at the broader edges of the world is not great. If Isa 49:6 is in the background, as is possible (see Acts 13:47), the point is that the message is going out to the world (but its reaching Rome is an important part of that task).

Moore notes that Luke uses Isaiah extensively, so that an allusion to it is likely. He cites eighteen texts with allusions to Isaiah in Luke-Acts.[48] Pao supports this view and regards the allusion to Isa 49:6 as solid, while observing that in Acts 13:47 (and Isa 49:6) the emphasis is on Gentiles, which rules out references to Ethiopia, Israel, or Diaspora Jews.[49] Pao also argues that the expression "the end of the earth" is not a stock phrase in Greco-Roman literature, as it appears only six times in the LXX, twice in Luke, and nowhere else in ancient Greek literature not influenced by Isaiah or Acts (although why Pao imposes this biblical limitation on the use of the expression in Greek sources is not clear). Moore notes six LXX texts—Isa 45:22; 48:20; 49:6; 62:10–11; Jer 16:19; 38[31]:8—but regards 49:6 as key.[50] In these LXX passages, the emphasis is on the extension into all the earth.

In *Pss. Sol.* 1:4, the phrase is parallel to πᾶσαν τὴν γῆν (*pasan tēn gēn*, "all the earth"), which indicates that the two expressions are synonymous or nearly so. Pao excludes Spain as not adequately attested in Greek sources. Schnabel adds that Spain has no role to play in Acts, so he prefers to see a reference to the edges of the empire.[51] Thus the expression is likely intended to refer primarily to the Gentiles, allowing an allusion within it to Rome as its center. Moore says it nicely: Rome "points to the end of the earth" and an "expansion of the gospel into the Gentile world without implying a final withdrawal of the gospel from the Jews."[52] An intended reference in the phrase to the Gentiles in the world is likely.

The phrase "the end of the earth," then, is geographic and ethnic in scope, inclusive of all people and locales. As Schnabel says, "The mission of the disciples is world mission."[53] The kingdom message will move out gradually and encompass all. The church's call is to be missionary in direction and eschatological in focus.

45. T. S. Moore, "To the End of the Earth: The Geographical and Ethnic Universalism of Acts 1:8 in Light of Isaianic Influence on Luke," *JETS* 40 (1997): 389–99.

46. David Pao, *Acts and the Isaianic New Exodus* (WUNT 2/130; Tübingen: Mohr-Siebeck, 2000), 93; Schnabel, *Early Christian Mission*, 372–76, studying the case for and against each option, opts for the farthest regions of the earth, bounded by Gaul-Britannia-Spain (west), the Arctic-Scythia (north), Ethiopia (south), and lands beyond India-China (east). He cites Strabo, Philostratus, and Philo for this

meaning, but these are all Hellenic or Hellenistic Jewish writers.

47. Barrett, *Critical and Exegetical Commentary on the Acts of the Apostles*, 1:80.

48. Moore, "To the End of the Earth," 389–99.

49. Pao, *Acts and the Isaianic New Exodus*, 84–86, 92–95.

50. Moore, "To the End of the Earth," 393.

51. Schnabel, *Early Christian Mission*, 375.

52. Moore, "To the End of the Earth," 397–98.

53. Schnabel, *Early Christian Mission*, 375.

The world is the end goal, pointing to complete deliverance that drives the present mission and gives it focus.

This does not exhaust the discussion, since at a literary level the involvement of Gentiles is not clear at this point in Acts. A reader of Acts must be open to the possibility of, and be sensitive to, the fact that what Jesus or Luke meant and how an expression originally might have been understood are not necessarily the same thing. The disciples probably originally thought of Jews everywhere. To Luke, it probably anticipates the offer of the gospel to all people. Such a double meaning is possible in literature and also in historical understanding that is developing. In fact, it will take the apostles and others time to realize that Jesus does not intend for the message to go just to Jews dispersed throughout the world but also to Gentiles. An indication of this double significance is how God must lead the church into Gentile mission in Acts 10–11. God's intention is the world; it is not to be implemented by merely bringing the nations to Jerusalem, as Israel's Scripture suggested.

Stephen Wilson rejects the idea that the passage could be understood ambiguously as referring to Diaspora Jews.[54] His reading fails to distinguish adequately between what Jesus or Luke meant by the Great Commission in Acts 1:8 as an introduction to the apostles' task and how the disciples may have originally heard it. The commission did have a universal thrust, but the disciples originally heard it in a limited, Jewish scope. God will clarify this realization, as Acts 8–11 shows, and it may well be that at a later point the significance of Isa 49:6 becomes more evident. Larkin rightly calls the verse a "command-promise."[55]

Thus, part of the concern of Acts is to show how the church came to be so inclusive of Gentiles. There was a commission from Jesus, but it took some time for its extent to be appreciated. Nevertheless, this mandate describes the church's key assignment of what to do until the Lord returns. The priority for the church, a mission of which the community must never lose sight, is to witness to Jesus "to the end of the earth." The church exists, in major part, to extend the apostolic witness to Jesus everywhere. In fact, the church does not *have* a mission; it is to be missional and *is* a mission.

The book of Acts follows that movement, as Judea and Samaria are mentioned in Acts 8:1, and as the missionary journeys of the book extend the church's outreach far into Gentile regions. Paul's long journey by ship to Rome in Acts 27 seems to highlight how difficult it was to get to the capital of the empire. Though Rome was a long way away, at the end of the earth from the perspective of Jerusalem, the message of salvation was penetrating the entire inhabited world. The move also indicated that the locus of salvation as moving out into the world, as Rome pictures outreach to all the nations. So the reference to "the end of the earth" is important.

---

54. Stephen G. Wilson, *The Gentiles and the Gentile Mission in Luke-Acts* (SNTSMS; Cambridge: Cambridge Univ. Press, 1973), 91–92.

55. W. J. Larkin Jr., *Acts* (IVPNTC 5; Downers Grove, IL: InterVarsity Press, 1994), 41.

I prefer a reference to Rome as the center of the extension to the world. It looks to a universal mission extending out to the world with Rome as its symbolic center.[56]

6.5.5 "It Is Necessary"

Perhaps no theme underscores divine design more than the Lucan "it is necessary" (δεῖ, *dei*, often translated "must") theme. This Greek word is used 99 times in the NT, of which 40 are in Luke-Acts. The references cover a wide variety of topics. Christ *must* be in the Father's house (Luke 2:49). He *must* preach the kingdom (4:43). He *must* heal women tormented by Satan (13:16). In looking at events associated with Jesus' death or return, certain things *must* precede the end (21:9). A Passover lamb *must* be sacrificed, as Jesus and the disciples gathered for a final meal (22:7). The Son of Man or the Christ *must* suffer, perish in Jerusalem, and be raised (9:22; 13:33; 17:25; 24:7, 26; Acts 17:3). The Scriptures *must* be fulfilled in that Jesus *must* be numbered with transgressors (Luke 22:37, quoting Isa 53:12), and certain events predicted of Christ *must* occur (Luke 24:44).

Judas's fall was a *necessity* according to Acts 1:16. The gospel *must* go to Gentiles after the Jews have rejected it (13:46). Entrance into the kingdom to come *must* come through trials (14:22). Christ *must* remain in heaven till the appropriate time (3:21). Paul *must* suffer for Jesus' name's sake (9:6, 16); he *must* stand trial before Caesar (25:10; 27:24); and he *must* go to Rome (19:21), where he *must* witness (23:11). Much in God's plan was carried out by commissioned agents, some of whom knew what they must do.

Other categories of necessity (δεῖ) do not reflect this plan, but they grow out of its nature as directed by God. Ethical necessity also exists. In critiquing the Pharisees, Jesus notes the *necessity* of justice (Luke 11:42) and the appropriateness of healing on the Sabbath (13:16). It was *necessary* to respond with joy to the prodigal son who repented (15:32). It is *necessary* to respond to Jesus with belief, since there is no other name under heaven by which it is *necessary* to be saved (Acts 4:12; cf. Luke 16:30–31). Persistent prayer is *necessary* (Luke 18:1). One *must* obey God, not human beings, when magistrates ask that believers not proclaim Christ (Acts 5:29).

---

56. This nuances the view of Brian Rosner in "The Progress of the Word," in *Witness to the Gospel: The Theology of Acts* (ed. I. Howard Marshall and David Peterson; Grand Rapids: Eerdmans, 1998), 217–21. He argues Rome cannot be meant, appealing to work by James Scott ("Luke's Geographical Horizon," in D. W. J. Gill and C. Gempf, eds., *The Book of Acts in its Greco-Roman Setting, Volume 2* [Grand Rapids: Eerdmans, 1994], 483–544, esp. 523) and the lack of such symbolism anywhere else. He prefers a reference to the full limits of the earth, the "widest possible geographical horizon" (p. 219). However, Luke's geographic emphasis and the effort told to get Paul to Rome as a goal of Acts speaks against detaching these two ideas too much and nuancing the association. See Michael Bachmann, "Jerusalem and Rome in Luke-Acts, in *Luke and Empire* (ed. David Rhoads, David Esterline, and Jae Won Lee; Princeton Theological Monographs; Eugene, OR: Pickwick, 2011), 68–83. He argues that Rome is seen as another religious center because in part the debate over Jesus is about another king, and the emperor in Rome was a figure of reverence, a point well taken and often forgotten in modern treatments of these volumes. So for Paul to reach Rome and bring his message of an exalted Jesus before this revered figure is a form of religious and social challenge. This prospective encounter from the perspective of the narrative is positive evidence of the gospel's advance. In this Bachmann sees a heavenly Jerusalem still in play because of themes of Jesus entering into glory and the contrastive picture of Stephen's critique of the temple being met with being raised to glory by Jesus (Acts 7:55). This is implicit, but possible. In this way, the kingdom of God is seen to cover the entire earth and to be rooted in the work of the raised Jesus who is Lord and the vindicating Son of Man.

Jesus promises that in times of persecution the Spirit will give what is *necessary* to speak (Luke 12:12). Again, Luke shows that the Lord is a God of design. God calls disciples to a relational integrity both in connection to God and to one's neighbor.

6.5.6 The Kingdom

Another key theme in Luke-Acts is the kingdom. This is a vast concept with many elements that relate to other areas. Here we will survey the major features.[57] Four points about God's kingdom program should be noted: the kingdom as present, the kingdom as future, the kingdom promise as political, and the kingdom promise as spiritual.

(1) The presence of the kingdom is suggested in Luke by the picture of John the Baptist as the bridge into the new era (Luke 7:28). John is pictured as the last prophet of an old age, and the new age of the kingdom has come, since the least in the kingdom is greater than John.

Jesus gives instructions to the seventy-two disciples to proclaim that the kingdom "has come near" (Luke 10:9). The debated term here is ἤγγικεν (*ēngiken*). Does it mean "to draw near" or "to arrive"? Lexically the term can carry either meaning.[58] But the use of the preposition ἐπί (*epi*, "to, upon") makes it likely that the sense in Luke 10:9 is "to arrive" or "to approach" (cf. Matt 26:45–46). This is confirmed by the fact that Luke normally uses the term this way (Luke 12:33; 15:1; 18:40; 22:47; 24:15; Acts 21:33).

The picture of a current ruling authority is presented in Luke 10:18–19. Jesus says he saw Satan falling like lightning, a clear image of his defeat. Jesus expresses this picture as a result of the miraculous activity of the seventy-two and relates it to the authority Jesus bestowed on them (v. 19). In Judaism there was the belief that with Messiah's coming Satan's rule would end (*1 En.* 55.1; *Jub.* 23.29; *T. Sim.* 6.6; *T. Mos.* 10.1).

The third passage dealing with this theme in Luke 10–11 is 11:20–23, where Jesus makes the point that if he casts out demons by the finger of God, then the kingdom of God "has come upon you" (v. 20, NASB; ἔφθασεν ἐφ᾽ ὑμᾶς, *ephthasen eph᾽ hymas*).[59] The allusion to the finger of God points to a formative era like the exodus, since the allusion is to Exod 8:19. Also, Luke 11:21–23 shows that arrival is meant, since Jesus is the stronger one who plunders Satan's house. This picture of victory and authority parallels other NT passages (Eph 4:7–10; Col 2:14–15). All these texts point to a plundering and victory that has already occurred.

In Luke 17:21, Jesus says that the kingdom is in the "midst" of the Pharisees (ἐντὸς ὑμῶν, *entos hymōn*); that is, the kingdom is in their presence. It is "within your

---

57. For more details, see Darrell L. Bock, "The Reign of the Lord Christ," in *Dispensationalism, Israel, and the Church: The Search for Definition* (ed. Craig A. Blaising and Darrell L. Bock; Grand Rapids; Zondervan, 1992); and idem, *Jesus according to Scripture: Restoring the Portrait from the Gospels* (Grand Rapids; Baker, 2002), 565–93.

58. Fitzmyer, *Gospel according to Luke X–XXIV*, 848.

59. The term clearly means arrival in this tense and context (Rom 9:31; Phil 3:16; 1 Thess 2:16). See W. Kümmel, *Promise and Fulfillment* (trans. Dorothea M. Barton; SBT 23; Naperville, IL: Allenson, 1957), 105–9. In the LXX, this verb with ἐπί means "to reach" or "to happen to" (Dan 4:24, 28). Thus, a past tense translation is justified here.

reach in the present."[60] The parable of the ten minas (19:12–27) is also instructive. Like the nobleman, Jesus has gone away to receive a kingdom, and, having already received that kingdom, he will return. In other words, his departure, not his return, initiates his reign. In 22:69 Jesus says that "from now on" the members of the Sanhedrin will see the Son of Man seated at the right hand of power (cf. Mark 14:62). The "right hand" alludes to Ps 110:1, which portrays investiture and especially the sharing of authority with God. This authority is indicated by God's vindication of Jesus in his resurrection-ascension. It pictures Jesus' rule at the side of God in a "coregency" in which Jesus is actively distributing salvation benefits to those who believe (Acts 2:30–36). Psalm 110:1 is a text that the NT relates to Davidic sonship and the promise to David, as Luke 20:41–44; 22:69; Acts 2:30–36 show (Heb 1:5–13).

(2) The distribution of the Holy Spirit as recorded in Acts 2 and Peter's explanation of that event show that Jesus is now at the side of God the Father. As Lord, he is exercising salvific authority and the prerogatives of rule from God's side. Thus in Luke's view, the kingdom is present not in its final form but in an inaugurated form. This commencing of the kingdom shows that the promises of the last days have begun to be fulfilled. Further fulfillment is anticipated in the future.

This second, future form of the kingdom receives detailed attention in several Lucan texts. Most crucial are the two eschatological discourses in Luke 17:22–37 and 21:5–38. Here the kingdom is still anticipated, and the passage depends heavily on Hebrew Scripture.[61] This is the kingdom of culmination foreseen in many OT prophecies. Peter speaks of the return of Jesus from heaven, when the Messiah will bring about the "period of restoration" (χρόνων ἀποκαταστάσεως, *chronōn apokatastaseōs*; Acts 3:21 NASB). This restoration involves all the things God has spoken through the mouth of the prophets. Here is hope for the world and particularly for Israel, since this verse recalls the disciples' question in 1:6 about the "time" of the "restoration" of Israel (χρόνῳ and ἀποκαθιστάνεις, *chronō* and *apokathistaneis*).

Peter's speech in Acts 3 is one undergirded by the Spirit of God as the one who enables the witness. The text shows that the question of Acts 1:6 was not wrong. Rather, the question about the timing of the restoration is something God was not answering at that time. The future kingdom is first and foremost the realization of OT kingdom promises. To know what the rest of the kingdom story will be and how it is also part of Israel's story, Peter argues that one need only read the Hebrew Scriptures and what it says about consummation.

(3) In certain verses, Luke describes the kingdom in political terms. Luke 1:32–33 points to Jesus' ruling from the Davidic throne over the house of Jacob

---

60. Marshall, *Gospel of Luke*, 476. Note also the present tense in this verse. The verse cannot mean the kingdom of God is "within you." Jesus would never have said this to Pharisees who were rejecting him.

61. The day of the Lord and kingdom imagery dominate these texts. For example, in Luke 21:2–27 alone, there are allusions to Isa 13:10; Ezek 32:7; Joel 2:30–31; Ps 46:2–3; 65:7; Isa 24:19 (LXX); Hag 2:6, 21; and Dan 7:13.

forever, and 1:51–55 relate the messianic task in direct terms to Israel, Abraham, and his seed. Mary's hymn is expressed in the tone of Jewish messianic national hope. In 1:69, Zechariah refers to salvation from a horn out of the house of David. That Davidic-led salvation combines political and spiritual elements is seen in the rest of the hymn (1:69–79). In this last hymn, the career of the promised Son of David is summarized. Some of what the Son of David does meets with fulfillment in his first coming (vv. 78–79), while other elements anticipate Jesus' activity in the future (vv. 71–75). This is yet another indication that blessing on the world is part of Israel's story. To include the nations does not mean excluding hope for Israel.

(4) Some aspects of the kingdom are spiritual rather than political. In the same infancy texts, Jesus' mission is described as a visitation from "the rising sun," which shines on those in darkness and those seated in the shadow of death (Luke 1:78–79). Jesus' coming is like the light of a new day. His task is to lead them "into the path of peace." This imagery comes from Isa 9:1–2; 58:8; 60:1–2; and Ps 106:10, 14 (LXX). It is spiritual in focus.

Some argue that the kingdom is not present until both political and spiritual elements are present, but Luke's view of the presence of forgiveness and the Spirit as kingdom realized speaks against this distinction. Luke's kingdom comes in two phases, "already" and "not yet." It has been "inaugurated," but it is not yet "consummated." The kingdom is present, but not all its promises have come. What is to come relates to the Hebrew Scripture and its covenant promises to the nation Israel. What is present now is related to the church and the exercise of her mission by the Spirit's power.

6.5.7 The Holy Spirit

Another key element in God's plan is the Holy Spirit's work. The Spirit's role indicates the inauguration of the fulfillment of God's promises (Acts 2:17–33 appeals to the fulfillment of Joel 2:28–32; cf. Acts 2:38–40). John the Baptist summarizes the OT hope and announces what the "more powerful" one to come will bring to show the arrival of the new era. John promises the coming of the Spirit with Jesus' coming as the Christ (Luke 3:15–18). In fact, the provision of the Holy Spirit is evidence of Jesus' superiority to John. With Jesus' own reception of the Spirit at his baptism comes one of two divine endorsements of Jesus (Luke 3:22, alluding to Ps 2:7, thus marking Jesus as the messianic Son, and to Isa 42:1, which pictures him as the beloved Servant).

The Spirit's activity extends to the community and includes a variety of functions. Luke does not emphasize the individual reception of the Spirit as much as he points to its corporate reception. This community reception is promised in Luke 24:49, which states that the Father's promise of the Holy Spirit looks back both to John the Baptist's pronouncement regarding the Christ to come and to the promise of new covenant hope. In Acts 1:4–5, Jesus repeats the promise. The initial bestowal in Acts 2 is so important to Luke that he alludes to it in numerous passages. Acts

10:44–47 notes a similar bestowal on the Gentiles, comparing it to the original provision in Acts 2 (cf. Acts 11:15–16; 15:8).

Acts 19:6 records another community reception of the Spirit that involves those who know only of John's baptism. It pictures the initial movement from the forerunner into the believing community. In Acts 19, the old age moves into the new as John's disciples catch up with Pentecost. The last of the transition groups comes in. This communal pouring out of God's Spirit not only shows the presence of the "last days" (Acts 2:17), but also indicates (when he is poured out again in Acts 10) that Gentiles and Jews are equal in God's plan (11:15–18). They participate in the same new community. The presence of the Spirit indicates a washing and acceptance by God as a result of forgiveness. In fact, 11:15 looks back to Acts 2 as "at the beginning" (ἐν ἀρχῇ, *en archē*). A new community, which has come to be known as the church, emerges from this special work.[62] The reception of the Spirit represents the presence of both blessing and enablement, since the Spirit is also called "power from on high" (Luke 24:49; cf. Acts 1:8). The beginning of a new period in God's work has dawned.

What functions does the Spirit have in this plan? The Spirit's primary activity is filling. The verb πληρόω (*plēroō*, "to fill") is a general Lucan term for presence and enablement. Before he was born, John the Baptist was filled with the Spirit (Luke 1:15). In fact, while still in the womb, he testified to Jesus with joy (v. 44). Filling here was enablement to testify to Jesus, the ability to function as a prophet. Elizabeth and Zechariah were filled and gave praise to God (vv. 41, 67). Filling was related to testimony and praise.

In Acts 2:4, all the believers are filled with the Holy Spirit. Again there is enablement to testify to Jesus and to offer praise (v. 11). Here filling also describes the Spirit's reception by the community, the Spirit's "outpouring" according to Joel 2. Later in Acts, the Spirit's filling again enables believers to testify to Jesus, whether through an individual like Peter (Acts 4:8) or by means of the entire praying community (v. 31). Another phrase, πλήρεις πνεύματος (*plēreis pneumatos*, "full of the Spirit"), is parallel in force. In 6:3, 5, the phrase refers to the mature quality of the Seven chosen to help the Hellenistic widows. This term speaks here of an abiding quality of spirituality.

Stephen, one of these men (Acts 6:5), is full of the Spirit at the time of his martyrdom, and in a vision he sees the standing Son of Man. He testifies to this vision as he dies (7:55–56). Though Stephen is stoned for blasphemy, he is full of the Spirit, is received by Christ, and is vindicated in heaven. Saul is enabled for ministry and filled with the Spirit through the laying on of hands by Ananias (9:17). Barnabas is described as full of the Spirit, as he shows maturity and ministers encouragement to believers (11:24). Paul, filled with the Spirit, pronounces judgment on Elymas

---

62. The term for "church" is not used in Luke's gospel, but it appears twenty-three times in Acts. The uses in 5:11 and 7:38 are ambiguous since they could simply mean "assembly," which is a common meaning for the Greek term *ekklēsia*. By 8:1, 3, the techni-cal meaning of "church" is more clearly present. Of the twenty-three uses in Acts, eighteen occur after Acts 10, when the gospel has gone to the nations.

(13:9–11). A variation of the phrase appears in the description of Apollos as "fervent in spirit" (ζέων τῷ πνεύματι, *zeōn tō pneumati*; 18:25).

The Lucan phrase "filled with the Spirit" describes an important role for the Spirit in God's plan. It is the gift of enablement, bestowed either initially, as in Acts 2:4, or in a later moment of special spiritual direction. Usually the gift describes enablement to testify to Jesus boldly. On a few occasions, the phrase describes an individual's general spiritual character. The words show that the Spirit is the driving power behind the early church's effectiveness. Jesus gives the Spirit not only to show that the promise is being fulfilled, but also to equip the church to perform its mission of taking the gospel message to the world.

The Spirit performs other functions in God's plan for his community. Through prophets the Spirit speaks to Israel (Acts 1:16: David; 4:25: David; 28:25: Isaiah) and to the church of the apostolic era (11:28; 21:10–11: Agabus; 21:4: disciples). These prophetic utterances of the church involve information about things like famines as well as exhortation and advice. In at least one instance, Paul seems to have had a choice about an issue the Spirit has raised, since the Spirit-led Agabus pleads for Paul not to go on to Jerusalem where he will face Jewish rejection (21:11). Paul decides to go anyway and the passage ends on the note, "the Lord's will be done" (21:14). Apparently, the Spirit's prophetic exhortation and warning here is something about which Paul can reflect. He chooses to go, knowing he will face rejection. Those present respond and agree that what lies in the future will be God's will.

In Acts 5:3, 5, the Holy Spirit guards the community from the lie of Ananias and Sapphira. In executing judgment in the community, the Spirit jealousy keeps the church's integrity. The Spirit sees what happens in the church.

The Spirit guides the believing community as she makes decisions and takes action. In the letter emerging from the Jerusalem Council, the leaders declare that the decision made is that of the community and the Spirit (Acts 15:28). The Spirit gives elders to the Ephesian community (20:28). The Spirit comforts or encourages the church as she grows (9:31). The Spirit enables obedience, especially under the pressure of persecution (Luke 12:12; Acts 5:32; 6:10). The provision of the Spirit is God's way of empowering the church to complete her task.

Whether leading the way in discipline, guidance, the supply of leadership, or encouragement, the Holy Spirit in Acts is a driving force in the new community. Along with the presence of the Holy Spirit, God calls those in the new community to lead lives honoring to him. In the emerging church, God through his Spirit is at work in molding a new, exemplary group of faithful people. That is a part of God's plan as well. The God of design and concern has called his people to a life of discipleship and service, a life that differs from the world's way of selfish living.

6.5.8 The New Community's Ethic

One of God's goals within the plan is to call his people to a righteous life, a life that honors him. Design and compassion provided the enablement, but with that provision comes a call for believers to live in light of God's goodness. The call to discipleship contrasts with the Jewish leaders' way to God. Most of these passages come in the "Jerusalem journey" section of the gospel (Luke 9:51 – 19:44). As Jesus heads toward the place of suffering, he instructs the disciples on what God desires of them and what God plans for them. When Jesus condemns the current ways of official piety, he issues a call to new piety and prepares his disciples for his approaching physical absence.

Luke's look at the Jewish leadership in Jesus' day provides the negative portrait against which Christian discipleship is defined. The note of trouble for those leaders comes early. John the Baptist states that the ax of judgment is sitting at the root of the tree, ready to be wielded against anyone who does not respond with repentance (Luke 3:7 – 9). Genealogy is no guarantee against judgment. God wants responsive people with hearts open to him.

No section is stronger in its condemnation of the old way than Luke 11:37 – 52. Here Jesus, like a classic OT prophet, rails against the hypocrisy of the Pharisees and scribes. They are morally filthy inside, no matter how clean they appear on the outside. They follow all kinds of tithing rules about herbs, but neglect justice and love. They love the attention of the first seats and think they lead others, but in fact their teaching is like an open grave, leading to death and uncleanness. They burden others with rules, but do not lift a finger to help those burdened. They think they have the key of knowledge, but instead their way of thinking is a wall that prevents entry. Their actions are like the nation's failure in earlier eras to heed God's message.

Jesus' imagery is strong here. This long condemnation destroys the popular portrait of Jesus as a mild-mannered teacher who avoids confrontation. Though not blatantly immoral, the Jews have a form of piety that does not honor God. That is what Jesus condemns here. By contrast, the new community is not to be selfishly and arrogantly pious.

Jesus' warning about the wrong way continues in Luke 14:7 – 14, where he admonishes his host and the guests at a meal not to seek places of honor. The next passage shows that many who think they will be present at the great banquet will miss it (vv. 15 – 24). Jesus also condemns self-righteousness (16:14 – 15), a flaw seen in the Pharisee in contrast to the tax collector-sinner (18:9 – 14). Here the humble sinner is commended. Jesus' confrontation closes with a word of weeping lament (Luke 19:39 – 44) and with his cleansing of the temple (vv. 45 – 48). The way to please God is not found in the Jewish leadership.

The way to God stands in contrast to the way sought by the Jewish leaders. God's way is a life of love and service, rooted in the great commandments to love God and one's neighbor. His followers are called to a unique kind of love. Luke 6:27 – 36 is a declaration to love in a way different from that of sinners. While Paul defined the attributes of love in 1 Corinthians 13, Jesus describes here in concrete terms what love is and how it acts. Love is giving. It reaches out to enemies as well as friends. It is vulnerable and sensitive to others, treating them as one wishes to be treated. Love exposes itself again and again to abuse by turning the other cheek in the hope of helping others. It is generous and expects nothing in return. In short, love continually and consistently displays mercy, compassion, and honesty. It is slow to judge others (6:37–42). It senses responsibility for others. It does not dictate to them, but aids them. This love recognizes that similar spiritual dangers and faults exist anywhere, especially in our own souls. The disciples' major responsibility is to deal with their own faults first and then to help others deal with theirs.

Love for one's neighbor is described in Luke 10:25–37. Here the issue is not who one's neighbor is. Rather, the challenge is to be a neighbor. Such was the Samaritan to the man who fell among the thieves. Love for Jesus is exemplified in Mary seated at his feet (vv. 38–42). This pictures the dedicated disciple, as does responding to the call to pray (11:1–13).

Love for God expresses itself in a variety of ways besides listening to and talking with God. Disciples give all of themselves to the Lord (Luke 9:57–62; 14:25–35). This means that generosity is a key characteristic of his life. In addition, that life is not defined by excessive attachment to material things (12:13–21; 16:1–32). The disciple is called to confess Christ and fear God (12:4–12), to seek the lost (15:1–32), to have faith (17:5–6), and to view his spiritual labor as his duty (17:7–10). Fundamentally, discipleship involves giving to God and to others.

The God of design and concern has devised a plan, in part, to produce such transformed people. Such ethics are to typify the community God has molded and saved through Jesus Christ. The Spirit whom Jesus gives enables this transformation. This is life lived as God designed it when he made people in God's image. Such a life pictures promise realized and enablement received. As seen in Luke 1:73–74, God made an oath to Abraham "to rescue us from the hand of our enemies, and to enable us to serve him without fear, in holiness and righteousness before him all our days." That is a key goal of the plan at an individual level.

6.5.9 God and Christ's Direct Intervention

A final way in which Luke reveals God's plan is through the direct intervention of God and his representative, the Christ. Early in Acts, an opponent, Gamaliel, states the driving observation of Luke's second volume as the Sanhedrin deliberates about how to handle the apostles (Acts 5:38–39). The respected rabbi states that if this movement is of human origin, it will fail of its own accord. But if it is of God, nothing can destroy it. To oppose it is to become an enemy of God. This statement poses the choice for the reader of Acts: the new movement is either divine or human in origin. Luke shows his preference even in the way the questions are framed. Luke has Gamaliel state the divine option with a first-class condition (εἰ plus a present indicative), a grammatical touch that has Gamaliel present the divine option with more certainty than the other alternative.

With this question posed, Luke describes a series of events that reveals God's hand in the activity and indicates the presence of a movement of God. Such activity extends beyond the numerous miraculous signs done in Jesus' name. For example, before Gamaliel's speech, the prison doors had been opened, so that Peter and his company were released (Acts 5:17–20). This act is probably what gives Gamaliel pause. Stephen's reception into heaven at the time of his martyrdom is yet another sign that God is with this movement and believers are on his side (7:55–56). God's direction of Philip also makes this point (8:26–29).

The reversal of Saul's life vocation from persecutor to persecuted witness for the Lord involves an appearance by Jesus (Acts 9:1–31). In fact, it takes a second appearance to Ananias to ensure that Saul is properly received (9:10–16). God directs in amazing ways and in surprising directions. The opening up of the door to Gentiles also requires a combination of visions, divine activity, and the public bestowal of the Spirit to make sure all see what God is doing (10:1–11:18). In a real sense, Luke's argument for the church's direction and activity in reaching out to the nations is simple: God has made us do it. This guidance requires engaging in such practices as giving the gospel to Gentiles. It also declares potential freedom from the Mosaic law's dietary restrictions for the sake of the gospel. In fact, in some cases when these visions initially come there is resistance (9:12–16; 10:13–16). But God insists, so the new community responds with obedience.

In the second half of Acts, such direction continues. God directly protects Peter and judges Herod in a picture of how divine judgment functions (Acts 12:1–23). Such direction continues in Paul's ministry. Whether in mission (13:1–3; 16:6–10, 26) or in travel (27:1–28:10), God actively directs and protects his witness. Luke is showing that this new movement is of God. This God stands behind the new community and has a plan. He has watched over this newly forming community and has sovereignly directed its mission, growth, and practice.

6.6 CONCLUSION

In examining how Luke portrays God's plan, it is important to see these themes as they are developed in Luke-Acts. Theophilus and others like him can be reassured as they examine what God has been and is doing in Christ (Luke 1:3–4). But details in the basic categories of the plan need examination as well. Who is this Jesus who saves (Christology)? How does Jesus bring salvation and the new era? How does one respond to the message of the sent one (soteriology)? Through which institution does God work, and what is that community's structure and task (ecclesiology)? Where is God's plan headed and how is it structured (eschatology)?

Our attention now turns to these questions to fill out this core picture of Lucan theology. Luke's theology paints a picture that focuses on the salvation of a caring, gracious God, who has sent Jesus to transform people's lives through the gift of salvation in the Spirit. God's ultimate desire is to bring people permanently back into healthy relationship with him, to seek and save the lost (Luke 19:10), and to call them to testify to God's goodness in promise (24:44–49).

Chapter 7

JESUS THE MESSIAH WHO IS LORD AND BRINGER OF THE NEW ERA: NARRATIVE ORDER

BIBLIOGRAPHY

Bock, Darrell L. *Proclamation from Prophecy and Pattern: Lucan Old Testament Christology.* JSNTSup. Sheffield: Sheffield Academic Press, 1987. **Buckwalter, Doug.** *The Character and Purpose of Luke's Christology.* SNTSMS. Cambridge: Cambridge University Press, 1996. Idem. "The Divine Savior." Pp. 107–23 in *Witness to the Gospel: The Theology of Acts.* Ed. I. Howard Marshall and David Peterson. Grand Rapids: Eerdmans, 1998. **O'Toole, Robert F.** "How Does Luke Portray Jesus as Servant of YHWH?" *Bib* 81 (2000): 328–46. Idem. *The Unity of Luke's Theology: An Analysis of Luke-Acts.* GNS 9. Wilmington, DE: Michael Glazier, 1984. **Rowe, C. Kavin.** *Early Narrative Christology: The Lord in the Gospel of Luke.* BZNW. Berlin: De Gruyter, 2006. **Strauss, Mark L.** *The Davidic Messiah in Luke-Acts: The Promise and Its Fulfillment in Lucan Christology.* JSNTSup. Sheffield; Sheffield Academic Press, 1995. **Tuckett, C. M.** "The Christology of Luke-Acts." Pp. 133–64 in *The Unity of Luke-Acts.* Ed. Joseph Verheyden. BETL. Leuven: Leuven University Press, 1999.

In this chapter, it is impossible to trace Luke's story of Jesus in sequence throughout the two volumes. That would result in a commentary. So we will trace key passages in narrative sequence as Jesus' mission and identity emerge. We move in this direction because many have claimed that Luke's Christology is haphazard and lacks coherence.[1] I argue the opposite, that Luke has a very nuanced and unified Christology.[2] After moving through Luke-Acts in this narrative manner, I will move in a more synthetic way to summarize Luke's Christology in the next chapter.

---

1. C. M. Tuckett, "The Christology of Luke-Acts," in *The Unity of Luke-Acts* (ed. Joseph Verheyden; BETL; Leuven: Leuven Univ. Press, 1999), 133–64.

2. In going this direction, I agree with the thrust of the work by C. Kavin Rowe, *Early Narrative Christology.* I do have some differences of nuance in how I see this unity, but Rowe is correct to proceed in a narratological manner, to see that "Lord" is a crucial title for Luke from early in his account, and that groundwork is laid not only for a high Christology but also for bridges to the idea of the Trinity. For this latter idea see Rowe's "Luke and the Trinity: An Essay in Ecclesial Biblical Theology," *SJT* 56 (2003): 1–26.

7.1 THE OVERTURE OF THE INFANCY NARRATIVE: INTRODUCING THE SENT ONE WHO IS MESSIAH-LORD

The first move Luke makes is through comparison. Luke's first two chapters juxtapose John the Baptist with Jesus. The manner in which this is done tells us about Jesus' uniqueness from the start. John is "a prophet of the Most High" (1:76) while Jesus is "great and will be called Son of the Most High" (1:32), "holy" (1:35), and "Son of God" (1:35). The repetition of Jesus' status makes the point more emphatically.

A look at the four titles tied to Jesus helps to indicate the direction things will go for Luke, although these titles in the infancy material are framed by a regal-messianic expectation. Luke 1:32 has two descriptions. The first is Jesus is "great." Often when this title is used by itself in the OT, it describes God (Pss 48:1; 95:3), though it also can describe people such as Moses (Exod 11:3) and Mordecai (Esth 10:3). In Mic 5:4, the coming Davidic figure is called "great ... to the ends of the earth." That text may be the one alluded to by Luke here.

The second title in Luke 1:32 sets up the fourth title in 1:35 and speaks of the "Son of the Most High." The name υἱὸς ὑψίστου (*huios hypsistou*) occupies an emphatic position because it precedes the verb. "Son of the Most High" is simply another way of saying "Son of God," since ὑψίστου is another way to refer to God's supreme authority as "the Most High." The title appears in the OT, in Judaism, and at Qumran (Gen 14:18–20, 22; Num 24:16; Ps 7:17 [7:18 LXX]; 2 Sam 22:14; Dan 4:24 [4:21 MT]; *Jub.* 16.18; *1 En.* 9.3; 10.1; 46.7; 60.1, 22; *T. Levi* 16.3; 1QapGen 12.17; 20.12, 16).[3] All but two of the NT uses of the genitive ὑψίστου are in Luke-Acts (Luke 1:32, 35, 76; 6:35; 8:28; Acts 16:17; cf. Mark 5:7; Heb 7:1).[4]

Some attribute this phrase to a Greek setting, but Qumran makes this description of the title's origin unlikely; it is a natural one for a Jewish setting.[5] The title "Son of the Most High" is clearly attested at Qumran in an Aramaic document that has several phrases parallel to Luke 1:31–35 (formerly 4Q243, now 4Q246 [= 4QpsDan ar^a = 4QpsDan A^a] 2.1). This passage is enigmatic because it is a fragmentary text containing only a few intriguing lines, but what is minimally present is the description of a regal figure.[6] The contemporary use of "Son of the Most High" for a king is therefore significant. A king is about to be born.

The phrase "Son of the Most High" also has parallels in the plural "sons of the Most High." Psalm 82:6 [81:6 LXX]; Matt 5:9; and Luke 6:35 show the phrase applying to special men of God. The psalm describes the OT judges, while the NT texts describe believers. Again, the term need not require a reference to deity. Rather, it describes someone with a special, intimate relationship to God.

---

3. Fitzmyer, *Gospel of Luke I–IX*, 347–48.
4. Marshall, *Gospel of Luke*, 67; Bertram, *TDNT*, 8:619–20.
5. Schweizer, *TDNT*, 8:381, n. 346.

6. Joseph Fitzmyer, "The Contribution of Qumran Aramaic to the Study of the New Testament," *NTS* 20 (1973–74): 391–94.

A regal reference to Jesus is also indicated by the description υἱός (*huios*, "son"). This term "son" occurs in various connections in the OT, including that of the Davidic king (2 Sam 7:14; 1 Chr 22:9–10; Pss 2:7; 89:26 [88:27 LXX]). It is also used regally and messianically at Qumran (4Q174 [= 4QFlor] 1.10–11).[7] As Jesus' birth is announced, regal imagery abounds to describe the coming Messiah.[8]

The third title (Luke 1:35) refers to Jesus' holiness, meaning that Jesus has been set apart for service to God. This sense conveys the basic meaning, but is there more significance to this term? Marshall argues that ἅγιον (*hagion*) leads into the description "Son of God" and should be taken as a reference to Jesus' divinity or at least his "divine relatedness."[9] This meaning depends on whether "Son of God" is taken as a term of divinity by Luke. Since the meaning of Son of God is the crux problem here, the exact force of *hagion* must wait until we have considered that title.

Until this verse, Jesus is clearly portrayed as the Davidic son, the regal messianic figure who is the hope of all Israel. The throne of David is specifically noted in Luke 1:32b, and the house of Jacob is named in 1:33. But does the addition of the title "Son of God" to the context mean the passage explicitly contains more than a simple declaration of Jewish regal hope?

The evidence offered for a deeper significance to the sonship reference is twofold. (1) The Holy Spirit's action on behalf of Jesus shows that his human origins are grounded in God's creative activity: Jesus is superior to John because of a superiority of position and the manner of his supernatural birth. (2) Verbally and linguistically there is a linkage between "Son of God" and "Son of the Most High" that makes them synonymous and points to a deeper role for Jesus than that of fulfilling the Jewish Davidic hope.[10] Initially, these arguments look compelling.

But historical linguistic factors and, more importantly, Luke's own usage raise questions about an explicit reference to a divine Son of God. The "birth from God" terminology appears at Qumran in 1Q28a [= 1QSa = Rule Annex] 2.11. The exact meaning of this passage is disputed, but it describes a nondivine child who is born with a special kinship to God through an anointing by God's Spirit. Thus, in contemporary Judaism, the phrase "Son of God" could describe a special human being without necessarily requiring ontological overtones.[11]

Luke's title "Son of God" is complex. The Davidic king can be seen as a "son" as 2 Sam 7:8–17 (esp. v. 14) shows. The special nature of Jesus' birth also points to this sonship and pushes us to see an additional element contributing to the framing of messianic-regal hope also proclaimed here by the angel. But again a careful look at details helps us see what Luke is doing. The most crucial factor is Luke's usage of the phrase. In Luke 1:32, Jesus is described as υἱὸς ὑψίστου (*huios hypsistou*, "Son of the Most High"), a phrase that anticipates 1:76, which, as noted above, is contrasted with John the Baptist as "a prophet of the Most High." That context, the hymn of

---

7. G. J. Brooke, *Exegesis at Qumran: 4QFlorilegium in Its Jewish Context* (JSOTSup 29; Sheffield: JSOT, 1985), 111–14, 197–205, especially 202–3.

8. Bock, *Luke 1:1–9:50*, 113–14.

9. Marshall, *Gospel of Luke*, 71.

10. Ibid., 67–71.

11. Bock, *Luke 1:1–9:50*, 123–24.

Zechariah known as the *Benedictus*, makes clear that the distinction is grounded in Jesus' Davidic office (1:69, 76). The contrast is one of role, not one necessarily of nature.

The same Davidic emphasis continues in Luke 2:26, 29–31. Jesus as Son is confessed at the baptism and, later, the transfiguration (9:35). The baptismal confession contains regal imagery (Ps 2:7), while the transfiguration follows a messianic confession (9:20). "Son" also appears in texts where exorcism is present or an attack by Satan is made (4:3, 9, 41; 8:28). Luke 4:41 is particularly significant because the verse is unique to Luke. There Luke explains the title "Son of God" by the following ὅτι (*hoti*, "because") clause, stating that the meaning of "Son of God" is that Jesus is Χριστόν (*Christon*, "Christ, Messiah"). Thus, Luke's usage consistently has a messianic thrust.

So Luke presents the title "Son of God" consistently as the Davidic deliverer, the regal and messianic Christ. For Luke, the Son of God is Messiah, at least at this point of his presentation. The presence of a divine element in Jesus' birth does not require or focus on an *explicit* statement of Jesus' metaphysical divinity; rather, it asserts that Jesus' origins are divinely grounded in the Spirit's creative power. Jesus is uniquely from God. This implies that there is more here than an earthly king, but the stress is not on ontology but on *office*. Luke has heightened the Jewish conceptual use of being born of God by tying it to a virgin conception. Jesus is from God in a unique way. His kingship is not only the reflection of a covenant relationship with God; it is rooted in God's direct act leading to incarnation. In this way, Luke is saying more than that Jesus is an earthly king, but the details are to be worked out in what Luke does in the rest of his narrative.

Luke's Davidic focus in the title "Son of God" implies an ontological conclusion, but the point here is simply that Luke does not emphasize ontology by his use of *this title*, as his later usage of "Son of God" also shows. One must distinguish between what Luke's language focuses on and what his language may give room for in terms of theological development. One cannot say that Luke does not believe Jesus to be divine. Luke's use of other titles reveals his high Christology. His use of the title "Lord" in Acts makes that clear, and Jesus' own portrayal of God as his Father in Luke 2:41–52 suggests that Luke did see Jesus in this deeper light. However, it seems that Luke does not seek to make this deeper christological point from his early usage of the title "Son of God." The nature of Luke's usage also explains why the hymns of Mary and Zechariah in Luke 1 concentrate on Davidic themes. It also serves to explain why at points Mary is troubled with the form of Jesus' ministry. She certainly is not portrayed as perceiving an announcement of a divine child here.

So, Jesus as a result of God's creative power comes as the Son of God. This portrayal views Christ's birth from the perspective of the start of his human existence. Luke builds his Christology from the ground up. Raymond Brown makes the point that there is no mention of Jesus' preexistence in Luke, a point that is correct enough, but neither is there a denial of such a role.[12] Luke portrays merely the earthly ministry and history of Jesus. The absence of a fully theologically developed presentation of Jesus in the infancy material is a defense of its authenticity. Luke makes no effort to Christianize or to theologically deepen Jesus' portrait to conform to what is later more clearly perceived about him.

Thus, this account fits the Jewish setting from which it emerges. The divine conception of Jesus is a supernatural work. His description as Son has a messianic and nativistic meaning.[13] The messianic thrust comes from the Davidic messianic context, while the nativistic or birth thrust comes from Luke 1:34 and 3:38. As Son, Jesus is a holy Messiah and possibly also is seen as True Man, the second Adam. Later texts will make it clear that his messiahship and sonship have even greater connections that transcend Jesus' earthly sonship ties. But Luke does not make such points explicit here.[14]

Jesus is a messianic figure with transcendent roots. This makes him far greater than John the Baptist. How much of a difference his position is from John's is shown in various ways. (1) Luke has John all but disappear once Jesus is introduced in the infancy story. (2) John is not directly connected to the events of Jesus' baptism in Luke 3. That event is told with the divine voice and Jesus as the only noted participants. (3) When John describes the one to come, he portrays himself as unworthy to untie the thong of his sandal (Luke 3:16). This is a significant thing for a prophet to declare, for in Jewish tradition, tying the thong of a master's sandal was prohibited as too demeaning an act for a Jewish slave (*Mekilta de Rabbi Ishmael, Nezekin* 1 on Exod 21:1). So if the difference between a prophet and the one to come is this great, then Jesus as the sent one to come is in a class by himself.

The second means Luke uses to point to Jesus' uniqueness is through the annunciation of a birth through a virgin and the note that this child is born by the agency of "the Holy Spirit" (Luke 1:26–35). Unlike Matthew, who points to Isa 7:14, Luke merely presents the announcement, saying to Mary at the key point that "the Holy Spirit will come on you, and the power of the Most High will overshadow you" (1:35). The association of the Spirit and the power of God will appear again in 24:49. This work of God through his Spirit opens the door to the close association between God, the Son, and the Spirit. This is the nativistic use of the idea of the Son. It does not make full an understanding of who Jesus is, but it does set the table for it. Jesus' birth is like no other.[15] He is great and uniquely sent from God.

The sonship of Jesus focuses on another central role that Jesus has in Luke. He

---

12. Raymond Brown, *The Birth of the Messiah: A Commentary on the Infancy Narratives in Matthew and Luke* (Garden City, NY: Doubleday, 1977), 291, 314, n. 48.

13. By "nativistic" I mean to say the term has a meaning rooted in his incarnational birth through divine activity.

14. Bock, *Luke 1:1–9:50*, 124–25.

15. There are resonances with births of other greats in the Greco-Roman world here, for Alexander the Great and Augustus were portrayed as birthed by the gods. However, in their case the impregnation by divinity was portrayed in a vivid manner involving snakes or portents. In contrast, Luke speaks only of an act of the power of God in the Spirit with no presentation of how Mary came to be pregnant. For these other portrayals of birth, see, for Augustus, Suetonius, *Augustus* 94; for Alexander, Plutarch, *Alexander* 2. What the existence of the parallels means is that the significance of the scene would be evident to Greco-Roman auditors of the story. Jesus is closely tied to heaven. Just how much is a part of the rest of Luke's story.

fulfills the promise of a "king" of the line of David who rules over Jacob's house in a kingdom to last forever (Luke 1:30–33).[16] This role, often tied to the idea of a "Messiah," explains the angelic declaration in 2:11 that Jesus is born in Bethlehem as "a Savior … he is the Messiah, the Lord." The juxtaposition of these titles is one way Luke uses to reinforce the close association between God and Jesus, one in which they are inseparable regarding how God's plan comes to fruition.

Luke's use of various images to set forth the idea that Jesus is Messiah rather than simple predication reflects how he presents his christological portrait. This variety means that simply looking for the use of a specific title may miss references to the concept and its development. The first direct words about Jesus in 1:31–35 are about his authority and call to rule. This introduces the kingdom and rule theme in Luke. Given how the announcement of John's birth was made to Zechariah (1:15–17), this is what the people were being prepared to participate in from John, who served as a forerunner preparing the way for God's salvation (1:16–17 with 3:4–6).[17]

The messianic thrust and base for Lucan Christology is affirmed again in Luke 1:68–79. Zechariah praises God for raising up a "horn of salvation" for us in the house of David (1:69). This reference comes from the OT, which pictures an ox with horns that is able to defeat enemies with a powerful thrust of its protected head (Deut 33:17). The image was transferred to the warrior who had a horned helmet to symbolize the presence of power (Pss 75:4–5, 10 [75:5–6, 11 MT]; 148:14 [in reference to the nation of Israel]; 1QH 9.28–29). The figure is also used to describe God himself (2 Sam 22:3; Ps 18:2 [18:3 MT]). In particular, the term was often used for a powerful regal figure. In some of these references the horn is specifically tied to the Davidic house, portrayed as delivering the nation (1 Sam 2:10; Ps 132:17; Ezek 29:21; Benediction 15 of the Jewish prayer *Shemoneh Esreh* [*Eighteen Benedictions*]). The nature of the powerful messianic deliverance is spelled out in the following

---

16. This is persuasively argued by Mark L. Strauss, *The Davidic Messiah in Luke-Acts: The Promise and Its Fulfillment in Lucan Christology* (JSNTSup 110; Sheffield: Sheffield Academic Press, 1995), 76–125. In a difference of nuance, it is C. Kavin Rowe's failure in his *Early Narrative Christology* to mention how the key announcement of Luke 1:31–35 sets up Luke's portrait of Jesus that causes him to highlight "Lord" at the expense of Messiah. He is correct to criticize me for underemphasizing the role of Lord early on in Luke in my *Proclamation from Prophecy and Pattern: Lucan Old Testament Christology* (JSNTSup; Sheffield: Sheffield Academic Press, 1987), but he missed my narrative point in his critique on p. 8. It was that "Lord" is introduced without as much development in the infancy material as the image of "Messiah" receives; Luke's initial emphasis is on Jesus' role as the promised Davidite. Rowe's treatment of 1:43 argues that Jesus is shown to be Lord as a result of a special birth, defining that role. I argued that the role of Jesus there was ambiguous. Narratively, Rowe is correct here, but the movement of the story in the understanding of the characters reflects the ambiguity I argued for. Mary, Zechariah, and Simeon praise

Jesus for his role as messianic deliverer, not something more. On another point, Luke is not engaged in effect in christological self-correction as Tuckett charges me as seeing in Luke ("Christology of Luke-Acts," 149–53). This is narrative development to gradually reveal who Jesus is, not an engagement with possible competing views from outside the narrative in Luke-Acts. The fact that Luke connects Messiah and Lord and relates them to each other means that one does not choose one title over another in Luke-Acts as in a correction, but comes to appreciate the relationship between these titles. Luke moves from the earth up in his portrayal with hints of something more at the start.

17. Another nuance difference with Rowe is that he sees a shift in the focus on Lord moving from the God of Israel to Jesus as we move from Luke 1:15–17 to 1:76 to 3:4 (*Early Narrative Christology*, 70–77). I would state this slightly differently. Luke is playing with the overlap, using Lord for both God and Jesus and making a crucial point about their intimate and shared authority, but the emphasis is on God as the main actor with Jesus as the agent of that deliverance.

verses (esp. Luke 1:71, 74). Zechariah portrays a Messiah of great power who will deliver God's people from their enemies.

The image of the "rising sun" functioning as light is also a messianic theme, from Isa 9:1 (Luke 1:78–79). Here the key image is of the ἀνατολή (*anatolē*). This Greek term (lit., "that which springs up") has a rich and varied OT background. In some passages it refers to "the branch" or "sprout" in dependence on the Hebrew term *ṣemaḥ* (Isa 11:1–10; Jer 23:5; 33:15 [not present in the LXX]; Zech 3:8; 6:12). It can also refer to the rising sun or star when the verbal form ἀνατέλλω (*anatellō*, "to rise up") is used (Num 24:17; Mal 4:2 [3:20 MT/LXX]). At Qumran and in contemporary Judaism, the former sense of "branch" was predominant and was understood messianically. Interestingly, both Philo (*Confusion* 14 §§60–63) and Justin Martyr (*Dial.* 100.4; 106.4; 121.2; 126.1) saw the term as messianic and tied it to the picture of a heavenly light.[18] *T. Judah* 24.1, 6 appears to mix the two images. Thus, the title was clearly messianic in the first century, though the picture in the term varied.

But which image is key in this text: branch or sun? The latter, for the context clearly marks the image of light as key. Ἀνατολή is qualified by the phrase ἐξ ὕψους (*ex hypsous*, "from on high"), a reference to the heavens. Moreover, Luke 1:79 goes on to speak of the light guiding in the midst of darkness, so that the picture is of a beacon from heaven. Nolland may be right in appealing to Isa 60:2–3 and 58:8–10 as important conceptual background.[19]

But many think that the first-century association of the term with the messianic Branch was so strong that double entendre is present—that is, that Luke intends to evoke both associations, though the rising sun association is the dominant idea.[20] By God's mercy, God's regal Messiah visits and serves people as a guiding heavenly light, leading them into God's way of peace. Marshall summarizes: "The imagery is thus that of the Davidic Messiah, the Shoot from Jesse (Is. 11:1ff.) and the star from Jacob (Nu. 24:17) who is to visit men from on high, i.e., from the dwelling place of God (2 Sa. 22:17)."[21] God sends his Messiah as the bright dawn of salvation shining on the face of people.[22]

This base declaration from the announcement to Mary and the hymn of Zechariah serves as a key to how Luke unveils who Jesus is. It places Jesus in a messianic regal context but as one who has transcendent roots in his birth.

Another key idea introduced early on is the idea of Jesus' position as "Lord." In Luke 1:43 Elizabeth addresses Mary as "the mother of my Lord" (ἡ μήτηρ τοῦ κυρίου μου, *hē mētēr tou kyriou mou*). The exact force of this is not clear from Elizabeth's point of view, but all the characters in Luke focus on the deliverance and realization of promise that Jesus represents. This is the most likely connection of the force of the passage. That is, Elizabeth is referring to "the mother of my king."[23]

---

18. Schlier, *TDNT*, 1:353.
19. Nolland, *Luke 1–9:20*, 90.
20. Bock, *Proclamation from Prophecy and Pattern*, 73.

21. Marshall, *Gospel of Luke*, 95.
22. Bock, *Luke 1:1–9:50*, 191–92.
23. So Strauss, *Davidic Messiah in Luke-Acts*, 95–96.

That the word "Lord" connects to the birthing work of the Spirit is not transparent (though it can be inferred), since in the earlier announcement Jesus is connected to sonship with God and the messianic role (4:41, a text unique to him; Acts 9:20, 22).

All of this initial ambiguity about exact relationships will be developed and clarified as Luke's narrative proceeds. He focuses on promise and Messiah in the infancy material but is also building narrative bridges to even more that he will say. In doing this, Luke sets up an unfolding story of who Jesus is so it can dawn on his readers as the story is told just how far all of this Christology goes. In this way he is reinforcing and assuring readers like Theophilus (Luke 1:4) that Jesus is who the church preaches him to be: both Christ and Lord.

Another theme here is Jesus as deliverer or "Savior." This is primarily what his work involves. Mary announces the victory to come in eschatological reversal and highlights a new, promised era that comes with this deliverance (Luke 1:46–55). The end of her hymn mentions promises to Abraham and his seed (1:55). Zechariah speaks of the already noted powerful horn of deliverance out of the house of David. This one frees people to serve God in fear and holiness, using the image of dawn coming to remove darkness to make the point (1:68–79). So here, although the title Savior is not used, the concept of deliverance is already clearly present.

All of this is summed up in the key title of "Savior" (σωτήρ, sōtēr) in Luke 2:11 with the angel's announcement. The sōtēr word group, when referring to people in the OT, describes a deliverer from enemies, such as a judge (Jdg 3:9, 15; 12:3; Neh 9:27). The only OT king related to this word group is Jehoahaz (2 Kgs 13:5). The primary OT reference of this term, however, is to God, who delivers from various types of peril: enemies who seek to destroy and diseases that seek to kill (Deut 20:4; Josh 22:22; Pss 24:5 [23:5 LXX]; 25:5 [24:5 LXX]; Isa 25:9). In the OT, Messiah is never called σωτήρ. In fact, Messiah as a technical term for the Davidic Anointed One is clearly developed in intertestamental literature (*Pss. Sol.* 17), though its roots go back to Ps 2:2. In Greek culture, σωτήρ referred either to gods who delivered or to humans who saved other humans from dangers (e.g., doctors, rulers, and philosophers). The term was popularly used of Roman rulers.[24] Luke intends the reader to see the meaning of σωτήρ in terms of rescue or delivery from peril, in both its physical and spiritual senses.

Again, overlap with a title for God takes place here. In Luke 1:47, it is the God of Israel who is "my Savior" (sōtēri mou). God's program is so intimately bound up with Jesus that they share roles and key titles. The emphasis continues with Simeon, who waits for the consolation of Israel and is told by the Spirit that he will live to see the Christ. When he holds the child, he sees God's "salvation" (σωτήριον, sōtērion, Luke 2:30), a salvation prepared in the presence of all the people, a light, which is "for revelation to the Gentiles and the glory of your people Israel" (2:31–32). The idea of someone's seeing God's salvation has OT echoes (Ps 98:2; Isa 40:5; 52:10; cf. Luke 3:6; conceptually 1QH 5.12; see also Luke 10:23–24). For Luke, Messiah's

---

24. Foerster and Fohrer, *TDNT*, 7:1003–21.

coming is at the center of salvation. The mood of joy in this text dominates the rest of the passage. Kingdom, deliverance, and salvation are linked together in the infancy material of Luke. This is the call and mission of Jesus the Messiah, who is Savior and Lord.

With all the triumph of these themes, the infancy material does hold one ominous note. Simeon again is responsible. He tells Mary that the child will be for "the falling and rising of many in Israel" (Luke 2:34). Jesus will divide Israel and will be rejected by many despite all that God has announced about him through a series of pious witnesses from the nation.[25] Two images appear in 2:34–35: Jesus will bring division and he will be a sign. Here is another set of themes, like Lord, that are introduced but left for development later in the narrative.

A closer look at Luke 2:34–35 shows the tension Jesus' coming introduces because of the different reactions he will generate. The first image of falling and rising is drawn from Isaiah, where God is portrayed as setting up a stone of stumbling over which some fall (Isa 8:14–15) but a precious cornerstone that will not disappoint those who trust in it (28:13–16, esp. v. 16). The use of these texts is common in the NT (Luke 20:17–18; Rom 9:33; 1 Pet 2:6–8).[26] The linking of Isa 8 with Isa 28 is possible either through recourse to the MT's use of the verbal element *ðâbar* ("to break") or through the LXX text's use of *piptō* ("to fall") and *syntribō* ("to break"). Since Messiah was the personification of God's deliverance and the agent of his justice, these texts were easily related to the Messiah.

The nature of the "falling and rising" picture is disputed. Is there one group that falls only to rise again—a reference relating only to the believers' suffering and vindication? Or are there two groups, unbelievers who fall and believers who rise on the basis of their response of faith to Jesus? Those who argue for one group make the point that in the OT the image of falling and rising refers to the same group (Prov 24:16; Isa 24:20; Amos 5:2; 8:14; Mic 7:8). In addition, the picture of falling only to rise sets up a perfect contrast to the image of the sign of contention later in the verse. Thus, it is argued that the image is of the humble (Luke 1:52), who start out low but are exalted by God.

Against this view is the context, which seems to suggest a note of deep pain in Mary in Luke 2:35b. If the note of this saying is evenly positive and negative for a single group, then the focus on her pain seems inappropriate. In addition, the normal force of the stone image in the NT is one of division (Luke 20:17–18; Rom 9:33; 1 Pet 2:6–8). Finally, a consistent NT note about Jesus' ministry is that it divides people into two groups (Luke 4:29; 6:20–26; 13:28–29, 33–35; 16:25; 18:9–14; 19:44, 47–48; 20:14–18; esp. 12:51).[27] Thus, it seems better to see an

---

25. There is a wonderful gender and age balance in these notes of praise and reflection. Zechariah is old and male. Elizabeth is old and female. Mary is young and female. Simeon is likely old and male, while Anna, who also looked for the redemption of Jerusalem (2:38), is old and female. These righteous Israelites are led to appreciate who

Jesus is. They are the first of Luke's witnesses to what God is doing.

26. Note that the image of a figure of division or of one who causes rising and falling also occurred at Qumran (1QH 2.8–10; 1QM 14.10–11).

27. Fitzmyer, *Gospel of Luke I–IX*, 422–23.

allusion to two groups in falling and rising, with those who reject Jesus headed for a fall, while those who accept him in faith are headed for vindication. The qualification "in Israel" shows the nationalistic perspective here. Jesus and the claims of his work will divide the nation.

The emphasis on opposition continues in the second image of the passage, namely, that Jesus will be a sign of contesting. Ἀντιλεγόμενον (*antilegomenon*, "that which is opposed") has a future sense, since Simeon is discussing how people will respond to Jesus. Humans will resist him. For them, Jesus will not be a hope of promise fulfilled, but a figure to be opposed. The sign is characterized best as one of contention, not only rejection, because the point of the context is division.[28] The incident in Luke 4:28–29 illustrates this situation as the people in Nazareth react against Jesus' synagogue speech and his mention of the low state of Israel's spiritual condition as he compares it to the era of Elijah and Elisha, where only Gentiles benefited from ministry. Simeon knows that although Jesus is God's hope, not everyone will respond positively to him. The raising of this aspect of Jesus' fate is Luke's first indication that all will not go smoothly for God's anointed.[29]

A final note from the infancy material comes from Jesus himself. It is the first place he speaks. When his parents discover that their twelve-year-old son is not with the returning pilgrimage caravan but later return to find him in the temple, Jesus declares that he "had to be in my Father's house" (Luke 2:49). The key Lucan term δεῖ (*dei*, "it is necessary")—used strategically in the gospel where elements of Jesus' mission are set forth—is included in the statement. This is the only use of δεῖ that suggests Jesus' relationship to the Father. His parents need to understand his mission.

A close look at Luke 2:49 shows the point. The thrust of Jesus' reply has been debated. The issue turns on filling in a missing element in the passage. The key phrase ἐν τοῖς τοῦ πατρός μου (*en tois tou patros mou*) is literally translated "in the ___ of my Father." Some translations read, "I must be about my Father's business" (KJV; NKJV; Erasmus).[30] This view can amass many parallel texts (e.g., Mark 8:33; 1 Cor 7:32–34; 1 Tim 4:15). The idea then becomes that God's ministry is paramount to Jesus and that his parents must understand this.

But this reading is contextually less than satisfying. The issue up to this point was his parents' pain in searching for Jesus. Why should Jesus raise the broad issue of the Father's business when Mary simply wants to know why he stayed behind at the temple? To put it another way, Jesus could do the Father's business in lots of places other than the temple, as his ministry will prove. Thus, this reading is not clearly supported from the context. Also, Luke 2:49 uses a grammatical construction (ἐν, *en*, and a neuter plural article) that is not used in the similar passages of Mark 8:33 and 1 Cor 7:32–34. First Timothy 4:15 does use ἐν, but with a neuter plural demonstrative pronoun. This "Father's business" view is unlikely to be correct.

---

28. Rengstorf, *TDNT*, 7:238–39.
29. Bock, *Luke 1:1–9:50*, 246–47.

30. See discussion in Brown, *Birth of the Messiah*, 476.

The most widely held view today is that the phrase translates, "I had to be in my Father's house" (NIV). Jesus must be involved with instruction in divine things, since the temple as presented by Luke is above all a place where instruction occurs (Luke 20–21). An additional point here is that Jesus' parents should have known where to look. The construction of ἐν with the neuter plural article followed by a genitive fits this view best. This is an idiom for being in one's house (Gen 41:51; Esth 7:9; Job 18:19; Josephus, *Ag. Ap.* 1.18 [118]; *Ant.* 16.10.1 [302]; P. Oxy. vol. 3 #523 line 3). Thus, Jesus declares the necessity of being in God's house, where God's presence is held to reside and where instruction about God is given.[31]

In other words, Jesus' first word about himself in Luke's gospel reveals both his sense of mission and a connection that is greater than family. The priority rests in his unique connection to God as his Father. This relationship to God reinforces the idea behind the picture of Lord and Messiah, who is Savior. Messiah has connections that transcend seeing Jesus as a strictly human agent and figure. It is on this note that the infancy portrait of Jesus ends, along with a human note about Jesus, that he grew in "wisdom" and "favor" (Luke 2:40, 52).

7.2 THE BODY OF LUKE'S GOSPEL: ACTIONS OF AUTHORITY AND THE ARRIVAL OF A NEW ERA

The work of Jesus as Messiah is connected to the Spirit in Luke 3:15–17. In a traditional passage whose framing is unique to Luke, John the Baptist is responding to speculation that people think he might be the Messiah. John's response uniquely tells us how we can know that Jesus is the Messiah. "The stronger one" to come (ὁ ἰσχυρότερος, *ho ischyroteros*) will baptize with the Spirit in contrast to John's water baptism.[32] This explicit tie of the Spirit's coming to the work of Messiah reflects a linkage of elements that normally were discussed separately in the Hebrew Scripture and Second Temple Judaism. The Spirit was associated with the new era in the new covenant as well as in other texts (Isa 32:15; 44:3; Ezek 36:25–27; Joel 2:28–32 [3:1–5 MT]; 1QS 4.20–21), while Messiah was a deliverer in that period who is Spirit-endowed (Isa 11:1–4; *1 En.* 49.2–3; 62.1–2). The writer of *Pss. Sol.* 17–18 looks to a purging for righteousness by a Messiah who is endowed with the Spirit, wisdom, and righteousness, but he does not tie that explicitly to the distribution of the Spirit to others (*Pss. Sol.* 17.22–25, 30, 35–37; 18.7).[33] So John as a prophet is putting pieces together in yet another linkage to develop the hope tied to Jesus.

The bringing together of Jesus and the Spirit takes place at his baptism (Luke 3:21–22). The saying of the voice from heaven consists of three parts: (lit.) a reference

---

31. Bock, *Luke 1:1–9:50*, 169–70.

32. We already noted the great difference in how John as prophet sees himself in reference to this stronger one by his note about not being worthy to untie the thong of the coming one's sandal.

33. Strauss, *Davidic Messiah in Luke-Acts*, 201 (see entire discussion on pp. 202–8). The image of fire is a combination of purg-

ing and judging that John sees in one act (Isa 4:4; Luke 12:49–50 breaks this up as something yet to come). There is no perspective of two comings here. The tradition Luke uses has preserved the unified look at the career of the one to come here. What John also foresees is a distinguishing within humanity that Messiah brings.

to the "Son" (υἱός, *huios*), a reference to the "beloved" (ἀγαπητός, *agapētos*), and a reference to God's being "well pleased" with the Son (ἐν σοὶ εὐδόκησα, *en soi eudokēsa*). The OT background to the saying is important. The reference to υἱός comes from Ps 2:7, and the reference to God's being pleased is from Isa 42:1. Only the source for ἀγαπητός is disputed. Three options have been suggested.

(1) A phrase in Gen 22:12, 16, τοῦ υἱοῦ σου τοῦ ἀγαπητοῦ (*tou huiou sou tou agapētou*, "your beloved son"), may be behind the reference. Thus, the idiom here in Luke 3:22 (ὁ υἱός μου ὁ ἀγαπητός) should be rendered "only Son." The emphasis is on the uniqueness of Jesus' sonship. (a) However, υἱός has a double meaning in this view, since it would be drawn from both Ps 2:7 and Gen 22:12 and would refer both to Messiah and to the Isaac typology. Such a multilayered allusion is possible, but it is complicated since two distinct types of sonship are in view. (b) Moreover, Luke has no Isaac typology clearly present in his material. In fact, in the NT, only Paul comes close to this allusion by his wording of Rom 8:32, though Heb 11:17–19 might also apply. (c) Luke does use μονογενής (*monogenēs*, "only begotten or unique") when he wishes to express the idea (Luke 7:12; 8:42; 9:38). (d) The shift from ἀγαπητός to ἐκλελεγμένος (*eklelegmenos*, "chosen") in Luke 9:35 speaks against the connection. That saying parallels this account and serves to give a clue as to the meaning of ἀγαπητός in 3:22. It does not suggest the Gen 22 reference.

(2) Isaiah 41:8 and 44:2 may be behind ἀγαπητός with their association of being chosen and being loved. Some argue for this approach based on the Targum on the Ps 2:7, which includes a reference to ἀγαπητός.[34] However, this targum is of a late date and its reference to sonship is too indirect to have been of influence.[35] In addition, Isa 44:2 cannot be a part of the connection since the reference to the concept of love is absent in that passage.

(3) It seems best to tie the reference to ἀγαπητός, if it has OT origin, to Isa 41:8. In this passage the ideas of servant, chosen, and beloved are tied together. This Isaiah passage links up with Isa 42 in that the ideas of servant and chosen are repeated. In Matthew, the concept of chosen in Isa 42 is translated as "beloved," which reflects this earlier linkage. It may be that the saying links only a targum-like rendering of Isa 42 with Ps 2, but if so, the hidden point of contact is still the concept of Isa 41. Thus, the reference to ἀγαπητός speaks of Jesus' intimate and chosen position. It also may imply that Jesus represents the nation, since Isa 41:8 refers to the nation.[36]

Thus, Ps 2:7, Isa 42:1, and possibly Isa 41:8 are the OT elements behind the voice's endorsement of Jesus in Luke 3:21–22. But what does the saying, with these allusions, tell us about him? Psalm 2 is a regal psalm that looks ideally at the king's total rule. The allusion to "my Son" in terms of Ps 2 says that Jesus is this regal figure. This allusion is essentially messianic, when it is placed alongside John the Baptist's declaration in Luke 3:16. This position is confirmed within Luke by the

---

34. Schweizer, *TDNT*, 8:368.

35. I. H. Marshall, "Son of God or Servant of Yahweh?—A Reconsideration of Mark i.11," *NTS* 15 (1968–69): 326–36,

esp. 333–34.

36. Bock, *Luke 1:1–9:50*, 341–43.

regal and rule images that appear in the other usages of the messianic concept. "My Son" appears in Luke 9:35, after a section where Jesus is confessed as "the Messiah" (the messianic concept also occurs in Acts 4:25–30, where similar "anointed" sentiments are expressed, and anointing is used with similar force in 10:36–38). Thus, a key part of the endorsement is a messianic one. In this it matches up well with the christological thrust of the infancy material.

For Luke, this event is more about Jesus' commission and enablement to begin ministry than the coming of the Spirit that Jesus previously lacked, since the Spirit is tied to Jesus at his birth. Again the Spirit in the Messiah link is strong in Jewish contexts (Isa 11:2; *Pss. Sol.* 17:37; 18:7; 1QSb 5.25; 4QpIsaᵃ 3.15–29). Luke makes the exchange a direct one between heaven and Jesus, for there is no direct mention of John within this event, although we can be sure that Luke is well aware of the tradition that John's baptism is in view here. More important to Luke than who performed the rite was what happened during it. The Spirit descends in bodily form, and a voice connects Jesus to a role as regal son (Ps 2:7) and as the Servant of God who declares and brings deliverance (Isa 42:1). Interestingly, the Servant is associated with the Spirit, just as Messiah was, because of Isa 42:1 and 61:1. So this scene brings yet more linkage to the concept of Messiah with other titles, repeating the Son-Messiah link of Luke 1:31–35 and adding the image of Servant to the portrait. The role of Scripture for Christology is important as the alluded texts carry the expositional weight. This heavenly endorsement points Luke's reader to a key revelatory moment about Jesus. When heaven speaks, we must hear.

The human side of Jesus as representative of humanity in terms of promise, kingship, and a tie to being Son of God appears next. This more representative sense comes from Luke's genealogy (Luke 3:23–38). Here the line runs through David for kingship, Abraham for promise, and uniquely back to Adam for the tie as "son of God" directly created by God to be human.

The Spirit's guiding of Jesus continues in Luke 4:1[37] and 14, as the key text of 4:16–30 follows immediately, where Jesus states both his mission and its fulfillment in the present at the synagogue in Nazareth. Here the text appealed to is a combination of Isa 61:1–2 and 58:6. Jesus is anointed by the Spirit as he realizes the commission of both prophet and king. The OT background of the passage is significant, as is the history of the interpretation of Isa 61. This Servant Song-like passage describes the prophet's role in terms used of the Servant of Isaiah (esp. in 42:1–4; 49:1–11). The figure of Isa 61 brings a message of God's deliverance to exiles suffering from the discipline of having been unfaithful to God. The deliverance imagery parallels the description of the Jubilee year (Lev 25: 8–17), when debts were canceled and slaves were freed every fiftieth year. It is a picture of forgiveness and spiritual liberation, which is at the center of Jesus' message.

---

37. Luke 4:1 continues the Adam-Christ typology as Jesus (in contrast to Adam) survives a test by Satan that the Spirit leads him into experiencing.

Isaiah 58 contains a prophetic rebuke of the nation for not exhibiting justice toward those in their nation who are in need. There God declares that the fast he prefers is one that treats one's neighbor properly. Isaiah 61 proclaims a time like that envisioned but not carried out by the nation in Isa 58. The two passages belong together because the release pictured in Isa 58 has Jubilee overtones and also describes release in Sabbath terms, an event much like the year of Jubilee. When Jesus applies the passage to himself, he is saying that the present time is like the message of comfort that Isaiah brought to the nation. In fact, the totality of the deliverance that Isaiah described is now put into motion with Jesus' coming. Jesus is the Servant par excellence, and the anointing he notes in the speech looks back to the regal emphasis in the remarks of the divine voice at his baptism.[38]

In this scene, Jesus connects his work to prophetic themes in the parallels to the time of Elijah and Elisha with references to the widow of Zarephath and Naaman the Syrian, as well as to the remark that a prophet has no honor in his hometown. However, the messianic theme is also present in the linkage back to the anointing and the voice of the baptism. Interestingly, in this event, it is not the christological claim of fulfillment that gives the Nazareth crowd the most pause, but the rebuke of Israel that a lack of faith means God may move to work with Gentiles. Thus this theme connects back to Simeon's remarks in Luke 2:25–35.

This passage completes the key explicit early texts in Luke's gospel framing who Jesus is. From here it is more actions that reveal who he is. Jesus silences demonic confessions because the demons know he is "the Holy One of God," "the Son of God," and "Messiah" (Luke 4:34, 41).[39] The first demon's confession here is important for what it suggests; it reveals the basis of his fear, that Jesus is not just a Nazarene, he is "the Holy One of God." He has a special anointing from God and is his Servant. In the OT, similar titles refer to Aaron (Ps 106:16 [105:16 LXX]) and Elisha (2 Kgs 4:9; cf. the description of Samson in Jdg 13:7). Thus, some suggest that Jesus is seen only as a prophet or a commissioned figure here.[40]

If one takes Luke 4:34 by itself, such an allusion might be possible, but this association ignores Lucan literary factors. Luke had made a connection between the Holy One and the Davidic Messiah in Luke 1:31–35. This connection appears again here in the conjunction of Son and Messiah in 4:41.[41] Luke clearly sees a messianic conflict. The Lucan connections also make likely the view of Procksch that the Holy One of God refers to Jesus as the bearer of the Spirit.[42] Thus, we have a battle between the "impure spirit" and the one who has the Holy Spirit. As James 2:19 notes, demons do have knowledge about God. They also appear to know who Jesus is and have some awareness of his power. This impure spirit is nervous about what Jesus will do. Evil has severe angst in the presence of righteousness ready to be exercised.

38. Bock, *Luke 1:1–9:50*, 405–6.

39. The juxtaposition of Son of God and Messiah in 4:41 is unique to Luke's account of this scene.

40. Fitzmyer, *Gospel of Luke I–IX*, 546.

41. Schürmann, *Lukasevangelium: Kommentar zu Kap. 1.1–9.50*, 249.

42. Procksch, *TDNT*, 1:101–2.

Jesus next calls Peter and those with him to "fish for people" (Luke 5:1–11). Here is Jesus' mission: not to overturn governments but to recover people. Then in 5:24 we have Jesus describing himself as "the Son of Man" with authority to forgive sin as only God does. This title is the one Jesus chooses most commonly as a self-reference.[43] He eventually will reveal that the designation comes from Dan 7:13–14, where "son of man" is simply a human figure in contrast to the four beasts. Yet his authority, derived from the Ancient of Days, is extensive, since this figure rides on the clouds and brings vindication to the saints. All of this background emerges explicitly through Jesus' later use and development of the phrase. In Luke 5, Jesus simply introduces the cryptic designation, a term that in Aramaic can also be an idiomatic way to say either "me" or "someone." By his actions, Jesus reveals himself as the Son of Man and indicates the extent of the authority he possesses. If the paralytic walks, the miracle talks about the Son of Man's authority to forgive sin. If the Son of Man possesses such unique authority, then who is the Son of Man other than God's unique agent of salvation? That is the question that this miracle raises.[44]

The Son of Man in Luke 5:24 can refer to Jesus as a representative man called by God to exercise authority over sin. That authority, however, is unique to Jesus and as such means that the representative himself is unique. In fact, if the healing evidences the verbal claim, then the divine prerogative is exercised uniquely by a man. Jesus' innovations with the Son of Man concept as they emerge from 5:24 and its later NT usage would be (1) the claim to be able to identify the authoritative, heavenly human figure (as himself!); and (2) the association of that figure with the Son of Man's right to forgive sins. This latter claim by Jesus is most certainly authentic, because the Son of Man's association with the forgiveness of sins is dissimilar to both Judaism's claims and the early church's language about Jesus. In other words, this term is one that goes back to Jesus himself, even if it was used in its most ambiguous sense. So the representative man is a "unique" man or "the" man through whom God works.

As a result, the NT is right to see a titular use for a specific figure, for that is the force of the saying in conjunction with the action. As Hooker points out, in this account the issue is not the title but the nature of the authority of the title bearer.[45] I would add that Jesus' actions underline this authority and define it. They also help to explain the force of Jesus' remark. Who "this" man is becomes clearer as Jesus' ministry proceeds and as the OT background of the phrase "Son of Man" emerges. The authoritative Son of Man is merged with the Suffering Servant portrait of Isa 52:13–53:12, which is yet a third innovation in Jesus' handling of the phrase. What eventually emerges is that heavenly and human authority are wed together in one unique person, who also suffers.

---

43. I will examine this title more in the synthesis of the next chapter.

44. A full development of this title and its use here is in my *Luke 1:1–9:50*, 924–30.

45. Morna Hooker, *The Son of Man in Mark: A Study of the Background of the Term "Son of Man" and Its Use in St. Mark's Gospel* (London: SPCK, 1967), 93.

Luke 5:24 is an initial glimpse of that union and a major clue to the eventual individual force of the title. The issue of uniqueness is effectively raised by the claim of authority to forgive sins. The claim itself receives confirmation by the paralytic's ability to get up in response to Jesus' call. If one puts together the remark and the event, one can know that Jesus is a unique figure. What one can see (a healing) points to what one cannot see (forgiveness of sins). In fact, Jesus as Son of Man exercises divine prerogatives. In the view of this pericope, either Jesus blasphemes (as the Jewish leadership claims) or he is uniquely related to God. Luke's readers are left to ponder the implications of the choice.

Let us return now to Jesus' key actions. His mission is to call the sick to repentance (Luke 5:27–32) as he brings a new era with new wineskins (5:33–39). The Son of Man is even Lord of the Sabbath (6:1–5) and does good on the Sabbath (6:6–11). Jesus calls the Twelve as he renews God's work on behalf of Israel (6:12–16). Luke juxtaposes disclosures of who Jesus is with declarations about his mission in this sequence of controversies tied to his work.

Jesus shows power over life in raising the widow of Nain's son and Jairus's daughter (Luke 7:10–17; 8:40–56). When John doubts and sends messengers to confirm whether Jesus is the one to come, Jesus does not answer with the confession of a title but points to his work in the eschatological language of Isaiah to say he brings the new era (7:18–23 with Isa 29:28; 35:5–6; 42:18; 26:19; 61:1). Jesus reaffirms his right to forgive sin with a sinful woman (Luke 7:36–50).[46] Jesus shows authority over nature in acts that recall what only God can do by calming a storm (8:22–25; see Pss 107; 89:26). Jesus shows authority over demons, disease, and death in a powerful linked sequence of miracles (Luke 8:26–56). He commissions preaching of the kingdom by his followers, giving them power and authority that is a foretaste of the Spirit to come (9:1–6; 10:1–24). This leads to Peter's recognition that Jesus is "God's Messiah" (9:18–20).

At this point, Jesus turns to explain that his messiahship, which he describes using the title Son of Man. His messiahship will involve suffering. Luke notes such predictions six times as Jesus sets his face to go to Jerusalem (Luke 9:21–22; 9:43b–45; 9:51; 12:49–50; 13:33; 17:25; 18:31–34). As he begins to make these points, a voice from heaven speaks a second time, that Jesus is "my Son, whom I have chosen; listen to him" (9:35). The reference to sonship alludes to Ps 2:7, just as the title "Son" at his baptism in Luke 3:22 was derived from Ps 2:7. In 3:22, the remark was messianic, especially as it is linked to two other Lucan texts (4:1–13, 16–30). The messianic thrust of the remark is confirmed by the second part of the declaration: ὁ ἐκλελεγμένος (ho eklelegmenos, lit., "the chosen one"). This wording is found only in Luke, probably as an explanatory reference to strengthen the regal

---

46. The two scenes where forgiveness of sins appears form a gender pairing as we have a male paralytic forgiven (5:17–26) and a sinful woman pardoned (7:36–50).

character of the remark, coming as it does after Peter's messianic confession of Jesus. It is God's "amen" to that confession.

Mark 9:7 (= Matt 17:5) has ὁ ἀγαπητός (*ho agapētos*, "the beloved"; see discussion above), as do all three Synoptics' reports of the utterance given at the baptism. Luke's change here explains his understanding of the wording and seems to derive from Isa 42:1, with its reference to the Servant as God's chosen instrument. When one puts the two titles together, Jesus is identified as the Messiah-Servant, the fundamental christological category that Luke has presented up to this point. The use of the perfect participle shows that Jesus has already occupied the position of the "chosen one"; enthronement is not the point here.[47]

Another key feature in the heavenly endorsement is the allusion to Deut 18:15. Unlike the Matthean and Marcan parallels, Luke's word order matches the LXX version of Deuteronomy ("listen to him"), which thus emphasizes slightly the focus of listening *to him*. This allusion is important because it marks out Jesus as a Leader-Prophet like Moses (Acts 3:19–24). It also indicates that the disciples need instruction from the one who leads the way to God. There are things that the disciples do not yet understand about the one whom they have confessed. Conzelmann is surely correct to say that the call is to hear Jesus' teaching about his passion and to recognize that Jesus will be a Messiah who suffers.[48] Jesus has much more to reveal about himself.

The reference to Deut 18 was not used in the voice's remark at Jesus' baptism (Luke 3:22). This new reference declares his role as revealer of God's way through a confession from heaven. Much of the rest of Luke involves the Prophet-Messiah's instruction to his disciples. In effect, the voice says to Peter, "Jesus is not equal to Moses or Elijah; he is greater than they."[49] God is saying, "Sit at his feet, so you can learn from him the way to me."

So the Messiah and the prophet like Moses (Deut 18:15) allusions appear here with the Servant image of being elect, as what is said here echoes and expands what was said at the baptism. Luke consistently portrays Jesus as the eschatological figure of the new era who brings the deliverance and power of God, something his work and ministry show. Jesus prefers to show who he is rather than to talk about who he is. So if Jesus casts out demons by the finger of God, then the kingdom of God has come upon the world (Luke 11:20). The long-promised kingdom is in their midst with Jesus and his work (17:20–21).

As Jesus and his disciples journey to Jerusalem, he also begins to discuss the judgment the Son of Man will bring, showing the accountability people have to him (Luke 12:35–48; 17:22–37). Jesus is a cause of division (12:49–53). People should discern the time and read well what is taking place (12:54–56). To know the Lord is to enter the narrow way (13:22–30). But Israel's hesitation to respond means she is in exile until she recognizes the one who comes in the name of the

---

47. Bock, *Luke 1:1–9:50*, 873–74.

48. Hans Conzelmann, *The Theology of St. Luke* (Philadelphia:

Fortress, 1982), 57–59.

49. Fitzmyer, *Gospel of Luke I–IX*, 803.

Lord (13:34–35). Luke is giving a running narrative about who Jesus is, how he is unique, and the new era he brings along. However, with the arrival of the new era comes an accountability to respond to what the Spirit of God is doing through him. This is why rejecting him is called blaspheming the Spirit, something that cannot be forgiven (12:10).

Nothing in this emphasis changes when Jesus becomes direct in his claims as he comes to Jerusalem. He rides into the city on a donkey amidst messianic praise about the blessed nature of the King who comes in the name of the Lord (an allusion to Ps 118:26). He refuses to stop his followers for proclaiming who he is (Luke 19:28–40). He laments that the bulk of ethnic Israel is missing the time of her visitation (19:41–44). He exercises authority over the most sacred space in Israel as he cleanses the temple, showing his authority over the most sanctified piece of earth in the world (19:45–46). When the authority to do this is questioned by the Jewish leaders, Jesus points to God's work through John the Baptist as testimony for how he has such authority (20:1–8). Jesus predicts the death of God's beloved Son through rejection in the parable of the wicked tenants (20:9–19).

In a crucial text, Jesus notes how David called Messiah "Lord" in Ps 110:1, which sets up what will be a move to develop the importance of this title (Luke 20:41–44). The issue here is how a descendant can be greater than an ancestor in a patriarchal society. "Lord" is a more significant title for Messiah than son of David. Just what Lord means Jesus does not yet say here, but that will be answered shortly when the Jewish leadership examines him.

Jesus' use of Ps 110 here is so important that it deserves a closer look. Verse 1 makes three points: (1) the recognition of authority that David, the author-speaker, gives to this figure by acknowledging him as "Lord"; (2) the picture of ruling in the figure of sitting "at my right hand"; and (3) the declaration of the presence of his rule until all enemies are removed. Though not addressed in Luke 20:41–44, the figure David addresses in Ps 110 rules until God finishes the job (cf. 1 Cor 15:25–28). It is not a passive reign that manifests itself as enemies are subdued, but the reign is in process until the rule is permanently established. In Luke 20:41–44, Jesus is only interested in the first point. David bows to this king's authority, even though he is a descendant of David.

Before developing Jesus' point, it is important to discuss how this psalm was seen in Judaism. Up to the time of Jesus there is no indication that this text was read messianically, though it was read regally (*T. Job* 33.3; 1 Macc 14:41; *T. Levi* 8.3; 18.1–3, 8, 12). It is important to recall that the Messiah is a king, so regal passages would apply to him and describe his role; but the point is that the text was not seen in exclusively messianic terms. It is broad, not narrow. The absence of this messianic use of the psalm has led many scholars to speak of a Jewish suppression of the messianic use of the psalm, probably as a result of the text's importance to Christianity.[50] Later Judaism saw the text referring to either Abraham or Messiah

---

50. Str-B, 4:452–65.

(Abraham in *b. Ned.* 32b and *Rab. Lev.* 25.6 on 19:23; both Messiah and Abraham in *Midr. Ps.* 110.1–4 on 110:1).

Given the nature of this evidence, Jesus' use of the psalm may be more focused than that of the Judaism of his era. But since the psalm was understood royally, it would also apply to Messiah, so Jesus' narrowing of the referent is not shocking. If the text were true of the king or the Davidic line, it would be especially true of Messiah. Of course, the Davidic root of messianic kingship was a given in the OT and in much of Judaism in this period (Ps 89:3–4 [89:4–5 MT]; Isa 9:7 [9:6 MT]; 11:1–2; Jer 23:5; 30:9; *Pss. Sol.* 17–18 [esp. 17.21, 32]). It also should be noted that this regal figure is referred to in ideal terms. This is the Davidite king in his most ideal form, which of course is what Messiah is. In fact, only Messiah meets the ideal, which is why the passage is uniquely suited to him.

Jesus' point is simple enough: How is it that David can call a son, a descendant, by the title "Lord"? This is a significant act in a patriarchal society, where a son is *under* his father. The answer is not a denial of Davidic sonship, but rather an implication that Messiah as David's Lord transcends him. It recognizes the key authority that is ascribed to the Davidic heir—an authority that David acknowledges. So the key title to be associated with this important figure is "Lord," not "son of David."

One question remains about the use of Ps 110 in this setting. Many argue that the ambiguity of the term "Lord" is possible only in the early church. In this view, this text does not go back to Jesus but is the christological work of the early church since the remark assumes the use of the LXX, with its ambiguous use of the term κύριος (*kyrios*) for "Lord." It is obvious that the Hebrew text of Ps 110 clearly distinguishes between God and this figure; Yahweh (*yhwh*) refers to God and Lord (*ʾâdôn*) to this regal figure. But this argument overstates the case and ignores the first-century practice of rendering texts orally and not pronouncing the divine name יהוה (*yhwh*). Thus, the ambiguity in the Greek text is possible in both Hebrew and Aramaic when the text was presented orally so that *ʾâdôn*-related words occur in both slots.[51]

This point is a key one, for it shows that Jesus is capable of making this remark in this setting. It is possible for him to raise this ambiguity. Jesus' point is how the great King David can reflect such submission to a descendant. Who can be greater than Israel's great king and founder of the regal line? The listeners are left to ponder the conclusion. This saying is thus authentic and goes back to Jesus. The passage and this reading of it are a key starting point for OT christological reflection about who Jesus is.

It is important to note that in this passage Jesus does not develop the citation in terms of himself, nor does he explain it. He simply raises a theoretical question here about why the Messiah is referred to in this way. The answer and rationale of the dilemma are not developed until Luke 22:69, so the explanation of the full significance of this passage must await that text. What is clear from Jesus' citation

---

51. Bock, *Proclamation from Prophecy and Pattern*, 130–31, 331.

and the question he raises in 20:44 is that the Messiah has the high title "Lord" and his authority is acknowledged by the great king David. Jesus raises it as a thought to ponder and breaks new ground in the thinking about who Messiah is.[52]

As Jesus looks to the judgment of Jerusalem as a picture of the end, he also discusses the return of the Son of Man to judge and consummate the deliverance he brings (Luke 21:5–36). Jesus changes the liturgy of Exodus and Passover by relating the elements to his own act of saving through his approaching death (22:1–23). This act also shows his authority over salvation. Who has the right to alter such central liturgy? Despite all of this authority, Jesus still serves as an example to his followers (22:24–27). He is not a messiah who merely exercises or will exercise raw power; he is a giver of grace and service. He also shares his rule with his Twelve (22:28–30).

Jesus goes to an unjust death. But this is all in God's plan. Even as Jesus is examined by the Jewish leadership, he tells them that "from now on, the Son of Man will be seated at the right hand of the mighty God" (Luke 22:66–71). Here is Jesus' answer to the dilemma he posed about Ps 110:1 in 20:41–44. The leadership may seek Jesus' death, but God will vindicate him and reveal who he is by giving him a place in sharing rule in God's presence. This is not the reception of an angelic figure; it is a place with and alongside God—sharing in his presence, power, and glory.

This answer to the question of whether Jesus is the Christ also leads into a recognition of Jesus as Son of God. The appeal to Ps 110:1 defines Jesus' lordship as one vindicated by God, giving him an inseparable place with God and the execution of divine power and authority. It forces a choice. Either Jesus is who he claims to be or he is a blasphemer. This image of divine vindication that shows Jesus to be "Lord" will become central to the proclamation of Jesus in Acts. This idea of divine vindication and endorsement in resurrection also stands behind the narrative use of the title Luke makes when he calls Jesus Lord in narrative asides. This narrative use is picked up from within the story and applied to Jesus by other characters starting in Luke 24:34. Luke is shifting the emphasis within his internal portrayal of the story from Jesus as Messiah to Jesus as Lord and Messiah.

Pilate sends Jesus to the cross as one who claimed to be king of the Jews (Luke 23, esp. v. 38). In this chapter, Jesus' innocence is declared at least six times, plus one more time in a figure, yet he is sent to the cross (v. 4: Pilate; v. 14: Pilate; v. 15: Herod; v. 22: Pilate; v. 31: pictured as green wood; v. 41: thief on the cross; v. 47: the centurion).

Luke 24 summarizes many of these themes. The angel reminds the women that Jesus predicted the Son of Man would be crucified and then be raised on the third day (24:5–7). Now seemingly disappointed since they do not yet appreciate the fact Jesus has been raised, the Emmaus disciples confess their hope that Jesus might have been a prophet mighty in deed and word before God and that he would be the

---

52. Bock, *Luke 9:51–24:53*, 1638–40.

one to redeem Israel (24:19–21). Jesus responds with a rebuke about being slow to believe what the prophets said about the Messiah's suffering and then entering into his glory. So Jesus expounds the Scripture starting from Moses (24:25–27). Here program, events, and Scripture come together for Luke.

Finally, the gospel closes with Jesus' expounding to the disciples that Moses, the Prophets, and the Psalms taught that "the Messiah will suffer and rise from the dead on the third day, and repentance for the forgiveness of sins will be preached in his name to all nations, beginning at Jerusalem" (Luke 24:46–47). All these things "must be fulfilled" (δεῖ πληρωθῆναι πάντα, *dei plērōthēnai panta*; 24:44). As we noted in the chapter on God and his plan, Luke uses language pointing to the divine design and necessity of God's program being realized as all the events behind Jesus have shown. It is here that the Spirit reenters the story as Jesus tells his disciples to await being clothed with power from on high in line with the promise of the Father (24:49). Luke 3:16 and its promise is the last key teaching note of the gospel.

The final act in Luke's gospel is Jesus' being taken up in ascension, an event unique to Luke-Acts. God's vindication of the Lord Messiah concludes the gospel. Those who know the story know what the vindication says about Jesus. This event shows God's vote in the difference of opinion Jesus had with the Jewish leadership that led to his innocent yet representative death. It is on this note that Luke's gospel presentation of Jesus closes.

7.3 THE PORTRAIT IN ACTS: THE LORD MESSIAH IN KERYGMA AND ACTION

Acts begins where Luke ends, repeating the ascension of Jesus as he calls the disciples to mission. The disciples are called as Spirit-empowered witnesses for the message of salvation to be taken "to the ends of the earth" (Acts 1:3–11). Now it is "the Lord Jesus" who went out among them, beginning with the baptism of John (1:21). This description, not present in Luke except at Luke 24:3, shows a deepened appreciation of Jesus because of his resurrection-ascension and divine vindication. This title for Jesus will now appear eighteen times in Acts, along with actions in the name of Jesus, who is Lord and Christ. This combination of titles shows Jesus' ultimate status that Luke wants his readers to embrace (1:21; 4:33; 7:59; 8:16; 9:17; 11:17, 20; 15:11, 26; 16:31; 19:5, 13, 17; 20:21, 24, 35; 21:13; 28:31, the last verse of Acts).

Jesus' share in divine power and his role in salvation are seen in his mediation of the Spirit, a fulfillment of the presence of the new era noted in Luke 3:16. Here the key portion of the text is Acts 2:30–36. These verses affirm that Pss 132:11 and 110:1 are realized in Jesus' receiving the Spirit from the Father and pouring him out onto his followers. The promise of the Spirit is from Joel 3:1–5. Key here is that people are to call "on the name of the Lord" to be saved (Acts 2:21). This looks as if one must call out to the God of Israel, but by the end of the speech, this calling out for salvation is associated with the name and authority of the Lord Messiah

Jesus, in whose name baptism takes place (Acts 2:21 with 2:36–39). His authority is active in the distribution of benefits of the divine promise of the divine program.

Healing also takes place in the name of Jesus Christ of Nazareth (Acts 3:1–4:22). Peter's explanatory speech develops what Acts 1 raised, noting that the God of promise (of Abraham, Isaac, Jacob, and the patriarchs) raised from the dead the one whom the Jewish leadership had slain. This holy and righteous one is "the author of life" (3:15), and through his name a lame man was healed. God told this story about the Christ in the prophets and calls on Israel to repent. In that turning, sins are blotted out and God can send the appointed Christ Jesus to complete his work for God's people. Heaven now receives him until the reestablishing of all that the prophets have told about this prophet like Moses. As the promised Leader-Prophet-Deliverer, Jesus must be heard. Failure to respond leads to destruction. All of the prophets have declared these things.

Peter notes that his audience is "heirs of the prophets" (Acts 3:25), with access to the covenant promise that all the earth will be blessed through Abraham's offspring. So the opportunity for blessing has come to Israel first, for blessing comes with turning to God. Jesus' career is now nicely broken up into inauguration of promise and consummation that comes with his return at a time only God knows (1:6–7). It will come because God promised it in the prophets. This is what Peter learned from the final exchange with Jesus in 1:6–11.

On the following day, Peter repeats the affirmation, noting that by the name of Jesus Christ of Nazareth the lame man was healed (Acts 4:9–10), despite the fact that the Jewish leaders had crucified Jesus. Jesus and his power are alive and present. The event also shows that salvation is in no one else, "for there is no other name under heaven given to mankind by which we must be saved" (4:12). Nothing can spell out Jesus' uniqueness more clearly that this affirmation that God's salvation is inseparably tied to Jesus. The Jewish leadership's efforts fail to prohibit the disciples from preaching the message, or what scholars call the *kerygma*, "in the name of Jesus" (cf. 4:17). This preaching takes place because the disciples are committed to obeying God (4:13–22).[53] The expression "in the name of Jesus" is also common in Acts, appearing seven times (2:38; 3:6; 4:18; 5:40; 9:27; 10:48; 16:18).[54] It points to his authority and reflects those who call out his name for deliverance.

The community then prays for enablement to speak about the holy servant Jesus and to heal in his name. This praying community understands that everyone in Jerusalem is gathered against the Lord God and his anointed (Acts 4:23–31). The prayer is uttered against the backdrop of Ps 2:1 being fulfilled.[55]

So the disciples testify to the resurrection of the Lord Jesus (Acts 4:33). Positive responses are described in terms of believing in the Lord as people are added to

---

53. The term κήρυγμα (*kērygma*) means "preaching" and refers to the message that Jesus' followers preached.

54. Numerous other references simply to "the name" also occur in Acts.

55. This kind of application of Ps 2 fits the way the psalm was often read as reflecting a pattern of opposition to those chosen agents of God. A look at the later midrash on Ps 2 shows this understanding of the text as deeply engrained in later Jewish tradition.

the number of the new community (5:14). When the Jewish leadership challenges preaching in Jesus' name again, Peter again responds that God must be obeyed over human beings (5:29). Here Peter uses the theologically significant term δεῖ (*dei*, "it is necessary") to show the necessity of following God's plan. God has raised this one up, Peter says, again pointing to the divine vindication of Jesus in exaltation to God's right hand as Leader and Savior to offer repentance and forgiveness of sins (5:30–31). So Peter and his colleagues are compelled as witnesses and as those who have received the Spirit to preach. The Spirit is given to those who obey God in terms of receiving this message (5:32). It is here that Gamaliel makes his ironically inspired statement that if this movement is of God, it cannot be stopped (5:39). The witnesses continue to testify that "Jesus is the Messiah" (5:40–42).

Stephen responds to charges that Jesus of Nazareth taught he would destroy the temple. He replies with a history of Israel's resistance to God's messengers and message. As a result, Stephen is stoned to death. Jesus as the Son of Man receives him, as Stephen reports a vision of seeing Jesus standing at God's right hand. As God vindicated Jesus, so Jesus vindicates the church's first martyr (Acts 6:7–7:60). As Stephen dies, he cries out to the "Lord Jesus" to receive his spirit and not hold the people's sin against them. Even in the midst of this authority of Jesus, the people who respond to him cry out for mercy to be shown to their opponents.

Philip preaches the Christ and the kingdom in the name of Jesus Christ to Samaritans (Acts 8:5, 12). Baptism takes place "in the name of the Lord Jesus" (8:16). Philip expounds the innocent suffering of Jesus in terms of Isa 53:7 (Acts 8:32–35)—a text that looks at the innocent, silent suffering of the Servant of the Lord and compares the figure to a sacrificial lamb, unjustly slain (Acts 8:33). The term for "lamb" (ἀμνός, *amnos*) is relatively rare in the NT, appearing just four times (John 1:29, 35–36; Acts 8:32; 1 Pet 1:17–21). This suggests a traditional source, since the NT use of this term is restrained and not limited to one writer. Philip will compare this description to Jesus (Acts 8:35). The comparison to a lamb might suggest atonement, but this is not the most emphasized idea. Luke makes such a point more clearly elsewhere in Luke-Acts (the substitution with Barabbas, Luke 23:18–19; Acts 20:28).

The death is described as being "taken from the earth" (Acts 8:33); it also is called here "humiliation" (ταπεινώσει, *tapeinōsei*). The Greek term is relatively rare in the NT, appearing four times (Luke 1:46–48; Acts 8:33; Phil 3:20–21; Jas 1:9–10). In its context, the Isa 53:8 passage refers to both submission and the idea of injustice. The text asks what kind of generation can take a life like this (Acts 8:33). The implied suggestion is that only a wicked generation can do so (Isa 53:8–9). The verb αἴρω (*airō*) in a context such as this means "to remove" something or "to take it out of the way."[56] Here it is justice that is removed, as the unjust death of an innocent takes place.

---

56. BAGD, 24 §4; 28–29 §3.

This was the major element of Jesus' death in Luke 23, and Isa 53:12 is used also in Luke 22:37, where Jesus is reckoned with the criminals. Jesus alluded to the servant in Mark 10:45 as well. The voice at the baptism pointed to Isa 42, another servant passage (the use of portions of Isa 52:1–53:12 appears in John 12:38; Rom 10:16; 1 Peter 2:21–25). The reading that justice was removed by an unjust death is more likely than the idea of a vindication. The issue of injustice fits with the Lucan portrait of Jesus' death as one suffered by one who was innocent. He died unjustly because he was who he claimed to be, the promised one of Israel. But there is irony here: in the generation's act of taking Jesus' life from earth, there is also, for Jesus, God's vindication of that death. This, in effect, nullified the judgment Jesus suffered on the cross. This tragic, unjust death, which at first looked as if it had resulted in all being lost, in fact resulted in everything being gained.

The Acts text, however, develops only one issue: Who is the text describing? This is the focus of the eunuch's question. The eunuch asks if the passage is about Isaiah or someone else. At the time, Jews may well have considered three candidates for the subject of the text: (1) the prophet; (2) Israel; and (3) another individual, such as an Elijah revived or a Messiah, but not one who suffered.[57] In asking the question this way, the eunuch may have thought the passage was about Isaiah. Philip explains that the passage is about Jesus, who is the servant who suffered unjustly (v. 35). This is the most developed text on Isa 53 in Luke; it also is one of the longest OT texts cited in Acts.

This brings us to the special calling of Saul in Acts 9. Here the exalted Jesus is active, appearing to Saul on the Damascus road and blinding him temporarily with his glory. Jesus is consistently addressed as "Lord" in this chapter, both by Saul and by Ananias. Saul's call is "to proclaim my name to the Gentiles and their kings and to the people of Israel" (9:15). The name of the Lord Jesus who is Messiah forms the consistent christological core of confession in Acts. So Saul preaches Jesus as Son of God, amazing the crowds who know he has previously wreaked havoc on those "who call on this name" (9:20–21), "by proving that Jesus is the Messiah" (9:22). The term "proving" (συμβιβάζων, *symbibazōn*) here is interesting as it means to unite things together, something said of ligaments in a body or of how evidence is brought together to make a case.[58] This is precisely what Luke is doing with his narrative: taking strands of hope and weaving them together to show that Jesus is Lord and Christ. So Saul preaches in the name of Jesus and in the name of the Lord (9:27–28).

Peter heals through Jesus Christ (Acts 9:34), and as a result of his work many believe in the Lord (9:42). At this point, God works to include Gentiles in his program, appearing to both Cornelius and Peter (10:1–23). Peter preaches to Cornelius's household about the earthly ministry of "the good news of peace through Jesus Christ, who is Lord of all" (10:36). This juxtaposition of titles is Luke's view of

---

57. Jeremias, *TDNT*, 5:684–89.   58. BDAG, 956–57 §3.

Jesus. He is Lord of all, so the gospel can go to all. God plays no favorites in terms of giving opportunity for access to the gospel. This Jesus was anointed by the Holy Spirit and with power as he did good works and healed those oppressed by the devil (10:38). He was crucified, but God raised him from the dead. So Jesus appeared to those who ate and drank with him, commissioning them to preach to the people and to testify that Jesus is ordained by God as judge of the living and the dead. Here the Lord Jesus is one to whom all are accountable (10:39–42). With faith comes forgiveness through his name (10:43).

At this point, the Spirit falls on the Gentiles, and they are "baptized in the name of Jesus Christ" (Acts 10:45–48). Later Peter defends the baptism of Gentiles, noting that "if God gave them the same gift he gave us who believed in the Lord Jesus Christ, who was I to think that I could stand in God's way?" (11:17). Here two crucial themes of Lucan theology converge. First is the gift of the Spirit as the sign of the new era and the evidence of God's cleansing. This looks back to Luke 3:16. In fact, Peter alludes to this passage as he presents how Jesus taught and reinforced it, something Acts 1:4–5 shows. Second is the summation of Luke's understanding of Jesus as Lord Jesus Christ or Lord Messiah. Jesus is the promised one with authority over salvation. God's program is inseparably linked to him.

Intense christological discussion and development tapers off in Acts once the message is extended to Gentiles. Summaries become the rule. The appeal to the Hebrew Scripture in explicit ways becomes less frequent. The narrative has established the key christological point that Jesus Christ is Lord of all so the gospel can go to all in his name.

Nevertheless, at Pisidian Antioch, Paul reviews Israel's history and moves from David directly to John the Baptist and to Jesus as the one whose sandal John is not worthy to untie. This is yet another allusion to the crucial Luke 3:16–17. Once again the death of Jesus by the cross and God's vindication of him are set forth. The good news is the forgiveness of sins, something that the law could not do. The message also highlights what the Son brings in accordance with what Pss 2:7; 16:10; and Isa 55:3 promised (Acts 13:16–41).

At the council of Jerusalem, the christological points are few but significant. Salvation is through "the grace of our Lord Jesus" (Acts 15:11). This salvation for the Gentiles comes in a manner that parallels how the first Jewish believers were saved (15:11). Appealing to Amos 9:11–15, James speaks of the rebuilding of the ruined tent of David, a rebuilding that allows humanity to seek the Lord. So Gentiles who are called by God's name can enter in (Acts 15:14–21). This shift back to "Lord" in v. 17 as a reference for God who oversees salvation (cf. v. 14) is an example of Lucan overlap in the use of the term Lord that indicates how connected God and Jesus are in God's program of salvation. God visits his people in the Messiah (Luke 1:68–69, 78–79; 7:16; 19:41–44). People who risk their lives "for the name of our Lord Jesus Christ" deliver the letter with the council's decision (Acts 15:26).

Jesus directs Paul's mission as it is his Holy Spirit that prevents Paul from going to Asia and turns him to Philippi (Acts 16:6–9). Here we see a close connection between the Spirit and Jesus in overlap, just as we have seen of God and Jesus in other texts. In Philippi Paul exorcises a demon from a slave girl "in the name of Jesus Christ" (16:18). He also urges the Philippian jailer to "believe in the Lord Jesus" (16:31) in order to be saved. In Thessalonica he preaches Jesus as the Messiah (17:3), as also in Corinth (18:5). Apollos will do the same in Achaia (18:27–28). In Athens, Paul sets forth Jesus as the one appointed to judge one day (17:31), but mention of resurrection is confusing to the Athenians and leads into a discussion that stops Paul's speech.

In Ephesus, Paul baptizes John's disciples and they receive the Spirit. They believe in the one John preached would come after him, Jesus (Acts 19:4). This is yet another allusion back to the crucial teaching of Luke 3:16. So these disciples of John are "baptized in the name of the Lord Jesus" (Acts 19:5). The spiritual battle in Ephesus is intense. The sons of Sceva try but fail to appeal to "the name of the Lord Jesus" as a means of exorcism (19:13). The name of the Lord Jesus is extolled in Ephesus as new followers burn their old magic books (19:17–20).

Later, to the Ephesian elders Paul describes his ministry as preaching "to Jews and Gentiles that they must turn to God in repentance and have faith in our Lord Jesus" (Acts 20:21). This is the same Lord who called him to this ministry (20:24). Paul serves the church, "which [God] bought with the blood of his own Son" (20:28).[59] This is the only verse in Acts to directly mention the means by which Jesus' death serves as a sacrifice. Luke is more interested in who Jesus is and what he does than in how salvation is achieved through Jesus' death. That emphasis is left to Paul's and Peter's epistles in the canon. Paul urges the elders to serve, as the Lord Jesus taught it was more blessed to give than to receive (20:35).

Paul is prepared to die in Jerusalem "for the name of the Lord Jesus" (Acts 21:13). At this point, the narrative in Acts turns from presenting Paul as missionary and preacher to discussing Paul as the one arrested for his faith. Defense speeches dominate the book from here to its conclusion, in which Paul retells his Damascus encounter with the Lord Jesus (chs. 22 and 26). In 22:14, he notes how God had appointed him to know God's will and see the "Righteous One" (τὸν δίκαιον, *ton dikaion*). This title recalls the confession by the centurion at the cross in Luke 23:47 (also using the word δίκαιος, *dikaios*). Jesus was just; God had vindicated him.

Later Paul says he is on trial for the resurrection of the dead. Here Paul means not only the hope of life after death, but the vindication of Jesus by God, showing who Jesus is. Later he speaks of a hope of a resurrection of the just and unjust (Acts 24:14–15) in line with all that the prophets taught. Felix and Drusilla hear Paul speak about faith in Christ Jesus (24:24). Festus, reflecting the way a Roman leader might think of the new religion, refers to it as a superstition. He describes how Paul refers to a certain Jesus who was dead but whom Paul asserted to be alive, an allusion to Jesus' resurrection (25:19).

---

59. In Luke's gospel, only at the Last Supper does this theme appear (Luke 22:17–20), where death for many and opening up the new covenant are the point. Note that I am adopting the textual reading of the NIV text note here.

Before Agrippa, Paul again retells his Damascus story, stating he is on trial for the hope of his ancestors (Acts 26:6). This connection to Israel's story and her hope for deliverance at the end of time is an explicitly new note in Acts, yet it reaches back to the infancy material. Paul himself had opposed "Jesus of Nazareth" (26:9). But now that very opponent, who he thought was dead, showed himself to be exalted and alive. That Jesus had appointed him to bear witness to this reality. Paul's mission was to open the eyes of both Jews and Gentiles to "turn them from darkness to light, and from the power of Satan to God, so that they may receive forgiveness of sins and a place among those who are sanctified by faith in [Jesus]" (26:16–18). What is interesting here is that what was said to be God's appointment in ch. 22 is now Jesus' commission in ch. 26. Again we have evidence of an inseparable overlap in task and action with distinction of persons at the same time.

Part of Paul's message was that he was obedient to this divine call. His teaching involved nothing other than to present what the prophets and Moses had said would come to pass. These Hebrew prophets had taught "that the Messiah would suffer and, as the first to rise from the dead, would bring the message of light to his own people and to the Gentiles" (26:22–23). Here the role of resurrection as tied to Christ becomes explicit as part of the hope. Paul's hope is not in resurrection as an abstract idea, but as part of what God had done in Jesus to open the door for people. Interestingly in preaching like Paul's, Jesus is said to speak. Paul is making a relational appeal to the role of resurrection. Jesus was raised to speak to us. Resurrection did not take place merely to show the fact that God can resurrect people.

The final scene of Acts brings Paul to Rome. Again Paul says that he is bound "because of the hope of Israel" (Acts 28:20). Paul seeks to convince the Jews there about Jesus "from the Law of Moses and from the Prophets" (28:23). When many of them reject that message, Paul notes that he will go to the Gentiles with this hope. The book closes with Paul welcoming everyone; "he proclaimed the kingdom of God and taught about the Lord Jesus Christ — with all boldness and without hindrance" (28:31). The rule of God offering his salvation through the Lord Jesus Christ is the message of assurance Luke seeks to give his readers in Luke-Acts.

7.4 CONCLUSION

The narrative presentation of Christology in Luke-Acts shows how Messiah and Lord dominate the portrait. Luke starts with an emphasis that Jesus is the promised "Messiah." But as his narration unfolds, the authority of this Messiah is shown to be comprehensive. It touches sin, relationships of acceptance by God, Sabbath, creation, liturgy, temple, disease, demons, and death. In the gospel, Luke shows who Jesus is more than presenting titles and declarations about who he is. The importance of Jesus as Lord emerges in the last week and early in Acts. Now salvation is in the name of the Lord Jesus Christ.

"Lord" shows an overlap with the God of Israel in terms of functions like forgiveness, the distribution of the Spirit, the offer of salvation in his name, and the coming exercise of judgment. Jesus' position at God's right hand shows an intimacy and inseparable connection between God and the one he sent. Jesus is shown as a "co-equal" and "co-regent" with God.[60] No other name yields salvation. Jesus shows the new era is present by giving the Spirit that the Father promised he would give to his people one day. Those who testify to Jesus act in the name of the Lord Jesus Christ. Lord becomes the dominating image—not at the expense of the title Messiah, but as an explanation and deepening of it.

It is now time to put all of this Christology together into a more synthesized portrait. Luke has presented and developed his understanding of Jesus by gradually revealing throughout the narrative who Jesus is. What does the total picture look like?

---

60. This is argued in detail by Doug Buckwalter, "The Divine Savior," in Marshall and Peterson, eds. *Witness to the Gospel,* 107–23, esp. 122–23. He speaks of Jesus as immanent deity in Luke-Acts. For another full treatment of Lucan Christology, see also D. Buckwalter, *The Character and Purpose of Luke's Christology* (SNTSMS; Cambridge: Cambridge Univ. Press, 1996).

Chapter 8

MESSIAH, SERVANT, PROPHET, SAVIOR, SON OF MAN, AND LORD: A SYNTHESIS ON THE PERSON AND WORK OF JESUS

BIBLIOGRAPHY

See chapter 7.

8.1 THE PERSON OF JESUS CHRIST: FROM MESSIAH-SERVANT-PROPHET TO LORD

In our narrative study of Lucan Christology, we saw that Luke consciously reveals who Jesus is with a step-by-step approach. He introduces a series of ideas in the infancy material and gradually connects these ideas to each other into a coherent portrait of Jesus. In this chapter, we review the sweep of this movement and fill in details about key points.

Luke's presentation of Jesus begins mostly in regal and prophetic terms and ends with an emphasis on his lordship and the authority of his name in Acts. In the infancy section, Jesus is described as Son and as King (Luke 1:31–35). There is ambiguity in this initial description of Jesus as "Son," since any Israelite king could be described as God's "son." In the Hebrew Scripture the Davidic successor was said to have God as his Father, as promised in the Davidic covenant (2 Sam 7:14). The dynastic Davidic ruler inherited the hope of this promise (Ps 2:7). This covenant is the core promise that led to a messianic hope later in Jewish expectation.[1]

But Jesus' unique birth by the Spirit makes it clear that "something more" is here. Exactly what is not explicitly clear in Luke 1–2 since the opening passage emphasizes Jesus as a Davidic, regal figure. Mary and those around her take the promise only in messianic terms. What that "something more" involves emerges as Luke develops his description of Jesus. In short, Luke built his Christology "from the earth up," though in the infancy section, it is suggested that this child is unique, since his birth comes directly from heaven.[2] Part of the plot built in Luke's narrative

---

1. Herb Bateman, Darrell L. Bock, and Gordon Johnston, *Jesus the Messiah: Tracing the Promises, Expectations and Coming of Israel's King* (Grand Rapids: Kregel, 2011).

2. I develop this "earth up" idea in my *Jesus according to Scripture*.

This chapter is an update of my section on Christology in "A Theology of Luke-Acts," in Zuck and Bock, eds., *Biblical Theology of the New Testament*, 102–17.

is to tell this story. It allows who Jesus is to dawn on the reader, much like many in Luke's time had experienced this growth in appreciating who Jesus is.

Other regal references in Luke 1–2 include the mention of the presence of the "horn of salvation" in the house of David (Luke 1:69). This title alludes to Ps 132:17, and with its reference to David's house brings in the hope of Davidic promise from 2 Sam 7 and the Davidic covenant. Psalm 132 will reappear in Acts 2:30–31. The picture of the "morning star" that shines in darkness (Luke 1:78–79) also indicates that fulfillment is present (Isa 9:1–2; 58:8; 59:19; 60:1–2). The grouping of three titles in Luke 2:11 — "Savior," "Christ," "the Lord" — sums up the descriptions in the infancy portrait. Of these titles, only "Lord" is not specifically defined through an appeal to the OT in this introductory section.

Luke 2:34–35 pictures Jesus as the one who divides Israel. Here the conceptual imagery comes from Isa 8:14. The pain that Jesus' ministry will cause Mary is the first hint of tension, alluding to Jesus' coming suffering. Jesus will be like a rejected prophet, as well as a rejected messianic King. This rejection, not normally anticipated for a messianic figure, is the hardest part of the portrait for the disciples to absorb. It will take them a long time to appreciate how this dimension in Jesus' work fits into the entire portrait of messianic expectation.

The first reference to Jesus' self-understanding comes in Luke 2:49. Here Jesus speaks of the necessity of being "in my Father's house." As we noted in the last chapter, the expression is unusual, since literally it reads "about the ___ of my Father." No clear noun is supplied. Contextually, the phrase refers either to the Father's business in general or to being in the Father's house, which also points to ministering with the Father. The latter seems more likely. Either way, Jesus' first words about his relationship to God point to an intimacy that reveals filial and familial self-consciousness. Luke thus shows early on that Jesus understands his special relationship to God. This is Luke's first indication of where things are headed. Only Luke presents this early self-disclosure, as much of what Luke tells us in these opening two chapters is unique to his presentation of Jesus.

As we also noted in the previous chapter, at Jesus' baptism, regal and servant categories come together. Here the divine voice speaks directly to Jesus for the first time (Luke 3:22). "You are My Son, whom I love; with you I am well pleased" refers to Ps 2:7 and Isa 42:1, which bring together the king and the servant imagery. The connection to the servant is a new element in Luke's portrayal.

This prophetic and regal marriage continues in Luke 4:18–19, where Isa 61:1–2 and 58:6 are cited in another passage that has detail unique to Luke's gospel. Luke is building on associations we already know about from Mark's gospel. Though strictly speaking Isa 61 is probably not a "servant song," the prophetic figure in that chapter serves much like the servant in earlier Isaianic passages, so the parallel can be made. The citation pictures Jesus in an anointed prophetic mode, as Luke 4:24–27 makes clear. However, the anointing by the Spirit, which Jesus declares was fulfilled, also alludes back to his baptism. This anointing was of Jesus as King-Prophet. In Luke

4, Jesus both proclaims and brings the deliverance he announces, also pointing to both a prophetic and delivering mission.

In Luke 3:21–22, Ps 2:7 points to the King, while Isa 42:1 looks to the servant who declares and brings God's deliverance. This union reflects the Lucan focus up to this point in his gospel. Efforts to limit Jesus to a prophetic category in Luke miss the influence of the infancy material's introduction of him as a regal figure as well as underestimate the importance of the baptism for the scene in Luke 4. The imagery of Luke 4 pictures the OT declaration of Jubilee, a release from debts and a declaration of freedom (Lev 25:1–12; Deut 15:2–3). It pictures one released to serve God because of who Jesus is. Jesus is the center of God's plan and brings the cancellation of spiritual debt.

Jesus is superior to the greatest figure of the old era, John the Baptist (Luke 7:18–35). Jesus is more than a prophet, though that is how the populace views him (9:7–9). He is the Christ (9:20). At Jesus' transfiguration, the divine voice returns and presents him, as in Jesus' baptism, as "Son," but the voice also calls him "elect" (the one "whom I have chosen," 9:35). In addition the heavenly voice calls for the disciples to "listen to him." Here Ps 2:7; Isa 42:1; and Deut 18:15 come together. Jesus is King, Servant, and Prophet, but not just any prophet. He is the "prophet like Moses," a leader-ruler-delivering-prophet who has ushered in a new era. The new salvation transcends the old even while being connected to it.

In Luke 9–19, predictions of the Son of Man's suffering are evident (9:22, 44; 18:31). But other descriptions of Jesus as the Son of Man also are present (9:58; 11:30; 12:10; 19:10 give descriptions of Jesus' present ministry; and 9:26; 12:8, 40; 17:22, 24, 26, 30; 18:8 describe Jesus' ministry when he returns). The title "Son of Man" is also ambiguous in Luke until Jesus' use in 21:27. In that text, Son of Man clearly refers to the image from Dan 7:13–14, where one like a "son of man" (a human figure who rides the clouds like God) comes to the Ancient of Days to receive authority. So this image, which Jesus turns into a title, pictures the authority Jesus has received from the Father to serve over a kingdom.[3]

The meaning of "son of man" in Dan 7 is debated. There it is not a title, but simply the image of a human being who rides the clouds in contrast to the four dynasties that precede him, which display various mixed animal characteristics. The association of the image in 7:18, 27 with the saints and the transcendent quality of the figure who rides the clouds lead many to suggest an angelic figure. But this does not work for two reasons: (1) the dynastic elements in the chapter point to nations and rulers; and (2) the description of this figure as being worshiped using the Aramaic term *pâlaḥ* points away from an angel. This term means worship as it is used in parallelism to giving homage in Dan 3:28, and the substansive use of a participle

---

3. Such a titular use was emerging elsewhere in Jewish contexts as the expression's use in *1 En.* 37–71. The date of this section of Enoch is disputed, but a good case can be made for the period of the turn from the first century before the time of Christ until early in the century of his ministry. This issue will be explored in a forthcoming work to be edited by James Charlesworth and myself, entitled *Parables of Enoch, Early Judaism, Jesus, and Christian Origins*, where the case is made for such a date and ideas about the Son of Man circulating in the Second Temple Judaism of Jesus' time.

means "worshiper" in 6:17, 21 [= 6:16, 20 in English]). This means that an exalted, transcendent figure is in view, who is distinct from an angel. So it is better to see Daniel's "son of man" as a reference to the "representative head" of a collective body of saints. In other words, there is a corporate-individual interplay in the figure, but the focus is on the king who heads the community. This honors the explanations of 7:18, 27, while also honoring the picture of that son of man as receiving homage.[4]

This authoritative position of Jesus as the Son of Man is made clear in the texts about Jesus' ministry, which state that the Son of Man can forgive sin (Luke 5:24), and in the texts that describe his return to judge (12:35 – 48; 17:20 – 37; 21:5 – 36). However, the "Son of Man" ministry texts also involve seeking the lost (ch. 15) and suffering rejection (9:21 – 22), as well as returning to judge the world. The texts on the suffering Son of Man point out that the road for Jesus leads to the cross. These images are still rather regal, since they look at rule, but such total authority also suggests something more about him. This something more is developed when, later in Luke's gospel, the imagery is tied to God's vindication of Jesus to God's right hand. This divine act raises the question about who can share God's presence and glory. The move also suggests why "Lord" becomes an important title for Luke.

Luke 19 and 20 include a series of parables in which Jesus is portrayed as Lord. In these parables Jesus functions as an intermediary with authority. He receives a kingdom and then grants authority to others (19:11 – 27). He is heir to the vineyard, "the son" who is slain, with the result that the vineyard goes to others after the original tenants (i.e., Israel's current leaders) have shown their unfaithfulness (20:9 – 19). Jesus' central role in God's program and his authority are clear in these parables as is the authority he passes on to those connected to him.

The key passages for Lucan Christology come in the middle of his two books as Jesus heads for death and then is raised from the dead. As we saw in the previous chapter, in Luke 20:41 – 44 Jesus had raised a question (cf. Ps 110:1) that stumped the religious leaders. He asked how Messiah could be called David's son, since David himself called Messiah his "Lord." The question is framed in a theoretical way here, so that a direct allusion to Jesus is only implied in the isolated scene. However, it is obvious who is meant in the flow of the narrative. As stated, the explicit question is a messianic query about what Scripture says about Messiah, not a christological question about Jesus. Jesus was asking, "Which title is best for Messiah?" He did not directly answer that question, but the context suggests that "Lord" is a better or more comprehensive title than "son of David." David called Jesus his Lord, an act unusual for an ancestor in a patriarchal society. Luke has affirmed Jesus as Davidic son in both the infancy material and the genealogy, so the remark is not a rejection of Davidic sonship. Rather, Jesus is probing the prioritization of emphasis between the idea of Davidic sonship and the idea of Messiah being Lord. The clear opting for Lord emerges as the story proceeds. Thus, this text shows Luke as moving the reader from seeing Jesus just as the promised Anointed One to seeing him as Lord.

---

4. Bock, *Luke 9:51 – 24:53*, 1685.

The answer began in Luke 22:69. Answering the question of whether he was the Christ, Jesus replied using the title "Son of Man." He said that "from now on" the Sanhedrin would see the Son of Man seated at the right hand of God (this also alludes to Ps 110:1). The picture is of Jesus being seated in authority at God's side, invested as a regal figure and ruling with God. The implications of this reply are staggering. In fact, Jesus' own response led to the leadership condemning him for blasphemy.[5]

Jesus' coming sovereignty is declared in his sitting at the right hand of God, a figure for rule (Exod 11:5; 12:29; 1 Kgs 1:17; 3:6; 8:25; 1 Chr 17:16). Drawn from Ps 110, this picture of rule from God's right hand answers the Sanhedrin's question: Is Jesus the Anointed One? He will be seated at God's side shortly, exalted as ruler. In fact, God will do this for Jesus. This claim had strong repercussions in a Judaism where God was so transcendent that angels had become the mediators between God and humans. Thus, in Luke 22:71, the council will argue that no other witnesses are needed, since Jesus in their view has made a damning statement. But what is the statement that condemns?

For most Jews, the idea of coming directly into God's presence and sitting with him in constant heavenly session without cultic purification or worship was an insult to God's uniqueness. It was the essence of blasphemy since a human seated by God diminishes God's stature. The later rabbinic dispute with Rabbi Akiva makes this clear, as does the leadership's response to Jesus. In that dispute, Akiva permits David a seat at God's side in light of Ps 110:1, but the rabbis rebuke him, asking how long Akiva will profane the Shekinah (*b. Ḥag.* 14a). Also, *3 Enoch* shows a reaction to the idea of comparing oneself to God as the angel Metatron describes himself as a "Lesser Yahweh," only to be punished by God for making the suggestion he can be at all like God (see *3 En.* 12–16). Biblical figures who go into God's presence are first cleansed (cf. Isa 6; Ezek 1).

In early rabbinic tradition, only God sits in heaven. The only exceptions to this come in a few earlier Second Temple texts. In the *Exagoge of Ezekiel* 68–82, Moses is portrayed as sitting on the "thrones" (Dan 7:9 is the only place in the OT where such a plural is used). This is a rhetorical depiction of Moses being "God to Pharaoh" (Exod 7:1). The image from *Exagoge* serves as a midrash on that text from the Torah. It is not an eschatological text. A second example is from *1 En.* 37–71, where the Son of Man sits at God's side and participates in the final judgment in numerous texts. Despite these exceptions, for most Jews, especially for the majority Sadducees on the council, one could stand before God, but one does not sit with him.[6] Anything else insults his person. Not until the fourth century were Abraham and David officially associated with Ps 110:1 (*Midr. Ps.* 110.1 on 110:1; 18.29 on 18:35 [18:36 MT]; cf. 1.2 on 1:1 and 108.1 on 108:1).

---

5. A full discussion of this scene in its Marcan form, which Luke mostly reflects, is found in my *Blasphemy and Exaltation in Judaism and the Final Examination of Jesus* (WUNT 2/106; Tübingen: Mohr-Siebeck, 1998). In it I trace the Jewish ideas of exaltation and blasphemy that collided in this event, as well as defend the event's historicity. That discussion is updated in Bock and Webb, *Key Events in the Life of the Historical Jesus*, 589–667. The latter update contains a full defense of the historicity of this scene.

6. It is important to remember that Sadducees resisted additions to the Torah.

Thus, when Jesus says that he can sit at God's side, he profanes God's person in the Jewish leadership's view. If, however, he is able to take the seat at God's side and God does vindicate him, then implications emerge about Jesus' person. The leadership understands these implications. The defendant claims to be the Judge. With strong irony, the Jews think that Jesus is on trial, but what they do to him does not matter, since he is the true Judge. The very remarks that the Jewish leadership thinks lowers God's stature, in fact, shows how exalted Jesus is.[7]

In effect, Jesus gives the testimony that leads him to the cross. Jesus is claiming that he can go directly into God's presence and sit and rule with God from the very side of the deity. In fact, God will do this for him, in an act of ultimate vindication and a heavenly display of his position on this dispute between Jesus and the leadership. This title "Lord" is a more important title than Messiah, for it pictures Jesus' total authority and his ability and right to serve as an equal with God the Father.

This emphasis is confirmed in Acts 2. Here as Peter reviews the events surrounding Jesus' death and resurrection, he also appeals to Ps 110:1 in Acts 2:32–36. Jesus is the Lord at God's right hand. Peter explains how the resurrection and exaltation of Jesus have led to his being seated at the right hand of the Father and to the distribution of the Spirit as promised in Joel 2. God has vindicated Jesus and shown him to be Lord and Christ as a result of his raising Jesus and giving him a place as mediator of the benefits of salvation. The citation of Joel 2:28–32 alludes to the initial fulfillment of the new covenant and the presence of the new era. Jesus is alive and active in the kingdom of God that has brought this new era. Joel urged men to "call on the name of the Lord" (Acts 2:21). The assumption had been in Hebrew Scripture that one was calling on the name of the God of Israel, but the association between Jesus and God is so tight in God's program that Peter argues that the "Lord" to be called on here is Jesus, as salvation benefits are celebrated in light of the authority of his name as the Christ (2:34–38).

In addition, Jesus' position at the right hand of God is an initial fulfillment of a promise made to David that one of his descendants would sit on his throne forever. Here Peter alludes to Ps 132:11, which in turn alludes to the promises of 2 Sam 7 and the Davidic covenant. In Acts 2, the Ps 132 allusion leads into the discussion of Ps 110 about the descendant of David. This Acts 2 text with Luke 22:69 answers Jesus' query of Luke 20:41–44. Jesus is Messiah, God's vindicated Lord, more than he is David's son. Psalm 110:1 tells us so. Peter linked Ps 132 and Ps 110 in fulfillment. Each of Peter's allusions to these psalms uses concepts tied to being seated ("place ... on his throne" in Acts 2:30 and "sit" in v. 34). So the two images are one and meet their initial realization in Jesus' resurrection-ascension.

Jesus is thus portrayed as ruling at God's side as the Mediator and the intermediary source of divine blessing, an act that is an initial realization of promises made long ago. In Peter's speech the title "Lord" in Acts 2:36 is in the emphatic

---

7. Bock, *Luke 9:51–24:53*, 1799.

first position (κύριον αὐτὸν καὶ χριστὸν ἐποίησεν ὁ θεός, *kyrion auton kai Christon epoiēsen ho theos*). Jesus' authority over salvation is absolute, and the title "Lord" is the comprehensive christological title that summarizes that total authority over salvation's benefits as the one who shares rule at God's side.

The observation that Jesus has gone to God's side, although expressed figuratively since God does not have a limited location or a right hand, leads to and reflects a high Christology, since it raises the question of who can sit in God's presence. Who is holy enough to do so? This description of Jesus' position suggests an intimate connection between Jesus and the Father and an equality between them. The vindication of Jesus is about more than merely that he lives and others will be raised. It explains who Jesus is and how God has shown him to be the Lord Christ. Here the title "Lord" has its full, heavenly authority because of Jesus' position.

It is sometimes suggested that such a Christology emerged late in the early church or that such an argument could have been made only from the Greek LXX.[8] But all the LXX did was to render the MT while respecting the unique name of God. As noted in the last chapter's discussion of Luke 20:41–44, the MT clearly distinguishes between Yahweh (*yhwh*) and David's Lord (*ʾâdôn*). Yet, in Second Temple Judaism, Jews did not pronounce God's personal name but replaced it with a form of "Lord," whether in Aramaic, Hebrew, or Greek, as the LXX did in its written form. Qumran shows that they may have inserted dots or an abbreviation to have the same effect of not pronouncing the sacred name (Isaiah Scroll at Qumran).[9] Thus, orally rendering the MT would produce a reading like that in the LXX.

What is important here is not just the use of "Lord" as a shared term but the event context in which the text was viewed. So this argument about "late" development is not adequate. Everything necessary to make the conclusion that Jesus is the Lord was in place as a result of the resurrection. Thus there is no need to insist on a later development by appealing to a later Christology or to the form of the LXX's reading. Between the resurrection and the ascension, all the factors to make this conclusion are in place, generating reflection about where Jesus might be as a result of resurrection and what that unique position would mean about him. Sharing God's unique glory points to Jesus' unique, divine position as Messiah, Lord, and Son. Nor is adoptionism present. Jesus did not become Lord but was shown to be Lord through the resurrection-ascension (see Rom 1:2–4).[10] As Acts 2:21, 36–38

---

8. With many others Jervell, *Apostelgeschichte*, 149, n. 257.

9. S. Byington, " יהוה and אדון," *JBL* 76 (1957): 58–59.

10. In Romans 1:2–4, Jesus is said to be (lit.) "marked out" or "horizoned" to be the Son of God by resurrection. The picture is of a display of a role, not an entry into it, except to note a shift of position that allows Jesus to execute the plan in a way he could not have done before his death and resurrection. The narrative flow of Luke-Acts argues for such a reading of Luke's Christology. In making this point, I challenge a view like that of Arie W. Zwiep in *Christ, the Spirit and the Community of God: Essays on the Acts of the Apostles* (WUNT 2/293; Tübingen: Mohr-Siebeck, 2010), 140–44. Zwiep argues that according to Acts 2:36, the resurrection-ascension made Jesus Lord and Christ. He contends that the choice of the verb in 2:36 is key here. Luke did not choose a verb that points to demonstration but to Jesus' being made to enter this role. There is a point to this in that Jesus' key function as Messiah and Lord cannot be executed until he has his full heavenly authority at the side of God so Jesus can perform central messianic tasks. However, this view still does not reflect Luke's perspective on Jesus. The argument is too based in a narrow linguistic reading and ignores the narrative context and flow of the christological argument in Luke-Acts. Jesus is declared Messiah in the infancy material. Peter confesses Jesus

suggest, the "Lord" to be called upon is Jesus—and only God saves.[11] He is Lord of all (10:36).[12]

The significance of Jesus' title of "Lord" appears again in Acts 10:36–42, where Peter makes the point that Jesus is Lord over all humanity (Rom 10:12 is similar in meaning). Therefore, Peter can proclaim to Cornelius and other Gentiles that the gospel is available to all. This is one of the most central points in Luke-Acts. Christology is the ground for the scope of the salvation message. One of Luke's crucial theological conclusions is that Jesus is Lord and that he has authority over salvation to distribute its benefits.[13] The movement from regal-prophetic categories to incorporation into the title "Lord" is one of the basic theological themes in Luke-Acts. It reveals that Jesus, being intimately related to God, functions with a full array of divine prerogatives.

In fact, the identity is so strong that one now acts "in the name of Lord Jesus Christ," as we saw so repeatedly in the last chapter's narrative survey. Jesus even bears the title "Lord," the title normally used of Yahweh in the LXX. His exalted position can be seen through a comparison with statements in the Hebrew Scripture about Yahweh. In those texts, such actions had occurred in the name of Yahweh; now they occur in Jesus' name. So the transition to "in the name of Jesus" is significant. As we saw, to act "in the name" is a major Lucan theme stressing Jesus' total authority to exercise divine prerogatives in salvation (Acts 2:38; 3:6, 16; 4:7, 10, 12, 18, 30; 5:40–41; 8:12, 16; 9:15, 27–28; 10:43, 48; 15:26; 16:18; 19:13,17; 21:13; 22:16; 26:9). Acts 15:17 speaks of the name of God in a similar way. Jesus' name means that when one deals with Jesus, that person deals with one who has the authority of God.[14] In short, to deal with Jesus is to deal with God.

---

as Messiah during Jesus' ministry. Jesus' lordship is shown in his exercise of authority over demons and over issues like the law and Sabbath. He is celebrated as Messiah in the entry into Jerusalem. During that time Jesus connects Messiah and Lord as related concepts. And in the trial scene before the Jews he makes the point that from now on this authority will be seen. Thus, to argue that Acts 2:36 shows Jesus to be Lord and Messiah fits this narrative development. It reflects Luke's view that Jesus was and is Messiah and Lord, but that the resurrection-ascension showed this in a way that made it clear this was the role God had given to Jesus. It also reflects a point made in Luke 3:16 in the presentation of John the Baptist that the way one could know the Messiah and new era had come was when the Spirit was distributed. This act showed who Jesus is. In making this point, I side with Rowe's argument about the point of the narrative flow in his *Early Narrative Christology* (esp. pp. 27, 44–58, 189–96). Zwiep's contention that Acts 2:36 is the Achilles heel for an emphasis on the narrative elevates one text at the expense of the presentation of the two volumes and fails to place that text adequately in its larger conceptual context. In his chapter on this text, Zwiep ignores messianic and lordship texts in the body of Luke's gospel, jumping from Luke 1–2 to Luke 24. What Luke has people say in between is important and raises questions about

the emphasis he gives to Acts 2:36.

11. Larkin, *Acts*, 57.

12. So Witherington, *Acts of the Apostles*,147–53: "It was not that Jesus became *someone* different from who he was before, but that he entered a new stage in his career, or assumed new roles after the ascension" (p. 149).

13. Here we see lordship presented and defined as the one with authority over salvation. When one calls on the name of the Lord Jesus for salvation in faith, it is the recognition of Jesus having such authority to deliver this grace that is invoked. See Darrell L. Bock, "Jesus as Lord in Acts and in the Gospel Message," *BibSac* 143 (1986): 146–54.

14. Luke never calls Jesus "God" directly. He presents Jesus' position more subtly through the use of the title "Lord." Luke shows that Jesus does what God does and carries the authority that God has. In contrast to John's gospel, where this identification is explicit, Luke shows this implicitly in Jesus' actions and God's vindication of him. The reader is led to draw the appropriate conclusion about who Jesus ultimately is. As Rowe argues in *Early Narrative Christology*, 27–30, Luke has a high Christology in which God and Jesus are bound together in identity and not mixed into one, so there is both identification and distinction in the role as Lord.

8.2 THE TITLES OF JESUS IN LUKE-ACTS

Having noted this fundamental christological progression in Luke-Acts, we must now examine the variety of christological titles in Luke, since Luke's portrait of Jesus is multifaceted.

8.2.1 Savior

Though it is popular today to refer to Jesus as Savior (σωτήρ, *sōtēr*), Luke rarely uses this title. It appears in the infancy summary in Luke 2:11, when the angel announces Jesus' birth. The deliverance alluded to in the title is clarified by the hymns and declarations of the infancy material. That deliverance is both national and spiritual (1:70–75, 77; 2:30–32). It reflects the coming of the consolation of Israel and the redemption of Jerusalem. It looks to a time when God's people are rescued from their enemies and are free to serve God in righteousness and holiness. That rescue involves both the challenges of destructive spiritual forces (11:20) and a life honoring God on earth. This God-honoring life emerges in the community's life in Acts and reflects Jesus' call in the Sermon on the Plain for disciples to live with integrity (6:20–49).

A similar picture surfaces in Acts 5:31 and 13:23–25, passages that present Jesus as the Savior of Israel. Jesus is the exalted Savior lifted up to the right hand of God to give repentance and forgiveness of sins to Israel. He is the Savior promised to David. Jesus is David's descendant and the one to whom John the Baptist pointed (Luke 3:15–18). For Luke, Jesus is the Savior and the Christ, the one to come who brings the Spirit. The offer of forgiveness and provision of the Spirit explains why Jesus can also be called Savior.

Luke reserves mention of Jesus as Savior in contexts where Israel as a nation is being discussed (Luke 1:47; 2:11; Acts 13:23).[15] In the OT, God is often the Savior (Isa 43:3, 11; 45:15, 21; 49:26; Jer 14:8; Hos 13:4; Ps 24:5 LXX); so also in the NT (1 Tim 1:1; 2:3; 4:10; Titus 1:3; 2:10; 3:4; Jude 25). God continues to appeal to his obstinate people. He is now saving and cleansing through a mediating Savior. Judaism believed that at the end there would be a need to receive cleansing from sin (*Pss. Sol.* 17.22–29; *Jub.* 4.26; 50.5; *1 En.* 10.22; *T. Levi* 18.9; *T. Jud.* 24.1).[16] This is the apostles' appeal. See what God is doing and believe. So for Luke the title Savior has particular reference to God's whole program of promised deliverance, in addition to being tied to Israel, to exaltation, to forgiveness, and to the offer of the Spirit.

8.2.2 Christ

Though the title "Lord" points up Jesus' ultimate authority as ruler, "Christ" (χριστός, *Christos*) is Luke's most frequent title for Jesus and serves as his foundation

---

15. Jervell, *Apostelgeschichte*, 208, n. 576.   16. Ibid., 208, n. 577.

point in building his "from the earth up" Christology. The title "Christ" refers to Jesus as the promised Anointed One ("Messiah" in Hebrew means "Anointed One"), the one at the center of God's eschatological program. The use of this title was so diverse in Second Temple Judaism that Jesus did not use it in public or emphasize the association until he was drawing near to Jerusalem at the end of his ministry. Those who embraced the title with any of its cultural meanings at the time would not have appreciated aspects of Jesus' messianic task. So in Luke we mostly see others making this connection. Still, Jesus accepts the title and role once it is understood on his terms as reflecting the one God has chosen to be at the center of his kingdom program, one who will suffer and then be exalted.

The first use of the title in Luke is in the angelic confession (Luke 2:11), and its force is clearly defined earlier in Luke by the description of Jesus' role in 1:31–35 and in the salvation Zechariah praises in 1:68–75, 79–80. Here is a regal deliverance figure promised to David. The hope Jesus stirred for the redemption of the nation was noted by Simeon (2:26).

John the Baptist refused the title for himself and spoke of one who would come after him (Luke 3:15–16). The promise that would reveal Messiah's presence is the distribution of the Spirit. A key usage of the word "Christ," unique to Luke, occurs in 4:41. Demons confessed that Jesus is the Son of God, and then Luke explained "that they knew that he was the Messiah." In this way Luke shows Jesus' sonship is linked to the promise of the Messiah.

"Christ/Messiah" was also the title Peter used in his confession in Luke 9:20. The role that the title plays in this scene shows its foundational character, since after this confession, Jesus began to reveal more about God's plan, especially his coming suffering. As already noted, in the last week the issue of Jesus' identity as Messiah was at the center of a key question asked by the Jewish leaders. It also was a key issue at Jesus' trial (22:67). In the narrative, this develops a question Jesus had raised earlier about the Christ as Lord and Son of David (21:41–44). The issue of Jesus as Christ the King continued to be central in his movement toward crucifixion (23:2, 35, 39). In reflecting on the resurrection, Luke made the point (in material unique to him) that Christ's suffering was necessary ($\delta\epsilon\hat{\iota}$, *dei*) and was foretold (24:26, 46).

In this concept of a suffering messiah, the Jesus movement's portrait of Messiah clashed with Jewish expectation, since Judaism had only anticipated a glorious, strictly victorious, and powerful figure. To Jews, a suffering messiah was incongruous, an impossibility. They thought that the nation might suffer, but not their deliverer. However, Jesus' suffering and death make it possible for the deliverer to purchase a people who will serve the Lord (Acts 20:28 does not use the term "Christ," but does use the image of purchase). Having been exalted as Christ, Jesus can bring both deliverance and forgiveness of sins.

In the book of Acts, a number of things are said to happen "in the name of … Christ": baptism (Acts 2:38), salvation (4:10), healing (9:34), peace (10:36), baptism of the Spirit (10:48), risking of life (15:26), and exorcism (16:18). Several things were predicted about the "Christ": resurrection (2:31), suffering (3:18; 17:3; 26:23), and being appointed for humankind (3:20). The Christ was the subject of the apostles' preaching (5:42; 8:5; 9:22; 17:3; 18:5; 28:31). Because of all Jesus is and all Jesus did, he is to be the object of trust (24:24).

8.2.3 Son of David

This title is another way of presenting Jesus as a regal authority. This emphasis is also part of the christological foundation Luke presents in the infancy material. Jesus' connection to David is noted numerous times early on in Luke, mostly in heavenly declarations (Luke 1:27, 32, 69; 2:4, 11). Of these passages, the most descriptive ones are 1:32, 69. Here one reads of Jesus' occupying the throne of David and emerging from David's house to rule and deliver. When blind Bartimaeus asks for healing, he addresss Jesus as "Son of David" (18:38–39). The relationship between a regal role and healing is not clear, though some have suggested that in Judaism Solomon was believed to have possessed miraculous skill in addition to wisdom.[17] The question Jesus raises about David's Son in Luke 20:41–44 focuses on Jesus' genealogical connection to David and yet subordinates this idea to that of Messiah being David's Lord; Jesus appeals to Ps 110:1.

In Acts 2:25–31, Peter makes the point that David as a prophet anticipated that his son would be resurrected (Ps 16:8–11). Peter uses this passage to explain that Jesus' resurrection is a part of God's promise. Acts 13:22–23 also refers to the promise to Israel of a Savior from David's lineage. Acts 13:34 adds a note, citing the promise of Isa 55:3. The promises given to David are also promises to the nation of Israel and to Paul's audience, since Paul notes that David's "holy and sure blessings" (τὰ ὅσια Δαυὶδ τὰ πιστά, *ta hosia Dauid ta pista*) belong to the nation. In Paul's exposition that follows, part of the holy things promised through the Messiah are the forgiveness of sins and justification. So part of the promises to David are inaugurated through Jesus' resurrection. The promised Messiah is active in giving to God's people things the new era promised.

The final passage relating to David is Acts 15:16, which refers to the promise of the rebuilt Davidic booth made in Amos 9:11.[18] Jesus' resurrection and recent events in the church show that God is rebuilding the Davidic house. So James argues that Gentile involvement in that process should not surprise anyone, for it is a part of the promise as well. Thus the title "Son of David" is a major link in the chain that points to God's completing his promise.

---

17. Josephus notes what looks to be an old tradition that Solomon was associated in his connection to wisdom with healing and incantations (*Ant.* 8.2.5 [45–49]). There is no eschatological element in this teaching or tradition, but it does show an association of a Son of David with healing. D. C. Duling, "Solomon, Exorcism, and the Son of David," *HTR* 68 (1975): 235–52; Klaus Berger, "Die königlichen Messiastraditionen des Neuen Testaments," *NTS* 20 (1973–74): 1–44.

18. In fact, though Amos 9 is cited, the introductory formula makes use of Luke's generalized appeal to the prophets ("the words of the prophets are in agreement with this"); this shows that Amos 9 is not the only text James could have appealed to in making his point. His use renders the LXX here, which differs from the MT, but James's point is that this is but one such text, and the prophetic teaching as a whole looks to such blessing of the nations in the Messiah. One can think of the promise to Abraham here as Luke already alluded to it in Acts 3:25–26.

8.2.4 Son of God and King

Another title of Jesus that Luke uses is "Son of God" (υἱὸς θεοῦ, *huios theou*). This full form rarely appears. As noted earlier, the title is used in Luke 1:35 in association with the virgin birth. There it has a nativistic force, tied as it is to his special birth. The term is a foretaste of Luke's high Christology, but its sense in 1:35 is so ambiguous that it is difficult to express its clear intent without the help of Luke's later development. In the original setting this title is surrounded by regal imagery, reflecting a royal association that "Son of God" can also bear (2 Sam 7:14: Ps 2:7). Later events push the force of the term into a deeper sense. Luke is gradually setting forth how Jesus came to be seen in the way the church now confesses Jesus. He does so with a gradual unveiling.[19]

The title is used by Satan at the temptations as the claimed title of Jesus ("If you are the Son of God"; Luke 4:3, 9). A significant use of the title appears in 4:41, where it is linked to and explained by the title "Christ." The linkage, given as an explanation, shows that the title does have regal overtones for Luke. Demons called Jesus the "Son of the Most High God" (8:28). This use pushes the force of the term some, although 4:41 points to a similar demonic confession context, and that earlier context reflects a messianic element. The title seems predominant when spiritual beings address Jesus. The use acknowledges that Jesus possesses a high level of authority. "Son of God" also is a position in dispute at Jesus' trial, as seen in 22:70. It was the title the high priest wanted Jesus to acknowledge.

The use of the simple title "son" is more complex. Sonship is associated with the virgin birth in Luke 1:31–32, expressing a unique origin of the "son." Jesus spoke of God as his Father (2:49). Again, here "son" suggests a unique relationship to God. "My Son" is the title in the heavenly voice at Jesus' baptism and transfiguration (3:22; 9:35). These are the only occurrences of this title in the gospel of Luke.

Acts 9:20 is the only place where the full title "Son of God" appears in Acts.[20] Early in Luke, the term "Son" may be ambiguous as to whether it stresses a regal position or unique sonship, but in Acts it clearly describes the exalted Messiah who sits next to God the Father with total authority. As such, it emerges as a title of high Christology. That Paul intends a high Christology in 9:20 is suggested by his sermon in 13:16–41. The title "Son of God" here is probably meant in terms of full "sonship," given its outgrowth from Saul's vision in seeing a glorified Jesus whom he had heard preached as the Son of Man at God's right hand by Stephen in 7:56.

However, the title also has a messianic thrust if Acts 9:22 and the speech of ch. 13 are guides. Romans 1:1–4 shows how Paul confessed Jesus as Son of God (see also Rom 8:3; Gal 4:4; Col 1:15–20; 1 Thess 1:10). "Son of God" in the OT refers to Israel as a people (Exod 4:22), to the king of Israel (2 Sam 7:14; Ps 89:26–27),

---

19. This may seem hairsplitting, but it is important. Luke is showing how it dawns on people who Jesus really is. They go from messianic hope to much more as a result of what God does through Jesus.

20. The use in Acts 8:37 looks to be later and not original to Acts; at least that is what the manuscript evidence on this verse suggests.

and to the king of the future (Ps 2:7 [seen as the covenantal ideal]; *1 En.* 105.2; 2 Esdr. [*4 Ezra*] 7:28–29; 13:32, 37, 52; 14:9; 4Q174 1.10–11).[21] Jesus is preached as the unique promised one of God; he is certainly seen in a glorified state, given Saul's experience of him.

This deeper understanding is confirmed by the reference to Ps 2:7 in Acts 13:33. This allusion looks back to the Father's voice at Jesus' baptism and transfiguration. An examination of Luke's two volumes shows that although "Son of God" is not used frequently in Luke, the title does ultimately express Jesus' unique relationship to God the Father, though in some contexts it may have been simply another way of saying Jesus is the King or the Christ.

Jesus is called the "king" (ὁ βασιλεύς, *ho basileus*) at the time of the entry into Jerusalem (Luke 19:38, which alludes to Ps 118:26). "King" is the title discussed in the legal proceedings surrounding Jesus' trial before Pilate (Luke 23:3: "Are you the king of the Jews?") and in connection with his death (vv. 37–38). Pilate had to be concerned about this claim, since in Rome's view, they appointed kings and Pilate was responsible to protect Caesar's interests in Judea. One thief recognizes he is dying with a king, for he asks to come into Jesus' kingdom (v. 42). Jesus promises him paradise that very day. Some Jews in Thessalonica accuse Christians by saying the believers call Jesus a king (Acts 17:7). The note on kingship, though not frequent, is important in the context of Jesus' trial, for it shows that kingship is the issue (and so messianism); Jesus is not being challenged for merely being a prophet.

8.2.5 Prophet

Still in the midst of the messianic Christology, one should be careful not to miss Luke's focus on Jesus as "prophet" (προφήτης, *prophētēs*). The outstanding example of this submerged category is Luke 4:16–30. Here Jesus presents his ministry as a fulfillment of Isa 61:1–2a, in which Isaiah described a prophet who would be anointed by God and would bring the message of hope to God's people. Jesus is presented as a servant-like prophet, fitting the pattern that Isaiah described. However, Jesus is also more than a prophet, for he brings the salvation he proclaims. Jesus' prophetic function receives confirmation in Luke 4:24, when he says that a prophet is without honor in his own country. In addition, the comparison to the period of Elijah and Elisha also makes the prophetic connection clear (4:25–27).

Luke 4:25–27 deserves a closer look. In pointing to the period of Elijah and Elisha, Jesus cites a low point in Israel's history. In this historical comparison, the threat is that those closest to Jesus, those within his nation, may miss God's blessing, while others, who are far away, will receive it. Luke 4:25–27, which alludes to the period of the evil king Ahab (see 1 Kgs 17–18), is unique to Luke's portrayal of the synagogue account. This OT text refers to a specific famine and judgment for covenant unfaithfulness. Such unfaithfulness brought Israel under judgment at this time, so God's provision and prophetic signs were absent from the land.

---

21. Bruce, *Book of the Acts*, 190.

Jesus notes that not a single widow received blessing except for a Gentile woman in Zarephath, a town located north of Israel between Tyre and Sidon (1 Kgs 17:9). In the OT account, the woman is described in terms of her faith (17:12, 16, 18, 24). This Gentile is an exception to the rule, and she is the last person one initially would have expected to be blessed by an Israelite prophet.

The parallelism with Elijah is popular in the NT and in Luke. In a dire period of Israel's history, Elijah ministered outside the nation. The exact point of the comparison can be stated in various ways.[22] (1) The comparison shows that Nazareth does not have exclusive claim to Jesus. This point, though true, is too narrow to develop the major idea. (2) Elijah and Elisha show that, because of Nazareth's refusal, Jesus will go elsewhere. This point also is true yet lacks specificity. (3) The prophetic example teaches that, although the homeland rejects him, others will respond and see God work. This approach is probably accurate, since not everyone in the homeland or in the nation will reject Jesus. Again, as in Luke 4:18, the language is in generalized form, but the warning is serious. Salvation will open up to all kinds of people. The comparison to this bleak time of famine and to Elijah's period certainly warns, through clear implication, that the consequences of rejecting Jesus may involve God's rejection.

The message is reinforced by a second illustration, this one about Elijah's successor, Elisha (2 Kgs 5:1–14), the only time he is named in the NT. No Israelite leper was healed. Rather, a Syrian Gentile named Naaman received God's cleansing in the Jordan River. The point about the danger of potential rejection is driven home through an illustration about a second category of needy people, lepers. God was working with those outside Israel and with the sick who were unclean (Lev 14:2–31). Those ostensibly distant from God could become the blessed, while those hearing his message now risked an experience like Israel of old. Those ostensibly near to God had better hear the warning.

Jesus' audience does react, but with something other than a positive response.[23] The crowd knows their biblical history and gets the point. The idea that Jesus might reach out to outsiders produces anger. In effect, Jesus is saying that the Nazarenes are worse than Syrian lepers and Phoenician widows. Luke uses the word θυμός (*thymos*, "anger") for angry reactions to speeches of major figures (Acts 19:28).[24] Like Paul's message about going to the Gentiles, this warning also leaves its audience displeased (13:46, 50; 22:21–22). Outsiders might end up being blessed, while insiders are left out. Jesus may have been a prophet sent to Israel, but her lack of response will cause God to turn to others who will respond.

Much popular speculation about Jesus centers in a prophetic confession. Luke 9:7–9, 19 shows the strength of such speculation, as does the popular reaction to Jesus' raising the son of the widow of Nain ("a great prophet has appeared among

---

22. Marshall, *Gospel of Luke*, 188.
23. The discussion of Elijah and Elisha reflects my treatment in

Luke 1:1–9:50, 418–19.
24. Büchsel, *TDNT*, 3:167–68.

us," 7:16). For many, Jesus is only a prophet. But even that is doubted by the Jewish leaders as Jesus' controversial associations lead them to question whether Jesus holds that position (7:39). Luke 7:36–50 is significant because Simon the Pharisee claims that Jesus' willingness to receive anointing from a woman of questionable reputation showed him not to be a prophet. And yet, as a prophet, Jesus knows all the while what Simon is thinking in this scene! The following parable that Jesus tells explains why he is open to this sinner who has responded to God's grace. This point of irony, expressed with literary flair, affirms that Jesus is a prophet.

The prophetic description of Jesus receives more emphasis as the narrative moves on. Luke 9:35 ("listen to him") points to Jesus as the "prophet like Moses" by alluding to Deut 18:15. The disciples need to hear what Jesus says, since he is the bearer of a new way, as was Moses. In particular, the message of the Messiah's suffering needs to be heard (Luke 9:43–45). The title "prophet like Moses" indicates that Jesus not only brings the message of God but also introduces a new era. These descriptions of Jesus receive more attention in Acts 3:22–23; 7:37.

One other point emerges from the prophetic theme. As a prophet, Jesus shares the fate of earlier prophets, namely, national rejection. Luke 13:33 brings this point out explicitly, and it is implicit in 11:47–51. It is particularly seen in the teaching of his journey toward Jerusalem (chs. 9–19), when Jesus, as a prophet, rebukes the Jewish leaders and calls disciples to righteousness. Many of the passages in chs. 9–14 are strong prophetic rebukes of current religious practice. There is a piety that is false and dishonoring to God, no matter how good it may seem outwardly. Such hypocrisy receives stronger judgment in this section than does blatant sin, possibly because hypocrisy is deception. Luke 11:39–52 presents Jesus at his prophetic best.

Disappointed that Jesus was crucified, one of the Emmaus followers called Jesus a "prophet, powerful in word and deed" (Luke 24:19). These men also hoped Jesus would redeem Israel (24:21). In this passage, the two Emmaus disciples share their personal view of Jesus: they are downcast because they hoped that he was going to redeem Israel. The imperfect ἠλπίζομεν (elpizomen, "we were hoping") expresses the ongoing character of this hope. The idea is like Jer 14:8, where Yahweh is called "the hope of Israel."[25] They hoped that through Jesus, God would work for the nation and deliver it into a new era of freedom. This is the only time that Luke uses λυτρόω (lytroō, "to redeem").[26] If this hope equals that expressed by Zechariah in Luke 1:68–79, then what is hoped for includes Israel's political release from Rome (a major Jewish emphasis: Isa 41:14; 43:14; 44:22–24; 1 Macc 4:11; *Pss. Sol.* 9.1). Luke loves to place Prophet-Redeemer themes side by side. Jesus is both, not one or the other.

The prophet like Moses receives his most detailed attention in Acts 3:22–23. That text deserves a closer look. The two verses are built around two OT citations. Peter cites Deut 18:15 with only three minor changes from the MT and LXX.

---

25. Fitzmyer, *Gospel according to Luke (x–xxiv)*, 1564.   26. Marshall, *Gospel of Luke*, 895; Büchsel, *TDNT*, 4:340–51.

(1) The second person pronouns are plural rather than singular to make a more direct connection with all the listeners in the audience. (2) This addition replicates the call at the beginning of the citation (ὑμῖν, *hymin*, "for you"), alludes to Deut 18:15, and includes the phrase "everything he tells you" as a summary of the point from 18:19. (3) Finally, the addition at the beginning of Acts 3:23 (lit., "it shall be") sets up the linkage to a second OT citation from Lev 23:29. The pronoun is moved forward (ὑμῖν, *hymin*, "for you") to make the point that God's action of raising up a prophet like Moses is for the benefit of the people, a clear example of a dative of advantage.

Peter makes clear that the promise of a great saving leader-prophet like Moses is something the OT has declared. Such a prophet God would "raise up" (ἀναστήσει, *anastēsei*, Acts 3:22). This verb, reused in v. 26, may well have a wordplay built around it (cf. 13:33). It means to bring someone onto the scene of history but could in this context allude to resurrection, to raising someone up, especially in v. 26.[27] In the original context, this promise of a prophet would have alluded to Joshua or others. Their presence as those who could speak for God would preclude the need to appeal to magic or divination. This passage came to be seen by first-century Judaism, however, as a typological promise of a prophet of the Mosaic leader-deliverer pattern, who is a part of the eschaton.[28]

The expectation of a Moses-like figure in the end times was common in Judaism (1QS 1.9–11; 4Q175 1.5–8; 1 Macc 14:41). Josephus (*Ant.* 20.5.1 [97]) shows the first-century Jewish figure Theudas trying to invoke Moses' parting of the sea to make the case that he is a prophet who could lead Israel.[29] The Samaritans pointed to this passage as describing a restorer figure known as the *Taheb* (*Memar Marqah* 4.3).[30] Luke repeats this pattern and connection to the Mosaic promise in Acts 7:22, 25, 30–39 and alludes to it in Luke 9:35.

The second OT citation that discusses the promise and the proper response to it comes from a mixture of Deut 18:19 and Lev 23:29. Here negative consequences for rejection appear as a prophetic warning. The concept of listening to the prophet is from Deut 18:19, and the penalty of destruction and separation from God's people comes from Lev 23:29. The patchwork nature of the citation is not common for Luke (but see Luke 4:16–18 using Isa 61:1 and 58:6; Acts 7:7 using Gen 15:13–14 and Exod 3:12). It suggests the presence of tradition.

The reference to "anyone" (lit., "every soul"; πᾶσα ψυχή, *pasa psychē*) provides the point of contact with Leviticus. Deuteronomy 18:19 appears in various Jewish texts with similar wording (*Targum Pseudo-Jonathan* on Deut 18:19b; Codex Neofiti I; 4Q175 [an eschatological *testimonia* text]). Another point of contact with Leviticus is the strong reference to the penalty of destruction for not listening to the prophet (ἐξολεθρευθήσεται ἐκ τοῦ λαοῦ, *exolethreuthēsetai ek tou laou*, "will be destroyed from

27. Larkin, *Acts*, 69.
28. Bock, *Proclamation from Prophecy and Pattern*, 191–94.
29. Witherington, *Acts of the Apostles*, 188.
30. Polhill, *Acts*, 136; Jeremias, *TDNT*, 4:848–73.

the people"). The verb used here depicts utter destruction ("completely cut off" in NIV).[31] This is the only use of this verb in the NT. In Leviticus the passage refers to not keeping the atonement, so there is an interesting parallel here. Failure to listen to (i.e., obey) this prophet and his career of suffering and glorification is like failing to heed the atonement. Given what Jesus went through, the association is significant in pointing to an implication of Jesus' death that enables sin to be blotted out (Acts 3:19; the association of the promise of Gen 22:18 in Acts 3:25 may also support this allusion). The remark warns of total judgment for failing to respond to the person and work of Jesus, who is *the* prophet like Moses. Peter declares that those who fail to respond will have no place among God's people.[32]

8.2.6 Son of Man

This key title (ὁ υἱὸς τοῦ ἀνθρώπου, *ho huios tou anthrōpou*) is the way Jesus prefers to speak of himself. Late in the gospel (Luke 21:27), Jesus indicates that "the Son of Man" alludes to the authoritative figure of Dan 7:13–14, who received authority from the Ancient of Days over the kingdom. In Daniel, the term is not a title but a description, "one like a son of man," that is, a human. However, this figure rode the clouds, an act of a deity in the Hebrew Scriptures (Exod 14:20; 34:5; Num 10:34; Ps 104:3; Isa 19:1). The title "Son of Man" is prevalent in the three Synoptic Gospels. Though Mark emphasizes the suffering Servant, Luke's treatment is divided between uses that describe Jesus' current ministry, suffering, and return.

As the Son of Man, Jesus has a wide variety of ministries. He has authority to forgive sins, a claim that stirs much reaction, since in the Jewish view only God can do that (Luke 5:21–24). The scribes see Jesus claiming a divine prerogative and therefore violating God's majesty by taking to himself something reserved for God. Forgiving sin is God's work only (5:21). Their reading of what Jesus is doing and claiming is largely correct, though there is some precedent for God's having an agent who communicates this forgiveness (Nathan in 2 Sam 12:13 or the priests' sacrificial work or the disputed reference in the *Prayer of Nabonidus*).[33] However, forgiveness itself is the work of God (Exod 34:6; Ps 103:12; Isa 1:18; 43:25; Jer 31:34). This claim shows the extent of the authority suggested in the title.

As Son of Man, Jesus is Lord of the Sabbath (Luke 6:5). This text deserves a closer look and a comparison to Mark's use. A literal rendering according to word order is, "Lord is of the Sabbath the Son of Man." The passage has its fullest development in Mark 2:27, which speaks about the Sabbath's being for people and not people for the Sabbath. Many see Mark's point to be humanity's authority over the Sabbath, with the "Son of Man" as a reference to humans in general, since the phrase can have this meaning in Aramaic. A later rabbinic statement is close to this remark in force; nonetheless, many regard Jesus' remark as a likely reflection of an ancient

---

31. BDAG, 351.
32. Schneider, *TDNT*, 5:171.

33. Marshall, *Gospel of Luke*, 214.

view: "The Sabbath is given over to you and not you to the Sabbath" (*Mekilta de Rabbi Ishmael*, tractate *Shabbata* 1 on Exod 31:13).[34]

But Marshall notes that this saying is not a broad reference to all people, but to Israel's special authority. So even here, the application is narrow. The point of Mark's text, which Luke does not have, is that the Sabbath is not to be a master over God's people, but is a service to them. The Sabbath was created for them and was not created as a burden against them. This approach to Mark 2:27 seems the best way to view its background, which in turn supports its authenticity and its meaning. The Marcan point in the next verse is a form of heightened argument. If the Sabbath is designed for God's people, if the Sabbath is created to serve people, then certainly the representative man, Jesus, has authority over it.

Luke does not record Mark's remark about the Sabbath and God's people. Rather, Luke has a more exclusive christological focus. Mark's intermediate argument is not made, but the deeper issue about Jesus is emphasized. The Son of Man's authority refers to that of Jesus. Even in Mark, however, this has to be the ultimate point. In chasing the background of the Son of Man, commentators have ignored the contextual clues. In fact, when one detaches this saying from its context because of form-critical or redactional concerns, the logic of the sayings becomes difficult and leads to challenges of the authenticity of Luke 6:5. Lindars seems to argue for the authenticity of Mark 2:27, but cannot accept Mark 2:28 = Luke 6:5 as authentic.[35] He argues that the point about David is not found in David's authority, for if the passage is taken with this christological force, then "Son of Man" must be taken as a messianic title. In Lindars's view a messianic force is unlikely at this early point in Jesus' ministry. Thus, Lindars argues that Mark 2:28 is a Marcan saying that is formed in dependence on 2:10.

However, the point becomes clear if we keep a unity in the Marcan remarks rather than create a division. The ability of the context to unify the argument strengthens the argument for authenticity. The key to the argument is the previous Davidic illustration, since the king is a *representative* figure. Jesus' claim to be Son of Man gives the term a representative sense through that contextual linkage. Son of Man need not be explicitly messianic to make the point; it needs only to be representative, which is how the reference to David functions in the analogy. There are, however, implications in the usage that suggest the nature of the authority referred to in the concluding remark. Danker sees this point clearly: the Son of Man is an authoritative representative on behalf of his people, much as a king would be.[36] Jesus, as this representative, has authority as Son of Man to evaluate and interpret tradition and law. This is why authority is stressed by the placement of κύριος in the emphatic position.

---

34. Ibid., 232.

35. Barnabas Lindars, *Jesus Son of Man: A Fresh Examination of the Son of Man Sayings in the Gospels in the Light of Recent Research* (London: SPCK, 1983), 103–6.

36. Fred Danker, *Jesus and the New Age: A Commentary on St. Luke's Gospel* (rev. ed.; Philadelphia: Fortress, 1988), 131; also discussed in Hooker, *Son of Man in Mark*, 100–102; Marshall, *Gospel of Luke*, 232–33.

Again, great claims for Jesus are alluded to here. Jesus uses the title "Son of Man" in this context and refers to himself as *this* man for a second time in Luke's gospel, with David providing here the additional backdrop to explain the point (Luke 5:24 is the first use). Jesus heightens the stakes with the appeal to David, for he suggests by the comparison that the present times are like the times of David. Jesus has such a high stature (1:32). He is an authoritative representative of the new way. Lindars takes an either/or approach that focuses on a messianic understanding of Son of Man as the only alternative that can really work. In so doing, he misses the unity of the argument that can be found by a more representative emphasis to the title. With the remark, Jesus argues that he is the authoritative representative of the new way (as David was in the old era?) and that he has authority over the understanding and administration of the Sabbath.[37]

In Luke 9:22 Jesus recognizes that the Son of Man will suffer, an announcement he makes immediately after being confessed as Messiah by Peter. Though Jesus has authority, some reject him. The Son of Man came eating and drinking, an allusion to his open lifestyle and particularly to his associating with tax collectors and sinners, another area where he differs from the leaders, who tend to separate from sinners (7:24). Rejection again is the note when Jesus laments that the Son of Man has nowhere to lay his head (9:58). Because of his rejection, it is hard to follow in the footsteps of the Son of Man.

In Luke 11:29–31, the Son of Man gives no sign to that generation except that of Jonah, a reference in Luke to preaching a call to repent and respond to God that is compared to the prophet's message to Nineveh and the wisdom of Solomon given to the Queen of the South. Verse 32 explains that this sign is the message to repent, not of Jesus' resurrection, for it was Jonah's preaching in Nineveh to which Jesus draws attention.

People may speak against the Son of Man, but if they speak against the Holy Spirit, that is, reject the Spirit's testimony about Jesus, they cannot be forgiven (Luke 12:10). This text is often discussed because of the difficulty of the concept of this blasphemy of the Spirit versus blasphemy against the Son of Man. Blasphemy of the Spirit is not so much an act of rejection as it is a persistent and decisive rejection of the Spirit's message and work concerning Jesus. When a person obstinately rejects and fixedly refuses that message or evidence, that person is not forgiven. Nolland says it well: blasphemy against the Spirit is "the denial or rejection of the manifest saving intervention of God on behalf of his people.... The one who hardens himself or herself against what God is doing as he acts to save places himself or herself beyond the reach of God's present disposition of eschatological forgiveness."[38]

The mission of the Son of Man is to seek and save the lost (Luke 19:10). This verse is a mission statement that explains Jesus' declaration of salvation to Zacchaeus.

---

37. Bock, *Luke 1:1–9:50*, 525–27.
38. John Nolland, *Luke 9:21–18:34* (WBC 35b; Dallas: Word, 1993), 679–80.

His transformation represents a fulfillment of Jesus' call. The picture of seeking and saving "the lost" (ἀπολωλός, *apololos*; 1 Cor 1:18; 2 Cor 2:15; 4:3; 2 Thess 2:10) recalls the shepherd imagery applied to God in Ezek 34. What God would do for the nation as its shepherd because it was leaderless, Jesus does now (esp. Ezek 34:2, 4, 16, 22–23; John 10).[39] In fact, Jesus becomes the instrument through whom God works. His mission is to initiate relationships with those who do not know God and call to them to come to him. Nolland sees a strand of Davidic hope in the OT background. Royal reform of the nation is part of Jesus' goal.[40]

Luke 19:10 stresses Jesus' initiative to proclaim salvation for those who respond with faith. Like 5:32, it emphasizes that one of the prerequisites of responding to Jesus is to realize that one stands in need of God. Like 5:24, it emphasizes the Son of Man's present ministry to forgive sin. Zacchaeus is like the prodigal, the lost coin, and the lost sheep (ch. 15). He is one who has been healed by the Great Physician. He is the rich person who responds to Jesus with faith, in contrast to the rich ruler (18:24–26). Some rich people do come to Jesus, but they do so on the same basis as others—in humility and responsiveness, recognizing their need. This mission to sinners will be extended to Gentiles (7:1–10; Acts 10:1–11:18). What Jesus does for lost Zacchaeus he also seeks for lost Israel (cf. Matt 10:6; 15:24).

Some question this statement's authenticity, arguing that the use of an apocalyptic title with a present ministry saying betrays church creation.[41] But authentic Son of Man sayings need not be limited to apocalyptic uses.[42] In addition, the saying's basic imagery has OT roots from Ezek 34, so that nothing in the saying prevents its coming from Jesus.[43] Luke does not create fresh Son of Man sayings. If the remark goes back to Jesus, it is unlikely that the title was added later to the saying. In short, the saying is a fitting climax to a paradigmatic account of Jesus' mission and ministry of salvation.[44]

Most of the Son of Man sayings that pertain to his suffering are predictions or point to the necessity of his suffering (Luke 9:22, 44; 18:31; 22:22; 24:7, a passage unique to Luke that notes the fulfillment did come). Jesus adds tension to the point of Judas's betrayal by noting the disciple is betraying the Son of Man with a kiss (22:48). Here the hypocrisy of the disciple stands in contrast to the submission of the Son to his calling, despite his high position. Luke 22:69 affirms that the result of Jesus' suffering is his glorification: "But from now on, the Son of Man will be seated at the right hand of the mighty God." Only Luke, among the Synoptic Gospels, omitted the reference to Jesus' coming back in the clouds; Luke's focus was on Jesus' current authority.

The apocalyptic Son of Man is a figure with great authority who judges. He

---

39. Jeremias, *TDNT*, 6:500; David Tiede, *Luke* (Augsburg Commentary on the New Testament; Minneapolis: Augsburg, 1988), 322.

40. Nolland, *Luke 9:21–18:34*, 907.

41. Rudolf Bultmann, *The History of the Synoptic Tradition* (trans.

J. Marsh; New York: Harper & Row, 1963), 152, 155.

42. F. H. Forsch, *The Son of Man in Myth and History* (NTL; Philadelphia: Westminster, 1967), 326.

43. Jeremias, *TDNT*, 6:492; Oepke, *TDNT*, 1:395.

44. Bock, *Luke 9:51–24:53*, 1523.

will be ashamed of those who are ashamed of him (Luke 9:26). Those who confess him, he will confess before the angels (12:8). He will come when he is not expected (12:40). Luke 17 includes several facts about his return. Many long to see his days (v. 22), yet when he comes it will be like lightning and the judgment in the days of Noah (vv. 24, 26). This passage makes the point that this coming will be quick and obvious. When Jesus is revealed, that is, when he returns, he will judge (v. 30). Later Jesus asks whether the Son of Man will find faith on earth when he returns (18:8). Will people continue to wait for his return? This suggests that a sufficient length of time will pass before the return so that some will lose heart. So the call is to persevere. Luke 21:27 notes Jesus will ride the clouds as he returns (cf. Dan 7:13–14). People are to watch so that they have the strength to stand before the Son in that day (Luke 21:36).

When Stephen is martyred, he sees Jesus, standing as the Son of Man to receive him (Acts 7:56). Here Jesus, functioning as judge, welcomes Stephen into heaven, showing that despite earthly rejection, Stephen is honored in heaven. The Son of Man for Luke is a title that allows Jesus to describe himself, since only he uses the title. Son of Man is an idiom that he uses as a self-reference, filled with content and tied to other images. Included in the title are authority, rejection, and reign.

8.2.7 Lord

The pivotal role of the key title "Lord" (κύριος, *kyrios*) has received much attention already. As a title for Jesus, the term is much more prevalent in Acts than in Luke. There are numerous uses of the term "Lord" in the gospel of Luke, but they occur as a title of respect to one who is viewed as socially superior, much as people today use the word "sir." The Lucan usage appears to do more than this, but it is not so clear early in Luke that the title has the full force it has later in the two volumes.

In everyday Greek usage, κύριος often referred to a master or to a leader who had authority over another. So it can point to the respect shown to a messianic figure or someone seen as a commissioned agent of God. However, Luke seems to be doing more than this. The christological use of the title first appears in Luke 1:43 and 2:11 and reappears in 24:3. Its use is ambiguous in certain gospel texts like 5:8, where Peter distinguished himself from the righteousness of Jesus. In 1:43, Elizabeth sees Mary as "the mother of my Lord," but what she exactly means beyond the sense of promised deliverer is not clear in this context where a messianic motif is dominant. Luke 2:11 associates the title with Christ and Savior. By 24:3, however, we are dealing with a raised and vindicated Jesus who we have been told is now at God's right hand. There the title begins to show its full force, although hints of this landing place show up when Jesus says things like the "Son of Man is Lord of the Sabbath" as early as 6:5.[45]

---

45. Although I think Rowe has made more of this than Luke does in the early passages in the gospel in his *Early Narrative Christology*, by failing to link the use of the title Lord to the introduction of Jesus as Messiah in Luke 1:31–35 as setting the background for its initial use for Jesus in 1:43, he is right to point to the title as most significant for Luke and ultimately an indication of Luke's high Christology. I also question his claim that John's going before the Lord in Luke 3:4–6 has Jesus in mind as well as God. The topic there is God's salvation, and John is set up in the infancy material with references that are about God in 1:15–17.

The force of the title is made clear in Acts 2:21, when Peter cites Joel 2:32, "Everyone who calls on the name of the Lord [κύριος, *kyrios*] will be saved." In that prophetic passage, κύριος translates the Hebrew *yhwh* ("Yahweh"). The call was the cry of one needing God to deliver him from peril, namely, the day of the Lord. In Acts 2:36–39, Peter makes the point that Jesus is the Lord to whom one calls. So "Lord" refers to Jesus' authority. Jesus' resurrection-ascension, revealed in 2:30–33, testifies to his lordship. The essence of his lordship is his authority over salvation and the right to distribute its benefits. He also has such authority over people of all races (10:35–36).

The centrality of the title becomes clear when one sees how many verses speak of people believing in the Lord (Acts 5:14; 9:42; 16:30–31; 18:8; 20:21). These texts show the title was appropriate to confess in response to the gospel, whether one was a Jew or a Gentile. The confession recognizes Jesus' right to distribute the benefits of salvation, his authority over them, and his authority over humanity. Jesus is worthy to receive honor and to be followed. To come to God, a person must come through Jesus (4:10 says the same thing, while not using this title).

8.2.8 Servant

The image of the "servant" (παῖς, *pais*) is one Luke makes occasionally, but in key places.[46] He works with passages (esp. from Isaiah) where the figure is present or describes the functions this figure has. Jesus' mission includes his work that reflects the Servant, a title alluded to in Jesus' call at his baptism (Luke 3:22) and at the transfiguration, when he is called the "chosen" one (9:35). Servant imagery of declaring the release of captives appears in 4:16–19. So this title is one that shows the prophetic dimension of Jesus' mission.

This title also points to Jesus' suffering as an innocent, since in Luke 22:20 his life is offered "for you" (ὑπὲρ ὑμῶν, *hyper hymōn*), a phrase that may allude to Isa 53:11–12.[47] In addition, 22:37 has Jesus reckoned with the transgressors as Isa 53:12 notes, while Philip expounds his innocent suffering in Acts 8:32–33 from Isa 53:7–8. In fact, this theme of Jesus' suffering as an innocent dominates Luke's passion account in Luke 23. This is why the potentially related title of "Righteous One" shows up in Acts 3:13–15, echoing the confession of the centurion at the cross in Luke 23:49. Such injustice is also what allows Jesus to be pictured as a servant in the prayer of Acts 4:24–30, where the term "your holy servant" is more generic and is not an allusion to the Isaianic servant. The language of being given over in the Son of Man suffering sayings also may allude to Isa 53:6, 12. So service is what characterizes Jesus' work (Luke 22:24–27).

Of course, specific imagery includes Jesus as "light for revelation to the Gentiles"

---

46. Robert F. O'Toole, "How Does Luke Portray Jesus as Servant of YHWH," *Bib* 81 (2000): 328–46. The term here, as noted, is παῖς, while the other common term δοῦλος, translated "servant," or better, "slave," is never used of Jesus. That latter term is used in Luke's parables for various servants, and Simeon calls himself God's δοῦλος (Luke 2:29), but it is never attributed to Jesus. Meanwhile, παῖς does have other uses, such as "child" or even general servants (12:45; 15:26).

47. The picture of the wine as representing the shed blood of Jesus that stands behind this reference looks to the idea of the Servant dying for others (esp. Isa 53:12).

(Luke 2:32 and Isa 49:6; also Acts 13:47, where Paul and Barnabas take up this calling). The appeal to Isa 61 in the programmatic Luke 4:16–20 is another key direct appeal to language of the Hebrew Scripture. Acts 26:18–23 returns to such imagery as Paul summarizes his preached message. In sum, "servant" is a term that summarizes Jesus' mission especially in the context of his suffering and offer of light to all.

Only in Acts does Luke use the specific term παῖς to refer to Jesus. He alludes to the servant passages in Isaiah. But before considering those passages, two other occurrences of this word are significant. (1) In Luke 1:54, Israel is called God's "servant." Having scriptural precedent (Isa 49:3), this use points to the special role Israel had as an object of God's grace and as his representative. God was helping his servant Israel by bringing justice to his people (Luke 1:52–53) and by being merciful (vv. 54–55) in bringing her promised one to her. (2) In 1:69, Zechariah called David God's "servant" for similar reasons. He was God's regal representative ruling over God's people, and he was the recipient of God's promises. Out of the lineage of this servant, the promised deliverer came. This is a more generic use of this term.

Interestingly, Luke presents Jesus in Acts more as the glorified Servant, not the suffering Servant. Jesus is God's Servant glorified (Acts 3:13) and exalted (v. 26). Exaltation (after suffering) is the overall emphasis in Isa 52:13–53:12 as well. For Luke, the fact that Jesus was vindicated and exalted to rule is as important as the fact that Jesus suffered. What good is his death without his exaltation? Nevertheless, as we already noted, Jesus as the rejected Servant is also a part of this theme.

Some observe that it is significant that the idea of substitutionary imagery from Isa 53 is not applied directly by Luke to Jesus. This is an insignificant complaint. What Luke stresses is the *person* of salvation more than the *means* of salvation. Luke is certainly aware of Jesus' substitutionary death (Luke 22:19; Acts 20:28), but he does not highlight it. Preferring to stress the position and person of Jesus, Luke does not detail the means of Jesus' work as much as Paul does. The two emphases show how various parts of the NT message supplement each other.

8.2.9 Less Frequently Used Titles

Other titles of Jesus appear in Luke-Acts with less frequency. Some refer to his authority. For example, Peter speaks of Jesus as the "Prince" or "author" (ἀρχηγός, *archēgos*; Acts 3:13–15; 5:31; cf. Heb 2:10; 12:1–2; Jdg 11:6, 11; *Pss. Sol.* 17.23–27; *Sib. Or.* 3.652–56). This depicts a royal figure who is leading the way for his people in redeeming them. The redemptive emphasis is seen in its use alongside the title "Savior" in 5:31. Ἀρχηγός refers to one who is given a preeminent position, a ruler or leader.[48] It is variously rendered ("Leader" in ESV, RSV, NET; "Prince" in NIV, NLT, KJV). The title points to the image of shared authority with God.

The exaltation also was an opportunity for the nation to receive repentance (see 2:38 for the verb) and forgiveness of sins (ἄφεσιν ἁμαρτιῶν, *aphesin hamartiōn*,

---

48. BDAG, 138 §1.

which appears four times in Acts: 5:30–31; 10:43; 13:38–39; 26:16–18; also in Luke 1:77; 3:3; 24:47). The exaltation has given evidence of divine support for Jesus, which the Jewish leadership has ignored. The word for "repentance" (μετάνοια, *metanoia*) appears six times in Acts (5:30–31; 11:18; 13:23–24; 19:4; 20:18–21; 26:19–20). Whereas 2:32–33 stresses the benefit of the Spirit as a result of exaltation, in the use of the title "Leader" it is Jesus' direct role in salvation that is stressed; he is prince, deliverer, and author of salvation.[49]

The demons confessed that Jesus is "the Holy One of God" (ὁ ἅγιος τοῦ θεοῦ, *ho hagios tou theou*; Luke 4:34). These spiritual beings are silenced by Jesus, who has authority over them. (A similar title was used in Acts 3:14–15.)

Jesus was called a "judge" (κριτής, *kritēs*) in Acts 10:42 (cf. 17:31). These remarks are made to a Gentile audience about the generic authority of Jesus over all.

Another title of respect is "Master" (ἐπιστάτης, *epistatēs*) used in Luke 5:5; 8:24, 45; 9:33, 49; 17:13. This title indicates little more than that Jesus is held in high regard.

A centurion referred to Jesus' innocence by affirming that he was "a righteous/innocent [δίκαιος, *dikaios*] man" (Luke 23:47). The exact force of the term is not clear, since the centurion could merely be reflecting on Jesus being innocent or on the result of such innocence, namely, that he is righteous. Ultimately, there is little difference since one implies the other. Note that Jesus' innocence is stressed in the chapter in which the remark appears.

In Acts 4:11, Peter spoke of Jesus as the "rejected stone," an allusion to Ps 118:22. Other parts of Ps 118 show up in other Lucan texts (e.g., Luke 13:35; 19:38). Here Jesus is portrayed as a suffering righteous figure, even as a regal figure.

Still another title referred to Jesus' role as instructor. Twelve times he was called "Teacher" (ὁ διδάσκαλος, *ho didaskalos*; Luke 7:40; 9:38; 10:25; 11:45; 12:13; 18:18; 19:39; 20:21, 28, 39; 21:7; 22:11). This title is the most popular title used by the scribes and Pharisees for Jesus, though others also use it occasionally. It describes Jesus as a "rabbi," at least of sorts (since he did not receive formal training). Luke never uses the Jewish term rabbi for Jesus. Teacher is a more common description of his function for Luke's largely Gentile audience.

In summary, Luke uses numerous titles to describe Jesus. Most suggested his authority or role as the promised regal Messiah. He also exercises a prophetic role. In addition, some day he will return and judge. He is at the center of God's plan. For Luke, the person of Jesus is as crucial as his work. Because of who Jesus is, he is able to save and is worthy of the people's trust. Because of who Jesus is, one must respond to him. Not only is he a prophet and the Messiah, but also he will return to judge all as they stand before him. In fact, even now he sits at the right hand of God, exercising authority and distributing the benefits of salvation, even the Spirit of God, to those who call on him for salvation. In Luke, when a person responds to

---

49. Bertram, *TDNT*, 8:609.

Jesus, it has as much or more to do with responding to who Jesus is than to what he has done. What Jesus does is also of importance to Luke, but Luke's priorities are shown by how little time he spends explaining how Jesus saves when the gospel is given. Nevertheless, an examination of Jesus' work reveals the ground of human salvation.

8.3 THE WORK OF JESUS: PAVING THE WAY FOR SALVATION AND THE NEW ERA

Luke stresses the authority in Jesus' work and the new era he has brought. The earthly ministry shows what Jesus is capable of, while the vindication of God leads to Jesus' mediating the salvation that God promised and Jesus preached as a part of the kingdom of God.

8.3.1 Earthly Ministry

Much of Jesus' ministry revolved around teaching and miracles. Several summaries in Luke's gospel, as well as a major summary in Acts, point up this fact (Luke 4:15, 31–32, 44; 6:17–19; 7:22; Acts 10:36–38). In particular, Jesus' teaching often included parables. The gospel of Luke has a concentration of parables in the "journey section" (Luke 9:51–19:44).[50] There are thirty-five parables or pictorial aphorisms in Luke, with eighteen of them unique to his gospel.[51]

Jesus' miracles serve as signs that attest to God's vindication of Jesus' identity and claims (Acts 2:22; 10:38). When John the Baptist's disciples ask Jesus if he is "the one who is to come" (Luke 7:20), an allusion to his messianic position, Jesus points to a series of miracles (v. 22) that Isaiah said would happen in the eschaton (Isa 29:18–19; 35:5; 42:6; 61:1). Jesus' reply indicates that his healing ministry marks the beginning of the eschaton.[52] Such activity also depicted the fall of Satan (Luke 10:18; 11:14–23). This event indicates that Jesus' coming impacts heavenly realities. It also represents the beginning of the display of the eschaton in pointing to the defeat of Satan and his forces. The new era is a special era for Luke, and Jesus' work is particularly unique.

The message of Jesus has two parts: a message of hope and a call to a life of ethical honor before God. Luke 4:16–30, which summarizes his message of hope, is a representative presentation of Jesus' preaching. Luke's presentation of this synagogue speech includes more than is found in the other gospels (cf. Mark 6:1–6). Jesus declares that the time of Jubilee is present and that the anointed one has appeared. Jesus has been commissioned to preach to the poor, proclaim release to the captives, give sight to the blind, release the oppressed, and offer forgiveness.

---

50. On where the journey section ends, see 4.1 ("An Outline of Luke").

51. These are named in the discussion in ch. 22.

52. The eschaton for Luke is presented in already-not yet terms. Some of what Jesus does is realized now, such as the Spirit and forgiveness, while other elements await Jesus' return.

"The poor" (πτωχός, *ptōchos*) refers especially to the materially impoverished and spiritually poor (cf. Luke 1:53; 6:24).[53] Luke establishes such a spiritual element in the definition when he refers to the humble in the context of covenant promise, who are exalted, while the proud are brought down (1:49–54). Luke's concern for such material categories is seen in 6:20–26 (1 Cor 1:26–29 is similar). This group is the most responsive to Jesus. Such people understand what it is to stand humbly before God. Jesus' concern is for a transformed life that leads into a new quality of living in this world, as well as hope for the age to come.

The Sermon on the Plain summarizes Jesus' ethical message (Luke 6:20–49).[54] The sermon closely parallels Matthew's Sermon on the Mount (Matt 5–7), except that Luke omits those elements that focus on Jewish issues especially as they related to the law. So, for example, Matthew's six antitheses (Matt 5:21–48) are mostly missing, with Luke only retaining and recasting one of them. Luke's including the sermon in a form that relates to Gentiles shows the message is timeless. The Beatitudes (Luke 6:20–22) stress the present situation of his disciples: poor, hungry, weeping now, and rejected. But all will be changed later (vv. 23–26). The ethic of love (vv. 27–36) is the cornerstone of the community's ethic, both as individuals and as a body. Jesus' new commandment to "love one another" is similar in force (John 13:34). Jesus' disciples are to display a slowness to judge and an awareness of one's own faults (Luke 6:37–42). A person's character is reflected in his or her actions, revealing the character of the heart, just as fruit reveals the nature of the tree (vv. 43–46). Foolishness is a failure to respond to Jesus' teaching, while wisdom means responding to it (vv. 47–49).

Part of Jesus' work is to reveal the way to God (Luke 4:17–19) and the will of God (6:20–49), but more detail comes from several of Jesus' parables. Some parables explain why Jesus spends time with tax collectors and sinners (15:1–32). God is committed to finding the lost. The way to God is open to all, but the message must go out so that all can hear. When Jesus associates with social outcasts, the Pharisees repeatedly grumble at these relationships (5:27–32; 7:36–39; 15:2–3); the parables of the lost sheep, lost coin, and lost son (ch. 15) form Jesus' apologetic for spending time with such people. His commitment and labor reflect God's love in seeking out the lost. This series of three parables is unique to Luke's gospel.

Other parables outline God's plan and the coming change of focus from Israel to the Gentiles because of rejection by the nation Israel. The parable of the wicked tenants (20:9–18) overviews the rejection of God's messengers all the way back to the prophets. However, the slaying of the son causes the owner to give the vineyard to others. The rejected stone is the capstone, and those on whom it falls are crushed (Ps 118:22; Isa 8:14; Dan 2:34, 44). Everyone knew against whom Jesus was speaking when he made that remark. In publicly challenging the leadership, he was forcing their hand to deal with him.

---

53. Chapter 17 presents the force of this term and its roots in the Hebrew Scripture.

54. Chapter 15 looks at the ethical teaching of Luke in both the gospel and Acts.

Other passages deal with key elements in the will of God and in discipleship. Another uniquely Lucan parable, the parable of the rich fool (Luke 12:13–21), teaches that Jesus' followers should avoid being overly dependent on wealth. At least twice Jesus stresses the importance of prayer for his disciples (11:1–13; 18:1–8). He often speaks of the crucial need for faithfulness among those who await his return (12:35–48; 19:11–27). Above all, Jesus makes it clear that discipleship is a total commitment of one's life and self to God. In terms of God's expectation and will, there is no minimal discipleship; what God desires is everything (9:23–26, 57–62; 14:25–33). In short, one is to love God with everything he or she has. Such a focus means his followers will also love their neighbor (10:27–28).

8.3.2 The Cross

Alongside Jesus' teaching stands his work on the cross. Often this is the only thing people consider when they speak of Jesus' labor to bring salvation. It also has an important role for Luke, though he does not give it the detailed attention Paul did.

Luke stresses that Jesus is "the righteous sufferer." This is indicated by allusions to the Psalter in Luke 23, where Luke applies psalms of lament about suffering to Jesus. He fit this pattern of suffering and fulfilled it (Luke 23:34–36, 46 allude to Pss 22:18; 31:5). All through this chapter Luke stresses that Jesus is innocent (Luke 23:4, 14–15, 20, 22, 47). Luke 23:47 is the climactic declaration that Jesus suffered innocently in that he suffered as a "righteous/innocent man."

Jesus' righteous suffering is also a major theme in the apostles' speeches in Acts. The sufferer is vindicated (Acts 2:23–24) since God raised Jesus from the dead and death could not hold him (Pss 18:4–5; 116:3–4). Other Lucan passages repeat this theme (Acts 4:10; 5:30). Acts 3:14–15 makes the point that he is "the Holy and Righteous One." Jesus was rejected, and that is clearly shown by the fact that his death occurred "on a tree" (5:30; 10:39; 13:29), a picture of rejection. In 13:29, the reference to the tree alludes to the cursed death described in Deut 21:23 (cf. Gal 3:13).

Two passages—Luke 22:20 and Acts 20:28—speak of Jesus' death in terms similar to Paul's. At the Last Supper Jesus shared a cup that commemorated "the new covenant in my blood, which is poured out for you" (Luke 22:20, accepting the longer reading of this verse).[55] Here several ideas come together. Jesus' death inaugurated the benefits of the new covenant. Jesus died on behalf of and in the place of his disciples. His death cleared the way for people to be rightly related to God, a relationship in which God also pours his Spirit on them through Jesus. Luke later alludes to this provision of the Holy Spirit as the "promise of the Father" (Luke 24:49; Acts 1:5). Jesus' death opens the door to many benefits to the one who comes to him.

---

55. There is a complex text-critical issue surrounding this verse, but I have defended its inclusion by Luke in *Luke 9:51–24:53*, 1721–22 (see also ch 2., above, fn. 19).

The second key text is Acts 20:28. Luke 22:20 looked forward to the cross, whereas Acts 20:28 looks back. The church has been purchased with Jesus' blood. Jesus is again portrayed as a sacrifice whose death makes possible the new community, "the church of God." Acts 20:28 deserves a closer look. Jesus "bought" the new community "with his own blood" (αἵματος, *haimatos*; cf. Eph 1:7, 14; Heb 9:12; 1 Pet 1:2, 19; Rev 1:5; 5:9 – 10). The verse does not explicitly mention the title "Son" but rather speaks of God's giving his own to gain the church. The image implies sonship. The picture is like what Abraham had been willing to do with Isaac (Gen 22), only here God carries out the offering so that others can benefit from the sacrifice (cf. Ps 74:2; Isa 43:21).

Thus the acquiring of the church has as its basis a substitution of God's own for those whom God would bring to eternal life. Such a sacred form of down payment for the church makes the responsibility of the elders in the Ephesian community sacred. It is clear that the death of Jesus, God's own Son, is described here. Behind the action stands the loving commitment of God to take the initiative and suffer sacrifice in order to restore a broken relationship with humanity. Wolves will deny this work in one way or another, challenging the work or denying the uniqueness of the one through whom it is done. But the precious nature of the sacrifice is to motivate the ministry to care for the community with faithfulness.

The Lucan treatment of the cross does not emphasize how the cross provides forgiveness. Luke simply points out repeatedly that the cross has made it possible for humans to be related to God, since death did not end the story. After death came vindication in Jesus' resurrection. Some have said that Paul saw "the Christ of the cross," whereas Luke saw "the Christ of glory." In this distinction the authors of Scripture complement each another.

8.3.3 Resurrection-Ascension

Jesus' resurrection receives strong emphasis in Luke-Acts. In addition, many of the speeches of Acts center on the significance of the ascension. Luke is the only NT author to describe the ascension. When he discusses it, he is also pointing up the significance of God's resurrection of Jesus, which is why we hyphenate the two events. For Luke they are distinct, but linked events. Jesus' reception into heaven to the right hand of God has a great impact on Luke's view of Jesus' work. In numerous passages in Acts the resurrection indicates divine vindication (Acts 2:23 – 24; 3:14 – 15; 4:10 – 12; 5:30; 17:31). Also, Jesus' resurrection results in his being positioned at God's right hand, so Jesus can pour out the Holy Spirit and exercise authority (2:30 – 34). As already noted, Jesus' resurrection is the basis on which his disciples can minister in his name. Jesus remains in heaven until his return (3:21). But when he returns, he will rule on earth and judge all humanity (3:20 – 21; 17:30 – 31).

A dead savior is no savior at all. If Jesus were still in a grave, he could do no one any good. But raised and ascended to the side of the Father, Jesus can empower his children and enable his church. He reigns, seeing all that everyone does and thinks. For Luke, the death and resurrection of Jesus are important, but more important is his reign, both presently and in the age to come. For Luke, Jesus is not passively sitting in heaven awaiting his return. He lives, administers the benefits of salvation, and rules in anticipation of a more visible rule to come.

8.3.4 The Two-Stage Kingdom Reign of Jesus

It is impossible to consider the work of Jesus without considering his rule. The basic outline of Jesus' rule has been discussed in relation to Luke's concept of the kingdom. Under the current heading, more specifics can be noted. The rule of Jesus is reflected in Luke's writing by what is done "in his name" or "through Jesus." To do something "in Jesus' name" is to do it in his authority—that is, in view of the fact that he reigns. Such texts are limited to Acts, which shows how important a turning point his resurrection is.

Numerous passages speak of salvation or forgiveness of sins in his name (Acts 2:21 [this refers to Jesus, cf. v. 38]; 4:12; 10:43). Others speak of baptism in Jesus' name (2:38; 8:16; 10:48; 19:5). These references to water baptism refer to the public confession of Jesus that expresses concretely the presence of inner faith in Christ. Water baptism pictures the spiritual washing that comes from forgiveness as well as the coming of the Spirit. This public identification with Jesus pictures God's saving act. This identification showed that the one who comes to be baptized acknowledges what God has done in Jesus. In the first century, the rite of baptism and what it represents are seen as a unit and are interchangeable (1 Pet 3:21–22 is similar in perspective). A third group of passages speaks of healing done in Jesus' name (Acts 3:6, 16; 4:9–10), and a fourth group refers to signs and wonders through his name (4:30). Some preach in his name (8:12) or speak boldly in his name (9:27–28).

Early in Acts, healing and other acts of ministry are the focus. But later the emphasis is on Jesus' followers suffering shame and imprisonment in or for his name (Acts 5:41; 9:14, 16; 15:26; 21:13). This suffering refers not to Jesus' activity, but to the consequences of identifying with him in a world that rejects him. Also, 15:14 does not mention Jesus, but the benefits of identifying with him are noted. The concept that the Gentiles are "a people for his name," where his name describes God the Father (cf. v. 17), shows that Jesus gives anyone who believes access to the Father. Jesus is active in dispensing the benefits of salvation and is involved in the rites where identification with him is demonstrated. The Spirit and forgiveness are the preeminent gifts Luke mentions as a result of one's coming to the Father through Jesus.

The kingdom program is already-not yet in Luke. Some texts point to its presence and arrival with Jesus. Others look to its consummation in his future return.

Two texts emphasize the kingdom's presence. Luke 11:20 deserves a close look. It is no exaggeration to see this passage as a crucial text for establishing Luke's view of the kingdom (see also 9:27; 10:9, 18; 17:20–21). The meaning of the passage is disputed.

Clearly the conditional clause alludes to God's work, as seen in the mention of God's finger. If God is acting through Jesus, then the kingdom has overtaken you. Interestingly, Matthew 12:28 agrees verbally with Luke except at this point, where he refers to God's Spirit. Luke, who normally emphasizes the Spirit, does not refer to him here. Their point is the same: God is the source of power for the exorcism. Most see in the reference to God's finger an allusion to Exod 8:19 [8:15 MT], where pagan magicians recognize divine work in their opponent Moses. The image is often used for God's activity and intervention, whether in creation, miracles, or the giving of the law (Deut 9:10; Ps 8:3 [8:4 MT]).[56] Jesus is suggesting here that if Satan is not behind his work, God is.

The main dispute involves the term ἔφθασεν (ephthasen). Does it mean "come near" or "arrive"? The difference is crucial.[57] Jesus is either teaching that the kingdom draws close in the present activity or that it arrives. At stake is whether an inaugural kingdom is present in Jesus' first coming or whether "kingdom" functions as it did in the OT and intertestamental Judaism as an eschatological term referring exclusively to the consummation of God's rule on earth through Israel. The idiom "kingdom of God" itself was not used in the OT, though the concept is found in the prophets. It was found later among the rabbis. But the concept of God's physical rule in a great age of fulfillment was expected both in the OT and in Judaism. This expectation took two forms: the prophetic hope that God would bring this promised age to pass on earth through sociopolitical rule, and the apocalyptic hope that he would usher it in with heavenly signs.[58]

Those who argue for the kingdom being "near" suggest that behind the reference is the same Aramaic term translated by ἐγγίζω (engizō, "to be near") in Mark 1:15. This verb can carry such a sense (Matt 26:45; Luke 15:1). In Judaism, "kingdom" is an apocalyptic, eschatological term, so the idea of its arrival without apocalyptic and political elements is not possible if traditional usage applies. However, against this understanding and in favor of the idea that the kingdom "arrives" is the normal meaning of φθάνω (phthanō) when linked to ἐπί (epi). Also for the idea of arrival is a passage such as Luke 10:18, which clearly ties Satan's fall to the disciples' miraculous activity. In addition, there is the immediacy of the image that follows in Luke 11:21–22.

Above all considerations, however, stands the prepositional reference in 11:20 to "upon you" (ἐφ' ὑμᾶς, eph' hymas), which because of its personal object cannot look at approach, but must refer to arrival. Jesus' activity gives evidence of the arrival of God's kingdom.[59] That arrival is vividly evident in his miraculous power, which his followers also exhibit. Jesus' work and demonstration of saving authority in their midst must be dealt with. It calls for decision. Twelftree brings out how Jesus' exorcisms and claims are unique, though he seems to underplay their messianic dimension, given their delivery and end-time character.[60]

---

56. Schlier, *TDNT*, 2:20–21.

57. Although Fitzer, *TDNT*, 9:91–92, minimizes it.

58. G. von Rad, K. Kuhn, and K. Schmidt, *TDNT*, 1:566–76, 580–89.

59. Schrenk, *TDNT*, 1:610.

60. G. H. Twelftree, *Jesus the Exorcist: A Contribution to the Study of the Historical Jesus* (WUNT 2/54; Tübingen: Mohr-Siebeck, 1993).

If the kingdom has come in an initial but not yet consummative form, what does its current form involve? The portrait of Luke-Acts provides a good answer. Jesus is perceived as ruling over God's many salvation benefits. He has authority to distribute them to anyone who responds to his message (Luke 3:15–17 [where "the more powerful" one brings the Spirit, which shows he is the Messiah]; Acts 2:16–39). In addition, he provides the Spirit as a sign of the arrival of the promised age and as a source of enablement and guidance over those he rules, which is why the Spirit is connected to the idea of power (Luke 24:44–49; Acts 2). The emphasis of the kingdom picture in the present phase is not on realm, but on rule.

Nonetheless, a realm is envisioned. Jesus' realm is the world as it is manifested in his scattered followers. The kingdom is contained in Jesus' total authority over salvific blessing, an authority that is present over everyone (Acts 10:42–43; 17:31). The presence of his rule in believers anticipates his coming to earth to rule physically, when he will exercise dominion and judgment over the earth. This theme of reign and authority is expressed in various ways in Luke-Acts. (1) Acts associates the concept of Jesus' universal lordship and rule with the fulfillment of Davidic promise (Acts 2:30–39; 13:32–39; see also Luke 1:68–79). (2) Acts 3:19–24 makes clear that the program is not yet consummated or completed but will come to pass as the OT prophets taught. (3) Acts 10:42–43 and 17:31 show Jesus' authoritative rule over salvation and his ultimate function as judge over all humans, living and dead. (4) Jesus' parables speak of the Son's going away to receive a kingdom and so look at his present authority.

The rule expressed in Luke 11 is the first phase of this kingdom program, what we might call the "invisible kingdom." The kingdom in Acts is expressed in the ministry of the Spirit during the time of Jesus' physical absence (thus the term *invisible*) from the earth. It is this rule that Jesus says is arriving now and that is pictured in his work of exorcism. The result of his presence is powerfully evident in the transformed people over whom he rules in the church, even though he is not physically visible.

The first phase of his rule is really put in place with the resurrection-ascension and the distribution of salvation's benefits (Acts 2:30–39), the roots of which are in the promise of the new covenant (Luke 22:19–20; 24:49; Acts 1:7–8). However, this power is also shown in Jesus' ministry, so that Jesus could speak of its presence with the divine activity that was worked through him in ministry. Still, the real benefits and provisions in forgiveness and the Spirit await his death and vindication to establish the covenant that will open up these core provisions of the new era. From the time of his divine vindication on, Jesus rules from God's right hand. He is not present on earth for all to see, but rules through the benefits he bestows on those who come to him to receive the life Jesus brings.

The Spirit reflects God's presence in people as well as God's work of power and his promise. Humans are now able to live as God would desire because they respond to his Spirit, so that his rule becomes evident in their lives. This group of disciples, which becomes the church, is not all there is to the kingdom, nor is it all there is to

God's plan and promise, but it is a microcosm of what the kingdom will be when OT promises are completely fulfilled at Jesus' return. The Spirit is the down payment of the redemption to come (Eph 1:13 – 14).[61]

Also significant is Luke 17:21. A closer look reveals an important exegetical issue. What does ἐντὸς ὑμῶν (*entos hymōn*) mean? Three options are available.

(1) Does it mean "inside of you"? Many, including numerous ancient interpreters, take the phrase to mean that the kingdom is "inside you" (Ps 39:4 [38:4 LXX]; 103:1 [102:1 LXX]; 109:22 [108:22 LXX]; Isa 16:11). This view has two major problems. Contextually, Jesus is addressing the Pharisees, who are the last group of people who Jesus would say has the kingdom in them (Luke 11:37 – 52, esp. 11:52). It would be strange if Jesus said this to the Pharisees and never to his disciples! Moreover, nowhere else in the NT is the kingdom spoken of in internal terms. Granted, the Spirit is sent as a token of God's promise and does relate people to the kingdom. Marshall, however, is right when he says that in the NT people enter the kingdom, but the kingdom does not enter people.[62] The Spirit is a sign that one has come into the kingdom, but his presence does not equal the kingdom. The kingdom is a community of residence, blessing, and enablement, while it is the Spirit who marks one for membership.

(2) Does it mean "in your grasp or reach"? Others argue on the basis of its usage in the papyri that the phrase means this — that the kingdom's coming is related to one's power to repent as a response to Jesus' message. This view is possible, but the case made for it from the papyri is challenged by Riesenfeld and Wikgren, who argue that the phrase could mean "in your presence or domain."[63] Also against this view is that it could be regarded as a nonanswer. On this view, Jesus has said it is not by signs that the kingdom comes, but it is within your grasp. But the essential question still remains, "Where is it so that I can obtain it?" Thus, this option does not really supply a sufficient answer to deal with the question. A clearer way to state that the kingdom comes through one's choice is to mention directly the need to repent, which Jesus often says to the Pharisees (Luke 5:31 – 32; 11:29 – 32). Meier rejects the reading, arguing that it puts the stress on human control and calculation when the context argues for God's manifesting his presence in his sovereign way.[64] In addition, to say that the kingdom is within one's grasp in the present is to say in effect that it is present, since one can reach for it now. Nonetheless this sense conceptually ends up being very similar to the next view.

(3) Does it mean "in your presence"? A final option argues that the phrase means "in your presence" or "before you" (Isa 45:14 ["God is among you"]).[65] The emphasis here would be that the Pharisees confront the kingdom in Jesus. They do not need

61. Bock, *Luke 9:51 – 24:53*, 1079 – 82.

62. Marshall, *Gospel of Luke*, 655.

63. H. Riesenfeld, "Ἐμβολεύειν – Ἐντός," *Nuntius* 2 (1949): 11 – 12; A. Wikgren, "Ἐντός," *Nuntius* 4 (1950): 27 – 28.

64. John P. Meier, *A Marginal Jew: Rethinking the Historical Jesus*,

vol. 2: *Mentor, Message, and Miracles* (ABRL; New York: Doubleday, 1994), 427.

65. Danker, *Jesus and the New Age*, 292; Marshall, *Gospel of Luke*, 655; Ellis, *Gospel of Luke*, 211.

to look all around for it because its central figure is in front of their eyes. Mattill objects that Luke has a more common phrase for this idea (ἐν μέσῳ [*en mesō*, "in the midst"] in Luke 2:46; 8:7; 10:3; 21:21; 22:27, 55; 24:36; Acts 1:15; 2:22; 17:22; 27:21).[66] But Mattill understates the synonymity of the phrases. Since Jesus and his authority are the major obstacles in the Pharisees' way, this view fits the context nicely. To see the kingdom, look to Jesus and what he offers.[67]

As noted earlier in the discussion on the kingdom, Jesus' future rule is described primarily in terms of his already noted work as judge, when he returns to gather his people (Luke 17:22–37; 21:5–36; Acts 1:11; esp. 3:19–23; 10:42; 17:31). Luke does not give much detail about God's future program other than to make one important point, namely, that Jesus will fulfill the rest of the promise in the Hebrew Scriptures about the restoration of all things at that time (Acts 3:20–21).[68]

8.4 CONCLUSION

Jesus' role in God's program is unique and indispensable. Jesus is bound inseparably to God's program as Messiah-Servant-Prophet-Son of Man-Savior, and above all as Lord. Luke presents Jesus as a divinely vindicated figure who now rules alongside God in a way that enables Jesus to mediate salvation. God's promises and plan are being realized. That is the assurance Luke's Christology seeks to give. The sign of the new era is found in forgiveness, the bestowal of the Spirit, and the presence of a new sanctified community. The role of the Spirit in Luke indicates the new era has arrived and energizes the community. That topic is next.

---

66. A. J. Mattill Jr., *Luke and the Last Things: A Perspective for the Understanding of Lucan Thought* (Dillsboro, NC: Western North Carolina Press, 1979), 196–97.

67. Bock, *Luke 9:51–24:53*, 1415–17.

68. The remarks in Acts 3:18–26 are the result of what Peter saw and heard in 1:6–11. Nothing about what is said in either text indicates that the restoration of Israel has been set aside, even though this is a popular position in expounding Acts 1. Peter in Acts 3 says that the program has already been revealed and can be read about in the Hebrew Scriptures.

Chapter 9

THE HOLY SPIRIT IN LUKE-ACTS: POWER AND ENABLEMENT FOR THE PROMISE AND WITNESS OF THE NEW ERA

BIBLIOGRAPHY

Green, Joel. "God as Savior in the Acts of the Apostles." Pp. 83–106 in *Witness to the Gospel: The Theology of Acts*. Ed. I. Howard Marshall and David Peterson. Grand Rapids: Eerdmans, 1998. **Jervell, Jacob.** *The Theology of the Acts of the Apostles*. Cambridge: Cambridge University Press, 1996. **Lampe, G. W. H.** *God as Spirit*. The Bampton Lectures. Oxford: Clarendon, 1977. **Menzies, Robert P.** *The Development of Early Christian Pneumatology with Special Reference to Luke-Acts*. JSNTSup. Sheffield: Sheffield Academic Press, 1991. **Turner, Max.** *Power from on High: The Spirit in Israel's Restoration and Witness in Luke-Acts*. JPTSup. Sheffield: Sheffield Academic Press, 1996. Idem. " 'Trinitarian' Pneumatology in the New Testament? Towards an Explanation of the Worship of Jesus." *Asbury Journal of Theology* 57 (2002–2003): 167–86. Idem. "The 'Spirit of Prophecy' as the Power of Israel's Restoration and Witness." Pp. 327–48 in *Witness to the Gospel: The Theology of Acts*. Ed. I. Howard Marshall and David Peterson. Grand Rapids: Eerdmans, 1998. Idem. "The Work of the Holy Spirit in Luke-Acts." *WW* 23 (2003): 146–53. **Varghese, P. V.** "The Holy Spirit and the Risen Christ in Luke-Acts." *Indian Theological Studies* 44 (2007): 245–74. **von Baer, H.** *Der Heilige Geist in den Lukasschriften*. Stuttgart: Kohlhammer, 1926.

The Holy Spirit plays a major role in God's program and in Luke-Acts. There are sixteen direct mentions of the Holy Spirit in Luke's gospel, plus a few other passages where he is the topic through a figure of speech (such as a reference to power). This compares to six references in Mark and twelve in Matthew.[1] In Acts, there are at least fifty-seven references to the Spirit.[2] The Spirit is a driving force for Luke's portrait of salvation, energizing and guiding events both in Luke and especially in

---

1. Max Turner, "The Work of the Holy Spirit in Luke-Acts," *WW* 23 (2003): 146–53. His entire article is a solid survey of the topic and stresses that enablement and mission are tied together in Luke's use of the Spirit. He speaks of the Spirit as "empowering for witness" (p. 147). He interacts in his many works on the Spirit in Luke-Acts especially with Robert P. Menzies, *The Development of Early Christian Pneumatology with Special Reference to Luke-Acts* (JSNTSup; Sheffield: Sheffield Academic Press, 1991).

2. There are a few texts, such as Acts 19:21, where it is not clear if the Holy Spirit is meant or the spirit within a person.

Acts. This has often been called the "Spirit of prophecy" in Luke-Acts, the forth-telling of the message of God.[3] However, it might be better to refer to the Spirit for witness, since the theme of the witness is so important to the two volumes (Luke 24:43–49; Acts 1:8). The picture of the Spirit's bestowal on Jesus launches his ministry. The Spirit directs the community in Acts at key points, so that witness is not the only function of the Spirit for Luke.[4] In this chapter, I will note both narrative sequence in references to the Spirit and do synthetic work as well.

9.1 THE SPIRIT IN LUKE'S INFANCY MATERIAL

For Luke, the move to the new era begins with John the Baptist. In the first mention of the Spirit, we see a theme that runs through many passages: John the Baptist "will be filled" with the Spirit (Luke 1:15). This filling, even from the womb, marks John out as a special prophet. The association of John with a permanent filling of the Spirit is not a Christianized account about John, since the association of God's Spirit with his prophets is strong (Isa 61:1; Ezek 11:5; Joel 2:28 [3:1 MT]). The point is, yet again, that a prophet is present. Luke commonly uses πίμπλημι (*pimplēmi*, "to fill") to refer to being filled with the Spirit (Luke 1:41, 67; Acts 2:4; 4:8, 31; 9:17; 13:9) or being filled with fear or anger (Luke 4:28; 5:26; 6:11); the verb can also refer to the fulfillment of a law, a time period, or a scriptural passage (Luke 1:23, 57; 2:6, 21–22; 21:22; Acts 13:33 [uses ἐκπληρόω, *eklēroō*]).

Reference to the Spirit's filling is largely absent from the rest of Luke's gospel, but it reappears in Acts. Such a contrast tends to indicate that John is a transitional figure, since he is regarded as part of the OT prophets (Luke 7:26–28). The Spirit's provision for him in this period is unique. This intensification may explain why Jesus calls him "more than a prophet" in 7:26. Luke's presentation of John as a transitional figure tends to dilute the attempt to make clean breaks in the "periods" of Luke's portrayal of salvation history. John represents a bridge between promise and fulfillment.

When the child leaps in Elizabeth's womb on the occasion of Mary's visit, this

---

3. G. W. H. Lampe, *God as Spirit* (The Bampton Lectures; Oxford: Clarendon, 1977), 65. There he says, "To Luke the Spirit means primarily the Spirit of prophecy" so that the Spirit's role is "to witness to Christ by empowering and inspiring the preaching of the gospel and by reproducing Jesus' own works of power." For a solid development of this idea and the work of the Spirit in Luke-Acts, see P. V. Varghese, "The Holy Spirit and the Risen Christ in Luke-Acts," *Indian Theological Studies* 44 (2007): 245–74. The end of his article argues against an absentee Jesus in Acts; he shows how bound up Christ's work is with and alongside the Spirit he sent (Acts 1:2, 8; 2:33, 38–39; 16:6–7; 18:9).

4. The foundational work here for the work of the Spirit in Luke-Acts is H. von Baer, *Der Heilige Geist in den Lukasschriften* (Stuttgart: Kohlhammer, 1926). The key role of the Spirit's work is traced and examined by Max Turner, "The 'Spirit of Prophecy'

as the Power of Israel's Restoration and Witness," in *Witness to the Gospel*, 327–48. This article by Turner surveys nicely various debates surrounding Luke's portrayal of the Spirit. Among key conclusions are (1) the teaching of the Spirit is rooted in Jewish and OT expression; (2) the Spirit legitimates the mission he leads; (3) the "Spirit of Prophecy" and empowering for witness represent the key functions of the Spirit; (4) little is said directly about individual renewal through the Spirit; (5) christological ties to the Spirit move his portrait beyond Jewish expectations; (6) miracles and community life are also a concern of the Spirit; (7) with exceptions that can be explained in Samaria and with John's disciples, the Spirit comes with conversion; and (8) the church is empowered by the Spirit beyond mission, reflecting the purging and restoring power of God in nurturing, shaping, and purifying the community (Acts 5:3, 9; 6:3; 11:28; 20:28).

remark points to a fulfillment of the child's being filled from its time in the womb (Luke 1:41). Being full of the Spirit is also attributed to Elizabeth (1:41) and Zechariah (1:67), while the Spirit is said to be with Simeon (2:25) — a different way to indicate basically the same thing although the reference with Simeon probably points to guidance as well. The pious witnesses to John's and Jesus' births speak and act through the direction of the Spirit. In doing so, they witness to the new era.

Mary also is the beneficiary of the Spirit's work, for the birth of Jesus happens when the Spirit comes on her and the power of the Most High overshadows her (Luke 1:35). The reference to power and the Most High shows the intimate connection between the Spirit and God. They share identity and yet are discussed distinctly. Power, which points to enablement from God, is another key attribute associated with the Spirit (24:49). Here the Spirit acts in an independent way distinct from being present with a person.

So in the infancy material, the Spirit appears as a figure who leads those called to serve God into witness. John, Elizabeth, Zechariah, and Simeon all testify to God's acts because of the Spirit's presence. The Spirit also is tied directly to the birth of Jesus. In addition, the Spirit reveals and directs at key points, such as when he tells Simeon that he will not die until he has seen the Lord's Christ (Luke 2:26). After this revelation, the Spirit directs Simeon to go to the temple, where he encounters Jesus (2:27). Luke 2:25 – 27 is the most clustered set of references to the Spirit in the infancy material. It shows the Spirit's moving to give witness to Jesus. Those who surround Jesus are pious, reflecting God's close presence.

9.2 THE SPIRIT IN THE BODY OF LUKE'S GOSPEL

Perhaps the most important text on the Spirit and its central role in God's program is Luke 3:15 – 16. Luke continuously alludes back to this text in Luke-Acts. In it John explains that he is not the Christ, and he declares that he baptizes with water, but there is a "more powerful" one to come who will baptize "with Holy Spirit and fire," one whose sandal he is not worthy to untie. We already discussed how a Christology emerged from this remark in that a prophet is not worthy to perform an act that Jewish tradition saw as too demeaning even for a slave. But the significance of the remark also touches on pneumatology and soteriology.

Luke 3:16 and what it says about the Spirit deserves a closer look. Scholarly discussion about the two-part description of Jesus' baptism is dominated by two issues: what John said in the original tradition, and the meaning of "fire."

On the first issue, there are two approaches. Some regard the reference to "fire" as a Lucan explanation of the significance of Spirit baptism, since Mark 1:8 does not mention fire.[5] Others regard the reference to a baptism in the the Spirit as an addition that must have been a part of the tradition since it occurs in all three

---

5. Ellis, *Gospel of Luke*, 90, citing a connection to Acts 2.

Synoptic Gospels. Those who argue that John predicted only a judgment and did not foresee the Spirit's coming use three pieces of evidence to support this view: (1) Acts 19:1–10 suggests that the disciples who knew John did not know of a coming Spirit baptism; (2) Luke 3:17 looks only to a judgment; and (3) the association of Messiah with the Spirit is not likely for Judaism in John's time.

Both approaches can be challenged. Against the view that Luke added a reference to fire are two points. (1) The appearance of "fire" also in Matt 3:11 shows that Luke did not add the phrase for the sake of Acts. (2) More important, the use of the image of fire in Acts 2:3 is exactly that, the use of a picture. It is not a description of the Spirit's baptism as a baptism of fire. Acts 2:3 does not say that the baptism associated with the Spirit's distribution is *of* fire, but that it spread through the crowd *like* a fire. Thus, the Acts image of fire discusses only the Spirit's spreading through the crowd and does not discuss the nature of the baptism itself. The attempt to appeal to the image of fire in 2:19 also fails, for there heavenly signs are in view. Thus, the baptism with fire in Luke 3:16 does not have literary contact with Acts.

Against the view that Luke added a reference to the Spirit are the following points. (1) Acts 19:1–10 does not argue that the disciples who knew John's baptism did not know about a Spirit baptism at all, despite the language, since the idea of a baptism of the Spirit comes from the OT (Ezek 36:25–27). Rather, it shows with hyperbole that they did not know that Spirit baptism had come.

(2) Luke 3:17 is not only about judgment, since there is mention that wheat is gathered by the "one who comes." That gathering is positive and looks to deliverance.

(3) One can assume that John the Baptist's ministry had positive notes as well as warnings. In declaring the kingdom's nearness or in announcing God's coming, John would be using terminology that noted the approach of God's promise.[6] The association of Spirit and the end times was strong in the OT (Isa 32:15; 44:3; Ezek 36:25–27; Joel 2:28–32 [3:1–5 MT]) and was also present at Qumran (1QS 4.20–21). Thus, an association of the Spirit with the end times is not at all unlikely for John. The theme was available to him from first-century Judaism (*Jub.* 1.22–25; *Sib. Or.* 4.162–70).[7] John could look forward to a baptism of the Spirit and fire. Since in Judaism both Messiah and Spirit baptism are associated with the end times, only some reflection on the OT hope is needed to put the two elements together.

Our second issue in Luke 3:16 is: What does the image of fire mean? All commentators agree that this image is the key to understanding the baptism. Four views exist:

(1) The reference is to Pentecost, and the distribution of the Spirit belongs to those who trust Jesus.[8] This view is old, going back to Chrysostom, *Homilies on Matthew* 11.6–7 (citing Luke 12:49–50; 24:32; Acts 2:3). The major problem with

---

6. James D. G. Dunn, *Baptism in the Holy Spirit: A Re-examination of the New Testament Teaching on the Gift of the Spirit in Relation to Pentecostalism Today* (SBT 2/15; London: SCM, 1970), 9–10; Ben Witherington, *The Christology of Jesus* (Minneapolis: Fortress, 1990), 41–42.

7. Green, *Gospel of Luke*, 164.

8. Ellis, *Gospel of Luke*, 90.

this approach is that it is too specific in linking up the promise to Acts 2. As was mentioned above, the fire terminology of Acts 2 does not support this view.

(2) Others see fire as referring only to judgment. The picture of the Spirit is seen as an allusion to a mighty wind that brings destructive judgment (Isa 40:24; 41:16; Jer 4:11 – 12; 23:19; 30:23; Ezek 13:11 – 13). The reference to the chaff in Luke 3:17 is seen as supporting this view.[9] The major problem with this approach is that it tends to limit the scope of John's ministry to a note of warning and thus conflicts with 3:18.[10]

(3) The reference is to two distinct baptisms, one of salvation (Spirit) and one of judgment (fire). This position goes back at least to Origen, *Homilies on Luke* 24.[11] By far the strongest argument for this view is that fire is a consistent image for judgment in the OT, especially the final judgment associated with the eschaton (Isa 29:6; 66:15; Ezek 38:22; Amos 1:4; 7:4; Zeph 1:18; 3:8; Mal 3:2; 4:1 [3:19 MT]), an imagery that continues in Jewish literature. The extent and consistency of this imagery make this view attractive. Of course, the mention of the Spirit refers to the provision of new covenant hope that associates the Spirit with the end times (Joel 2; cf. Isa 32; Ezek 36; esp. Jer 31:31 – 33). The fulfillment of this element is not seen so much in Pentecost as in the provision of the Spirit to all who come to Messiah. However, two points seem to be against the two-baptism view. (a) There is only one grammatical object (ὑμᾶς, *hymas*, "you"), which speaks against a division into two groups according to two distinct baptisms.[12] (b) Two explicit baptisms would seem to require ἤ (*ē*, "or") and not καί (*kai*, "and") in Luke 3:16. Thus, this view, though initially compelling, does have problems.

(4) View 3 musters strong rationale, but the best option seems to be a reference to a single baptism. The Spirit purges and thus divides humankind.[13] The key OT text here is Isa 4:4 – 5, which sees a purging of peoples so that some may dwell in God's presence. The key connection is that the Isaiah passage is the only OT text to use Spirit and fire together. Some who hold this view tend to discuss the purging of the righteous at the expense of the judgment concept, but it seems best to keep both in view in light of Luke 3:17 and the nature of OT fire imagery. The Christ comes with the Holy Spirit. The more powerful one will test all people and divide them. This approach to the passage is also supported by other texts in Luke: 12:49 – 53 speaks of the division by fire that Jesus came to bring; 17:29 – 30 speaks of the day of the Son of Man as a day of fire that divides people; and 12:10, which mentions the blasphemy against the Spirit, may well belong here in that the failure to respond to the offer of the Spirit creates an irreversible division among people, with some ending up rejected. So the offer of the Spirit divides people into two camps. One

---

9. R. I. Eisler, *The Messiah Jesus and John the Baptist according to Flavius Josephus' Recently Discovered "Capture of Jerusalem" and the Other Jewish and Christian Sources* (trans. A. H. Krappe; New York: Dial, 1931), 274–79.

10. Fitzmyer, *Gospel of Luke I–IX*, 474.

11. See also Lang, *TDNT*, 6:943.

12. Fitzmyer, *Gospel of Luke I–IX*, 473.

13. Marshall, *Gospel of Luke*, 146–47; Dunn, *Baptism in the Holy Spirit*, 12–13. Green, *Gospel of Luke*, 181–82, is not clear as to whether he prefers view 3 or 4.

baptism is offered to the world, but it has two consequences. Which consequence a person experiences depends on the individual's decision in regard to the baptism.

Thus, the baptism of Spirit and fire represents two sides to Jesus' offer of God's promise. It divides people into two groups. Those who accept it, by accepting the one who brings it, are purged and taken in. Those who do not accept it are thrown to the wind, as 3:17 suggests. The offer of this decisive baptism, revealed at Pentecost but offered continuously thereafter, shows Jesus' superiority to John. The offer of the Spirit began with the message of salvation, which was preached at Pentecost. With acceptance come the gift and the presence of the Spirit, who protects one from judgment (Acts 2:38–40). John is only a precursor to him who brings this baptism.[14]

John is saying that the way one can know the new era has come is when the stronger one to come baptizes with the Spirit. In light of Luke 3:15, that is a reference to the work of the Messiah. So not only is the Spirit the sign of the new era; he is the indicator of Messiah's presence.

Luke 3:16 casts its shadow across the two volumes. The Spirit-Christ-new era connection is precisely the point Peter will make in his speech in Acts 2: the coming of the Spirit is the indication that God has made the crucified but raised Jesus both Lord and Christ (2:30–36). Other texts also echo this idea. Luke 24:49 has Jesus tell the disciples to await being clothed with power from on high as the Father promised. This idea is reiterated in Acts 1:4–5, when they are told to wait for the promise of the Father, and then Jesus notes the contrast between John's water baptism and being baptized by the Spirit before many days. So Acts 1:4–5 connects back to Luke 3:16. Pentecost and Peter's remarks in Acts 2 are the realization of this promise.

Luke 3:16 extends even further into Acts. In Acts 10–11, the theme returns as Peter and his entourage realize that the distribution of the Spirit shows Gentiles can participate in salvation and the new era because the Spirit would only be given where God has cleansed. The Spirit is poured out on Gentiles even as it was on them (Acts 10:45–47). The verb "has been poured out" (ἐκκέχυται, *ekkechytai*) in Acts 10:45 recalls the language of Acts 2 (see 2:33: ἐξέχεεν, *execheen*).

In Acts 2:33, the aorist verb form of ἐκχέω (*echeō*) recalls the verb in 2:17 (ἐκχεῶ in the Joel 3 citation) and links the two passages in another example of Jewish *gezerah shewa* (or linking two passages together through one term). The image in 2:17 is rich. It is of a torrential downpour that is poured out on a parched earth.[15] The use of this verb with the Spirit summarizes Joel's key promise—that the Spirit would be poured out "on all people." The use of ἀπό plus the genitive (lit., "of/from the Spirit") is partitive here, pointing to the distribution of the Spirit. The universality of the distribution is one of the main elements of the promise. Before this new period, the Spirit had been distributed to a few people on special occasions for special enablement (see Luke 3:4–6 [Isa 40:3–5], 16–17). Universal distribution is a key sign that the new era has come. Jesus has now done what Joel promised. Thus,

---

14. Bock, *Luke 1:1–9:50*, 321–24.   15. Larkin, *Acts*, 53.

Peter argues in Acts 2 that the Spirit's outpouring fulfills the promise pointing to the last days and to the Messiah's mediation of salvation from God's side.

When Peter defends his actions later in Acts 11:15–17, he says, "As I began to speak, the Holy Spirit came on them as he had come on us at the beginning [an allusion to Pentecost and Acts 2]. Then I remembered the Lord had said, 'John baptized with water, but you will be baptized with the Holy Spirit.' So if God gave them the same gift as he gave us who believed in the Lord Jesus Christ, who was I to think that I could stand in God's way?" The reaction to Peter's report was to give glory to God because "even to Gentiles God has granted repentance that leads to life" (11:18). The Greek of this verse is emphatic in placing the reference to Gentiles at the front of the remark. This gift had come to Gentiles! Here God is directing the mission and the giving of the Spirit to Gentiles—a key point. Gentile inclusion in the new era has taken place because God did it through his Spirit.

Luke 3:16 reappears yet again in Acts 13. Here Paul is preaching at Pisidian Antioch and reviewing step by step Israel's history from the patriarchs to David (Acts 13:16–22). Then Paul leaps over a thousand years of Israel's history to John the Baptist. He notes that from David's seed God has brought to Israel a Savior, Jesus, just as God had promised (v. 23). Paul notes how John had preached a baptism of repentance to all the people of Israel (v. 24). Then Paul, alluding back to Luke 3:16, notes what John said toward the end of his ministry, "Who do you suppose that I am? I am not the one you are looking for. But there is one coming after me whose sandals I am not worthy to untie." Anyone reading Luke knows the rest of that passage: John baptized with water, but the one to come will baptize with the Spirit.

This gifting of the Spirit Peter calls bearing witness to the Gentiles in Acts 15:8. Again, the evidence is that God gave "the Holy Spirit to them, just as he did to us." This Peter describes as an act where God "purified their hearts by faith." So the work of the Spirit is an act of cleansing, picturing a washing like baptism.

The final allusion back to Luke 3:16 occurs in Acts 19:4. When Paul is discussing the baptism that some disciples of John had experienced, he says to them, "John's baptism was a baptism of repentance. He told the people to believe in the one coming after him, that is, in Jesus." Again, the new era comes when Messiah brings the promise of the new era, the Spirit.[16] For Luke, this is the hope of the presence and kingdom of God providing the dynamic for God to rule in his people. It is what Acts 11:18 called "life." So this string of texts tied to Luke 3:16 shows not only the importance of these verses for Luke's teaching of the Spirit; it also summarizes the major function the Spirit has in Luke-Acts: enablement for witness and life that shows the new era has come through the Christ.

---

16. This idea is severely understated by Jervell, *Theology of the Acts of the Apostles*, 47, when he argues that Acts 2 does not introduce anything new and unheard of in the people of God. He sees this distribution of the Spirit to be only one of greater degree. However, to say this is to ignore the new era emphasis Luke gives to this event and the need the disciples have to wait for the Spirit coming in this form. Yes, this is a greater presence of degree of the Spirit than in times past, but it also is of such a greater dimension that the top figure of the old era is at the bottom of ranking in the new era he pointed to (Luke 7:27).

The picture of the baptism's coming with Spirit and fire is rooted in Isa 4:4 and 11:1–4. It pictures a sifting and purging as the following illustration of separating wheat and chaff in Luke 3:17 indicates. This purging process stretches out over the entire kingdom period for Luke, so what John summarizes as an act in an instant takes place over time for Luke with consummation in judgment at the end. The result finds people freed to serve God in holiness and righteousness in the context of fearing God as Zechariah proclaimed (1:74–75). This completes Luke's development of the theology of the Spirit emerging from the key text of 3:16.

After Luke 3:16 points to the importance of the Spirit, Luke's narration of the Spirit's roles continues in 3:21–22. The association of the Spirit with God's program appears again when the Spirit comes on Jesus at his baptism (cf. Acts 10:38). In describing what took place in the baptism, some have spoken of adoption; that is, Jesus is made Messiah at this point in his life. In fact, some argue that the time of Jesus' entry into his messianic office has been pushed back in the tradition from its original locale at the resurrection to this time of baptism. But it is better to speak of legitimation for Luke. Jesus does not become Messiah at his baptism.[17] This point is especially clear in Luke's presentation, where Jesus' position as a promised Davidic ruler is clear from the start in 1:31–35. Rather, what is present is the first testimony to Jesus from heaven, as God's agent prepares to embark on his mission. The baptism is like an inauguration, a call to begin the mission for which Jesus was always headed. That work takes place in conjunction with God's Spirit.

When one sees the voice in this light, one also can speak of the Spirit's anointing not just in terms of wisdom, power, and enablement, but also in terms of endorsement and confirmation. The power that Jesus exhibits in Luke-Acts is attributed to his own authority, person, or name, and not solely to the Spirit (Luke 4:36; 5:12, 17; 6:19; 8:46; 9:1; 10:19; Acts 3:12, 16; 4:7). Even the power that the disciples receive is sent to them by Jesus, for he has authority over it (Luke 9:1 and 24:49 with Acts 2:32–34). Nevertheless, the Spirit is associated with power in Acts 2:38, not so much because the Spirit is the source of the power, but because the Spirit shows that God is with Jesus (Acts 10:38).

The same "chosen by God" emphasis is seen in Luke 4:18–19, a passage that speaks of Jesus' anointing and looks back to this baptism. After the baptismal confirmation come the presence and direction of God's Spirit into the task (4:1, 14). The Spirit leads and confirms more than he empowers Jesus in Luke. Both ideas—power and confirmation—are present, but the emphasis is on direction, identification, and support for Jesus rather than on provision. This distinction is important, because the disciples have a fundamentally different relationship to the Spirit than does Jesus. The disciples are totally subject to the Spirit, who comes to them through the agency of Jesus (Acts 2:32–34). Thus, Jesus' baptism is an endorsement and confirmation of him in terms of his Messiah-Servant mission. Jesus is the Coming One to whom John looked. Spirit, call, and mission meet with this role.

---

17. Schürmann, *Lukasevangelium: Kommentar zu Kap. 1.1–9.50,* 191–95.

Guidance and encouragement leading to joy are other things the Spirit does. So the Spirit guides Jesus into the wilderness to meet his temptation (Luke 4:1) and takes him to minister in Galilee (4:14). In this second reference the Spirit is again described in relationship to power as Jesus goes to Galilee in the power of the Spirit. Later when Jesus prays to God thanking him for those who have responded, he prays rejoicing in the Holy Spirit (10:21). This parallels the note of praise that Zechariah gives in his hymn earlier in the gospel (1:67).

God is gracious to those who desire wisdom and gives the Spirit to those who seek it from God (Luke 11:13). For Luke, the Spirit is the good gift that God can give. The saying here differs from Matthew's version, where the gifts given are simply good things (Matt 7:11). Matthew's remark is in a distinct context, but the difference does show Luke's regard for the unique value of the Spirit.

The Spirit's testimony to Jesus is so important that blasphemy against the Spirit cannot be forgiven (Luke 12:10). This idea is in contrast to a single remark against the Son of Man. Blasphemy against the Spirit is when one walks away from all the Spirit shows about who Jesus is. In that case, forgiveness is not possible because this judgment is a slander against God's decisive work as testified to by his Spirit.

The Spirit also gives aid in terms of our facing persecution. So the disciples need not worry about what to say when they are brought before rulers and authorities, since the Spirit will teach them what they ought to say (Luke 12:12). Luke shows the realization of this promise in how Jesus' followers respond to such situations in Acts.

One can see by these references in Luke just how tied to the new era, mission, and witness the Spirit is. Nothing says this as much as Jesus' last reference to the Spirit in Luke's gospel, when he tells his disciples to wait for the promise of the Father when they will be clothed with power from on high (Luke 24:49). Interestingly, the Spirit is not mentioned directly from 12:12 until here. With Luke 24 the issue of the Spirit's enablement for mission and transformation into boldness come to the fore.[18] One need only contrast the timid Peter who denies Jesus three times in Luke 22 to the bold Peter who preaches Jesus after the Spirit comes in Acts 2. This text shows that the Spirit's power transforms people. The Spirit will enable a new kind of life in the community. Those filled with the Spirit will engage in mission and lead the community. Two scenes showing this are the call of the Spirit-filled men in Acts 6 and the call by the Spirit in Acts 13:1–4 that causes Barnabas and Saul to move into mission.

9.3 THE SPIRIT IN THE BOOK OF ACTS

There are almost four times as many references to the Spirit in Acts as in Luke's gospel. Although many of these texts are descriptions of people as Spirit-filled or Spirit-directed, the increase shows how the Spirit is now active in the community

---

18. Turner, "Work of the Holy Spirit in Luke-Acts," 150.

Jesus formed and how the coming of the promise enables the community to carry out its mission. The Spirit is now widely distributed across the whole of the community, not just in a few people as earlier.

Several references involve the setting up of the coming of the Spirit. This coming is important. For Luke this Spirit's internal presence is a sign of the new era, something that had not existed previously for the faithful, which is why they have to wait for the Spirit to come in order to engage in mission. The Spirit may have indwelt here and there in the old era, but the kind of outpouring into indwelling for all who come to God did not exist previously. The Spirit's fresh coming is part of what makes this eschatological era new. Speaking of the coming of God's promise means something new has come that involves God's fresh administrative activity for his people.

So Jesus had reminded the disciples by the Spirit about their commission (Acts 1:2). The detail is shown in 1:4, when Spirit baptism is contrasted with John's water baptism. The commission includes receiving power when the Holy Spirit will come upon them, making them witnesses in Jerusalem, Judea, Samaria, and to the ends of the earth (1:8). This remark by Jesus came in response to the disciples' query about whether the restoration of Israel was near. Jesus reprioritizes their concerns by getting them to focus on mission and what God would have them do now versus being overly concerned about when the consummation will be. The community has a job to do. So God will send the Spirit to enable them to do it.

The Spirit also is a part of the revelatory process of the promise of Scripture. So Peter describes the work of the Spirit in foretelling Judas's betrayal through Ps 69:26 (Acts 1:16, 20). Similar texts include a reference to the Spirit's speaking through David in Acts 4:25 and through Isaiah in 28:25. So the Spirit directs the community through his presence but also instructs through pointing out the relevance of the Scriptures. The Spirit also leads them to seek boldness in their witness, something both Peter and the community show in Acts 2–4 (also Stephen in 7:51).[19]

The Holy Spirit runs throughout Acts 2. Six of the explicit references in the book take place here, plus a few more implicit associations. The disciples are filled with the Spirit when he is poured out on them (2:4). As a result, people hear the message of God in their own languages as tongues break out (2:4, 8, 11). This fulfills what God promised about the last days through Joel, for twice Peter speaks of the Spirit being poured out as he cites Joel 2:28–29 (cf. Acts 2:17–18).

Acts 2:17–18 deserves a closer look. The events that Peter by the Spirit uses Scripture to explain are part of God's long-awaited promise in fulfillment of new covenant hope. It is better to say that Luke sees the start of the decisive eras of fulfillment as happening in these recent events. As with the other three OT texts that will be raised in his Acts 2 speech, this event is seen as fulfilled, at least initially, by what God has done and declared. The apostles read such texts as last-day, kingdom

---

19. Jervell, *Theology of the Acts of the Apostles*, 50.

texts. The new community saw themselves as residing in the last days (1 Cor 10:11; 1 Tim 4:1; 2 Tim 3:1; Heb 1:1–2; 9:26; 1 Pet 1:20; 1 John 2:18). Since the day of the Lord is also alluded to in this citation, what Peter is really saying here is that the coming of the Spirit is the beginning of "the last days." An era of righteousness will conclude them, and that era comes with the day of the Lord. At the end of his speech, Peter will use the coming of judgment as an appeal for the people to repent and thereby experience the blessings of the new era (Acts 2:38–40). People must remember that they are accountable to the living God, so that an appeal to judgment is an appeal to reality as Peter sees it.

It is the pouring out of the Spirit that they are seeing and that Joel declares will take place in the last days. Later Jewish interpretation connected the Joel citation to other OT texts that explained the Spirit's coming in the eschaton, a link that was conceptual in nature (Isa 32:15; Jer 31:31–33; Ezek 34–37, esp. 36:22–32; *Midr. Pss.* 14 §6 [57b]; *Midr. Rab.* 203a on Deut 6:14, where Ezek 36:26; Joel 2:28; and Isa 54:13 are used side by side as God's presence is said to rest on God's people).[20] Qumran also expressed the idea of how the Spirit enables discernment in this eschatological community (1QH 15.6–7 [= 7.6–7]; 1Q35; 4Q428.6–7; 1QS 4.2–4).[21] This access to the Spirit fulfills the wish, expressed in Num 11:29, that God would put the Spirit in all God's people. *Numbers Rabbah* 15.25 declares that in the "world to come all Israel will be made prophets," while citing Joel 2. So the declaration may not be all that surprising, if this late text reflects earlier Jewish tradition. The background to Acts 2:17–18 shows Luke's view fits well into the Jewish context in which it was preached.

Later in his speech, Peter speaks about how Jesus received the promise of the Spirit from the Father before pouring him out (Acts 2:33). This particular text has implications. The Spirit is distinct both from the Father and from the Christ who sits at the right hand of God. This means the Spirit is not an impersonal force for Luke.[22] God promises the gift of the Spirit to those who respond and are baptized in the name of Jesus Christ (2:38). That promise is for any whom God calls to him, whether near or far off (2:39). Here we see that the Spirit is a key gift of the new era, growing out of the forgiveness Jesus provides. In fact, one can say that God cleanses through Jesus in order to bring us into ongoing fellowship with him. For Luke, nothing can better summarize the gospel than this combination of forgiveness, cleansing, Spirit, and life—all received when one believes.

In the next few chapters of Acts, the bulk of the Spirit references shows the impact of the Spirit's coming. Many who lead the church and even the community as a whole act as a result of being filled with the Spirit: Peter (Acts 4:8), the community (4:31), the Seven (6:3), Stephen (6:5; 7:55—at his martyrdom), Saul (9:17;

---

20. Str-B, 2:615–16.

21. Larkin, *Acts,* 52, note on 2:17.

22. So correctly Max Turner, "'Trinitarian Pneumatology in the New Testament? Towards an Explanation of the Worship of Jesus,"

Asbury Journal of Theology 57 (2002–2003): 178–79, who criticizes Jervell's description of the Spirit as impersonal for Luke; Jervell, *Theology of the Acts of the Apostles,* 44.

13:9), and Barnabas (11:24). Mission takes place through Spirit-filled leaders and through a Spirit-directed community. That is where the Spirit takes people. Spirit-directed people are not able to be resisted (6:10) and insist on doing what God has called them to do, not what human beings require (5:32). So they can boldly proclaim that those who reject the testimony are resisting the Holy Spirit (7:51). All of this is a function of the witness and enabling role of the Spirit, whom Peter notes God gave to people who obey God so that they will stand up and testify for what God is doing (Acts 5:32).

In contrast stand those who lie to the Spirit. Ananias and Sapphira do so and face an instant judgment as they misrepresent themselves by pretending to give their entire proceeds to the community (Acts 5:3, 9). Peter says they are lying to the Spirit and testing the Spirit of the Lord, respectively. Here we see the Spirit as that which makes the community special. To give to the church is to give to the Spirit's community. To lie about such service leads in this case to a shocking judgment to let the church know the Spirit knows what is happening in his community. Fitzmyer calls it "a lie to *koinōnia*," and thus it is an act against fellowship.[23] As the end of the passage indicates, Ananias has followed human ways, not the ways of God.

This final remark makes clear that the responsibility for the act, though influenced by Satan, is Ananias's directly, for it is out of his heart that he has acted, and it is his heart, apart from God, that Ananias has obeyed. The deceit and allegiance represented here reflect the personal characters of Satan and the Spirit respectively—one reflecting deceit and the other honesty and faithfulness to God. Nevertheless, the sin is Ananias's because he left himself open to follow Satan. There are implications here for the person of God, since to act against the Spirit is to act against God.

Seven references to the Spirit show up in the scene in Samaria involving Simon Magus and the Ethiopian eunuch in Acts 8. Again, the concern from this concentration of references is that the Spirit is sovereignly given and is not to be purchased or manipulated. So Peter and John pray for the Samaritans to receive the Spirit (8:15) since he has not yet come to them (8:16), and the Samaritans do receive the Spirit as a result (8:17). Simon Magus sees the Spirit given by the laying on of hands (8:18) and asks to purchase such power so he, too, can give the Spirit by the laying on of hands (8:19). This elicits Peter's rebuke. Part of the point of this scene is that Simon is seen as a master magician with great power himself (8:9–10), but that power cannot touch what God does sovereignly through the Spirit. Those to whom God has given the Spirit have a power greater than other power in the world.

In the next scene, the Spirit both directs Philip to and then away from the Ethiopian eunuch, to whom he witnesses (Acts 8:26, 39). This passage indicates the Spirit's role in directing people into opportunities for witness. It also serves as a precursor to the work that the community will do far outside the land of the nation.

The Holy Spirit's work is responsible for the community's growth, offering

---

23. Fitzmyer, *Acts of the Apostles*, 323.

"encouragement" to the fellowship as it grows (Acts 9:31). Here a term related to an important term in John's gospel (παράκλητος, *paraklētos*) shows up (John 14–16 and the mention of the *Paraclete*).

A cluster of eight references to the Spirit appears in the Cornelius episode. The Spirit directs Peter concerning the three men Cornelius has sent as a result of his divine vision (Acts 10:19). The interaction and interconnection between God's work and that of the Spirit in this event show how important it is for Luke. In his speech to the group Peter notes how the Spirit anointed Jesus during his ministry (10:38). Of course, the Spirit comes on the Gentiles gathered there; this is the significant result of the meeting (10:44). The believing Jews with Peter are amazed that "the gift of the Holy Spirit" is poured out on Gentiles as well (10:45; cf. Joel 2:28–32; Acts 2:17–21; 8:16; 11:15). God is leaving no doubt that this initiative is his (11:15–17).

This event has correctly been called the "Pentecost of the Gentile world." The Gentiles' reception of the Spirit means that they can now be baptized (Acts 10:47). The presence of tongues and the praise of God clearly show the Spirit is present (v. 46). The verb ἐξέστησαν (*exestēsan*, "were astonished," v. 45) describes the surprise of the believing Jews that the Spirit has been given to Gentiles. This verb (ἐχίστημι) appears in several key passages to denote a reaction to what is taking place (2:7, 12 [to the coming of tongues]; 8:9, 11, 13 [to the work of Philip and Simon]; 9:21 [to Paul's preaching Christ after having persecuted the church]; 12:16 [to Peter's escape from prison]). Acts 2:12 is important here, for the description in 10:45 matches the reaction ("amazed" in NIV) that took place at the original Pentecost.

Peter recognizes that the Spirit will only enter a vessel that God has cleansed and forgiven (see Acts 11:9). In his retelling of this event, Peter notes that the Spirit had instructed him to go to the Gentiles and that he should make no distinction among people (11:12). He notes how the Spirit fell on the Gentiles as he was speaking (11:15), a fact that led him to recall the Lord's teaching about the coming baptism with the Spirit (11:16). So Peter could not resist God, and the Jews to whom Peter is reporting rejoice that God has allowed the Gentiles to experience repentance unto life (11:17–18).[24] This last remark is important, because some argue that the Spirit of prophecy is all the Spirit is for Luke. This text and others that tie the Spirit to the new era of life and covenant indicate that the Spirit is also associated with salvation and is a key gift of the new era (cf. also 2:39).

After noting the work of a Spirit-filled Barnabas (Acts 11:24), Luke tells how Agabus as a prophet is led by the Spirit to predict a coming famine (11:28). As in a few other places in Acts, the Spirit speaks through a direct communication or through prophets.

---

24. The force of this text argues against a simple equation of the Spirit simply connected to the kingdom of God as primarily for proclamation, as important as that idea is for Luke. The Spirit is the gift of the new era that purges and enables the people of God to be the people of God. So against Youngmo Cho, "Spirit and Kingdom in Luke-Acts: Proclamation as the Primary Role of the Spirit in Relation to the Kingdom of God in Luke-Acts," *Asian Journal of Pentecostal Studies* 6 (2003): 173–97. He is correct to criticize James Dunn's view that kingdom and Spirit are almost interchangeable ideas, but reacts too far in the other direction. The role of the Spirit in enablement extends beyond proclamation into life and evidence of a key benefit of the new era.

The Spirit also leads into mission. So the first missionary journey of Paul comes as a result of the Spirit's calling out Barnabas and Paul (Acts 13:2), with the result that they are said to have been sent out by the Holy Spirit (13:4). Early in this journey Paul is said to be full of the Spirit (13:9). In a summary after rejection at Iconium, the disciples on this journey are said to be filled with joy and the Holy Spirit (13:52). So one can be faithful to God and one's call, meet rejection, and still be full of the Spirit, rejoicing at having been faithful and used by God.

Peter's retelling of the Cornelius episode at the Jerusalem council yields another mention of the Gentiles' reception of the Spirit (Acts 15:8). The letter emerging from the deliberations at the Jerusalem Council is said to be a product of the work of the Spirit in terms of not laying on any burden beyond the four practices that the letter notes (15:28).

In another example of direct guidance, the Spirit prevents Paul from going to Asia, sending him to Phrygia and Galatia instead (Acts 16:6). In the next verse, the Spirit of Jesus prevents him from going to Bithynia, so he ends up in Macedonia instead (16:7). So the Spirit is active in the middle section of Acts in directing where the witness goes.

In an event we already noted, Paul discusses with some disciples of John the Baptist whether they have received the Spirit, and he provides the Spirit to them (Acts 19:2, 6).

The direction one should take again becomes the point in a series of references that one can deliberate over in terms of its force. These references involve Paul's desire and even insistence that he go to Jerusalem after leaving Achaia. In these references to the Spirit Paul is told he will find trouble, so much so that others in the community, including the prophet Agabus (Acts 20:22–23; 21:4, 11), urge him by the Spirit not to go.[25] This incident shows that in some cases what the Spirit reveals in terms of what will happen can be discerned and includes a choice to go and face the consequences. What Agabus and others try to prevent, Paul chooses to face. When he does so, they all agree that the Lord's will should be done (21:14). This remark closes the matter on a positive note and seems to be Luke's recognition that Paul did the will of the Lord, especially since the Jerusalem incident is what causes Paul to reach Rome, a destination that is divinely and providentially directed as well.

That the Spirit directs in terms of leadership selection surfaces in Paul's remarks to the Ephesian elders (Acts 20:28). Paul notes that the Spirit has made them overseers in order to shepherd the church of God, which God obtained with the blood of his own Son.

The debate within Judaism about spirits in general shows up next during Paul's defense speech in Acts 23. Here Luke notes that the Sadducees insist that "there

---

25. It is in this sequence of texts that Luke refers to Paul's resolve to go to Jerusalem (Acts 19:21). This passage has a reference to the *pneuma* that could refer either to the Holy Spirit or to Paul's inner resolve of spirit. The fact that this text opens a sequence of texts where the direction of the Spirit is being discerned may well speak for a reference to the Holy Spirit here, especially given how this sequence of texts ends up affirming the trip to Jerusalem.

are neither angels nor spirits" (23:8). Given the mention of angels, this could be a reference to the Holy Spirit, but the fact that Paul is discussing resurrection makes it more likely that the spirit of Jesus is meant. The Pharisees, who accepted such beliefs, reply that they do not find it implausible in principle that an angel or spirit has spoken to Paul (23:9).

The final reference to the Spirit in Acts looks at his role in giving revelation through Isaiah in Isa 6:9, where God rebukes the nation for being slow to hear (Acts 28:25).

With this Acts 28 reference, the mention of the Spirit in Luke-Acts comes to an end. His key role is as the sign of the new era, the giver of life that enables and directs the community. One key association is especially important to Luke, namely, that of the Spirit's association with power.

9.4 SPIRIT AND POWER

In our survey, we have noted in a few key places where the Spirit is tied to the idea of power. Key texts we discussed already include Luke 1:35 and Jesus' birth, and 4:14, where the Spirit leads Jesus to Galilee. Other texts might also belong here. For example, in 4:36 Jesus is said to minister with authority and power as he casts out demons. In 5:17 the power of the Lord was with Jesus to heal; in this passage we may well have a convergence of God, Jesus, and the Spirit at work. Luke 6:19 also mentions the power to heal, as does 8:46. That unusual text describes Jesus as sensing power going out from him as the woman with an issue of blood touched him. Since Acts 10:38 associates the anointing of Jesus with his power to heal and exorcise, it is appropriate to see the Spirit in the background here. Jesus shares such power in Luke 9:1 with those whom he sends out to declare the kingdom of God is near.

Of course, the key text here is Luke 24:49, which speaks of the coming of the Spirit in terms of being clothed "with power from on high," something that Acts 1:8 also affirms when they "will receive power," for the Spirit comes upon them. According to the NT, this is the promise of the new covenant (Jer 31:33; Ezek 36:26–27; Acts 2; 2 Cor 3; Heb 7–10). This permanent indwelling is a bestowal of power that enables believers to give evidence of God's presence, to appreciate the will of God (John 14:25–26; 16:12–15; 1 John 2:27).

In an example of Lucan overlap, it is the power of Jesus that heals the lame man in Acts 3–4 (also 4:7–12). Yet it is the coming of the Spirit that allows signs to be performed (2:16–18). Again, Jesus and the Spirit are seen as working in a connected manner through the image of power.

9.5 CONCLUSION

The work of the Spirit in Luke-Acts reveals the new era and equips the new community with enablement for witness. As a result, her leaders are bold and wise in testimony. The Spirit also guides the community at key points. He sometimes reveals what the church is to do in mission and where one should go.

Before the coming to the believing community, the Spirit was an anointing power tied to Jesus in birth and ministry. He also was a source of inspiration for the writings of Scripture. The key text of Luke 3:16 and the many following allusions to it show that this equipping is part of what Luke sees as not only evidence of the new era but the presence of a saved life. The Spirit's coming reflects the result of the promise of the Father and allows life to be lived as a result of the cleaning work of God through Jesus (Acts 11:9, 18).

So what does the Spirit do? The short answer is many things. He anointed Jesus and energized his birth (Luke 1:35; Acts 3:21–22; 4:16–18; 10:38). He is the giver of dreams and visions (2:17; 7:55–56). He gives revelatory words and inspires Scripture (1:2; 1:16; 4:25; 7:51; 28:25). He gives wisdom and discernment (Luke 21:15; Acts 5:3; 6:3, 5, 10; 9:31; 13:9; 16:18). He leads into praise for what God has done (Luke 1:67; Acts 2:4; 10:46; 19:6). He leads into witness (Acts 1:4, 8; 4:8; 31; 5:32; 6:10; 9:17), as well as teaching (9:31; 13:52).[26] In sum, the Spirit directs the new community in the new life as he clothes it with power from on high (Luke 24:49).

---

26. This list slightly expands the one in Turner, "Spirit of Prophecy," 334–35.

Chapter 10

The Salvation of God through Christ and the Healings That Picture It: Narrative Order

Bibliography

Adams, Dwayne. *The Sinner in Luke.* Evangelical Theological Society Monograph Series. Eugene, OR: Pickwick Publications, 2008. **Dupont, Jacques.** *The Salvation of the Gentiles: Essays on the Acts of the Apostles.* Trans. John R. Keating. New York: Paulist, 1979. **Franklin, E.** *Christ the Lord: A Study of the Purpose and Theology of Luke-Acts.* London: SPCK, 1975. **Green, Joel B.** "God as Savior in the Acts of the Apostles." Pp. 83–106 in *Witness to the Gospel.* Ed. I. Howard Marshall and David Peterson. Grand Rapids: Eerdmans, 1998. **Maddox, R.** *The Purpose of Luke-Acts.* Edinburgh: T&T Clark, 1982. **Marshall, I. H.** *Luke: Historian and Theologian.* Grand Rapids: Zondervan, 1970. **Pilgrim, Walter.** *Good News to the Poor: Wealth and Poverty in Luke-Acts.* Minneapolis: Augsburg, 1981. **Stenschke, Christoph.** *Luke's Portrait of Gentiles Prior to Their Coming to Faith.* WUNT. Tübingen; Mohr-Siebeck, 1999. Idem. "The Need for Salvation." Pp. 125–44 in *Witness to the Gospel: The Theology of Acts.* Ed. I. Howard Marshall and David Peterson. Grand Rapids: Eerdmans, 1998. **Turner, Max.** *Power from on High: The Spirit in Israel's Restoration and Witness in Luke-Acts.* JPTSup. Sheffield: Sheffield Academic Press, 1996. Idem. "The 'Spirit of Prophecy' as the Power of Israel's Restoration and Witness." Pp. 327–48 in *Witness to the Gospel: The Theology of Acts.* Ed. I. Howard Marshall and David Peterson. Grand Rapids: Eerdmans, 1998. **Witherington, Ben.** "Salvation and Health in Christian Antiquity: The Soteriology of Luke-Acts in Its First Century Setting." Pp. 145–66 in *Witness to the Gospel: The Theology of Acts.* Ed. I. Howard Marshall and David Peterson. Grand Rapids: Eerdmans, 1998.

We now turn to survey the salvation program of God.[1] Here we look especially at words in the σῴζω word group (σῴζω, σωτήρ, σωτηρία, σωτήριος, *sōzō, sōtēr, sōtēria, sōtērios*). These terms appear forty-seven times in Luke-Acts, with the verb σῴζω taking up thirty of those uses. Alongside these direct references we will summarize the acts of healing that picture this deliverance and give a sense of its

---

1. A helpful chapter on this theme in Acts comes from Joel B. Green, "God as Savior in the Acts of the Apostles," in *Witness to the Gospel, 83–106, and a solid monograph is from Robert Maddox, The Purpose of Luke-Acts* (Edinburgh: T&T Clark, 1982).

scope. Here the dominant terms are θεραπεύω (*therapeuō*) and ἰάομαι (*iaomai*; used nineteen and fifteen times respectively).

Also examined is the relationship of promise to covenant, the commitments God had already made in terms of how he will relate to Israel and the world. The Abrahamic covenant had promised blessing to the world (Gen 12:1–3). The Davidic covenant promised a line of kings that by Jesus' time had led the people to expect a singular deliverer. The new covenant had promised forgiveness of sins and the presence of the "law in the heart" as an internal dynamic for responding to God. All of these covenant commitments play a role in Luke's portrait of salvation. Again we will keep an eye on narrative order before coming back to a more synthetic look in ch. 11. One difference in our synthetic chapter is we will introduce a few themes tied to salvation, such as Israel, the Gentiles, and the law.

10.1 SALVATION IN THE INFANCY MATERIAL

To invoke the arrival of the new era and a forerunner figure who comes in the spirit and power of Elijah is to invoke the arrival of the eschaton and the salvation of Jewish hope (Luke 1:17; cf. Mal 3:1; 4:5; Sir 48:10). To follow it with a reference to the Davidic king over Israel is to point to Davidic hope and Messiah (Luke 1:31–35).

But what will this hope entail? This is set forth in the hymnic materials of the infancy material. Mary, for example, describes how God's looking on those who are humble like her involves a reversal of fortune for the haughty and powerful in contrast to those in need. Here is God acting as her Savior (Luke 1:47). The reversal of social position will occur in the final exercise of God's power.

Who is described in this hymn? Luke 1:52–53 gives us a clue. Ταπεινούς (*tapeinous*, "humble") stands in contrast to δυνάστας (*dynastas*), a term that refers to rulers (Gen 50:4). That rulers are removed "from their thrones" makes the nuance of ταπεινούς clear. The powerful are governing rulers; the humble are those oppressed by these rulers. Mary has in mind God's covenant people (see 1:54–55 and the mention of "those who fear him" in 1:50).

R. Brown sees a reference to the spiritually oppressed, a reference that is correct in light of the emphasis on God-fearers in the hymn.[2] All the injustice of the ruling classes against God's people will be reversed as the humble are lifted up by God. God will deal with the rulers' oppression and lack of compassion; he wants people to treat their neighbors with compassion. These rulers deny God and oppress his people. Mary has in mind the Romans and those like them, who use their secular power to keep God's people at bay. Those who think they have authority do not have ultimate authority. A major theme of the OT is the oppressed people of God described as poor and humble (Pss 9:11–12, 17–20 [9:12–13, 18–21 MT]; 10:1–4, 17–18; 12:1–5 [12:2–6 MT]; 18:25–29 [18:26–30 MT]).[3] These few references are part of a consistent theme of the OT, especially in the Psalter.

---

2. Brown, *Birth of the Messiah*, 363.   3. A closer look at this category takes place in ch. 17.

The idea of the removal of rulers is expressed in the OT and in Jewish hope (Job 5:11; 12:19; 1 Sam 2:7; Sir 10:14; Jdt 9:3; 1QM 14.10–11).[4] The exaltation of the humble is also a key OT and Jewish theme (1 Sam 2:7; Ps 147:6; Sir 10:14). Mary uses the language of the faithful. She trusts God's just vindication in the approaching messianic reign. She is anticipating, in the child she bears, total vindication. The way God will accomplish this vindication has other intermediate requirements of which she is not aware, such as Messiah's suffering. First Peter 1:11 summarizes the emerging career of Jesus in two stages: "the sufferings of the Messiah and the glories that … follow." Mary longs to share in the days of glory, but Luke will show how before the glory comes the clearing of the way for it in suffering and sacrifice. Thus, this salvation emerges with a social dimension right at the start (Luke 1:46–55). Relationships are reconfigured as a result and rooted in God's mercy as he spoke to Abraham and his posterity. There is an undercurrent of God's justice at work in this portrait of salvation. All who turn to God will be lifted up by him.

Zechariah portrays salvation as rescue from enemies and from those who hate God's people by a Davidic "horn" who visits and redeems his people. This deliverance allows the delivered to serve God without fear in holiness and righteousness before him all the days of their lives (Luke 1:69–75). This salvation is tied to the forgiveness of sins, which John will introduce. The sent one to come is pictured as light that dawns and drowns out the darkness and the shadow of death in which people sit; this will lead to peace (1:76–79). Salvation is comprehensive, including spiritual elements and the restoration of justice. To remove either is to shortchange what God does when he acts to save in a comprehensive way that changes people and the world.

As God is a Savior, so is Jesus (Luke 2:11). The Spirit-inspired Simeon, who holds the child Jesus, confirms this understanding when he says that his "eyes have seen [God's] salvation"; to see Jesus is to see that salvation (2:30). Light is repeated as a characterization of Jesus' work. Jesus represents glory for Israel, probably in completing the promises of covenant through her. Jesus also is revelation for the Gentiles as they will be included in what Jesus does—an allusion to the Abrahamic promise to bless the world through the seed even as Isa 42:6 and 49:6 are invoked. So salvation completes promises, brings peace, establishes justice, changes the social order, and leads into deliverance.

10.2 SALVATION IN THE BODY OF LUKE'S GOSPEL

The coming of John the Baptist invokes Isa 40:3–5, a text Luke lengthens in comparison to Mark and Matthew (Luke 3:4–6). John prepares for the arrival of the Lord. The image used is that of creation leveling itself like a red carpet for the welcome. That welcome requires repentance (see John's preaching in 3:7–14). Luke

---

4. Schneider, *TDNT*, 3:412 §3.

mixes material unique to him and traditional material in these verses (vv. 7–9 are paralleled in Matt 3:7–10; vv. 10–14 are unique to Luke). He reminds those present that descent from Abraham is not enough, and he calls on people to relate to others as an indication of repentance. So this text shows that a responsive heart that considers social relationships not only to God but to one's neighbor is wrapped up in being responsive to God (3:7–14).

When the crowd, tax collectors, and soldiers ask what should they do (Luke 3:10, 13, 14), John calls for a response in terms of practice in life. They understand that John is not calling them to participate in an efficacious rite, but he is calling on them to respond with action from a changed heart. They are asking John in effect, "What sort of product reflects true repentance?" The crowd wants to know what repentance entails. John responds by telling them it involves generosity (his message to the crowds), integrity by not collecting more than is required (to the tax collectors), and not abusing power but being content with one's wages (to the soldiers). The impact of welcoming God's coming salvation with repentance is that the dynamic in relationships with others changes.

The coming of the Spirit as a sign of the new age is also suggestive of the fact that its purging work will move one toward the goal that repentance embraces (Luke 3:15–17). All of this is involved in the salvation of God that Luke declares all flesh will see (3:6). The universality of the visibility of salvation points to the fact that it will extend out to Gentiles.

Pictures of salvation flood Jesus' ministry. The terms used for these events include the σῴζω word group ("save": Luke 6:9; 7:3; 8:36, 48, 50; 17:19; 18:42) as well as terms like θεραπεύω ("heal": 4:23, 40; 5:15; 6:7, 18; 7:21; 8:2, 43; 9:1, 6; 10:9; 13:14 [2x]; 14:3) and ἰάομαι ("heal": 5:17; 6:19; 7:7; 8:47; 9:2, 11, 42; 14:4; 17:15; 22:51). The overlap suggests an association between what Jesus does in his ministry and its role in picturing what he really is about in healing.

Numerous texts in the early portion of the gospel speak of this healing or "saving." The coverage has a broad range as paralytics, the blind, the diseased, the possessed, and the dead receive healing. When Jesus is asked if he is the one to come, it is to these acts that he appeals (Luke 7:22–23); he sees them as pointers to the arrival of the new era and his role as the one to come. The OT background to the list of miracles involving the blind, lame, lepers, deaf, and dead is found in various Isaianic passages: Isa 35:5–6; 26:19; 29:18–19; 61:1.[5] In addition, a resurrection has just occurred with the widow of Nain's son. The remarks in Luke 7:22–23 are intended to refer to literal acts of healing and restoration (e.g., healing the blind: Luke 18:35–43; Matt 9:30; 12:22; 15:31; 20:33; Mark 8:25; John 9:10, 25; lame: Luke 5:17–26; lepers: 17:11–19; dead: 7:10–17; 8:40–56).[6] These events show the presence of the eschaton. Isaiah 35:5–6 is a picture of paradise, when God's rule is fully manifested, for that is the period to which all these Isaianic passages allude.[7]

---

5. Bock, *Luke 1:1–9:50*, 112–13, 321; Schürmann, *Lukasevangelium: Kommentar zu Kap. 1.1–9.50*, 410, speaks of a "cry of Jubilee" or a "song of salvation" here.

6. Schrage, *TDNT*, 8:287 §E.II.1.

7. Jeremias, *TDNT*, 5:772.

These OT texts look for God's deliverance, and the events described in them point to such a decisive time. So this text makes it clear that these events are indicators of the wholeness that salvation brings.

Similar is Luke 11:20, where Jesus notes that if he casts out demons by the finger of God, then the kingdom of God has come. This text we covered earlier in the discussion on Jesus' teaching on the kingdom.[8] Such events also picture how one should act before God in compassion, so that healing is not a violation of the Sabbath (6:9). In fact, there is no better day to deliver a person (13:16). So this stream of texts shows God's care for people through Jesus and pictures his deliverance. It is why later Jesus' work will be called signs (Acts 2:22).

A special study of exorcism accounts in Luke-Acts by Todd Klutz shows how this kind of material contributes to Luke's message.[9] Klutz argues that these kinds of texts ascribe a degree of authority to Jesus that compares him "not to some merely human deliverer but rather to 'the Most High,' the Lord God of Israel himself."[10]

Faith is important in all of this. Jesus commends the faith of a sinful woman who anoints him out of gratitude for forgiveness from her sin (Luke 7:50). Jesus tells a parable to underscore this point in 7:41–43 and explains why he takes the initiative with sinners in calling them to salvation. The parable deserves a closer look. It is introduced simply; two debtors are present, one with ten times the debt of the other (500 denarii versus 50). A denarius was a soldier's or laborer's daily wage (Matt 20:2; Tacitus, *Annals* 1.17). To put these numbers in perspective, one can note that Cicero made 150,000 denarii per year; officeholders under Augustus, 2,500–10,000 denarii per year; and procurators like Pilate, 15,000–75,000 denarii per year.[11] So the wages in Luke are middle class at best. Given the fluctuating values of money across time, it is better to figure the debt in relative terms of basic wages than to figure its current monetary equivalent: about two months' wages versus one-and-three-quarter-years' wages (assuming a six-day work week). The picture prepares us to see how great God's forgiveness is.

Then comes the twist to the story. It is often a characteristic of Jesus' parables that they have some striking feature. The twist supplies the element that Jesus uses to make his point. The moneylender, rather than forcing the debtors to pay, freely forgives the debt. A modern analogy might be the cancellation of a house mortgage or a debt on a car. The verb used for forgiving the debt, χαρίζομαι (*charizomai*), was a common business term for remitting debt and is the verb that will be used later in

---

8. See ch. 8.

9. Todd Klutz, *The Exorcism Stories in Luke-Acts: A Sociostylistic Reading* (SNTSMS 129; Cambridge: Cambridge Univ. Press, 2004).

10. Ibid., 267. Later on the same page, Klutz notes Jesus "looks less like a shaman than like the ultimate source of theraputic power in the entire cosmos." He "uniquely bears in his own person the power of God" (p. 268). Ultimately, Klutz argues that this sets up part of what Luke does in Acts with Paul and his exorcism in Acts 16. It links Paul to Jesus' authority, showing Paul "could not have been connected with a higher source of authority and status than

that with which Luke identifies him" (p. 268). The goal of the entire exercise is to give reassurance "that Paul and the Jesus he preached were loyal to Jewish ancestral custom and legitimate heirs to the heritage of Israel" (p. 265). All of this suggests an audience that was partly Jewish and/or composed of Gentiles who had sympathized with Judaism before becoming connected to the new movement, people such as Lydia in Acts 16. All of these comments by Klutz express Luke's intentions well.

11. Nolland, *Luke 1:1–9:20*, 355.

Scripture for the free offer of God's grace.[12] The verse describes the act of a money-lender that is totally out of character for the average debt collector. The forgiving of the debt is unexpected, but it would be welcome news to someone with no money to pay it off. The remitting of debt should be seen as extraordinary, despite efforts to appeal to OT precedent (Lev 25:8–17; Deut 15) for forgiving such debts.[13] It is the unmerited character of the act that is the basis for the gratitude.

Jesus makes this point by raising a question: Which of the two debtors will respond with greater love? Simon answers the question correctly in the next verse by noting that the larger the debt that is forgiven, the larger the gratitude and love that emerge in the response. The joining of love and gratitude in this way through the term ἀγαπάω (agapaō, "to love") is indicated in the rest of the parable (Luke 7:44–46). Jesus argues the greater the sense of what has been forgiven, the deeper the love and gratitude that results. Salvation is seen as removing a great debt that is to make one deeply grateful to God.

The presence of salvation also brings a risk because of spiritual opposition to it. So Jesus warns that the devil takes the seed of the word of the kingdom from some lest they believe and be saved (Luke 8:12). The only seed that bears fruit comes when the word of the kingdom is received with patient endurance (8:15).

A woman healed of a flow of blood is saved by her faith, even though her faith is less than perfect, since Jesus stops her to lead her to disclose what she had hoped for (Luke 8:48). Jesus calls on Jairus to believe and his daughter will be saved (8:50). This cluster of texts in the midst of Jesus' ministry shows how the call of salvation involves a call to trust the one who brings it. The theme is repeated shortly before Jesus enters Jerusalem with the faith of the blind man who seeks healing from the Son of David—who sees with the eyes of faith (18:42).

The giving of one's self over to faith in God is seen as the essence of discipleship. So Jesus notes that to seek to save one's own life means one will lose it, but to lose one's life will mean one will be saved (Luke 9:24). This remark should be seen in the context of Jesus' suffering and rejection, an idea he has just introduced in 9:21–22. To seek to save one's life is to seek the world's acceptance. To lose one's life is to identify with Jesus and face rejection by the world for making the choice.

In Luke 13:23, Jesus is asked if only a few will be saved. This generates a reply that speaks of the need to enter by the narrow door. The issue is that the doorkeeper will not know some who knock at the door. A glimpse at the room shows many from east and west, north and south, who are there along with Abraham, Isaac, Jacob, and the prophets. So many will be saved from all the nations, but some of those with the closest opportunity to be saved will not be there. The question becomes not whether many are saved but whether the one asking will be saved. In other words, the question is not will the saved be few, but will the saved be you?

Another challenge to salvation is wealth, a point already noted in the seed choked

---

by the thorns (Luke 8:14). Jesus notes that it is easier for a camel to go through the eye of a needle than for a rich person to enter the kingdom. Because of the common association of wealth with blessing, the disciples inquire who then can be saved (18:26). Jesus answers that with God it is possible, and then he encourages the disciples that they have done what God has asked to enter into eternal life.

In one of a handful of mission statements Jesus makes in the gospel, he notes how the Son of Man came to seek and save the lost (Luke 19:10). Here the emphasis is on how God takes the initiative to save. Earlier Jesus had said his mission was to do the Father's business (2:49), to preach the kingdom in various locales (4:44), and to call the sick to repentance (5:32). The goal of this mission is nicely stated in the Luke 19 remark about seeking the lost. Some rich people do come to Jesus, but they do so like others—in humility, recognizing their need. The picture of seeking and saving the lost recalls the shepherd imagery applied to God in Ezek 34. What God was to do for the nation as its shepherd because the nation of Ezekiel's time was leaderless, Jesus does now. Invoking Ezek 34 suggests a Davidic backdrop to this declaration.

The last uses of "save" in Luke's gospel are ironic. Jesus is mocked as he hangs on the cross by those who taunt him to save himself, especially since he "saved others" (Luke 23:35). The irony is that Jesus is in the business of saving others before God saves him in vindication through resurrection. The unbelieving thief on the cross continues the taunting saying, "Aren't you the Messiah? Save yourself and us!" (23:39). It is with this irony surrounding Jesus' death that the idea of salvation is last explicitly expressed in Luke's gospel. Luke 24 speaks of forgiveness of sins and hope of redemption, but the word "saved" is not used there (24:41–47).

Salvation in Luke's gospel is about responding in faith and trust to what God offers everywhere to people through Jesus. It is pictured in the acts of healing that Jesus brings. It is prepared for through a humble response of repentance before God that looks to reorient the way one relates to God and others. Wealth and acceptance by the world can get in the way of response. But God takes the initiative to reach people. He does so through the irony of Jesus' suffering and death, a death that is not permanent because God vindicated Jesus in his resurrection.

10.3 SALVATION IN THE BOOK OF ACTS

Salvation first emerges in Luke's second volume in Acts 2. Here one who "calls on the name of the Lord will be saved" (2:21). Peter's use of Joel 2:32 to make this point also has an important development from its use in the Hebrew Scripture. When Peter initially makes this remark in his speech, the listener would assume that one calls on the God of Israel for this salvation, but by the time his speech ends, it is clear that it is the name of Jesus Christ, who is Lord as well as Messiah, that is invoked (Acts 2:30–38).

Acts 2:38 deserves a closer look on this point. The person who turns toward God calls on the name of the Lord by being baptized "in the name of Jesus Christ."

This phrase reflects the language of the speech in 2:21. So Peter's remarks draw on what he has already proclaimed in Acts 2. The rite is not magical but pictures what repentance is asking God to do, to give forgiveness (5:31; 10:43; 13:38; 26:18). To agree to baptism is to affirm in a public act what the heart has already done to come into relationship with God. "Baptism is a natural part of the much more important conversion" and a "self-evident expression of conversion."[14]

Thus, baptism is the representation of the cleansing that belongs to salvation. This washing signifies the forgiveness of sins that Jesus brings and the emergence into a new, clean life with fresh enablement that his work provides (Rom 6:1–11). Peter calls for each person to be baptized in order to express a personal, visible turning to God. That baptism takes place in the name of Jesus Christ shows the authority Jesus has at God's side in heaven. Now one appeals to God through this formerly crucified one. One calls on him to be saved (Acts 2:21). This interchange between God the Father and the Messiah as the one called upon shows the unity of the work between God and the Exalted One. This reflects the tight overlap and linkage that Luke has between God and the sent one. Salvation is their joint work.

In the midst of Peter's speech connection is also made to David and the promise to him of one to be set on his throne, an allusion to Ps 132:11. This psalm in turn alludes to the Davidic covenant of 2 Sam 7. God's salvation is connected to his covenant promises.

Peter also stresses the need for this salvation in light of the plight of a world inhabited by a perverse generation from which people need to be saved (Acts 2:40). The reference to a "corrupt generation" appears only here in the NT and alludes to a generation that is ethically crooked, spiritually off the path to God, and thus subject to judgment. With an ethical force, it refers to "social and ethical misconduct which is rooted in ungodliness and unbelief."[15]

The full phrase does not appear in the LXX, but the shorter one without the articles is found in Deut 32:5 and Ps 78:8 (77:8 LXX). Both are allusions to the rebellious generation that wandered in the wilderness.[16] Peter urges his audience to experience salvation and deliverance from the coming judgment. The context of this remark is the shadow of the coming day of the Lord with the judgment of God that comes with it (Acts 2:20). Salvation is not an entitlement that is automatic. It must be embraced on God's terms.

The community that responds can be called the "saved." In Acts 2:47, God was adding daily to the number of the saved.

The stages of salvation are featured in Acts 3, though the term does not appear. In this speech Peter sets forth the offer of salvation as a result of repenting and turning (Acts 3:19). He then goes on to speak of heaven holding Jesus until a time to come that the Scriptures describe, the establishing of all things that God spoke by the mouth of his holy prophets of old. The point is that the rest of the story is revealed

---

14. Schweizer, *TDNT*, 6:413–14.
15. Bertram, *TDNT*, 7:406–7.

16. Larkin, *Acts*, 60; also in the NT, Phil 2:15; conceptually, Luke 9:41; 11:29; Heb 3:10.

in Scripture. This period is called both the "times of refreshing" and "the time ... to restore everything" (3:19–21). So Peter has taken what he has heard in 1:6–11 and now speaks of a return of Jesus as kingdom blessing comes in two phases.

As in the gospel, signs of healing picture the deliverance. So a lame man is made whole through the name of Jesus Christ of Nazareth, the rejected stone, yet the only one through whom salvation comes (Acts 4:9–12). The appeal here is to Ps 118:22 and the welcome God gave to the rejected one. Vindication shows who saves.

Numerous texts in Acts speak of healing in a way that pictures and points to Jesus' role in deliverance (Acts 4:14; 5:16; 8:7; 9:34; 12:11; 14:9, where the point is the person has faith to be delivered). In Peter's speech in Acts 3, he makes an appeal to Torah teaching, the prophet like Moses, and the Abrahamic covenant in calling on people to embrace Jesus, the one whom God exalted as a part of what salvation entails (3:11–26). Blessing comes to the world through Abraham's seed (3:25–26). Those who turn to God from their wickedness experience this blessing. This idea is repeated later in the debate surrounding this healing when Peter notes that God exalted Jesus as Leader and Savior to give repentance to Israel and forgiveness of sins (5:31). It is clear from several texts that repentance is a key component of responding to the offer of salvation. We will consider this theme in more detail in the next chapter.

God was in the business of deliverance in the past (Acts 7:10, 25, 34). One has the sense that Stephen is setting up a parallel between Moses and Jesus, but he never gets there since his speech is interrupted when he accuses the people of always resisting God's Spirit.

Peter is sent to Cornelius to bring a message by which he and his household can "be saved" (Acts 11:14). That salvation comes becomes apparent when the Spirit dscends on his house. This theme is picked up at the Jerusalem Council in Acts 15, where some argue that one cannot be saved without circumcision (15:1). Peter, however, replies that "it is through the grace of the Lord Jesus that we are saved" (15:11). In making this point, he notes how salvation is the same for Jew and Gentile since both have received the Spirit.

Part of the key here is that Gentiles received the Spirit while still being uncircumcised. This divine act showed that God had cleansed them without their being required to be circumcised (Acts 15:9). In the ensuing explanation, James invokes Amos 9:11–12 LXX and points to the rebuilt tent of David that paves the way for Gentiles to be called by God's name and so become members of God's people (15:14–17). The idea that Gentiles can "bear [God's] name" is stated twice in these verses. This idea is significant, for salvation is about being incorporated into a unified body of God's people. This points to a reconciliation that Peter highlighted when he said that God makes no distinction between people (10:34).

Paul preaches the message of salvation about a Savior, Jesus, a descendant of David (Acts 13:23, 26). This fulfills the promises of Davidic hope (as Ps 2:7 shows). It also fulfills the hope of the people to share in that promise as the citation about "the holy and sure blessings promised to David" from Isa 55:3 shows. In several speeches Acts highlights different covenant commitments Jesus fulfills. In this speech as well "forgiveness of sins" and "justification" are invoked (13:38–39). The realized promise of salvation deals with covenant hope and leads to one being declared righteous by God.

A most significant text is Acts 13:46–47. Here Paul and Barnabas turn to the Gentiles after being rejected in Pisidian Antioch. They cast themselves in the role of the servant of God as followers of Jesus. Their mission statement is to be "a light for the Gentiles, that you may bring salvation to the ends of the earth" (cf. Isa 49:6). The verse deserves a closer look.

Three points dominate verses 46–47. (1) They (the Jews in Pisidian Antioch) have rejected the message (see ἀπωθεῖσθε, *apōtheisthe*, lit., "you thrust out"). This is a graphic term for pushing something away forcefully. As a group, the Jews have taken God's Word and have pushed it aside or repudiated it (1 Sam 12:22; Pss 61:5; 76:8; 77:60, 67 LXX [62:4; 77:7; 78:60, 67 Eng.]; Jer 23:17; Acts 7:27, 39).[17]

(2) These Jews have judged themselves not to be "worthy of eternal life," which is another way of describing what salvation is by highlighting its content. So rejection and their lack of salvation are their responsibility. This passage (here and in v. 48) is the only place in Acts that "eternal life" appears. Acts 5:20 and 11:18 are close with references to "life" (Luke 10:25; 18:18, 30; Gal 6:8; 1 Tim 6:12; in the OT and Judaism: Dan 12:2; Sir 37:26; 4Q181 1.4, 6; 1QS 4.7; CD 3.20; 4Q511 2.1.4; 6Q18 2.2).[18] The message of salvation is now equated with the hope of eternal life.

(3) Thus, finally, Paul will "now turn to the Gentiles." This is the first of several places in Acts where Paul goes to the Gentiles after being rejected by most Jews (Acts 18:6; 28:28). This turning away is not absolute, however. In each place Paul subsequently goes, he always starts by preaching to Jews (14:1; 18:4–6, 19; 19:8–9; 28:28 followed by vv. 30–31, where he speaks to all; this is explained in Rom 9–11). Paul repeatedly faces violent resistance in many synagogues (2 Cor 11:24), but he continues to preach to Jews. In this he turns the other cheek, as Jesus commanded in the Sermon on the Mount (Matt 5:39).

In Acts 13:47, Paul turns to Scripture, explaining how the Lord commands the missionaries' response. This alludes to Paul's commission noted in 9:15 and what is reported in 22:18, that Paul will be called as the apostle to the Gentiles. The entire series of remarks connects to things said earlier in Acts and parallels to Luke's gospel. This shows how important this event is to the book. Paul's ministry mirrors that of Jesus and the apostles. He is also obedient to the commission God has given him. He perseveres, modeling the commitment of the church to all people as the church brings a message of salvation to the world.

Not only does this key passage repeat the language of Luke 2:32 and Acts 1:8, but it stresses that salvation will go out to all of humanity, using the language of the Hebrew Scripture to support the move and call. The inclusion of Gentiles in blessing is a part of Israel's story according to Luke. God is not forcing a choice

---

between Gentiles and Jews; rather, he is reaching out with the offer of salvation to both of them.

A curious use of the idea of being saved and a rejection of its public use occurs when the Philippian slave girl follows Paul and declares that he is proclaiming "the way to be saved." This leads to Paul's rebuke and his casting out of the demon (Acts 16:17). Most likely the association of this woman with spirits and divination causes Paul to act in silencing her, even though ironically what she says is true.

An important exchange takes place with the Philippian jailer. When he asks, "What must I do to be saved"? (Acts 16:30), Paul replies, "Believe in the Lord Jesus, and you will be saved—you and your household." Here the response to salvation is summarized as faith in the Lord Jesus, the one who has authority over salvation. Luke emphasizes who saves far more than he outlines how salvation occurs (which Paul describes in greater detail).

Several remaining uses of the picture of being saved come in the rescue from the storm of Acts 27 and the following events in Malta (27:26, 31, 34; 28:1, 4, 8–9). These uses are not technically theological, but they do reflect a common everyday use of the term. Yet even these scenes are relevant. For in them it is shown how responding to Paul and believing him lead to deliverance. Much as healings point to salvation, so this scene shows how Paul's connection to God authenticates his message of salvation, as well as showing him to be a trustworthy messenger. This is not to say all who survive the shipwreck are saved in an ultimate sense. It is merely to argue that Luke pictures salvation and the credibility of Paul through this event.

The final use of being saved comes in yet another announcement of turning to the Gentiles with the salvation of God in Acts 28:28. Yet even with this Paul continues to share the gospel with any who will hear. In 28:30–31, Paul welcomes all who come to him; he preaches the kingdom of God and teaches about Jesus openly and unhindered. Acts ends on this triumphant note of the word of salvation going forth in the capital city of the Roman empire. The word of salvation is reaching the ends of the earth.

10.4 CONCLUSION

Salvation in Luke is a broad concept. It is about comprehensive deliverance and restoration. It is pictured in the signs of the scope of Jesus' healings as well as those of the apostles. It frees people from sin, from Satan, and from darkness, and it results in forgiveness, the gift of the Spirit, and incorporation into a people of God made up of all nations. It reorients how one sees justice. It changes how one conducts relationships as it reverses the way people are seen. It means being ready to face rejection by the world. It is received as one repents, turns, or exercises faith—all descriptions of the same fundamental embrace of God and his sent agent, Jesus Christ. Ironically, it becomes possible through a death that God vindicates in the resurrection-ascension. In other words, one calls out for God's salvation by calling out in the name of Jesus Christ, the Lord.

Chapter 11

THE MANY DIMENSIONS OF SALVATION IN LUKE-ACTS: A SYNTHESIS

BIBLIOGRAPHY

See chapter 10.

L ooking at Lucan salvation in a more synthetic way takes us in many directions. Soteriology is a vast field in Luke's writings. Some see it as the theme of the two volumes.[1] I prefer to see it as a key element in the larger theme of the legitimization of the new community as reflecting God's work of salvation to bring Jew and Gentile together. Either way, salvation is a central element of Luke's discussion.

In discussing salvation, two categories are basic. "Objective salvation" refers to what God has done as well as the delivery of the message about that work, and "subjective salvation" refers to the responses of people that permit them to share in the benefits God has provided. We will first examine the act of proclaiming the good news, giving attention to the scope of salvation, including both Jews and Gentiles and other mentioned groups. Also requiring attention is the means by which God supported the message and gave it authentication.[2]

With such background in place, the treatment of objective salvation follows first. Then we will examine subjective salvation. The benefits received in salvation will be discussed next, followed by a consideration of some tangential issues in soteriology (e.g., How does the salvation message relate to promise? What is Luke's view of the law?).[3]

11.1 THE ACT OF PROCLAIMING GOOD NEWS

11.1.1 The Gospel

In Acts, the word "gospel" (εὐαγγέλιον, *euangelion*) occurs only twice. Peter notes that the "message of the gospel" went to the Gentiles through him (Acts 15:7). The good news is about the grace that comes through faith in Jesus Christ (15:9–11).

---

1. Green, *Gospel of Luke*, 21; Marshall, *Luke: Historian and Theologian*.

2. See Ben Witherington, "Salvation and Health in Christian Antiquity: The Soteriology of Luke-Acts in Its First Century Setting," in *Witness to the Gospel*, 145–66. He discusses this theme

in part in the context of ancient views of benefaction and closes by noting that it is not the emperor who is the source of greatest blessing but Jesus Christ, because his largesse is both temporal and eternal (p. 166).

3. Chapter 18 is a full chapter on Luke's view of the law.

Acts 10:34–43 is a good example of the gospel message Peter preached to Gentiles. Paul says that his life is given over for the testimony of "the gospel of God's grace" (20:24). So the gospel is tied to God's work of grace, the gifting of salvation to those who respond to the divine work through Jesus.

The use of the verb "proclaim the good news" (εὐαγγελίζω, *euangelizō*) occurs more often in Luke-Acts than elsewhere in the NT. Angelic announcements of John's and Jesus' births are said to be "good news" (Luke 1:19; 2:10). John's message of repentance in preparation for the coming of salvation is the preaching of good news (3:18). This verb is especially used of Jesus' message to the poor (4:18; 7:22), his preaching the message of the kingdom (4:43; 8:1; 16:16), or his preaching the gospel (9:6; 20:1). Many of these uses come in texts summarizing Jesus' ministry.

In Acts, the content of the good news is more specific. The apostles proclaim the message that "Jesus is the Christ" (Acts 5:42). Other verses also point out that Jesus is the focus of the apostles' preaching (8:35; 10:36; 11:20; 17:18). Some passages call this message the preaching of the word (8:4; 15:35), while others refer to the promise of the fathers (13:32). Still another speaks simply of the kingdom and Jesus (8:12). However, the most common expression is simply to preach the gospel (8:25, 40; 14:7, 21; 16:10). Most of those uses also involve summary declarations.

Acts 10:36 is a representative text on this theme, where Peter reviews the gospel and its Jewish roots. He observes that God sent the word to Israel, offering peace through Jesus Christ. The syntax is complex. The term "word" (λόγον, *logon*) is placed forward in the Greek sentence for emphasis ("the word that he sent to the sons of Israel, preaching good news …"). It also is assimilated to the accusative relative pronoun that follows, which in turn is in apposition to the thought of 10:34–35 and expresses what Peter realizes, namely, that "God does not show favoritism but accepts from every nation the one who fears him and does what is right." The point is that the extension of the word of this salvation to Gentiles is something Peter knows is taking place.[4] The word here refers to the apostolic, preached message about Jesus and the gospel.[5]

The gospel message contains an opportunity for "peace" (εἰρήνην, *eirēnēn*). This is the concept of shalom from the OT (Pss 29:11; 72:7; 85:8–10; Prov 3:17; Isa 48:18; 54:10; Ezek 34:25–29), a well-being of relationship between a person and God, which now seems to express itself in peace between people as well (Eph 2:11–22). The idea of preaching peace recalls OT ideas (Isa 52:7; Nah 1:15). When Peter says "you know" about these things, he suggests that Cornelius is likely to be aware of this ministry, possibly because Cornelius has associated himself with the synagogue as a God-fearer. Indeed, such a report went about the region of Judea from the time of John's baptism. It was a spreading verbal communication (ῥῆμα, *rhēma*) of what God did through Jesus, as Acts 10:38–41 shows. This term is dis-

---

4. Fitzmyer, *Acts of the Apostles*, 463; BDF, §295.
5. Kittel, *TDNT*, 4:120.

tinct from the earlier term for "word" in v. 36 (λόγον, *logon*). So Jesus is a topic of public discourse.

What makes Jesus important is what God is doing through him. God has brought peace through what Jesus did, and this Jesus is described as Lord of all (Acts 2:36; Rom 10:12). This title presents the christological theme of the speech. The exalted Jesus is Lord over all people. Therefore, the gospel can go to all people, including Gentiles such as Cornelius. Jesus' authority is described in the next few verses as a function of his work that came through God's anointing him with the Spirit and power so that he could do good and heal those oppressed by the devil. Even though the remark is parenthetical grammatically, it is the theme of the speech conceptually. Jesus has authority to deliver the peace that comes from God to those of every nation. His activity and God's vindication of him show this. God takes the initiative here, as is always the case in Acts. The message comes from God.

Salvation surfaces again as a theme in the ministry of Barnabas and Paul. The emphasis shifts slightly as they preach to Gentiles with no background in the synagogue. Here it is idolatry that is addressed most directly by what salvation brings. So according to Acts 14:15, Barnabas and Paul present themselves as mere mortals in light of claims they are gods. They preach that the gospel means turning from "worthless things [idols] to the living God, who made the heavens and the earth and the sea and everything in them."

Paul asks why the crowd seeks to offer sacrifices when Paul and Barnabas are mere mortals (ὁμοιοπαθεῖς, *homoiopatheis*, lit., of like passions; Jas 5:17; similarly, Acts 10:26). They are no different from anyone in the crowd; they are simply creatures of the Creator God.

The question "Why are you doing these things?" is really a request to stop.[6] The only goal of Paul and Barnabas is to bring the good news to the crowd that they should turn from vain idols (Rom 1:21) to the living Creator God. This is classic prophetic Jewish natural theology (as in Isa 40 – 41).[7] This also is the first speech to purely pagan Gentiles in Acts, for Cornelius had an acquaintance with the God of Israel as a God-fearer.[8] To this audience, Paul preaches that they must change orientation from vain and dead idols to the God who lives and is the Creator of heaven and earth and everything in them (cf. Luke 1:16 – 17; Acts 3:19; 17:25 – 26). It is God as Creator who makes his creatures accountable to him. This point is the foundation stone of Jewish thought about the relationship between God and his creatures.

Beyond this there is something new in God's relationship to Gentiles. In the past, God let the nations go their own way, but not so anymore. That former time is what Acts 17:30 will call the times of "ignorance." In other OT and Jewish texts,

---

6. BDF, §299.1.

7. Bruce, *Acts of the Apostles*, 323; Acts 17:24. See also Exod 20:11 – 12; 1 Kgs 16:2, 13, 26; 2 Kgs 17:15; Esth 4:17 LXX [Add. Esth 13:8 – 14 Eng.]; Ps 145:6 LXX [146:6 Eng.]; Jer 2:5; 8:19; Neh 9:6; 3 Macc 6:11 (addressed to the living Creator God); 4Q521 2.2.2; in the NT: 1 Thess 1:9 – 10, but the 1 Thess 1:10 point is not

in Acts. Also Johnson, *The Acts of the Apostles*, 249.

8. B. Gärtner, "Paulus und Barnabas in Lystra: Zu Apg. 14,8 – 15," *Svensk exegetisk årsbok* 27 (1991): 83 – 88; F. G. Downing, "Common Ground with Paganism in Luke and Josephus," *NTS* 28 (1982): 546 – 59.

such vain pursuit of idols is called foolishness (Isa 2:20 LXX; 30:7; 31:2; Ezek 8:10; Wis 13:1; 3 Macc 6:11). In Rom 1:20, Paul suggests that the nature of this new revelation about salvation among the Gentiles leaves them without excuse for not responding to the Creator God, a point Paul is now trying to drive home but with a more gentle emphasis (Rom 2:14–16; 1 Cor 1:20–21).[9]

The absence of any mention of Jesus in the Acts 14:15–17 message is striking but not surprising, since first there must be established that there is only one God (Deut 6:4), to whom all are responsible and whose will stands revealed. The "living" God stands in contrast to and implies "dead" idols (Isa 37:4, 17; Hos 2:1 LXX [1:10 Eng.]; 4:15; Dan 5:23; 6:27).[10] God is the Creator, who shows mercy and yet reveals much kindness in the creation.

Polhill argues that the message is cut short; this is possible.[11] Jervell calls the unit not a full missionary speech of the kerygma, but simply a polemical response to stop the sacrifice; this also is a likely reading of the unit.[12] The chaotic nature of the scene may prevent a full missionary speech. Paul rejects polytheism here, especially an effort to worship mere mortals.[13] Paul and Barnabas hold to one God and one message of salvation. So that is what Paul preaches because he believes that the view is rooted in the activity and revelation of God. One cannot discuss Jesus without first establishing that God is one. That the early church worshiped Jesus in light of such feelings about the worship of humans is significant, for it shows that Jesus clearly was seen as more than a mere mortal.

Paul declares that God is now more actively engaged with the nations than in years past. In Acts 14:16 the dative ταῖς παρῳχημέναις γενεαῖς (*tais parōchēmenais geneais*, lit., "in past generations") is temporal here.[14] During past generations he allowed the nations to walk in their own way, but this is no longer the case. The verb εἴασεν (*eiasen*, "let") speaks of God's lack of direct, active spiritual engagement with the nations. God allowed them to go "their own way," where ταῖς ὁδοῖς (*tais hodois*) is a dative of rule, indicating a standard of orientation.[15]

There was no special revelation for the nations as Paul is giving now, although there was general revelation and providence, as Paul notes in Acts 14:17. God gives the rain, the seasons, and "plenty of food." God's provision of enough food "fills" your hearts with joy (ἐμπιπλῶν, *empiplōn*). This verb means "fill" to the full (Luke 1:53; 6:25; John 6:12; Rom 15:24 are the other NT uses).[16] The grace of the care of creation in rain, seasons, and fruit is also a prevalent idea in the OT (Gen 8:22; Pss 4:7; 145:15–16; 147:8–9; Isa 25:6; Jer 5:24; Eccl 9:7; cf. Luke 12:22–34). In other words, God gives abundant care to all. Paul's speech barely restrains the crowd from sacrificing to the apostolic messengers (Acts 14:18). Nevertheless, the speech

---

9. Polhill, *Acts*, 316; Bruce, *Acts of the Apostles*, 324; against Haenchen, *Acts of the Apostles*, 428.

10. Fitzmyer, *Acts of the Apostles*, 532.

11. Polhill, *Acts*, 316.

12. Jervell, *Apostelgeschichte*, 376–78.

13. Hans Josef Klauck, *Magic and Paganism in Early Christianity:*

The World of the Acts of the Apostles (Minneapolis: Fortress, 2003), 60.

14. BDF, §200.4.

15. BDAG, 269 §1.

16. BDAG, 323.

shows how the early community preached salvation to those with no background of believing in a single God or in the promise of Scripture.

In such a speech, the gospel is an invitation to come to the living Creator God and to enter into a dependent relationship with him. At the center of the gospel in most of the speeches of Acts stand the person and work of Jesus. Those speeches that do not mention him serve to introduce the one God, setting the stage for later mention of Jesus. The longer version of the type of speech we see in Acts 14 takes place in Athens in Acts 17. There Jesus is referred to (17:31), even though that speech also is not a full presentation, since it is also interrupted by the discussion that ensues about resurrection. Jesus is the promised one, the Christ, to Jews (2:36). The promise of the fathers finds fulfillment in him (3:13–14). The kingdom is bound up with him. Peace is through him (10:36). To Gentiles, he is the judge of the living and the dead (10:42–43; 17:31). Accountability to God is what gets the attention in these speeches to non-God-fearing Gentiles on salvation.

In these various speeches about salvation and through a myriad of images, the gospel points to Jesus as people are invited to come to know God through forgiveness. This call to be related to God through Christ summarizes the gospel as presented in Luke's writings. It is the offer of forgiveness and then life, life given through the Spirit of God, the sign of the new era.

11.1.2 Preaching

The noun "preaching" (κήρυγμα, kērygma) is rare, appearing in Luke's writings only in Luke 11:32, where the message of repentance Jonah preached is compared to Jesus' message. The verb "to preach" (κηρύσσω, kēryssō) is more frequent. John the Baptist preached a baptism of repentance (3:3). Jesus preached in the synagogue about the arrival of "the year of the Lord's favor," a picture of forgiveness made through Jesus' appeal to the OT image of Jubilee (4:18–19; cf. Lev 25, esp. v. 10). Jesus preached the good news of the kingdom in the synagogues of Judea (Luke 4:43–44; 8:1). The disciples also preached the kingdom (9:2). On occasion, the verb κηρύσσω is used to describe how others told people about what Jesus had done for them (8:39). As such, the term means the same as giving testimony. Jesus also notes that a day will come when everything people said secretly will be preached from the rooftops (12:3). This does not refer to the preaching of salvation, but to judgment in the eschaton.

In Acts, Christ is the one preached. Acts 10:42–43 gives a significant summary of the apostles' preaching. As witnesses they are commissioned to testify that Jesus is the one God "appointed as judge of the living and the dead," i.e., of all people. That Jesus is judge is what his resurrection attests to. This role partially explains why he is called Lord (John 5:22, 27; Rom 14:9; 2 Tim 4:1; 1 Pet 4:5; *2 Clem.* 1.1).[17] He is the ultimate eschatological judge, possessing full authority over life and death. In

---

17. Fitzmyer, *Acts of the Apostles*, 466.

Judaism the Son of Man had such an exalted role (*1 En.* 38–71 [e.g., 46:4; 48:2; 62:7], drawn from Dan 7:9–14). This title was Jesus' favorite self-designation. In Greek, Jesus' judging role as Lord (Acts 10:36) expresses the same idea as Son of Man. This idea will appear again in 17:31.

In Acts 10:43, all the prophets bear witness that "everyone who believes in him receives forgiveness of sins through his name." Barrett suggests that the allusion here is to the new covenant (Jer 38:34 LXX [31:34 MT and Eng.]), whereas Fitzmyer thinks that this is another example of Luke's general appeal to the OT (Luke 24:25–27, 44; Acts 8:35).[18] Marshall speaks of allusions to Isa 33:24; 53:4; Jer 31:34; Dan 9:24.[19] Here Peter underscores that it is faith in the Jesus he has just described that brings the forgiveness. So the way of salvation is through the judge of the living and the dead, by appealing to him to forgive sin, which leads into the way of peace through the gospel (Acts 10:35). Everyone who believes in this forgiveness receives this salvation. Christians are described as "those who believe," a key response in Acts.[20] Both apostolic witness and OT prophetic witness testify to Jesus.

A nonsoteriological use of κηρύσσω is in Acts 15:21, which refers to the fact that Moses was being preached every Sabbath in the synagogues. And, of course, Paul presents Jesus or the kingdom (19:13; 20:25; 28:31). As Luke-Acts progresses, the message of salvation becomes more focused on Jesus than on anything or anyone else.

11.1.3 Teaching

Jesus is described as one whose "teaching" (διδαχῇ, *didachē*) brought astonishment because of its authority (Luke 4:32). Of course, illustrations of his teaching occur throughout the gospel of Luke. He taught with sayings, parables, and prophetic actions, along with several major discourses (4:16–30; 6:20–49; 11:37–52; 15:1–32; 17:20–37; 21:5–36; 22:14–38). The topics range from salvation from sin to life with God, from Jesus' current ministry to his return. Jews saved on the day of Pentecost followed in the apostles' "teaching" (Acts 2:42). The consternation of the Jewish leadership (5:28) and the astonishment of the synagogue audiences (13:12) greeted the apostolic message as well. In Athens, Paul's message of the resurrection was called a "new teaching" (17:19).

Like the noun διδαχή, Luke uses the verb "to teach" (διδάσκω, *didaskō*) to summarize Jesus' and the apostles' teaching. Jesus taught in the synagogues on the Sabbath; in public settings as on a boat by the shore, in towns, and in villages; and in the temple (Luke 4:15, 30; 5:3, 17; 6:6; 13:10, 22, 26; 19:47; 20:1; 21:37). Luke is particularly fond of Jesus' teaching at meals (5:29; 7:36; 9:16; 11:37; 12:37; 13:29; 14:1, 8–9; 22:14; 24:30). Luke is concerned to show that teaching takes place in settings where a sense of intimacy with the teacher is established. Only once is teaching requested of Jesus, when his disciples ask him to teach them to pray (11:1). Jesus'

---

18. Barrett, *Critical and Exegetical Commentary on the Acts of the Apostles*, 1:528; Fitzmyer, *Acts of the Apostles*, 466.

19. Marshall, *Acts of the Apostles*, 193.

20. Passages referring to those who believe: Acts 9:42; 11:17; 14:23; 16:31; 19:4; use of the verb "to believe," 5:14; 8:12; 16:34; 18:8; 24:14; 26:27; 27:25.

opponents acknowledge that he is a teacher, though they accuse him of stirring up trouble in Judea and Galilee (20:21; 23:5). Jesus tells his disciples that the Spirit will teach them what to say when they face persecution (12:12).

In Acts, the emphasis on teaching sometimes looks back at Jesus the teacher (Acts 1:1). The apostles teach the people about the resurrection and the name of Jesus, which annoys the authorities (4:2, 18; 5:21, 25, 28, 42). Barnabas and Saul teach the disciples in Antioch, where disciples are first called Christians (11:26; 15:35). Some Judaizers wrongly teach that Gentile Christians must be circumcised (15:1). Paul teaches in various locales, including Corinth (18:11) and Ephesus (18:25), where he teaches "the way of the Lord." Later, he offers the Ephesian elders a summary of his teaching of repentance toward God and faith in the Lord Jesus (20:20). Paul's opponents charge him with teaching against the people and Moses (21:21, 28). Acts closes with Paul teaching about the Lord Jesus Christ (28:31).

Teaching in Luke-Acts is a broad term encompassing much more than the offer of the gospel, whereas preaching in Luke-Acts tends to be limited to the salvation message. As Luke-Acts progresses, Luke's presentation of the gospel message becomes more focused on Jesus. That message is still one message and one hope because of its link to God's promise, but the center of the promise residing in Jesus emerges most clearly after his resurrection. Prior to that, the kingdom and the salvation that came with the new era formed the key topic. But Jesus and the kingdom are still being preached in Acts right up to the end; thus, the difference is one of emphasis, not of substance (8:12; 28:30–31).

11.2 THE SCOPE OF SALVATION

11.2.1 The Promise for Jews and Gentiles

Luke emphasizes that what Jesus provides is available to everyone. This point gradually emerges in the infancy narrative's overview of salvation. Zechariah speaks of Jesus, the "horn" in David's house (Luke 1:69), as a rising light (Num 24:17; Isa 9:2–7) that will shine on those who sit in darkness and death (Luke 1:78–79). Such activity is a fulfillment of God's promises. Angels tell the shepherds that Jesus has come to bring peace on earth for all those who are the object of God's good pleasure (2:14). Not every person automatically receives these benefits, but God in Jesus makes them available to those who respond and are a part of his people.

Those of God's good pleasure he calls to himself (Acts 2:39). The scope of this provision becomes clearer still in Luke 2:30–32, where Jesus is said to be a light given on the one hand for revelation to the Gentiles and on the other for the glory for Israel. This language is rooted in Isaiah (Isa 42:6; 46:13; 49:9). Thus the universality of God's work is noted early in Luke's introductory section in language that recalls OT promises about Messiah and his rule.

The body of Luke's gospel makes the same point. In an extended citation unique to Luke, the gospel writer includes Isa 40:3–5, which describes John the Baptist's ministry. The ending of the citation provides the emphasis with the words "all people will see God's salvation" (Luke 3:6). Here the scope of salvation becomes clear. The wording itself is not a direct citation but rather a summary of Isa 40:1–12, drawing on the imagery that comes from Isa 40:10–11, since the reference to "God's salvation" summarizes the picture of 40:10–11 in the Masoretic text, while Isa 40:5b in the LXX has already made the summarizing translation. This universal note occurs also in Luke 24:47, where the message of the new community is the preaching of repentance to all the nations. This message is said to be present in the Hebrew Scripture of Moses, the Prophets, and the Psalms (vv. 44–47). In extending salvation to the Gentiles, God's promises about the Messiah are being initially realized.

Acts continued this Gentile emphasis by citing Jesus' words that the message is to go "to the ends of the earth" (Acts 1:8). Geographically Acts presses forward to this goal as the message moves from Jerusalem, to Judea, to Samaria, and then on to Rome as a picture of its reaching into the world. The dramatic vision given to Peter (10:9–16) shows God's direction and intervention to guarantee and endorse this expansion, while Peter in his speech in Cornelius's house says that "God accepts from every nation the one who fears him" (10:35) and that salvation through Christ is available to "everyone who believes in him" (10:43). Acts 28:28 also makes explicit the fact that the message is for Gentiles.

This Gentile inclusion is a key theme in Luke. Its tie to the hope of the Hebrew Scriptures strikes a note of continuity in God's plan. To Jews in the community, this inclusion was a difficult point, since Israel had been God's special people. Therefore Luke spends much time on this theme. His point is that Israel's story always looked to include the blessing of the nations, beginning with Israel since that was the promise God made to Abraham (Acts 3:25–26) and to Isaiah (Luke 2:30–32; Acts 13:47).

Numerous texts picture this expansion of the gospel to Gentiles. Luke 7:1–10 describes a Gentile centurion whose faith exceeds anything found in Israel (7:9). That centurion's faith pictures what occurs in Acts: Gentiles respond to Jesus while many Jews reject him. Moreover, Luke shows that pious pagans can understand Jesus, who offers the path to God.[21]

What does Jesus commend as unique in the centurion's faith? It cannot be his recognition of miraculous power, for that had drawn wide response (Luke 4:40–41). This unique faith recognizes Jesus' authority and the power of his word, not only over illness but also in the face of his physical absence and distance. Magical presence or touch is not required for healing—only the power of Jesus' command and will. The centurion recognizes that God's power works through Jesus without spatial limitations. Jesus is entrusted with great authority. It is clear that entrusted power is in view because of the illustration of 7:8, where Jesus, like the centurion, is a man who has authority.

---

21. Bock, *Luke 1:1–9:50*, 642–43.

In addition, the centurion recognizes personal unworthiness. Humility mixed with deep faith describes what Jesus praises. The soldier approaches the man of God on proper terms. In the commendation, Jesus makes an indirect call to others to trust him in a similar way. Joel Green summarizes this faith this way: "Unlike Israel, he [the centurion] recognizes Jesus' authority and trusts that Jesus will exercise it on his behalf, even though, as a Gentile, even as one who acted on behalf of Israel, he does not deserve such treatment."[22] This lack of entitlement is part of the humility of faith that makes it something so commendable to Jesus. The question in effect is, "Will you trust as the centurion has?" Such faith brings Jesus' approval.

Jesus also ministers on occasion to Gentiles, as his trip into the Decapolis area east of the Jordan River shows. There Jesus exorcises a demon from a man in the Gentile region of Gerasene (Luke 8:26–39). Jesus also leads a mission to Samaria, a region of a mixed race (9:51–56). Samaritans are often seen positively in Luke's gospel. In the parable of the good Samaritan, a man regarded by Jews as a rank outsider responds to God's will properly in the treatment of others (10:25–37). Jesus speaks of people coming from east, west, north, and south to dine at the banquet table in the kingdom to come (13:22–30). In another parable, people from the highways and hedgeways were invited to share in the banquet that Jesus brings (14:15–24). In the episode of the ten lepers, only the Samaritan leper responded with gratitude for the healing he received (17:11–19). In the parable of the tenants (20:9–19), the vineyard will be given to others after the son is slain (v. 16). Jesus goes so far as to call the current age the "times of the Gentiles" (Luke 21:24).

Acts continues this emphasis. Acts 9:15 describes the call to Saul to bear Jesus' name before the Gentiles. Acts 10–11 shows how God directs Peter to Cornelius. God is the one who brings in the Gentiles. Of course, much of the rest of Acts shows how Gentiles are receptive to the gospel. If anyone was disturbed by the expanded racial breadth in the new community, there was only one figure to blame: God himself. He was the one who had orchestrated the effort on both sides, directing Cornelius and Peter to come together. Luke's emphasis on the universality of the gospel is an effective apologetic claim against any who think the gospel message in the church has become too broad, too generous, or too gracious.

11.2.2 To the Poor, Sinners, and Outcasts

Special attention is given to the poor in Luke's gospel.[23] Mary's hymn in Luke 1:46–55 sets the tone for this theme. Her reference to God's lifting up and blessing the poor (vv. 52–53) does not mean all the poor. It refers primarily to the ᶜᵃnâwîm of the OT, those pious poor who humbly relied on God (vv. 50–55; cf. Ps 9:18; 22:26; 37:11; Isa 11:4; 61:1; Zeph 2:3). This distinction is an important one for Luke, since

---

22. Green, *Gospel of Luke*, 288.
23. Walter Pilgrim, *Good News to the Poor: Wealth and Poverty in Luke-Acts* (Minneapolis: Augsburg, 1981), walks through this theme in detail. See also David Peter Seccombe, *Possessions and the Poor in Luke-Acts* (SNTSU; Linz: A. Fuchs, 1982); and S. John Roth, *The Blind, the Lame, and the Poor: Character Types in Luke-Acts* (JSNTSup 144; Sheffield: Sheffield Academic Press, 1997). Our study returns to it in more detail as well in ch. 17.

the focus on the poor was not primarily a political manifesto. However, the gospel does have social consequences insofar as social status should not matter in the new community. This passage indicates that often the poor are more dependent on God and in tune with his will than the rich are.

The focus on the poor is reinforced in three representative presentations of Jesus' preaching (Luke 4:18; 6:20–23; 7:22). In these passages, salvation is offered specifically to the poor. Jesus mentions the poor explicitly when he thanks the Father for those who are his ministering disciples (10:21–22). The poor are those who should be invited to the eschatological banquet table (14:13, 21–24). Here the social implications of responding to God are made clear. Salvation for Lazarus adds to the focus on this theme (16:19–31), while the widow with her small copper coin of contribution also reinforces it (21:1–4). For Luke, the "lowly people" are especially noted as candidates for God's grace (cf. the book of James).

Sinners also received special mention in Luke.[24] Jesus' opponents frequently complain about Jesus' making himself available to such people (Luke 5:27–32; 7:28, 30, 34, 36–50; 15:1–2; 19:7). Each time Jesus vindicates his behavior by word and/or deed. Such grumbling shows that the Jewish leaders misunderstood Jesus' mission. His mission is to call the spiritually sick to be healed through repentance (5:30–32). Luke 15 with its three parables of the lost sheep, the lost coin, and the forgiving father to his prodigal son shows God's initiative to recapture the lost that motivates the direction of Jesus' ministry.

Another group of rejected people are the tax collectors, regarded in that culture as social outcasts and traitors. The passages dealing with this group often overlap with passages dealing with Jesus' treatment of sinners: Luke 5:27–32 (Levi); 7:29, 34; 18:9–14 (prayer of the publican); and 19:1–10 (Zacchaeus). These passages show that the gospel penetrates the hearts of those living on the fringe of humanity. Whether rich in sin (the tax collector) or poor in life (the ⁿâwîm), the gospel can transform the lives of those who respond to it.

11.3 THE AUTHENTICATION OF THE MESSAGE

11.3.1 Three Levels of Authentication

Along with the message comes authentication. By what authority does Jesus perform his works and proclaim his message? When this question is raised by the Jewish leaders, Jesus does not reply other than to point to the same authority as John the Baptist had (Luke 20:1–8). Other evidence demonstrates that Jesus is who he claimed to be. Jesus is authenticated (1) through his fulfilling of promises given in the Scrip-

---

24. On this theme, see Dwayne Adams, *The Sinner in Luke* (Evangelical Theological Society Monograph Series; Eugene, OR: Pickwick, 2008).

tures; (2) through miracles often called signs and wonders (Acts 2:22; 10:38); and (3) through the presence of the Holy Spirit.

(1) The subject of scriptural fulfillment has been discussed already, but a key passage for this theme is Luke 4:18–21, in which Jesus publicly proclaims that the Scriptures attest to his ministry; he points specifically to Isa 61:1–2 and 58:6. Luke 24:44–47 is similar in force, where Jesus appeals to Moses, the Prophets, and the Psalms. Acts 3:24 speaks of "beginning with Samuel, all the prophets who have spoken have foretold these days."[25]

(2) Jesus' work and message are authenticated through miracles. When John asks whether Jesus is the coming one, Jesus answers by pointing to the miracles of his ministry (Luke 7:18–23). These actions allude to passages in Isaiah that point to the eschaton and God's day of deliverance (Isa 26:19; 29:18–19; 35:5–7; 61:1). Jesus' work indicates the nature of the time and the nature of his person. He is the promised coming one. Luke 11:14–23 explains what his miracles mean. If Jesus has cast out demons by the finger of God, then the kingdom has come upon the people. God the Father exercises his power through Jesus, a power that demonstrates his superior strength to malevolent spiritual forces. So in this passage Jesus portrays himself as the strong man pilfering Satan's house (11:21–22).

In Luke 11:21–22, Jesus illustrates his point with a picture of war, for his battle with Satan is a cosmic struggle. When a man, strong and armed, makes preparations to defend his home, his possessions are "safe" (lit., "at peace").[26] In this context, Satan is the strong man whose home is secure, but Jesus is the stronger man who overruns him.[27] Such eschatological imagery is not without precedent in Judaism: "Beliar shall be bound by him [an eschatological priest], and he shall give power to his children to tread upon evil spirits" (*T. Levi* 18.12).[28]

Only Luke introduces this illustration of Jesus. In fact, this illustration goes its own way and looks like an abbreviated summary of other things Jesus taught, for Matt 12:31–32 = Mark 3:28–30 agree by each mentioning the blasphemy of the Spirit, a teaching that Luke has in 12:10. In addition, Matthew and Mark speak of an οἰκία (*oikia*, "house") whereas Luke uses αὐλή (*aulē*), often translated "castle, palace, fortress, court." A secure abode is in view.

Jesus notes that his miracles mean a fall for Satan, whose formerly secure abode has been overrun. From the initial image of security, Jesus moves to the portrait of defeat. Exorcism means that Satan has been "overpowered" (Luke 11:22).[29] Defeat comes when the stronger one arrives, lays siege, and gains victory. Victory is graphically portrayed as Satan's entire "armor" stripped away. Satan's armor pictures his power, while the seizing and defeat picture what Jesus accomplishes through his ministry as the more powerful one (3:15–18).

---

25. Chapter 21 will take a close look at how Scripture frames what Luke declares in his two volumes, as well as how Luke works hermeneutically.

26. Foerster, *TDNT*, 2:411.

27. Grundmann, *TDNT*, 3:399–400.

28. Ellis, *Gospel of Luke*, 167.

29. Bauernfeind, *TDNT*, 4:944.

It is important to remember that though the more powerful one is Jesus, it is a Jesus who works by God's power (Luke 11:20). To the victor go the spoils, which in turn are divided among those who fight alongside him. Note that among the gospel writers, Luke alone mentions the distribution of the spoils.[30] This dividing of spoils recalls Isa 53:12, but the presence of a definite allusion is uncertain, since other texts share this imagery. But Satan is no longer in control. Victory belongs to Jesus, who has cast out demons by the finger of God. Paul later uses other victory images with reference to the cross (Eph 4:7–10; Col 2:14–15).[31] The spoil is the whole of salvation benefits: forgiveness, the Spirit, his gifts, and living eternally with the king.

This picture of authority over Satan as a picture of victory in salvation appears elsewhere as well. It is extended in the ministry of the disciples, who gain their power from Jesus. Jesus gave authority to the Twelve (Luke 9:1–2) and to the seventy-two (10:1) to heal and cast out demons. The defeat of Satan was seen in Judaism as evidence of the new era (*T. Mos.* 10.1–5). The Eleven received unique authority in relationship to the present kingdom; they will also receive it over Israel in the kingdom to come (Luke 22:29–30). Such authority causes the disciples to marvel and rejoice (10:17–20). Jesus' reference to Satan falling like lightning shows the current victory that this authority represents (Luke 10:18; Eph 1:19–23; 1 Pet 3:20–21).

Similar authority exists through the apostles and others in the early church. God performed miracles through a number of individuals: apostles (Acts 2:43; 5:12), Peter and John (4:16, 22), Stephen (6:8), Philip (8:6, 13), and Paul and Barnabas (14:3; 15:12). Such healings occurred in the name of Jesus (3:6, 16; 4:10) and demonstrated that there is no other name under heaven by which people can be saved (4:12). The apostles (4:33), Stephen (6:8), Philip (8:13), and Paul (19:11) are said to have miraculous "power" (δύναμις)—a power that stems not from within themselves but from Jesus (3:12; 14:8–18).

(3) A third authentication of the gospel message is the presence of "power from on high," that is, the Holy Spirit (Luke 24:49; Acts 1:8; cf. 2:14–22, 32–36; 10:38; 11:15–16). Pentecost authenticates not only Jesus' resurrection but also the presence of the promise of God. The Spirit's activity and testimony declare that Jesus is alive and that God is at work through his church. Tied to this is the ultimate authentication, God's vindicating resurrection and ascension, which have made the distribution of the Spirit possible since cleansing through Jesus' death has taken place (Luke 22:18–20; Acts 20:28).

11.3.2 The Miracles of Jesus and His Disciples

As we traced in the previous chapter, what Jesus offered in his person and message is pictured in the miracles he and his followers performed. The nature of miracles as "picture" as well as event emerges most clearly in Luke 5:1–11, where a miraculous

---

30. Bock, *Luke 9:51–24:53*, 1083.

31. A. Plummer, *A Critical and Exegetical Commentary on the Gospel according to St. Luke* (ICC; Edinburgh: Clark, 1896), 303.

catch of fish prompts Jesus' remark that the disciples "will fish for people" (v. 10). That miracle portrays a deeper reality and inspires wonder. Miracles for Jesus are power points, showing his authority over salvation. To appreciate the extent of salvation, it is important to look at the theology of this aspect of his ministry, which authenticates, pictures, and explains what Jesus is doing.

The scope of Jesus' healing can easily be regarded as part of his work and could have been discussed earlier. However, the truths about salvation pictured by his miracles show their importance to the present theme. Jesus' healings covered a vast range of situations: the sick (Luke 4:18, 40–41; 5:31–32; 7:22), evil spirits (4:31–37; 8:26–39; 9:42; 11:14–20; 13:32), fever (4:38–39), leprosy (5:12–16; 7:22; 17:11–19), paralysis (5:17–26), a withered hand (6:6–11, on the Sabbath), epilepsy (9:37–43a), dropsy (14:1–6, on the Sabbath), blindness (4:18; 7:22; 18:35–43), a constant flow of blood (8:43–48), deafness (7:22), and resuscitation from the dead (7:11–17, 22; 8:40–42, 49–56). All these maladies picture the destructive presence of sin and chaos, whereas the healings show Jesus' power to reverse these effects and to declare the healed one saved (5:24). The scope of Jesus' miraculous work is unlike anything that had come before in Israel. Only the work of Moses and Elijah-Elisha comes close to covering this kind of range. Moses had several nature miracles in which he called on God to show his power. Elijah and Elisha had a string of mostly healings. Jesus has both kinds of signs.

So Jesus' authority goes beyond dealing with human misery. He also controls creation; he directs his disciples into finding a large catch of fish (Luke 5:1–11), calms a storm (8:22–25), and feeds five thousand people from only a small amount of food (9:10–17).

In Luke 8:22–56a, Jesus brings restoration in a variety of ways. In a succession of four miracles, he calms the storm, exorcises demons, heals a flow of blood, and resuscitates a girl from the dead. Whether over nature, spiritual forces, disease, or death, Jesus has the authority to deliver and overcome those forces that harm or destroy people. This section of miracles shows the range of Jesus' miraculous activity, a kind of A to Z of his saving power. These miracles review the character of his ministry that leads to Peter's great confession.[32] Only one more miracle, the feeding of the five thousand (9:10–17), intervenes between the miracles in Luke 8 and Peter's confession in 9:18–20. The miracles of Luke 8 also reflect an escalation, since they progress from external threats to more internalized threats, culminating in the threat of death itself. Jesus can deal with all such attempts to overwhelm humankind. Schürmann describes these miracles as functioning in much the same manner as the "signs" in John's gospel: they show who Jesus is and reassure the reader because of the power they reveal.[33]

The reactions produced by his miracles are significant. Usually the reaction is

---

32. Marshall, *Gospel of Luke*, 332.
33. Schürmann, *Lukasevangelium: Kommentar zu Kap. 1.1–9.50*, 472–73.

in the form of a question or an emotional response. Seeing a man exorcised of a demon, the crowd asked, "What words these are!" and "With authority and power he gives orders to impure spirits and they come out!" (Luke 4:36). Reacting to the catch of fish with a sense of his own sinfulness, Peter asks Jesus to depart (5:8 – 9). After Jesus heals a man with leprosy, news about him spreads (5:15); and after Jesus heals a paralytic, people glorify God (5:26). Some think Jesus' power to restore the widow's son to life points to the presence of a prophet as well as a visitation from God (7:16). When confronted with the calming of the storm and knowing that God controls the weather, the disciples ask, "Who is this? He commands even the winds and water, and they obey him" (8:25). This is precisely the kind of question Luke warns his readers to ask as they see Jesus exercise delivering power.

Another crowd is gripped with fear after the demoniac is healed (Luke 8:37). The parents of a resuscitated child are amazed (8:56). After another exorcism by Jesus, multitudes marvel (11:14). A large crowd gives praise to God when a blind man receives his sight (18:43). Even demons confess Jesus' authority (4:34, 41). Clearly the people are impressed that someone of unusual authority and power is present, though many never think he is more than a prophet (9:18 – 19).

Equally impressive is the scope of the disciples' work. They also heal the sick (Luke 9:1 – 2; 10:9) and exorcise demons (9:1, 42, 49; 10:17). Yet Jesus keeps this work in balance when he tells the disciples not to be impressed with their power to cast out spirits, but that their names are written in heaven (10:18 – 20). That is, Jesus wants his disciples to focus on and to rejoice in their gracious and secure standing before God. "Rejoice" (χαίρετε, *chairete*, 10:20) is a present imperative and speaks of continual rejoicing.[34] The statement is given weight by the use of the perfect tense in ἐγγέγραπται (*engegraptai*, "are written"). In everyday Greek, ἐγγράφω (*engraphō*) refers to making a list in a public register or census.[35] The disciples' names stand written in heaven, the census of life.

The gospel of Luke indicates that the disciples are personally known by God and that their eternal presence before him is certain. Therefore, this final word is one of comfort and encouragement, for in this context it means that the evil one's power cannot remove their secure position before God. Disciples can rejoice in this important truth. While Satan is cast down from heaven, the disciples are a part of the heavenly census.[36]

In Acts, God heals a lame man through Peter and John (Acts 3:1 – 10, 16; 4:8 – 12) and another cripple through Paul and Barnabas (14:8 – 18). Saul regains his sight (Acts 9:17 – 18). Aeneas, a paralytic, walks (9:32 – 35), while Dorcas is resuscitated (9:36 – 43), as is Eutychus (20:7 – 12). Exorcisms occur (16:16 – 18). Publius's father is cured of a fever (28:7 – 10). The power of Jesus authenticates the ministry of those who preach Jesus. Alongside these miraculous works of ministry come other

34. Plummer, *St. Luke*, 280.
35. Schrenk, *TDNT*, 1:769 – 70.
36. Bock, *Luke 9:51 – 24:53*, 1008 – 9.

authenticating signs. On three occasions, angels deliver the apostles from prison (5:17–26; 12:6–11; 16:24–34). Apostolic judgment brings death or other consequences (5:1–11; 19:13–20). People survive shipwreck and snakebites (27:23–44; 28:3–5). The scope of this exercise of power is impressive.

The important point is not so much the miracles themselves as what they portray (Luke 10:18–20). In Jesus' ministry, God is present, exercising power through the one he has sent. In Acts, Jesus' power is expressed through his appointed messengers, which shows that he has been raised and is active. The forces that oppose people meet their defeat and death through Jesus. He can deliver. In other words, physical salvation portrays spiritual salvation. The account of Acts 3:1–4:21 makes this connection clear as Peter moves from discussing physical healing to declaring spiritual salvation. Jesus and his disciples indicate what God is doing. The message of hope they bring in the gospel was (and is) true.

11.3.3 The Work of Salvation: The Cross and Jesus' Resurrection-Ascension

Luke highlights who Jesus is more than how he saves, but the basic outline of his work is still present. Many of the points to be made here were discussed earlier in connection with Jesus' work on the cross. Here the focus is on the OT allusions, since they vividly explain various aspects of Jesus' work.

There are two probable allusions to Isa 53 in Luke's passion material. It is explicit in Luke 22:37, which portrays Jesus as the innocent sufferer ("And he was numbered with the transgressors," Isa 53:12). The force of this image in Isaiah is highly disputed. Corporate Israel and the true remnant are clearly referred to in Servant Songs such as Isa 49:3–6, while Isaiah himself is sometimes individually referred to, as the discussion between Philip and the eunuch in Acts 8:34 suggests. The individual, messianic reference to the Servant of the Lord has a long history in both Judaism and Christianity.[37] The rendering of Isa 53 by Aquila, Theodotion, and the Targum suggests a messianic element. But it should be noted that the idea of a *suffering* Messiah is not present in these ancient Jewish texts. Rather, Judaism understood these verses to refer to an exalted Messiah.

In other words, ancient Judaism did not have a suffering messianic Servant. In Judaism the exalted Messiah delivers a suffering people. The suffering aspect of NT use is unique in the early history of interpretation. In regard to the OT sense of the servant, C. R. North defends a view that seems the most balanced: the servant was initially a broad reference to the nation but narrows to an individual reference in Isa 53.[38] The persistence of the messianic view within Judaism in the face of Christian

37. Jeremias, *TDNT*, 5:682–700.

38. C. R. North, *The Suffering Servant in Deutero-Isaiah: An Historical and Critical Study* (2nd ed.; Oxford: Oxford Univ. Press, 1956). More recent discussion of issues tied to this important text can be found in William H. Bellinger Jr. and William R. Farmer, eds., *Jesus and the Suffering Servant: Isaiah 53 and Christian Origins* (Harrisburg, PA: Trinity International, 1998); Bernd Janowski and Peter Stuhlmacher, eds., *The Suffering Servant: Isaiah 53 in Jewish and Christian Sources* (Grand Rapids: Eerdmans, 2004); and Darrell L. Bock and Mitch Glaser, eds., *The Gospel according to Isaiah 53: Encountering the Suffering Servant in Jewish and Christian Theology* (Grand Rapids: Kregel, 2011).

use shows how strongly Judaism held to an individual reading of this text, even though its suffering elements were applied to the nation, not to the Servant.

In Luke, the Servant is Jesus, but Jesus' servant imagery does not explicitly stress Jesus' substitutionary work. Rather, the use reflects themes of both exaltation and suffering (cf. Luke 24:44–47; Acts 8:32–33). In stressing exaltation, Luke follows the emphasis of Isa 53, which moves past suffering to exaltation (Isa 52:13–15; 53:12). In Luke 22:37, the focus is on Jesus' suffering like a rejected one, though there is no explicit substitutionary picture here. Jesus' point in citing the text is that he will die a shameful death between criminals as anticipated by the Scripture (Luke 23:32, 39–43).[39] Jesus notes that his fate was a necessary part of God's plan. In addition, Luke notes that he died a cursed death on a tree (Acts 5:30; 10:39; 13:29, using Deut 21:23).

The second passage alluding to Isa 53 is more debated because it is conceptual and also involves a passage that is missing in some Greek manuscripts of Luke's gospel.[40] On the cross, Jesus intercedes for the forgiveness of his enemies (Luke 23:34). This also recalls Isa 53:12, which says that the Servant "made intercession for the transgressors." The connection between Luke 23:34 and Isaiah 53:12 is not verbal, but nonetheless it is likely. The text is probably original to Luke, since it has a parallel in Acts 7:60, where Stephen intercedes for his enemies. Such parallelisms are frequent between Luke and Acts. It is more likely that Stephen mimics Jesus in the original narrative than that Stephen showed such graciousness alone.

These two allusions to Isa 53 relate Jesus to the figure of Isaiah's Suffering Servant, especially in portraying his death as unjust. Jesus died like a sinner, numbered with transgressors. Yet in the midst of it all, Jesus' compassion for his enemies shone forth in his prayer for them. In praying for his enemies, Jesus applies the principle he enunciated in Luke 6:27–36, namely, to love one's enemies.

Repeatedly, Luke 23 affirms Jesus' innocence. Pilate mentions it three times (vv. 4, 14–15, 22), and in one of his references Pilate reports that Herod too found Jesus innocent (v. 15). In addition, a centurion at the cross proclaims Jesus' innocence (v. 47, a remark unique to Luke, although the other gospels have him confessing Jesus as Son of God). The term chosen by the soldier is δίκαιος (*dikaios*), which can be translated "innocent" or "righteous." Either term makes good sense here, but the slightly more common contextual force "innocent" seems preferable.

---

39. Bock, *Luke 9:51–24:53*, 1747–48.

40. If Jesus' prayer forgiving his executioners is original, then it is unique to Luke. Many Alexandrian and Western witnesses omit the prayer (p[75], א[1], B, D*, W, Θ, Syriac), while א*,2, (A), C, D[2], L, Byz, and some Syriac include it. External evidence leans toward rejecting the prayer, but internal factors also enter into the decision: (1) The parallel prayer of Stephen in Acts 7:60 argues for inclusion, since Luke frequently notes parallelism between events. (James the Just is said to utter a similar prayer in Eusebius, *Eccl. Hist.* 2.23.16.) (2) The absence of a parallel in the other gospels speaks for inclusion here (i.e., there is no good reason to explain why a copyist would add such a remark). (3) The motif of ignorance is common in Acts (3:17; 13:27; 17:30) and finds endorsement here. (4) It is easier to explain the prayer's omission than its insertion. A scribe might have omitted it if he considered the remarks too forgiving of the Jews (Brown, *Birth of the Messiah*, 979) or if he regarded the prayer as unanswered in light of AD 70 (Jerome, *Letter* 120.8.2 says it delayed the judgment). (5) Each major subunit in Luke's crucifixion narrative contains a saying. If the prayer is omitted, then a saying is lacking from this subunit (Marshall, *Gospel of Luke*, 868). These internal reasons suggest that the reading is original to Luke and should be included in his text.

Nevertheless, the soldier is probably not interested in just the legal status of Jesus, but in his character. So the implication of the remark is that Jesus died although he was innocent/righteous. According to the lips of one of his executioners, Jesus died as a righteous man. The testimony of an enemy is often worth more than the affirmations of many friends.

Luke's record of the crucifixion reflects imagery from the Psalter and from Isaiah. Five such allusions exist. Jesus not only requests forgiveness for his enemies (Luke 23:34, alluding to Isa 53:12), but Luke notes that they cast lots for his clothes, recalling Ps 22:18 (21:19 LXX). In Luke 23:35, the onlookers' mocking cry that Jesus save himself recalls Ps 22:6–7 (21:8–9 LXX). The offer of wine (Luke 23:36) finds a parallel in Ps 69:21–22 (68:21–22 LXX). Psalms 22 and 69 are psalms of lament, portraying an innocent sufferer's cry to God for vindication from his enemies. These allusions show that Jesus died in the pattern of suffering like that of the saints of old.[41] It also shows that Jesus trusts in God the Father for vindication.

The fourth allusion to the Psalter is in Luke 23:46. This one records Jesus' final words in which he commits his spirit into God's hands. The language recalls Ps 31:5 (30:5 LXX). The prayer contains an address and a statement of faith. The address "Father" (πάτερ, *pater*) is frequent in Luke (10:21; 11:2; 22:42; 23:34) and shows the special familial appeal that Jesus makes. Jesus is giving over his spirit to God's care. "Hand" (χείρ, *cheir*) indicates God's care (John 10:29; Acts 4:28, 30; 1 Pet 5:6). Interestingly, Ps 31 was used in later Judaism as an evening prayer. God is asked to care for and protect during sleep (*b. Ber.* 5a).[42] Jesus submits to his death. He "sleeps" and leaves his vindication to God.

This "last word" of Jesus in Luke from Ps 31 differs from the record in the other Synoptics (Mark 15:34–37; Matt 27:46), where Jesus quotes Ps 22:1 (21:2 LXX), though Mark notes that Jesus made two cries. Only Luke records the details of the second cry. Psalm 22:1 expresses a painful cry of anguish that Jesus offered from the cross. Psalm 22 is another psalm of lament. Psalm 31 is also a psalm of lament, but verse 5 from that psalm is an expression of trust. Thus, Jesus knows that his fate and vindication are in God's hands. With this cry, he rests himself in the care of the Almighty. The vindication, if it is to come, must come from almighty God, who cares for his own.

Of course, the vindication does come in Jesus' resurrection. The enemies mock Jesus by urging him to get down from the cross (Luke 23:33–38). God does something more; he takes him out of death. With vindication come benefits bestowed on those allied to him. Numerous verses indicate that with Jesus' resurrection–ascension comes the opportunity for forgiveness. Forgiveness is included in the message (Luke

---

41. The use of the OT here is a case of typological-prophetic fulfillment, where Jesus fits the patterns of earlier suffering, but in a unique way because of the nature of his work. Many NT uses of the OT reflect this type of usage. For more on this see my essay "Single Meaning, Multiple Contexts and Referents: The New Testament's Legitimate, Accurate, and Multifaceted Use of the Old," in *Three Views on the New Testament Use of the Old* (ed. Kenneth Berding and Jonathan Lunde; Grand Rapids: Zondervan, 2008), 105–51.

42. Marshall, *Gospel of Luke,* 876; Str-B, 2:269.

24:47), is pictured in baptism (Acts 2:38), results from repentance (3:19), is offered to Israel (5:31), comes through Jesus' name as the prophets promised (10:43), comes through one by faith (22:16), and is a result of turning from Satan to God (26:18). According to Luke, forgiveness is the key emphasis that Jesus' work on the cross brings. Resurrection makes it possible. When Jesus cries out, it is as if he intercedes for all. To gain access to that forgiveness, all one needs to do is to respond to his offer.

Other benefits of Jesus' resurrection-ascension include the outpouring of the Holy Spirit (Acts 2:30–36), the offer of the "times of refreshing" along with the yet-future times of restoration (3:19–21), the realization of the Abrahamic covenant (3:25–26), the offer of salvation in his name (4:12), the availability of justification (13:23, 38–41), and the appointment of Jesus as Judge (17:31). God is at work through Jesus.

According to Luke 22:19–20, the new covenant has been inaugurated by Jesus' death.[43] The supper portrays a broken body and life's blood shed on behalf of "you," a reference to the disciples. The church is a community purchased by the blood of "his own" (Acts 20:28), that is, the blood of God's Son. As such, the community is precious, and those who are elders must care for it as a special gift. Rich benefits come from the hand of the innocent one who was vindicated by God and now rules at God's side as Lord.

11.4 THE OBJECTIVE ASPECT OF SALVATION

11.4.1 Words for Salvation

Luke-Acts uses several words to speak of salvation. The best way to summarize this subject is to review the salvation word group we surveyed in the last chapter. The term "Savior" (σωτήρ, *sotēr*) is used three times of Christ (Luke 2:11; Acts 5:31; 13:23); once it refers to God (Luke 1:47). God saves through the promised and exalted Savior, Jesus.

The verb "to save" (σῴζω, *sōzō*) means to deliver from calamity. Numerous miracles picture this concept. When Jesus heals the man with the withered hand, he asks the Pharisees and teachers of the law whether it is lawful on the Sabbath "to do good or to do evil [harm], to save life or destroy it" (Luke 6:9). For Jesus the answer is to save life, which is what the miracle of physical deliverance pictures. The same is true of the demon-possessed man (8:36), the bleeding woman (v. 48), Jairus's daughter (v. 50), the Samaritan leper (17:19), and the blind beggar (18:42). These miracles are audiovisuals of God's power and authority.

The sinful woman who anoints Jesus' feet is saved because of the attitude reflected in her action (Luke 7:50). The woman must depart with a sense of God's

---

43. There is a major textual issue here about whether these verses are original to Luke's gospel. See discussion in ch 2, fn 14.

blessing, as Jesus tells her to go in peace (Mark 5:34 = Luke 8:48). She is to be secure in the knowledge that God has seen her faith.[44] The wording has a parallel in 1 Sam 1:17 (Jdg 18:6; 2 Sam 15:9).[45] God has seen her faith and has reconciled her to himself (Luke 2:14).[46] She can be sure that her relationship to God has changed.

In the parable of the sower (Luke 8:4–15), Jesus explains that rejecting the word, i.e., the message of the kingdom (v. 10), results in lack of salvation (v. 12). To save one's life, a person must lose it (9:24). Those who place their lives in his hands can be delivered. The description of discipleship in 9:24 continues with the "lose life to gain life" saying. In fact, this verse explains the previous images of taking up one's cross daily and following Jesus (note the use of γάρ [gar, "for"] at the start of v. 24). They "draw out the meaning of the summons to discipleship in v 23."[47] If one wishes to control one's life, it will be lost because of refusal to submit to God's way. If one wishes to save one's life through the world's acceptance, it will be lost because of a refusal to come to a rejected Jesus, who does save (John 12:25).[48]

The context foresees persecution. One might be inclined to court acceptance with the world by distancing oneself from Jesus (see Luke 14:25–33, esp. v. 26), but such distancing is disaster. A person might seek to save life by surrounding it with the comforts and protections of life, but this, too, is dangerous (Luke develops the idea of excessive attachment to wealth in 12:13–21; 16:19–31; 18:18–30). The point is that life's comforts and the threat of losing them might keep one from coming to Jesus (8:14). If one gives up life for the sake of Jesus, if one gives one's spiritual and physical welfare over to him, that person will receive life. Orientation to Jesus (i.e., "for me," 9:24) is a prerequisite for saving life. Though some disciples fulfill this passage in martyrdom, the image of the entire section is figurative and so is the remark here.

Luke later describes this change in attitude with two terms: repentance (μετάνοια, metanoia) and faith (πίστις, pistis; Acts 11:18; 13:38–39; 20:21; 26:18). In turning to God for the forgiveness of sins, one recognizes that one must not live life as in the past and that one cannot approach God on human terms. Rather, one must live in light of God's offer of forgiveness and life. Thus, a person's spiritual welfare is to rest in God's hands. Paul speaks of faith in describing this reorientation of perspective toward the things of God (Rom 1:4–5; 1 Thess 1:9–10). The issue is fundamentally one of attitude and allegiance, though there may be failure in its execution at individual points.[49]

After hearing Jesus' teaching, some conclude that few will be saved. Thus, a listener asks Jesus about this (Luke 13:23). Jesus answers that entry is through a "narrow door"—a reference to responding to the message on God's terms, not on human terms. This imagery suggests that fewer will enter than expected. There is

---

44. Marshall, *Gospel of Luke*, 314; Foerster, *TDNT*, 2:413.

45. Schürmann, *Lukasevangelium: Kommentar zu Kap. 1.1–9.50*, 439, n. 59.

46. Danker, *Jesus and the New Age*, 172.

47. Green, *Gospel of Luke*, 374.

48. Ellis, *Gospel of Luke*, 141.

49. Bock, *Luke 1:1–9:50*, 854–55.

no automatic entry. The "narrow door," like the narrow way, pictures the way of righteousness or entry into God's presence and blessing (Jer 21:8; 2 Esdr. [= *4 Ezra*] 7:3–7, 12–14; John 10:7).[50] Getting through the door presupposes a favorable response to Jesus' message (Luke 13:3, 5).[51] A door is often an image of entry into the banquet of eschatological blessing at God's palace or is related to the image of the great wedding (Matt 7:7–8, 13; 22:12; 25:10, 21, 23; Luke 14:23).[52] The Lucan stress is not only that the door is narrow so that people must come in the right way, but also that it is only open for a short time (Luke 13:25).[53] Jesus adds that people will come and enter in from all directions (13:29, an allusion to all races), yet some who expect to sit at the banquet table with the patriarchs and prophets will be missing (13:24–30).

Another parable speaks of a filled house (Luke 14:23), which also suggests that though many reject the gospel, many others will respond. The point of the remarks in both Luke 13 and 14 is that though many Jews will miss out on the promise they expect to share in because of a failure to respond to Jesus, the place of God's blessing will be full of God's people.

A similar question from one of the disciples raises the issue of who can be saved (Luke 18:26). This question is asked in response to Jesus' remark that a rich man entering the kingdom is like a camel passing through a needle's eye (v. 25). Here Jesus notes that what is impossible for human beings is possible with God. Peter then remarks that the disciples have left all for Jesus. In turn, Jesus responds positively, describing the rich reward that will be theirs for their response, a reward that includes eternal life (vv. 27–30).

Though Peter has said that the disciples have forsaken "all," they, including Peter himself, fail at certain points to be "total" disciples. Nevertheless, basic dependence on God is there, so Jesus responds positively to the claim that the disciples have left all. What Jesus' reply here means is "to leave all" is to put God first in terms of salvation and to rely on him alone. These disciples, along with people like Zacchaeus, picture what the mission of Jesus is about, namely, to seek and save the lost (Luke 19:10).

There is irony in the final use of the verb "to save" in Luke's gospel. As Jesus is crucified, people mock him, calling on him to "save" himself (Luke 23:35, 37, 39). Of course Jesus' death is laying the groundwork by which he can save sinners. He is doing what they mock him for not doing!

In Acts, the use of the term "save" (σῴζω, *sōzō*) for physical deliverance occurs in Acts 27:20, 31 (and perhaps 16:30). Most uses of this term are summary descriptions that occur along with acts of healing or preaching (2:47; "no other name under heaven ... by which we must be saved," 4:12; about the house of Cornelius, 11:14; of the lame man at Lystra, 14:9; of Gentiles like Cornelius, 15:11). In his message

---

50. Danker, *Jesus and the New Age*, 264; Bertram, *TDNT*, 7:605–6.

51. Fitzmyer, *Gospel of Luke X–XXIV*, 1024–25.

52. Jeremias, *TDNT*, 3:174, 178.

53. Bock, *Luke 9:51–24:53*, 1234–35.

on the day of Pentecost, Peter says those who call "on the name of the Lord will be saved" (2:21), a quotation of Joel 2:32 (cf. Rom 10:13). This Lord to whom one calls, Peter explains, is Jesus (Acts 2:36). He saves by providing forgiveness, sparing from wrath, and giving the Holy Spirit (vv. 38–40).

Another key summary occurs in Acts 16:30–31. The Philippian jailer is overwhelmed by his circumstances and asks what he needs to do to be saved. All he may have meant is how his physical life can be spared. Paul responds by speaking of spiritual life, by calling for faith in "the Lord Jesus" (v. 31). Paul explains that faith in the Lord Jesus will save the jailer and his household. This brief confession expresses the core of what a saving response is—to trust in Jesus' salvation authority and work. "Lord" is the title chosen here to summarize that authority (κύριος, *kyrios*; see Acts 2:36). The use of this title reflects tradition (Acts 5:14; 9:42; 11:17; Rom 10:9; Phil 2:11). Clearly, Luke is summarizing here. The jailer has the meaning of such a confession explained to him (cf. Acts 16:32). The theme of Jesus' authority is what is highlighted in a first-century Gentile context in the church's preaching (Acts 10:42; 17:30–31). At a literary level in the unit, faith in Jesus is the answer to the way of salvation (Luke 16:17).[54] This response is the theological point that the scene in Acts 16 is driving toward as well as the goal of the early church kerygma. Ultimately, life is retained through faith in Jesus, so Paul answers a question even more fundamental than the one the jailer has asked.

Thus the verb "to save" is used in a variety of ways. (1) Some occurrences refer only to physical deliverance (Acts 27:20, 31). (2) Other occurrences suggest both physical and spiritual deliverance. Often miracles of physical deliverance picture spiritual deliverance. Though Luke 5:17–26 does not use the term "save," the incident recorded there pictures this connection when Jesus heals the paralytic. Jesus asks whether it is easier to tell the man to get up and walk or to tell him his sins are forgiven (v. 23). There is irony in the question. In one sense it is "easier" for Jesus to say one's sins are forgiven, since that cannot be seen, while making a man walk can be observed. And yet, forgiving sin in reality is the "harder" thing to achieve. But how can one show that forgiveness is present? Such a claim can only be pictured. So to show his authority to forgive, Jesus performs the "harder and more visible" act, physical healing. One reality pictures the other. Miracle becomes a metaphor for salvation. All Jesus' miracles should be seen in this light. (3) Still other verses refer directly to spiritual salvation (Luke 19:10; Acts 2:40; 4:12). When spiritual healing is present, Jesus stands active at the center of salvation.

The meaning of the nouns for "salvation" (σωτήριον, *sōtērion*; σωτηρία, *sōtēria*) differs little from that of the verb σῴζω. When the prophet Simeon sees Jesus, he can say he has seen God's "salvation" (*sōtērion*, Luke 2:30). Luke 3:4–5 cites Isa 40:3–5 to describe John the Baptist's ministry, noting the forerunner's activity of clearing the path so that "all people will see God's salvation [*sōtērion*]." Salvation has come

---

54. Fitzmyer, *Acts of the Apostles*, 589.

to the Gentiles in the message about Jesus (Acts 28:28). So from the first of Luke to the last of Acts, God's saving activity is in view.

The other noun (*sōtēria*) is rarely used in Luke-Acts, but its usage is significant. In Luke 1:69, 71, 77, the focus is on the Davidic "horn of salvation," who delivers from all enemies and who is associated with the hope of forgiveness and the arrival of peace with God, through rescuing people out of darkness (cf. Col 1:12–14). Luke 1:74–75 summarizes the results of deliverance. There Zechariah describes the messianic salvation that delivers God's people so they can serve God. The desire to be rescued from one's enemy has OT roots; it is also a theme of Judaism (2 Sam 22:18; Pss 18 superscription [18:1 MT]; 97:10; Jer 30:8; *Pss. Sol.* 17.30, 45; 3 Macc 6:10). The enemies in view here are opponents of God's nation and people (cf. Acts 4:25–31). In Zechariah's time the enemy was primarily the foreign domination of Palestine by Rome. God will rescue God's people through Messiah from the hands of these enemies. Zechariah anticipates physical deliverance as a part of messianic salvation. Such expectation belongs to the salvific perspective of those who trust Messiah.

Luke will explain in his two volumes how this expectation works itself out. It will press beyond the political circumstances and speak instead of cosmic opposition by Satan. This turn in the narrative comes with the naming of Jesus as "the son of Adam, the son of God" in Luke 3:38, followed by Jesus' successful overcoming of the temptations by Satan. This act qualifies Jesus to represent humanity in a way that Adam failed to do. It also shows how Luke builds on what Zechariah says to extend the scope of what God is doing through Jesus.

The idea of being rescued is subordinate to Zechariah's key idea of serving God. The "holy covenant" (Luke 1:72–73) has been made and granted to the faithful in order that once the faithful are rescued, they may fearlessly serve God. The term ἀφόβως (*aphobōs*, "without fear"), even though it begins the verse, modifies λατρεύειν (*latreuein*, "to serve"), so that the hymn speaks of "serving God fearlessly." The position of this word at the start of the sentence means that the reference to fear's absence is emphatic. It reflects a life without the distraction of oppression. In turn, λατρεύειν is tied to the infinitive δοῦναι (*dounai*, "to grant") in 1:73 as an epexegetical infinitive. It explains precisely what God has granted his people to do. Thus, God fulfills his covenant so they can serve him fearlessly.

So God saves for service. The verb "serve" refers to the total service one gives to God, not just to the worship or sacrificial service that a faithful Jew would render in the temple or synagogue. In the NT, the term is used exclusively of service given to a deity, whether to God or, in pagan settings, to the gods (Luke 2:37; 4:8; Rom 1:25; cf. Exod 3:12; Deut 11:13).[55] God's deliverance enables one to serve God with one's life—at least, that is Zechariah's desire.

In regard to Zechariah's hymn's original setting, the political emphasis, alongside the spiritual emphasis, is interesting. Godet asks the following penetrating

---

55. Strathmann, *TDNT*, 4:62–63.

question: "How, after the unbelief of Israel [as portrayed in the rest of the gospel account] had created a gulf between the expectation and the facts, could a later writer, attributing to Zacharias just what words he pleased, put into his mouth these fond hopes of earlier days?"[56] What Godet suggests is that the only appropriate setting for such unqualified hope is one involving an expectant Jew, a Jew looking at messianic events before Jesus' life made the picture more complex. The hymn is appropriately attached to Zechariah.

The purpose of Messiah's deliverance is to allow continuous service before God, but such service is not merely activity on behalf of God. There is a moral quality to this worship. God's people are to serve "in holiness and righteousness before him" (Luke 1:75). This combination reflects an attitude that respects God's moral demands in obedience and conforms to his call to righteousness. The essence of worship is responsiveness to God's demands. Zechariah desires undefiled, undistracted worship of God, a worship that is both personal and moral. It is conducted with the realization that all service is done before God. Such worship is not tied to a locale but is related to all of life. In addition, it is a continuous worship that spans the lifetime of the delivered faithful; thus, the reference to service is given as "all our days." Zechariah wishes to be a useful servant of God. Deliverance, in his mind, will make fulfilling this desire more possible; that is why he rejoices at its prospect.[57]

In Zechariah's key description of salvation, physical and spiritual deliverance are discussed side by side as part of Jesus' messianic task. Jesus brings both. This usage also links national and spiritual hope. Personal salvation ultimately results in peace on earth.

This kind of ethical response within faith Luke describes elsewhere. Zacchaeus, rejected by society, responds to Jesus' teaching with a faith that also seeks to compensate for sins previously committed, and so he is welcomed before God and commended by Jesus (Luke 19:1–10, especially vv. 8–10).

As already noted, Acts 4:12 points out that salvation is only through Jesus. The hope of deliverance for Israel is expressed in Paul's apostolic message in Antioch of Pisidia (Acts 13:26). In fact, Paul's entire speech recorded in 13:16–41 is representative of a Pauline message on salvation, just as Luke 4:16–30 is an example of Jesus' preaching. Paul's mission is to bring salvation to the Gentiles and to the ends of the earth (Acts 13:47 alludes to Isa 49:6). The remaining two uses of σωτηρία in Acts (7:25; 27:34) refer to physical deliverance.

Without doubt, salvation is a key concept in Luke. Salvation is centered in Jesus. It possesses spiritual qualities, but eventually it will impact the human structures on earth because it changes the way people live (Luke 1:68–79). It is offered to all races (Acts 10–11). Only those who respond to Jesus possess it. It is at the center of the apostolic message, and in it is everlasting life.

---

56. F. Godet, *A Commentary on the Gospel of St. Luke* (2 vols.; trans. E. W. Shalders and M. D. Cusin; Edinburgh: Clark, 1875), 1:113.

57. Bock, *Luke 1:1–9:50*, 185–87.

11.4.2 Mercy and Judgment

This combination of ideas is important in Luke-Acts. It juxtaposes two attributes of God that speak to his compassion and yet to the accountability Luke describes as a part of salvation.[58] Mercy is shown especially to the needy and the poor (Luke 4:18; 7:22). If the marginalized can be saved, then God's mercy is underscored. But note that God can be merciful to the rich as well (18:24 – 27; 19:1 – 10). More than that, he is merciful to sinners as a whole (6:36). God as merciful is stressed in the infancy material (1:50, 54, 58, 72, 78). Luke also underscores judgment by making the point that one is accountable to God. To ignore God's message leaves one exposed to the judgment Jesus will bring one day (11:50 – 51; 12:20, 45 – 48, 57 – 59; 13:1 – 9; 16:19 – 31; 17:26 – 37; Acts 10:42; 17:31).

11.5 THE SUBJECTIVE SIDE OF SALVATION

The subjective aspect of salvation refers to the personal appropriation of salvation. Luke uses a variety of concepts to express this fundamental response. Each term he uses helps focus on a different aspect of one's response. Salvation itself should not be seen as the accumulation of these various responses. Rather, Luke wishes to show the multidimensional character of a true response to the message, with each term highlighting an ingredient within that response. The three key terms are repentance, turning, and faith.[59] Luke wants his readers to appreciate what God graciously offers, how simply it can be received, and how deep the response itself is.

11.5.1 Repentance

A key concept for Luke is repentance, whether expressed by the noun "repentance" (μετάνοια, *metanoia*) or the verb "to repent" (μετανοέω, *metanoeō*). Luke is a theologian of repentance since his eleven uses of the noun comprise half of the uses in the NT. The verb appears in Luke-Acts fourteen out of the NT's thirty-four uses. It means "to change one's mind," but in its Lucan usage it comes close to the Hebrew verb for repent, which literally means "to turn, turn around" (*šûb*). That the Hebrew sense of the term is primary is clear from Luke 24:44 – 47, where the message of repentance is seen as fulfilling the OT promise that such a message would be preached to all the nations.[60] So repentance is a reorientation, a total shift of perspective from where one was before repenting.

This prophetic force is introduced in the section where John the Baptist preached "a baptism of repentance for the forgiveness of sins" (Luke 3:3). This term calls for a

---

58. I. Howard Marshall, *New Testament Theology* (Downers Grove, IL: InterVarsity Press, 2004), 144 – 45.

59. This point about the acceptability of the use of a variety of summary terms for responding to the gospel is important since some today like to insist that only one term (faith) is acceptable. This sets up a standard the NT authors do not follow, especially Luke. Luke is important here because he is the one figure who gives us detailed

evangelistic speeches from the early church. Those speeches reflect this variety. For more on this topic in the NT, see Darrell L. Bock, *Recovering the Real Lost Gospel: Rediscovering the Gospel as Good News* (Nashville: Broadman & Holman Academic, 2010).

60. So correctly Leonhard Goppelt, *Theology of the New Testament* (2 vols.; trans. John Alsup; ed. Jürgen Roloff; Grand Rapids: Eerdmans, 1981), 1:34 – 36.

change of perspective involving the total person's point of view. In fact, John called for the Israelites to bring forth fruit worthy of repentance (3:8). This passage is significant in that it separates repentance from what it produces, and yet it also expresses a link between repentance and fruit. One act (repentance) leads to the other (fruit).

That this change of perspective finds concrete expression in life is clear from the dialogue that follows in Luke 3:10–14, a passage unique to Luke's gospel. When people asked what they must do in response to John's call to repent, he told them to live with kindness and compassion toward others. John's message only prepared one for the gospel, so it is illustrative, not defining. Nevertheless, the passage reveals the basic character of repentance, though the gospel makes the ultimate basis of repentance clearer by pointing toward forgiveness of sin found through Jesus.

A central passage picturing repentance is Luke 5:30–32. Here Jesus describes his mission as calling sick "sinners" to repentance. Though this passage has parallels in Matthew 9:13 and Mark 2:17, only Luke mentions repentance here. Jesus uses the term to describe his own mission, thus showing that it is an appropriate concept to use today in looking for a response to his mission and work.[61] To repent includes an awareness that as a sinner one has an unhealthy relationship with God that needs the "medical attention" of the Great Physician. Repentance involves recognizing that a person is spiritually sick and impotent, unable to help oneself. Repentance is turning to Jesus for spiritual healing, for treatment of one's heart and life, for one knows that only Jesus can give "the cure."

A person goes to a physician in order to be diagnosed and treated for a disease. Repentance is similar with regard to sin. Sin corrupts one's standing before God, but repentance seeks God's help to deal with sin in God's way. Jesus makes it clear that humankind has a disease and that only he can treat it. Part of the change of perspective in repentance is to see sin differently and to recognize that it is deadly if left untreated. So the sinner who repents to receive salvation comes to Jesus, knowing that only he can heal the relationship to God and deal with sin and its consequences. The term Jesus uses in his Great Commission to the disciples about their future message is repentance (24:47). Such transformation in a sinner causes Jesus and the angels to rejoice (Luke 15:7).

Acts reinforces this point. According to apostolic preaching, repentance is available for both Jews and Gentiles. It is for Israel and is related to Christ (Acts 5:31); it is for Gentiles, leading to life (11:18); and it was prepared for by John's baptism of repentance (13:24; 19:4). So repentance is offered to Jews and Greeks though Jesus (20:21). In fact, in 26:20 Paul tells Agrippa that those who repent should "demonstrate their repentance by their deeds," a comment similar in tone to that of John the Baptist in Luke 3:3–14. This parallelism shows a continuity between John the Baptist and Paul.

Acts 26:20 is a key verse about what Paul asked for when he preached. He asked the same from both Jews and Gentiles, namely, that they repent (i.e., change their

---

61. Another mission statement similar to this in terms of Jesus' work is Luke 19:10: "for the Son of Man came to seek and to save the lost."

minds) and turn (i.e., change the direction of their life). These responses can also be called faith directed toward Jesus (see v. 18). All these ideas are related to each other. Faith in Jesus is where the process ends, but to get there, a person changes his or her mind about sin and God and turns to God to receive the offer of salvation through Jesus. So each of these terms ("repent," "turn," "believe") is adequate for expressing the offer of the gospel.

Acts 26:20 shows that Paul is not an antinomian. He does not believe that someone who has faith can do whatever her or she wishes without concern for God's moral standards. Thus, Paul also exhorts his audience to live, in response to grace, in a way that produces fruit reflecting the change of direction called for by forgiveness. This is not a third responsibility, since the term πράσσοντας (*prassontas*, "perform-ing") is a present participle, making the performance of deeds something that hap-pens alongside, and simultaneously with, repenting and turning (cf. Luke 3:8; Eph 2:8–10; Titus 2:14; 3:8; Gal 5:22–23; 2 Cor 13:5–7). This response is wrapped up in the ideas of repenting and turning, just as repenting and turning are wrapped up in faith. One who turns to God follows in God's way and produces fruit.

John's gospel calls this process loving God, knowing God, or abiding in God (John 14–16). Polhill summarizes, "Works can never be the basis of salvation. They are, however, the inevitable result of a genuine experience of turning to God in Christ."[62] Deeds are the natural, expected product of genuine repentance.

The verb "to repent" is similar in force. Repentance is the natural response to the miracles Jesus performed (Luke 10:13). Jesus' message is compared to Jonah's call to the Ninevites, showing that repentance in the NT has OT roots (11:32). Jesus warns that people will perish if they do not repent (13:3, 5). But joy in heaven results when anyone does repent (15:7, 10). The rich man in Hades held out the hope that a mes-senger from the dead would convince his brothers to repent of the way they treated others, that is, to respond with a different way of life (16:30). Abraham, however, replies that a resurrection would not be convincing. Nevertheless, the discussion shows the centrality of repentance as an appropriate summary term for response.[63]

In Acts, the verb "to repent" is used in summary calls that invite one to enter into forgiveness (Acts 2:38; 3:19; 17:30; 26:20). Peter urges Simon the sorcerer to repent and seek forgiveness (8:22). Excluding Simon from sharing in the benefits of the Spirit may well indicate that Simon is lost and that the belief he exercised earlier (v. 13) is less than genuine. The force of this text is debated, but Peter's rebuke is severe, and the early church viewed Simon negatively, making it likely that Simon's faith is seen as inadequate.

Three portraits of repentance exist in Luke's gospel. Already noted is that of the physician calling the sick to repent (Luke 5:30–32). A second portrait is the prodigal son returning to his father (15:11–32). The attitude of the son is the key. He comes pleading no rights, no entitlement; he simply seeks his father's mercy. He

---

62. Polhill, *Acts*, 505.
63. Luke 17:3–4 uses "repent" in a nonsoteriological sense (repentance of personal acts done to another).

asks to be received not as a son, but only as a servant. Recognizing that what he had done was wrong, he entrusts himself to his father's mercy and care. There is no bargaining, only the seeking of mercy. That humble reliance is a change of perspective, and it reflects the essence of repentance.

The third portrait is that of the tax collector in contrast to the Pharisee (Luke 18:9–14)—a picture similar to the prodigal. Standing before the throne of heaven and realizing he cannnot bring anything to commend himself to God, the tax collector rests on God's mercy. The beating of his breast graphically portrays his sense of regret for his sin and of need for that mercy. This is the prayer of a penitent, a plea for mercy from a self-confessed sinner.[64] The prayer asks God to show mercy through atoning forgiveness (Add Esth 4:17 [= NRSV 13:17]; Lam 3:42; Dan 9:19 [Theodotion]). The ἱλάσκομαι (hilaskomai, "to propitiate") word group is used in the LXX to translate the important Hebrew verb kpr ("to cover," the OT term for atone).

In referring to himself as a sinner, the tax collector makes no comparison to others, unlike the Pharisee.[65] The tax collector is concerned only with improving his own spiritual health, and he knows the only way to do so is to rely totally on God's mercy. Not an emotion, repentance in Luke is a change of perspective. What the emotive picture evidences is that this man knew he was in need of God's mercy, but the attitude, not the emotion, is the point.

In summary, Luke sees repentance as a change of perspective that transforms a person's thinking and approach to life. It applies to Jews and Gentiles. It summarizes the appropriate response to the message of Jesus and the apostles. Bringing forth fruit is a natural outgrowth of repentance. Just as a good tree brings forth good fruit, so genuine repentance produces change in one's life (Luke 6:43–45).

11.5.2 Turning

Another key term in Luke pertaining to the response to salvation is "turning." The noun "turning" (ἐπιστροφή, epistrophē) is used in Acts 15:3, where it refers to the act of conversion by Gentiles. The report alludes back to the results of Paul's first missionary journey. The verb "to turn" (ἐπιστρέφω, epistrephō) is more frequent. John the Baptist's ministry was to turn Israel to God (Luke 1:17). Luke 17:4 speaks of a brother who turns ("seven times comes back [turns] to you") to seek forgiveness for sin. This example does not refer to initial salvation.

In predicting that Peter will turn from his failure of denying Jesus, Jesus then calls on the apostle to "strengthen" the brothers (Luke 22:32). Here again, "turning" refers to how a believer rebounds from sin. "Turning" is the reversing of estrangement as one recognizes and accepts that he has done wrong. In this sense it is similar to repentance, but it is a more vivid term, since it portrays a reversal of direction.

The word "turn" is used similarly in Acts. In Acts 3:19, turning is associated with repentance: "Repent, then, and turn to God, so that your sins may be wiped out." In the OT, the term appears in texts like Isa 6:10; 9:13; 55:7; Hos 5:4; 6:1; Joel

---

64. Plummer, St. Luke, 419.   65. Büchsel, TDNT, 3:315.

2:12 – 14; Amos 4:6.[66] It is important to note that whereas "faith" was highlighted in Acts 3:16, now Peter calls for repentance and turning. Thus, the NT uses a variety of terms to describe properly responding to Jesus' message.

Forgiveness is the result. The expression used in Acts 3:19 is "to blot out" (ἐξαλείφω, *exaleiphō*) sin.[67] This is another way to describe obtaining forgiveness (see also Col 2:14 – 15; Rev 3:5; 7:16 – 17; 21:3 – 4). In the LXX, this verb is used to describe being blotted out of God's book if one is not forgiven (Exod 32:32), blotting out sin (2 Macc 12:42), a request to blot out sin (Ps 51:9 [50:11 LXX]), and a request not to let the sin of an unrighteous one be blotted out (Ps 109:14 [108:14 LXX]; Jer 18:23; cf. also Isa 32:15 [Symmachus]; 43:25).[68]

The term "blot out" means "wipe away, erase, obliterate."[69] It was used of washing papyri to remove letters written in ink. In ancient times ink did not soak into the paper but remained on the surface, so removing writing was simply scraping the surface. This became the metaphor, denoting an obliteration that leaves no trace. Peter offers the opportunity to have the penalty of sin removed completely. Acts 3:19 points up a slight difference between repentance and turning. Repentance is the change of perspective and turning follows, as one's core direction changes as well.

Other summaries in Acts also use the term. Gentiles, seeing Aeneas healed by Peter, "turned to the Lord" (Acts 9:35). Gentiles in Antioch "believed and turned" to the Lord (11:21). In this passage, "belief" functions in a manner similar to repent in 3:19. These terms are used interchangeably to refer to the same saving act, though they highlight different elements of that response. Whether by repentance or faith, the product is a turning to God. That entire single act saves and produces a reorientation toward God.

So Barnabas and Paul urge the Gentiles in Lystra to turn from idols to God (Acts 14:15). Again, this passage shows the reversal of direction necessary for the salvation of unbelievers. The focus of turning always comes back to God. Gentiles are said to be "turning to God" in 15:19, where the term alone is sufficient to describe the response that saves.

The most important passage on turning to God is Acts 26:18, 20. Paul relates the Lord's call for him to turn the Gentiles from Satan to God, to receive forgiveness of sins and inheritance that come by faith in God. This passage is important in that all the terms mentioned thus far appear together here. Jews and Gentiles must "repent and turn to God" (v. 20), so they can receive benefits from God that come by faith; the result is that they perform deeds worthy of repentance (cf. John the Baptist's words in Luke 3:10 – 14).

Repentance for Luke is to express itself concretely and visibly in the life of the responder. That Paul presents this as a part of his gospel message shows that such exhortation is appropriate in an evangelistic setting. Fruit shows the presence of a life-giving root. That root can be biblically described as planted by faith, repentance, or

---

66. Johnson, *Acts of the Apostles*, 68.
67. BDF, §402.5.

68. Larkin, *Acts*, 68, note on 3:19.
69. BDAG, 344.

turning. Each of these three terms points to approaching God and resting in his provision and mercy. "Repenting" emphasizes what is left behind as one looks at life, sin, and God in a new way; "turning" alludes to a person's taking up a new direction; and "believing in God" focuses where one's attention ends up as one has a new orientation.

A negative use occurs in Acts, when Luke describes the Jews' failure to "turn" because of the hardness of their hearts (Acts 28:27). Failure to turn is the result of a refusal to respond.

11.5.3 Faith

Two other terms used frequently in Luke-Acts are "faith" (πίστις, *pistis*) and "to believe" (πιστεύω, *pisteuō*). Luke's usage of these words varies between the act of trust and the trust that saves. All occurrences suggest a reliance on another to provide something one cannot provide for oneself. The paralytic's friends had faith in Jesus that he could heal their friend (Luke 5:20). Because of the centurion's "great faith" (7:9), he understood Jesus' authority to heal (vv. 7–8). Jesus spoke of the faith of the sinful woman who washed his feet (7:50). Each act of faith expressed itself in concrete action. By contrast, the disciples' lack of faith showed that they questioned God's ability to watch over them. As a result, they were nervous and panicked (8:25). The woman with the continual flow of blood understood that Jesus could heal her, and in faith she touched his garment (8:48). Jesus challenged Jairus to believe (8:50).

Faith can be increased, as indicated by the apostles' request, "Increase our faith!" (Luke 17:5–6). This request means faith can always have more depth, though Jesus' reply emphasized the importance of faith's presence, no matter how small. The Samaritan leper (17:19) and the blind beggar (18:42) also acted out of faith in approaching Jesus.

Peter's faith failed, as Jesus had predicted (Luke 22:32). The possibility of lapsed faith in the face of persecution was so real that Jesus asked if faith would be found on earth when he returns (18:8). The faith described in these last two examples refers not to initial faith but to the continuation of faith. Lapses of faith can and do occur, but ideally faith should be constant. Such faith involves a fundamental orientation and trust that a person possesses, a basic recognition that if provision for deliverance in any situation is to come, Jesus must provide it. So faith is to continue; if it does not, spiritual catastrophe is the result.

The use of the noun "faith" in Acts is similar. Faith comes through Jesus and was the basis of the lame beggar's healing by Peter (Acts 3:16) and of Paul's healing of the man in Lystra with crippled feet (14:9). Stephen was "full of faith," a spiritually mature man, whose faith was exemplary and constant (6:5). At times, the Christian movement was actually called "the faith" (6:7; 13:8; 14:22; 16:5). Gentiles had faith (14:27) and were cleansed by faith (15:9). Faith's object is Christ (20:21; 24:24), and faith is the subjective means that sanctifies (26:18).[70]

---

70. One unusual use of faith is in Acts 17:31, where it means proof or assurance.

In Luke's gospel, the verb "to believe" is similar in force. Positive and negative examples abound. Zechariah did not believe the angel Gabriel about what God could do (Luke 1:20), but Mary did believe (1:45); as a result, she became a vessel for God's use. In the parable of the sower, the devil is said to prevent belief (8:12), while faith on the part of others is portrayed tragically as short-lived (v. 13). Luke notes that many people believed John's message (20:5). Jesus declared that whatever he might say in his defense, the Jewish leaders would not believe (22:67). Jesus asked the Emmaus travelers if they believed all that the prophets spoke (24:25). Faith responds to content and results in concrete reaction. It includes perception, but this perception produces a product, a reliance on God and what he promises.

Most uses of the verb πιστεύω in Acts are summaries of people's responses of belief. In a few passages the church is described as a community that believed (Acts 2:44; 4:32). The participle describes the respondents as "believers" (5:14; 15:5). Usually, the word refers to someone or something that is trusted: belief was in the message (4:4); in the good news (8:12–13); in the Lord, with faith in him produced by a miracle (9:42); in the Lord, with forgiveness as a result (10:43); in Christ (11:17); in the Lord (11:21; 14:23; 16:31); in God (16:34; 27:25); in Jesus (19:4); in the OT promise (24:14); and in the prophets (24:14). Those who believed included the Bereans (17:12), Athenians (17:34), Corinthians (18:8), Ephesians (19:18), Jews (21:20), and Gentiles (21:25). In 13:12, no object of faith is mentioned, but the proconsul of Cyprus believed as a result of the sorcerer Bar-Jesus being blinded. Belief justifies (13:39), but those who do not believe will perish (v. 41). All those whom God has ordained to eternal life believe (v. 48). And believing comes by God's grace (15:11; 18:27).

Faith, that is, simple belief, expresses itself concretely. Numerous pictures provided in Jesus' ministry are illustrative. They show that faith acts. Faith is the recognition and persuasion that God has something to offer that one must receive and embrace. So in Jesus' miracles, individuals receive what he offers. Faith is not passive. It understands, receives, and embraces. The one who welcomes God's message receives what God offers and responds to the gospel. He or she acknowledges that God through Jesus has dealt with the effects of sin and that only God can provide what is needed to reverse sin's presence and eradicate its penalty.

11.6 THE BENEFITS OF SALVATION

11.6.1 Forgiveness of Sins

Besides the presence of the indwelling Spirit, Luke enumerates numerous benefits that come from salvation. The first is "forgiveness" (ἄφεσις, *aphesis*).[71] In Luke the

---

71. This theme receives more detailed treatment in Christoph Stenschke, "The Need for Salvation," in *Witness to the Gospel*, 125–44. His essay is a look at Lucan anthropology and why people need to be saved. Accountability to God is Luke's starting point (Acts 10:42–43; 17:26). The fact one is a sinner in need of repentance for any number of reasons is another base (Luke 5:1–11, 32; 19:10; Acts 2:40, a reference that connects to the Lucan idea of the evil generation that inhabits the world; Luke 11:29, 50; 17:25 with Noah's and Lot's generations, as the prototype, 17:27–29).

knowledge of forgiveness is available through the preaching of the prophet of the Most High, namely, John the Baptist (Luke 1:76–77), who in turn points the way to the Davidic "horn" (v. 69), who will bring salvation to the nation of Israel (v. 68) and light to all who sit in darkness (v. 79). This knowledge and experience of salvation comes through embracing the forgiveness of sins.

John's baptism for the forgiveness of sins (Luke 3:3) was not the same as Christian baptism, since it could not yet picture the cleansing provided by the cross. Rather, John's baptism represented a turning to God as a preparation for the arrival of the promised Messiah. The humility reflected in the partaking of this baptism paved the way for divine forgiveness.

To the synagogue crowd, Jesus proclaimed a "freedom" or release (ἄφεσιν, *aphesin*) for the captives and liberty for those who are oppressed (Luke 4:18). Here Jesus' words hark back to the imagery in Isa 61:1 and 58:6. This "second exodus" imagery, as Jesus announced in the synagogue, pictures God's people released from enemies, which include Satan and sin, as Jesus' later mission makes clear (Luke 10:9, 18; 11:20–23; 22:20). Luke 24:47 summarizes the disciples' message, a message about repentance and the forgiveness of sins. In Acts 2:38 forgiveness is related to repentance and pictured in baptism; in 5:31 forgiveness is available to Israel; in 10:43 forgiveness is based on faith; in 13:38–39 forgiveness is available through Jesus based on the faith that frees one from bondage, a freedom that the law could not provide; and in 26:18 those who turn from Satan to God receive his forgiveness.

11.6.2 Life

Another key benefit of salvation is "life" (ζωή, *zōē*). A scribe asked Jesus about inheriting eternal life (Luke 10:25); he wanted to be assured of participating in the final resurrection (Dan 12:3). Jesus replied that he should love God and his neighbor, a reply that summarizes the message of God's law. To do this brings life (Luke 10:28). This reply, though soteriological in nature, reflects to a degree the pre-cross setting it depicts. The scribe's failure to respond to Jesus' message shows that he erroneously thought he could earn salvation through his own achievements. If he had loved God, he would have responded to Jesus as God's agent, let Jesus deal with his sin, and been led into the life he asked about. This need leads Jesus to continue his answer and press him when the scribe asks who his neighbor is. The scribe was really asking if some people were not his neighbor and could be ignored; in other words, he loved only some neighbors! Jesus responded with the parable of the good Samaritan, calling on the scribe to be a neighbor, showing that love for God means responding to those around him.

Jesus offers a negative statement about life in Luke 12:15. Life does not consist in one's possessions. The parable of the rich fool (vv. 16, 21) illustrates this truth and calls on one to be rich toward God.

Luke 18:18 repeats the question of 10:25, "What must I do to inherit eternal life?" In his answer in 18:29–30, Jesus says that anyone who leaves all for the sake of the kingdom will receive many benefits in this life and eternal life in the age to come. Jesus indicates that the disciples have already done this and so they have received these benefits. This response, together with Jesus' remarks in 10:25–28, shows the ultimate point of where the kingdom is designed to take people, namely, into a genuine love relationship with God fueled by the faith and gratitude of experiencing God's forgiveness with the response of a life that seeks to love God and one's neighbor, meeting needs as one is able. One does not earn salvation but must come to God for it. The goal of the kingdom message is not merely to offer salvation, but to reflect the care and character of God in response to it. Total sacrifice for Jesus does pay off.

Total sacrifice is also in the pictures of faith where one is told to set aside even family priorities (Luke 9:59–60; 14:26). Note that in 14:26, the call to "hate" is not literal but rhetorical. Otherwise, Jesus' command to love one's neighbor as oneself as a summation of what God desires makes no sense (10:25–37). The call to hate simply means to "love less" (Gen 29:30–31; Deut 21:15–17; Jdg 14:16). The image is strong, but it is not a call to be insensitive or to leave all feeling behind. Marshall suggests "renounce," which is possible depending on how it is defined.[72] Following Jesus is to be the disciple's "first love." This pursuit must have priority over any family member and even one's own life; that is, other concerns must take second place to following Jesus (Luke 8:19–21; 9:59–62; 12:4, 49–53; 16:13). Matthew 10:37–39; Luke 9:24; and John 12:25 make a similar point, though Matthew speaks of loving family more, rather than hating, thereby softening the remark's emotive force.

This saying needs to be set in the context of its first-century setting. At that time, a Jewish person who made a choice for Jesus would alienate his or her family. If someone desired acceptance by family more than a relationship with God, one might never come to Jesus, for rejection would inevitably follow. In other words, there could be no casual devotion to Jesus in the first century. A decision for Christ marked a person and automatically came with a cost.[73]

The modern Western phenomenon where making a decision for Christ is popular in the larger social community was not true of Jesus' setting; this complicates our understanding of the significance of a decision in the NT to associate with Christ. Today one might associate with Christ simply because it is culturally appropriate. Such a "decision" was impossible in the first century. Anyone who chose to be associated with Jesus received a negative reaction, often rejection from within one's own home, since most Jews were rejecting Jesus.[74] Thus, if a person feared family more than God, he or she would refuse to come to Jesus. To give over everything meant being willing to leave all earthly ties behind for a new set of relationships, namely, the ones God calls for through Jesus. So Jesus noted in Luke 18:29–30 that although a disciple lost a family, that person gained a new family, along with eternal life.

---

72. Marshall, *Gospel of Luke*, 592; Michel, *TDNT*, 4:690–91.

73. Contemporary comparisons may be seen in certain formerly Communist Eastern European settings, in Muslim countries, or in tight-knit Asian families.

74. This idea I have developed in my article, "Embracing Jesus in a First Century Context: What Can It Teach Us about Spiritual Commitment?" in *Journal of Spiritual Formation and Soul Care* 3 (2010): 128–39.

In Acts, life is viewed as the result of resurrection (Acts 2:27–28). What Jesus provides allows him to be called "the author of life" (3:15). The apostolic message is called "this new life" (5:20), and repentance leads to life (11:18). Paul states that since the Jews refused to respond to his message, they did not consider themselves worthy of eternal life (13:46). So he turned to Gentiles, who were appointed to it (v. 48). In 17:25, "life" is probably not soteriological but refers instead to the physical life God gives all human beings, since the verse also speaks of God's giving "life and breath and everything else" to all.

11.6.3 Gift

A number of times Luke refers to "the gift" (δωρεά, *dōrea*), by which he means primarily what the Holy Spirit supplies (Acts 2:38; 8:20; 10:45; 11:17). Particularly significant here is the already frequently noted parallel between Acts 2 and Acts 10–11, since what was given to the Gentiles is also what the disciples received at Pentecost.

11.6.4 Peace

Another benefit of salvation is "peace" (εἰρήνη, *eirēnē*). Like a rising star, Jesus, as the promised one from the house of David (Luke 1:69), shines as light and reveals "the path of peace" (v. 79). That is, Jesus makes possible a reconciled relationship between God and humanity. Jesus, as Savior, Christ, and Lord, brings "peace to those on whom his favor rests" (2:14). The offer of peace is part of the kingdom message (10:5–6). In a counter-note, Jesus said that he came not to bring peace but division (12:51). This remark is simply a recognition that some will accept what he offers and others will not. With that reality is the recognition that division within families will come (12:51–52; see sec. 11.6.2 on "Life"). Peter said his message was "the good news of peace through Jesus Christ" (Acts 10:36).

11.6.5 Grace

"Grace" or "favor" (χάρις, *charis*) is another salvation benefit, though Luke uses the word with some variation of force. Grace refers to unmerited favor, a gift one receives from God at the moment he or she genuinely believes. Mary was the object of God's "favor" as God prepared to use her as a vessel through whom Jesus would enter the world (1:30); this was based solely on God's initiative, freely bestowed.[75] Only Luke among the Synoptics uses the noun *charis*. It also becomes a key term in Acts to describe what God does for his people out of his good pleasure (Luke 2:40; Acts 7:10, 46; 11:23; 13:43; 14:3).[76]

The expression of finding favor or grace with God is a Semitism (Gen 6:8; 18:3; 39:21; 43:14; Jdg 6:17; 1 Sam 1:18; 2 Sam 15:25).[77] It is also common as a secular OT expression (Gen 33:9–10). Whether the person showing favor is blessed because

---

75. Bock, *Luke 1:1–9:50*, 111.
76. Conzelmann, *TDNT*, 9:392–93.
77. Marshall, *Gospel of Luke*, 66.

of an earlier action by the favored one or whether the one giving the favor simply chooses freely to display kindness depends on the context. As an expression of divine working, favor signifies God's gracious choice of someone through whom God does something special (Noah is spared from the flood; Gideon is chosen to judge Israel; Hannah is given a child in barrenness; David receives back the ark of the covenant). In the OT, the phrase often involves a request granted on the condition that someone had favor with God (so Gideon, Hannah, and David).

In two verses that describe Jesus' growth (Luke 2:40, 52), grace (i.e., God's favor) is said to rest on him. In a nontheological use in 6:32–33, the term "grace" is understood as "credit." Here Jesus questions the merit of a person loving only those who love him or her.

In Acts, grace rests on people and communities. Acts 4:33 speaks of grace resting on all the believers. Stephen is full of grace (6:8) and speaks of God's favor on David (7:46). Paul and Barnabas have been committed to God's grace by the church at Antioch for their first missionary journey (14:26). Later they are sent to Antioch (15:40). The most common use of the word "grace" is as a description of salvation or its message (11:23; 13:43; 14:3; 15:11; 20:24, 32). Acts 18:27 speaks of belief through grace; that is, God enabled people to believe. Salvation is a gift of God in which he bestows rich blessings and favor on those who seek his aid. Those who come to him humbly in faith for deliverance receive his unmerited favor, realizing they cannot supply what God can give. When that happens, heaven rejoices at the provision of the gift (Luke 15:7, 10).

11.6.6 Justify

There is one text where the verb "justify" (δικαιόω, *dikaioō*) appears in a nontechnical sense, but it illustrates how Luke sees a key component of the term.[78] It is in the scene from Luke 18:9–14. Jesus notes that when the tax collector walks away from his prayer, he is "justified." The commendation is for the humility of the tax collector in contrast to the Pharisee, who is proud. The Pharisee distorts a praise psalm by thanking God for all his own work. God commends the humility of the tax collector, for he senses his need for God's mercy without any sense of entitlement.

Other texts not using the term reinforce this emphasis. In Luke 7:1–10, the centurion who asks to have his slave healed has a similar attitude, which leads Jesus to say he has not seen such faith anywhere in Israel. The prodigal returns from his waywardness knowing he has no right be a son, yet he is received by the father as a full son (15:11–31). Jesus compares his own mission to that of a physician who seeks to heal those who need his work by calling them to repentance. Thus, the appeal for God's mercy and turning in repentance are what justifies, for one merely seeks mercy and understands there is no entitlement.

---

78. By nontechnical I mean that this is not yet "Christian" justification as a result of Jesus' work. This use merely means God has accepted the plea for mercy of the tax collector in the parable. A more technical sense of justify appears in Acts 13. That text looks to being declared righteous in light of Christ's work and contrasts with what the law cannot do. Here faith does accomplish being justified (Acts 13:38-39)

11.7 OTHER POINTS OF SOTERIOLOGY

11.7.1 The Message of Salvation and Promise

Much of this subject has already been discussed in connection with other themes about salvation. The purpose of this section is to review the idea that in Luke-Acts God's promise is portrayed as already-not yet with a judgment tied to what remains. Acts 2 emphasizes what is already fulfilled and Acts 3 discusses what is yet to come. In the review, we pick up with texts in Acts, whereas our earlier treatment focused on key kingdom texts in Luke.[79]

Jesus' message focused on the offer and approach of the kingdom. He coupled that offer with exhortations about the ethic that was appropriate for those associated with the kingdom.

The apostles' message emphasizes the realization of God's array of promises, particularly as they relate to Jesus Christ, the Lord. Salvific benefits are available through him now, and judgment and consummation are yet to come. This is all in line with the hope of the Hebrew Scripture as discussed in the sections on God's plan, the kingdom, and the fulfillment of the sacred texts. In addition, Paul argued in his defense speeches that he was simply preaching the hope of the Scriptures and the hope of resurrection (Acts 23:6; 24:14 – 16; 25:8; 26:6 – 7, 22 – 23). The scope of this message includes all people. Therefore, there should be no bigotry in the church or in the offer of the gospel.

In the face of promise, one other contrasting dimension merits discussion. It is that the hope of the gospel is offered in the face of approaching judgment. Speaking of an ax lying at the root of a tree, John the Baptist warns that judgment is imminent (Luke 3:7 – 9). Though the actual judgment to which John refers will come later, the fate of one's relationship to that judgment is decided in this life. So judgment is encountered directly in the message, along with the opportunity for deliverance from it.

When Jesus' message is rejected or when he anticipates rejection, he pronounces woes on his hearers to make the consequences clear (Luke 6:24 – 26; 10:13 – 15; 11:42 – 44, 46 – 52). Without repentance, Jesus says, deliverance is impossible (13:3 – 5). In the story of the rich man and Lazarus, judgment is seen in the fate of the rich man (16:19 – 31). Vultures hovering over dead bodies graphically depict the death and judgment that come with Jesus' return as the Son of Man (17:37). Similar warnings in Acts invoke the imagery of the day of the Lord (Acts 2:40) and of the "covenant curses" of the Torah that promise being "cut off" (3:23, taken from Lev 23:29). In addition, two texts refer to Jesus as the judge (Acts 10:42; 17:30 – 31).

With the offer of salvation, each individual faces life or death. A person may choose to be related rightly to God or to face eternal judgment. Jesus gives opportunity to receive life, forgiveness, peace with God, and the presence of his Spirit. His death and resurrection have shown that Jesus died for others and is ruling at God's

---

79. See the earlier discussion of the kingdom in ch. 6.

right hand, ready to distribute salvific benefits to those who come to him. As already discussed, Luke uses three terms to describe the appropriate response: "repent," "turn," and "believe." Any one of these terms can summarize the response that gains life as one humbly comes to God for deliverance that only he can give. When a sinner repents, heaven rejoices and God receives the sinner with open arms, for to seek and save the lost is at the center of Jesus' mission (Luke 15:7, 10, 18–24; 19:10).

11.7.2 The Law

An examination of the law in Luke-Acts is related to soteriology, because a dispute over the relationship of the law to grace was a central conflict in the early church (Acts 15).[80] The law does have certain points of value for the church. The law does not have only one function, nor is it simply abrogated. What is said about the law depends on the perspective from which it is addressed. Luke-Acts can refer to law as a moral guide that still has instructive value, to law as containing promise that is fulfilled, or to law as regulating membership and offering guidance within the community. Acts 15 shows that some laws are abrogated. Gentiles do not need to be circumcised or to change their choice of food (i.e., to become Jews) to come to Christ.

Certain Lucan passages emphasize continuity between the old era and the new era introduced by Jesus. According to Luke 10:25–28, the moral essence of the law is to love God and one's neighbor. Here is life. The law, having an ethical goal, is concerned with how others are treated. All the law is summed up in this focus, and Jesus endorses it as a message worthy of the one who wishes to have a right relationship with God. Such a description fits what other NT texts say when they describe a believer who has embraced God's grace (John 21 with Jesus' questions to Peter; 1 Cor 2:9; Jas 2:5; 1 John 4:19). Of course, if one loves God, he or she will respond to Jesus' call to enter into a relationship with God by responding to Jesus' message.

In Luke 16:17 Luke affirms that the law has abiding value; it will not fail. Here the focus is on law as promise, since the verse follows a remark about John the Baptist's message and the newly arrived kingdom announcement (v. 16). In another example, Moses and the OT prophets reveal the type of moral life God desires (v. 29). If one is to respond to God and examines the law carefully, one can see the hope (and accountability to God) it proclaims. The law indicates promise, since Moses and the prophets witnessed to Christ (24:27, 44). The continuity of the new era to the law is found in its ethical call to love and in its anticipation of God's promise.

Other passages, however, point to discontinuity between the law and the present age (though in some cases the discontinuity pertains to how the law was interpreted in the Jewish tradition). The Pharisees and teachers of the law thought that the authority to forgive sin was limited to God, but Jesus notes that he, as the

---

80. A more detailed treatment of this theme appears in ch. 18. The discussion here only orients us to that discussion as it touches on salvation.

Son of Man, possesses such authority (Luke 5:17–26). In 5:27–32, Jesus challenges how the Pharisees and teachers of the law viewed associating with sinners. He shows that the person who is sensitive to the message of God's hope can and should relate to sinners the hope of God's promise, as his own example has proved (see also ch. 15).

An explanation for the difference in perspective about sinners comes in Luke 5:33–39, when Jesus responds to questions about his associations with sinners by using proverbs that show how what he is teaching is new. It cannot be mixed with Judaism, the old cloth or old wineskin. He also notes that those who like the old (i.e., Judaism) will not like the new, the message of Jesus. The two approaches cannot be syncretized, for they are distinct. That Jesus' objection here is with the interpretation of the law as opposed to law itself is clear from 16:19–31, where the law should have taught the rich man to care for those in need (cf. Deut 14:29). When the rich man wished to warn his relatives, it was to tell them, in part, that they should not respond as he had by failing to help Lazarus, who had sat outside his door reachable and in need (Luke 16:24–29).

Another key pair of texts pertains to laboring on the Sabbath, where two aspects of the law are more directly challenged (Luke 6:1–11). In vv. 1–5, Jesus points out that David was allowed to do what the law specifically prohibited when he and his companions ate the consecrated bread (Lev 24:5–9; 1 Sam 21:6). Jesus then affirms that he and his disciples can pick the heads of grain (Sabbath labor in Jewish tradition) because he, the Son of Man, has authority over the Sabbath.[81] Jesus is like David and more than David. Verses 6–11 affirm his right as Lord over the Sabbath to "labor" on the Sabbath in order to heal, to save a life. There is irony and vindication when God honors Jesus' "labor" of commanding the woman to straighten up or the man with the withered hand to "stretch out" his hand (cf. 13:10–17; 14:1–6).

In Luke 11:41–42, Jesus argues that the Pharisees' perception of the law is distorted. By tithing herbs and neglecting justice and love, they are ignoring the law's ethical thrust. Luke 16:16 teaches discontinuity, for here Jesus notes that the law and the prophets were until John. In contrast to the era of law stands the present era of proclaiming the kingdom. The law is viewed as a period that has passed away, even though 16:17 makes it clear that the law does not fail, in the sense that it reaches its realization in the kingdom preaching about Jesus. Thus Luke 16:16–17 places discontinuity and continuity side by side.

The picture in Acts is similar. Law is juxtaposed as both continuous and discontinuous. What the new community preached stirred the charge that the disciples did not uphold the law (Acts 6:11–14, against Stephen; 18:13 and 21:21, against Paul). The church's reply was that the law is upheld because the promise of the law is proclaimed, either in resurrection or in hope in general (23:6; 24:14–21). What

---

81. For the tradition that indicates what Jesus did was seen by pious Jews as a Sabbath violation, see *m. Šabb.* 7.2.

Paul preached is what the law and the prophets teach (24:14; 25:8; 26:22). Paul is highlighting the law as read in light of the prophets. The law reflects the moral will of God and anticipates that deliverance and justice will someday come from him.

Paul even emphasizes that he says nothing against the Jews, and so he calls on his listeners to consider his message and ask themselves if they believe the prophets (Acts 26:26–28; 28:17). Seeing the law as promise is evident in 3:12–26, where Peter declares the hope of Jesus by appealing only to passages from the Torah (3:13, the promise of the God of Abraham [Exod 3:6, 15]; Acts 3:22, citing Deut 18:15–20; Acts 3:23, citing Lev 23:29; Acts 3:25, citing Gen 22:18; 26:4). In highlighting the promise of the second Moses, Peter declares that in Jesus a new era has come.

Nevertheless, the church, at least in Jerusalem, kept portions of the law as a means of staying in contact with Jews, for the sake of the gospel. The apostles frequented the temple (Acts 3:1). They went to the synagogue on the Sabbath (13:14). Jewish believers were sometimes circumcised (16:3). Paul took vows and honored them (18:18; 21:23–24). In fact, they advised all believers, both Jews and Gentiles, to refrain from certain items. Such action was to "do well," for it avoided giving offense (15:23–29).

The law, however, is not binding on Gentiles, since Peter affirms that to insist that believers keep the law places a burden on their necks (Acts 15:10). Peter argues that even their ancestors, the patriarchs of Israel, were not able to bear this burden. The law is not a way of salvation. It might instruct and guide, but it is not binding for the church. Nothing makes this distinction clearer than the vision from God himself. In that vision, God shows Peter that all foods are to be considered clean. This vision stands in clear contrast to what the law taught (Lev 11; Acts 10:9–16). Peter's hesitation to believe the vision only underlines the contrast contained in this instruction. The fact is that the "end of the law's reign" in this kind of an area is something God insists on, despite the apostle's objection.

In short, the Mosaic law has ended because God has brought its role to an end! God as Lord of the law indicates dramatically that the law has served its purpose. The hope now realized in Jesus, the resurrection, and the inauguration of the kingdom program has changed everything. The law no longer plays a central role in marking out what the people of God should eat or do to establish their association to Christ. The only function remaining for the law is its call to love God and to love one's neighbor, which also means responding to Jesus, the one who embodies the message of God's offer of peace to the fallen world (Luke 1:68–79, esp. vv. 78–79). Coming to Jesus means embracing light and entering a new era of relating to God.

11.8 CONCLUSION

Salvation is virtually on every page of Luke-Acts. God is at work completing his promise, working through Jesus, bringing the Spirit, and forgiving sin. Salvation means reestablishing a lost relationship with God and finding peace with him. In repenting, turning to or believing in Jesus, the person receives the benefits of forgiveness, the Spirit and life. That presence of grace through faith leads to a changed life. So now the call is to love God fully and love one's neighbor as a reflection of God's own work. In gratitude for the grace tied to salvation, one will love deeply. So we turn now to look to the various groups who heard this message of hope and promise. Their responses are also a key part of Luke's narrative and theology, showing us the array of reactions this word generated.

Chapter 12

ISRAEL IN LUKE-ACTS

BIBLIOGRAPHY

Bachmann, Michael. "Jerusalem and Rome in Luke-Acts." Pp. 60–83 in *Luke-Acts and Empire: Essays in Honor of Robert L. Brawley*. Ed. David Rhoads, David Esterline, and Jae Won Lee. Princeton Theological Monographs. Eugene, OR: Pickwick, 2011. **Brawley, Robert.** *Luke-Acts and the Jews: Conflict, Apology, Reconciliation.* SBLMS. Atlanta: Scholars Press, 1987. **Evans, Craig.** "Prophecy and Polemic: Jews in Luke's Scriptural Apologetic." Pp. 171–211 in *Luke and Scripture: The Function of Sacred Tradition in Luke-Acts.* Ed. C. A. Evans and J. A. Sanders. Minneapolis: Fortress, 1993. **Fuller, Michael E.** *The Restoration of Israel: Israel's Regathering and the Fate of the Nations in Early Jewish Literature and Luke-Acts.* BZNW. Berlin: DeGruyter, 2006. **Jervell, Jacob.** *Luke and the People of God.* Minneapolis: Augsburg, 1972. Idem. *The Theology of the Acts of the Apostles.* Cambridge: Cambridge University Press, 1996. **Moessner, David.** *Jesus and the Heritage of Israel: Luke's Narrative Claim upon Israel's Legacy.* Harrisburg, PA: Trinity International, 1999. **Rese, Martin.** "The Jews in Luke-Acts: Some Second Thoughts." Pp. 185–201 in *The Unity of Luke-Acts.* Ed. J. Verheyden. BETL. Leuven: Leuven University Press, 1999. **Rhoads, David, David Esterline, and Jae Won Lee**, eds. *Luke-Acts and Empire: Essays in Honor of Robert L. Brawley.* Princeton Theological Monographs. Eugene, OR: Pickwick, 2011. **Seccombe, David Peter.** "The New People of God." Pp. 349–72 in *A Witness to the Gospel: The Theology of Acts.* Ed. I. Howard Marshall and David Peterson. Grand Rapids: Eerdmans, 1998. **Tannehill, Robert.** *The Narrative Unity of Luke-Acts.* 2 vols. Minneapolis: Fortress, 1986, 1990. **Tiede, David.** *Prophecy and History in Luke-Acts.* Philadelphia: Fortress, 1980. **Tyson, Joseph, ed.** *Luke-Acts and the Jewish People: Eight Critical Perspectives.* Minneapolis: Augsburg, 1988. **Tyson, Joseph.** *Images of Judaism in Luke-Acts.* Columbia: University of South Carolina Press, 1992.

In the next few chapters, we will work in narrative order with separate topics involving Israel, the Gentiles, the church, discipleship and ethics, women, the poor, and Luke's view of the law. Then we will synthesize all this in a chapter on ecclesiology.

We start with Israel ('Ισραήλ, *Israēl*) because for Luke the story starts here and the gospel goes out first to this nation. On this point, Luke is like Paul (Rom 1:16–17). In fact, for Luke the entire story of Jesus is Israel's story.[1] We consider both the term "Israel" and references to "the Jews." God gave the promise to Israel originally. That plan was designed especially for her to be a beneficiary and through her for divine benefits to be given to the world, as the promise to Abraham shows (Gen 12:3). In effect, Luke argues that a good Jew will embrace the Messiah whom God has sent and become a member of the new way. When one does so, the world witnesses and receives divine blessing.

Luke also emphasizes that the church was not formed with the intent of Jesus' followers would become something distinct, but they were forced to become distinct when significant Jewish rejection set in. This is where the term "Jew" (Ἰουδαῖος, *Ioudaios*) becomes important, for we will see a divided people with many opposed to what God has done in Christ. Indeed, the term "people" (λαός, *laos*) is also important for this topic in some of its uses. This theme is especially prominent in Acts and in its treatment of Paul. Nonetheless, to the very end Paul defends himself as a Jew (Acts 21:39; 22:3). He argues that he has done nothing against the Jewish people (25:8), whom he calls "our people" (26:23; 28:17).

12.1 ISRAEL IN THE INFANCY MATERIAL

References to Israel are not that common in Luke's gospel after the infancy section. Of the twelve references in the gospel, seven appear in these first two chapters. Acts has fifteen references. Still, the term is important because it shows up so much in these key early chapters.

The first reference describes part of the ministry of John the Baptist. He "will bring back many of the people of Israel to the Lord their God" (Luke 1:16). This turning involves working in the spirit and power of Elijah, so that children and fathers are brought together along with the disobedient and the just. Here we see an emphasis on reconciliation between people that results from responding to God. This ethical triangle is a product of salvation.

The hope reflects texts like Mal 3:1; 4:5 and Jewish hope expressed in Sir 48:10. So Luke's remarks fit issues tied to Israel's hope and to her being moved out of spiritual exile. The result brings in the key term λαός (*laos*, "people"), since those who respond for the Lord's coming are "a people prepared" (1:17). The passage as a whole argues that out of Israel will come some who are responsive to God, but this also implies others will not be responsive, pointing to a divided people, where ancestry is not an automatic guarantee of blessing (see also 3:7–9; 14:15–24).[2]

---

1. John T. Carroll, *Response to the End of History: Eschatology and Situation in Luke-Acts* (SBLDS 92; Atlanta: Scholars Press, 1988), 84, says that Luke's presentation of the kingdom is "inextricably bound to the motif of Israel." Michael E. Fuller, *The Restoration of Israel: Israel's Regathering and the Fate of the Nations in Early Jewish Literature and Luke-Acts* (BZNW 138; Berlin: De Gruyter, 2006), 204, n. 30, notes how the nations are never "isolated subjects of interest, but are connected to *Israel's* narrative" (emphasis original).

2. Jervell, *Theology of the Acts of the Apostles*, 34–43. He stresses that Israel does not go away in Luke-Acts. Israel continues its life in those who respond to Messiah. There is both a rejecting Israel and an accepting Israel. The church includes those who accept, i.e., the Jewish Christians. They are rightful heirs of Israel's promise and complete what the Hebrew Scriptures had hoped for. The relationship between Israel and the church is complex in Luke-Acts. Israel is old and is rooted in promises of old. The church is new, forced

Mary's hymn, the *Magnificat*, also appeals to God's promise to Israel. She praises God for how he responds to the humble, the needy, and those who fear him through his divine mercy. She looks forward to the justice of eschatological reversal that will bring down the proud, the mighty, and the rich while raising up the hungry and others of low status (Luke 1:46–53). All of this is said to be a help to Israel as God recalls his mercy in a commitment he made to Abraham and his seed (1:54–55). This mercy is then shown in justice and faithfulness. It is a key part of what Mary anticipates comes with salvation.

A similar expression of gratitude for God's faithfulness comes in the *Benedictus* of Zechariah. His praise is for a "horn of salvation" out of the house of David that is the visit and redemption of God. This deliverance frees up God's people to serve him in righteousness and holiness (Luke 1:67–75). This praise is extended to "the God of Israel" (1:68). In this salvation as initially mediated through the message of John the Baptist, God's people receive knowledge of the forgiveness of sins (1:77) in preparation for the coming of the dawn that is Messiah (1:78–79). It is no surprise that Zechariah's remarks echo themes we saw when John the Baptist's birth was announced. Israel is in need of renewal, and Messiah brings it. It is no wonder that the note on the growth of John the Baptist ends with the remark about his being in the wilderness before he "appeared publicly to Israel" (1:80). This is because the wilderness is a place where revelation occurs and Israel can replay the exodus.

In the third hymn of the infancy section, the *Nunc Dimittis*, Simeon declares joy at the arrival of Messiah and God's salvation as one who was awaiting "the consolation of Israel" (Luke 2:25), precisely what Luke 1–2 were describing. Simeon is righteous, making him another pious witness to Jesus. "The consolation of Israel" (παράκλησιν τοῦ Ἰσραήλ, *paraklēsin tou Israēl*) was a key element in many strands of OT and Jewish eschatology, referring to the hope of deliverance for the nation (Isa 40:1; 49:13; 51:3; 57:18; 61:2; *2 Bar.* 44.7). Later, the rabbis would refer to Messiah as *Menahem* ("comforter") because they saw him as the one who would bring this consolation (*y. Ber.* 5a [2.4]).[3]

In the OT, various agents brought God's consolation, but a primary agent in eschatological contexts was the Servant of God.[4] This desire for consolation characterizes the believer or God-fearer in Luke (Acts 17:22–37; 21:25–36). Interestingly, while Luke associates consolation with Messiah, John will associate it with the Spirit (John 14–16). One also can associate this hope with the idea of messianic comfort given to those in darkness (Luke 1:79).[5] God was expected to complete his promise, and Simeon was looking forward to the arrival of that day — a day that meant blessing for the world, not just for Israel.[6]

---

to emerge out of the rejection of so many in Israel, but it is still tied to these old promises. What Paul calls "the remnant" in Rom 9–11 is the link between what was old and what was new. Jews who responded never saw themselves as having left Israel even as they became a part of what became the church. They saw themselves as faithful to God's promises and the hope of Messiah and resurrection. This complexity between Israel and the church will demand its own chapter (see ch. 14).

3. Schmitz and Stählin, *TDNT*, 5:793; Str-B, 1:66, 83, 195.

4. Schmitz and Stählin, *TDNT*, 5:789–90, 792–93; Str-B, 2:124–25.

5. Plummer, *St. Luke*, 66.

6. Bock, *Luke 1:1–9:50*, 238–39.

Simeon has a more universal scope in his remarks as he speaks of salvation "which you have prepared in the sight of all nations" (Luke 2:31). He also speaks of how this event is "light ... [and] glory for your people Israel" (2:32). Yet it also includes the Gentiles, for whom the light of salvation in Jesus is a "revelation" (ἀποκάλυψις, *apokalypsis*; 2:32). The entire closing looks to the light as blessing for both Israel and the nations. In other words, Messiah's coming both is Israel's story and looks to the inclusion of the nations. When that happens, nationalism is subsumed under divine universal blessing and reconciliation, or at least the opportunity for this in the community Messiah will form. This is part of what being light means.

Yet there is division in God's people. As in Israel, Messiah's coming means "the falling and rising of many in Israel, and ... a sign that will be spoken against" (2:34).[7] This is the story Luke tells, when we see how the Messiah, authenticated by God, is rejected. In Acts, we see how those whom God has commissioned face intense resistance. Here is the theme of the divided people. So God's program is doing two things at once. It is dividing Israel as we know her, but it is also forming a new people made up of Israel and the nations. This new thing is what Luke will refer to as the church, a church that still has roots in God's old promises because of the faithful in Israel who respond to Messiah. What is new also is really old.

The theme of the hope of the nation closes when an old prophetess Anna issues a pronouncement regarding Jesus. She is described as speaking about him to those "looking forward to the redemption of Jerusalem" (Luke 2:38). Anna represents a gender pairing with Simeon, and her hope for the nation is described in similar terms. The phrase "redemption of Jerusalem" (λύτρωσιν Ἰερουσαλήμ, *lytrōsin Ierousalēm*) refers to the redemption of the entire nation of Israel, since the capital stands for the nation. Equivalent to the phrase "consolation of Israel" (2:25), it has OT background in that it refers to God's decisive salvific act for his people (Isa 40:9; 52:9; 63:4). The focus is on the Redeemer and the special time of salvation that comes with him.[8]

In Luke, Anna's expectation is like that of Joseph of Arimathea, who "was waiting for the kingdom of God" (Luke 23:51). It also parallels the description of the Emmaus travelers, who were disappointed at Jesus' death because they were awaiting Israel's redemption (24:21).[9] In addition, the content and mood of Anna's remarks parallel ideas already expressed in the *Magnificat* and the *Benedictus* (1:46–55, 68–79; also Acts 1:6; 26:6–7).[10] For Luke, the ultimate expectations for Jesus' ministry change little between the start and finish of the gospel.[11] Jesus' story is Israel's story.

12.2 ISRAEL IN THE BODY OF LUKE'S GOSPEL

There are not many Israel texts in the rest of the gospel. Two uses appear in a key scene, Jesus' exposition of an Isaiah passage in the Nazareth synagogue (Luke

---

7. We took a close look at this text in ch. 7.
8. Büchsel, *TDNT*, 4:351.
9. Danker, *Jesus and the New Age*, 72; Schürmann, *Lukasevange-*

lium: Kommentar zu Kap. 1.1–9.50, 131.
10. Tiede, *Luke*, 78.
11. Bock, *Luke 1:1–9:50*, 253.

4:16 – 30). Here Elijah and Elisha are noted as prophets who had come to Israel (4:25, 27), but given the spiritual state of the nation they ended up being able to bless only two Gentiles, the widow of Zarephath and Naaman the Syrian. The teaching met with intense anger as Jesus contended that a prophet is without honor in his own home. The reference back to these prophets of old was a warning not to be like Israel of old, when God sent messengers but Israel missed blessing because of a hard heart. The crowd did not miss the point that the period of these prophets came at a spiritual low point in Israel's history. Their reaction to the warning shows their rejection of Jesus' assessment of their spiritual condition and points to a fissure that his teaching brought to Israel.

Another interesting note along the lines of Gentile responses versus that in Israel comes with the faith of the centurion whose slave is healed. Jesus commends this soldier's faith. As he moves to heal the centurion's slave, Jesus says that "I have not found such great faith even in Israel" (Luke 7:9). Again, note how Gentiles are showing openness to God's agent.[12]

Jerusalem gets an important mention in Luke 13:31 – 35. Here Jesus declares that the "house" (i.e., "the nation") is desolate until she says, "Blessed is he who comes in the name of the Lord" (Luke 13:35). This is the declaration of an exilelike judgment using the language of desolation from Jer 12:7 and 22:5. Israel's desolation will remain until she recognizes the one whom God has sent, a phrase using the language of Ps 118:26. This psalm appears several times in Luke and Acts, referring to the rejected stone God honors as well as to the reception of him as sent by God (Luke 19:38; Acts 4:11).

The OT declared the possibility of exile for the nation if it did not respond to God's call about exercising justice (Jer 22:5 – 6).[13] Therefore, Jesus' use of "house" (οἶκος, oikos) in Luke 13:35 does not allude to the temple. Jesus is more emphatic than Jeremiah in his statement of the potential rejection of the nation. He states that a time of abandonment has come. Rather than being gathered under God's wings, their house is left empty and exposed. The now-empty house is the nation. The tree is being cut down (13:6 – 9).

Jesus adds a note about the duration of this judgment: they will not see God's messenger until they recognize the one "who comes in the name of the Lord," a citation of Ps 117:26 LXX (118:26 Eng.). The original psalm alluded to the priests' blessing of those who came to worship in the temple — in all likelihood pilgrims led in procession by the king. In a parallel manner, Jesus says that until the nation acknowledges him as blessed by God, it will be judged.

The question arises as to what office Jesus possesses according to this allusion: prophet, Messiah, or both? The pericope itself and Jesus' actions in the passage (esp. Luke 13:32 – 33) suggest that he is acting only as a prophet. However, Luke's earlier use of certain terminology and the general use of Ps 118 by Jesus suggest a messianic

---

12. Matthew's gospel also makes a similar point in that the Magi in his infancy account are more sensitive to Jesus' birth than Herod the Great and the Jewish leaders. He also includes the centurion miracle.

13. Tiede, *Luke*, 259.

force.[14] The key term "he who comes" (ὁ ἐρχόμενος, *ho erchomenos*) has already been given a technical force in Luke. In 3:15–16 and 7:19, this phrase alludes to the coming messianic figure who brings God's deliverance. So Luke's use of the phrase here has a clear messianic flavor. Luke 19:38 also has a messianic force in its use of Ps 118: the nation is depicted as missing another opportunity to respond to the king's coming; a lament follows in 19:41–44. Israel must accept Jesus as its deliverer. Until it does so — like the priests of the psalm received the leader of the worshipers' entourage — it stands alone, exposed to the world's dangers.

It is debated whether Luke by this remark holds out hope for Israel's future. Luke 21:24 and the speech of Acts 3 show that Jesus and the church continue to extend hope to Israel. They believe that God will restore the nation in the end. In fact, the NT suggests that such a response will precede Christ's return — thus, Luke's later reference to the current period as "the times of the Gentiles" (Luke 21:24; see also Rom 11:11–32 [esp. 11:12, 14, 25–27, 31–32]; and probably Rev 7:1–8). The triumphal entry of Luke 19 cannot be the fulfillment of this remark since a note of rejection is present in 19:41–44. Neither is Jewish conversion throughout the age a fulfillment, since this can hardly explain the NT and the Lucan phrase "the times/fullness of the Gentiles," which appears in other passages. Still another faulty explanation is that Jews will be forced to recognize him at the second coming.[15] The quotation from Ps 118 is positive and anticipates a positive recognition, not a forced one.[16]

This scene is set up by a parable in Luke 13:6–9, where a vineyard owner representing God threatens to dig up a failed vine, which is given only a little more time to bear fruit. Jesus' entry into Jerusalem accompanied by praise also from Ps 118:26 (Luke 19:38) is a chance for the nation to respond, but her leaders refuse the chance, causing Jesus to weep at her having missed her time of visitation (19:41–44). A reference to God's "coming" (ἐπισκοπή, *episkopē*) can refer either to a gracious act (Ps 8:4 [8:5 MT]) or to judgment (Jer 44:13).[17] Here the reference is to God's gracious visit. The expression is common in contemporary Judaism (Wis 3:7; *Pss. Sol.* 3.11; 10.4; 11.6; 15.12; *T. Levi* 4.4; *T. Asher* 7.3; CD 1.7) and is also found in the OT (Gen 50:24–25; Exod 3:16; 4:31; 13:19; 30:12; Isa 23:17; Pss 80:14 [80:15 MT]; 106:4; Ruth 1:6).[18] The theme of visitation is important to Luke (Luke 1:68–69, 79; 7:16; Acts 15:14). This important sequence of texts shows that the division in Israel is deep and that much of the nation has missed the opportunity to enter into blessing.

The relationship between the old era and the new shows up in the next direct reference to Israel (Luke 22:30). Here the Twelve are appointed to judge the tribes of Israel in the future. This note about rule over Israel shows the extent of the Twelve's authority, thus providing a continuity of leadership in the structure of God's plan.

---

14. Bock, *Proclamation from Prophecy and Pattern*, 118–21.

15. But so W. Hendriksen, *Exposition of the Gospel according to Luke* (New Testament Commentary; Grand Rapids: Baker, 1978), 711, citing Isa 45:23; Rom 14:11; Phil 2:10–11.

16. Bock, *Luke 9:51–24:53*, 1250–51.

17. Marshall, *Gospel of Luke*, 90; Beyer, *TDNT*, 2:605.

18. Brown, *Birth of the Messiah*, 371; Nolland, *Luke 1–9:20*, 86.

The "thrones" imagery recalls Ps 122:4–5 and perhaps Dan 7:9.[19] The apostles, who are the foundation of the church, are those who will lead Israel. This statement is significant, given its setting. Jesus faces rejection by the nation's "leadership," but the nation will continue to exist. The disciples will have a continuing role under "new management," in an administration to be revealed in the future but having validity now. Though God's plan for Israel might look derailed, it is not. The Israelite focus in this remark shows that Israel has a future and recalls the remark about eating the Passover in the kingdom (Luke 22:15–16).

These Israelite touches should not be interpreted to refer exclusively to the church. These remarks look to the final wedding of events in God's plan when promises to Israel are fully realized and when Jesus rules both heaven and earth. In that day Jesus' authority will be clearly visible in both spheres. Promises made to Israel long ago will be fully carried out, such that God's grace and word are shown to be fully true. Jesus is indicating that the promise is a testimony to God's faithfulness.[20] This is Israel reconstituted for Luke, but in such a way that an Israel that rejects is still accountable to God and a part of his program.

Jesus goes to the cross as the "King of the Jews" (Luke 23:3, 37, and esp. 38, where the inscription notes the charge). Jesus' relationship to Israel as more than a prophet but as a king claimant is what gets him crucified as far as Rome is concerned.

The final reference to Israel in Luke comes with a note of disappointment. The Emmaus disciples tell the story of Jesus' death. In it they say that they had hoped that Jesus would be the one "to redeem Israel" (Luke 24:21). Of course, this is precisely part of what will be proclaimed in Acts once the message of the now raised and vindicated Christ is set forth.

12.3 ISRAEL IN THE BOOK OF ACTS

Thus, in Luke we see Israel divided and reconstituted, and her hope is realized in what is said about the nation. What does Acts add? An important and often misread text appears in Acts 1:6. The disciples ask Jesus if now is the time he will "restore the kingdom to Israel." Many see this as an erroneous question, but nothing in the context suggests this, and Peter's speech in Acts 3 is against such a reading.[21] Jesus simply redirects their concern to the mission God will give to them. Then the angel promises a return like Jesus' ascended departure that will bring the consummation, something Peter affirms clearly in his speech in Acts 3.

---

19. Marshall, *Gospel of Luke,* 818; Tiede, *Luke,* 385–86, suggests that *1 En.* 62 and 1 Cor 6:2 are conceptually related to this passage in Luke.

20. Bock, *Luke 9:51–24:53,* 1741.

21. Against Carroll, *Response to the End of History,* 123–28, who speaks of Acts 1:8 as redefining the content of restoration. Instead, I see a reprioritization that says, in effect, the timing of this restoration is not your business but that of the Father; in the meantime concentrate on the mission God will give to you. Nothing in the reply suggests that the question is flawed. The only critique is that they are not to be privy to the issue of the timing. The language of Acts 3, which points back to the prophets and speaks of times of refreshing and the establishment of all things they proclaimed, tells us we still are engaged with Israel's story, hope, and restoration. So correctly Fuller, *Restoration of Israel,* 258.

The possibility of being removed from the people is something Peter warns about in the Acts 3 speech. Those who do not listen to Jesus, the prophet like Moses, will be removed from the people of God ("cut off from their people," 3:23). As we noted earlier, this affirmation is rooted in Lev 23:29 and Deut 18:15.[22]

Acts 2 also underscores that this message is for Israel. Not only is the audience of the speech made up of dispersed Jews from all over the world (Acts 2:9–11), but "all [the house of] Israel" is to know that God made Jesus Lord and Christ by the resurrection-exaltation (2:36). This divine program involves her Messiah and promise. God's vindication means Jesus is Lord.

Similar in force is the picture of the authority of Jesus in healing a lame man that Luke presents through Peter's remarks in Acts 3–4. Once again, it is declared to all of Israel that "by the name of Jesus of Nazareth . . . this man stands before you healed" (Acts 4:10). Opportunity knocks with this show of authentication.

But the next scene shows that something surprising appears to have taken place. In Jerusalem, various groups are gathered together against the Lord and his anointed. Using Ps 2 as the basis for a prayer, the new community notes how what is taking place was predicted as nations and peoples, kings and rulers, Herod, Pilate, the nations, and the people Israel oppose the one sent by God (Acts 4:25–28). This was a part of the plan. But even as a part of the plan, there is a surprise of sorts. For in the Jewish use of this psalm, those praying it would *never* have seen themselves as part of the problem, but rather as those victimized.[23] That is distinct from Luke's reading of this psalm. For Luke, this faithful remnant sees Israel divided with the people as part of those opposed to the one God has anointed. They are part of the people who plot foolish things. Israel is explicitly named as part of the conspiracy. God planned it this way, but it was not what many would have expected. So the community asks to be faithful and bold in the midst of this opposition, using the Psalter as a basis of their understanding and appeal.

Acts 5:31 makes the point that Israel has been called to repentance by the exalted Leader and Savior Jesus. Here a call to repentance is tied to a fresh offer of forgiveness of sins. It is not too late. These texts show the tension a divided Israel is under. The call is not to reject the opportunity, something Stephen's speech also looks to be setting up before it is interrupted. He traces the history of Israel's resistance to those God has sent at various points in her history (7:23, 37, 42, as well as references to the people in 7:17, 34).[24] Surely what would have come next had the speech not been interrupted by martyrdom was an appeal to respond to God.

---

22. See the discussion in ch. 8.

23. A reading of the Midrash on Ps 2 makes clear that those opposed to Israel are the problem.

24. We should note that theologically significant mentions of the land and temple are rare. Stephen speaks of the temple as a place that cannot contain God (Acts 7:47–49). A similar idea is found in 17:24, where God is said not to live in temples made by human hands. Despite this, the believers in Jerusalem frequent the temple both early in the book, with the healing there in Acts 3,

and late in the book in Acts 21, showing their connection with the ancient faith. The land is referred to as the country where Jews now live in confirmation of promises made to Abraham (7:4). It also is described as an inheritance in 13:19. Beyond these brief notes little more is said. Even in the Olivet Discourse, which looks in part to the destruction of the temple, Luke has Jesus speak of the city's destruction as a picture of the approach of the end, and not of the temple specifically nor of the abomination of desolation as Mark and Matthew do (Luke 5:5–37, esp. v. 20). Some issues tied to these

Peter describes Jesus' earthly ministry as a preaching of "the good news of peace" to Israel, even as Peter notes that this one "is Lord of all" (Acts 10:36). As a result, believers are to preach to all the people to testify that he is ordained by God to be the judge of the living and the dead. Everyone who believes in him receives forgiveness of sins through his name, something concerning which all the prophets bear witness (10:42–43). As the gospel goes out to Gentiles, its relationship to Israel's hope is still noted.

Paul also reviews Israel's history as rooted in the fathers whom God chose (Acts 13:17) as he formed a people, delivered them, and gave them a land for their inheritance (vv. 18–19). According to promise, he has sent "to Israel" a Savior, a descendant of David (13:23), just as John preached a baptism of repentance "to all the people of Israel" (v. 24). Israel's story starts with the patriarchs and ends with Jesus. Nothing shows this more powerfully in this Acts 13 speech than where Paul works step by step through Israel's history until he gets to David and then he leaps a thousand years directly to John the Baptist and Jesus.

The last direct reference to Israel in Acts comes in Acts 28:20, where even at the very end after all the Gentile inclusion, Paul says that he is bound in chains "because of the hope of Israel." Jesus' story is Israel's story.

This completes the survey of the use of the term Israel in Luke's two volumes. Also of importance is what is happening with references to "the Jews" in Acts.[25] The use of this term shows the divided nature of the people. Not every reference needs to be examined to see the point Luke is making. In fact, there is a pattern in the book repeated several times as Paul goes from city to city. The Pauline mission is the context where the references to Jews cluster the most.[26] He goes to the synagogue and preaches. Some respond. Others react against him. That reaction often becomes violent. Then Paul either flees the city or turns to the Gentiles.

There has been some debate whether Luke is anti-Semitic in this kind of generic use of the term "Jews."[27] This conclusion is unlikely since Luke advocates continued outreach to the Jews. Note too that what Luke is describing took place in an environment of contention and polemic. Luke continues to have his characters plead for Jews to respond to Jesus.[28]

The pattern starts right after Paul's conversion in Acts 9:22–23. In the meantime, Peter learns that God does not accept the common idea of a Jew not associating

---

topics will be treated when eschatology is examined in ch. 20. In Luke-Acts, the temple is a place for teaching and pilgrimage (Bachmann, "Jerusalem and Rome in Luke-Acts," 60–68, esp. 63–66). Bachmann also notes how the two versions of spelling of Jerusalem reflect the fact that speakers from Jerusalem tend to use the more Semitic form of spelling and may point to the use of traditions.

25. The plural "Jews" appears five times in Luke and seventy-nine times in Acts. Only John's seventy-one uses come close to this number of references. On this theme, see Martin Rese, "The Jews in Luke-Acts: Some Second Thoughts," in *The Unity of Luke-Acts* (ed. J. Verheyden; BETL 142-; Leuven: Leuven University Press,

1999), 185–201. My view on the Jews in Acts is different than his. Where he sees anti-Semitism and ultimate rejection of Israel, I see the polemics of conflict and the continuing hope and expectation that the nation will embrace her Messiah.

26. Rese, "The Jews in Luke-Acts: Some Second Thoughts," 188.

27. This view is most strongly advocated by J. T. Sanders, *The Jews in Luke-Acts* (London: SCM, 1987).

28. My claim that Luke continues to argue for outreach to the Jews stands in contrast to Ernst Haenchen's contention that the Jews are written off (*Acts of the Apostles*, 128, n. 5).

with Gentiles (10:28–29). Nevertheless, for a time others were only sharing with Jews (11:19), even as many Jews were rejecting the message. Peter even had an angelic visit in prison that rescued him from Herod and from all that the Jewish people were expecting, namely, the hope of executing Peter (12:11).

This is where the pattern really begins to set in. Paul preaches in a synagogue (Acts 13:5). Resistance comes from one whom Luke calls a magician and a Jewish false prophet, Bar-Jesus (13:6). This encounter leads Paul to call for judgment on the magician, one of the few places we get a judgment miracle.

In Pisidian Antioch, Paul preaches, leading many Jews to believe (Acts 13:45). However, there is a reaction as Jews incite devout women and high-standing men in the city to react against Paul's message (13:50). In the meantime, Paul and Barnabas have gone to the Gentiles (13:46–47). In Iconium and Lystra, the same thing happens as those reacting come from Iconium and Antioch (14:2, 19). In Thessalonica, Jews again are jealous and set the city in an uproar (17:5). The Jews of Berea are more noble than those in Thessalonica and respond (17:11), only to end up having to deal with Jews from Thessalonica, who stir up the crowds (17:13). In Corinth, Paul is reviled by the Jews (18:6), leading him to go to the Gentiles. In Ephesus, Paul engages the Jews (18:19). Here the reaction comes from silversmiths, whose work for Artemis is threatened (19:21–40). Luke does not always blame the Jews.

Paul reviews his fate in the face of "plots of my Jewish opponents" when he speaks to the Ephesian elders (20:19). The same result takes place when he is in Macedonia, as a Jewish plot causes him to take a different route (20:3). Yet Paul continues to preach to Jews and Greeks (20:21). As he nears Jerusalem, he is told he will be bound up and opposed by the Jews (21:21). James urges Paul to participate in the temple to refute charges that Paul teaches all Jews to forsake Moses (21:21). When Paul is arrested, his defense is: "I am a Jew!" (21:39; 22:3). Paul is accused by the Jews (22:30). Later some Jews conspire to kill him (23:12). This comes after the Roman soldier in charge of Paul noted that the Jews had seized Paul initially, which had caused the Romans to intervene and take charge of him (Acts 23:27).

The opposition continues at Paul's trials (Acts 24:5, 9; 25:7), despite Paul's defense that he believes everything written in the Law and Prophets (see 24:14; 25:8, where he says he has not sinned against the Jews, temple, or Caesar; 25:10: "I have not done any wrong"). Yet the charges from the Jewish leadership continue (25:15, 24; 26:2), just as Paul continues to argue that he is on trial "because of my hope in what God has promised our ancestors" (26:6). In Paul's view, they have seized him for preaching this hope and calling them to repent and turn to God (26:21).

Paul repeats this defense when he gets to Rome and speaks to other Jews. In his last remarks on this topic he says, "I have done nothing against our people or the customs of our ancestors, [yet] I was arrested in Jerusalem and handed over to the Romans" (Acts 28:17). Up to the end of Acts, Paul still identifies with Israel even in the face of this consistent and intense opposition. Israel is divided from Luke's perspective. God's protection in all of this is called a deliverance "from your own people and from the Gentiles. I am sending you to them" (26:17). Here the people referred to are Israel. The nation stands divided by Paul's message on behalf of God's program through Jesus. Yet even to the end Paul preaches to "all."[29]

12.4 CONCLUSION

So Luke's story about Jesus is Israel's story. The promises are hers. The Messiah is hers. The hope is hers. The inclusion of Gentiles is rooted in promises to her. Yet she is a people divided. Some respond; others do not. All through the two volumes, those who preach the message present it as Israel's story and identify with Israel's God and hope. Nothing in any of this shows that Israel has been set aside. What is seen instead is a persistent effort to continue to reach out even in the face of intense opposition and rejection. It is for Israel's hope that Paul contends at the end of Acts even as he preaches a message many Jews reject. For Luke, Israel is still to be reached, and her restoration is a hope yet to come, even as God reaches out and turns to Gentiles. The church, filled with a believing remnant, is doing in outreach what Israel's story also had always promised, being people out of Israel who became a blessing and light to the world (Acts 13:46–47).

---

29. There is debate about whether "all" means both Jew and Gentile here. Haenchen, *Acts of the Apostles*, 726, n. 5; and Rese, "Jews in Luke-Acts: Second Thoughts," 200, argue no. But an inclusive reference is likely not only because of Paul's heart as we see it in Rom 9–11, but also because of the pattern of Acts, as well as the emphasis Luke has that this story is about Israel's hope. See Robert Brawley, "The God of Promises and the Jews of Luke-Acts," in R. P. Thompson and T. E. Philips, eds., *Literary Studies in Luke-Acts: Essays in Honor of Joseph B. Tyson* (Macon, GA: Mercer Univ. Press, 1998), 279–96, esp. 294, n. 12, and his "Ethical Borderlines between Rejection and Hope: Interpreting the Jews in Luke-Acts," *CurTM* 27 (2000): 415–23, where he argues the close of Acts is open-ended toward the Jews. He stresses how the announcement of the accomplishment of such promises starts in Luke 1:16 and drives the narrative in such a way that failure of this announcement is unlikely. Also in contrast to Rese is Richard Bauckham, "The Restoration of Israel in Luke-Acts," in his *The Jewish World around the New Testament, Collected Essays I* (Tübingen: Mohr-Siebeck, 2008), 325–70. A full list of recent works on this theme appears on his p. 327, n. 8. Bauckham sees Luke's hope as very much in line with Second Temple Jewish expectation. The essay traces the connection to such themes at a series of individual points in detail. Bauckham makes the point with a key caveat, namely, that in Luke's story there are surprises for exactly how this hope works itself out in the two volumes. Bauckham argues that this leaves what is ahead in the future also somewhat more open-ended. He sees Acts 28 as a rejection reflecting only this portion of Paul's mission, but not to all Jews. I would add that this would fit the pattern of other such texts in Luke-Acts (Acts 13:46–48; 18:6; see ibid., 367). Correctly David Seccombe, "The New People of God," in *A Witness to the Gospel*, 367. Nothing in the context suggests limiting this remark to all who hear Paul. The idea that hearing with καί (*kai*) in Acts 28:28 means "also" hear makes such a meaning most likely.

Chapter 13

THE GENTILES AND THE EXPRESSION "THE NATIONS" IN LUKE-ACTS

BIBLIOGRAPHY

Dupont, Jacques. *The Salvation of the Gentiles: Essays on the Acts of the Apostles.* Trans. John R. Keating. New York: Paulist, 1979. **Maddox, R.** *The Purpose of Luke-Acts.* Edinburgh: T&T Clark, 1982. **Stenschke, Christoph.** *Luke's Portrait of Gentiles Prior to Their Coming to Faith.* WUNT. Tübingen; Mohr/Siebeck, 1999. Idem. "The Need for Salvation." Pp. 125–44 in *Witness to the Gospel: The Theology of Acts.* Ed. I. Howard Marshall and David Peterson. Grand Rapids: Eerdmans, 1998. **Tannehill, Robert.** *The Narrative Unity of Luke-Acts.* 2 vols. Minneapolis: Fortress, 1986, 1990. **Wilson, Stephen G.** *The Gentiles and the Gentile Mission in Luke-Acts.* SNTSMS. Cambridge: Cambridge University Press, 1973.

Like the term "Israel," the ἔθνος (*ethnos*) word group is also prominent in Luke-Acts, pointing to how Luke saw the Gentiles and dealt with national entities. This term appears fifty-six times in the two volumes: thirteen times in the gospel, and forty-three times in Acts. The fact that it appears far more often in Acts is the first indication of a shift of emphasis as Luke's two volumes tell their story.[1] Moreover, there are references to specific Gentiles that fill out the portrait. Some of these texts we covered in discussing the Jews, for often the two groups are discussed side by side. Only one text appears in the infancy material, so we will cover the use in Luke's entire gospel and then in Acts.

---

1. A complete and focused study of the issue of Gentiles before they come to faith is found in the monograph by Christoph W. Stenschke, *Luke's Portrait of Gentiles Prior to Their Coming to Faith* (WUNT 2/108; Tübingen; Mohr-Siebeck, 1999). A full treatment of the theme of Gentiles and mission is found in Wilson, *Gentiles and the Gentile Mission in Luke-Acts.* Wilson argues that Luke's theology of the Gentiles is inconsistent. His view confuses Luke's presentation of a variety of themes tied to Gentile inclusion as showing the lack of a consistent answer with the complexity of what motivated this move. Luke's associations with the promise of Scripture, the work of the Spirit, the teaching of Jesus, the initiative of God, the affirmation of the confirming role of miracles, and the impetus of Jewish rejection are all part of the puzzle that Wilson traces so well in noting such themes. No one explanation suffices for Luke. Wilson's effort to argue that Luke's practical emphases cancel out any historical or unified theological concerns makes too much of a break between these two categories, arguing for an either-or approach where both-and are in play. Also overdrawn is the claim that Luke idealizes this expansion into the Gentile world, making it look like a growing expansion versus what Wilson sees as a more haphazard process. However, the growth of this movement to the point where it is a source of concern in the empire may have more the look of Luke's portrayal than Wilson admits. All of this impacts Wilson's judgment that Luke is neither totally reliable nor a tendentious writer but somewhere in between, who still has left us much of great historical value (p. 267). I am more confident of Luke's trustworthiness in setting forth this key part of his account about Gentiles.

13.1 GENTILES AND NATIONS
IN THE GOSPEL OF LUKE

The first reference to the Gentiles comes in Luke 2:32, a text already treated several times. The coming of Jesus as Messiah is a "revelation to the Gentiles." God's eye has moved beyond Israel to act on behalf of the nations. As Simeon holds the child Jesus, he makes the point that God's salvation will extend to the nations. Similar to this is 3:6, where Luke extends the citation of Isa 40 as seen in Matthew and Mark to make the point that "all people will see God's salvation." In addition, the genealogy of Jesus at the end of Luke 3 extends itself to Adam to show a concern for the human race.

That God has touched Gentiles before is indicated in Jesus' remarks in Luke 4:25–27. He points out how the spiritual vacuum in Israel at the time of Elijah and Elisha meant that God's ministry extended itself only to a widow from Zarephath and to Naaman, a Syrian. Thus, in the past, Gentiles have experienced God's grace. Jesus will show it to them more intentionally. All of this is taking place in light of promises made from the time of Abraham and Isaiah (Abraham: Acts 3:25–26; Isaiah: 13:47).

Another Gentile viewed with respect is the centurion in Luke 7:1–10. To his credit, he loves the nation of Israel so that Jews ask Jesus to intervene on behalf of his sick slave (Luke 7:5). Here Luke uses the term "nation" (ἔθνος, *ethnos*) to refer to Israel as a distinct people. This man's faith is unlike any faith seen in Israel since he trusts that Jesus' power requires only his word—that Jesus can act from a distance. He also believes he is not worthy of Jesus' acting but trusts in his mercy. Thus, the centurion is a model of response that stands out in contrast to so many in the nation who were failing to respond.

The portrait of Gentiles is mixed in Luke's gospel. Texts such as Luke 10:12–14 point to judgment to come for places like Tyre and Sidon. Other texts are more positive, such as Nineveh's positive response to Jonah in terms of repentance or the Queen of the South's search for the wisdom of Solomon (11:30–32). Judgment to come will take place in the midst of a flow of life (17:26–29). The nations often pursue wealth and the things of the world in a way that distracts from God (12:30). Prophets existed from the beginning of the world but were not heeded (11:50). This portrait of life simply running its course with little or no attention to the one true God forms a basis for a message of repentance going to the nations. These texts for the most part look to the past. The coming of Jesus can change this, but only if people respond.

Gentiles are predicted to have a hand in Jesus' death as he will be handed over to them (Luke 18:32). This theme is picked up in Acts 4:24–29, when the nations' role in Jesus' death is placed alongside Jewish involvement. In an early Christian prayer, the believers interpret Ps 2 to read the Gentiles and nation of Israel as arrayed against God and his Messiah. In the original reading of Ps 2, most Jews would have argued that these opponents are exclusively Gentiles. The prayer's point, however, is that once one sees who the enemy of God's Messiah is, one can identify God's enemies, who here explicitly include both Gentiles and Jews, for v. 27 names Herod, Pilate, the nations, and the people Israel. This hermeneutical key to reading this psalm shows that this is not a misreading of the psalm.[2] Also important here may be the thrust of the entire psalm, namely, that opposing this plan is ultimately futile.[3]

The opposition Jesus faced is now extended against the new community he formed, so they pray. It is often claimed that Luke does not show Roman opposition to Jesus but places blame on the Jews. Such a view is wrong. All ethnic groups in Jerusalem do nothing (Luke 23:1–25) to stop the injustice Jesus experiences, so they share the responsibility for his death.

On the one hand, "the nations rage" (ἐφρύαξαν ἔθνη, *ephryaxan ethnē*, Acts 4:25). This verb for raging appears only here in the NT. It refers to being insolent. In its everyday use, it refers to "spirited animals," such as snorting horses before a race (2 Macc 7:34; 3 Macc 2:2).[4] The term for "nations/Gentiles" reappears in v. 27 as part of the exposition identifying who is meant in the prayer. The word-link form of explanation in this verse is another example of the Jewish interpretive technique of *gezerah shewa*.[5]

On the other hand, "the peoples plot in vain" (λαοὶ ἐμελέτησαν κενά, *laoi emeletēsan kena*). The plotting here involves the mindless attempt to do something to God's Messiah and to try to stop God's plan.[6] This refers to Israel according to the word linkage with v. 27 (λαοί, people). If Jesus is the Messiah (Acts 4:18; 10:38) and is opposed, then Ps 2 applies to his opponents, whoever they may be. It was this combination of kings (Herod) and rulers (Pilate and the Jewish council; see Acts 4:5, 8), as well as those they represented, who have "banded together" (συνήχθησαν, *synēchthēsan*) to oppose God's way. The occurrence of this verb in v. 27 identifies how the early Christians read Ps 2 and whom they viewed as sinning against God. Four terms are linked between the citation and the explanation: "nations," "people," "band together," and "anointed one."

The psalm asks, "Why" does this illogical opposition take place? At one level, it makes no sense. On another level, it shows how out of tune many are with God's ways. Given the fact that God is working out his plan, the tone of the prayer is calm, but the implication in the prayer is that many Jews and Gentiles need to see what God is doing and to change their approach to Jesus. In the meantime, as the predicted opposition works itself out, the community will seek to be what God has called it to be, faithful and bold.

Verse 27 explains the theological rationale for this understanding of Ps 2. The use of the phrase "indeed" (ἐπ' ἀληθείας, *ep' alētheias*) seems to be Lucan (Luke 4:25; 20:21; 22:59; Acts 10:34; cf. LXX of Deut 22:20; Job 9:2; 19:4; 36:4; Isa 37:18;

---

2. Against Barrett, *Critical and Exegetical Commentary on the Acts of the Apostles*, 1:246.

3. Bruce, *Acts of the Apostles*, 99, points to Acts 2:23; 3:18 as speaking about the plan directly; Marshall, *Acts*, 105, says the effort to oppose is "fruitless."

4. BDAG, 1067.

5. Johnson, *Acts of the Apostles*, 85, notes that the technique shows up at Qumran in several texts: 1QpHab; 4QpNah; 4QpPs 37.

6. BDAG, 627 §3.

Tob 8:7).[7] Those gathered together against God's plan through Jesus included Herod, Pilate, the Gentiles, and the people of Israel.

Only Luke details a role for Herod Antipas in Jesus' trial. Herod is seen as a Jewish leader in Luke 23:6 – 12, as he is portrayed in his role as a Jewish king, the chief Jewish political ruler (Herod was half Jewish).[8] The Roman governor Pilate is portrayed with a degree of sympathy in Luke 23, but is pressured by the Jewish leaders. He succumbed to the pressure and allowed the death of an innocent man, regardless of his own personal judgment, and thus became a member of those whose acts opposed Jesus. There is no inconsistency in Luke's portrayal here, just a difference of focus in terms of motivation for the action. The Jewish leadership wished Jesus removed, and Pilate opted to follow those who had advised him on Jewish affairs over the years rather than to follow his sense that Jesus was innocent.

These rulers and others are arrayed against God's set-apart "holy servant" (τὸν ἅγιον παῖδα, ton hagion paida), Jesus, the one "whom you [God] anointed" (ὃν ἔχρισας, hon echrisas). This opposition is against the Messiah (on Jesus as servant, see Acts 3:13). Jesus is like the "servant . . . David" (v. 25). Kilgallen effectively argues that the unusual phrase "your holy servant Jesus, whom you anointed" shows Jesus to be the Messiah, who also is the servant.[9] "Messiah" points to Davidic messianic authority especially as it relates to the arrival in power of the kingdom and the defeat of evil. "Servant" points to one who, like David, obeyed God and was fully at his disposal, and it points to his suffering as well.

Just as David had enemies, as Ps 2 notes, so did Jesus. Both figures, however, were God's chosen and anointed. This reference to anointing shows that Jesus is the Messiah and is ready to begin his mission. It does not argue that God made Jesus Messiah at some point in time, since the infancy material (Luke 1:31 – 35) and Jesus' baptism (Acts 10:38) rule out such a reading for Luke. Barrett, however, suggests this kind of adoptionism in these verses.[10] Fitzmyer focuses on the terminology only and the baptism as a point of reference for sonship, but this is too limited a reading for Luke.[11] An adoptionist reading also is an unlikely view for the early church to have held when placed in a context where God is described as having a predestined plan and Jesus is presented as the Lord at God's side. Jesus experienced a call with a symbolic anointing at the baptism but did not become Messiah then. He simply began his messianic ministry then.

The presence in Luke of an infancy narrative shows that Jesus' status as Messiah was something he possessed before his birth, not something conferred at his baptism or birth. The debate among scholars about early church Christology is over how far back such a Lucan understanding goes in early church theology. If Jesus saw his messianic calling in the context of designed suffering, then all the features necessary for

7. Haenchen, *Acts of the Apostles*, 227.

8. On Herod's career, see Bruce, *Acts of the Apostles,* 158.

9. J. J. Kilgallen, "Your Servant Jesus Whom You Anointed (Acts 4,27)," *RB* 105 (1998): 185–201.

10. Barrett, *Critical and Exegetical Commentary on the Acts of the Apostles*, 1:247.

11. Fitzmyer, *Acts of the Apostles*, 309.

this kind of declaration existed by the time such a speech was made. In other words, nothing prevents this declaration from having roots in the church's earliest period.

The human rejection Jesus experienced falls within God's plan and the activity of God's "hand," that is, his will and power (Luke 1:66; 23:46; Acts 4:30; 7:25, 50; 11:21; 13:11). Jesus' arrest is expressed as his being given over into the hands and power of others (in the OT: Exod 3:20; 13:3, 14, 16; 15:6; Ps 55:20 [54:21 LXX]; conceptually, Acts 2:23; 3:18). This opposition is not seen as a surprise but as something God had planned and "decided beforehand" (προώρισεν, proōrisen). This verb appears six times in the NT but only here in Luke-Acts (Acts 4:27–28; cf. Rom 8:29–30 [2x]; 1 Cor 2:6–8; Eph 1:3–6, 11–12).

The term for God's "will" (βουλή, boulē) appears twelve times in the NT, with the bulk of occurrences in Luke-Acts (nine times; Luke 7:30; 23:51; Acts 2:23; 4:28; 5:38; 13:36; 20:27; 27:12, 42; cf. 1 Cor 4:5; Eph 1:11; Heb 6:17). Some are going to oppose what God is doing. So the question becomes how members of the new community will face such opposition. They will not cower to it and become silent. They seek God's power to be bold in their declarations.[12] Acts 4:25–26 is an important Lucan text that frames how Gentiles are seen. They also are a divided lot, as Israel is. Some respond, but others stand in opposition to Jesus and even form a conspiracy of opposition against him.

Nations opposed to God's plan will also have a role in the chaos that precedes both the fall of Jerusalem and the end. Nation will fight against nation (Luke 21:10), and eventually they take people captive and trample Jerusalem as "the times of the Gentiles are fulfilled" (21:24–25). This designation of the "times of the Gentiles" (καιροὶ ἐθνῶν, kairoi ethnōn) points to a period when Gentiles dominate world affairs (cf. Dan 2:44; 8:13–14; 12:5–13). It would seem that a period for Israel follows that period (Ezek 39:24–29; Zech 12:4–9), for why else would one mention a seemingly limited time of the Gentiles to come? It may be that the note in Mark 13:10 that the gospel must be "preached to all nations" before the end comes may also help explain the expression, since the domination is not only political in terms of Jerusalem, but spiritual in terms of the gospel making an impact on nations in the world.

The phrase "times of the Gentiles" suggests three things. First, the city's fall is of limited duration; why else mention a time limit?

Second, there is a period in God's plan when Gentiles will dominate, which implies that the subsequent period is of a different nature.[13] Jesus' initial coming and return represent breaking points in God's plan. Arndt denies this implication about the phrase and points to a limited time of Gentile domination, wanting to be noncommittal on the verse, since "the times" has six possible senses: "seasons" (1) for executing divine judgments; (2) for Gentiles lording over Israel; (3) for existing as Gentiles; (4) for Gentiles becoming subject to divine judgments; (5) for

---

12. Bock, *Acts*, 197–99.
13. Ellis, *Gospel of Luke*, 245, says that "times of the Gentiles" equals Gentile possession of Jerusalem that extends to the parousia (Zech 8; 12–14).

a "opportunities" for Gentiles to turn to God; or (6) to possess privileges that Israel forfeited.[14] But the question remains: Why describe this period this way unless there is an intended contrast between Israel and the Gentiles? In his detailed discussion, Giblin argues that the phrase refers to a time of judgment on the world, but with no reference to a future for Israel (view 4).[15] Giblin speaks correctly of a time of judgment on the nations and of the event as a fulfillment of the Scripture. But his descriptions seem to be limited to events at the end of the period, which is too narrow in focus. More likely, "times of the Gentiles" is a general way to describe the current period in God's plan, when Gentiles are prominent but that will culminate in judgment on those nations. Giblin can deny restoration for Israel only by failing to relate this verse to Paul, Mark, and especially to other portions of Luke-Acts.[16]

Third, it would thus seem that this view of Israelite judgment now but vindication later suggests what Paul also argues in Rom 11:25–26: Israel has a future in God's plan. Israel will be grafted back in when the fullness of Gentiles leads it to respond (cf. 11:11–12, 15, 30–32). Considered with the more developed picture of Rev 20, it seems that the early church held to a kingdom hope that included Israel's reincorporation into God's program as an expression of God's faithfulness.[17] Thus the phrase "times of the Gentiles" seems to imply a time after this period that will again involve Israel.

Jesus sometimes uses the lifestyle of the nations as a point of contrast about how to live. So how the rulers of Gentiles live in the world with an air of pride, power, and patronage serves as a contrast to Jesus' teaching on humility and service by disciples, especially the community's leaders (Luke 22:25). Unlike the way in which these rulers lord their power over people, the disciples are called to serve, as their example in Jesus shows.

Another use of "nation" for Israel comes in the charge against Jesus that he is subverting "our nation" (Luke 23:2). This charge was important in the leadership's view. Pilate should care about what Jesus is doing to the public order, since Rome was interested in keeping the peace.[18]

The final text involving Gentiles in Luke's gospel is the commission to take a message of "repentance for forgiveness of sins … to all nations" (Luke 24:47). This is a key part of the story that will drive Acts.

In sum, the scope of salvation extending to the nations and those on the fringe in Luke's gospel is seen in a series of ideas, some connected to Luke's treatment of other groups on the fringe in Jewish eyes. There is (1) the already noted key remark

14. W. F. Arndt, *The Gospel according to St. Luke* (St. Louis: Concordia, 1956), 422.

15. C. H. Giblin, *The Destruction of Jerusalem according to Luke's Gospel: A Historical-Typological Moral* (AnBib 107; Rome: Pontifical Biblical Institute Press, 1985), 89–92.

16. Ibid., 91, n. 45.

17. Bock, *Luke 9:51–24:53*, 1680–81. Revelation 20 speaks of a millennium and appears to see a period of direct earthly rule

involved here before the period of the new heaven and new earth, a view known either as chiliasm or premillennialism.

18. This point about Jewish concerns for public peace and preventing any sense of revolution is a key argument in the essay by Edwin Judge defending the authenticity of the social context of Jesus' trial. This argument appears in David M. Scholer, ed., *Social Distinctives of the Christians in the First Century: Pivotal Essays by E. A. Judge* (Peabody, MA: Hendrickson, 2008), 44–47.

in Luke 2:32; (2) John the Baptist's ministry including Roman soldiers in 3:1 and 14; (3) the use of Isa 40:5 in Luke 3:6; (4) Jesus' allusion to Gentiles in 4:25–27; (5) Jesus' associations with tax collectors and sinners throughout the gospel, a group often associated with the rejected nations; (6) the prominence of women throughout the gospel; (7) and the interest in Samaritans, another fringe group (9:51–56; 10:25–27; 17:11–19).[19]

So in Luke's gospel, we see hints of what is to come for the nations. God's salvation will go to them. In the meantime, they are portrayed as only here and again being associated with what God has done up to the present. God has touched Gentiles either during times when Israel was in spiritual decline (Elijah-Elisha) or at points where some responded either by God's initiative (Nineveh) or on their own (Queen of the South, centurion). Most of the descriptions of Gentiles are of people who merely lived life while pursuing wealth and power with little or no attention to God.

13.2 GENTILES AND NATIONS IN THE BOOK OF ACTS

Another reference to the Jewish nation opens these references in Acts as Jews from every nation are gathered at Pentecost and witness the outpouring of the Spirit (Acts 2:5–10). This key event has an international stage for Luke, but it is still "in house" at this point of the story. As just examined, when the new community suffers persecution, she sees herself as surrounded by a conspiracy of the nations and Jewish opposition, appealing to Ps 2 as a way of understanding what God is doing. The community asks for boldness to witness, not for revenge.

Israel's conflict with the nations in her history is mentioned next. Egypt is a nation God punished for enslaving the Jews (Acts 7:7). Later Israel dispossessed the nations during the time of the tabernacle (7:45). These brief notes of conflict are but a hint of why Jews were nervous about associating with Gentiles. There had been a long history of conflict with them, most recently in the Maccabean struggle of 167–64 BC and their being overtaken by the Romans in 63 BC.[20]

The expansion of the gospel into Samaria, as Acts 1:8 had predicted, comes with Philip's trip into Samaria, where Simon the magician had "amazed the people [ἔθνος, *ethnos*] of Samaria" (Acts 8:9) before Philip's arrival. Here we see the sense of distinct identity that a Jewish perspective gave to those from Samaria. Their response to a magician like Simon portrays them as somewhat gullible. In fact, the Acts 8 scene with Simon, Philip, Peter, and John is a power encounter where the gospel shows itself superior to such magic.

With Saul's conversion the number of references to Gentiles accelerates. Ananias is told that Saul will carry Jesus' name before the nations and kings and the

---

19. Rosner, "Progress of the Word," 220.
20. The pain of the Maccabean conflict and the threat of complete assimilation to Hellenism are expressed powerfully in 1 Macc 1–2.

sons of Israel (Acts 9:15). The Cornelius episode generates twelve uses of the term by itself between Acts 10–11 and 15. Cornelius is described as well spoken of by the Jewish nation (10:22). In a key text making a central affirmation on the theme, Peter declares that people from every nation who fear God and do righteousness are acceptable to him (10:35). In 10:45, the key evidence of cleansing appears as the Holy Spirit is poured out "on Gentiles." So "Gentiles . . . had received the word of God" (11:1). After some discussion about whether this was correct without requiring Gentiles first to be circumcised, the community rejoiced that "even to Gentiles God has granted repentance that leads to life" (11:18).

When the issue is rejoined in Acts 15, Paul and Barnabas retell the story of the conversion of the Gentiles (15:3). Peter notes how God chose him to be the one to preach to the Gentiles (15:7). Paul and Barnabas again note the signs and wonders God did through them among the Gentiles (15:12). A key text is 15:14, where James speaks of how Peter related God's visitation among the Gentiles. This idea is important insofar as Israel has missed on her visitation (Luke 19:40–41) and Messiah's visit was an early topic of praise (1:68, 78–79). Gentiles are now incorporated into the name and community of God. All this, James says, is a part of the promise in Amos 9:11–12, regarding the rebuilt tent of David, leading the rest of humanity (i.e., all Gentiles who are called by God's name) to seek the Lord (Acts 15:17). So Gentiles should not be troubled with issues of the law and circumcision except for a few concerns related to cultural sensitivity such as idolatry, fornication, things strangled, and things with blood (15:19). Thus, a letter informing the churches of these issues is sent to the Gentile brothers (15:23). Clearly, this Cornelius scene and its aftermath are a key turning point in the book, as well as being central to the theme of Gentile inclusion.

At Pisidian Antioch, Paul's review of Israel's history leads into another key text. After noting how God had destroyed the seven nations and given Israel their land as an inheritance (Acts 13:19), Paul notes how Jewish opposition has now caused him to take his message elsewhere and "turn to the Gentiles" (13:46). This is the first of three such notes in Acts (see also 18:6; 28:28). The move is supported by an appeal to the Scripture and the picture of the Servant of Isaiah. Paul and Barnabas are to be a "light for the Gentiles that you may bring salvation to the ends of the earth" (13:47; cf. Luke 2:30–32; Acts 1:8).

This citation of Isa 49:6 in Acts 13:47 is closer to the MT than to the LXX, which mentions God's servant being set up as a covenant for the people, an allusion to the covenant for the Jews.[21] Paul says that the Lord has commanded Barnabas and Paul to undertake this role of being a guide to the nations concerning the way to God. This task is much like the way that "a light" illumines a path.

What is surprising is that in Acts 13:47 Paul and Barnabas are cast in the role of the servant of Israel. The servant was normally an image tied to Jesus in the NT. Now Paul and Barnabas are the light (a term that describes Jesus in Luke 1:78–79;

---

21. Fitzmyer, *Acts of the Apostles*, 521.

2:29–32, using Isa 49:6; 2 Cor 4:3–6; servant and Jesus: Isa 42:1–4 in Matt 12:17–21; Isa 53:12 in Luke 22:37; Isa 53:7–8 in Acts 8:32–35).[22] They bring salvation to the "ends of the earth" (cf. Luke 3:6). So Paul and Barnabas are now seen as an extension of the work of the Servant of the Lord, who was Jesus.

The hermeneutic used here is the "one in the many," which is a basic way of connecting themes between the OT and NT. One can compare the use of "servant" in Luke-Acts to the use of "seed" in Gen 12:3 and Gal 3, where it is about both Jesus and those incorporated into him. The task of Jesus continues in his commissioned servants.

Their call is to be a light to the Gentiles and go to the end of the earth. This verse echoes Acts 1:8, which alludes to Isaiah 49:6 as well. The goal of God's plan of salvation is to take the message to the ends of the earth, to extend it to all nations in every part of the world. These echoes link the text to earlier declarations showing the importance of the remark (Luke 24:47). When the Gentiles heard this, they rejoiced (Acts 13:48).

However, all is not well when it comes to the response of the nations, since they are divided about Jesus just as Israel is. In places like Iconium, the Gentiles are stirred up by the presence of the message, often at the instigation of some Jews, which leads to the potential mistreatment of Paul so that he departs (Acts 14:2, 5). At Lystra, where initially Paul and Barnabas are mistaken as gods, these messengers of the new hope note how in the past God had cared for the nations but had allowed them to go their own way in idolatry (14:16). Idolatry is something Luke wants the Gentiles to turn from in Acts, as the speech in Athens in Acts 17 will make clear.[23] When this first missionary journey ends, Paul and Barnabas report on what God has done through them and how he has "opened a door of faith to the Gentiles" (14:27).

What is said briefly in Lystra is elaborated on in Athens. Here the appeal is also to God as Creator in a reaction to idolatry. So God made "all the nations ... [to] inhabit the whole earth" (Acts 17:25). The hope is that they will seek God and realize that God is not found in a representation or man's imagination because the deity has fixed a day when he will judge the world through a man he appointed. When Paul mentions the resurrection, his speech is interrupted so he is not able to finish his point.

At Corinth, Jewish rejection again causes Paul to say he is going "to the Gentiles" (Acts 18:6). Later, as Paul nears Jerusalem, he is warned about what will happen there. He will be handed over "to the Gentiles" (21:11). The language is very much an echo of Jesus being handed over to the Gentiles, for Paul suffers just as his Lord did (both Acts 21:11 and Luke 18:32 use the same verb (παραδίδωμι, *paradidōmi*, "to hand over").

---

22. Marshall, *Acts of the Apostles*, 230.

23. This is the first major text of five scenes where paganism and idolatry in one form or another are challenged in Acts. See David Peterson, "The Worship of the New Community," in *Witness to the*

Gospel, 382–84. These scenes are Paphos in Acts 13:6–12; Lystra in 14:8–20; Athens in 17:16–34; Corinth (imperial cult) in 18:12–17; and Ephesus in 19:23–27.

In Jerusalem, Paul tells James what God has done through him among the Gentiles (Acts 21:19). James, for his part, reviews the earlier Jerusalem Council letter sent to the Gentiles as he asks Paul to participate in a vow to show his respect for the law (21:25).

Paul's defense speeches follow his arrest in Jerusalem. Here he speaks of his calling, given at the Damascus road, to be sent "far away to the Gentiles" (Acts 22:21). There is much jockeying for position in these scenes before the leaders, so Tertullus praises Felix for the reforms he introduced into "this nation" (a reference to Israel), to ingratiate himself to Felix (24:2). Paul responds by saying he recognized Felix had been a judge over the nation (24:10). He tells the story of his arrest, noting he simply was bringing to "my people [*ethnos*] gifts for the poor" (24:17); note how Paul still identifies himself with the Jewish people and Israel.

Even later to Agrippa, Paul notes that from the beginning he lived his life among "my own nation [*ethnos*]" (26:4). God called Paul as a witness, and he would need to be delivered both "from [his] own people [*laos*] and from the Gentiles [*ethnōn*]" to whom he was sent (26:17). So he preached to those in Jerusalem and Judea and to the Gentiles that they should repent and turn to God and perform deeds worthy of repentance (26:20). One can hear the echo of the Great Commission to take this message to all the nations in this summary (Luke 24:47). So according to his call Paul proclaimed light both to the people of Israel and to the Gentiles (Acts 26:23).

At the end of Acts in his last full speech, Paul is still taking the message to any who will hear (28:25–28). He explains his situation to Jews in Rome, and he has no charge to bring against his nation (28:19). But since the nation is rejecting his message because of their hard-heartedness (cf. Isa 6), Paul will take God's message "to the Gentiles" (Acts 28:28). Paul clearly speaks to all who come to him about the kingdom and the Lord Jesus Christ (28:30–31). The rebuke of Israel is exactly that, a rebuke; Paul does not shut the door against her. In each case in Acts where Paul turns to go to the Gentiles, he still addresses Israel in line with his call.

So the use of the term "nation[s]" shows several interesting things in Acts. Sometimes it is a reference to "this" nation, that is, to Israel. Most often, however, it refers to Gentiles. They are a split community as Israel was when it came to Jesus. Some respond; others react as they sense a threat to the way they have lived. The key note is that God has taken the initiative to bring the nations the message of forgiveness and hope that Jesus first had brought to Israel.

13.3 CONCLUSION

Acts describes how the gospel went out to the Gentiles, who needed salvation because of their association with idolatry. This inclusion did not take place at the expense of mission to Israel but out of it and alongside of it. Paul exemplifies this mission. Whether in the synagogue or the marketplace, he took the message as a faithful witness to all. Part of Israel's story was the inclusion of Gentiles in line with promises to Abraham and commitments discussed in prophets like Isaiah and Amos. The Spirit's coming showed the community that God had cleansed the Gentiles and called out from them a people for his name. They also had access to life through repentance and the work of Jesus Christ.

Chapter 14

THE CHURCH AND
THE WAY IN LUKE-ACTS

BIBLIOGRAPHY

Bolt, Peter. "Mission and Witness." Pp. 191–214 in *Witness to the Gospel: The Theology of Acts*. Ed. I. Howard Marshall and David Peterson. Grand Rapids: Eerdmans, 1998. **Dupont, Jacques.** *The Salvation of the Gentiles: Essays on the Acts of the Apostles*. Trans. John R. Keating. New York: Paulist, 1979. **Hengel, Martin.** "Die Ursprünge der christlichen Mission." *NTS* 18 (1971–72): 15–38. **Hume, Douglas A.** *The Early Christian Community: A Narrative Analysis of Acts 2:41–47 and 4:32–35*. WUNT 2/298. Tübingen: Mohr-Siebeck, 2011. **Marshall, I. H.** *Luke: Historian and Theologian*. Grand Rapids: Zondervan, 1970. **Rapske, Brian.** "Opposition to the Plan of God and Persecution." Pp. 235–56 in *Witness to the Gospel: A Theology of Acts*. Ed. I. Howard Marshall and David Peterson. Grand Rapids: Eerdmans, 1998. **Roth, S. John.** *The Blind, the Lame, and the Poor: Character Types in Luke-Acts*. JSNTSup. Sheffield: Sheffield Academic Press, 1997. **Seccombe, David Peter.** "The New People of God." Pp. 349–72 in *A Witness to the Gospel: The Theology of Acts*. Ed. I. Howard Marshall and David Peterson. Grand Rapids: Eerdmans, 1998.

References to the "church" (ἐκκλησία, *ekklēsia*) are not as common as one might expect in Luke and Acts. In fact, there are no references to the church in Luke. In Acts, the term appears only twenty-three times. However, Luke has a unique motif tied to the church, that of a community being called "the Way." This will lead us not only to look for places where the term for church is used but to examine where the term ὁδός (*hodos*, "way") appears. Also included for discussion are the two places where the term "Christian" appears (Χριστιανός, *Christianos*).

What we see is a group developing a distinct identity. They are gathering in various locales, most often in homes, but they also still connect to Israel and her story. So the social institution is new and distinct, functioning as its own community with its own leadership.[1] This community is forced to be distinct, operating outside of

---

1. A look at this theme makes for a more nuanced presentation than found in Seccombe, "New People of God," 349–72. Much in his chapter is excellent, especially his description of the setting of Acts and identity issues on p. 368, but we find him not doing enough to nuance the newness of the institution of the church with the continuity of the people of God. In my view, he stresses the latter while understating the former.

social-religious Israel and the synagogue because most in Israel reject it. Yet, at the same time, its roots are sunk into promises that God made to Israel long ago. The community's message teaches that if that promise of Israel's God is appreciated, those who respond will be a part of the new movement that is faithful to the old promises. In other words, if one were a good Jew following what God has done in Christ, one would join the Way. This summary reflects the complexity of how the church emerges according to Acts. Paul's defense speeches also show this complexity, because Paul argues that he still operates with Israel's hope and promises, yet is a member of the Way.

14.1 THE THEME OF THE WAY IN THE GOSPEL OF LUKE

"The way" initially is an image from Isaiah and Malachi. Its first use involves an allusion in Luke 1:17 where John the Baptist is said to go before the Lord in the spirit and power of Elijah and to make ready for the Lord a prepared people (allusions here are to Mal 3:1; 4:5; and Isa 43:7). In the context, the Lord here is clearly the God of Israel. John sets the table for the arrival of God's salvific work. In Luke 1:17, the expression "the way" is not present, but the next reference to John's ministry develops the image of John going before the Lord in preparing a people and turns it into a metaphor of "preparing the way."

The key passage here is Luke 3:4b–5, which presents Isaiah's picture of preparing for God's salvation by pointing to a supernatural preparation of a highway (Isa 40:3–4). The leveling of geographic obstacles is a way of portraying God's coming as powerful and without obstruction. Just as God parted the sea in the exodus, so he will remove all of creation's obstacles for his people as he delivers them. There are several key passages in Isaiah that use one or another of these images. The highway as a means of access to God and his city is found in Isa 57:14–17 and 62:10. The first of these is especially important, since the image of clearing the way for God's people is present alongside a picture of his people as humble and lowly. Thus, a way is cleared for a humble and righteous people; the imagery has ethical dimensions.

Other passages give background. Isaiah 2 presents the fundamental picture of the Lord's mountain raised up for all to see. All nations are to come to the mountain to learn the ways of God. There will be a period of peace and harmony, which pictures the total salvation that God brings. But in the latter portion of the chapter, the haughty and proud are brought low, as the Lord shakes the earth (Isa 2:6–22). Thus, the geographic leveling not only clears a path for God's entry, it pictures the severity of God's coming as well. It shows the prospect of judgment for the proud. The expression "brought low" in Isa 2:9, 11, 12, 17 is the same term used in Isa 40:4 for the laying low of the mountains.

The clearest passage on geographical reorganization is Isa 42:14–17. God clears a path to lead the blind, as he will not forsake his people. But those who pursue idols will be put to shame. Isaiah 42:16 repeats an image of 40:4 in making the rough places smooth (see also 63:11–14, for God's clearing a path in the exodus).

These texts in Isaiah explain the image. God is preparing to clear a highway for his people as he comes in power to redeem them. Total victory is in view. Those who share in the victory are the humble and the blind, those who recognize a need for God and who depend on him. But such leveling of obstacles also will crush the proud and destroy those committed to idolatry. Physical and ethical images merge. The images call the hearer of John's message to realize that God is coming in judgment and only the humble who rely on him will be spared.[2]

The first explicit use of the image comes earlier in Luke 1:76 and 79. Zechariah declares that John the Baptist "will go on before the Lord to prepare the way for him [ὁδοὺς αὐτοῦ, *hodous autou*]" (v. 76). Zechariah goes on to speak about the Messiah who as the rising light of dawn will "guide our feet in the path of peace [εἰς ὁδὸν εἰρήνης, *eis hodon eirēnēs*]" (v. 79). The hymn is about what God will do through John and the Messiah, so God is the primary actor, and it is his way that is being prepared. But that way is inseparable from what Messiah as light brings to it. God's way is prepared through the illuminating work of Messiah. That way leads to peace because it is the way of salvation and deliverance (cf. 1:68–69; note also 1:78).

The theme is repeated in Luke 3:4, where Isa 40 is explicitly cited. This passage from the Hebrew Scripture was a well-known text of expectation, appearing at Qumran (1QS 8.14–15; 9.19–20).[3] John is presented in terms of this text as he ministers in the desert with his call to prepare for God's arrival in salvation and judgment. The picture of clearing the way in Luke 3:5 was just noted above as a key passage using this imagery. This ministry enables all flesh to see God's salvation (v. 6).

The idea is repeated again in Luke 7:27. Here Luke cites Isa 40 again as Jesus connects John's ministry to this text. This text also includes an allusion to Exod 23:20, so that John goes before the people (as God did in the wilderness in the exodus) to prepare their "way." This ministry is what made John the greatest born of woman in the old era (Luke 7:28). Yet the difference between the old era and the new is so great that the least in the new era is greater than John! Thus the way John opens up is a great way of salvation that elevates people to a new status before God.

The final allusion to this image comes with irony in Luke 20:21. It surfaces in the midst of controversy between Jesus and the leaders in his last week in Jerusalem. The leaders present Jesus with the dilemma of paying taxes to Caesar and open the questioning with the remark that Jesus teaches "the way of God [τὴν ὁδὸν τοῦ θεοῦ, *tēn hodon tou theou*] in accordance with the truth." This is an attempt at flattery for

---

2. Bock, *Luke 1:1–9:50*, 293–94.

3. On this citation at Qumran, which is applied to that community in a context of justifying their separation from society and their community life in the desert, see Hengel and Schwemer, *Jesus und das Judentum*, 303 and n. 36; see also James H. Charlesworth, "Intertextuality: Isaiah 40:3 and the Serek Ha-Yahad," in *The Quest*

for Context and Meaning: Studies in Biblical Intertextuality in Honor of James A. Sanders (ed. Craig A. Evans and Shemaryahu Talmon; Biblical Interpretation Series 28; Leiden: Brill, 1997), 197–224; and Klyne Snodgrass, "Streams of Tradition Emerging from Isaiah 40:1–5 and Their Adaptation in the New Testament," *JSNT* 8 (1980): 24–45.

they really do not believe this. Still, Luke uses the image ironically to show Jesus' connection to the idea of the way, as the way of God that Jesus reveals.

14.2 THE CHURCH, THE WAY, AND CHRISTIANS IN THE BOOK OF ACTS

In looking at how Luke portrays the church, we will examine the generic, nontechnical use of the term, some actions reflective of the church without the use of the term, and passages that use the term itself.

The term ἐκκλησία (ekklēsia) in its most generic usage means "assembly," referring to a general gathering of people. We see this use in Acts 7:38, where Israel is gathered as an assembly of people in the desert as Moses receives the commandments of the Lord at Mount Sinai. Some have argued this is a technical use of the term that points to a church in the time of Israel, but this makes far too much of a generic use.[4] The absence of the term "church" in Luke and the use of *ekklēsia* in Matt 16:18 looking forward to what Jesus will do on the foundation of Peter's confession of Jesus as the Christ makes it far more likely that this term describes a *new* work of God in a fresh institution that Jesus generates.[5] Another common use appears in Acts 19:32, 39–40, where a mob gathers in Ephesus in reaction to Paul.

In a few key places, we see the church at work without the term being used. No text does this as prominently and crisply as Acts 2:42–46. Here the community gathers around four key activities: "the apostles' teaching ... fellowship ... the breaking of bread and ... prayer." We also read they held their possessions loosely, sharing all things in common and meeting one another's needs (2:44–46). Yet they also continued to frequent the temple together (v. 46). So in gathering as their own community, they had not yet separated from Israel and her worship.

The depiction also has ethical dimensions. Douglas Hume has argued for a full depiction of the virtues of friendship present in this text, which he calls friendship with God and with one another. That idea could just as easily be called love for God and for one another. Hume shows that the idea of friends being one soul and holding all things in common was a frequent note in Greco-Roman writing.[6] In Acts 2:42–47, he argues, friendship is pursued in the context of trusting in God; in persevering in learning, community, worship, and hospitality; and in sharing possessions.[7] Acts 4:32–35 presents the same ideas, emphasizing boldness in testifying to Jesus and in sharing with each other.[8]

---

4. See, e.g., Seccombe, "New People of God," 358.

5. Also for this understanding is the image of the *new* man in Eph 2:11–22 where the bringing together of Jew and Gentile starts something new and fresh, even though it is connected with Israel and her promises. This imagery from Ephesians is much like the idea Luke puts forward through his complex portrait in Acts.

6. Douglas A. Hume, *The Early Christian Community: A Narrative Analysis of Acts 2:41–47 and 4:32–35* (WUNT 2/298; Tübingen: Mohr-Siebeck, 2011), 44–77. The sources Hume notes

in the Greco-Roman context are Aristotle's *Nicomachean Ethics* (esp. 1168b.7–9); Plutarch's *Advice to Bride and Groom* (esp. 141F, where they hold all things in one pot); three biographies from Diogenes Laertius (Bion, Pythagorus, and Epicurus; esp. *Pythagorus* 8.10, where friends hold all things in common; also *Epicurus* 10.11); and Iamblichus's *On the Pythagorean Way of Life* (esp. 6.30).

7. Hume, *The Early Christian Community*, 98–116.

8. Ibid., 119–39.

Another glimpse of the church in action appears as she reacts to persecution by going to prayer in Acts 4:23–30. This prayer does not ask for judgment or revenge but seeks to remain bold in the face of the opposition. The request is to be faithful to the call God gave in the midst of being surrounded by opposition. The community sees their experience in light of Scripture, pointing to a conspiracy that Ps 2:1 had indicated often takes place against the Lord and his anointed, as was taking place in Jerusalem.

The first use of the term "church" (ἐκκλησία, *ekklēsia*) occurs as the community reacts in fear to the judgment of Ananias and Sapphira in Acts 5:11. The accountability before God strikes an emotional cord. It gets the attention of the community. This judgment calls on the believers to fear God more intently since he knows what is taking place in his church.

"Church" again surfaces when Luke describes "a great persecution [that] arose against the church" in Jerusalem at the time of Stephen's martyrdom (Acts 8:1b). This ironically leads to the scattering of many outside the city and leads to new directions for the Way. This diaspora causes those scattered to witness into Judea and Samaria as Acts 8–9 shows, even setting the stage for Saul the great persecutor to head to Damascus to pursue those of the Way (9:2; 22:4) and to try to "destroy the church" (8:3). This verb in Acts 8:3 is graphic. It describes someone who damages or spoils something.[9] Its imperfect tense highlights Saul's ongoing act, possibly carrying an ingressive force. Saul either is "trying to destroy" (conative force, NET) or beginning to seek to damage the church (ingressive force). This is the only time this verb occurs in the NT.

According to later texts in Acts (9:1–2; 26:10–11), Saul worked with the approval of local Sanhedrin officials. However, his journey to Damascus was interrupted as the Lord Jesus stopped him and called him in a new direction. In a kind of irony, Saul traveled on the way against the Way, yet he was stopped on the way to join the Way (9:17, 27). Ananias gives him his calling in 9:17 by noting he will be filled with the Holy Spirit. In 9:27 Barnabas defends Saul to others, noting how Saul had preached boldly in the name of Jesus after the Lord spoke to him. So Saul receives his direction to become a key figure in the early church.

In a summary, Luke describes the church in Judea, Galilee, and Samaria as experiencing peace and being strengthened through the Word of God and the comfort of the Spirit as it increased in numbers (Acts 9:31). What we see about the church so far in Acts are the dynamics that drove the church to be effective in this period: sitting under the Word with respect for apostolic teaching, fellowship, the Spirit, prayer, community to the extent of sacrifice and sharing, and bold witness.

These churches are also connected through communication and mutual support. When the church in Jerusalem hears about what has taken place in Antioch, they send Barnabas there with Saul to see what God is doing (Acts 11:22). On their

---

9. BDAG, 604.

arrival, Barnabas and Saul meet with the church over the period of a year and teach them there (11:26).

It is here that the community begins to gain a distinct identity, and they are called "Christians" for the first time by those who oppose them (Acts 11:26). This term E. A. Judge calls "bafflingly peculiar" and "a Greco-Roman hybrid." It appears to have been coined by Latin speakers, possibly out of the Roman community in Antioch. It classified the followers as partisans of a political leader as the *-ianus* suffix indicates, on analogy with the name Herodians. It was their loyalty to the Christ that generated the name.[10] This term is another piece of evidence that the loyalty of the early church surrounded Jesus as the Christ, not merely Jesus as a prophetic figure.

Meanwhile in Jerusalem the church is still under pressure as Herod lays hands on some in the church, including Peter (Acts 12:1). Again, the church responds with prayer (12:5), and their request is granted with Peter's miraculous release. So support in the church involves teaching, resources, and prayer.

Mission also drives the dynamic community Luke describes. There are prophets and teachers in the church in Antioch, including Barnabas (Acts 13:1). Barnabas and Saul are then set apart by the Spirit to leave this community and engage in a larger mission, which they do with enough success that in various locales they appoint elders to lead the new churches that are formed (14:23). They also commit these leaders to the Lord with prayer and fasting. Here the church is described as an individual community, the most common usage found in Acts. Whereas "the Way" refers commonly to the movement as a whole, in general within Acts "the church" refers to the local community. On their return to Antioch, Paul and Barnabas report to the gathered church there what God has done through them and how a door of faith has opened up to the Gentiles (14:27).

When controversy arose, the community's leaders gathered to sort out if Gentiles had to be circumcised. The church at Antioch sent Paul and Barnabas as its representatives (Acts 15:3). They, in turn, were received by the church in Jerusalem and given an opportunity to report on all God had done with them (15:4). At the end of the deliberations, the apostles, elders, and the church decide it is best to inform other communities of their decision, and they send men with a letter to report the results (15:23). In all of this, there is a sense of linkage and connectedness among the churches. Thus as Paul begins the second journey, Luke summarizes here that "the churches were strengthened in the faith and grew daily in numbers" (16:5).

Part of this success might be as a result of hearing about the kind of power encounter that Paul had in Philippi, where a possessed slave girl shouted that Paul was declaring the "way of salvation," a statement that was true, but one that Paul silenced with an exorcism (Acts 16:17). Luke shows how the Way is more power-

---

10. On this background, see E. A. Judge, *The First Christians in the Roman World: Augustan and New Testament Essays* (ed. James Harrison; WUNT 229; Tübingen: Mohr-Siebeck, 2008), 609–10.

ful than demonic or magical forces.[11] In another summary, he notes how Paul on his return to Antioch at the end of this journey greeted the church in Caesarea (18:22). In a side note, Priscilla and Aquila explained the way of God to Apollos more accurately, showing how in private community and support all could teach or learn (18:26).

Paul continued by ministering in Ephesus. Here some opposed him, "speaking evil of the Way before the multitudes" (Acts 19:9). Later a mob formed in reaction to Paul's success as those who responded had burned their magic books. So the silversmiths who made idols of Artemis and other gods reacted, nervous at what it meant for them in business terms. This reaction Luke describes as "no little stir concerning the Way" (19:23). Here was a ministry where the transformed lives of believers of the Way made a social impact.

As Paul made his final missionary journey in Acts, he sent for the elders of the church in Ephesus to meet him at Miletus (Acts 20:17). He reviews his faithfulness in ministry and then commends them to the Lord to live out their call. They are to "keep watch over yourselves and all the flock of which the Holy Spirit has made you overseers. Be shepherds of the church of God, which he bought with his own blood" (20:28). Here we see the leadership being called to watch out first for one's own spiritual welfare and then for that of the community they serve. This is an overseer role, where the welfare of the community is their concern. In the context, proper teaching and living are the focus of this concern. The church is precious, purchased by God's own act in giving the blood of his own Son to secure it. This alludes to the sacrifical and substitutionary death of Jesus. The only mention of this theme in Acts about how Jesus' death works makes the point about the means by which God has secured the cleansed status of the new community. The church has come into existence at great cost. Its integrity is to be preserved by leaders who appreciate what God did to bring it to life.

By the time we get to Acts 21, Paul's support of the new community gets him into more trouble as he is arrested for his commitment to the movement. Paul, who had opposed the Way (Acts 22:4), has come to confess it (22:14) and has done so to such effect that he ends up being arrested through the Jewish leadership's effort to try and stop him. It is here that the last mention of the church or the Way appears in Acts. In the defense speeches, Paul notes the movement, which is known as the Way (24:14), is called a sect of Judaism by the Jewish leaders.

The second and last mention of "Christians" in Acts occurs in Acts 26:28 during the final defense of Paul recorded in Acts. Agrippa blurts out that if Paul keeps talking, he might shortly make him into a Christian. The term is important because it shows a people identified and gathered around the idea of Jesus as the Christ. These are people who identify with Jesus as the anointed one of God. Also

---

11. The same power was shown in Acts 8 in the encounter with Simon Magus. The importance of these texts is shown in Klauck, *Magic and Paganism in Early Christianity*.

interesting is that both uses in Acts appear to be from what other people called them, not self-designations. When those outside saw what these people believed and preached, it was their connection to the Christ that identified them. This assumes a witness and the carrying out of a mission, something that makes a community most dynamic. This emphasis is precisely what Luke has noted as the impact of the church.

14.3 CONCLUSION

For Luke, the church is a new entity with connections to old promises. What he highlights in describing it, however, is not its roots but its dynamism. The early churches were engaged in active mission.[12] There were internal dynamics that kept them active, even as they looked outward to mission. (1) They sat at the feet of solid teaching from the apostles and Scriptures; (2) they engaged in meaningful community and fellowship; (3) they worshiped and broke bread together; (4) they supported one another across locations; (5) they prayed when they faced pressure; and (6) the leadership kept a careful watch over their spiritual health. They were a community that formed a new household of God. So this is how the Way grew along the way, drawing on the dynamics the Spirit among them provided. The community focused on what they were called to do: to engage in mission and to represent in the world the Lord who so graciously had paved the way for them. They garnered the name "Christians" as a result.

---

12. This point is also stressed in the article by Peter Bolt, "Mission and Witness," in *Witness to the Gospel*, 191–214. He looks at the important witness motif that runs from Luke 24:48 through Acts as well as the term mission and the role of the Twelve plus Paul.

Chapter 15

DISCIPLESHIP AND ETHICS
IN THE NEW COMMUNITY

BIBLIOGRAPHY

Bolt, Peter. "Mission and Witness." Pp. 191–214 in *Witness to the Gospel: The Theology of Acts*. Ed. I. Howard Marshall and David Peterson. Grand Rapids: Eerdmans, 1998. **Clarke, Andrew C.** "The Role of the Apostles." Pp. 169–90 in *Witness to the Gospel: The Theology of Acts*. Ed. I. Howard Marshall and David Peterson. Grand Rapids: Eerdmans, 1998. **Cunningham, Scott.** *"Through Many Tribulations": The Theology of Persecution in Luke-Acts*. JSNTSup. Sheffield: Sheffield Academic Press, 1997. **Peterson, David.** "The Worship of the New Community." Pp. 373–95 in *Witness to the Gospel: The Theology of Acts*. Ed. I. Howard Marshall and David Peterson. Grand Rapids: Eerdmans, 1998. **Pickett, Raymond.** "Luke and Empire." Pp. 1–22 in *Luke-Acts and Empire: Essays in Honor of Robert L. Brawley*. Ed. David Rhoads, David Esterline, and Jae Won Lee. Princeton Theological Monographs. Eugene, OR: Pickwick, 2011. **Plymale, Steven F.** *The Prayer Texts of Luke-Acts*. American University Studies. New York: Peter Lang, 1991. **Rhoads, David, David Esterline, and Jae Won Lee**, eds. *Luke-Acts and Empire: Essays in Honor of Robert L. Brawley*. Princeton Theological Monographs. Eugene, OR: Pickwick, 2011. **Rosner, Brian.** "The Progress of the Word." Pp. 215–33 in *Witness to the Gospel: The Theology of Acts*. Ed. I. Howard Marshall and David Peterson. Grand Rapids: Eerdmans, 1998. **Seccombe, David Peter.** *Possessions and the Poor in Luke-Acts*. SNTSU. Linz: A. Fuchs, 1982.

This chapter will not proceed consistently in a narrative order. This is because the character and dynamic of the church was already examined in the previous chapter. This survey starts with a look at how the church functioned as disciples. Then we focus on Jesus' teaching about discipleship to show the roots of these ideals in the church. The term "disciple" (μαθητής, *mathētēs*) is used thirty-seven times in Luke and twenty-eight times in Acts. Most of the scenes in Acts involve texts where the term "disciples" serves as another name for "believers," so we will not cover those texts in this section (Acts 6:1, 7; 9:1, 19; 9:26 [2x], 38; 11:26; 13:52; 14:28; 16:1; 18:23, 27; 19:1, 9; 20:1; 21:4, 16). However, numerous scenes involve instruction without using this term, so those will be included in the final section on ethics.

15.1 THE NEW COMMUNITY AND ITS ACTIVITY AS FOLLOWERS OF JESUS

After Pentecost, believers were identified with Jesus in ways that had not been possible previously, for the Spirit our Lord sent now lives in them. After reviewing the activity of Jesus' followers in the new community, we will survey the use of the term "disciple" in narrative order and then consider specific instructions on key ethical themes given to Jesus' followers.

15.1.1 The New Community's Activities

The early church was an active community.[1] Many of the believers' activities have already been discussed. Missionary activity and the proclamation of Jesus as the Christ are the outstanding features of Acts. This preaching moves from Jerusalem (Acts 2–5), into Samaria (ch. 8), then to Gentiles (chs. 10–11), into various missionary journeys (chs. 13–20), and finally by trial to Rome (chs. 21–28). Along with the message comes authentication by miracles. Various summary statements underline the church's proclamation role as a bearer of the word and/or as believers are responsive with faith (2:47 in light of 2:42–46; 5:14; 6:7; 9:31; 11:21; 12:24; 13:49; 16:5; 19:20). That word is about the message of the gospel. In various ways, these verses speak of the word growing or the community growing as a result of the church's activities.

Besides proclamation, the church also enjoys communal life. The believers become a caring community, who worship, study, and pray together. Acts 2:42–47 summarizes the variety of activities in which the church engages. The believers share possessions, meet needs, break bread in their homes, praise God, share in apostolic teaching, have fellowship, and pray. Acts 4:23–35 records the early church's exemplary prayer for boldness in speaking the word.

The belivers also care for each other. Acts 4:32–37 indicates how they share possessions with each other to meet their needs. Acts 6:1–6 portrays how they creatively accept appropriate criticism about the treatment of widows and then let those who raised the problem assist in solving it. Even physical needs are the object of the church's attention. One local community in Antioch sends material aid and food to another needy community in Jerusalem (11:29). The church prays, supports, and commissions a missionary endeavor (13:1–3). The church is active in outreach and in supporting the growth of its members.[2]

The church also engages in instruction, which leads to theological reflection about what God is doing through them. In Acts 11:1–18 Peter submits an oral report about what God has been doing for the Gentiles. Later, in Acts 15, further

---

1. There is an excellent survey of this theme by Peterson, "Worship of the New Community," 373–95. He highlights homage to the ascended Lord, serving and worshiping the Lord (noting that the term "worship" only appears in Acts 13:1–2), teaching, fellowship, eating together, prayer, and praise.

2. As Rosner, "Progress of the Word," 215–33, shows, the themes of the growth of the community and the progress of the Word are tied closely together in Acts. He is also correct to note that this portrait is not triumphalistic but reflects growth through struggle and persecution (233).

questions about this same issue need further reflection. Here the church comes together and hammers out a solution to a difficult theological and social problem. The discussion involves a reflective evaluation of experience measured by the Scriptures, and God's clear actions and Scripture come together in the solution. The decision also reflects sensitivity to all concerned.

The church disciplines her members. This is graphically portrayed in the experience of Ananias and Sapphira, who lie to the Spirit and are struck dead (Acts 5:1–11). Peter, functioning like a prophet, describes their deceit as against the Spirit of God, a reference to the fact that the community is indwelt by God and thus is special in his sight (vv. 3, 9). The penalty's immediacy probably has more to do with the young age of the church than anything else. But here God goes to great lengths to show how important honesty, purity, and accountability are to him. God sees everything that happens in his church. Sin and deceit are an offense to him.

The church seeks to minister to her members and reach out to the world. Ministry involves meeting both physical and spiritual needs. Individual churches and communities linked together even from a distance care for the whole person. In addition, the church preaches the gospel whether locally or by missionaries sent to faraway lands. The believers in the churches in Acts do not limit their vision to their own neighborhoods. The call is to preach the gospel to the ends of the earth (Acts 1:8; 13:47), and each community seeks to do so. Alongside are activities such as preaching, worship, and a desire to represent the Lord boldly. This requires a clear message, an active communal life, theological reflection, and support for righteous living. The many dimensions of church activity create an effective community that accomplishes much despite initial small numbers.

15.1.2 Functions in the New Community

Luke mentioned five church functions, which are either offices or other organized roles. Some were permanent; others were temporary. Luke discusses the first, that of *apostle*, most frequently. The Twelve who were chosen for this role are named in Luke 6:12–16. [3] They are not all successful, since Judas Iscariot was in their midst. He represents someone who participates in the community but is not a genuine member. Such people can even reach prominence in the church.

When the church replaces Judas, Peter describes the qualifications of an apostle (Acts 1:12–26). [4] This office is not to continue into succeeding generations, since a requirement is that one must have been with Jesus and seen him after the

---

3. Andrew C. Clarke, "The Role of the Apostles," in *Witness to the Gospel*, 169–90. He notes how they functioned as a bridge between Jesus and the mission of the church. Their first-hand knowledge of Jesus is what qualified them for this role. It was not one that was passed on, as their appointment to judge the twelve tribes of Israel in the future and the requirement of a direct experience with Jesus shows (Luke 22:29–30; Acts 1:21–22). They formed the nucleus of restored Israel, served as witnesses to Jesus' resurrection, and were authoritative teachers and missionaries. The NT is a product of their

presence and influence. Paul and Barnabas were added to their number (Acts 14:4, 14).

4. There is no indication that the appointment of Matthias was an error by the church. Acts 1 has no hint of criticism about it. The discussion before the vote is bathed in Scripture, prayer, and dependence on the Lord. Luke also closes the scene noting Matthias was added to the eleven. Luke solved the issue of Paul's authority another way. He pointed to the Lord's specific appointment of him (Acts 9) and showed him doing what the apostles did in ministry.

resurrection (vv. 21 – 22). These authoritative representatives lay the foundation of the church and exercise oversight over the various communities. But with the passing of the Twelve, this office passes away in its most technical sense. Paul and Barnabas are also called apostles in Acts 14:4, 14, but this use is not the narrowest use of the term as referring to the Twelve. This slightly broader use is indicated by the fact that Barnabas is included in the Acts 14 listing (cf. 1 Cor 9:1 – 6). Luke makes no effort to argue that Paul is the twelfth apostle. In Acts 14, the term "apostle" refers to authoritative representatives who plant churches in new areas. Nevertheless, their role is like that of the Twelve in overseeing the start of a new community.

The second function, the role of *witness*, has been discussed earlier. This is a major Lucan category and is often used along with the title of apostle in describing one of their functions. But others are also witnesses. Stephen and Paul are singled out (Acts 22:15, 20; 26:16). The disciples are commissioned as witnesses (Luke 24:48), and the Lord's commission is repeated in Acts 1:8 to show its importance. These witnesses attest to Jesus' miracles (Acts 2:22), resurrection (v. 32), crucifixion and resurrection (Acts 3:15; 5:30 – 32), and post-resurrection appearances (13:31).

Third, Luke briefly mentions *prophets*. Agabus predicts famine in Judea and warns Paul about traveling to Jerusalem (Acts 11:27 – 30; 21:7 – 14). Philip's four unmarried daughters are prophetesses to the church (Acts 21:9). Though not members of the new community since they precede it, Simeon and Anna are also prophets who speak to all who pass by about the baby Jesus (Luke 2:25 – 38). They represent pious Jews waiting for the time of promise who respond to Jesus. Finally, Peter calls the praise associated with the tongues-speaking of Acts 2 prophecy (vv. 17 – 18). So sometimes the activity is present without the office being present.

Fourth, the seven men of Acts 6:1 – 6 are *servants* who play a role in support of the apostles and in meeting the needs of a specific problem. They probably are not deacons, since Luke does not mention that connection anywhere. Still these men represent those who minister to believers' physical and other needs so that the leaders of the Jerusalem church can concentrate on ministering the Word.

Fifth, Luke mentions the *leaders/elders* of a local community in Ephesus (Acts 20:17 – 35). These elders are charged with oversight in a local area. That oversight comes with a responsibility to serve believers. [5] There are several such leaders. This points to a clear level of mutual accountability and the sharing of authority. No one person holds all the power and has absolute control. They must instruct and lead the local congregations. They also give the church a structure for accountability, as well as instruction and direction.

As the church grows, new functions emerge and organizational structure develops for the sake of efficient, effective service. Such development is seen in Acts 6:1 – 6. Leaders of spiritual quality develop. However, Luke spends little time discussing the structure of the church. Instead, he stresses her activities and effectiveness.

---

5. Probably these elders supervised believers in a given area rather than over "one congregation" in Ephesus. Ancient house churches could hold only about fifty or so people, so it is possible there were numerous meeting areas around a city the size of Ephesus.

15.1.3 Descriptions of Community Members

Luke has a few titles by which he refers to those who follow Jesus. By far the most common title is "disciple" (μαθητής, *mathētēs*), which simply means "learner" or "pupil." [6] It reflects the fact that one who responds to the gospel is walking with Jesus and is learning from him. Some disciples (e.g., Judas) are not real believers. There are false disciples and poor disciples. But the term itself describes a person who is dependent on and instructed by Jesus, or who at least appears to be in such a position.

Another common title used by Luke is "believers" (οἱ πιστεύοντες, *hoi pisteuontes*), a term that becomes equivalent to "disciples." Eventually "believers" replaces "disciples" in other NT writings because the former focuses on the fundamental characteristic of trust. The words "believe" and "believers" occur with this force in Acts 2:44; 4:32; 10:43; 11:21; 13:39; 18:27; 19:18; 21:20, 25; and 22:19. Most of the thirty-seven uses of the term simply speak of a reaction of faith or belief.

As we saw in the previous chapter, outsiders use the title "Christian" to describe believers. The members of the community have so identified with Jesus Christ that they are given his name; at least this seems to be the implication of the passive verb ("were called") in Acts 11:26. Agrippa also uses the term (26:28). As we have noted in ch. 14, the final title for the movement is "the Way." This title expresses the notion that this movement points the way to God and salvation (Acts 9:2; 18:25–26; 19:9; 22:4; 24:14, 22).

Note, however, that the church's faith and commitment, not her titles, are the important issue for Luke. That, along with her ethics, marks the church out as a unique institution. Both her deliverer and her messengers are light to a needy humanity (Luke 1:78–79; Acts 13:47).

Finally in a few texts, believers are called "saints" (ἅγιοι, *hagioi*). There is no elaboration here, just the description (Acts 9:13, 32, 41; 26:10). They are simply people set apart to God. This title parallels Paul's common description of believers.

15.2 DISCIPLES IN LUKE-ACTS

Most of the passages about disciples in Luke treat scenes where they accompany Jesus or are reacting to events he has generated. So the first appearance of the term involves a complaint that the Pharisees and scribes make about Jesus' associations (Luke 5:30). In a sense, these are discipleship texts because they show what Jesus taught about following him, even in the midst of controversy. Jesus pursued association with sinners because his mission was to call the sick to repent like a physician who gives a cure (Luke 5:32).

Another lesson in controversy has to do with the practices of Jesus' disciples. Their expression of religious faith is unlike that of John the Baptist's followers or the

---

6. BDAG, 609.

Pharisees. They do not fast or offer public prayers (Luke 5:33), practices well established in Second Temple Judaism. By grouping the Pharisees' disciples and John's disciples, Luke makes clear that an issue of the larger Jewish community is at stake.

Fasting was highly regarded during this period. The OT discusses fasts for specific occasions (Lev 16:29–34; 23:26–32; Num 29:7–11). [7] Individual fasts were taken for differing reasons: some fasted in hope of God's deliverance (2 Sam 12:16–20; 1 Kgs 21:27; Pss 35:13; 69:10 [69:11 MT]), while others hoped to turn aside calamity (Jdg 20:26; 1 Sam 7:6; 1 Kgs 21:9; 2 Chr 20:3–4; Jer 36:6, 9). By combining prayer and fasting, the participants hoped that God would answer, since often fasting accompanied confession and intercession (Ezra 8:21, 23; Neh 1:4; Jer 14:12). The one who fasted reflected a mourner's mood (1 Kgs 21:27; Esth 4:3; Isa 58:5; Dan 9:3; Joel 2:12–13). The usual fast lasted one morning and evening (Jdg 20:26; 1 Sam 14:24; 2 Sam 1:12). More severe were the three-day fast (Esth 4:16) and the weeklong fast (1 Sam 31:13), where food was forbidden only during the day (2 Sam 3:35). The three-week fast described in Dan 10:2–3 belongs to this latter type of severe fast. Needless to say, such fasting had an influence on the body (Ps 109:24).

National fasts occurred on the Day of Atonement and the four-day memorial to recall Jerusalem's fall. Thus, fasting held a high place in Judaism's psyche. It occurred frequently and had great significance. In fact, fasting prepared one for all kinds of activity in Judaism. Many apocalyptic materials mention that fasting preceded their visions (2 Esd. [= *4 Ezra*] 5:13, 19–20; *2 Bar.* 9.2; 12.5). A vow often was confirmed with a fast (Acts 23:12, 14). Fasting was often regarded as a virtue (*T. Jos.* 3.4–5; 4.8; 10.1). It even was regarded in some circles as meritorious (*1 En.* 108.7–9; Philo, *Special Laws* 2.32 [197]). Only here and there do voices warn that fasting without actual turning from sin is useless (Sir 34:31 [according to NRSV numbering]). The zealous fasted twice a week, usually on Monday and Thursday. *Didache* 8.1 shows that some in early Christianity took up this practice. Fasting was not permitted on Sabbaths and festival days (Jdt 8:6; *Jub.* 50.10, 12). Clearly, this activity had a major role in first-century religious life, so one can see why Jesus' lack of emphasis raises questions.

When Luke focuses on prayer and fasting, the issue is thus not on the periphery of religion. It is a central act of great piety. Luke alone mentions prayer with fasting, probably because the two activities went together. One fasted in order to spend focused time with God. The remark concerns a serious issue in ancient spiritual life. Still, Jesus defends his disciples' seemingly irreligious practice. [8] Despite the role of such practices in Second Temple Judaism, Jesus teaches the arrival of the new era as something new and fresh, something that could not be patched on to what was old. This is new wine. Those who like the old wine will not want the new. In the Sermon on the Mount, in a portion Luke does not include, Jesus notes that prayer and fasting must not be done in public to draw attention to one's practice (Matt 6:1–8, 16–18).

---

7. Danker, *Jesus and the New Age*, 127; Behm, *TDNT*, 4:928–29.   8. Book, *Luke 1:1–9:50*, 515–16.

A third lesson that involves disciples in controversy is about the Sabbath (Luke 6:1). Here the Pharisees complain about the disciples plucking grain on the day of rest. Jesus replies in two ways. First, Jesus points to the precedent of Scripture with the example of David and his men eating forbidden bread. Second, he makes the even more controversial point that he is Lord of the Sabbath. The first reply makes the point that the Sabbath is not designed to be excessively restrictive. The second argues that Jesus has the authority to decide what is right for the Sabbath. This is a claim to extensive authority, for the Sabbath is a part of the Ten Commandments, is in the Torah, and is modeled on God's rest on the seventh day of the creation. These kinds of teaching points in front of the disciples set the stage for their activity in Acts after Jesus has departed.

Jesus also built in leadership among his disciples since he chose Twelve out from among them (Luke 6:13). The ethical core of love the disciples should have is recorded in the Sermon on the Plain (6:20). Here Jesus stresses a love superior to what one normally finds in the world among sinners, as he issues a call to love one's enemies. The example given is God's care for the unrighteous. Such love shows one to truly be a child of God in action. It also means not judging but being accountable in a healthy way, taking care as to what teaching one follows and building on the rock of Jesus' teaching (6:20–49). No disciple is greater than his teacher, so the model of teaching matters (6:40).

The disciples witness Jesus' miraculous acts. For example, they are with him when he raises the widow of Nain's son (Luke 7:11). Others also witness this when John's disciples report to John what Jesus is doing (7:18). This leads John to ask for confirmation that Jesus truly is the one to come. Jesus' actions in healing the blind, lame, deaf, and others are the evidence he gives to answer the question positively (7:22–23).

The disciples ask Jesus to teach them as they ask for an interpretation of the parable of the sower. Jesus points to the different kinds of reactions the word of the kingdom generates, depending on a person's heart (Luke 8:9). So the disciples learn that Satan grabs the word before some have a chance, others have a short-lived faith but persecution causes them to fall away, while the concerns and riches of life choke the word in the lives of still others. Finally, there are those who with an honest and good heart hold fast to the word and bear fruit with patience. Disciples are to have the heart of the good soil.

Jesus' power is displayed to the disciples when he calms the storm (Luke 8:22), causing them to ask, "Who is this? He commands even the wind and the water, and they obey him" (8:25). Events like this make the disciples witnesses to Jesus' authority, an authority like God's ability to control the seas (Ps 107:27–29). Another display of Jesus' ability to provide is the multiplication of the loaves and fish, which the disciples witness (Luke 9:16).

With his disciples alone, Jesus asks who people say he is (Luke 9:18). The disciples answer that the crowds wonder if he is some sort of prophet. Peter, however, speaks for the disciples and proclaims Jesus as "God's Messiah." Jesus is not simply one among many. These disciples who have spent time with Jesus appreciate that he has a unique role in God's program.

Jesus then tells the disciples that he will suffer and that they too must be prepared to take up their cross daily and lose their lives to gain them, not being ashamed of the Son of Man (Luke 9:23–27). He soon repeats the idea when he notes that the Son of Man is going to be betrayed (9:43–44). Here is the kind of Messiah Jesus will be — one who serves and suffers. Jesus explicitly tells this to Zacchaeus when he says the Son of Man came to seek and save the lost (19:10). To the disciples he notes that he has not been a figure of power with them but one who serves as an example (22:24–27). So this theme runs throughout the gospel.

The disciples still have much to learn, for they fail to exorcise a demon from a boy (Luke 9:40) and respond poorly to the rejection by some in Samaria; they want to bring judgment immediately rather than continuing to witness in the face of rejection (9:54). The disciples James and John want to rain fire down from heaven. Jesus just moves on after rebuking them. Discipleship is not about power, but about service and suffering.

Jesus then notes how they must be ready for such rejection since the Son of Man has no place to put his head (Luke 9:57). Discipleship in the context of such rejection allows nothing to get in the way, not even family obligations or longing for attachment to the world (9:58–62).

Let's take a closer look at the three key points Jesus makes. The first incident involves a volunteer who commits to follow Jesus wherever he goes. We know nothing about this man or how he came to this decision. Since his declaration is so openended, Jesus responds with equal openness about what such a commitment means. In the parallel (Matt 8:18–19), the man offers to be Jesus' student and follow him, since there he calls Jesus "teacher" (διδάσκαλε, *didaskale*). But, of course, Jesus wants more than a student. Students of Judaism lived with their teachers in order to learn the Torah, but what Jesus offers is a more compelling and dangerous course (Luke 6:40).[9] It is a reorientation of life, involving suffering and perhaps death. If one is to go wherever Jesus goes, one must be ready for rejection (9:51–56). Jesus' claims challenge commonly held views.

Jesus describes what disciples can expect when he is their example. His situation is worse than that of beasts: foxes and birds have places to stay, but the Son of Man has no home. Bultmann argues that the Son of Man reference is generic and applies to people in general, but this contradicts the conception of Scripture that God loves and cares for people more than he does other creatures.[10] Most people have homes, so the reference must be to Jesus.[11] "Homelessness" has been Jesus' fate from his birth.[12] A disciple of Jesus must realize that following him means living as a stranger in the world, because a choice for Jesus is a choice rejected by many in the world.

9. Plummer, *St Luke*, 265; Ellis, *Gospel of Luke*, 153.
10. Bultmann, *History of the Synoptic Problem*, 28, n. 3.
11. Marshall, *Gospel of Luke*, 410.
12. Hengel, *TDNT*, 9:55.

Jesus then asks a second man to follow him. Unlike Levi (Luke 5:28), who immediately left all to follow Jesus, this man comes up with a reason not to follow, at least initially: he wants to take time to bury his father. The request seems reasonable, as this responsibility was one of the most important a family member could perform (Tob 4:3–4; 12:12). Jesus' teaching often has a surprising twist to portray emphatically what God desires. The twist in this passage causes the reader to reflect on Jesus' reply.

Proper burial was a major concern in ancient culture. That cultic purity was regarded as less important than burying the dead shows that burying the dead was a Jewish ethical priority.[13] The language of the request follows 1 Kgs 19:19–21, where Elisha asked Elijah for permission to kiss his parents good-bye. Sirach 38:16 expresses the sentiment of this would-be disciple: "My child, let your tears fall for the dead.... Lay out the body with due ceremony, and do not neglect the burial." So in refusing this man's request, Jesus describes a demand that is greater than this important familial responsibility, rooted in the commandment to honor one's parents. In fact, the remark may point to Jesus' bringing in the new era. The ability to set priorities that go beyond the Ten Commandments suggests the presence of messianic authority.[14] The new Moses has come. Following Jesus is top priority.

Is the remark as harsh as it seems, or is the father already dead and awaiting burial? Arndt argues that the man is asking to wait until his father has passed away—whenever that may be.[15] If that is the request, then discipleship is delayed indefinitely and the rebuke seems more reasonable. Adherents of this view note that ἀκολούθει (akolouthei, "follow") is a present imperative that means "be my follower." They also argue that it is unlikely that a man with a dead father awaiting burial would be out traveling about town. Those who prepared a body for a funeral were unclean for a week and therefore would not be out in public, except for the funeral (so Luke 7:12; cf. Num 19:11). If this view is correct, the son wants to postpone devoting himself to Jesus until basic familial duties are behind him, putting commitment to family ahead of service to the kingdom. Jesus' response shows that his call has priority.

However, the parallel Luke 14:25–27 makes a similar point with hyperbolic language. More important, the request is parallel to 9:61–62, where an immediate request is in view. Plummer also seems to reject Arndt's explanation, though he allows that perhaps the father is very ill.[16] Rejecting this "down the road" option regards the effort to press the present imperative as unlikely and argues more correctly that Jesus' reply about burial becomes unnecessary if a later burial were in view. The demand appears much too urgent for this view. So in the second request, Jesus highlights the urgency of the demands of discipleship. They are a first priority.

The pericope closes with a third figure, who also volunteers to follow Jesus.

13. Ellis, *Gospel of Luke*, 153.
14. Witherington, *Christology of Jesus*, 139–40.
15. Arndt, *Gospel according to St. Luke*, 277.
16. Plummer, *St Luke*, 266.

He also wishes to introduce a proviso before starting. He asks for the right to tell his family that he is leaving and to bid them farewell (Luke 9:61–62). Only Luke includes this third scene, while the previous two examples have a parallel (Matt 8:19–22).

Again, the request seems reasonable. It parallels Elisha's response to Elijah's call (1 Kgs 19:19–21), a passage that also had some conceptual parallelism to the previous request to Jesus.[17] Elisha, an OT "disciple," asks to kiss his mother and father before joining the prophet, and Elijah grants that request. As in other Lucan texts, the story of Elijah supplies the background (cf. Luke 1:15–17; 4:25–27; 7:27; 9:30–32, 54). It may well be that the nature of Jesus' response is purposefully contrastive to this OT text, which suggests a greater urgency in the present situation because this is a greater era in God's program. As with the first man, this volunteer indicates he will follow Jesus. And Jesus similarly replies in terms of what that volunteer's commitment really requires. One cannot follow after two things at the same time; following Jesus means making him the compass of one's life. It is easy to miss what discipleship demands. Jesus makes sure this commitment is clear.[18]

Jesus' reply is a warning, since he sees a danger in the request. One may follow him initially, only to long for the old life later. Such looking back does not promote spiritual health. If one is going to follow Jesus, one needs to keep following him and not look back. Jesus' reply here is not so much a refusal as it is a warning.[19] The nation of Israel looked back after the exodus (Exod 16:3). Lot's wife looked back after departing Sodom (Gen 19:26; cf. Luke 17:32). Once we commit to Jesus, we are to hold fast our confession. If one confesses Jesus, only to renounce permanently that confession later, then the apparent confession is false, and one's position is as perilous after the "departure" as before the profession (Matt 7:21–23; 22:11–13; Luke 13:25–27; 1 Cor 15:2; Col 1:21–23; cf. the warnings in Hebrews).

Perhaps in the desire to bid farewell, the heart never leaves the attachment to old values and the old way of life. It is this lack of a clean break against which Jesus warns here. To follow Jesus means not to look back to the way life was before one came to follow him. Good service requires undivided loyalty.[20] Discipleship is not an emotional decision of one moment, but a walk of life.[21]

In sum, these key verses on discipleship show how Jesus presents discipleship as a full vocation. Nothing else comes ahead of it.

Jesus is grateful for his disciples as they engage in mission. So he prays to the Father with gratitude that God has revealed himself to them and tells the disciples they are blessed for having seen what prophets and kings had longed to see (Luke 10:24–25).

The disciples are learning and ask Jesus to teach them to pray. He does give them

17. Marshall, *Gospel of Luke*, 412.
18. Rengstorf, *TDNT*, 4:450.
19. Arndt, *Gospel according to St. Luke*, 278.
20. Ellis, *Gospel of Luke*, 154.
21. K. Schmidt, *TDNT*, 1:588; Bock, *Luke 9:51–24:53*, 977–83.

a corporate prayer that affirms God's uniqueness, submission to his will, an acknowledgment of daily needs, and a prayer for spiritual protection (Luke 11:1–4).[22] The disciples' prayer is intercession that communicates complete dependence on God in every key sphere of life.

In contrast to such dependence is the hypocrisy of the Pharisees, which Jesus warns the disciples about (Luke 12:1). In this section of Luke where Jesus is journeying to Jerusalem to meet his divine destiny, Jesus is preparing his disciples for his absence in a world that will treat them as it did him. Acceptance and seeking the approval of others are things to avoid.

These disciples can trust the Father to provide whatever they need, just as he does for the birds and wild flowers (Luke 12:22–31). They are not alone, and what their heart pursues will say where their treasure is. So they should be watchful, knowing they are accountable for the gifts God has given them, something Peter asks Jesus to explain (12:35–48, esp. v. 41). In doing so, Jesus calls them to faithfulness.

Discipleship demands counting the cost and even loving God over family (Luke 14:26). Again, Jesus notes that one must be ready to carry one's cross (14:27). This verse stresses the process of discipleship in carrying the cross, not the decision to enter into it. This emphasis is indicated because βαστάζει (bastazei, "bears") and ἔρχεται (erchetai, "comes") are both present tense: "whoever is not bearing and is not coming after me." Βαστάζω (bastazō) means "to carry an object" or "to bear a burden" (Luke 7:14; 10:4; 11:27; 22:10; Acts 3:2; 9:15; 15:10).[23]

Counting the cost is a picture Jesus uses to describe discipleship in Luke 14:28–30. Jesus describes starting a building and not finishing it as a negative example not to follow. Before building, the wise person assesses the expense. One does not build the tower, despite its benefits, until one knows it is affordable and can be brought to completion. The wise decision involves reflection, not reaction. Sitting and calculating the cost mean a reasoned assessment. So, Jesus suggests, it should be with discipleship: one should assess whether one is ready to take on the personal commitment and sacrifice required to follow Jesus.

Danker cites a similar teaching from Epictetus 3.15.10–13, a portion of which says, "Look these drawbacks over carefully, and then, if you think best, approach philosophy, that is, if you are willing at the price of these things to secure tranquility, freedom, and repose." The object for Epictetus is different, but the attitude is similar.[24] Jesus' teaching is in common with the moral exhortations of the day. A decision to pledge allegiance to Jesus is one of great moment and is to be entered into with sober reflection.[25]

A second picture about discipleship points to the picture of settling differences with a stronger king in Luke 14:31–32. This second parable differs slightly from the first in that the builder makes up his own mind whether to start a project; in

---

22. This prayer is discussed in detail in my *Luke 9:51–24:53*, 1050–56.

23. Büchsel, *TDNT*, 1:596; Bock, *Luke 9:51–24:53*, 1286.

24. Danker, *Jesus and the New Age*, 273.

25. Bock, *Luke 9:51–24:53*, 1287–89.

the second, a decision is forced on the king by a stronger power. Both pictures are important and show the slight difference between the parables of 14:28–30 and 14:31–32. The first pictures coming to Jesus; the second deals with following after him. First, consider what discipleship will cost. Second, consider what refusing the "more powerful one" will mean. Can you enter battle against him? In short, consider the cost of entry and the benefits of allying with the one who carries the power.

This discipleship also includes the renunciation of possessions, which means that God is more important than what we have and own (Luke 14:33; see 18:28–30; 19:1–10).

Disciples must be careful with how they handle resources, doing so generously as the unjust steward did when he was facing being fired (Luke 16:1–13). Jesus warns them not to be a stumbling block to the little ones of the kingdom (17:1–2). He notes they will long to see the days of the Son of Man, but they will not yet come (17:22). That day will come suddenly, but only after Jesus is rejected.

Jesus rebukes the disciples when they try to prohibit little children from being brought to him; he insists that the kingdom is made up of such little ones like these (Luke 18:15–17). The picture is of simple trust and dependence.

After sending two disciples (Luke 19:29) to prepare for Jesus' entrance into Jerusalem and to procure an animal for him to ride, Jesus enters the city to the praise of his disciples, crying out in the language of Ps 118 about the king, the one who comes in the name of the Lord (Luke 19:37–38). When the Pharisees ask that Jesus rebuke his disciples (19:39), he refuses. The disciples know who Jesus is.

As the pressure of rejection in Jerusalem mounts, Jesus tells his disciples to beware of the scribes, who like attention but are full of hypocrisy, taking advantage of those in need (Luke 20:45–47). They stand in contrast to a poor woman who gives everything she has by giving a mere two lepta. By doing so as a poor woman, she gives her very life (21:1–4).

Jesus tells the disciples both about the destruction of the temple and about the return of the Son of Man, not by giving its exact timing but by telling them what will come with it. He assures them that their redemption is drawing near as they persevere (Luke 21:5–37). They will need to be strong, but the Spirit will help them when they are examined by those who have arrested them. This promise is also something we see realized in the book of Acts.

Jesus gathers his disciples for a special meal (Luke 22:11), where he expounds on his upcoming death using the picture of the exodus and Passover as a means of speaking of the new deliverance of the new covenant. He also calls them to serve and promises them a role in the judgment to come (22:7–30). Yet there will be failure as well, for even Peter will deny Jesus. They must understand that Jesus is numbered among the sinners, and they will need to fend for themselves (22:31–38).

So the disciples follow Jesus to the Mount of Olives (Luke 22:37), and there they fail again, for they are sleeping when he has told them to watch (22:45). Peter also fails as predicted, denying Jesus three times (22:54–62). This group is well meaning, but they need what Jesus will provide, the Spirit of God.

In Luke 24, we see a series of disappointed disciples who struggle to believe the report of the women about the empty tomb or who are still processing what has taken place in Jerusalem (as the Emmaus disciples show). Only appearances by Jesus reverse their sense of despair; he reminds them of what he and the Scriptures have taught. Jesus then gives them a commission to go into the world with the message of repentance after they have been clothed with the Spirit of power from on high. Jesus has taught them well about what to expect. Now they need the enablement.

In Acts, we see a Spirit-enabled and bold community (see speeches of Acts 2–4). We also see them obedient as they wait for the Spirit, gathered together in prayer and reflection on Scripture in Acts 1. As disciples are again explicitly mentioned, we see them engaged faithfully in various tasks as disciples; they have learned what Jesus has taught them.

So Luke portrays disciples growing in number as they engage in mission (Acts 6:1, 7). They work together to resolve problems in the church, such as the solution to the issue involving the Hellenistic widows (6:2–3). We see them under threat as Jesus said they would be but also faithful in taking the word out as they are scattered by persecution (8:1). A number of disciples protect Saul when his embrace of the Lord brings him under threat (9:25). They give of their resources and send relief to a church in need because of a famine (11:30). Luke presents the leaders urging that the law not be handled in a way that puts disciples under a yoke that the nation has never been able to bear (15:10). Finally, we see disciples as elders instructed to take care that false teaching and perversions of the truth not lead them astray (20:30).

Here are followers of Jesus who live life with a character of strength and dependence as well as a commitment to respond to the truth of the teaching of Jesus and his apostles. This combination of faithfulness and a willingness to be instructed is what makes the disciples so dynamic in Acts. All that Jesus taught the original disciples has been passed on faithfully to others. The result is that the church grows as it continues to be faithful in discipleship.

15.3 THE ETHICS OF THE NEW COMMUNITY

15.3.1 Total Commitment

The ethics of the church community find expression in discipleship. At salvation, a believer becomes a disciple, but discipleship is a walk that lasts the rest of one's life. Since each Christian must still deal with the presence of sin, his or her walk has successes and failures. As we have just seen, for Jesus, the life of a disciple requires total commitment (Luke 9:23: lose one's life to gain it; 14:25–33: count the cost). This is something the disciples struggle to learn, but Jesus makes it clear that an absolute commitment is a requirement for being successful at discipleship.

Nevertheless, Jesus deals graciously with his followers' lapses. Intention and core orientation are the point, not perfection (Luke 18:24–30). On numerous occasions, the disciples fail to understand what Jesus is doing, and he rebukes them; but he calls them to learn and respond more appropriately the next time (8:24–25; 9:46–50, 51–55). The disciples are also willing to learn. They are committed to Christ, for which he commends them (18:28–30).

15.3.2 Love for God and for One's Neighbor

Jesus' basic commandment to his followers is for them to love God and others. This ethic has always been a part of God's plan and revelation, since it is called the essence of the law (Luke 10:25–28). In one significant passage, Jesus juxtaposes a discussion of love with the issue of faith, showing how closely these two ideas are tied together (Luke 7:37–50; cf. 1 Cor 2:9; 9:21; an idea called "the law of Christ" in Gal 5:2–6:5; Jas 2:5, 8; 1 John 4:18).

Another section of Luke's gospel is particularly clear in setting forth a focus on love for God and for others. In three consecutive passages, Luke details loving one's neighbor (Luke 10:25–37), showing devotion to Christ (10:38–42), and speaking to God (11:1–13). The parable of the good Samaritan is Jesus' response to an attempt by a scribe to limit his own ethical responsibility by asking, "Who is my neighbor?" Jesus tells the parable to make one point: the question is not to determine who one's neighbor is, but rather one is called to be a neighbor to everyone. Loving others has no limitations, something Jesus has elaborated on in 6:27–36, where one must love even one's enemy. This love, because of its unusual quality, is different from the way the world ("a sinner") loves (vv. 32, 33, 34). As Jesus says, a distinguishing mark of sonship is this unusual kind of love (v. 35).

When Martha is preparing a meal for Jesus, she is disturbed that Mary is not helping. She complains to Jesus, but he rebukes her, noting that Mary has made the better choice (Luke 10:38–42). It is better to sit and dwell on his teaching, for that reflects devotion to him, even in the context of worthy activity such as Martha was pursuing.

Sensing that communicating with God is a key to their spiritual walk, Jesus' disciples ask him how to pray (Luke 11:1–13). Jesus' model prayer reflects a respect for and reliance on God for every daily need. Although known as the Lord's Prayer, this is really the Disciples' Prayer. The manner of address is important here, since the prayer is in the plural ("our, us"), not just an individual request for oneself. This is a community prayer in the full sense of that description. It also shows that the only way to be protected from sin is if one asks for the Father's help in avoiding temptation. Following him will take one out of temptation. Jesus also urges them to trust God to give them what is best. Together these three passages (10:25–37; 10:38–42; 11:1–13) emphasize treating others well, being in contact with Christ, and praying often to God the Father.

15.3.3 Prayer

Besides the focus on prayer recounted in Luke 11, other passages have this empha-sis.[26] In Luke 18:1–8, Jesus tells a parable to stress that his disciples should pray for God's justice and not lose heart. Just as the judge has decided to give the persistent widow justice, so God will execute justice when he returns. The passage is often read in a general way, but its focus is on keeping an eye out for God's vindication of the saints at his return. But Jesus wonders whether many, in fact, will be waiting in faith for his return (v. 8).

Luke 18:9–14 contrasts two attitudes in prayer, one of which is commended and the other rejected. The Pharisee prays proudly, almost as if his relationship with God does the deity a favor. The Pharisee's prayer is a distortion of a praise psalm, where one praises God for what the deity has done, not what the petitioner has done (as the Pharisee prays). Jesus condemns such arrogance. By contrast, the tax collector prays humbly, approaching God on the basis of his grace and knowing that one cannot demand anything of God. God honors such humility.

Jesus urges his disciples to pray that they "will not fall into temptation" (Luke 22:40), a phrase that recalls a petition of the Lord's Prayer. They fail to learn the lesson during Jesus' passion (vv. 41–46), but in Acts 4:23–31, the believers are praying, showing that they are ready through the power of God to stand up for the Word and boldly proclaim the message.

Luke also underscores the importance of prayer by showing how significant events are associated with prayer. Jesus' baptism (Luke 3:21) and one of his miracles (5:15–16) are accompanied by prayer. The choice of the Twelve comes after Jesus spends an evening in prayer (6:12). The transfiguration is accompanied with his praying (9:29), as is the return of the seventy-two (10:17–21). Both at Gethsemane and on the cross, Jesus expresses humble dependence on God through intercession (22:39–46; 23:34, 46).

The church learns from Jesus' example of prayer. The descent of the Spirit comes through prayer, even though it was promised (Acts 1:7–14). Decisions are made alongside prayer (1:23–26). Miracles are done in conjunction with prayer (3:1). The vision about the mission to the Gentiles comes to Peter as he prays (10:9–11). Peter's deliverance from prison comes during prayer (12:5). Paul and Barnabas's mission to the Gentiles is bathed in prayer (13:2–3). Prayer is clearly of supreme importance to Luke.

---

26. Steven F. Plymale, *The Prayer Texts of Luke-Acts* (Ameri-can University Studies; New York: Peter Lang, 1991). He notes on p. 105 that "Luke consistently demonstrates the significant role prayer plays in the working out of the divine plan in each of the four stages of salvation history [Israel, Christ, Church, Con-summation]. Through prayer, individuals and the community at large receive direction and support. By means of prayer the power to fulfill responsibilities is given the human participants. Prayer is God's way of guiding and implementing the accomplishment of His will." Later Plymale notes prayer prepares one for service, rejoices at God's saving activity (something to be done habitu-ally at set times and spontaneously), is involved in commission-ing for service, attends key events, involves intercession, seeks to accept and implement God's will, and can be done with confidence (pp. 110–14).

15.3.4 Perseverance in Suffering

Jesus fully expects his disciples to suffer rejection for their association and identification with him.[27] He constantly calls on them to persevere in the face of such rejection. One of the obstacles that may prevent them from bearing fruit is the pressure of the world. But fruit may appear as they receive the Word with patience (Luke 8:13–15). The exhortation for them to take up their cross daily (9:23) has already been noted. This figure points to suffering, and Luke alone has the note of being ready to do this "daily." The question of whether the Son of Man will find faith on earth when he returns has already been noted (18:8). The remark suggests that there is enough of a delay in the return that some will not hold on to their faith. The call to endure to the end is made also in the Olivet Discourse (21:19). The road of Jesus' followers is difficult, and so they should be prepared to experience opposition, as should any believer. More than that, they should continue to trust him through all the adversity.

15.3.5 Watchfulness, Patience, and Boldness

Jesus tells his followers that pressure against them will be intense. This was especially true in the first century, for if a person within a Jewish family decided to follow Jesus, one could be dismissed from his or her family and be excommunicated from the synagogue. Therefore Jesus tells believers to be bold and patient.

He exhorts them not to fear those who kill the body, but rather to fear the one who can cast into hell (Luke 12:1–12). In addition, Jesus promises the aid of the Holy Spirit to help believers give the right kinds of responses when they are brought before government or synagogue leaders. They must be prepared to stand before earthly authorities and confess him. Peter (Acts 3–4), Stephen (Acts 6–7), and Paul (Acts 21–26) do so.

Jesus also tells various parables on stewardship to warn those associated with the church to be faithful in carrying out their responsibilities. Luke 12:35–48 records a parable in which Jesus teaches that people will be accountable to him when he returns. Three levels of punishment will be meted: dismemberment (v. 46); "many blows" (v. 47); and "few blows" (v. 48). Those who are faithful will be rewarded with more responsibility (vv. 43–44).

Luke 12:46 is an important text. The master's reaction to the slave's behavior is swift and strong. Some translations do not properly render the key term διχοτομήσει (*dichotomēsei*). The RSV says that the master will "punish" the slave, but the term is

---

27. Scott Cunningham, *"Through Many Tribulations": The Theology of Persecution in Luke-Acts* (JSNTSup 142; Sheffield: Sheffield Academic Press, 1997). He notes how persecution is in the plan of God, involves rejection of God's agents by those who supposedly are God's people, places believers in continuity with the rejected prophets of Israel, is an integral part of following Jesus, and is an occasion for Christian perseverance (pp. 295–327). See also Brian Rapske, "Opposition to the Plan of God and Persecution," in *Witness to the Gospel*, 235–56, esp. 255–56. He notes three themes tied to persecution: (1) Believers are exhorted to stand because trouble does not stop the gospel witness. (2) Special fillings of the Spirit embolden the witness in the face of opposition. (3) God directly intervenes on the believers' behalf, affirming their cause.

stronger and more emotive than this: "to dismember, to cut in two."[28] Beating the servants produces judgment in kind, only it is more severe. The steward receives a "mortal blow," a "declaration of judgment or prediction of cursing."[29] God's smiting the servant depicts punishment of the most severe type.[30] Dismemberment figuratively speaks about the severe punishment given to the person who denies Christ by actions that blatantly disobey what he asks for from those who profess him. It pictures being cast out with the unfaithful into hell.[31] Many lashes will be given to those who do not obey but have knowledge. Few lashes will be meted to those who do not obey but who are ignorant. The obedient will receive the reward of additional responsibility.

A similar parable is that of the ten minas (Luke 19:11–27). Here, too, Jesus urges his hearers to watch and be faithful. Those who do something with the opportunity they have from the Lord will receive blessing. Those who do not trust God and fail to see him as gracious will end up with no blessing (v. 26). When the Lord returns, he will require accountability. One should be bold, patient, and obedient.

Steadfastness in praying for the Lord's return is also stressed in the parable of the persistent widow, already noted (Luke 18:1–8). Being able to read the weather but not the signs that Jesus performed points up the need for all to be watchful spiritually (12:54–56). These words rebuke the majority of people's refusal to see Jesus' authority in his works. Finally, Jesus warns the disciples to read the times that point to the approach of the end much as one "reads" the leaves of a fig tree (21:28–36). All these passages stress the importance of living in light of the end. One could place such texts in a discussion of the believer's response to eschatological hope. But for Luke the believer is called to live his or her life in light of the approach of the end, so placing this subject here in the context of discipleship is also important.

15.3.6 Faith and Dependence

Individuals must approach God humbly, recognizing that because of their sin they are "sick" and in need spiritually (Luke 5:31–32). Having come to the Father for help, the believer must not be anxious but rest in the care of the gracious Father (Luke 12:22–34). Here Jesus states that God's children are much more important to the Father than the other parts of creation. In fact, since the Father knows his children have need of things, they need not be anxious. Faith helps remove anxiety.

Another picture of faith is the example of the prodigal son who returns to his father, asking nothing but to rest in his mercy (Luke 15:17–21). The response of the father as he runs to meet his son is as important as the turning of the son to him. Here the humility of genuine repentance and return are met with total acceptance.

---

28. Marshall, *Gospel of Luke*, 543; Stählin, *TDNT*, 3:852–53; Plummer, *St Luke*, 332–33; Schlier, *TDNT*, 2:225–26.

29. Stählin, *TDNT*, 8:267–68.

30. Bock, *Luke 9:51–24:53*, 1182.

31. In the parallel, Jesus said that these individuals will be cast out among the "hypocrites," where there will be "weeping and gnashing of teeth" (Matt 24:51), a Matthean figure depicting the reaction of being rejected by God (Matt 8:12; 13:42, 50; 25:30).

One can trust the heavenly Father, who runs to the penitent to meet the one who turns to him.

A prime example of humility is Jesus' prayer at Gethsemane (Luke 22:39–46). Jesus desires for events to be different from the death he is facing, but in the end Jesus asks for the Father's will, not his own. He trusts in God's sovereign care. Equally exemplary is Paul's willingness to die (Acts 21:13–14). Those who know they are in God's hands can face any opposition.

15.3.7 Joy and Praise

Luke frequently mentions praise as the appropriate response to God's work. John the Baptist's birth is a cause for praise, as is the birth of Jesus (Luke 1:14; 2:10). Joy is an initial response of some people to God's word (8:13). The seventy-two return from their mission with joy (10:17). Heaven rejoices when sinners repent (15:7, 10). The disciples are filled with joy when they see the resurrected Jesus (24:41) and witness his ascension (24:52). Philip's ministry in Samaria is a cause for joy (Acts 8:8). Peter's release from prison brings joy to the servant girl Rhoda (12:14). Paul's converts rejoice (15:3). God's works bring joy; believers are to enjoy what God is doing in drawing people to himself.

15.3.8 Testimony and Witness

This theme has already been examined in the previous chapter. It is at the center of the church's mission; all believers are called to share in witnessing about Jesus' work. Basic passages here are Luke 24:44–49; Acts 1:8; and 13:47.

15.3.9 Wealth and Possessions

Luke has written more on the topic of wealth than any other NT writer. The first mention of this topic is Luke 1:50–53, where the hymn of Mary contrasts the powerful and the humble. God will bring blessing on the poor and judgment on the rich. This first reference is given in the context of God's covenant with his people (vv. 50, 55). God's promises come to those who fear him; therefore, the hymn is not saying that God blesses all the poor without regard for their spiritual condition. Only certain poor, the pious poor, can claim these promises. Mary's references to the poor allude to the ʿⁿâwîm, the pious poor described in the Psalter and elsewhere (1 Sam 2:5; Job 5:11; 12:19; Pss 89:10; 103:11, 13, 17; 107:9).[32]

The poor are mentioned again in Luke 4:18, in which Jesus said he came "to proclaim good news to the poor" (εὐαγγελίσασθαι πτωχοῖς, *euangelisasthai ptōchois*). In addition, Jesus' beatitudes focus on the poor and the deprived (Luke 6:20–23); they suggest that the poor may have an inherently clearer understanding of what it means to depend on God for needs.

Luke also writes about wealthy and poor people whose generosity is commend-

---

32. Chapter 17 develops this portrait of the poor.

able. The women who support Jesus' ministry receive brief mention in Luke 8:1–3, a passage unique to Luke's gospel. The wealthy Zacchaeus, standing in contrast to the wealthy young ruler of 18:18–23, is commended when he declares that he has changed the way he handles his tax collecting (19:1–10). A poor widow is said to have given more than anyone else because she gave of her life when giving two copper coins worth little more than a few pennies (21:1–4). In Acts 4:32–37, Luke applauds the sharing that occurred in the church, singling out wealthy Barnabas for special attention.

Three passages focus on money directly. Luke 16:1–13 records the parable of a shrewd manager, who, faced with dismissal, becomes generous and forgives some of the debts of those who owe his master money. Jesus lauds this generosity as wise (v. 8). Then Jesus adds that a person cannot serve both God and money (v. 13). He calls the disciples to be generous with their resources, for generosity makes friends (v. 9). He also notes how the handling of money is an indicator of responsibility and trustworthiness (vv. 10–12).

The failure of money is precisely the point of the parable of the rich fool in Luke 12:13–21. Here a farmer experiences a great harvest. Initially there is no greed in him, only good fortune. Yet when fortune comes, he plans selfishly and foolishly. He naturally wants to preserve his crops, but there is a hint of a problem in his perspective, for throughout these verses the major stylistic feature is the presence of the pronoun μου (*mou*, "my"), not to mention the numerous first-person singular verbs.[33] The fruit of the land and other elements of the parable are repeatedly described with μου: *my* fruit, *my* barn, *my* goods, *my* soul. Such language suggests exclusive self-interest, a focus that is often the natural product of "earned" wealth. When God requires the man's soul, he is rich toward himself but not toward God. In his death he is left with nothing. Such are the dangers of attachment to wealth. They can leave us self-focused and detached from God, thinking we can live well on our own apart from God.

A negative example appears in Luke 16:19–31. Here the rich man who showed no concern for the beggar Lazarus ends up in Hades, where he suffers torment. In contrast the poor man, Lazarus, is at Abraham's side enjoying fellowship and comfort with his ancestors. Because "a great chasm" (16:23) separate the two, it is impossible for them to change places. The passage warns the rich to be generous, for God knows what one does with his or her wealth (16:19–23). In the OT, God declared his desire for people to be generous to the needy (Deut 14:28–29; 15:1–3, 7–12; 22:1–2; 23:19 [23:20 MT]; 24:7–15, 19–21; 25:13–14; Isa 3:14–15; 5:7–8; 10:1–3; 32:6–7; 58:3, 6–7, 10; Jer 5:26–28; 7:5–6; Ezek 18:12–18; 33:15; Amos 2:6–8; 5:11–12; 8:4–6; Mic 2:1–2; 3:1–3; 6:10–11; Zech 7:9–10; Mal 3:5). The picture of eschatological reversal between the poor and the rich, like that found in this parable, is also seen in Luke 1:53 and 6:20–26.

---

33. Plummer, *St Luke*, 324.

Yet another negative example regarding wealth is Ananias and Sapphira, who lie about their donation and incur the swift and total judgment of God. He takes their lives (Acts 5:1–11). Wealth can be a potential obstacle to discipleship, as is pictured in the seed that fell among the thorns (Luke 8:14).

Money, like any other God-given resource, must be used wisely and generously. Having money is a risk, for it can give a false sense of power and security as well as lessen one's dependence on God. Money can create an excessive attachment to the world and greed, both of which Jesus condemns (Luke 9:57–62; 12:13–21). It also is a barometer of whether one wishes to serve self or others. The statements in Luke about money are not unique, for Paul's advice is similar (1 Tim 6:6–10, 17–19). It is far better to trust God than money (Luke 12:22–34).

15.3.10 Hindrances to Discipleship

Besides money and attachment to the world, Luke comments on other hurdles to discipleship. When the cost of discipleship is not counted sufficiently, failure results (Luke 9:23–26, 57–62; 14:25–35). God must be first. Because suffering is a potential reality (12:1–10; 21:12–17), it takes patience and endurance for believers to stand for the Lord (8:15). Much of 9:51–19:44 is dedicated to explaining what the disciples' walk with him should be like. In fact, this section exists to explain how the disciples should live in light of the reality of Jesus' coming departure (setting up the section, 9:22, 44–45; then 9:51, 58; 13:33; 17:11, 25; 18:31–34; 19:41–42). The disciples' piety is to stand in contrast to the false piety displayed by the Pharisees and scribes. Those whose walk pleases God love selflessly and serve constantly, suffering rejection and loving those who reject him. The believer's distinctive walk with the Lord and their love are to stand out in contrast to the self-directed love of the world (6:27–36).

15.3.11 Commitment to the Lost

Another key to discipleship is the believer's role in helping the church to accomplish her mission. Luke 24:46–47 and Acts 1:8 record Jesus' commission to the church, while Luke 3:6 promises that in Jesus, the world will see God's salvation. God's commitment to the lost is noted in his consistent concern for outcasts and sinners, even when others object (Luke 5:27–32; 7:28–35; 15:1–32). When the church was slow to take up her task to reach all nations, God took the initiative by giving a vision to guide her (Acts 10:9–22). He also used persecution to spread the church out to locales beyond Jerusalem, where the word of God grew (chs. 6–8). Members do not cower at the adversity; they ask for boldness to stand in the face of it (4:23–31). Individuals walking with God desire to make him known to those who need him. This is the challenge and call of the disciple: to share him with others.

This ministry is shared by all the people, and all types of people participate in its benefits. Peter, a self-confessed sinner, is a major leader (Luke 5:8). Lepers, paralytics, tax collectors, the blind, lame, deaf, and poor are included (5:12–16,

17 – 26, 27 – 32; 7:22 – 23). A woman of suspect reputation responds to the Lord (7:36 – 50). This is a beautiful account of the sacrifice of response, faith, and love. In the account, this woman says not a word, yet her anointing of Jesus speaks volumes about the gratitude she feels for receiving forgiveness. Anyone can be included in God's blessings. This woman is one of four "silent witnesses" in Luke, whose acts speak more than a thousand words could (the others are Mary, 10:38 – 42; Lazarus, 16:19 – 31; and the widow, 21:1 – 4).

Luke also notes the active role women have in Jesus' ministry.[34] Elizabeth and Mary exchange notes of praise (Luke 1:39 – 45). Anna the prophetess announces to all at the temple about Jesus as Israel's hope (2:36 – 38). Women offer monetary support to Jesus, including Joanna, a woman from inside Herod's palace (8:1 – 3). A poor widow who gives little actually gives everything (21:1 – 4). Women go to Jesus' tomb to anoint his body, and they are the first to hear that he has been raised from the dead (24:1 – 12).

In the book of Acts, other women have important roles in the church's mission. Mary, the mother of Mark, hosts a house church (Acts 12:12). Rhoda announces Peter's release (12:13 – 17). Lydia helps plant a church and hosts it (16:14 – 15). Priscilla, with her husband, aids a community and corrects Apollos, explaining to him "the way of God more adequately" (18:26; cf. 2:18). Philip's daughters are prophetesses (21:9). Nowhere in Luke does a woman have an official role in the church's organizational structure, but they are active and effective in many aspects of the church's work.

15.4 LUKE AND EMPIRE

When one puts all of these ethical exhortations together, one sees a contrast between the way people functioned in the Roman Empire and how Christians are called to function ethically.[35] In this is Luke's challenge to how the world lives. So Luke's concern for the poor is in contrast to the way the empire lifts up the elite. Luke's emphasis on generosity contrasts to the more *quid pro quo* approach of the Roman culture of patronage. The values reflected in these exhortations do not represent a political challenge to the empire, but they do represent a distinct ethical lifestyle about how to live and challenge the common cultural way of life. This difference more subtly undercuts some of the empire's rationale for claims on people's lives.

This is especially seen in the monotheistic base of the Christian's ethical commitment to the one God that challenges both the surrounding polytheism and the veneration of the emperor as Lord and Savior. This difference is a more local and practical form of cultural challenge than the seeking of a political and revolutionary

---

34. This theme receives more detail in ch. 17.

35. Raymond Pickett, "Luke and Empire," in Rhoads, Esterline, and Lee, eds., *Luke and Empire*, 1 – 22. The volume as a whole considers how Luke addresses and subtly challenges the empire from a postcolonial perspective. It overplays the way in which empire is the focus of such exhortations, but many points are made about how ethical exhortations distinct from the surrounding culture are valid.

change of government. It means that Christians are seen as cultural outsiders who will not participate in the social events on the Roman cultural calendar. These beliefs, along with hope in resurrection, lead various Romans to call the Christian faith a superstition (Acts 25:19: Festus; see also Tacitus, *Annals* 15.44.4; Suetonius, *Nero* 16.2).[36] Those on the outside sense that Christianity is something different.

15.5 CONCLUSION

Discipleship is both demanding and rewarding. According to Luke, it is people-focused, showing love for God and then treating others with love that parallels the love of the Father. In Acts, one sees little of the church serving itself and much of the church reaching out to those who need the Lord. For Luke, the people in the highly effective early church look outward. They are not cloistered; they penetrate the world and share the gospel, even though it involves great risk. The church does not withdraw from those outside her; rather, the church engages the world. Trusting God, believers are not afraid of what that path means for them. Persecution may come, but boldness is what is desired.

Such is the picture of the effective, exemplary community of Acts, which takes the message of God's plan and promise to a dark and dying world (Luke 1:79). The picture of the church in Acts is not so concerned with structures, strategies, and offices as with attitudes, allegiances, growth, character, and outreach. What Jesus preached about disciples in the gospel, the church of Acts becomes, showing herself to be full of effective disciples.

---

36. On superstition and Christianity in the Roman view, see Judge, *First Christians in the Roman World*, 434–37.

Chapter 16

HOW RESPONSE TO JESUS DIVIDES: THE OPPONENTS, THE CROWDS, AND ROME AS OBSERVER OF EVENTS IN LUKE-ACTS

BIBLIOGRAPHY

Carroll, John T. "Luke's Portrait of the Pharisees." *CBQ* 50 (1988): 604–21. **Cook, Donald E.** "A Gospel Portrait of the Pharisees." *RevExp* 84/2 (Spring 1987): 221–33. **Cunningham, Scott.** *"Through Many Tribulations": The Theology of Persecution in Luke-Acts.* JSNTSup. Sheffield: Sheffield Academic Press, 1997. **Gowler, David.** *Host, Guest, Enemy, and Friend: Portraits of the Pharisees in Luke and Acts.* New York: Peter Lang, 1991. **Rhoads, David, David Esterline, and Jae Won Lee,** eds. *Luke-Acts and Empire: Essays in Honor of Robert L. Brawley.* Princeton Theological Monographs. Eugene, OR: Pickwick, 2011. **Tyson, Joseph.** *Images of Judaism in Luke-Acts.* Columbia: University of South Carolina Press, 1992. **Walton, Steve.** "Trying Paul or Trying Rome? Judges and Accused in the Roman Trials of Paul in Acts." Pp. 122–41 in *Luke-Acts and Empire: Essays in Honor of Robert L. Brawley.* Ed. David Rhoads, David Esterline, and Jae Won Lee. Princeton Theological Monographs. Eugene, OR: Pickwick, 2011. **Weatherly, J. A.** *Jewish Responsibility for the Death of Jesus in Luke-Acts.* London: Sheffield Academic Press, 1994.

Besides the disciples and Rome, there are two other major groups that pay attention to Jesus: the Jewish leadership and the crowds. We can sense the reaction Jesus generated by seeing how Luke portrays them. So we will examine them together and the interaction they create with Jesus. For the most part, the bulk of Jesus' interaction with the Jewish leadership involves Pharisees and teachers of the law until we get to Jerusalem, when the chief priests take a major role, in part because Jesus' entry into Jerusalem forces their hands to act.[1] They are mostly Saduccees. The crowd swings in its reaction, especially in Acts, where it is often incited to react by the initiative of Jews who oppose the new movement.

---

1. A monograph dedicated to this topic is J. A. Weatherly, *Jewish Responsibility for the Death of Jesus in Luke-Acts* (London: Sheffield Academic Press, 1994).

16.1 OFFICIAL JEWISH REACTION TO JESUS

16.1.1 Jewish Groups in Luke and Acts

The "Sadducees" appear only in Luke 20:27 in the gospel, where they ask a question about resurrection, a doctrine they do not accept (cf. Josephus, *Ant.* 18.1.4 [16]). In Acts, they are only referred to in Acts 23 (also a setting where resurrection is the issue) and in the arrest of Peter in 4:1; 5:17. Their predominance in Jerusalem fits where their presence was most dominant. Herodians are not mentioned, unlike in Mark 12:13, where they are among those who ask about paying taxes to Caesar.

Interestingly, the term "priest" is fairly neutral in this gospel. It appears five times. Once it describes Zechariah (Luke 1:5). Twice Jesus says to someone to show themselves to the priest (5:14; 17:14). Once it refers to the consecrated bread David took that was for the priests (6:4). The only negative reference is to the priest in the parable of the good Samaritan, where he does not offer help (10:31). In Acts, this term appears three times. Priests help with the arrest of Peter (Acts 4:1–3); many of them believe the gospel (6:7); and one reference is to a pagan priest of Zeus (14:13).

The "chief priests and teachers of the law" or "elders" are combined in a number of texts in both volumes as those who oppose or lead the challenge to the church. In Luke 9:22, Jesus predicts their opposition. When Jesus gets to Jerusalem, they lead the opposition against him (19:47; 20:1–2, 19; 22:2, 4, 52, 66; 23:4, 10, 13). In 22:52, for example, they arrest Jesus with the temple guards. Then in Acts they are a frequent combination of opposition (Acts 4:5, 23; 6:12; 23:14; 24:1; 25:15).

If we ask what got Jesus into trouble, a look at his ministry and the observations of the "Pharisees" tell us where things start to garner a reaction; they are mentioned twenty-seven times in the gospel. This compares to fourteen mentions of the "teachers of the law" (γραμματεύς, *grammateus*), six mentions of "experts in the law" (νομικός, *nomikos*), one mention of "teacher of the law" (νομοδιδάσκαλος, *nomodidaskalos*, Luke 5:17), three mentions of elders, and twelve mentions of the high priests as a group (with all but one of those in Luke 19–24). So during Jesus' ministry before he gets to Jerusalem, it is the Pharisees and teachers of the law who interact the most with Jesus among representatives of official Judaism.

In fact, the Pharisees and teachers of the law are often paired up in texts (Luke 5:21, 30; 6:7; 11:53; 15:2). These are all controversy passages, where Jesus' actions generate a reaction. For example, Jesus forgives sin, and they react by insisting that he blasphemes (5:21). Jesus' associations with tax collectors and sinners elicit a question from them (5:30). Jesus' prospect of healing on the Sabbath leads them to want to accuse him (6:7). After Jesus' rebuke of both the Pharisees and teachers of the law at a meal in 11:37–52, they bitterly oppose him (11:53). This confrontation was triggered when the leaders were surprised that Jesus did not wash his hands as ritually required in the tradition. The Pharisees and teachers of the law question his associations again in 15:2. These texts show the kinds of public acts Jesus did that brought opposition from these Jewish leaders.

The rest of the references to teachers of the law in the gospel sees them as among those who will reject the Son of Man (Luke 9:22) or have them paired with the chief priests in their opposition (20:1–2,19; 22:2, 66; 23:10). The role they play in Luke is very much as supporters and accompanists to the actions of other leaders. In Luke 11, when Jesus rebukes the Pharisees, a teacher of the law joins in and notes that this insults them as well; this leads Jesus to rebuke them at the same time. Only when Jesus defends the resurrection do the teachers of the law compliment Jesus (20:39). So Jesus warns about the hypocrisy of Pharisees and teachers of the law at various points (12:1; 20:46–47) and rebukes them at a meal (11:37–52).

It is the Pharisees who interact with Jesus the most, sometimes alone, sometimes with the teachers of the law.[2] Already noted are the controversies over Jesus' claim to forgive sin, his associations with tax collectors and sinners, and his Sabbath healings. They also inquire about Jesus' lack of fasting and public prayer (Luke 5:33, where the use of "they" looks back to the previous scene where Pharisees and teachers of the law ask the question). A Pharisee at a meal watches Jesus interact with a sinful woman and decides he surely is not a prophet (7:36, 39). Six references appear in the infamous meal where Jesus rebukes the Pharisees for a variety of sins, including not being clean inside, neglecting the justice and love of God, and drawing attention to themselves (11:37, 38, 39, 42, 43, 53). Another meal with a Pharisee leads to major teaching on humility and associating with those who cannot pay you back (14:1–24). The Pharisees ridicule Jesus when he urges people to be generous with money (16:14). They ask when the kingdom is coming (17:20), a question that leads Jesus to note the kingdom does not need to be hunted down.

Such exchanges lead Jesus to warn people about the Pharisees (Luke 12:1; 20:45–47); in addition, Jesus tells a parable in which a Pharisee takes an arrogant posture before God by praising his own life and work (18:9–14). When Jesus enters Jerusalem being praised as king, the Pharisees want him to rebuke his disciples (19:39); he refuses. This is the final reference to Pharisees in the gospel.

These texts show the Pharisees as the key foil for Jesus until he gets to Jerusalem. Then the chief priests and teachers of the law take over that role with much more hostility. The confrontations show that a variety of actions and claims upset the Pharisees. Their opposition is part of the picture of a divided Israel for Luke.

In Acts, the Pharisees are mentioned only nine times. Six of those appear in Acts 23, when Paul notes to the Pharisees present that he is a Pharisee, something to which they can testify (23:6 [3x], 7, 8, 9). Gamaliel is identified as a Pharisee and speaks with some openness to the movement in allowing that it might be of God (5:35). Some Pharisees among the believers want to argue that Gentiles should be circumcised (15:5). And Paul again mentions in 26:5 how he lived as a Pharisee. In

---

2. John T. Carroll, "Luke's Portrait of the Pharisees," *CBQ* 50 (1988): 604–21; Donald E. Cook, "A Gospel Portrait of the Pharisees," *RevExp* 84/2 (Spring 1987): 221–33. Cook speaks of a moderating read of the Pharisees by Luke since many scenes where Mark or Matthew identifies Pharisees as the opponent Luke omits the reference (Luke 3:7–9; 10:25; 11:14–23; 11:29–32; 16:18; 20:9–19; 20:20–26; 20:41–44). He argues that Luke notes the hostility between the groups without being bitter.

effect, in Acts the Pharisees are open to resurrection and the Christian movement. This is an open portrait in contrast to the conflict that Luke described in the gospel. However, this is not surprising in that the possibility of someone turning back to God is always there for Luke.[3]

16.1.2 Conclusion on Jewish Groups

The portrait of Jewish groups shows that Jesus engendered controversy because of the authority he claimed in a variety of areas. He claimed authority over sin and Sabbath—two major issues of theology. He was open to sinners and tax collectors. His opponents saw this as being insensitive about sin. Finally, there was the controversy that some of his public practices caused regarding issues associated with law and tradition. Jesus' new way brought reaction from those who liked the old wine (Luke 5:33–39).

16.2 CROWDS AND THE MULTITUDES

16.2.1 Crowds and Multitudes in the Gospel of Luke

The crowds form a different kind of foil in Luke. The crowds are Luke's primary way to show how the public responds to Jesus. Although the term "multitudes" (πλῆθος, *plēthos*) is sometimes used for the public, "crowds" (ὄχλος, *ochlos*) is much more frequent.

Plēthos occurs eight times in Luke's gospel, two of which appear in the infancy section. They refer to the group gathered as Zechariah is in the temple and to the multitude of angels appearing to the shepherds (Luke 1:10; 2:13). Another occurrence refers to a multitude of fish the disciples caught (5:6). None of these is theologically significant, other than the gathering of angels in 2:13, where the angelic "host" (*plēthos*) testifies to Jesus' birth as a heavenly witness.

A multitude does gather to hear Jesus preach on loving one's enemy at the Sermon on the Plain (Luke 6:17). A multitude of the Gerasenes asks Jesus to leave their region after he heals the demoniac (8:37). And a multitude of disciples enters Jerusalem with Jesus in 19:37. A multitude of Jewish leaders take Jesus to Pilate (23:1). And a multitude of people follow Jesus, especially of women, as he bears the cross (23:27). This survey of uses shows it is not a term used for Jesus' interaction with the public.

References to *ochlos* are far more important. The term appears forty-one times in the gospel and twenty-two times in Acts.[4] The rest of this section traces the use of this term in both Luke and Acts.

---

3. Thus I read disputes about whether Luke's portrait of the Pharisees is distinct and in conflict in Luke and Acts as misguided, failing to see Luke as always open to the possibility one may respond to the gospel. For the view that Luke is inconsistent here, see David Gowler, *Host, Guest, Enemy and Friend: Portraits of the Pharisees in Luke and Acts* (New York: Peter Lang, 1991).

4. *Plēthos* appears sixteen times in Acts, often to speak of a multitude who believed (Acts 4:32; 5:14; 14:1; 17:4), but sometimes the author notes a division of opinion among the multitude (14:4; 23:7). Other times the multitude is a gathered group (2:6: 5:16; 6:2, 5; 15:12, 30; 19:9; 25:24). Once it is an unruly mob (21:36). So the term shows some sense of the division the gospel generates among people.

Interaction with the crowd starts with John the Baptist, who challenges the crowd to flee the coming wrath of God (Luke 3:7); this leads them to ask what they should do (3:10–14). This more generic audience differs from Matthew, where John challenges the Pharisees and Sadducees and has no indication of any response that leads into a question about what to do. In other words, 3:10–14 is unique to Luke's gospel. John tells the crowd to produce fruit worthy of repentance and to show it by treating others well, sharing coats with them, giving food to those in need, not collecting more tax than they should, and not wielding power as soldiers while being content with one's wage. This answer is important, because it shows that responding to God changes the way we relate to others. It pictures the reconciliation that John's ministry had as a way of preparing for the Lord (1:15–17). It shows the ethical thrust in Luke's teaching about responding to God with repentance.

Crowds often note Jesus' presence or press upon him in his ministry. These activities form the bulk of the references to crowds. Jesus gains public attention, even if it is short of gaining massive amounts of adherents (Luke 4:42; 5:1, 15, 19; 6:17, 19; 7:11; 8:4, 19, 40, 42, 45; 9:11, 37; 11:29; 12:1; 14:25; 18:36; 19:3; 22:6; 23:48). In places, Jesus warns the people not to be deceived by the numbers and challenges them either to respond (11:29–32) or to be careful of courting popularity through hypocrisy (21:1).

On a few occasions, teaching is generated when someone speaks from the crowd and evokes a response from Jesus. Jesus stops and singles out from the crowd the woman who has touched him for healing (Luke 8:45). A man asks Jesus to heal his son when the disciples could not (9:37–40). A women cries out that Jesus' mother should be blessed, which leads him to say those who do God's word are blessed (11:27–28). Jesus refuses to help a brother who asks him to intervene about dividing up the family inheritance (12:13). Jesus uses the occasion to tell the parable of the rich fool, issuing a warning about being too attached to possessions. A synagogue leader tells the crowd there are six days to be healed (13:14); Jesus responds by saying there is no better day to heal than on the Sabbath. A blind man asks the crowd what is taking place, and when he hears Jesus is present, he calls out to the Son of David for healing (18:36–38).

This last text is christologically important and underscores how Luke shows that those on the fringe are often more sensitive to Jesus' work and importance. The blind man cries out to the "Son of David" (υἱὲ Δαυίδ, *huie Dauid*), a messianic confession of great significance (4Q174 [= 4QFlor] 1.11; 4QPBless 1.3–4; 2 Esd. [= *4 Ezra*] 12:32; *Pss. Sol.* 17.21).[5] This is the only Lucan use of this confession, though Jesus' association with David is common in this gospel (Luke 1:27; 2:4; 3:31; 20:41) and in the NT (Matt 9:27; 12:23; 15:22; 21:9, 15; Mark 12:35; John 7:42; Acts 2:29–32; Rom 1:3; 2 Tim 2:8). Many argue that the idea of the Son of David healing is evidence that this story and the use of this title are late, since, it is argued,

---

5. BAGD, 171.

the Son of David was not seen as a messianic healer.[6] However, such a tradition is found in ancient material (Wis 7:17–21; Pseudo-Philo, *Biblical Antiquities* 60.1 [David as exorcist]; slightly later, Josephus, *Ant.* 8.2.5 [42–49] [the Jewish exorcist Eleazar and a tradition about Solomon as a healer and writer of incantations because of his wisdom]).[7]

There is no doubt that the messianic period was seen as one of restoration and healing. In fact, Jesus' own use of Isa 61:1 in Luke 4:17–18 indicates this perspective, as does his reply to John the Baptist in 7:22. The blind man probably had heard reports of Jesus' miraculous work and now realizes that he might be the Messiah because of the public stir Jesus has created. The man's confession shows great faith, for which Jesus will commend him (18:42). For the blind man, Jesus is the promised helper. He sees clearly what others cannot. He is an exemplary member of the crowd.

The blind man's plea for mercy is a request for compassion and healing. Such cries were common (Matt 9:27; 15:22; 17:15; Mark 5:19; Luke 16:24; 17:13). The need for mercy is often associated with sin, and sometimes mercy is needed because the plight is particularly desperate. The Lucan examples of the cry of the lepers (Luke 17:13) and of the rich man's plea from Hades (16:24) show the emotional impact of this cry. The cry is reminiscent of David's plea in his penitential lament of Ps 51:1 [50:3 LXX] (cf. Pss 6:2 [6:3 LXX]; 9:13 [9:14 LXX]; 41:4, 10 [40:5, 11 LXX]; 123:3 [122:3 LXX]). The blind man sees that only Jesus can meet his need.[8]

Some Pharisees from the crowd request Jesus to rebuke the crowd praising him as he enters Jerusalem (Luke 19:39). He replies that the stones will cry out if he does so and so he refuses. This is one of a few places where creation is personified and shows its understanding of Jesus (darkness and the tearing of the temple veil are other examples, although in these latter two examples there is testimony about what God is showing through these events).

On other occasions Jesus teaches the crowds (Luke 5:3; 9:11) or they seek him for healing (5:15; 6:19; 9:11). In one important scene, Jesus tells the crowd that nowhere in Israel has he seen such faith as in the centurion whose son he heals (7:9). He teaches the crowd about John's being a prophet of God (7:24–27). He teaches them the parable of the sower about the different responses to the word of the kingdom (8:4). Jesus calls people to obey that word when his family shows up and has trouble reaching him because of the crowd (8:19). He teaches the disciples about provision in the feeding of the crowd (9:12–16).

Despite all of this teaching, the crowd as a group thinks of him only as a prophet (Luke 9:18), a category that comes up short in contrast to Peter's recognition that Jesus is the Christ. He tells the crowd after healing a mute man that his power is not from Beelzebul (as his opponents claim) but reflects the finger of God acting to show that the kingdom of God has come (11:14–20). The allusion to the finger of God

6. Ferdinand Hahn, *The Titles of Jesus in Christology: Their History in Early Christianity* (trans. Harold Knight and George Ogg; London: Lutterworth, 1969), 253–55.

7. Str-B, 4:533–34; Duling, "Solomon, Exorcism, and the Son of David," 235–52.

8. Bock, *Luke 9:51–24:53*, 1507–8.

is to the power of God to deliver in the exodus (Exod 8:19). He warns the crowds to read the spiritual signs of the times, similar to how they can read the weather (Luke 12:54 – 55). In Palestine, a cloud from the west meant moisture riding in from the Mediterranean Sea, i.e., rain. Then Jesus describes a second weather phenomenon: southwesterly breezes (νότος, *notos*) that come from the desert and bring heat. This heat is so scorching that it wilts plants. Everyone in Judea or Galilee would know the weather that these conditions produce. In a similar way, the crowd should be able to read what God is doing through Jesus and the kind of special time to which it points.

As Jesus travels to Jerusalem to face rejection, he challenges the crowd to have faith and repent, warning people both individually and as a nation (Luke 13:1 – 9), telling parables about the kingdom's growth (13:18 – 19), and warning all about the cost of discipleship (14:25 – 35). He reinforces his teaching on associations with his parables of Luke 15 of the lost regained. He shows his point about associations in calling out to Zacchaeus, who cannot reach him because of the crowds (19:1 – 10, esp. vv. 2 – 3).

The crowds are an issue for Judas, who seeks to betray Jesus when a crowd is not present; ironically, however, he brings a crowd to arrest him (Luke 22:6, 47). Pilate tells the chief priests and crowds that he finds no basis for their charges against Jesus (23:4). And crowds are but one audience at the cross (23:48). At the end, many in the crowd beat their breasts at Jesus' death. Luke 23 and its portrayal of Jesus' death are significant in that this story is told with many people reacting in a variety of ways. Women weep (23:27); others mock (23:35, 37, 39); some believe (23:40 – 43: thief on the cross). Creation goes dark (23:44). The temple reacts (23:45). A centurion affirms Jesus (23:49). This scene summarizes well what has happened with the crowds taught by Jesus. They are divided in their opinion, with some for him, others against him, and some sitting on the sidelines.

16.2.2 Crowds in the Book of Acts

Generally in Acts, the crowd is more easily swayed. A few times a crowd simply gathers to observe an event. So it is for the 120 disciples who await the coming of the Spirit in Jerusalem (Acts 1:15). Crowds hear Philip and respond to his miracles (8:60). "Great numbers" (*ochlos hikanos*, "a great crowd") are objects of Paul's teaching in 11:26.

In a few cases as well it is a crowd of people who respond to the gospel (Acts 6:7 of priests; 11:24 of people responding to Barnabas). In one case, the crowd in Lystra misunderstands Barnabas and Paul and regards the apostles as gods (14:11, 13, 14, 18). This is the one chapter where Paul and Barnabas are called apostles. It may be to highlight that they are God's agents, not gods. Here the pagan crowd is portrayed as ignorant of the way of God and the uniqueness of Israel's deity, especially being tied to his role as the Creator of all.

However, the bulk of the references are to a crowd being incited or worked up to oppose the new movement. Here we see various instigators. Jews are responsible in Pisidian Antioch (Acts 13:45). After the initial success at Lystra, Jews from Antioch and Iconium stir up the crowd, resulting in Paul's being stoned (14:19). In Philippi the same result takes place as magistrates beat Paul and Silas (16:22). Here it is not Jews but the owners of the possessed slave girl who incite others to react. She had followed Paul and Silas, causing Paul to rebuke the spirit out of her. This made her owners angry at the prospect of lost business. A crowd is stirred up in Thessalonica, when people complain that Paul, Silas, and those following him, like Jason, are acting against Caesar's decrees and call Jesus a king (17:8). This claim disturbs the crowd. In Berea, Jews from Thessalonica arrive and incite the crowd (17:13).

In Ephesus it is those who make idols for the lucrative religious trade surrounding Artemis who react and incite the crowd against Paul (Acts 19:24–26, 33, 35). Only a word from a civic official calms them. A few chapters later, Paul ends up arrested after Jews from Asia see him in the temple and wrongly accuse him of bringing a Gentile into the sacred area (21:27). The charge is that Paul teaches against the people, the law, and this place (i.e., the sanctuary; 21:28). So the crowd reacts to something that Luke readers know is not true. They yell as a mob for Paul to be taken away (21:34–36).

The final reference to the crowd has Paul explain to Felix what happened in Jerusalem. He had not stirred up the crowd and had gone to the temple without causing a disturbance (Acts 24:12, 18). So in Acts the crowd is subject to the direction of others who oppose the movement. Those of the believing community do not cause violence, but are victims of it.

Thus in Acts, for the most part the crowd is portrayed as reactionary to the nervousness that the new movement has generated. This may well reflect the popular perception of the movement as Luke writes, explaining why Theophilus needs assurance. Those who have the ear of the masses have stirred them up against the believers.

16.3 THE ROLE OF ROME AS OBSERVER OF EVENTS IN ACTS

How Rome responds to all of this tension is an important backdrop for Luke. On the one hand, Rome's consistent core reaction to the presentation of Jesus or Paul for trial is that this has little to do with Roman politics and concerns. So Pilate wishes to free Jesus initially in Luke 23 and declares him innocent with respect to any capital crimes against Rome. Similarly, the Roman governmental leaders are perplexed as to what to do with Paul, as the letter of Claudius Lysias in Acts 23:26–30 typifies. In the Roman judgment in Acts, the dispute is about "questions about their law" (23:29), or as governor Festus later puts it, "some points of dispute with [Paul] about their own religion and about a dead man named Jesus" (25:19), or as Gallio said it earlier, the controversy is "about words and names and your own law" (18:15b). So those who investigate these issues argue that the new faith does nothing that demands a response from Rome. At one point, when Paul is transferred in Acts 23, the ruler Felix makes a point to be sure Paul is adequately protected. There is no political threat present, but neither is there justice from Rome, a major Lucan point.

The judgment that Christians are not out to be a political threat to Rome does not suffice for Luke's view of Rome, although it is argued that this Lucan view of Rome shows his favorable view of Rome. But things are not so simple. Rather than releasing those judged to be innocent, the Romans lead Jesus to death and put Paul in prison. This suggests an injustice in the Roman system, something Acts 4:23–31 makes explicit in seeing Pilate as part of the conspiracy against Jesus and Christians.[9] One ruler, Felix, even expects a bribe for freedom (24:26). The unwillingness to engage the gospel seriously in these exchanges between Paul and the leaders also reflects poorly on Rome from within the narrative. In this take on Rome there is the suggestion of a serious injustice against the new faith that God will deal with one day.

In sum, the portrait of Rome and her rulers in Luke-Acts is mixed. After Jesus, her actions protect the Christians from the hostile desires of the Jewish leadership, but do so with an injustice that will not recognize their rights or release them. For Luke, Rome does not have completely clean hands, but neither need she fear anything politically. The most danger the faith presents is in changing the way people live, which will be different from the way the culture functions—a topic covered in the previous chapter. Nothing the believers in the new movement do is a threat to Rome's political role.

One other role for Rome fits the Lucan emphasis on God's central place in his volumes. They are often the unseen agent of providence in their acts. The Romans become a source of protection for the disciples in the leaders' failure to release Paul. They refuse to get trapped into an ambush in moving him from one prison to another. When Paul is moved, it is done in secret as a way to protect him.

The one place where there is tension in the portrait of Rome and the belief of the community is in the believers' challenge to the popular worship of many gods. This is because in the larger society, so much of what was done to bring solidarity in Roman society included sharing in the worship activities and holidays given over to the gods or emperors who were so honored. A look at a religious calendar such as the *Fasti* shows that up to 150 days in a year were given over to a variety of celebrations, many dealing with the gods. Luke does not address this directly, but he implies the idea in speeches where God is said not to be like a human or in the judgment Herod experiences in Acts 12 when he allows himself to be equated to a god.

---

9. Steve Walton, "Trying Paul or Trying Rome? Judges and Accused in the Roman Trials of Paul in Acts," in *Luke and Empire*, 122–41.

16.4 CONCLUSION

Jesus' coming generated a reaction. From official Judaism, Jesus' handling of issues like Sabbath, forgiveness, associations, and practices of the law caused a reaction, initially of scribes and Pharisees, but eventually of the chief priests and Saduccees, who ran the religious business in Jerusalem. No doubt Jesus' entry into the city and his cleansing of the temple, as well as his telling the parable of the wicked tenants, sealed his fate with them. His challenge of them in their most sacred site meant the leaders had to respond in faith or reaction.

The crowds are drawn to Jesus, but they also manifest a variety of positions regarding him as their reactions at his death poignantly show. In Acts, the opposition continues and even stirs up the crowds against Jesus; opponents are both Jews and Gentiles. In this there is a divided people as Simeon had predicted of Israel (Luke 2:34–35)—only now in the world as a whole. The coming of the Spirit in fire has created a separation (3:15–17). Jews react to the challenges made to their customs and temple, while Gentiles react either because their commerce associated with idols is challenged or they think loyalty to Caesar is at stake. Luke tries to show this Gentile view is wrong by noting no effort at violence or revolution on the part of the new movement. More complex is the charge associated with the law, our subject after we examine the special place of women, the poor, and the social portrait of society in Luke-Acts.

Chapter 17

WOMEN, THE POOR, AND THE SOCIAL DIMENSIONS IN LUKE-ACTS

BIBLIOGRAPHY

Arlandson, James M. *Women, Class, and Society in Early Christianity: Models from Luke-Acts.* Grand Rapids: Baker, 1996. **Bauckham, Richard.** *Gospel Women: Studies of Named Women in the Bible.* Grand Rapids: Eerdmans, 2002. **Bode, Edward L.** *First Easter Morning: The Gospel Accounts of the Women's Visit to the Tomb of Jesus.* Chicago: Loyola University Press, 1970. **Boff, Leonardo.** *Jesus Christ Liberator: A Critical Christology for Our Time.* Maryknoll, NY: Orbis, 1978. **Cassidy, Richard J.** *Jesus, Politics, and Society: A Study of Luke's Gospel.* Maryknoll, NY: Orbis, 1978. Idem. *Society and Politics in the Acts of the Apostles.* Maryknoll, NY: Orbis, 1987. **Clark, Stephen.** *Man and Woman in Christ: An Examination of the Roles of Men and Women in Light of Scripture and the Social Sciences.* East Lansing, MI: Tabor, 1980. **Corley, Kathleen.** *Private Women, Public Meals: Social Conflict in the Synoptic Tradition.* Peabody, MA: Hendrickson, 1993. **Foh, Susan T.** *Women and the Word of God: A Response to Biblical Feminism.* Phillipsburg, NJ: Presbyterian & Reformed, 1978. **France, R. T.** *Women in the Church's Minstry: A Test Case for Biblical Interpretation.* Grand Rapids: Eerdmans, 1997. **Gutiérrez, Gustavo,** *A Theology of Liberation.* Maryknoll, NY: Orbis, 1973. **Horsley, Richard A.** *Jesus and the Powers: Conflict, Covenat and the Hope of the Poor.* Minneapolis: Fortress, 2011. **Kim, Seyoon.** *Christ and Caesar: The Gospel and the Roman Empire in the Writings of Paul and Luke.* Grand Rapids: Eerdmans, 2008. **Kramer, Ross S.** *Her Share of Blessings: Women's Religions among Pagans, Jews, and Christians in the Greco-Roman World.* Oxford: Oxford University Press, 1992. **Liefeld, Walter, and Ruth A. Tucker.** *Daughters of the Church.* Grand Rapids: Zondervan, 1987. **Rhoads, David, David Esterline, and Jae Won Lee**, eds. *Luke-Acts and Empire: Essays in Honor of Robert L. Brawley.* Princeton Theological Monographs. Eugene, OR: Pickwick, 2011. **Schottroff, Luise, and Wolfgang Stegemann.** *Jesus and the Hope of the Poor.* Maryknoll, NY: Orbis, 1986. **Segundo, J. L.** *The Liberation of Theology.* Maryknoll, NY: Orbis, 1976. **Seim, T. K.** *The Double Message: Patterns of Gender in Luke-Acts.* Edinburgh: T&T Clark, 1994. **Witherington, Ben.** *Women in the Ministry of Jesus: A Study of Jesus' Attitudes to Women and Their Roles as Reflected in His Earthly Life.* SNTSMS. Cambridge: Cambridge University Press, 1987. **Yamazaki-Ransom, Kazuhiko.** *Roman Empire in Luke's Narrative.* London: T&T Clark, 2010.

In this chapter, we examine primarily two key categories in Luke-Acts and in contemporary discussion about Luke's theology: women and the poor. These two topics raise issues about the social dimensions of Luke's work. Women and the poor connect to his emphasis on Jesus' care for those on the edge of society. For example, women were not qualified to give testimony in a legal case unless they were the only witness or in a case of being the only witness for their own condition of purity after an arrest.[1] Other texts argue a woman cannot bring evidence at all. It appears she could do so only in exceptional situations. For example, *m. Šeb.* 4.1 reads, "An oath of testimony applies to men but not to women." In addition, *Roš. Haš* 1.8 reads, "Any evidence a woman is not eligible to bring." Later *b. B. Qam.* 88a reads, "A woman … is disqualified from giving evidence." All of this shows how significant it is that women bring the evidence of the empty tomb. This cultural context of the secondary role of women argues against such an event being created by the community, since one would not choose to use nonwitnesses (women) to make the case for a culturally controversial belief (resurrection).

We begin with Luke's presentation of women and then turn to the poor and any social implications they may or may not have. Finally we briefly look at other groupings of a similar type: the lame and the blind.

17.1 WOMEN IN THE GOSPEL OF LUKE

Luke notes several women the other gospels do not mention. Thirteen women appear here and nowhere else. They are often examples of deep piety and run the gamut from humble women (the widow who gives the mite) to those from wealthy backgrounds (Joanna) to those with a past now transformed (the sinful woman who anoints Jesus' feet).

17.1.1 Women in the Infancy Narrative

Women are present from the beginning of Luke. Elizabeth, Mary, and Anna all play key roles in the infancy material.

Elizabeth expresses her joy at bearing a child by declaring that the reproach of barrenness has been lifted from her; she also rejoices when she meets Mary, "the mother of my Lord" (Luke 1:24–25, 41–45). Elizabeth expresses both relief and joy that God has removed this source of public shame (barrenness was commonly viewed this way).[2] Expressing thanks to the Lord for the provision of a child is a common OT theme (Sarah in Gen 21:6; Rachel in Gen 30:23). Everything about Elizabeth's reaction tells us she is pious, as does her introduction in Luke 1:6, where she is said to be "blameless" with respect to the law.

---

1. Josephus, *Ant.* 4.8.15 [219]. says, "From women let no evidence be accepted, because of the levity and temerity of their sex." Women could be witnesses if they were the only ones present at a crime, as when a woman claimed she was not assaulted while taken captive. However, even this exception indicates a secondary status. If her testimony was challenged, she was automatically doubted. See *m. Yebam.* 16.7; *m. Ketub.* 2.5; *m. ʿEd.* 3.6.

2. Str-B, 2:98.

Mary is a person of faith when she accepts the announcement of the virgin birth with all it entails for her socially (Luke 1:38). Her trust, despite what would have been public shame, is not explicitly addressed but is clearly understood to come with her acceptance of her role. Her praise in the *Magnificat* underscores the picture of her as pious. Her self-description as humble in terms of social status sets the tone for God's care for those without power in society (1:48, 52). God sees what society does not.

In her hymn, Mary describes herself as God's "servant" (the repetition of δούλη, *doulē*, connects Luke 1:48 to 1:38). This acknowledges her subordinate position before God. She does not expect or assume that she should be the object of such special attention from God, so she is grateful for the attention. She also describes herself as of "humble state," a term (ταπείνωσιν, *tapeinōsin*) that many see as a more natural reference to barrenness. Seeking support from OT parallels in 1 Sam 1:11; Gen 16:11; and esp. 29:31–32, they argue that the term is more suitable for Elizabeth. But the expression can also naturally refer to one's low social position, as Luke 1:52 makes clear. In fact, the social terminology throughout the hymn argues for a broader reference here and supports an original reference to Mary.[3] As we noted earlier, ταπείνωσις as social-status terminology has OT parallels to describe both Israel and individuals (Gen 29:32; Deut 26:7; 1 Sam 9:16; 2 Sam 16:12; 2 Kgs 14:26; Pss 9:13 [9:14 LXX]; 25:18 [24:18 LXX]; 31:7 [30:8 LXX]). This use also has parallels in Judaism (Jdt 6:19; 2 Esd. [= *4 Ezra*] 9:45).[4] Mary is able to praise God her Savior, because he looked upon her low social state and yet in love let her bear the Messiah. What God did for her is like what he does for others in the same state (Luke 1:52).

Mary recognizes that God has given her a special place by having her bear the Messiah. She explains (see γάρ, *gar*, "for") that generations of all time will bless her. They, too, will perceive her fortune in receiving this special role. She is an example of one graced by God, an example of faith (cf. Gen 30:13).[5] Elizabeth's blessing in Luke 1:45 is the first blessing that Mary receives as an exemplary servant touched by grace (11:28–29 is another). Luke presents Mary as an example of faith in God, a humble servant who is willing to do what he asks.

There are scenes where the role of the woman in Jewish society does reflect secondary status. For example, when Elizabeth names John, using a name without family precedent, the assumption is that she has acted independently and in a manner inappropriate for her culture (Luke 1:57–62). Only confirmation from Zechariah removes the doubt. Later when Peter's mother-in-law is healed, she immediately serves them after her healing (4:38–39). This represents her reentry into society by returning to her former expected role.

Anna is a pious prophetess who witnesses to Jesus as one who hopes for the redemption of Jerusalem (Luke 2:38). The women surrounding Jesus are pious and

---

3. Grundmann, *TDNT*, 8:21. See the longer discussion in ch. 10.   5. Fitzmyer, *Gospel of Luke I–IX*, 367.

4. Nolland, *Luke 1:1–9:20*, 69.

are given place to testify to him. Their witness stands alongside that of the men of the infancy material, like Zechariah and Simeon. This pairing of male and female is something Luke will often do.[6]

17.1.2 Key Women in Jesus' Galilean Ministry

Several key stories in Jesus' Galilean ministry involve women (Luke 4:14–9:50). After the healing of Peter's mother-in-law in 4:38–39, we encounter the need of the widow of Nain. After the death of her only son, she is socially isolated and at risk. Jesus' healing of her son not only pairs with the later healing of Jairus's daughter, but also restores her family and gives her a means of support (7:10–17). The event leads the crowd to proclaim Jesus as a prophet.

Few women are as important to Luke's story as the sinful woman who at a meal anoints Jesus' feet in the home of Simon the Pharisee (Luke 7:36–50). She speaks not a word in the scene, but her actions evoke reaction all around. The Pharisee is sure this shows Jesus is not a prophet. Ironically, while the Pharisee makes this judgment, Jesus prepares to tell a parable that shows he knows about Simon's doubts. Jesus takes her act to be a sign of gratitude in response to grace and forgiveness, as the parable stresses how love emerges from forgiveness. She then is reassured as Jesus declares her sins forgiven. Jesus therefore turns the sinful woman into a spiritual example of a proper response of gratitude to him and God's grace. She is the one who is forgiven much and so loves much. This reversal is significant, for normally the pious Pharisee would be such an example in society. Once again, God sees things differently than society often does. Not status nor title, but action from the heart is what counts for God.

The three women who support Jesus are also important to Luke (Luke 8:1–3). Mary Magdalene will be a witness at the cross and at the empty tomb. Joanna has a high social status as the wife of Herod's steward, and she is also a witness to the empty tomb (24:10). We know nothing more about Susanna than her place in this list. The mix of a woman who was possessed and healed in an exorcism with one of some status shows the reach of Jesus across the entire social stratum. The issue is not social position but responsiveness. As financial supporters of Jesus, they help make his work possible and show the partnership Luke values as an important contribution. A poor widow in 21:1–4 will also show that women can handle what means God gives them to offer support for the worship of God.

Some women have a timid faith but are still beneficiaries of Jesus' ministry. The woman with a flow of blood tries to gain healing without gaining notice (Luke 8:42b–48). When she touches Jesus, he stops and brings her story out. He does not rebuke her but says her faith has made her well. Jesus acts in a way that grows the woman's faith. Once again, a woman testifies to what God has done for her. Finally, Jairus's daughter is brought back from the dead, considered as valuable as any son.

---

6. T. K. Seim, *The Double Message: Patterns of Gender in Luke-Acts* (Edinburgh: T&T Clark, 1994), studies this pattern in detail.

17.1.3 Women in the Journey to Jerusalem Section

There are several examples of women in the journey to Jerusalem section of Luke (9:51–19:44). They often appear in parables and frequently point to a parallel pairing with men.

The contrast between Martha and Mary should be seen as the contrast between a woman performing her normal social duties and a disciple seated at Jesus feet and learning from him (Luke 10:38–42). Martha assumes, in asking for Jesus' help, that he will tell her sister to perform her social duty. The Greek here is important. Martha asks for Jesus' help in v. 40 in a way that assumes he will intervene, using the particle οὐ (*ou*), which anticipates a positive reply to her question. Instead, Jesus affirms the picture of Mary at his feet, saying she has chosen the one thing that is needful. Discipleship with Jesus is a priority, even over the normally commended category of service. This priority of discipleship applies even to women.

A woman from the crowd seeks to commend the mother of Jesus, who raised and nourished him (Luke 11:27–28). But Jesus will have none of it. Blessing comes to those who do God's will. Even more important than life is obedience to God.

A woman is a beneficiary of a Sabbath healing in Luke 13:10–17. This becomes another pairing when Jesus heals a man with dropsy on the Sabbath in 14:1–6. The woman's healing brings the synagogue leader's rebuke and instruction to heal on the other six days of the week. Jesus responds that no better day exists to heal a "daughter of Abraham, whom Satan has kept bound," than the Sabbath. The value of the well-being of a woman is greater than the Sabbath.

In this passage, Jesus contrasts the leader's indignation at the woman's being healed on the Sabbath with a Jew's readiness to untie cattle, feed them at the manger, and lead them to water on the Sabbath. All are overt acts of labor and compassion. The Mishnah allowed cattle to be moved on the Sabbath as long as they did not carry a load (*m. Šabb.* 5) and to be tied up on the Sabbath lest they wander (*m. Šabb.* 15.2). The Mishnah also describes the wells at which cattle can drink without violating the Sabbath (*m. ʿErub.* 2.1–4). At Qumran, CD 11.5–6 allowed travel up to two thousand cubits (three thousand feet) for pasturing.[7] Jesus' question is rhetorical, a statement that the Jews often labored for their cattle's sake. They cannot dispute that this is common practice, which raises the issue of how and why an animal can fare better than a human on the Sabbath.

Thus the leaders are condemned by their own practice. They show compassion to animals but not to humans. It is this issue of inconsistency and priority in creation that Jesus raises. Some interpreters miss Jesus' point by arguing that his retort is not relevant, since he could indeed have waited a day to heal.[8] Jesus' point, however, is relevant: How can an animal be treated with more concern on the sacred

---

7. Marshall, *Gospel of Luke*, 558–59.

8. C. G. Montefiore, cited in J. M. Creed, *The Gospel according to St. Luke* (London: Macmillan, 1930), 183.

day than a person? Such an attitude is a reversal of the created order (Luke 12:6–7; cf. 1 Cor 9:9).

Jesus explains why he acted as he did: just as some feel free to aid animals on the Sabbath, one should feel the same moral necessity (ἔδει, *edei*) to aid this ailing daughter of Abraham on the Sabbath (cf. Luke 16:22; 19:9). Most see a minor-to-major argument here: what is true of animals is even truer for people. Satan had bound the woman for eighteen years, and she should be loosed from this bondage, even more than the ox should be loosed on the Sabbath to eat. Jesus is arguing that the woman's relationship to Abraham, the man of God's promise, makes her healing on the Lord's Day not wrong but appropriate, even necessary. What better day to reflect on God's activity than the Sabbath?

The passive infinitive λυθῆναι (*lythēnai*, "to be set free") suggests that someone frees the woman. Since only God can exercise such power, the healing is another evidence of God working through Jesus and a token of the struggle in which God is engaged to reclaim and restore people. Such activity is ideal for the day when people are to rest and offer worship to God, the good Creator. In effect, Jesus argues that his act does not violate the Sabbath but fits the very spirit of the day. What better way to celebrate the Sabbath? The difference in the views of Jesus and the synagogue leader could not be greater. So everything in Jesus' argument affirms the value of the woman.[9]

A woman who places leaven in bread is a picture of the growth of the kingdom; Jesus pairs this woman up with the man who plants a mustard seed (Luke 13:18–21). Another pairing comes in 15:1–10. Jesus first refers to the shepherd who recovers a lost sheep and then to a woman who recovers the lost coin. In both is the representation of how God seeks the lost and why Jesus seeks tax collectors and sinners. He takes the initiative in regaining the lost.

A negative example comes in Lot's wife, who in looking back to Sodom pictures someone whose tie to the world keeps a hold on them and damages their spiritual growth (Luke 17:32). She pairs up with Noah and Lot in the discourse. These examples involving women show Jesus' spiritual concern for their well-being. He tells parables that involve women as a way to communicate that the gospel is for everyone. Their status is as important as that of men.

The final scene involving a woman in the journey section of Luke is of the nagging widow who seeks justice from a judge (Luke 18:1–8). She represents a believer who must pray to God for justice and be assured that God hears. God will vindicate the righteous. It is her persistence about justice in prayer that is commended as an example.

17.1.4 Women in the Passion Week

Women with a heart to worship God are affirmed in the example of the poor widow who gives two small coins at the temple (Luke 21:1–4). She gives of all her life and stands in contrast to those who trumpet their gifts and ministry. Lepta were

---

9. Bock, *Luke 9:51–24:53*, 1217–19.

small copper coins, the smallest currency available, whose value was one-eighth of a penny. Ellis computes the value as one one-hundredth of a denarius—thus, one one-hundredth of the average daily wage (a very small sum indeed).[10]

No doubt most people would say that the gifts of the rich were more significant. Jesus explains why he says the widow gave the most even though she only contributed two lepta. All those who preceded her donated their gifts out of excess income; what they gave to God cost them little. In contrast, the woman gave, not from her abundance, but from her very life. As Jesus puts it, she gave "all she had to live on." But this did not stop her from giving. She did not say, "I do not have enough to live on, so I will postpone my giving." In fact, she could have given just one lepton, but instead she gave more. She gave "out of her poverty" (ὑστέρημα, *hysterēma*; elsewhere in the NT at 1 Cor 16:17; 2 Cor 8:14 [2x]; 9:12; 11:9; Phil 2:30; Col 1:24; 1 Thess 3:10).[11] Her use of resources is the second example of women using financial resources well (Luke 8:1–3). Other such examples are rare in Luke's gospel, with Zacchaeus as the other important example. Barnabas is an example of this in Acts.

Some women weep for Jesus as he bears the cross (Luke 23:27–31). Jesus uses their compassion as an opportunity to warn that if this judgment is what happens to green wood that is alive, what will happen to dead wood? Their compassion becomes an occasion for Jesus to warn again about the importance of spiritually responding to him and the consequences of rejection.

The women who follow Jesus are faithful. Some from Galilee are present and watch what takes place at the cross (Luke 23:49). These Galilean women also watch as Joseph of Arimathea buries Jesus. They use the next day as a day of preparation to gather their own spices and ointments to take to the tomb after the Sabbath (23:55–56).

Surprisingly, these women are the ones to whom God first reveals the resurrection (Luke 24:1–11). This part of the story gives a strong indication of historical authenticity. No one in that culture, if they were to make up the story of resurrection, would have written down women as the first witnesses. That would have been a credibility hurdle. The women are there because they were there at the event. However, the act also affirms the role of women as witnesses and those who can give testimony to what God has done through Jesus. They are shown to be quicker to believe than many men around them.

In Luke, women play a key role as witnesses to what God is doing. They are also beneficiaries of God's grace. They often display exemplary behavior and deep faith. Paired with men, they are beneficiaries of Jesus and can testify to him.

17.2 WOMEN IN THE BOOK OF ACTS

Women are not as prominent in Acts as in Luke. Its focus on communities and on Paul is responsible for this. Often it is the community role that is in view when they

---

10. Ellis, *Gospel of Luke*, 239. 11. Bock, *Luke 9:51–24:53*, 1645–46.

appear. We divide the book in half, the first half being when Jerusalem is mostly the focus and the second half involving the ministry of Paul.

17.2.1 Women in Acts 1–12

Women are among those who wait for the Spirit to come on them in Jerusalem (Acts 1:12–14). They are gathered along with the Twelve among the 120 present. They appear to be the witnesses from Galilee. Mary, Jesus' mother, is among them.

These women are among those receiving the gift of the Holy Spirit at Pentecost. Acts 2:17–18 speaks of the gift being poured out on both sons and daughters and on men and women servants. Acts 2:17 is clear here. The distribution is open with respect to gender. Joel promised that in this new era "your sons and daughters will prophesy." This is one of three parallelisms in Acts 2:17–18: sons/daughters, young/old men, male/female servants.[12] This third parallel shows that no class is excluded from those who will be gifted in "those" days (i.e., the last days of 2:17). This fits with the category we will consider next, the poor.

In this verse "prophesy" alludes to the tongues, which are immediately intelligible to the audience. The message declares "the wonders of God" (Acts 2:11). The idea is repeated for emphasis in an addition to the Joel citation at the end of v. 18 ("and they will prophesy"). There was precedent for including women, as in the Hebrew Scriptures Sarah, Miriam, Deborah, Hannah, Abigail, Huldah, and Esther were regarded as prophetesses (*b. Meg.* 14a; Exod 15:20; 34:22; note also Anna in Luke 2:36). There is no gender or status differentiation in who is indwelt by God's Spirit. This promise of the Spirit is at the hub of the gospel. It is for anyone who repents and so receives the forgiveness of sins (Acts 2:38–39).[13]

The next woman provides a negative example. Sapphira, along with her husband Ananias, pretends to give all their proceeds from the sale of a field to the church, whereas they actually keep some of it for themselves (Acts 5:1–11). After her husband suddenly dies as he is confronted, Sapphira comes forward and makes the same claim. She, too, is struck dead for lying to the Spirit, one of the few judgment acts in this book. Everyone is accountable to God, who knows what is taking place. This event also strikes fear into the community, both inside and outside of the church. With giftedness comes accountability before God.

In one of the summaries about response in Jerusalem, Luke notes that multitudes of "men and women … were added to their number" (Acts 5:14). The apostolic healings seem to be an element in this expansion, as in the context note is made of that work.

Another issue in the church rotates around an initial inequity of treatment, namely, how Hebrew and Hellenistic widows were being cared for by the body (Acts 6:1–6). This kind of racial preference did not fit the model of church care

---

12. The third parallel reads "servants, men and women alike" in NLT; "servants, both men and women" in NIV; "bondslaves, both men and women" in NASB.

13. Bock, *Acts*, 119–20.

and ethical concern for one's neighbors, whoever they might be (Luke 10:25–37). So the apostles urge those making the justifiable complaint to select men from their group to deal with the issue. They do so, resolving the problem in the process. The scene shows how widows were at risk in the society and so the church moved to make sure they were cared for.

When the church is persecuted, there is no distinction made between believing men and women (Acts 8:3). Saul's persecution in Jerusalem drags off both genders to prison. Suffering for identifying with Jesus sees no difference. Anyone who confesses Jesus is subject to arrest.

In Samaria, men and women respond to Philip's message about the kingdom of God and the name Jesus Christ (Acts 8:12). Again, the presence of signs is a factor in this response, even impressing a magician like Simon Magus.

As in Luke's gospel, we have a gender pairing. Peter's healing of Aeneas in Lydda is followed by his healing of Tabitha, also known as Dorcas, in Joppa (Acts 9:32–43). Dorcas is described as a woman "always doing good and helping the poor." Peter raises her from the dead. The healing draws much attention, so many in the area come to the Lord.

When Peter is miraculously released from Herod's prison, it is the servant girl Rhoda who greets him at the door of Mary's house and excitedly tells the group that Peter is present (Acts 12:13). As with the women at the tomb, her report is not initially believed, and the believers accuse her of being out of her mind. When she insists it is true, they attribute what she saw to an angelic appearance. Only when they see Peter do they believe Rhoda has told the truth.

Women are a natural part of the new community, gifted and participating in all that is taking place, from receiving the promised Spirit to experiencing persecution. Some are the beneficiaries of apostolic miracles. But there is no direct teaching about any administrative role for women.

17.2.2 Women in Acts 13–28

As the mission moves out from Antioch with the journeys of Barnabas and Saul, women continue to respond and react to their work. In Pisidian Antioch, the Jews incite prominent women and leading men to stir up persecution (Acts 13:50). If other texts in Acts are a guide (16:21; 17:6–7; 18:13), it is the claim that these missionaries teach against the customs of the culture that brings the reaction. Those in power have the most to lose from a change in the cultural direction and habits of a city. This kind of difference plays itself out later in Ephesus.

A positive example comes with Lydia during Paul's visit to Philippi (Acts 16:11–15). There at a place for Jewish prayer, Paul explains the gospel to a group of women. Lydia, a worshiper of God and a seller of fine goods made of purple, responds. Paul ends up experiencing her hospitality by staying with her household.

Also in Philippi, Paul exorcises a demon from a young fortune-telling girl, whose talents are being exploited by those who own her (Acts 16:16–24). This act leads the owners to seek Paul's arrest on the charge that he is advocating customs it is not lawful for Romans to practice, a charge that is not true since religious freedom to worship any gods existed in Rome. It may be that the Jewish roots of the new faith are being attacked here. Paul and Silas are beaten and arrested. What these scenes involving women tell us is that they are responsive to the gospel, but that response also could generate a counterreaction from those who do not wish to see things change.

In Thessalonica, leading women are among those who respond to Paul (Acts 17:4). This capturing of the city, including some elites, brings the reaction of Jews in the city to stir up the crowd, claiming these men are turning the city upside down and acting against the decrees of Caesar (Acts 17:6–7).

In Athens, one of the people who respond to Paul is a woman named Damaris (Acts 17:34). This is the most abstract of Paul's speeches, appealing to God as Creator and Jesus as Judge, yet it also meets with some reception.

Perhaps the major female figure in Acts is Priscilla, who is paired with her husband Aquila. She appears in two scenes. Paul stays with them in Corinth, as they share the same trade of tentmaking (Acts 18:1–4). Later in Ephesus, the couple ministers to Apollos (18:24–28), explaining to him the way of God more accurately by noting that the Spirit of God has come. Priscilla is explicitly included in the teaching of Apollos, albeit in private. Here is a woman who exercises gifts that edify the body, even though it is done in a discreet way.

We get a passing mention of Philip's four daughters in Caesarea who are prophetesses (Acts 21:9). We are told nothing else about their ministry; only their gift is noted. It is the prophecy of Agabus about what will happen to Paul in Jerusalem that Luke presents.

In Acts 22:4, Paul tells the story of his encounter with the risen Jesus and notes that he persecuted men and women. Now at his examination, he preaches before governors and kings, as well as before leaders' wives, such as Drusilla and Bernice (Acts 24:24; 25:23; 26:30).

There is not much development of the role of women in Acts. Their responsiveness and presence in the community are mostly described. Clearly they receive the indwelling and empowering Spirit for witness. They are participants in the community. Some teach in certain contexts and prophesy. This fits the tone set in Luke, where women are included in what Jesus does. Unlike many social contexts in the first century, they are neither dismissed nor forgotten.

17.3 THE POOR IN LUKE-ACTS

The treatment of the poor (πτωχός, *ptōchos*) in Luke-Acts takes place mostly in the gospel. The ten uses of this term occur in Luke, while one other text in Acts alludes to the poor. This group receives special attention in the gospel, for God consciously reaches out to them. The gospel is said to be for them. It is a way of showing that those whom society forgets are special to God; the gospel is truly for everyone.

The example of Mary had already indicated that God cares for the humble and lowly, as she praises God in her hymn (Luke 1:46–55). God also holds the powerful accountable, while reaching out to the poor. Both ideas are noted in this hymn.[14] Mary looks forward to God's vindication of those who fear God and regards it as a matter of faith that it will come to pass (Luke 1:45, 50). This vindication involves the scattering of the proud, those who see no need for God or for treating fellow humans with compassion. The idea of God's dispersing the proud (ὑπερηφάνους, *hyperēphanous*) — people who are consistently viewed negatively in the NT (Luke 1:51; Rom 1:30; 2 Tim 3:2; Jas 4:6; 1 Pet 5:5) — or having sovereignty over social status is a popular OT theme (Num 10:35; 1 Sam 2:7; Pss 68:1 [68:2 MT]; 89:10 [89:11 MT]).[15]

The arrogance of the proud is described in the phrase "in their inmost thoughts" (διανοίᾳ καρδίας αὐτῶν; *dianoia kardias autōn*; lit., "[proud] with respect to the thoughts of their heart"). The heart is seen as the center of feeling (1 Sam 16:7; Prov 4:23) and as the base of reasoning power (1 Chr 29:18; Job 12:3).[16] This pride is deep-seated and reflects one's innermost being. God will judge such pride. Luke 18:9–14 can be seen as a commentary on the contrast between the proud and the humble, which serves as testimony concerning those whom God accepts and those whom he does not. God will scatter those who feel no need for him but are proud of their spiritual or material attainments and capabilities.

The reversal of social position will occur in the final exercise of God's power. God will lift up the "humble" (ταπεινούς, *tapeinous*), who stand in contrast to δυνάστας (*dynastas*), a term that refers to "rulers" (cf. Gen 50:4), who are removed "from their thrones." That is, the powerful are governing rulers, whereas the humble are those oppressed by these rulers. Mary has in mind God's covenant people, which is evident from Luke 1:54–55 and the mention of God-fearers in 1:50. R. Brown sees a reference to the spiritually oppressed, a reference that is correct in light of the emphasis on God-fearers in the hymn.[17] All the injustice of the ruling classes against God's people will be reversed as the humble are lifted up by God. The rulers' oppression and lack of compassion will be dealt with by God, who desires that people treat their neighbors with compassion.

Mary probably has in mind the Romans and those like them, who use their secular power to keep God's people at bay. Those who think they have authority do not have ultimate authority. A major theme of the OT is the oppressed people of God described as poor and humble (Pss 9:11–12, 17–20 [9:12–13, 18–21 MT]; 10:1–4, 17–18; 12:1–5 [12:2–6 MT]; 18:25–29 [18:26–30 MT]). These few references are part of a consistent theme of the OT, especially in the Psalter.

The idea of removing rulers is expressed in the OT and in Jewish hope (1 Sam

---

14. Parts of Luke's treatment and description of the humble in these verses were already treated earlier in the chapter and in ch. 10. Here we examine how the theme of the humble and arrogant are played off against each other.

15. Bertram, *TDNT*, 8:528.
16. Behm, *TDNT*, 3:612 §D2b.
17. Brown, *Birth of the Messiah*, 363.

2:7; Job 5:11; 12:19; Sir 10:14; Jdt 9:3; 1QM 14.10–11).[18] The exaltation of the humble is likewise a key OT and Jewish theme (1 Sam 2:7; Ps 147:6; Sir 10:14). Mary uses the language of the faithful. She trusts God's just vindication in the approaching messianic reign. Hendriksen makes reference to how the humble were lifted up in the past, but this passage shows only that what God will do is like what he has done.[19] Mary is looking to the future, not to the past. She is anticipating, in the child she bears, total vindication. The way God will accomplish this vindication has other intermediate requirements of which she is not aware, namely, Messiah's suffering. First Peter 1:11 summarizes the emerging career of Jesus in two stages: "the sufferings of the Messiah and the glories that … follow." Mary longs to share in these days.

The social consequences of God's work are now set forth. God will fill the hungry with good things, a promise paralleled in the OT (1 Sam 2:5; Pss 107:9; 146:7) and Judaism (*Pss. Sol.* 5.8–11).[20] In the beatitude of Luke 6:21, Luke returns to the theme of the poor being filled, and in 11:13 he mentions that God will give the Spirit to those who ask for good things (Ps 34:10 [34:11 MT]).[21]

In contrast, God will send the rich away empty, another theme with OT precedent (1 Sam 2:5; Job 15:29; Jer 17:11). Luke is strong in his denunciation of the independent rich (Luke 6:24–26; 12:19–20; 16:25; 21:1–4). Luke 12:21 is clear that independence from God tends to characterize the wealthy, making them an object of condemnation. Danker argues that Luke (6:20–26; 16:19–31) expresses traditional Jewish hope for political vindication, a hope that is redefined by Jesus when those inside the nation are warned.[22] But one must be careful not to interpret the eschatological reversal solely in a spiritualized form, so that the context of the national hope is lost (1:54–55). Luke 16:19–31, with its contrast between poor Lazarus and the unbelieving rich man, serves as a commentary on this passage's ultimate teaching of the reversal at the time of judgment. The rich man's self-focus reflects his lack of faith and his spiritual insensitivity toward the God to whom he is responsible. Such self-focus produces a lack of concern for one's neighbor, which God condemns. Nevertheless, the reversal also applies to national hope. It is the nation that is helped (1:54).

Luke's point is that one should keep material things in perspective and use them generously to serve one's neighbor. Two errors of interpretation must be avoided. One is to spiritualize the material references to the point where the warning about excessive attachment to riches and the dangers it can hold is ignored.[23] On the other side, one can ignore the hymn's covenant background and context to such an extent that the spiritual element in the context is lost. The hymn exalts God-fearers. When one ignores this background, the temptation is to make the hymn a manifesto for

18. Ibid., 337; Plummer, *St Luke*, 33; Danker, *Jesus and the New Age*, 44; C. Schneider, *TDNT*, 3:412 §3.

19. Hendricksen, *Exposition of the Gospel according to Luke*, 108.

20. Plummer, *St Luke*, 33.

21. Hauck, *TDNT*, 4:389.

22. Danker, *Jesus and the New Age*, 45.

23. Marshall, *Gospel of Luke*, 85; Nolland, *Luke 1:1–9:20*, 72.

political action, devoid of any spiritual content. This empties the teaching of its central thrust, the need to turn to God.

The context requires that both of these extremes be avoided. Luke 1:53 looks to the ultimate eschatological reversal that God will bring in the end times. But care with regard to material things and power is what his followers ought to pursue with good spiritual balance. Such an attitude reflects what God desires in light of what he will judge. Everything said here forms the narrative and theological background for the next key passage that mentions the poor, Luke 4:16–20.[24]

In his synagogue address in Luke 4:16–20, Jesus' gospel is said to be for the poor. This remark has engendered an entire theology, known as liberation theology.[25] There is a reinforcement of this idea of God's concern for the poor in many Lucan texts. What Luke lacks, however, is the full political emphasis that many give to these texts. The "poor" in these passages are rooted in OT texts, those who are the $^{c a}$nâwîm, the pious poor of the Hebrew Scriptures who are exploited, in part because of their association with God. The $^{c a}$nâwîm background is present both in the Isa 61 text Jesus cites here and in the theme of the Psalter to which Jesus alludes in his beatitudes in Luke 6 (Pss 41:1; 72:4, 13; 82:3; 140:12). There is a social dimension and justice dimension to how the poor are mistreated or ignored in the background to Jesus' usage that also needs to be recognized.

What we have in these passages is something that falls between the full political agenda of a liberation perspective and the ignoring of the poor that often is the approach of the alternatives to liberation. Our survey of these texts helps to show this in-between position in Luke-Acts. Jesus' release in Luke 4 is compared with a spiritual jubilee in the reference to the acceptable year of the Lord (Lev 25; Isa 61:2). In drawing near to God and the community he forms, the poor come into a new family and care. This is part of what God promises will be a concern of his people.

This is why Jesus issues a beatitude for the poor in Luke 6:20. It is clear from the woes that follow that this use of "the poor" is not merely or exclusively spiritual. This is not Matthew's "poor in spirit." There is a social dimension to this group as the woes to the rich that follow in Luke 6:24–26 are not to the "rich in spirit" but to the materially wealthy. Guelich's summary definition is helpful: "*The poor* in Judaism referred to those in desperate need (socioeconomic element) whose helplessness drove them to a dependent relationship with God (religious element) for the supplying of their needs and vindication. Both elements are consistently present, although ^{c}nwm does place more stress on the latter."[26] As we have seen in Luke, responding to the gospel changes the way people relate not only to God but to their neighbors

---

24. Bock, *Luke 1:1–9:50*, 156–58.

25. This theology was developed in the context of poverty and concerns about justice in Latin America. See Gustavo Gutiérrez, *A Theology of Liberation* (Maryknoll, NY: Orbis, 1973); Leonardo Boff, *Jesus Christ Liberator: A Critical Christology of Our Time*

(Maryknoll, NY: Orbis, 1978); and J. L. Segundo, *The Liberation of Theology* (Maryknoll, NY: Orbis, 1976).

26. Robert Guelich, *The Sermon on the Mount* (Waco, TX: Word, 1982), 69.

(1:16–17; 3:10–14; 10:25–37). This also assumes change in values. The result is that concerns for those in need are heightened (14:12–24). That is part of what Jesus affirms here. God and his community care for such as these and share with them.

Luke 7:22 repeats to John the Baptist what Jesus said in 4:18. The gospel is preached to the poor. The extension of God's grace includes those whom society has set to the side. In fact, the gospel makes a priority of them according to Jesus. This reversal of values from the world is part of what shows the gospel to be transformation of life in the world.

So in other texts we see Jesus exhorting people to sell what they have and give the proceeds to those who are poor (Luke 12:33; 18:22). These exhortations reflect the new values and reorientation that the gospel gives when it comes to human need and one's neighbor. They show one turning to depend on God and not one's own resources. The passage points to a spirit of giving appreciation that the gospel engenders. So Jesus urges associating with the poor and inviting them to the table of banquet fellowship, and he even illustrates the point with a parable (14:12–24, note esp. vv. 13 and 21).

The parable of the rich man and Lazarus also illustrates the danger of ignoring the needs of the poor. Many read this parable as simply about resurrection, but it also is about heeding Moses and the prophets regarding how to live. It emphasizes caring for one's needy neighbor who is within one's reach (Luke 16:19–30). The rich man had ignored the one who was without in his earthly life. The rich one who had everything and more to spare had done nothing to help, and God had seen the injustice.[27] A heeding of what the Hebrew Scriptures had taught about care for those in need should have made an impression on the rich man.

Zacchaeus stands in contrast to the rich man. He vows to make restitution for his past wrongs and to give to the poor (Luke 19:8). This move gains Jesus' commendation and approval, along with praise that here is a true son of Abraham.

The example of the poor widow who gives all when she places two small copper coins in the temple treasury also affirms these values. What little a poor person can give is seen and appreciated as a lot by God.

The term "poor" does not appear in Acts. Instead we see actions of community in the pooling of resources, in bringing alms, or in providing relief to those in need. So the Jerusalem community pools resources (Acts 2:45; 4:32–36). This is mentioned more than once, something Luke does when he wishes to emphasize something. This is not an ancient form of communism because it was not required of the community, but was spontaneous. What it reflects is a deep sense of community that generates mutual care and is rooted in a deep friendship.[28]

The community in Antioch sends food goods to Jerusalem during a famine (Acts 11:27–30). Paul takes alms to the temple (24:17), only to get arrested. We get

---

27. This issue is developed in detail in my "The Parable of the Rich Man and Lazarus," *SwJT* 40 (1997): 63–72.

28. Hume, *Early Christian Community*, 111–12.

glimpses of a people whose values yield generosity. The gospel has transformed them into a giving people, generous with their possessions. This change of perspective and the consequent action are what Luke emphasizes as he speaks of care for the poor and as he notes that the gospel goes out to them.

In sum, Luke's portrait of the poor is an important part of his gospel and theology. Few things show the change the gospel brings more than how people in the community are to view the poor. Those whom society has cast aside and treats with contempt, Jesus urges, are special objects of compassion and mercy. Much like the pursuit of reconciliation and love for God and one's neighbor, the treatment of the poor indicates the effective presence of God and his values in the community, a witness that is to stand in contrast to the world's lack of care for some of God's creatures.

17.4 OTHER GROUPINGS: THE LAME AND THE BLIND

Other groupings of those on the fringe are also mentioned, but less frequently and often in conjunction with the poor. The lame (χωλός, *chōlos*) show up in Luke 7:22 in the discussion with John the Baptist about Jesus' work pointing to the eschatological era. This is one of six uses of this term in Luke-Acts. Here the lame walk and the blind see (Isa 29:18; 35:5–6). Curing blindness is significant, since in the Hebrew Scriptures the healing of a blind person never occurs. In Luke 14:13 and 21, Jesus urges that one invite the poor, crippled, lame, and blind to one's table. These are the only texts where the term for crippled is used (ἀνάπειρος, *anapeiros*). Healings of the lame occur in Jerusalem in Acts 3 and in Lystra in 14:8. A summary about healing in Samaria also points to the lame.

The term "blind" (τυφλός, *typhlos*) occurs nine times in Luke-Acts, with eight of the uses in the gospel. Several of these texts we have already discussed (Luke 4:18; 7:21–22; 14:13, 21). In Jesus' preaching at the synagogue in 4:18, the blind are able to see (so also in 7:21–22), and the blind are among those to be invited to the banquet in 14:13 and 21. Luke 6:39 has a negative example in the warning not to allow the blind to lead the blind since they are not able to guide. This is a reference to not following the Jewish leadership. The healing of a blind man in Jericho is the topic of 18:35–43. In a rare miracle of judgment, Bar-Jesus is struck blind in Paphos for trying to prevent Paul from sharing the gospel with Sergius Paulus (Acts 13:11).

These two groups add to the portrait of Jesus' outreach to those on the edge of the society. The gospel is for them, even especially for them. God reaches out to those in need. Often it is those in dire straits who better sense their need for God, lacking any false sense of security or a misguided trust in their own ability.

17.5 CONCLUSION:
THE SOCIAL DIMENSION IN LUKE-ACTS

The social dimensions of Luke show no effort at revolution or political overthrow. What the texts do evidence is an outreach to those on the edge of society. Appreciation for God's way leads into values that care about such people in contrast to the way the world has cast them aside. Jesus' involvement of and concern for the women, the poor, the lame, and the blind show that God cares for the entire spectrum of people. The community Jesus forms must also care about such people, even giving special attention to them. This is one of the ways the new community's values contrast with those of the world.

The role of women is particularly affirmed in terms of being community participants. They also have an important role in testifying to Jesus. We do not see them as among the Twelve or in other places of leadership in the community, but otherwise they are there as full and equal participants in the giftedness that comes through the gospel.

The poor are singled out as of special concern for the gospel and the kingdom message Jesus brings. God lifts up the humble. The picture of a vindicated Lazarus may show this most vividly. Jesus urges care for the poor, lame, crippled, and blind. This shows a special concern about those in human need. This kind of equalizing of societal expectation and concern is revolutionary, not at a political level, but in an important social way. It testifies to God's care for people, even people whom other people tend to ignore.

Chapter 18

THE LAW IN LUKE-ACTS

BIBLIOGRAPHY

Bachmann, Michael. "Jerusalem and Rome in Luke-Acts." Pp. 60–83 in *Luke-Acts and Empire: Essays in Honor of Robert L. Brawley.* Ed. David Rhoads, David Esterline, and Jae Won Lee. Princeton Theological Monographs. Eugene, OR: Pickwick, 2011. **Blomberg, Craig.** "The Christian and the Law of Moses." Pp. 397–416 in *Witness to the Gospel: The Theology of Acts.* Ed. I. Howard Marshall and David Peterson. Grand Rapids: Eerdmans, 1998. Idem. "The Law in Luke-Acts." *JSNT* 22 (1984): 53–80. **Brawley, Robert.** *Luke-Acts and the Jews: Conflict, Apology, Reconciliation.* SBLMS. Atlanta: Scholars Press, 1987. **Jervell, Jacob.** *Luke and the People of God.* Minneapolis: Augsburg, 1972. Idem. *The Theology of the Acts of the Apostles.* Cambridge: Cambridge University Press, 1996. **Moessner, David.** *Jesus and the Heritage of Israel: Luke's Narrative Claim upon Israel's Legacy.* Harrisburg: Trinity International, 1999. **Peterson, David.** "The Worship of the New Community." Pp. 373–95 in *Witness to the Gospel: The Theology of Acts.* Ed. I. Howard Marshall and David Peterson. Grand Rapids: Eerdmans, 1998. **Wilson, Stephen G.** *Luke and the Law.* SNTSMS. Cambridge: Cambridge University Press, 1983.

Luke's handling of the law in Luke-Acts has been disputed over the last several decades. Two positions contend for supremacy. One argues that Luke presents the end of the law and an emphasis on salvation in Christ and freedom from the law.[1] The other sees Luke viewing the law most conservatively but still with some value for believers.[2] I argue for a position somewhat between these two options, noting that each side has a point, although in the end law-abiding for Luke is only a consideration for Jewish believers, while Gentiles must be sensitive to certain practices tied to the law. Law-abiding is an acceptable option for Jewish believers as they seek to reach out to other Jews, but in no case should it get in the way of Jew-Gentile unity in the church or the gospel of salvation by faith through Jesus Christ alone. This is why circumcision is no longer a covenantal requirement for Gentile believers.

This may sound like the first option, but as I will suggest, that option underestimates the point of certain texts in Acts: the note in Acts 22:12 about Ananias being

---

1. The position is most vigorously defended by Craig Blomberg in "The Law in Luke-Acts," *JSNT* 22 (1984): 53–80, and in "The Christian and the Law of Moses," in *Witness to the Gospel*, 397–416.

2. Jacob Jervell, *Luke and the People of God* (Minneapolis: Augsburg, 1972); Stephen G. Wilson, *Luke and the Law* (SNTSMS 50; Cambridge: Cambridge Univ. Press, 1983); R. L. Brawley, *Luke-Acts and the Jews: Conflict, Apology, Reconciliation* (SBLMS 33; Atlanta: Scholars Press, 1987).

a law-observant believer; the mention of the role of the law in the weekly reading of Moses as an explicit concern for the Acts 15 decree; the significance of Paul's taking a vow in Acts 18; and the claim that in Acts 21 James's suggestion to Paul of sacrificing "backfires" because of its outcome.[3] This last suggestion is particularly unpersuasive, since the example of suffering and rejection goes back to Jesus' example on the cross — and surely he did nothing wrong. For Luke, Paul's arrest in Jerusalem is seen as God's will.

Paying attention to the fact that Gentiles have no real obligations to the law while Jewish believers seem sensitive to it helps us see how Luke nuances this discussion. In the end, the way even Jewish Christians handle the law would not be persuasive to the most scrupulously observant Jews, since the way Gentiles are involved in the new community would be seen as forcing violations in terms of diet and purity. Nevertheless, the continual presence of Jewish believers at the temple and the type of request James makes shows that the temple is more than a place of prayer and teaching for them, as the first view claims about Acts 3.[4]

On the other hand, the way Luke handles the law with issues such as the Sabbath, hand washing, and diet indicates that there is more freedom than generally law-sensitive Jews had accepted. This speaks against some of the scholarly emphasis on Luke's "conservative" stance toward the law. What is important to see is that much of that positive language toward the law comes in contexts where promise is being evoked (Luke 16:17; 24:43–47; Acts 24:14; 28:23). This does suggest that the law has force in pointing to promise. Law as realized promise is important for Luke. One thing both views mostly share correctly is that Luke saw no salvation benefit for the law.[5] So let us look at these texts in Luke's two volumes.

18.1 THE LAW IN THE GOSPEL OF LUKE

The first note about the law in the gospel of Luke shows that John and Jesus come from a pious background. Not only are Zechariah and Elizabeth described in terms of being righteous regarding the law, but they circumcise John, as was common among Jews (Luke 1:6, 59). Jesus' parents also keep the law and have Jesus circumcised (2:21–24). These two scenes are the only two references to circumcision in Luke's gospel.[6] Simeon affirms Mary in the midst of this law-keeping (2:27) and a narrative remark in Luke explicitly makes the point (see 2:39: "when Joseph and Mary had done everything required by the Law of the Lord").

3. I also doubt the suggestion that Paul's angry reaction to the high priest in Acts 23 is ironic. More likely it is Paul catching himself and recalling his ultimate goal is to try to be a Jew to Jews (1 Cor 9:19).

4. Peterson, "Worship of the New Community," 374–77, notes that the relationship of believers to the temple is complex. Here is where they could bear testimony, yet they also meet separately. As a faithful remnant they cannot disengage from the temple. Stephen's remarks are not against the temple, but against an attitude that "assigned permanence and finality to it" (p. 378). The vow incident

of Acts 21 and the description of Ananias as a devout man of the law (Acts 22:12) are important here as well. See also Bachmann, "Jerusalem and Rome in Luke-Acts," 60–68.

5. A few of those defending Luke as conservative with respect to the law argue that in Acts 13 Paul has a partial justification view of the law, but this is correctly refuted by Blomberg, "Christian and the Law of Moses," 404–6.

6. The term appears eight times in Acts. This count involves both the verb (περιτέμνω) and the noun (περιτομή, *peritomē*).

When we turn to Jesus' ministry, we see him send healed lepers to the priests as the law requires (Luke 5:12–14; 17:11–14). He refers the questioner back to the law when the scribe asks what he must do to inherit eternal life (10:25–26). Jesus also speaks, in a context of promise, about not one stroke of the law becoming void (16:17). The previous verse is significant for understanding what this means, for 16:16 says that the Law and the Prophets were in force until John. This crucial text is underappreciated and shows two things: (1) the law had a central role until John pointed to the kingdom (and thus to the Messiah); and (2) the law as discussed in 16:17 is placed in this context about law being in place until the promise comes.

In this passage, as elsewhere in Luke and Acts, Luke sees two parts in God's plan: promise and fulfillment (Luke 1–2; 3:1–6, 15–20; 7:18–35; Acts 10:37; 13:34–35). John the Baptist is consistently portrayed as the transition figure and belongs to the era of promise as a forerunner to the era of fulfillment (Luke 1–2; 3:1–18; 7:22–28). Luke reasserts this basic division here. Jesus speaks of the Law and the Prophets existing until or through John the Baptist. Is John in the era of fulfillment? Luke 7:18–35 and 3:1–6 (where John only prepares the way) suggest not; but Luke 3:18 and Acts 1:22 make the issue debatable (see Luke 7:27–28).[7] In a sense, as a transition figure John has one foot in each era. But as the pointer of the way, he really belongs to the old era in terms of his function. He is its end.

Perhaps the key is that John announces the arrival of Jesus, who is the only one who preaches the kingdom. This observation separates John from the message of the new era. Since his time, however, the kingdom is preached, which suggests that the new era has come and that the old era of the Law and the Prophets, as the era of promise, now ceases to exist. The period before Jesus was regulated through the Law and the Prophets. They operated in a context of promise, as Luke 24:44–49 and Acts 3:11–26 show. That old era proclaimed the promise and program of Messiah. The frequent temporal marker ἀπὸ τοῦ νῦν (*apo tou nyn*, "from now on") is a key phrase used by Luke to denote significant turning points in the sequence of events (Luke 1:48; 5:10; 12:52; 22:18, 69). God's plan has turned over a new leaf with Jesus' coming. The preaching of the kingdom's message is no longer a matter of declaring a distant promise, but the kingdom can be preached in terms of nearness and arrival. A new era has come—with new realities and new authority.

But what of the remark about the law not failing in Luke 16:17? Various answers have been given about what this remark means.

1. Jervell argues that for Luke the law is "eternally valid."[8] This is part of Luke's conservative view of the law that shows Christians are to be faithful to it. For Jervell, whatever 16:16 means, it does not mean the passing away of the period or epoch of the law. This view has problems. Seen in isolation, 16:17 might be able to sustain such a meaning, but given the previous verse where

---

7. Marshall, *Gospel of Luke*, 628, sees John in the new era; but in Luke it depends on which passage one is discussing, so seeing him as a transition figure more clearly affects Luke's usage.

8. Jervell, *Luke and the People of God*, 140–41.

delineations of epochs are present, Jervell's meaning cannot be right. Texts such as 6:1–5 raise questions about this reading. Some contextual qualification of what the law means is necessary for the passage to make sense.

2. Manson takes the verse by itself and argues that Luke uses it as bitter irony.[9] The scribes view the law in such a way that it is easier for creation to pass than for the law to fail at any single point. But to isolate the verse like this is unwise. Neither Matthew's nor Luke's usage requires such an alteration.

3. Blomberg distinguishes between the law in this age and the Mosaic law, which has lost its validity and become superfluous.[10] The law that is still valid accomplishes everything it intends. This explanation goes in the right direction in seeing law used with a special force, but it places the emphasis in the wrong category, that of moral law. The sense is broader than this.

4. Banks and Luce ("absolutely and completely fulfilled in . . . Jesus") argue that the law points to the kingdom and so does not fail. It is transformed and fulfilled in Jesus.[11] It does not fail because its goal is Jesus and its authority is expressed through him. Wilson objects to this view, arguing that it really means that the law has been set aside.[12]

5. Wilson offers his own explanation in terms of Jesus' authority: the law's demands are valid and have been intensified and extended in Jesus' teaching, as Luke 16:18 illustrates.[13] But he also argues that there is ambiguity in Luke's position, since the full extension of the law is not being followed. Is this explanation precise enough? How can all the demands of the law be valid, when Jesus appears to challenge some laws (6:1–5)? The resolution through Jesus' authority appears helpful, but in what sense is the law appealed to, if not in its demands?

What makes determining the best view difficult is that Luke 16:17 is the only verse in Luke's gospel that directly concerns the law as a whole. When one looks at Luke-Acts, then both views 4 and 5 have merit. But Wilson's view fails to distinguish clearly how the law is seen by Luke, though his note on Jesus' authority is helpful. There is no doubt that Luke holds that the law functions as part of the period of promise and that it points to Christ and his activity (16:19–31; 24:44–47; Acts 3:11–26). This is the emphasis of the Lucan introduction in Luke 1–2 and, less directly, of the circumcision debate in Acts 15. The Law and the Prophets point to God's final activity in Christ. View 4 as articulated by Banks is most satisfactory: the law does not fail only in this salvation-historical sense.[14] The limits of the remark mean that Wilson's objection to this view does not hold.

9. T. W. Manson, *The Sayings of Jesus: As Recorded in the Gospels according to St. Matthew and St. Luke* (London: SCM, 1949), 135–36.

10. Blomberg, "Law in Luke-Acts," 60–61.

11. R. J. Banks, *Jesus and the Law in the Synoptic Tradition* (SNTSMS 28; Cambridge: Cambridge Univ. Press, 1975), 214–15;

Luce, *Gospel according to S. Luke*, 267.

12. Wilson, *Luke and the Law*, 50.

13. Ibid., 50–51.

14. Fitzmyer, *Gospel of Luke X–XXIV*, 1116 (law is vindicated in the demands of the kingdom); Marshall, *Gospel of Luke*, 627.

In this Lucan context, the point is a powerful one to the Pharisees, who are lovers of the law. If they are to keep the law, they must embrace Jesus' kingdom message to which it points. Responding to Jesus represents fulfilling the law, and so receiving him brings its intention to pass (Rom 9:31 – 10:13). They must respond and adhere to the teaching of the one sent to present the message of God's rule. The statement underlines Jesus' authority.

The similar statement in Matt 5:18 about the law not failing is in a greatly different context: it is part of Jesus' exposition of the law's real force and meaning. The Matthean remark is followed by six illustrations, one of which is marriage and divorce. Jesus also says there that the law does not pass away and that he comes to fulfill it, a meaning similar to Luke, though Luke presents the nature of the law's ethical application less comprehensively than does Matthew.[15]

Luke 10 and 16 are the only texts within Jesus' ministry in Luke's gospel to use the term "law" (νόμος, *nomos*), outside of Luke 24:44, where the law is part of the promise about the Messiah, reaffirming what 16:16 already said.[16] So these are all the explicit texts on the law in Luke's gospel.

Moses (Μωϋσῆς, *Mōusēs*) is also sometimes referred to in a way that points to the law. Of the ten uses in the gospel, only two refer to him as a figure (Luke 9:30, 33, where he appears at the transfiguration). Every other reference involves the law; more importantly, many of those eight references have the christological thrust of promise we just noted for the law.

Luke 2:22 is a traditional use, simply describing how Jesus' parents obeyed the law of Moses about the firstborn. In 5:14, Jesus commands the healed leper to do as Moses commanded and show himself to the priest. Luke 16:29 and 31 appear in the parable of the rich man and Lazarus and point to the ethical thrust of the law and the need to care for those in need. In this scene the rich man in Hades asks that someone be sent from the dead to tell his brothers not to follow his now-condemned example. The reply is that they have Moses and the Prophets and if they do not listen to them, they will not hear even if someone rises from the dead. This use of the law shows its ethical value and thrust. The passage affirms that ethical role for the relational parts of the law, just as the reference to the scribe about eternal life evoked the command to love God completely and one's neighbor as oneself. This core value of the law Luke affirms through Jesus in ch. 10.[17] These last two texts show the law affirmed in terms of promise and ethical thrust, which Jesus calls the justice and love of God in 11:42.

Moses also defends resurrection according to Jesus as he counters the levirate marriage problem the Sadducees raise in Luke 20:28. Here Jesus replies that at the burning bush, Moses spoke of the God of Abraham, Isaac, and Jacob. So these figures must be alive since God is a God of the living. This conclusion argues

---

15. Bock, *Luke 9:51 – 24:53*, 1351 – 56.

16. This term appears nine times in Luke and seventeen times in Acts.

17. Of course, if the man loves God fully, he will heed his agent Jesus and what he says about what God is doing through him.

that resurrection is taught in the Torah, the one section of the Hebrew Scripture Sadducees respect. So the law points to the hope of resurrection, a point that has christological value and also points to hope and promise.

Finally, in Luke 24:27 and 44, Jesus uses Moses and the Prophets (and in v. 44 the Psalms) to point to himself and the work of the Messiah to die, to be raised, and to have forgiveness preached to all the nations. This is an explicit use of Moses and appeals to the law in relationship to promise. Luke's emphasis about the law in his gospel lies here with the idea of promise, since it is a closing note.

This leaves us with passages in the gospel where Moses or the law is not mentioned but its practices are described. Here two scenes are especially important. One is the entire set of Sabbath scenes (Luke 6:1–11; 13:10–17; 14:1–6); the other is the dispute over Jesus not washing his hands in 11:37–38 along with the rebuke Jesus gives in vv. 39–52.

The Sabbath scenes are important for here we see the ethical thrust of the law as a basis for Jesus' practice.[18] David and his men can eat the bread of the Presence, which the law allowed only the priests to eat (Luke 6:3–4). It is right to heal on the Sabbath and save a life (6:6–10). In fact, there is no better day on which to have a daughter of Abraham healed than the Sabbath (13:10–16). Even an ox is saved on the Sabbath. These three examples show that the law has an ethical thrust that negates any charge against Jesus. But Jesus makes an even more compelling point in one of these scenes: he is Lord of the Sabbath (6:5). He stresses that his coming and role in the new era give him authority over the Sabbath. Christ trumps law in terms of interpreting how it is to be implemented. Nothing in what Jesus says here nullifies the Sabbath, but it does challenge some Jewish views of it and argues that if one understands the ethical and eschatological dimensions of what is taking place, the law will not be read as it is by many.

The hand washing incident is also important because it challenges the traditions tied to purity that grew out of the law but were not explicit in it (Luke 11:37–44). As with the Sabbath, Jesus emphasizes relational issues as he rebukes the Pharisees and scribes for being so concerned with the keeping of the law but bypassing the justice and love of God, as well as leading people to death by their hypocrisy. Once again we see a reading of law that is not in line with the most scrupulous Jewish practices of the time, fed as they are by tradition.

We also see a concern for people that drives how the letter of the law should be read. When we place this alongside Acts 10 and the direct challenge to dietary practices in the vision to Peter as a picture for moving into Jew-Gentile relations, we do see a relativizing of the law in terms of diet and other purity practices that had served as obstacles between Jews and Gentiles. It is here where Luke's portrait of the law is not so conservative and seems at least to challenge how those who observed the law sought to practice it. To note this does not mean the law is abrogated for

---

18. On these scenes in the gospels and their authenticity, see Hagner, "Jesus and the Synoptic Sabbath Controversies," 251–92.

Jewish believers; rather, it is relativized and placed on a less central level than either the ethical thrust of the law or its role in moving us to the promise of kingdom and Messiah.

18.2 THE LAW IN THE BOOK OF ACTS

The law in Acts initially appears in Acts 3, although it may well be in the shadows in Acts 2. In Acts 2, the day of Pentecost takes place on the day on which, according to Jewish tradition, the law was given to Moses. Luke says nothing explicitly about this connection, but it may well be one of those things that were so much a given nothing needed to be said.[19] If that is in play in Acts 2, then we have another scene that shows the overshadowing of the law by promise through the christological lens of the coming of salvation.

The promise emphasis also appears in Acts 3 — a speech completely rooted in the Torah. Here the God of the patriarchs is the God of realized promise (Acts 3:13–14). In 3:22 Peter appeals directly to Moses in his promise in Deut 18:15 about the prophet like Moses. And the promise to Abraham of blessing is mentioned last of all (3:25–26). So once again the law points to the new era and the Messiah.

That the law is an issue between the new community and the Jewish leadership is clear in the Stephen episode in Acts 6–7. Stephen is charged with speaking blasphemy against Moses and against God (6:11), as well as speaking against the holy place and the law (6:13) and arguing that people should change the customs that Moses handed down (6:14). Stephen's speech in Acts 7 is an historical overview of God's action for Israel and her consistent disobedience to his revelation. Stephen does not engage the charges directly, but paints a picture that argues that if one understood the law, they would see the coming of promise and recognize that God cannot be contained in the temple.

Stephen starts with Abraham and mentions the covenant that led to circumcision (Acts 7:8). He ends with the nation in disobedience and engaged in idolatry. So Israel has consistently rejected God's messengers when they rejected Joseph and Moses, not to mention the prophets whom Israel persecuted or the golden calf they built in the desert. They have resisted all of the prophets and do not obey the law the angels gave (7:52–53). So their resistance now is not surprising. This is one of Luke's ways to show why there is rejection and that it is misguided. The nation has habitually not responded to the message of God.

In this way Stephen also shows his respect for the story of Israel and the law. He knows where it is supposed to take people in terms of promise, even if those who accuse him do not see it. In the speech Moses is a key figure, mentioned nine times (Acts 7:20, 22, 29, 31, 32, 35, 37, 40, 44). This comprises almost half the nineteen

---

19. Turner, "Spirit of Prophecy," 345–46, speaks of Acts 2 as echoing Jewish accounts of the Sinai theophany and notes the Targum of Ps 68:18 and Josephus, *Ant.* 3.5.1 [77–78], as relevant background.

references to Moses in Acts. The way the lawgiver was treated by Israel in the past and the pattern it reflects means the charges against Stephen lack credibility.

This brings us to the crucial text in Acts 10–11, where promise and the Gentiles meet. Here the distribution of the Spirit on uncircumcised people shocks the circumcised who witness his coming on the Gentiles (10:45). The event leads those of the circumcision not present at the event to question how Gentiles could avoid being circumcised since it is the sign of the covenant with Abraham and is in Moses' law (11:2). Peter's reply is simple. God has acted by giving the Gentiles the Spirit without first being circumcised. Although Peter does not say this directly here, this is his point (as 15:7–9 later argue). The Spirit was given to Gentile hearts that God had already cleansed and sanctified. This act of God speaks to promise and how it trumps previous practice. So the leaders in Jerusalem rejoiced that the Gentiles had been given life.

The issue will come up again from some of the circumcised in Judea and among believers from the Pharisees in Acts 15:1 and 5. The reply will be the same. God did it and showed that blessing and the sign of the new era can come without circumcision. The decree that comes from the Jerusalem Council emerges out of a concern for sensitivity to the fact that Moses is proclaimed in every town since ancient times and is read each Sabbath (15:21).

The decree of Acts 15 and what drives it are much discussed. Is this the continuation of the law for Gentiles? This seems unlikely given what Luke has said about the law and Gentiles. The very principle that they need not keep the core sign of the Abrahamic covenant indicates this is not the point. If the law were in force, this stipulation would top the list of what should be kept. Neither is Lev 17–18 the key, as some claim.[20] What appears to be the case, if we keep all of Luke-Acts in mind, is a relational concern and sensitivity that mean one should be slow to do things that can cause the wrong kind of offense where a principle about salvation is not at stake. Thus, immorality, other practices tied to pollution with idols and blood, and strangled things, all of which might be part of pagan rituals, are to be avoided out of this relational concern. Though the roots of such sensitivity are in the law, it is not the law that is being kept but a concern that religious offense not be engendered in a way that can obscure the gospel message to Jews. Thus we have the mention of the reading of Moses in these communities.

The last two references about circumcision in Acts follow the meeting of Acts 15. In the first text, Paul takes Timothy, whose mother was Jewish, and circumcises him to prevent any issue from getting in the way of his mission (16:3). This is different than his refusal to circumcise Titus, noted in Gal 2:3, because Titus was a Gentile.[21] It shows an ethnic demarcation in practice that Luke is sensitive to note. It also shows how Paul applies a principle stated in 1 Cor 9:19. He is a Jew to the

---

20. For such a connection, see Seccombe, "New People of God," 366. But so correctly Stephen Wilson, *Luke and the Law*, 71–102, who in his full discussion of the three key views on this text shows the problems with seeing this as the point. The three views are Lev 17–18, a concern for pagan cults, and ethical rules. Wilson prefers

the last category but notes that the view would be easier if there were no mention of "strangled things" (πνικτός, *pniktos*). This term is very enigmatic as it is not in the Leviticus text or the Noahic laws, which some see in the background.

21. Wilson, *Luke and the Law*, 64–65.

Jews, when it comes to issues of practice, which means he shows respect for such practices at those times.

In the second text, James raises the Jewish charge against Paul that as ardent believers in the law, Paul was teaching Jews living among the Gentiles to abandon the law. The claim is that Paul specifically teaches them not to circumcise or to live according to Jewish customs (Acts 21:20–21). Note how the issue is ethnically driven. The issue of Gentile practice is not a concern; Jewish practice is in view here. Note also how James calls these "our" customs. James is a hero for Luke, giving the clinching speech in Acts 15. So any claim this idea is seen as negative by Luke ignores how James is seen in Acts. The issue is the practice of Jewish believers and showing sensitivity to the law for them, though not as a requirement of salvation. Paul accepts this proposal.

We have jumped ahead in the story, but the links between Acts 10–11, 15, 16, and 21 are important to see in sequence. They bring to the surface the ethnic concerns that are making this an issue in special contexts.

Back in Acts 13, the law and promise surface again alongside the one summary statement about the law in Acts in terms of being able to justify someone. In 13:15, the reading of the Law and the Prophets in the synagogue in Pisidian Antioch leads to an invitation for someone to speak, which Paul takes up. In his speech, he traces Israel's history step by step from Abraham to David. Then he leaps over a millennium to the realization of the promise in John the Baptist and Jesus. Here again, the Law and the Prophets point to the promise as their key idea. In the exposition that follows, Paul says that through Jesus forgiveness of sins is proclaimed, from which they could not be justified in the law of Moses (13:38). Luke could not be clearer here that the law is unable to justify anyone and that salvation is tied to Jesus. Here law and promise meet in the most explicit way in Acts. That this event frames what is said in Acts 15 and that decision is important as well.

After Acts 15 and the circumcision of Timothy in Acts 16, reference to the law appears again Acts 18. Here the dispute over Jewish law perplexes a Roman ruler, Gallio, who refuses to rule on such religious matters. The charge is that Paul is "persuading the people to worship God in ways contrary to the law" (18:13). Gallio's response is that "since it involves questions about words and names and your own law—settle the matter yourselves. I will not be a judge of such things" (18:15). This is Luke's view on how Rome sees this dispute; she has no need to get involved. It is a religious dispute among people debating practices from the Hebrew nation.

Later in Acts 18, Paul takes a vow (v. 18). It is not clear whether this is a Nazirite vow.[22] There is no mention of a sacrifice in Jerusalem tied to it, but Luke does not

---

22. Bock, *Acts*, 527–28. The two best options for what is taking place assume a Jewish background. (1) Plausibly, it may be a Nazirite vow (Num 6:1–21). Or (2) it may be a mere vow of thanksgiving for preservation as God promised in v. 10. If this vow were Nazirite, then Paul for the duration would abstain from alcohol and uncleanness, such as touching a corpse. In addition, he would need to complete this vow by offering a sacrifice in Jerusalem, assuming that he is following the law and tradition on this matter. It is also possible to cut one's hair before offering the sacrifice to denote the vow's end (*m. Naz.* 3.6; 5.4; Josephus, *J.W.* 2.15.1 [309–14], relates a vow made in Jerusalem). The absence of the mention of a sacrifice makes a thanksgiving vow likely. But Jewish pious practice is in view in either option.

tell us everything about Paul's itinerary. The very adoption of such a Jewish practice is significant. Paul is portrayed as a faithful, pious Jew.

In Acts 21, with James's request to Paul we meet a text where law and Moses are mentioned together four times ("law" three times: 21:20, 24, and 28; "Moses" once: 21:21). As already noted, the charge is that Paul teaches that Jews living among Gentiles should abandon their practice of the law. James argues that to show that this is wrong, Paul should accompany four men to the temple and support their vow. Again, what exactly is present is not clear. Is this the end of a thirty-day Nazirite vow, a ritual act tied to some type of uncleanness these men had, or is Paul simply supporting the completion of a vow these men had made?[23] It seems unlikely this is tied to Paul's vow in 18:18, since so much time has passed. In any of these options, this act will involve sacrifices, not tied to salvation but to worship. Respect for Jewish practice among the Jews is the point. When Paul is seized at the end of this event, some in the crowd shout, "This is the man who teaches everyone everywhere against our people and our law and this place" (21:28). Luke has done everything he can to show this charge is false.

When Paul defends himself in Acts 22, he declares his innocence. He notes that he grew up under the law (22:3) and persecuted the Way (22:4). A devout observer of the law, Ananias, well spoken of by all Jews, testified to him and helped him regain his sight (22:12–13). Again, the pious Jew receives Paul.

In Acts 23, we see Paul in an emotional and awkward dispute with the high priest. He insults the high priest, as Paul calls him a "whitewashed wall" (23:3). In effect, Paul is saying the high priest is violating the law in having commanded some to strike Paul. In reply, Paul says God will strike the high priest. When confronted Paul steps back from this remark, based on a challenge from the law (23:4–5). Efforts to argue that Paul is being ironic here do not persuade. Here his temper temporarily gets the best of him and the reminder of the law and of respect for the high priest causes him to renew a relational sensitivity to the situation. There is nothing about keeping the letter of the law in this reaction other than to show an appropriate respect as others who suffer in Acts do.

In Acts 24, Paul's defense continues with his note that he is on trial for simply worshiping "the God of our ancestors" and believing "everything that is in accordance with the Law and that is written in the Prophets" (24:14). Paul identifies with Israel's hope here, including resurrection to judgment and accountability (cf. 14:15). Paul's allusion to judgment is no accident. In the end, he is faithful to God. So here also the law is seen in terms of promise.

Another protestation of innocence comes in Acts 25, when Paul notes that when he was arrested, he was not sinning against the Jewish law, the temple, or Caesar (25:8). Similar in emphasis are remarks in Acts 26, when he declares that he is simply testifying to both great and small, saying nothing but what the Prophets and Moses said would happen (26:22). This message was that the Messiah would suffer and

---

23. Bock, *Acts*, 581–82, discusses the options.

rise from the dead. His obedience to the call meant that Paul proclaimed light to his people and the Gentiles (26:23). This summary is much like Luke 24:43–47. It is yet another christological appeal to the law and promise that saturates Luke-Acts.

The final scene using the law appears together with the term kingdom and is like the previous use in Acts 26, pointing to law as it relates to promise. In 28:23, Paul testifies to the kingdom of God, trying to convince his Jewish audience about Jesus from both the Law and the Prophets. A christological promise note closes the reference to the issue of the law, fitting the key emphasis for the topic in Luke-Acts.

18.3 CONCLUSION

The complex overlap between Israel and the church is seen in Luke's handling of the law. Those of Jewish background in the new community still identify with their Jewish roots, speaking of our God, our customs, our law, and our hope. Key to appreciating the law is knowing that in the new era, the promise and hope of the law come to fruition. Yet the law still teaches ethically and relationally. It calls for justice and love. Yet some practices of the law are not to be undertaken, as they were in the past. So challenges to Sabbath practice, the washing of hands, and diet are seen. Salvation is not present in the law. That comes through faith in Jesus.

However, sensitivity means that Jewish believers are free to practice the law. Gentiles should avoid acts that offend Jews because of their association with idolatry or immorality. Luke shows respect for the law among Jewish believers and total freedom from its requirements for Gentiles. The law does not justify, but it can teach and instruct. So he calls on those who belong to the community to show it some respect, provided they do not exalt it to a place where its goal in promise is lost.

Chapter 19

ECCLESIOLOGY IN LUKE-ACTS

BIBLIOGRAPHY

Bock, Darrell L. "A Theology of Luke-Acts." Pp. 140–62 in *A Biblical Theology of the New Testament*. Ed. Roy B. Zuck and Darrell L. Bock. Chicago: Moody Press, 1994. **Cassidy, Richard J.** "Paul's Proclamation of *Lord* Jesus as a Chained Prisoner in Rome: Luke's Ending Is His Beginning." Pp. 142–53 in *Luke-Acts and Empire: Essays in Honor of Robert L. Brawley*. Ed. David Rhoads, David Esterline, and Jae Won Lee. Eugene, OR: Pickwick, 2011. **Clarke, Andrew C.** "The Role of the Apostles." Pp. 169–90 in *Witness to the Gospel: The Theology of Acts*. Ed. I. Howard Marshall and David Peterson. Grand Rapids: Eerdmans, 1998. **Fuller, Michael E.** *The Restoration of Israel: Israel's Regathering and the Fate of the Nations in Early Jewish Literature and Luke-Acts*. BZNW. Berlin: De Gruyter, 2006. **Jervell, Jacob.** *Luke and the People of God*. Minneapolis: Augsburg, 1972. **Wilson, Stephen G.** *The Gentiles and the Gentile Mission in Luke-Acts*. SNTSMS. Cambridge: Cambridge University Press, 1973.

A look at Lucan ecclesiology requires an examination of the relationship between Israel and the church. After this study, there will be a survey of the major ecclesiological characters in Luke-Acts. Such an inquiry is necessary because Luke often reveals his theology through the examples of the individuals he discusses. He lets actions speak in place of claims. We have already looked at the activities and structure of the church in the chapter on the church in Luke-Acts,[1] so now we concentrate on the church's identity in relationship to Israel and the shining examples that come from that new community.

19.1 THE CHURCH: OLD AND NEW

A consideration of Israel's relationship to the church requires defining the church. Then we will consider the role of the apostles and what is actually said to Gentiles and to Israel about God's promise.

The church in Luke's thinking relates to some things old and new. It is tied to old things because it shares in promises made in the Hebrew Scripture and offers

---

1. See ch. 14.

that old promise to the world. It is tied to things new because God is now working through an entirely new structure. The apostles proclaimed in the synagogues that Jesus is the fulfillment of the promise of the Hebrew Scripture, including the law, so any Jew responding to promise and believing in the law should come to Jesus. The apostles' contention was that the natural end of Judaism is to be found in Jesus.

The apostles, early in Acts, do not appear to see themselves as called to be separate from Israel. They go to the temple and meet there (Acts 3:1–10; 4:1–2; 5:12). Their practices are sensitive to Jewish concerns (15:1–35; 21:17–26). Later in Acts, Paul preaches in the synagogues to Jews everywhere he goes (13:14–48; 28:17). Even when Paul turns his back on the Jews to go to the Gentiles, he still goes to the synagogue in the subsequent cities to which he travels or to the temple in Jerusalem (13:46–14:1; 18:6 with 21:26; 28:28, 30). The point of continuity is the message of promise-fulfillment, whose roots reach back into the Hebrew Scripture and the nation of promise (Luke 24:44–49; Acts 3:13–26; 10:42–43; 13:23–39). The Jews who hear Paul are being told that if they follow through on their commitment to God, they will embrace the message of inaugurated promise and become members of the new community.

19.2 THE CHURCH BECOMES DISTINCT

However, events force the church to become distinct because of the depth of Jewish rejection. As a result, the church emerges as an independent community outside the synagogue. In Luke's view, Christians do not leave the synagogues; they are forced out. Acts outlines this development and shows that Christians do not turn their backs on Israel; rather, the synagogue has failed to embrace the promise given to the Jewish fathers. In fact, even after being rejected, the new community still engages Jews in the hope that they might respond. These preachers even experience and accept intense persecution in the process. Such argumentation about responding to the promise is especially central to Peter's and to Paul's apologetic in their speeches (Acts 2:42–47; 4:23–37; 13:1–3; 20:17; 23:6; 24:14–16; 25:8; 26:6–8, 22–23).

Luke sees the new community as something novel. This is why in Acts 11:15 Peter can refer to the events in Acts 2:1–4 as "the beginning" (ἐν ἀρχῇ, *en archē*). Now in Lucan terms, it is the beginning of the realization of promise, as Peter's remarks relate to the first distribution of the Spirit (2:14–36), an act that recurs for Gentiles in Acts 10. So what emerges is that Luke sees the church having its origin in the coming of the Holy Spirit, the key marker of the arrival of the new era in terms of its benefits for those who respond. Acts 11:15–18 makes the bestowal of the Spirit the starting point for this new era and this new group of faithful people.

This beginning has to come after Jesus' work on the cross with its provision of forgiveness, which sanctifies people and allows the Spirit to enter a cleansed vessel (15:9). Luke explains how this group has become distinct from Judaism and yet has the right to proclaim promises that used to be the unique property of the synagogues. God is present in this new community. The additional point about this new people in Acts 11 is that God has included Gentiles in this circle of blessing through direct intervention (vv. 11–18). The events of the founding of the church in Acts 2 have a parallel in the events at Cornelius's house in 10:1–11:18, which thus shows beyond dispute that God has acted to include the Gentiles.

Such inclusion was suggested in remarks earlier in Acts (i.e., before ch. 10), even though their full force was not realized at the time by the speakers. The promise was for Israel and also for "all who are far off" (πᾶσιν τοῖς εἰς μακράν, *pasin tois eis makran*; Acts 2:39; cf. Eph 2:11–17). In fact, it is for "all the families of the earth" (πᾶσαι αἱ πατριαὶ τῆς γῆς, *pasai hai patriai tēs gēs*; Acts 3:25 NASB). Even Jesus spoke of the teaching being rooted in Moses, the Prophets, and Psalms, which taught that the message of repentance would go to all nations (Luke 24:47). In this sense, there is continuity between the new community and the Hebrew Scripture, yet there is discontinuity as well.

God had to press the point to make discontinuity clear and to show that Gentiles were to be included. He had to use a vision to show Peter that no man is unclean and that the church is to show no partiality (Acts 10:28, 34). All are welcome and have access to the Spirit, whether Jew or Gentile (10:35, 47; 11:18). But Gentiles do not have to become Jews first and then Christians (15:1–29). The new institution, having a beginning, does not require a total link to the old era other than to share in the promise to which it always looked. This promise stands inaugurated, but it is not completed. God still has work to do.

19.3 A New Thing: The Church As a Spirit-Indwelt Community

In the section on the bestowal of the Holy Spirit, the Spirit's provision was seen to be central in Luke's theology.[2] The Spirit's coming is clearly central to the church. John the Baptist alluded to it (Luke 3:15–18), and Jesus told the disciples to wait for it (24:49). The event is described in Acts 2:1–4 and explained later by Peter in vv. 17–21, where he cites Joel 2:28–32. Here is a sign of the inauguration of the last days. The Spirit's bestowal is the essence of the new covenant promise. In his exposition, Peter makes clear that the events of Acts 2 initially fulfill Joel. Peter uses a strong fulfillment formula to introduce the citation, saying of the present event that "this is what was spoken" (τοῦτό ἐστιν τὸ εἰρημένον, *touto estin to eirēmenon*; v. 16) by God through Joel long ago. This fulfillment formula would be familiar to Peter's Jewish audience as indicating fulfillment, as its use at Qumran to indicate fulfillment shows (several places in 1QHab).

When Peter cites Joel, he also adds within the citation an additional reference to prophesying (Acts 2:18c) to highlight the connection to what is occurring and to

---

2. See ch. 9.

describe what has just resulted from the pouring out of the Spirit. In 2:18, the verb for pouring out, ἐκχεῶ (*ekcheō*), is used again in 2:33 with ἐξέχεεν (*execheen*), thus linking the citation's fulfillment to the event at Pentecost. Peter is using the Jewish link-word hermeneutical method of *gezerah shewa*, where text and event or a set of texts are linked by using the same word to show the connection. Because Jesus has ascended, the promised Holy Spirit has been poured out. This promise of God has now come for those near and those far off (vv. 30–33, 38–39).

The centrality of the Spirit's bestowal is also indicated in two other outpourings: 10:45 ("the gift of the Holy Spirit had been poured out [ἐκκέχυται, *ekkechytai*]," the same verb as Acts 2) and 19:6 ("the Holy Spirit came on them"). The repetition of the event shows its importance to Luke.

Thus, the essence of the church is that she is a Spirit-indwelt community. This indwelling is not limited to her leaders and is not something that comes and goes. Instead, it includes the entire membership and continues permanently, just as Joel said the Spirit would do "in the last days" (Acts 2:17). The indwelling described here is new and unprecedented in that Peter says it is now taking place, though it was anticipated in Joel.

The church is something new and something old. It is new because of its quality and scope, and old in that God said the Spirit would come and relate the new era's gifts and blessings of forgiveness to existing covenants and promises tied to the hope of the Messiah and his resurrection. When significant Jewish rejection follows, the new community begins to have its own structure and identity, although Jesus' selecting of the Twelve shows he anticipated all of this. The Twelve have a key leadership role in the new community, will judge the tribes of Israel one day, and mostly are tied to the land in their work within Acts.[3]

19.4 THE CHURCH AND JESUS' RULE

One other feature makes the church new. The Spirit's indwelling comes because of Jesus' rule "*in absentia*," which means that the Messiah is ruling now from God's side in heaven, not on earth from a national throne. A future, earthly rule is not excluded by this new dimension, as Acts 3:19–21 shows. Peter's remark about "times of refreshing" (καιροὶ ἀναψύξεως, *kairoi anapsyxeōs*) of all that the OT prophets promised shows that the development of OT promise in Jesus' ministry does not cancel out what had been promised earlier. The program of promise as presented, explained, and expanded by Jesus and the apostles complements earlier Hebrew Scripture revelation and anticipates the decisive rule of Christ on earth (what Rev 20 defines as the millennium). This future period will bring in the final phases of the

---

3. Fuller, *Restoration of Israel*, 239–67, focuses on the Twelve and their role in Luke's portrait of regathering Israel from her exile. He argues a key turning point is when the Spirit is provided in Acts 2 when those who follow return from the "wilderness" of exile (p. 263). This fits what was said about the Spirit and the new era in the discussion on the Spirit.

promise's realization that Luke alludes to in Acts 3:21, a realization that eventually will culminate in the new heavens and new earth.

So the church age represents a sneak preview of Christ's coming earthly rule. The transforming presence of God's Spirit in his people shows that God is active in fulfilling his promise to vanquish the enemies of God's people, as he enables people to serve him in holiness, gives them life, and spares them from the judgment to come (Luke 1:74–75, 78–79; 3:7–18; 11:14–23; Acts 2:30–39). The Spirit-indwelt community pictures to some degree, but not fully, what the greater kingdom and rule of Christ will be like when Jesus returns to earth to bring all righteousness. However, only in this coming return will Jesus' foes and the enemies of the people of God be totally vanquished, as the restoration of all things comes and Israel's promises are fully realized (Acts 3:21).

So Luke sees two phases of rule, of which the church is the first. The two periods, though distinct, are related. The church, though it lives in an era of fulfillment, also awaits the consummation of God's promises. For Luke, the uniqueness of the church is not so much that she is Spirit-indwelt, for that was anticipated by the new covenant. Rather, she is Spirit-indwelt *in a way that includes Gentiles* (cf. Eph 3:4–6; Col 1:24–29), something the Abrahamic promise anticipated (Gen 12:3) but did not spell out in detail. This "Spirit in the Gentile" work caught Jesus' disciples by surprise when it came in Acts 10:45. It was a new detail. In this new institution, the church, the Mediator Jesus Christ rules from heaven through the work of his Spirit to bring righteousness to people on earth. Though Jesus is not directly manifest on earth in this period, he is active and dispenses blessings to his children. The next phase of God's rule will differ because the Mediator will be present on earth and his rule will be comprehensive, including the redemption of all earth's social institutions and national entities. In this way, Luke periodizes his eschatology with some of it being already and the rest being not yet here.

It is interesting to note that in Acts the term for church (ἐκκλησία, *ekklēsia*), when it refers to this new community, appears almost always in narrative notes and summaries (Acts 8:1, 3; 9:31; 11:22, 26; 12:1, 5; 13:1; 14:23, 27; 15:3–4, 22, 41; 16:5; 18:22; 19:32, 39, 41; 20:17). The one exception comes in Paul's remark to the Ephesian elders (20:28). The new community's identity emerges slowly as her distinctness becomes clearer through the movement of events. Even the name "Christians," as we saw,[4] comes after the church has spread to Antioch (11:26), and another frequent term refers to her as a "sect" (αἱρέσεως, *haireseōs*) of the Nazareans (24:5; the term "sect" was also used for groupings within Israel, e.g., 5:17; 15:5; 26:5, so it is not necessarily negative). It simply notes that a distinct group is emerging. Even outsiders have trouble noting that the distinction between Jew and Christian is becoming a chasm (23:27–29). Acts notes the growing division with sensitivity and tries to explain what factors have created it.

---

4. See ch. 14.

19.5 THE APOSTLES AND THE CHURCH

The importance of the present church age is underscored by various authenticating signs, as discussed in the section on soteriology.[5] Here we consider the twofold role of the apostles as overseers and witnesses to the formation of this new entity.[6] The function of overseeing is evident in the passages that refer to the presence of the apostles at new phases of the community's expansion. Acts 8:14–25 records Peter's and John's approval of Philip's work in Samaria. Paul contacts the apostles after receiving his call from Jesus (9:26–27). Peter carries the gospel to Gentiles (10:23–48). The apostles send Barnabas to Antioch (11:22). The Jerusalem Council is mainly an apostolic gathering, though others (including James, Paul, and Barnabas) are involved (15:1–35). Paul reports to James and the elders of Jerusalem about his Gentile mission (21:17–19). From the beginning, the church has structure, authority, and accountability. In Acts this authority is mostly in the hands of the apostles.

Luke 22:29–30 also shows a distinct feature about the apostles' role. Here Jesus offers the Eleven kingdom authority, with the opportunity to sit at his banquet table and additionally to "sit on thrones, judging the twelve tribes of Israel." This passage looks ultimately to the coming consummation, when Messiah will reign on the earth. The seat at the banquet anticipates a kingdom celebration after Jesus' victorious return. Though the apostles have authority in the early church, they will also have authority in the kingdom to come.[7] Their authority then will expand and extend over all Israel. This expanded exercise of authority is future because such a banquet or such "apostolic rule" over Israel's twelve tribes is not seen in Acts. No allusion to a current apostolic rule over Israel appears there. The apostles have oversight over the church, but one day, interestingly, they will help rule Israel. Here is their role as forming a nucleus of restored Israel, and it serves also as a bridge into the new community that connects the new community to the promise and people of old.[8]

The apostles are qualified to exercise leadership over the church because they have been appointed to be witnesses (μάρτυς, *martys*) to Jesus. Luke 24:48 anticipated this development, and Acts 1:8 formalizes this call to be witnesses. The qualifications for this special function include being personal acquaintances with Jesus and his ministry and being witnesses to his resurrection (Acts 1:21–22). References to witnesses abound as they testify to various events in Jesus' life, including his resurrection (2:32; 3:15; 13:31); his death, resurrection, ascension (5:32); and his ministry, crucifixion, and resurrection (10:39).

---

5. See ch. 11.

6. Clarke, "Role of the Apostles," 169–90. Their roles include forming a nucleus of a restored Israel, being authoritative teachers and serving as missionaries to Israel. Miracles accompany them. They commission and confirm expansion of the promise, and give key speeches to explain what is taking place.

7. Though one could speak of the millennium here canonically, Luke does not use the term here, so I prefer in a biblical theology to speak simply of the kingdom to come.

8. In noting these roles, there is no indication of any apostolic succession. The role of the Twelve is unique and is tied to their eyewitness role and direct involvement with Jesus.

Not all witnesses are apostles in Acts, though most are. Though Paul was a witness (22:15; 26:16), his "apostolic" role is a much-discussed issue in Acts.[9] Stephen also receives the title of "witness" and he clearly is not an apostle (22:20). Despite these minor exceptions, the church expands under the leadership of the apostles, who have oversight over the church. As reliable witnesses of what they had seen firsthand, they proclaim the message about Jesus. They take the message to a broader audience and form a new community by God's direct intervention.

19.6 ISRAEL AND THE CHURCH

In the early chapters of Acts, the Jews' reception of the gospel message is strong and troubles the Jewish leaders. But later, Jewish reaction and persecution surface so that the church is scattered. In some locales the message is taken out of the synagogue and offered directly to Gentiles, who respond favorably (Acts 13:46; 18:6; 28:28). This pattern of mixed Jewish reception, persecution, and turning to the Gentiles is especially common in Paul's ministry. The apostles begin in the synagogues because they believe the message of Christ is for those in Israel.[10] Local churches develop by necessity, the necessity of survival in the face of rejection. These realities cause Luke to speak repeatedly in Acts of the church's messengers turning to the Gentiles and warning Israel. These themes often appear side by side, as we noted in earlier chapters of this book,[11] and they dominate the last third of the book of Acts. They show how the church is not Israel, at a cultural structural level, and how that distinction becomes a reality historically.

From the start God's plan is to include Gentiles. Luke 2:32 and 3:6 appeal to Isaiah to make the point that God has sent Jesus to bless Gentiles too. First, the appeal to Isa 42:6 means that Jesus will be a light to the Gentiles. This servant-light image pictures the inclusion of Gentiles in the blessing of the light (cf. Luke 1:78–79). The quotation of Isa 40:5 in Luke 3:6 shows that God's salvation will be available to all. John the Baptist's ministry will prepare the way for God's coming in Jesus so that all people might have the opportunity to come to God.

Illustrations of this universally available salvation abound. The centurion is commended for having a faith greater than anything seen in Israel (Luke 7:9). Gentiles are pictured as parading to the banquet table, even as some of those invited first (i.e., many Jews) miss out (14:16–24). In a particularly significant parable overviewing God's plan, the vineyard of promise and blessing is described as taken from Israel and given to others (20:9–18). The fact that the current period is called "the times of the Gentiles" (21:24) also points to God's present focus on the Gentiles.

Two facts show that Israel has a future as well. Jesus' eschatological discourse in Luke 21:5–36, with its day of the Lord imagery, points to Israel's future vindication,

---

9. I will discuss this when I discuss Paul specifically later in this chapter.

10. This is "first to the Jew," as we also see in Rom 1:16–17.

11. See esp. chs. 12–13.

since that is what the day is all about. Also Peter's speech recorded in Acts 3:12–26, which refers to the future fulfillment and completion of all the promises from the holy prophets (v. 21), indicates that she is only temporarily set aside. But the current focus on Gentiles also helps show that a distinction exists between Israel and the church.

The apostles are slow, however, in turning to the Gentiles, though Jesus commanded the disciples to preach forgiveness of sins to all the nations starting from Jerusalem (Luke 24:47). What the disciples seem to understand by this is a call to preach the message in every nation to Jews of the diaspora. However, that is not what Jesus meant. So God seizes the initiative in Acts 10. Through a vision to Peter, God shows that Gentiles are intended.

This vision is important because it is Luke's (and God's) answer to the Jewish charge that what the church offers is not really God's promise, since that promise is for Israel. God's offer of salvation and of a share of his promise to Gentiles needs explaining, because some Jewish Christians are nervous about opening the gospel to Gentiles without making them respond to the law and because many Jews have rejected the Christian claims outright. Acts 15 shows the concern of Jewish Christians, while the persecution of the church in Acts comes mainly from Jewish sources. At the same time, Gentiles may have been disturbed too. Having entered into God's blessings, they see the violent response of Jews to something that was originally for Jews. That reaction may have suggested that something foreign is emerging in the culture. Some Gentile believers may have concluded they are in the wrong place at the wrong time, or at least, in the wrong way. Or they may have thought Jesus is not for them, or that they need to heed the law. Luke's answer to this problem is short and simple. God makes disciples go to the Gentiles. It is in the plan all along.

As a result, Gentiles, starting in Acts 10, become more and more the center of evangelistic success. Four times Luke highlights Paul's turning to Gentiles (Acts 13:46–49; 14:27; 18:3–11; 28:25–29). Sometimes Jewish unbelief precedes this turn in Paul's ministry, but the call to the Gentiles is a part of the church's mission regardless of Jewish response. Nevertheless, the juxtaposition of Jewish rejection and Gentile reception recalls an element in Pauline theology, the turning to Gentiles as a means of making Israel react (Rom 11:11–14).

Warnings to Israel are also frequently given. John the Baptist speaks of the ax at the root of the tree, warning that having the right racial ancestry is not enough (Luke 3:7–9). In bitter pronouncements of woe against the Jewish leaders Jesus tells them they are not on the path to life and are preventing others from getting there (11:37–52). In the parable of the barren fig tree Jesus threatens to cut down the tree of Israel, which has not borne fruit (13:6–9). The judgment is delayed, but its potential reality still is present.

That threat is carried out later. The first hint is Jesus' declaration that Israel's house is desolate (Luke 13:35). This language recalls the judgment of the exile stated in Jer 22:5 (cf. Jer 12:7). When Israel rejects God's way and lives under sin, the prospect of covenant curse—God's judgment—can only follow. However, this does not mean that Israel is permanently rejected, just as the exile was not permanent. But those in the period of judgment will have no hope unless they respond to the Lord. The nation's history of rejection of the Lord is evidenced by the fact that they had slain prophets and God's messengers even before Jesus came to them (Luke 13:31–33).

This critique of the nation's habitually rejecting God's messengers is common in Luke and recalls the message of the prophets against the nation. This historical critique of the nation means that Luke shared the "deuteronomistic perspective" of Israel's history, because the appeal for judgment is based on the covenant curse that will come on the nation for unfaithfulness, as promised in Deut 28–32. The OT declared the possibility of exile for the nation if it did not respond to God's call about exercising justice (Jer 22:5–6).[12]

Jesus does not relish such judgment. He weeps over Jerusalem because she has not recognized that in Jesus, God is coming to her in a "visitation" (Luke 19:41–44, v. 44 NASB: τῆς ἐπισκοπῆς σου, tēs episkopēs sou). Similarly, as he journeys to the cross, Jesus warns the daughters of Jerusalem to weep and mourn because judgment is coming on the nation (23:27–31). This passage, unique to Luke, alludes to several OT passages in painting the horror of judgment in terms that recall the day of the Lord (Isa 54:1; Jer 19:9, 41, 43; Hos 10:8).

The image is built around the contrast between green wood (Jesus) and dead wood (the nation). If God will not spare Jesus, how much more will the impenitent nation not be spared when divine judgment comes? In Luke 23:31, the use of "they" (ESV) is an oblique third-person plural reference to God (cf. 12:20). The concept of wood consumed in judgment also occurs in Isa 10:16–19 and Ezek 20:47 [21:3 MT]. Although Luke does not have the concept of burning found in these two references, it seems implied in the figure. This is Jesus' last lament for the nation in Luke's gospel. It is easier to burn dry wood than lush, moisture-filled green wood. Jesus presents a lesser-to-greater argument: if this is what happens to a living tree, what might happen (a deliberative subjunctive) to a dead one? The allusions refer to the approaching fall of Jerusalem in AD 70. The vineyard, given to others, fits this theme as well (20:9–18).

Luke makes the same point in Acts. In Acts 3:23, Peter spoke of the curse of being "cut off," citing Lev 23:29. Failure to heed the apostles and prophets results in judgment. Stephen's dying words relate how the nation has always resisted God and, as a result, brought judgment on herself (Acts 7:51–53). Stephen's remarks recall Jesus' stinging rebuke in Luke 13:31–33.

Too much, however, should not be made of this emphasis that the nation is cut off. Throughout Acts, the apostles always go to the Jews first and then to the Gentiles (Rom 1:16). The offer to enter into participation in the promise is always made

---

12. Tiede, *Prophecy and History in Luke-Acts*, 259.

to the nation Israel, despite her rejection of Christ. Nowhere is that offer withdrawn in Acts. Opportunity to receive the message still exists. However, the pattern of response is clear. Usually the offer is rejected, though others respond (2:41, 47; 4:4; 5:14; 6:7). Those who respond picture a faithful remnant in the nation who clings to the nation's hope. In fact, it can be argued that this Jewish remnant is a point of connection between the promise of the old era and the realization of the new, since this group most clearly has moved from one period into the other. They represent those Jews who have clearly seen what God is doing and so have responded to the gospel message.

So the new community sees herself as called to obey God by continuing to preach the message of Jesus to the people of the Jewish nation, even in the face of the leadership's opposition. In fact, much of Acts 3–5 shows that God has given an endorsement to those being persecuted for preaching Jesus. Peter notes that the new community will obey God, not humans (4:19). Rabbi Gamaliel notes that if this movement is of God, the Sanhedrin will not be able to stop it, while if it is not, the movement will die out on its own (5:38–39). The new community's growth and survival in the narrative form Luke's answer to these alternatives. Even while the apostles are in prison, God directs them through the angel to take the message to the people of Israel in the temple (5:19–20). The church considers it an honor to be able to share the message and asks for boldness to do the job (4:23–30; 5:41).

However, since most Jews do not respond, the messengers of the gospel turn to others. In Acts 13:41–45, Paul offers a warning to Jews. Jewish jealousy and persecution will not stop the message, but it does mean danger for those who reject it. Paul and Barnabas shake the dust from their feet (v. 51), a sign of judgment (cf. Luke 10:11–15). Shaking the dust from one's feet was a symbolic act against one's opponents (Mark 6:11 = Luke 9:5; Luke 10:10–11 = Matt 10:14). This custom is a way of signaling that responsibility for an action is with the people or town.[13] It portrays leaving defilement behind and moving on. In other words, no trace of their presence is left, even on their feet. Jesus himself commanded this response in Luke 9:5. Other texts where Paul notes the judgment for rejection are Acts 18:6 and 28:25–27.

Later Paul leaves the synagogue in Corinth to continue his evangelistic work (Acts 18:5–11). In 28:25–28, Paul turns again to the Gentiles, explaining to the nation his move by using the language of Isa 6:9–10 to describe the dull hearts of many (or even of most) in the nation. Though not a rejection of the nation or of Jewish mission, Paul's remark does warn of severe obduracy and thus of possible judgment that the nation faces, like that during the period of the prophets.

Luke is saying to his readers that the gospel might not be going to Israel as much as it seems it might, but that is not the church's fault or intention. Such a failure has not halted God's plan, nor does such failure represent a departure from his plan. The Gentiles are also included. They are responding. God is building a new institution,

---

13. Str-B, 1:571.

the church, which now proclaims the promise and in which both believing Jews and Gentiles are blessed (Eph 2:11–22). The new community has offered the promise to Israel. That new community had taught and preached in her synagogues, but the church has met mostly with persecution and expulsion.

God has presented his message to Israel through Jesus and his commissioned witnesses, but the nation, especially as represented in her leadership, has rejected it. Since Israel is failing to embrace the divine message, God has left the nation, leaving her house "desolate" (Luke 13:35). In its place has come a new house, the church, in which God's Spirit indwells all who come to seek refuge in salvation through Christ. Jew and Gentile alike share in God's benefits. The temple is no longer a place to go see the Shekinah. Rather, the Shekinah has come to indwell believers. God is not through with Israel; he has just set her aside for a time. In her stead has come a new entity whose origin is traced in the momentous events recorded in Acts 2. The Holy Spirit, once promised to Israel, still came, despite the nation's refusal. That promise resides in the church until Jesus returns to set all things straight again and bring Israel back into the fold (3:19–21).

19.7 KEY PERSONALITIES IN THE EARLY CHURCH

19.7.1 Peter

Undoubtedly, the key disciple in Luke's writings is Peter. He is the representative disciple, as well as the leading apostle. A key incident early in Jesus' ministry occurs in Peter's boat (Luke 5:1–11). The miraculous catch of fish causes him to confess his sinfulness and to ask Jesus to depart, since he considers Jesus too holy to be in their presence. But Jesus communicates reception, mentioning that the fish caught in the net are nothing compared to the people Peter and others like him will catch for God. They will become fishers of people. The recognition of sin's presence and its consequent respect for holiness enables one to serve. Peter represents confessing disciples who enter humbly into service for God and are accepted by his grace. Jesus takes the faith and humble attitude exhibited in Peter and turns it into a call to serve. Peter's attitude reflects an openness that allows Jesus to transform the sinner.

Peter's responsiveness and humble approach to Jesus' word reflect exemplary attitudes about how people should respond to God's message. In other words, Peter reflects the essence of faith that operates with humility at its core. Luke does not so much emphasize responsiveness to personal sin as stress that one should change one's mind about Jesus and thus become humbly obedient to him. Jesus can transform the sinner's life and vocation, as the disciple comes to serve God.[14] Joel Green observes that this is Luke's first use of the term "sinner."[15] This is no accident. The

---

14. Bock, *Luke 1:1–9:50*, 459–60.

15. Green, *Gospel of Luke*, 233–34. He goes on to note that Jesus brings "good news to the unworthy."

scene shows what Jesus can do for a sinner who knows he is in the presence of God and his power.

Another indication of Peter's leading position is his confession of Jesus as the Messiah (Luke 9:18–20). Here Peter typifies the follower who appreciates who Jesus is.

In another incident, Peter speaks for the disciples by raising a question about the meaning of a parable (Luke 12:41). He begins to show the qualities that will lead him to become a key spokesperson for the Twelve and the new movement. In this same vein, Peter recognizes the difficulty in what Jesus has asked a rich man to do, in telling him to sell all and follow him (Luke 18:22); so Peter probingly affirms that the disciples have done that very thing (18:28). Responding positively, Jesus speaks of the rewards such a response brings both now and in the age to come (v. 30). Jesus' remark showed that the "giving all" language of the call to the rich man does not mean that the absolute standard is impossible to attain since the disciples have done it. As Jesus said, "What is impossible with man is possible with God" (18:27). The disciples, despite their many moments of failure and lack of faith, have a fundamental association with and commitment to Jesus that God recognizes. Peter typifies all of this and becomes the spokesperson for the responsive follower.

Another incident showing that failure does not mean disqualification is Peter's denial of Jesus (Luke 22:31–34, 54–62). Here is an example of a disciple in severe failure who regrets his fall and is enabled by God to continue to serve. This reaction is in contrast to Judas. Peter has a failure of nerve, while Judas has a failure of the heart. Peter has learned that assuming one will always remain faithful can lead to spiritual failure. One must recognize the strength of sin and the necessity of dependence for the disciple.

Peter is a representative disciple. He learns about his sin. He confesses Christ. He makes fundamental commitments to Jesus in the midst of a world with other values. He sometimes fails. But in it all he recognizes that Jesus is the answer. There is nowhere else to turn. He learns to rely on the Jesus he has confessed as the Messiah. In this focus, Peter is exemplary.

Peter also is the leading apostle. He preaches to the unsaved, exercises apostolic oversight among believers, and witnesses to Jesus. He is the key leader in many early church events, including the choosing of a replacement for Judas (Acts 1:15–22), explaining Pentecost (2:14–40), speaking of a healing (3:12–4:12), or exercising judgment against members of the community (5:1–11). He challenges the religious authorities, who try to prevent Peter and others from speaking about Jesus (5:29–32). He takes the gospel to the Gentiles and defends this expansion before Jewish believers (10:1–11:18). Peter models carrying out God's will boldly and bearing God's message powerfully.

19.7.2 Stephen

Stephen is a key transition figure whose ministry is told briefly (Acts 6:8–7:60). He is the first Hellenistic Christian whose words are recorded in Acts. He has less patience for the veneration of the temple than perhaps did his Jewish Christian colleagues, but his understanding of Israel's history parallels that of Jesus in terms of seeing the nation as often rejecting God's messengers (Luke 11:47–52; Acts 6:9–12). Stephen knows that God cannot be confined to a single location, something the prophets also knew (Isa 66:1). In Acts 7, Stephen outlines Israel's history of rejection of God's appointed messengers, an act ironically repeated by the nation when the people stone Stephen.

In Acts 6, Stephen is a part of a group that raises questions about the church's treatment of widows. He then becomes part of the solution to the problem as he serves the widows in the church. His bold preaching and selfless service are models to the church of an active member filled with God's Spirit (Acts 6:3, 5; 7:55), wisdom (6:3), faith (v. 5), and grace and power (v. 8). His martyrdom shows the length to which a disciple should be prepared to go in proclaiming Jesus. Jesus' standing to greet him at his death (7:55–56) shows heaven's welcome of such a saint, where Jesus as the reigning Son of Man receives him. The idea that the Son of Man functions as judge is a key point of the imagery (Luke 12:8).[16] Jesus appears as an advocate for Stephen, a vindicator of his claims.[17] This also implies that the Jewish judgment against Stephen will serve to leave the audience subject to the judgment of God and the Son of Man. Stephen models the faithful disciple who witnesses to Jesus even to the point of martyrdom.

19.7.3 Philip

Another Hellenist prepared to share Christ is Philip. An active witness for Christ in Samaria (Acts 8:5–13), he explains Christ from Isa 53:7–8 to the Ethiopian eunuch (vv. 26–40). The cameo descriptions of figures like Stephen and Philip indicate what God can do with people among the multitudes in the new community. Such people grow into maturity and benefit the church through active service, including evangelism.

19.7.4 Barnabas

Barnabas is the exemplary encourager, witness, and servant. Nothing he does is for himself. He freely gives of his resources to the church (Acts 4:36–37) and thus provides an example of how one with material means can serve the church. He confirms Paul to the disciples, when some doubt Paul's sincerity (9:26–27). He was an encourager and teacher at Antioch (11:22–30). He engages in a missionary work with Paul (13:1–15:12). Even when Paul has doubts about John Mark, Barnabas continues to offer encouragement that eventually bears fruit (15:36–40; 2 Tim 4:11). In a church under pressure, where it would be easy for some to complain or blame, Barnabas, by example and word, continually encourages others to serve.

---

16. Polhill, *Acts*, 208; Bruce, *Book of the Acts*, 156.   17. Witherington, *Acts of the Apostles*, 275.

19.7.5 James

By Acts 15, James, the half brother of the Lord, has become the leader of the Jerusalem church and the representative of Jewish Christian interests. He plays a crucial role at the Jerusalem Council (15:13–21). His citation of the teaching of Amos, as one example among the prophets about Gentile inclusion in God's blessing, seals the decision that Gentiles need not be circumcised. The citation of Amos 9:11–12 is a clear stroke of genius. Besides mentioning the rebuilding of the Davidic house and Gentiles seeking the Lord in a context of fulfillment, James cites the text in its Greek form, showing his desire to reach an agreement with those concerned about the Gentiles. James has a spirit that desires a thought-through, theologically sound unity. Lest anyone at the council object about the use of Amos with this emphasis, he introduces the citation by noting that many prophets have taught the same thing.

When James says, "the words of the prophets are in agreement with this" (Acts 15:15), he affirms not only what Amos taught, but also what the prophets as a whole taught. The verb "are in agreement" (συμφωνοῦσιν, *symphōnousin*) literally means "share the same sound/voice," and thus "match" or "agree."[18] Its only other occurrence in Acts is when Ananias and Sapphira agree to deceive the church (5:9; other NT occurrences are Matt 18:19; 20:2, 13; Luke 5:36). The reference to the prophets is important. James's point is not just about this one passage from Amos; rather, this passage reflects what the prophets teach in general. Other texts could have been noted (Isa 2:2; 45:20–23; Jer 12:15–16; Hos 3:4–5; Zech 2:11; 8:22).

James is stressing fulfillment, for the prophets agree with what Peter has described. This is not an affirmation of analogous fulfillment but a declaration that this is now taking place. God promised Gentile inclusion; now he is performing it. Paul cites a string of OT texts on this theme in Rom 15:7–13. So Amos is but one rendering that could be used to teach the theme. Thus James, representing the theologically conservative Jewish camp, supplies the final touch that results in a resolution to the problem.

When Paul returns to Jerusalem, James advises him to carry out purification rites (Acts 21:17–24).[19] Taking the advice, Paul reflects sensitivity to Jewish Christian concerns. In this way Paul follows principles contained in his own writings (1 Cor 9:19–23). James is the representative of traditional Christian interests, but he is not a hard-nosed, stubborn leader. He examines what God is doing and studies the Scriptures to determine the best way to proceed. His commitment is not to rules or to blind tradition, but to God's message and will. He wishes it to be carried out in the church with sensitivity to others. He works for unity. Here is another example of leadership, in which cooperation is exercised in the midst of recognizing nonessential differences of emphasis.

19.7.6 Paul

The major personality in the second half of Acts is Paul. Converted while an archrival of the church, Paul represents the truth that God can transform even the most

---

18. BDAG, 960–61 §1.   19. This event was covered in the previous chapter on the law.

hostile heart. As a young Jewish leader, he took delight in Stephen's martyrdom and sought to put Christians in jail (Acts 7:58–8:3). Saul (as he was called then) thought he was protecting God's honor from being defamed. But, ironically, God, taking the initiative yet again in Acts, transforms this archenemy of the gospel into one of its chief proponents. Paul ends up honoring God in a way Saul had never imagined. That is what coming to God can do. The account of Paul's conversion from persecutor to persecuted is so crucial to Luke that the story appears three times (Acts 9:1–19; 22:6–16; 26:12–18). Paul's conversion illustrates the dramatic reversal that God's grace can achieve. He also represents the church's mission to Gentiles (9:15–16). Carrying out the commission Jesus gives to him is the burden of Acts 11–20, while the theological basis that vindicates his mission appears in Acts 15.

In fact, the account of Paul's ministry has two parts: his journeys (Acts 11–20) and his trials (Acts 21–28). His journeys describe what he did, while his trials explain why he did it. Through Paul's arrest and persecution, the gospel goes to Rome. The movement shows that even events that on the surface seem to be hindrances to the gospel help accomplish its advance. Paul arrives in Rome, despite great risk. His long journey depicts the gospel getting to the symbolic location of the hub city that reaches to the ends of the earth and thus into all the world through God's sovereign protection (Acts 27).

In his mission, Paul preaches Christ, plants churches, and performs miracles. This combination shows that he is engaged in all the groundbreaking activities of the apostles. In fact, Paul may well be the key to the otherwise enigmatic Acts 19:1–7 episode, in which the Spirit comes on those who know only about John the Baptist. God uses Paul in bestowing the Holy Spirit on them (v. 6). This shows him to have an authority and role similar to the apostles, who took part in other earlier distributions of the Spirit into new realms (Acts 8 in Samaria and Acts 10 with Cornelius).

Scholars have discussed whether Luke considers Paul to be an apostle. In Acts 14:14, Paul shares this title with Barnabas, but this is not necessarily conclusive, since all that may be meant here is a broader use of the term, which suggests Paul is an authoritative representative of the church who plants churches. Luke answers the question of Paul's position and role not by giving him titles, but by showing how Paul's ministry is like that of the other apostles. Again, for Luke actions tell the story. Paul's miracles and events such as those in 19:1–7 make this point about the extent of Paul's authority. Appointed directly by the Lord, he acts and does things only apostles do.

So Paul preaches the promise of the resurrection (Acts 23:6; 24:15; 26:6–8, 22). From the early days of his conversion, he shares Jesus (9:27–29). In his trial, Paul declares his innocence and affirms that he has suffered innocently with a good conscience (23:1; 24:12–21; 25:8). He is guilty of no offense, and none of the charges against him can be proved. As with Jesus, others also declare Paul's innocence, including scribes (23:9), Claudius Lysias (23:29), Festus (25:25), and Agrippa (26:32). Paul is an innocent sufferer, just as Jesus was as he went to the cross in Luke

23. Justice may not always be carried out on earth, but the Lord notes Paul's faithfulness. Acts ends triumphantly, even though Paul is in prison, because the message still goes out openly. Paul's own words in Phil 1:12–19 describe the mood in which the book of Acts concludes. Even in chains, Paul can rejoice because the gospel is being preached. As a witness and a sufferer for Christ, Paul is an example to all believers, especially those who face negative reaction to the gospel. In fact, the book ends in a way that shows Paul to be to a consummate faithful witness, preaching the kingdom boldly with Jesus as Lord in the city of Rome, where the emperor is seen as Lord. Even chains do not restrain Paul.[20]

Paul's speeches differ, depending on his audience. His message in Pisidian Antioch, as summarized in Acts 13:16–41, is a typical synagogue speech, in which the emphasis is on God's promise to the nation about a future Son of David and the opportunity for Jews to share in the fulfillment of Davidic hope given to the people (Paul cites Isa 55:3). Acts 17:22–31 records a representative speech to pagans for whom the gospel is a new idea.

In Athens, Paul begins by speaking of the sovereign God, who is Creator and Judge of all humans. He is interrupted, so no one can know exactly how his message would have ended, though one can be sure he is headed toward mentioning Jesus Christ, whom God has "appointed" as the coming Judge (Acts 17:30–32).

Later Paul addresses the elders of the Ephesian church. The contents of this speech (Acts 20:18–35) look most like portions of his letters. Here he exhorts the leaders to be faithful in their oversight of the church, just as he had been with them. They are to guard the truth, watch for error, and offer gentle care to the flock. The church is precious, having been purchased with Christ's own blood. They are to lead it accordingly, knowing that God's grace will strengthen them for their tasks. They are to help the weak, for as Jesus taught, it is more blessed to give than to receive. Paul's three messages recorded in Acts 13, 17, and 20 picture him in three distinct roles: preacher-evangelist, apologist-evangelist, and church leader.

Paul's defense speeches differ from his earlier discourses. He gives defenses to the Jews (Acts 22:1–21), to the Sanhedrin (23:1–10), to Felix (24:10–21), to Festus (25:8–11), and to Agrippa (26:1–32). In them he speaks of his faithfulness to God and to his racial heritage. He has upheld the Law and the Prophets. He believes, as the Hebrew Scriptures teach, in promise and resurrection. He did not ask for the role he has, for God called him in a vision. He was compelled to preach Christ as the fulfillment of promise and to carry out a mission to Gentiles. If Paul is "guilty" of anything, it is that he has been an obedient vessel for God, faithfully proclaiming God's promise.

Paul's career is a capsule portrait of grace. The opponent of God's people has become their servant. He is a Jew burdened for saving Gentiles, picturing the rec-

20. Richard J. Cassidy, "Paul's Proclamation of *Lord* Jesus as a Chained Prisoner in Rome: Luke's Ending Is His Beginning," in Rhoads, Esterline, and Lee, *Luke and Empire*, 142–53.

onciliation that is at the hub of the effects of the gospel and kingdom message. He is victorious in persecution. Though he has been imprisoned, the Word of God is free. Paul pictures the triumph of God's sovereign direction.

Paul also pictures, with Barnabas, the messenger of God who is a light to the world through the message preached to it (Acts 13:47). Interestingly, in this passage the task of Isaiah's servant, normally associated with Jesus (8:32–35), extends to those who represent Jesus and preach the message about the one God sent.

19.8 STRUCTURE, ACTIVITY, AND WORSHIP IN THE CHURCH

With as much time and energy as we give to the structure and the makeup of church leadership and worship, it is somewhat surprising that Luke says so little about this topic in Acts. The already noted Acts 2:41–47 and 4:32–37 show us the activity of the church.[21] The believers gather at the temple and in homes sharing fellowship, being devoted to the apostles' teaching, breaking bread, and praying. They hold their possessions with loose hands, giving to the body where there is need. The apostles and others preach Jesus in public locales, such as synagogues and other public meeting places, in a manner common to the time. We are told nothing about what a worship service looked like, how long it was, or what kind of hymns were sung. It is bare bones in terms of such detail. Luke is far more interested in how the church engages their calling to take the message of the gospel into the world. Almost all the activity we just traced in the key personalities moves in this direction.

When it comes to leadership, we are hardly informed. The apostles play a key role, and the activity of missionaries like Barnabas and Paul is presented in some detail. We know that James leads the community in Jerusalem and that the apostles have an overseeing role, with Peter and John taking the lead and noting especially when the gospel goes into fresh locales. We know of elders, mainly because Paul speaks to a group from Ephesus at Miletus. They are told to guard the flock from false teaching and to serve humbly and faithfully as Paul served them. We hear nothing about deacons, although we do see a special group appointed to take care of a particular problem in Acts 6, so the apostles can focus on preaching. Maturity is the key qualification for appointment to such roles; Jesus had selected the Twelve and the choice of Judas's replacement is left to God and the drawing of lots after worthy candidates are set forth.

So when it comes to church organization, Luke-Acts mostly highlights how the Spirit empowered the community to live, engage, pray, and preach with faithfulness and boldness. Even the one act of church discipline is performed through an apostle and act of judgment by God's Spirit. The dynamic of the church is driven by the Spirit and their commitment to carry out the call of Jesus to take the gospel into the world.

---

21. There is more detail on many of these activities in ch. 15. We summarize these areas here.

19.9 CONCLUSION

Events in the early church and the difficult lives of the church's major early characters do not seem on the surface to favor the spread of the gospel. But every apparent setback is a catalyst to the church's growth. Suffering is not to be shunned, and neither is rejection. It is part of how the gospel spreads. The early church understands this lesson for when she prays, the community asks not to be spared of suffering, but to have boldness in speaking the Word of God (Acts 4:24–31). The lessons in the lives of the believers and leaders of the book of Acts can be summarized in the call to be strong, faithful, generous, and unified as the church seeks to fulfill her mission of proclaiming Jesus in the strength of God's Spirit.

Chapter 20

Eschatology, Judgment, and Hope for the Future in Luke-Acts

Bibliography

Carroll, John T. *Response to the End of History: Eschatology and Situation in Luke-Acts*. SBLDS. Atlanta: Scholars Press, 1988. **Chance, J. Bradley.** *Jerusalem, the Temple and the New Age in Luke-Acts*. Macon, GA: Mercer University Press, 1988. **Conzelmann, Hans.** *The Theology of St. Luke*. Philadelphia: Fortress, 1982. **Kümmel, Werner Georg.** "Futurische und präsentische Eschatologie im ältesten Urchristentum." *NTS* 5 (1958–59): 113–26. Idem. *Promise and Fulfillment*. Trans. Dorothea M. Barton. SBT. Naperville, IL: Allenson, 1957. **Marshall, I. H.** *Luke: Historian and Theologian*. Grand Rapids: Zondervan, 1970. **Nielsen, Anders E.** *Until It Is Fulfilled*. WUNT. Tübingen: Mohr/Siebeck, 2000. **Nolland, John.** "Salvation History and Eschatology." Pp. 63–81 in *Witness to the Gospel: A Theology of Acts*. Ed. I. Howard Marshall and David Peterson. Grand Rapids: Eerdmans, 1998. **Tiede, David.** *Prophecy and History in Luke-Acts*. Philadelphia: Fortress, 1980.

This chapter will not contain a narrative overview because most of the key texts have already been treated. However, it does consider several key themes related to Luke's eschatology. The most important aspect of his handling of eschatology is that the last days have already arrived. Eschatology is not merely an issue about the future. Fulfillment of the end comes with Jesus. His coming has opened up the last days, and the Spirit's coming is the proof of its arrival (see Acts 2:16–18). So the key themes include the basic structure of Luke's eschatology, the visit and the battle with Satan, the tension between imminence and delay, the issue of hope, and personal eschatology.

20.1 The Basic Structure of Luke's Eschatology: The Kingdom Comes in Fulfillment

20.1.1 A Two-Part Structure to the Era of Fulfillment: Already-Not Yet

A look at Luke's eschatology shows a fundamental two-part structure, with the second half divided into three parts. The basic division is between promise and fulfillment (Luke 7:28; 16:16). In the "period of anticipation" are the OT promise and the ministry of John the Baptist.[1] John's ministry is a bridge into the new era. It represents a transition preparing for Jesus and the arrival of kingdom hope, but technically he is the last of the old era. The forerunner was a part of the promise period (see Luke 7:19–20, 28; 16:16). Luke 7:28 reads, "I tell you, among those born of women there is no one greater than John; yet the one who is the least in the kingdom of God is greater than he." The difference between the two core eras of promise and fulfillment is that great. Here is the best evidence of the Lucan breakdown of history into two core eras.

Luke 16:16 reads in a similar way, "The Law and the Prophets were proclaimed until John. Since that time the good news of the kingdom of God is being preached, and everyone is forcing their way into it."[2] Again, a twofold breakdown appears with the kingdom now preached as present and available. These two texts are the most important passages when it comes to showing the structure of Luke's view of eschatology.

With Jesus' ministry one enters the "period of realization" for kingdom promise. This fulfillment has three parts: (1) transition tied to Jesus' earthly ministry (where Jesus' authority is established and his message of arrival and invitation goes out); (2) the "already" (church age of the indwelling Spirit); and (3) the "not yet" (Christ's return to reign).[3]

(1) The transition period into arrival and authority is shown in passages such as Luke 11:20 and 17:21.[4] Luke 11:20 reads, "If I drive out demons by the finger of God, then the kingdom of God has come upon you." Luke 17:21 says, "Nor will people say, 'Here it is,' or 'There it is,' for the kingdom of God is in your midst." God's current activity for his people has taken on a new level of intensity with Jesus' coming. The kingdom is within their present reach; it has arrived. One can speak of

---

1. This reading of Luke's structure having two parts and not three stands in contrast to the famous reading of Lucan eschatology by Conzelmann, *Theology of St. Luke.* He has a period of promise, the church, and the end. He sees Luke's major concern as the delay of the return, arguing that Luke opted for salvation history in place of eschatology. This reading requires that Conzelmann ignore the infancy material of Luke 1–2. It also misreads the position of John the Baptist presented as a bridge figure between only two periods, the old era and the new. Luke 7:28 shows this most clearly with John being connected to the old era and differentiated from all who are a part of the new era, which shows fulfillment's fundamental unity as an era for Luke. Luke 16:16 also has this core twofold breakdown. Nor do we accept the idea that Luke wished to arouse end-time hope of a return as John Carroll argues in *Response to the End of History.* This makes too much of consummative eschatology in Luke. Our position is that Luke uses eschatology to motivate for mission and ethical accountability. This motivation occurs in the context of a present and future dimension to eschatology that looks ahead to vindication by God in the end. This position is rooted in the treatment by Kümmel, *Promise and Fulfillment,* and his article, "Futurische und präsentische Eschatologie im ältesten Urchristentum," *NTS* 5 (1958–59): 113–26. This position is most recently argued for by

Anders E. Nielsen, *Until It Is Fulfilled* (WUNT 2/126; Tübingen: Mohr/Siebeck, 2000). His study looks at eschatology through the lens of the farewell discourses of Luke 22:1–39 and Acts 20:17–35. See also John Nolland, "Salvation History and Eschatology," in *Witness to the Gospel,* 63–81, esp. 68–70. As Nolland notes, the claim of a present initially realized kingdom would seem empty if it were not linked to the comprehensive victory to come in the future. Our look at hope will cover similar ground.

2. The meaning of βιάζεται (*biazetai,* "is forcing") is much discussed but not directly relevant to this discussion on eschatology. The term normally describes struggle but in a middle/passive can refer to being urged in with a note of struggle. For details, see BAGD, 140–41, and my discussion of this term in *Luke 9:51–24:53,* 1351–53.

3. For Luke, there are no stages to the consummation. He simply presents it as a unit. Differentiation of this final stage of the eschatological calendar is something Paul reveals in the Thessalonian letters, which is why he speaks of a word of the Lord in 1 Thess 4:16. Such periodization also gains detail in Rev 20, as well as in much of the rest of the Apocalypse.

4. Chapter 8 has treated these key texts in more detail.

the kingdom arriving, in that the King was exercising his power and reflecting his authority. The presence of the kingdom reflects a transition at this point, because the covenant's salvific blessings (most notably the forgiveness of sins and the coming of the Father's promise of the Holy Spirit) have not yet been distributed. Jesus' coming requires his death to provide for the forgiveness that in turn cleanses so that the Spirit can occupy clean, sanctified vessels.

These benefits were not yet available to any who believed and had to await the key work Jesus would do in death and in God's resurrection of him (Luke 3:15–18; 24:49). So the promise of the new covenant (22:20) could not be realized until the covenant was activated by Jesus' sacrifice. The arrival of the central promised blessings of the period of realization did not come until the Spirit arrived and the rule of God could be enabled from within his people. The Spirit's arrival completed the period of transition, in terms of bringing initial fulfillment of the promised blessings. These blessings were for those who acknowledged that Jesus is the promised Messiah and sought the forgiveness and enabling life he offered.

(2) The descent of the Holy Spirit on Pentecost, made possible by Jesus' resurrection-ascension, marks the arrival of the "already" period of promise. Jesus functions now as Lord-Messiah, distributing blessings promised in the Hebrew Scriptures and holding all people accountable for responding to him.[5] Acts 11:15 referred back to the event on the day of Pentecost as "the beginning." Here the hope of the new covenant was inaugurated, made possible by Jesus' death (Luke 22:20; Acts 20:28). These current blessings are part of the eschaton because in Luke's view they represent the initial line of OT promises that God fulfilled. In the Holy Spirit, God is at work in his people. Jesus rules with sovereignty over these benefits as the Mediator of divine blessing.

This is the point Peter makes in his speech, that Israel can know God has made Jesus both Lord and Messiah (Acts 2:36), because the Spirit has come to God's believing people. This verse says: "Let all the house of Israel know with assurance that both Lord and Christ God has made him, the Jesus whom you crucified" (pers. trans.).[6] The kingdom has come because the power of God is expressed through Jesus by means of the Holy Spirit working in his people.

(3) But there also is a "not yet" element in Luke's eschatology. Here Luke presents the hope of consummation, in which God's promises will be brought to full realization. All the prophetic promises made to Israel will be fulfilled (Acts 3:19–21) as God will restore everything: "Repent, therefore, and turn for the washing of your sins, so that times of refreshing might come from before the Lord and he might send the Christ appointed for you, Jesus, whom it is necessary that heaven receive until the times of restoration of all things which God spoke about through the mouth of his holy prophets of old" (pers. trans.). Note how the prophets speak with a singular

---

5. "From now on," Luke 22:69; "exalted to the right hand of God" as Ps 110 promised, Acts 2:32–36; the pouring out of the Holy Spirit as Joel promised, 2:1–4, 16–21; and coming to judge, 2:40; 10:42; 17:30–31.

6. I have kept the word order in the translation to show the emphasis with which the point is made.

voice (note it is one "mouth"). God speaks through them about his program. Also important is that what is left to be done is already described in the prophets. To see what God will do one need only to go back and read them. There is no hint here of a reconfiguration of anything as a result of Jesus' coming. He realizes what was always promised and revealed.

In Acts 3:20, "the times of refreshing" (καιροὶ ἀναψύξεως, *kairoi anapsyxeōs*) is a NT *hapax* expression. It looks to a period of time that includes rest and refreshment. The term ἀνάψυξις (*anapsyxis*) refers to a "cooling" to relieve trouble or to dry out a wound ("refreshment" in NLT; "refreshing" in NIV, RSV, NET; BDAG, 75).[7] In the LXX, the only use of ἀνάψυξις is in Ex 8:11 LXX (= 8:15 Eng.), where it refers to relief from the plague of frogs. The verb ἀναψύχω (*anapsychō*, "to refresh") is used of the Sabbath rest of slaves and animals and the soothing of Saul by David's music (Exod 23:12; 1 Sam 16:23).[8] The arrival, then, is of a period of messianic refreshment, the "definitive age of salvation."[9] The idea has parallels in Judaism (2 Esd. [*4 Ezra*] 7:75, 91, 95; 11:46; 13:26–29; *2 Bar.* 73–74; *1 En.* 45.5; 51.4; 96.3) and is traditional in its origin.[10] It refers to entry into a new and unending eschatological life before the Lord. The closest parallel in the NT is the concept of "rest" in Heb 3–4.[11] One wonders if ἀνάψυξις alludes to the Spirit's washing work in the messianic age that points to spiritual refreshment.

The reference to times and seasons contains terms that appear in Luke 21:24 ("times [καιροί, *kairoi*] of the Gentiles" — the current era) and Acts 1:6–7. The question in Acts 1 receives a reply that it is not for Peter's hearers to know the "times or dates" — a reply that uses both terms for "time" (χρόνοι, *chronoi*, and καιροί). In other words, their repentance opens up the possibility of both times of refreshment and times establishing all things God promised.[12] All of this takes place before the Lord, before his presence.

Along with this entry into refreshment is the completion of God's plan with Christ's return. Peter urges repentance so that one can participate in God's entire planned program from start to finish. A key aspect of that program is Jesus' return, when the Christ will exercise judgment on behalf of righteousness and complete God's promise already outlined in the prophetic teaching of the Hebrew Scriptures. Nothing Peter says indicates that anything promised there has been changed. There may be additions and expansions of those ideas in light of revelation in the period tied to Jesus, but in the rest of what Jesus brings he will complete what also was already revealed.[13] The timing of the consummation comes down the road, but what

---

7. Schweizer, *TDNT*, 9:664; Fitzmyer, *Acts of the Apostles*, 288; "to cool by blowing" is the idea of the related verb.

8. Johnson, *Acts of the Apostles*, 69.

9. Schweizer, *TDNT*, 9:664.

10. Bruce, *Acts of the Apostles*, 144. This is against the argument of Kremer that the language is Lucan (see his discussion in *EDNT*, 1:95).

11. R. Pesch, *Die Apostelgeschichte (Apg 1–12)* (EKKNT 5/1; Zurich: Benzinger/Neukirchen-Vluyn: Neukirchener, 1986), 155.

12. Barrett, *Critical and Exegetical Commentary on the Acts of the*

Apostles, 1:205.

13. This point is made against those who argue Jesus reconfigured the end events by what he said and did in his initial coming. What Jesus did was to add to an existing portrait, not change or reconfigure promises that had been made already to a specific people. The implication of this observation is that hope for Israel remains as the completion of promises at the end of time will include her as it also does the reconciliation of the world. That plan for her is revealed in the Hebrew Scriptures.

will happen has been and remains described in those texts. Peter speaks of God's sending the Christ "appointed" (προκεχειρισμένον, *prokecheirismenon*) for all of them (Acts 3:20).[14] The two other occurrences of this verb in Acts are about Paul as a "chosen" servant of God (22:14–15; 26:16–18).

This Christ is received in heaven for now. Here is another way to portray the experience of ascension. Heaven holds Jesus at God's side until the day he is revealed to the world in power in his return (Luke 21:25–28). He is not passive until the return, however, for Acts 2 shows that Jesus is active now in salvation by distributing the Spirit, and Acts 3 shows him as the source of the healing of the crippled man. This is executive messianic, kingdom authority that Jesus is exercising from heaven as he blesses those who come to him with forgiveness and the Spirit. As Bruce notes, "Jesus must reign at God's right hand until all hostile powers are overthrown" (1 Cor 15:24–28).[15]

Nevertheless, with his return come "the seasons of the restoration of all things" (lit. trans. of 3:21; χρόνων ἀποκαταστάσεως πάντων, *chronōn apokatastaseōs pantōn*), yet another NT *hapax* expression. The term ἀποκατάστασις (*apokatastasis*, "establishment") does not appear in the LXX.[16] The anticipated end is seen as establishing again the original creation's pristine character. This restoration is what Jesus will bring with his return, an idea given later development in Rev 19–22 but whose roots Peter declares here are already evident in that which "God promised long ago through his holy prophets." The relative pronoun ὧν (*hōn*, "of which") could refer back to "the seasons" of which God spoke[17] or to "all things" of which God spoke.[18] Acts 3:24 appears to highlight the period of time being addressed by the promise ("these days"), but it is the content that is being highlighted here—that all things will be restored (i.e., taking πάντων as the antecedent of ὧν).[19] The new world and the messianic creation appear in a final and complete restoration.

In the NT, this idea is discussed in Matt 19:28; Rom 8:18–23; and Heb 2:5–8. The point is that God has already indicated what the end will be like. So, to learn about the future, Peter urges the people to note what God has already said through the prophets about the new era that the eschaton will bring. The expression about the prophets is like Luke 1:70. Texts such as Isa 65–66 are in view, where Israel is restored to fullness (also Isa 34:4; 51:6; Jer 15:18–19; 16:15; 23:8; 24:6; Ezek 17:23; Amos 9:11–12).[20] The two expressions for time—καιροί and χρόνοι—probably look at one period, as opposed to distinct periods of time. However, it is seen as one great, extended period (thus the plurals) whose high point is Christ's return, and so the stress is on what participation in the period of messianic blessing ultimately will yield.[21]

---

14. Note that the second-person pronoun "you" (ὑμῖν, *hymin*) is plural.

15. Bruce, *Book of Acts*, 185.

16. Müller, *EDNT*, 1:130.

17. Otto Bauernfeind, *Kommentar und Studien zur Apostelgeschichte* (WUNT 22; Tübingen: Mohr-Siebeck, 1980), 69.

18. Conzelmann, *Acts of the Apostles*, 29; Barrett, *Critical and Exegetical Commentary on the Acts of the Apostles*, 1:206. It is the nearest referent.

19. So Oepke, *TDNT*, 1:391.

20. Jervell, *Apostelgeschichte*, 167, n. 358.

21. Marshall, *Acts of the Apostles*, 93–94.

In sum, three blessings are offered in Acts 3:19–21: the forgiveness of sins, the promise of times of refreshing, and the opportunity to participate in the return of the Messiah. Jesus brings all of this over time.

20.1.2 The Timing of the Consummation

The promise of a period of the restoration of all things in Acts 3 recalls the language of the disciples' question in 1:6, about whether this was the time "to restore the kingdom to Israel." Jesus defers answering the question at that time, saying the exact timing is the Father's business. Yet Peter answers the question in his Acts 3 speech by noting that Israel's full restoration comes when Messiah returns. This is the promise of salvation for Israel, expressed in Luke 1:69–75. Yet it is also a salvation that covers the nations, for Israel's story is also that of the nations (2:28–32; 3:4–6).

All of this helps to explain where Jesus' rule over Israel (Luke 1:31–35) is headed. He will return to the earth to rule directly over all, reconciling Israel and the nations to each other. He will exercise his sovereignty, not only in salvific benefits but also as "judge of the living and the dead" (Acts 10:42; cf. 17:31). At that time, another promise will arrive, namely, the realization of Jesus' promise to the apostles that they will rule over the twelve tribes of Israel, as they help administer righteousness and justice (Luke 22:29–30). That promise reads, "And I confer on you a kingdom, just as my Father conferred one on me, so that you may eat and drink at my table in my kingdom and sit on thrones, judging the twelve tribes of Israel."

Jesus personalizes the kingdom here. It is his banquet table and his kingdom. He shares that authority with the twelve. Authority over Israel and her twelve tribes is a part of this promised package. The numerous pictures of the banquet table celebration relate ultimately to this yet-future age, when those who will share in the consummation of the promise will rejoice in rich fellowship in the presence of God and share in the vindication that is a part of the justice and peace to come (Acts 13:22–30; 14:15–24; 22:16, 20). This hope motivates behavior in the present, including the willingness to persevere under suffering. The fact that Jesus makes this point at his final meal as he looks to his own suffering and rejection is important. It sets the context for the remarks and shows how eschatology motivates one in the context of a world not yet fully redeemed, even though the kingdom is initially present.

Luke 22:16 is particularly significant here: "I tell you, I will not eat it again until it finds fulfillment in the kingdom of God." There is a committal of the kingdom to those who have followed him until the consummation comes, something Paul also does in Acts 20 with the Ephesian elders.[22] The first "it" in Luke 22:16 refers to the Passover lamb. Jesus will not eat the Passover meal again with his disciples until he does so in the kingdom. This remark suggests that Jesus anticipates that promises to Israel will be fulfilled, that her major feast (the Passover) will continue to be celebrated, and that the apostles will be present at the celebration.

---

22. Nielsen, *Until It Is Fulfilled*, 200.

Details about establishing this period are given in Luke 17:22–37 and 21:5–33. However, even these texts contain little detail about what takes place there other than the establishment of this justice and peace. In Luke 17 and 21 the coming final judgment is compared to what will happen soon, namely, the fall of Jerusalem in AD 70. In Luke 21, Jesus discusses what will happen first "before the end" (vv. 5–9) and what will occur "before" those events that come "before" the end (vv. 12–19, i.e., the events of vv. 12–19 come before those of vv. 5–9 as Jesus comes back in time toward the time of the Twelve). This period will be one of confusion, conflict, and chaos. It will include persecution of those who believe in Jesus. The book of Acts depicts how the promised Spirit will help the persecuted stand up for their faith.

Jesus also declares what will happen to Jerusalem until the times of the Gentiles are fulfilled. The Gentiles will trample her down. Yet this set of events also serves as a pattern for what the chaos of the end-time consummation is like (Luke 21:20–24). Then Jesus summarizes what the end will look like in 21:25–28. Those verses point to a final vindication of those who have responded to Jesus. His return is the believers' "redemption" (21:28: ἡ ἀπολύτρωσις, *hē apolytrōsis*).

In this Luke 21 speech, there are two judgments with one picturing or patterning the other. Jesus layers his account about the end with a pattern prophecy where one event mirrors and foreshadows the other. The first judgment involves Jerusalem and her fall for missing the messianic visitation (Luke 19:41–45). That judgment, then, pictures what the final judgment on the world will be like (see more on Luke 21 below). Jerusalem's fall is a guarantee that the plan is moving ahead. To see the one event is to know the other judgment will come. In this way, Jesus also connects the new era at its start with the arrival of the consummation, linking them together as one period in two parts.

An inauguration (of the present age) is related to Jesus' ascension, and the consummation (in Jesus' future reign) is related to his return. Jesus is at the center of these plans. His return, followed by the consummation, provides perspective on how one should live now. For in the consummation, there is accountability, judgment, and reward. Judgment will be for those who do not know Jesus or who blatantly disregard him (Luke 12:45–46; 13:25; 17:37; 19:24–26; Acts 10:42; 17:30–31). Reward is for those who obey, while punishment is for those who fail to respond to the call of the Master (Luke 12:42–44, 47–48; 14:14; 19:17–19).

20.2 ESCHATOLOGY AND ACCOUNTABILITY: MOTIVATION TO FAITHFULNESS

There are two motivations for faithfulness in Luke-Acts. One is the love generated by the grace of God. This is shown by Jesus' remarks about the sinful woman who anoints Jesus in Luke 7:36–50, especially the parable he tells in conjunction with her act. To be forgiven much leads into loving much. Jesus also highlights the duty of service. Luke 17:7–10 says this directly: the servant does his duty. No thanks are to be sought or expected. Part of what motivates this duty is the relationship one has to the master and the accountability that Jesus teaches as a part of his presentation of eschatology. This is an often neglected theme of Scripture, so a careful look is needed.

The parable of Luke 12:36–50 shows this in detail. Jesus' call here is to be faithful until the return takes place, however long it takes. Four categories of response are possible for those connected to Jesus, with the first category being particularly difficult and important to determine. The expressions must be examined because of the range of accountability it suggests is present among any connected to Jesus.[23] (1) First are those who do not believe and do the opposite of what the Lord asks. They are "cut . . . into pieces and assigned . . . a place with unbelievers" (12:46). This is a picture of total rejection by the Lord.

The action of the unfaithful servant is severely judged upon the master's return. Ἄπιστος (*apistos*) usually means "faithless," but in contrast to the faithful steward in Luke 12:42, and in light of the severe nature of the punishment, it should be understood to mean "unbelieving." The servant is totally unconcerned about his master's return or his master's instructions. The key to the image of accountability is pictured in the master's return when he appears at an unexpected hour. The return's surprise is highlighted by the repeated reference to the unknown day and hour of his return. The reference to the "day" of the return recalls OT day-of-the-Lord imagery (Joel 2:31 [3:4 MT]).[24] It is judgment day.

The master's reaction to the slave's behavior is swift and strong. Some translations do not properly render the key term διχοτομήσει (*dichotomēsei*). The RSV says that the master will "punish" the slave, but the term is stronger and much more emotive than this: "to dismember, to cut in two."[25] Beating the servants now produces judgment in kind, only it is more severe. The steward receives a "mortal blow," a "declaration of judgment or prediction of cursing."[26] God's smiting the servant depicts punishment of the most severe type, but it is figurative, despite the opinion of some that it is literal.[27] A figurative sense emerges from the next line, which shows that the servant is to be placed among another group of people. Figuratively speaking, he is chopped beef. This pictures rejection.

The reprimand and punishment are total, since the servant is placed with the "unbelievers" (ἀπίστων, *apistōn*) because of his complete lack of faithfulness. This is a picture of exclusion. In fact, dismemberment is the most graphic way possible to express rejection. This is not a matter of dismissal or demotion, but departure. A high calling does not protect from the consequences of total unfaithfulness,[28] for

---

23. As I am about to argue, connection to Jesus in stewardship (and even in ministry) does not equal having faith on Jesus and being a genuine member of the community. The presence of a figure like Judas among the Twelve tells us of a category of people who associate with Jesus and even minister in his name but do not know him.

24. Fitzmyer, *Gospel of Luke X–XXIV*, 990.

25. Marshall, *Gospel of Luke*, 543; Stählin, *TDNT*, 3:852–53; Plummer, *Gospel according to St. Luke*, 332–33; Schlier, *TDNT*, 2:225–26.

26. Stählin, *TDNT*, 8:267–68.

27. Plummer, *Gospel according to St. Luke*, 332; Creed, *Gospel according to St. Luke*, 177.

28. Arndt, *Gospel according to St. Luke*, 322.

with the call must come some kind of obedience that is not reflected in acting in a manner completely contrary to what the Master has instructed. Such a warning is necessary, because Judas is among the disciples. The passage is addressed to anyone associated with Jesus who has undertaken responsibility in the new community. Such a profession may be taken at face value by those around such a person, but Jesus will evaluate the genuineness of it on the day of judgment and warns that not all who associate with him are really connected to him. A similar evaluation is found in 1 Cor 3:10–17 (esp. 3:17), where to destroy the temple of God is to risk one's own destruction.

Matthew 24:51 is parallel to this parable in Luke 12, except that the slave there is placed among the "hypocrites" (ὑποκριτῶν, hypokritōn) rather than among the unbelievers (ἀπίστων). To be placed with the hypocrites is to receive their punishment (Matt 6:2, 5, 16; 23:13–19; on the terror of divine judgment, see Job 23:13–17; Isa 17:14). In addition, Matthew notes that "there will be weeping and gnashing of teeth" in the place where the slave goes. This image appears frequently, especially in Matthew (Matt 8:12; 13:42, 50; 22:13; 25:30; cf. Luke 13:28). The Matthean figure also indicates total rejection, since it is often associated with being cast into outer "darkness" (25:30). Outer darkness does not mean being on the edge of the kingdom or being on the edge of light. It does not mean being excluded only from participating in kingdom administration. It means being cast totally outside. The kingdom is light, so one cannot be in darkness and in the kingdom at the same time, much less in outer darkness! The point for both writers is the same: the unfaithful slave is rejected by the master for being an utterly irresponsible steward. Given the setting, it would seem that false teaching and a double life are the points of the allusion, since the essence of a leader's stewardship is found in the teaching and guiding role.

Grundmann notes that this unfaithful servant is treated and addressed as the scribes and Pharisees were (Matt 23:13, 15, 23, 25, 27, 29).[29] Efforts to argue that this person is "saved, but disciplined" ignore the force of ὑποκριτής in Matthew's parallel, which, though distinct from Luke, is related to this Lucan account. Such efforts also ignore the picture of dismemberment and weeping and gnashing of teeth. Both accounts picture total rejection.[30] The detail shows how accountability and eschatology merge in Luke. Allegiance to Jesus in faith means one does not move in an opposite direction from what he commands.

The three other categories in this parable are easier to discern. (2) Others do not obey, but they have knowledge (Luke 12:47). They are severely disciplined for disregarding the command, but they do not do the exact opposite. They simply fail to carry out what was asked. (3) Still others do not obey out of ignorance (12:48). Their punishment is even less. These two categories look at discipline for those who genuinely are a part of the community.

---

29. W. Grundmann, *Das Evangelium nach Lukas* (THKNT 3; Berlin: Evangelische Verlagsanstalt, 1963), 268; Wilckens, *TDNT*, 8:568.

30. Bock, *Luke 9:51–24:53*, 1182–84.

(4) Finally, those who obey are honored and served by the Master (Luke 12:37–38). This is the category to which faithful believers belong. This is how to respond to the accountability that one has to Jesus as a member of his community. Here also is how eschatology functions for Luke; it means hope and accountability. To Luke, all of this is eschatology, not merely what relates to the future of Jesus' coming. Blessing now should lead to responsiveness of faith and obedience, but there is a stewardship that will reflect whether real faith has been present, as well as the quality of each person's service to the Lord.

20.3 THE MESSIANIC VISIT AND THE BATTLE WITH SATAN

Another key eschatological theme can be described in terms of the visit and the battle. The visit is the arrival of blessing in terms of the sending of the promised Messiah. This theme was already traced in the discussion of God's plan.[31] It was introduced in Luke 1:68–79 with the picture of the visit of delivering redemption by the horn of David and the image of the rising sun shining into darkness and illuminating the path to peace. It is a cause of mourning when Jesus weeps over Jerusalem because she is missing her time of visitation (19:41–44). Zechariah's hymn in 1:73–75 best explained what the hope was that was tied to this arrival when he said that now God's people can look to deliverance from the enemy and serve in holiness and righteousness in line with an oath God has given to his people. The visit is designed to free God's people to serve him faithfully.

The battle with enemies is something Zechariah also describes. Here one might think the enemies are primarily the social and political opponents of those who believe, but Luke's story tells us otherwise. Jesus' battle is with cosmic forces. Thus Satan tempts Jesus in an effort to thwart him at the start (Luke 4:1–13). Luke presents these as tests that Jesus overcomes in contrast to the last son of God, Adam, whose name frames this scene from the previous verse (3:38).[32] Jesus' exorcisms point to the arrival of the kingdom of God and the defeat of one whose house has been overrun by Messiah (11:20–23). This short parable of the overrun house appears right after Jesus makes the point about the kingdom's coming as a result of casting out demons. This connection tells us that the enemies Jesus fights are spiritual and transcendent forces of evil. Jesus overcomes those elements that attack within a person.

The demons' goal is to steer allegiance away from God. So Luke 11:22–23 reads, "But when someone stronger attacks and overpowers him, he takes away the armor in which the man trusted and divides up his plunder. Whoever is not with me is against me, and whoever does not gather with me scatters." Jesus is the stronger one who gains the cosmic victory.[33] But only those who identify with him share in the plunder. The devil does try to thwart Jesus again by entering Judas, leading to the

---

31. See ch. 5.

32. Fuller, *Restoration of Israel*, 233.

33. For these verses in more detail, see ch. 11.

disciple's betrayal (22:2). Satan also "sifts" Peter into denial (22:31–32). But divine vindication in resurrection-ascension means defeat for the devil. Acts 26:17–18 affirms this conclusion. There Paul describes his mission as turning people from Satan to God, showing the cosmic dimensions of the battle and the victory that comes through the one God has sent.

As Fuller argues, restoration tied to eschatology pays much attention to Israel as Luke treats the vindication of God, but the field of view is much broader. Restoration encompasses a victory over transcendent forces, Satan, and evil.[34] Enthronement in heaven pictures the scope of the rule. Jesus is a heavenly Davidic Messiah. The pouring out of the Spirit allows God's people to experience and mediate God's rule to the world. Again, eschatology issues a call to mission and motivates to faithful response. What starts in the land of Israel moves out into the world and impacts the cosmos (Acts 1:8). Israel's story is the world's story as well. It is also creation's story. Eschatology covers the cosmos.

20.4 THE TENSION BETWEEN IMMINENCE AND DELAY

One of the great tensions in NT eschatology is the fact that Jesus' return, which is said to be soon, is placed alongside the fact that the church has a mission to the whole world. The goal is to bring this cosmic victory to as many as possible. Added to this is the reality that Jesus has not yet returned, neither by the time Luke writes, nor even in our own time.

This tension is reflected in Luke's two volumes. For many scholars, Luke expected a return within a generation.[35] For other scholars, Luke treats the delay of the return as a problem and supposedly substitutes salvation history for the hope of a soon-to-come return.[36] However, despite the popularity of these two options and their contradictory claims, a third option seems a better reflection of Luke's position. This third explanation also helps us to see how these first two alternatives can each be advocated. Luke's view of imminence, delay, and mission is that a tension exists between the near hope and not knowing the exact time of the return and a period long enough to allow for worldwide mission, a temporal frame long enough to sow doubt.

The key text reflecting this tension in full is Luke 18:8.[37] In v. 8a, Jesus speaks of the speedy vindication that will come to God's children: "I tell you, he will see that they get justice, and quickly." This highlights the theme of imminence that Luke associates

---

34. Fuller, *Restoration of Israel*, 268.

35. So argues Nolland, "Salvation History and Eschatology," 65–67. See also J. Bradley Chance, *Jerusalem, the Temple and the New Age in Luke-Acts* (Macon, GA: Mercer Univ. Press, 1988), 90–95.

36. The most famous advocate for this view is Conzelmann, *Theology of St. Luke*. This point is the major thesis of his entire study. As already noted earlier in this chapter, to make his case, Conzelmann has to ignore the infancy material and underplay texts that do point to a sense of imminence in Luke-Acts.

37. Interestingly, this is a text Nolland does not treat. Yet it contains the key tension we are arguing for as Luke's view. Nolland argues four theses in "Salvation History and Eschatology." Two are questionable, namely, the near hope and his claim that Luke does not delineate clearly the periods in salvation history, preferring a more repetitive view of history. Luke 7:18–35; 16:16; and Acts 3:18–22 are against this idea of a lack of defining the boundaries of the periods. This may be an overreaction to challenging Conzelmann. Two of his theses— (1) that eschatology is present and future and (2) that Jewish rejection is not a cause of Gentile mission—do reflect Luke's emphases.

with Jesus' return. Yet even in this one verse there is tension in this text because Jesus also asks whether the Son of Man will find faith when he returns. Verse 8b reads, "However, when the Son of Man comes, will he find faith on the earth?" This suggests the return is delayed enough that some will lack faith and not be looking for his return. This imminence and delay theme, and its extant tension, is something Luke is concerned to address as he encourages believers to persevere until the Son of Man returns.

Perhaps Luke 18 sees imminence and vindication at two levels. One set of events lays the groundwork for ultimate vindication. Jesus' current rule means that he is present to give aid to his children now, as they face opposition from the world. Final vindication will come, but Jesus' presence with his own now means that the foundation of vindication is already present, since victory is guaranteed.

This reality, and tension, is seen in two "death scenes" in Luke-Acts. One involves a thief crucified with Jesus and the Lord's promise that "today" the thief will be with him in paradise (Luke 23:42–43). In the other scene, Jesus welcomes the martyr Stephen (Acts 7:55–56). Strictly speaking, this is not the full vindication spoken of in Luke 18:8, since the enemies are not yet completely dealt with, but it does represent an initial form of vindication. End-time vindication is both "soon" and "not yet." Those who know Jesus are present with him now, but the enemies are not dealt with completely until the judgment comes. Only then will the restoration of all things be complete, along with the justice and peace that come with it.

Another text often thought to teach imminence (and particularly problematic, if it has that sense) is Luke 21:32, where Jesus said that "this generation" will see God's promises being completed: "Truly I tell you, this generation will certainly not pass away until all these things have happened." The "generation" in view may be the generation of the end (looking back to events about Jerusalem's end in v. 20 or to the events of v. 25). That is, once the end-time events start, it will take only one generation's duration to establish his rule. When Jesus comes, the end will come quickly. Thus, in this view, the text teaches how "instantaneous" the return is, not how imminent.

Another, slightly more likely way to take the verse is to see the reference to "generation" not as chronological in force, but moral or ethical. So this "evil" generation, which is what the unredeemed creation consists of, will not pass away until Jesus returns. Such a use of "generation" occurs in Luke 9:41 and 11:29. If this is the sense, then imminence is not in view either; instead what is emphasized is that at the end, judgment comes and justice as vindication follows. Either view of this verse is possible, but the point we have seen about vindication in judgment tied to the eschaton might slightly favor an ethical reading here.

20.5 THE FALL OF JERUSALEM AND THE END: TYPOLOGY OF THE END

We noted that Luke uses the coming judgment of the nation and the fall of Jerusalem in AD 70 as a picture and type of the consummation, while noting also that everything from the time of Jesus' first coming to that ultimate consummation is full of eschatological significance for Luke. Luke 17 and 21 are key and complicated major texts that give as much detail about the end as anything in Luke-Acts.

Luke 21:5–36 shows this typological reading about the consummation. As already discussed above, two events are described simultaneously in the first part of the discourse, because one event is like the other. Luke 21:5–24 covers two periods in an overlapping manner. Verses 5–19 describe mostly the situation that came with the fall of Jerusalem in AD 70. This fall was also discussed in Luke 19:41–44. Its grisly judgment in turn pictures the chaos of what the end will be like. The earlier judgment "patterns" what the period of the end time return will be like, providing an illustration of it.

Luke 21:20–24 describes both events as one. Luke clearly includes the earlier event when he, alone among the Synoptic writers, refers to Jerusalem's "desolation" and does not mention "the abomination that causes desolation" (cf. Mark 13:14). The shorter term in Daniel refers to a variety of desecrations, as opposed to the specific desecration by the abomination (Dan 9:27; 11:31; 12:11). All the desecrations involve the temple, but Dan 11:31 refers to temple destruction and a cessation of sacrifices, as opposed to a desecrating sacrifice. Luke's version broadens the allusion to include the fall of Jerusalem. However, Luke 21:25–36 describes the events of the end only.

The details about the suddenness of the end and its visibility are discussed more fully in Luke 17:22–37. The return of the Son of Man to earth will take place instantly and in a way that is obvious to all (like lightning; 17:24). It will come after the Son of Man suffers (17:25). Again, judgment is near, but not so near that other things will not happen first. Suddenly, as judgment comes, some will be taken and others will be left. Some will be preserved; others will be judged. The vultures (17:37) indicate that the major picture of this aspect of the return involves judgment. If one asks, as the disciples did, where those who are taken go (v. 37), the reply is only that vultures are there.

In Luke 21, Jesus spoke of two events, both future when he spoke, but one of which (the destruction of Jerusalem in AD 70) is now past and one of which is yet future. In good prophetic style, Jesus united two events that picture the same reality. One mirrors the other. The fall of Jerusalem, occurring in the lifetime of many of the disciples, guaranteed the coming reality of the end-time judgment on the world. As such, the fall of Jerusalem indicated that God's program was on track.[38] The events are so similar; it is easy to see how they could be confused. In fact, describing

---

38. The thesis of Chance, *Jerusalem, the Temple and the New Age in Luke-Acts*, is that Jerusalem and the temple are viewed as renewed by Luke because of Jesus' work and believers' activity in mission emanating from there. This reading views the temple activity too positively. The temple is hardly renewed when Israel is seen as under exililike judgment until she recognizes her Messiah (Luke 13:34–35; 19:41–44). Neither is Jerusalem seen so positively. It is a city where the case for God's program is a highly contentious issue and believers are persecuted. It is true that the new community represents the presence of divine renewal in the heartland of Israel, but the presence of conflict shows that Luke does not see these sacred locales so positively. In fact, the movement of Acts toward Rome also makes this point. Jerusalem is no longer the hub of divine activity.

the two events together would have made it difficult to distinguish the two events until one of them had occurred. But the mixing together of these events also means that this discourse was very relevant to the disciples. They would need to stand firm in persecution, but they also could know that when the Lord returns, those who stand opposed to God's people will be judged. Vindication for the saints will come, and so will a restoration for Israel as the times of the Gentiles come to an end.[39]

Other verses state that a time of delay will come. In Luke 19:11, the people expected the immediate arrival of the consummated kingdom. But in the parable of the ten minas that follows (vv. 12–27), Jesus makes the point that in the interim between his departure and his return the disciples are to be faithful. Again, the distance in the parable between the departure of the nobleman to receive the kingdom and his return points to a period of delay before the end comes. Any sense of delay should not lessen the call to be faithful.

Also indicative are warnings in the Olivet Discourse itself. Luke 21:8–9 shows that the events described in the first section of Jesus' speech are not yet part of the time of the very end, because "the end will not come right away." Verses 20–24 suggest that Jerusalem will fall before the end comes. Only with the cosmic signs and the Son of Man's return will the end come (vv. 25, 28, 31). Then redemption draws near. In fact, v. 24 refers to the entire present age after Jerusalem's fall as "the times of the Gentiles." This reference also suggests that a time is also coming when Israel is back in the picture. This idea that Israel still has a future also fits with 13:35, where Jesus taught that Israel's house is desolate until she says, "Blessed is he who comes in the name of the Lord."

Similarly within the canon, Peter later declares that delay is actually evidence of God's patience and desire to save (2 Pet 3:9). The return of Jesus and all the events associated with it are next on God's calendar (and so at least in this sense they will occur "soon"), but also in the interim believers are to be faithful and to watch for his return (Luke 21:34–36).

Luke's treatment of eschatology is not exhaustive. Other NT writers described events that Luke does not mention. Luke's eschatology focuses on the saints' final vindication in terms of OT promises. His focus on the authority and victory of the returning Son of Man shows where the resolution of all things resides. Similarly, Paul remarks that God has summed up all things in Christ (Eph 1:9–10). Salvation moves toward its completion, which means not only deliverance for the saints but also vindication before their opponents as well.

---

39. David Tiede, *Prophecy and History in Luke-Acts* (Philadelphia: Fortress, 1980), 65–96, shows how the conflict in Jerusalem is a key theme and that out of the judging vengeance of God comes vindication. Luke's use of a deuteronomistic theology means that purging takes place, so that judgment precedes grace and restoration for Israel. Jerusalem is judged but will be purged in the process (Zech 12:3; 1 Macc 3; *2 Bar.* 67–68; 4 Macc 4:11, esp. Deut 32). Tiede says, "But in spite of the dire fate of Jerusalem and the severe reproof it represents, it has not even been considered that the Gentiles have replaced Israel or that God's long-standing promises to Israel will fail to be fulfilled" (p. 95). In all of this, God is shown to be just and faithful. With the end of the times of the Gentiles comes a time when Israel finally will say, "Blessed is he who comes in the name of the Lord" (Luke 13:34–35). Acts 3:18–22 argues that what the prophets promised will come to pass in Jesus' return.

20.6 HOPE

The term "hope" (ἐλπίς, *elpis*) appears only in Acts, not in Luke, even though the concept is wrapped up in the entire program and promise of God in the Messiah. All that is said about Messiah's coming and what he will do in the two volumes informs Luke's concept of hope. There are six theological references to this theme in Acts.[40] These references help to frame how Luke views the consummation of eschatology.

Resurrection as vindication and hope is the point of the first text using the term (Acts 2:26). Here the body of Messiah is said to reside "in hope" (quoting Ps 16:9, cited as a text to argue for the promise of the resurrection of David's descendant). The soul of this holy one will not be left in Hades, and so "my body also will rest in hope." This hope was realized when God raised Jesus, showing that he is both Lord and Christ (Acts 2:36). So God's work for Jesus stands at the hub of hope for Luke.

The rest of the references to "hope" appear in Paul's defense speeches. In Acts 23:6, he states that he is on trial "because of the hope of the resurrection of the dead." The subsequent context makes it clear that Paul is alluding to his Damascus road experience and what that showed about Jesus being alive. What the Sadducees and Pharisees debate is whether someone could actually have appeared to Paul (v. 9), with the Pharisees open to such a possibility. So the theme linking hope and resurrection here matches Acts 2.

Acts 24:14–15 speaks of believing all the Law and Prophets have taught, having "the same hope in God as these men themselves have, that there will be a resurrection of both the righteous and the wicked." Here the hope is of justice, since in this judgment there will be a distinction made between the righteous and unrighteous. Judgment means vindication. That is what the consummation will produce.

In Acts 26:6 Paul declares that he is on trial "because of my hope in what God has promised our ancestors." This is Israel's hope, for Paul goes on to mention the hope of the twelve tribes in v. 7: "This is the promise our twelve tribes are hoping to see fulfilled." Verse 8 then speaks of resurrection from the dead, and the subsequent discussion points to Jesus' call of Paul on the Damascus road. So once again resurrection and a living Jesus are the key to why hope exists. It is the raised Jesus who is the hope.

In Acts 28:20 Paul is in Rome, speaking about the fact he is bound in chains "because of the hope of Israel." This summarizes what Luke has already said in the earlier texts. What is important to note is that it is Israel's story that is still being told even at the end of the two volumes. Israel's story of hope is also the world's story of hope. So Acts ends with Paul speaking to anyone who will listen about the kingdom of God and the Lord Jesus Christ (28:30–31). This is where Luke's eschatology takes us—to the kingdom of God and to Jesus as its Lord Messiah. Deliverance, vindication, justice, hope, and peace are found here for Luke.

---

40. Two secular uses of the term appear. In Acts 16:19, those in Philippi who benefit financially from the girl of divination complain they have lost any hope of profit after Paul exorcizes the demon. In 27:20, those on the ship are losing hope they will survive the storm.

Jesus' career has two stages that point to the fulfillment of God's promises to Israel for the sake of the world. Those promises contain the realization of hope for the world. This corporate dimension of salvation is important to Luke. Eschatology means reconciliation between people as well as with God. Much in our theology today has lost this more corporate view of the importance of salvation and where it takes the world. In our overindividualized sense of personal salvation, we lose the scope of what salvation and the eschaton means for the whole of creation and all the nations.

Nevertheless, eschatology does have its personal dimensions. We turn to that part of Luke's teaching next.

20.7 PERSONAL ESCHATOLOGY

In Luke's "personal eschatology," Jesus briefly describes in two passages what happens when people die: Luke 23:42–43 and Acts 7:55–56. These texts speak of people at death who are immediately aware that they are entering God's presence. Luke gives no other details besides noting this sense of hope from realizing Jesus is with a believing person from the moment they die.[41]

In Luke 23, the thief who confesses Jesus while hanging on the cross hears the promise that "today" he will be with Jesus in paradise. The thief asks to be remembered when Jesus comes into his kingdom. He is likely referring to the resurrection of the righteous at the end of time, as was the common Jewish view.[42] Jesus' reply is more than what the thief requests, since Jesus assures him that even in this very day he will share in the life to come: "Today you will be with me in paradise" (23:43). Even as Jesus dies on the cross, the Messiah draws people to himself and promises them life in God's presence, even in the face of death.

The second passage is similar. In Acts 7:55–56, Stephen, filled with the Holy Spirit, sees heaven open up and Jesus, standing as the Son of Man, waiting to welcome him. The arms of heaven are open to receive his children. Death is consumed by eternal life (1 Cor 15:54–55). Here the point also involves vindication, a core element of Luke's idea of hope. Eschatology and its hope motivate one to persevere. Justice and peace will come one day. Eschatology is not an abstract doctrine. It is practical and builds a perspective that solidifies allegiance to God.

20.8 CONCLUSION

Luke's eschatology is now-not yet in terms of the realization of promises God made of a Lord Messiah to come. This Messiah brings the rule of God in stages. Believ-

---

41. There are important elements of personal eschatology reflected in the parable of the rich man and Lazarus. They point to a permanent separation between the righteous and the judged, with no second chance for salvation for those who are judged. That is the point of Abraham's reference to a chasm that those judged cannot cross.

42. This hope is common in many strands of Judaism, expressed as hope in the world to come and associated with resurrection in *m Sanh.* 10.1. Biblical roots are Ezek 39 and Dan 12:1–3. See also Wisdom 3:1–9; 5:1–5; *T. Job* 40:3; *T. Abraham* 11.

ers live in between the two comings of the Lord with provision made for them to reflect what God can do for those who turn to him. The consummation comes at an unspecified time like a thief in the night. In the meantime, believers are to be faithful and keep watch for his return, not so much to figure out when it will come, but to represent him well in their stewardship before God. They are to be faithful until the hope of vindication, justice, and peace comes in the return.

Chapter 21

THE SCRIPTURES IN LUKE-ACTS

BIBLIOGRAPHY

Bock, Darrell L. *Proclamation from Prophecy and Pattern: Lucan Old Testament Christology.* JSNTSup. Sheffield: Sheffield Academic Press, 1987. Idem. "Scripture and the Realisation of God's Promises." Pp. 41–62 in *Witness to the Gospel: The Theology of Acts.* Ed. I. Howard Marshall and David Peterson. Grand Rapids: Eerdmans, 1998. Idem. "Single Meaning, Multiple Contexts and Referents: The New Testament's Legitimate, Accurate, and Multifaceted Use of the Old." Pp. 105–51 in *Three Views on the New Testament Use of the Old.* Ed. Kenneth Berding and Jonathan Lunde. Grand Rapids: Zondervan, 2008. **Clarke, W. L.** "The Use of the Septuagint in Acts." Pp. 66–105 in *The Beginnings of Christianity. Part 1: The Acts of the Apostles*, vol. 2. Ed. F. J. Foakes Jackson and K. Lake. London: Macmillan, 1922. **Evans, Craig**. "Prophecy and Polemic: Jews in Luke's Scriptural Apologetic." Pp. 171–211 in *Luke and Scripture: The Function of Sacred Tradition in Luke-Acts.* Ed. C. A. Evans and J. A. Sanders. Minneapolis: Fortress, 1993. **Green, Joel.** "The Problem of a Beginning: Israel's Scriptures in Luke 1–2." *BBR* 4 (1994): 61–85. **Holtz, Traugott.** *Untersuchungen über die alttestamentliche Zitate bei Lukas.* TUGAL 104. Berlin: Akademie, 1968. **Kimball, C. A.** *Jesus' Exposition of the Old Testament in Luke's Gospel.* JSNTSup. Sheffield: Sheffield Academic Press, 1994. **Litwak, Kenneth Duncan.** *Echoes of Scripture in Luke-Acts: Telling the History of God's People Intertextually.* JSNTSup. London: T&T Clark, 2005. **Rese, Martin.** *Alttestamenliche Motive in der Christologie des Lukas.* Gütersloh: Gütersloher, 1969. **Strauss, Mark L.** *The Davidic Messiah in Luke-Acts: The Promise and Its Fulfillment in Lucan Christology.* JSNTSup. Sheffield; Sheffield Academic Press, 1995.

The last summary citation of Scripture in Luke-Acts reads, "But God has helped me to this very day; so I stand here and testify to small and great alike. I am saying nothing beyond what the prophets and Moses said would happen — that the Messiah would suffer and, as the first to rise from the dead, would bring the message of light to his own people and to the Gentiles" (Acts 26:22–23).[1] This is but a variation on Luke 24:43–47, which makes much the same point. What has taken

---

1. This chapter is an update of my earlier chapter on Scripture in Luke-Acts entitled "Scripture and the Realisation of God's Promises," in *Witness to the Gospel*, 41–62. This work for a British publication reflects that origin in the title. For this version, I will use American spelling. The last citation in Luke-Acts is from Isa 6 in Acts 28:26–27, but the above citation is the last of Luke's summary citations where he notes what Scripure as a whole teaches.

place in Jesus is a realization of what God revealed would happen both for Israel and the nations. In everything Luke does, a key frame is the teaching and promise of Scripture, for Luke's claim is that this seemingly new faith realizes promises of old that God made to his people.

This citation serves as both an adequate introduction to, and summary of, Luke's use of Scripture. It notes three central themes: (1) the message of the newly emerged Christian teaching spans the full array of scriptural hope from Moses to the prophets; (2) at the center of that hope is the Christ event, especially his death and resurrection-ascension; and (3) God's vindication of Jesus becomes the occasion for his new appeal both to the Jews and the nations to enter into divine promise and life (light). Paul speaks as a representative of a mission where the raised Christ speaks for God through people such as this directly commissioned messenger of God (Acts 10:36, 42–43; Eph 2:17). These historically significant claims are the basis of Paul's defense before Rome. Paul is simply playing his role in the call of God to bring the light of God's truth in Christ to the people and the nations (Acts 26:15–18). Luke's story in Acts and his use of Scripture travel the same highway.

New movements in the ancient world, like the emergence of "the Way," were often viewed with interest but with skepticism as well (Acts 17:18–21). A great disadvantage of a new movement was that it appeared to lack a history and roots spanning the generations. The claim for heritage means being rooted in history and legitimacy, an ancient sociological necessity for obtaining cultural credibility, where what was older and tested was better, especially when making claims about what God had done in history.[2] This chapter examines Luke's scriptural claim for this new Christian movement. One way to make a significant religious claim was to appeal to ancient, sacred writings. The new movement had emerged out of Judaism, so that is where it found its sacred roots. This final summary text, like many others in Luke-Acts, does not reflect taking on the burden of a specific citation, but presents a broader summary claim appealing to the swath of teaching from the entire corpus of Scripture.[3] The consideration of Luke's broad use of Scripture should show how pervasive his appeal is.

This chapter proceeds in two steps.[4] First, some hermeneutical axioms reveal how Luke saw divine history and thus how he read Scripture. Also treated is a current critical debate over whether Luke appeals to promise and fulfillment. Then we move to the description of Luke's five major scriptural themes that support his claim for the new movement.

---

2. On ethnography as an ancient apologetic genre, see Sterling, *Historiography and Self-Definition*, 103–310, 389–93. See also the ancient works of Berossos, Menathon, and Josephus's *Antiquities*.

3. Other summary citations appear in Luke 24:26, 43–47; Acts 3:22–23; 17:2–3. A reference to Moses and the prophets also appears in Acts 28:23, but as an introduction to a specific citation, not a summary claim.

4. For the issue of Luke's use of the Hebrew Scripture, especially the LXX, see W. L. Clarke, "The Use of the Septuagint in Acts,"

in *The Beginnings of Christianity, Part 1: The Acts of the Apostles*, vol. 2 (ed. F. J. Foakes Jackson and K. Lake; London: Macmillan, 1922), 66–105; and Traugott Holtz, *Untersuchungen über die alttestamentliche Zitate bei Lukas* (TUGAL 104; Berlin: Akademie, 1968). Luke uses a version of the text akin to the LXX. Holtz argues the presence of another version is evidence of a source, especially in the Twelve Prophets and Isaiah. He sees more variation in the way the Torah and Psalter are cited.

21.1 HERMENEUTICAL AXIOMS DEFINED

Various themes in Luke's gospel show his perspective. They set the historical horizon from which he works with Scripture and history. Some have questioned anew the unity and legitimacy of the designation Luke-Acts.[5] But the testimony of Luke's gospel is crucial in setting the stage for Acts when it comes to the use of Scripture. The question is also important, because it shows how Luke sets the table for his claim of fulfillment.

In appealing to hermeneutical axioms, I am making a case for Luke much like Richard Hays's appeal to the "grand narrative of election and God's righteousness" as an influence for Paul's reading of Scripture, but with two major differences.[6] First, the hermeneutical appeal to these axioms is not as free and haphazard as Hays's reading argues, but serves rather as a very thought-through, fundamental claim about Scripture considered from the perspective of a prioritized theology grounded in the Christ event.

Second, Hays's rejection of midrashic technique fails to distinguish hermeneutical axioms from hermeneutical techniques. The reason the early church's (and Paul's) conclusions were so different from those of Judaism is not that their procedures of reading were so different.[7] Rather, the interpretive grid, the axioms to which those procedures were applied, produced the difference in the readings. Both Luke's and Paul's apparent "revision" of the meaning of the ancient Hebrew Scriptures is really a claim that the ancient narrative, representing only promise, was incomplete without Jesus' coming and the revelation that accompanied him. Now that he has come, we can understand God's plan more clearly, because the events tied to his coming reveal the priorities and relationships in that ancient plan, in terms of issues like the law, the covenants, and the nations. These events set new priorities, witnessed to by the Spirit, but not as a denial of the function of how older elements in revelation prepared for the promise's arrival. In this perspective, the NT writers are one. So the enumeration of these axioms is important to understanding the grid through which Luke read Scripture and the events tied to Jesus.

21.2 AXIOM 1: GOD'S DESIGN AND A NEW ERA OF REALIZATION

This theme emerges in Luke 1:1. The point surfaces clearly by comparing two recent translations as Luke describes his effort to compose a narrative. The RSV reads

---

5. See the earlier discussion of the work of Pervo and Parsons in ch. 3. Another important evaluation of their thesis is found in Marshall, "Acts and the Former Treatise," 163–82.

6. For Hays's approach and the claim for Pauline charismatic freedom, see his *Echoes of Scripture in the Epistles of Paul* (New Haven: Yale Univ. Press, 1989), esp. ch. 5.

7. Various studies of Luke's use of Scripture show how similar procedures to Judaism were used. See my *Proclamation from Proph-*

ecy and Pattern; Martin Rese, *Alttestamenliche Motive in der Christologie des Lukas* (Gütersloh: Gütersloher, 1969); C. A. Kimball, *Jesus' Exposition of the Old Testament in Luke's Gospel* (JSNTSup 94; Sheffield: Sheffield Academic Press, 1994); Strauss, *Davidic Messiah in Luke-Acts*; and Kenneth Duncan Litwak, *Echoes of Scripture in Luke-Acts: Telling the History of God's People Intertextually* (JSNTSup 282; London: T&T Clark, 2005).

v. 1b as "a narrative of the things that have been accomplished among us," while the NRSV reads "an orderly account of the events that have been fulfilled among us" (περὶ τῶν πεπληροφορημένων ἐν ἡμῖν πραγμάτων, *peri tōn peplērophorēmenōn en hēmin pragmatōn*). The NRSV is more precise. The key term is πεπληροφορημένων, referring to the presence of designed events, acts that stand fulfilled in the midst of Luke's audience. The events of Luke's gospel are "designed" as part of God's plan, bringing a necessity with them, as Luke 24:43–47 points out, using δεῖ (*dei*) while appealing both to events and Scripture.

The earlier gospel volume, according to Acts 1:1, refers to what "Jesus began to do and to teach," but Acts tells the rest of that story. Even the preaching of Paul is represented as the preaching of Jesus (26:22–23). As 1:4 argues, the promise of the Father, that is, the enabling Spirit who will help them testify to the work of God, must be dispensed in Jerusalem (cf. Luke 12:11–12). The Spirit's coming into the community in Acts 2 is told with appeal to a series of scriptural texts as event, sacred text, and preaching take place side by side. This combination of designed events and enabled preaching from the Spirit sets a backdrop for the appeal to Scripture. God is at work in events revealed in Scripture. The Spirit from Christ explains these designed events through representatives like Peter and Paul. So Paul can speak for Jesus. Luke wishes his readers to view their citations and declarations as tied to the realization of Scripture.

The design is not stated in general terms; it has a structure. Four texts are crucial: Luke 7:28; 16:16; Acts 10:42–43; 17:30–31. The first two of these texts were treated in the previous chapter. They show how John the Baptist is, in one sense, the end of an old era. As the greatest man born among women, this forerunner prophet has a unique role in the old era. Until he came, the Law and the Prophets were at the center of God's plan. But now everything is different. The least in the kingdom Jesus brings is greater than the man who was the greatest of the old era. Now the gospel of the kingdom of God is preached. The gospel is the presence of something new and something old. The old era of expectation leads to the new era of realization. That is part of the design. To understand where the story of the new community begins, one must understand that John, as the forerunner whom Malachi promised, is part of a divine design whose roots go back to scriptural hope (Luke 1:14–17; 7:27).[8]

---

8. A debate has emerged as to whether this reflects prophecy and fulfillment. This is a question I will treat below, but for the claim that prophecy and fulfillment are not what is being emphasized by Luke, see Joel Green, "The Problem of a Beginning: Israel's Scriptures in Luke 1–2," *BBR* 4 (1994): 61–85; and Litwak, *Echoes of Scripture in Luke-Acts*, esp. pp. 11–12 and n. 40, as well as pp. 15–17. Litwak appeals to discursive framing of narrative as to how Luke uses Scripture. This focus includes within it a way to deny Luke's use of promise-fulfillment or any appeals to pattern to support such a promise-fulfillment view in Luke-Acts. To do this, Litwak ignores three key points. (1) The reading of texts out of Judaism saw history in recurring patterns, something my study in *Proclamation* showed through its examination of Jewish texts that Luke

appeals to and something Litwak's study does not engage. Litwak claims my definition of "pattern" is so broad that almost anything can work as fulfillment, but this ignores the Jewish background and *Wirkungsgeschichte* study I did on how individual texts were being read in Judaism. For many of the texts I was able to trace how Jews read history in cyclical ways that point to pattern and how pattern was a kind of hermeneutical axiom. (2) As a result, his limiting of prophecy and fulfillment to predictive texts (pp. 15–17) is historically flawed in how the category was seen in an ancient context. I hope to show this in what I say in this chapter. Promise can proclaim without predicting and still be seen as prophetic. Promise is a form of speech act that functions in an open-ended way into the future. (3) As a result, his claim that discursive framing and prophecy and

A similar emphasis emerges in Acts 10:42–43 and 17:30–31. Here the apostolic preaching centers on "the one whom God appointed as judge of the living and the dead." Thus in Acts 10:42–43 the divine plan is mentioned first, then the reference to Scripture: "All the prophets testify about him that everyone who believes in him receives forgiveness of sins through his name." The plan's presence is corroborated and declared in Scripture. The movement, new in execution, is old in planning. Event and Scripture are placed side by side. God's plan is what Scripture records.

When Paul makes the same point to a strictly pagan audience (Acts 17:30–31), the Scripture is less explicitly present, but he still refers to a plan and presents a biblical theology with reference to idolatry and the creation. This text reads, "In the past God overlooked such ignorance, but now he commands all people everywhere to repent. For he has set a day when he will judge the world with justice by the man he has appointed. He has given proof of this to everyone by raising him from the dead." What was for Jews the era of law and prophets, for pagans was the era of ignorance—more specifically, a rejection of God's presence in the creation. A new era in the plan has come involving all nations more directly with special revelation and showing through resurrection that Jesus is the one to whom all are accountable. Acts 17:30–31 notes how fundamental the plan was in Luke's mind. Scripture addresses and establishes that the new community has rich roots connected to the living God's ancient promises. What was revealed and promised long ago has come.

21.3 AXIOM 2: CHRIST AT THE CENTER

This axiom needs little development. It is already evident in reading Luke and from the earlier discussions of Jesus' person and work in Luke-Acts.[9] Whole works expound the theme, though with differing concerns.[10] But it is important to place it in proper reference to the more encompassing theme of God's activity and plan. Christology is not the sole goal of Luke's use of Scripture. It is an important port of call on the way to more comprehensive claims about God's plan and the promise's subsequent realization. The literary flow of Luke's use of Scripture reveals that once Jesus' messianic and lordship credentials are established ("He is Lord of all and judge of the living and the dead"), then scriptural attention can concentrate on how Gentiles are included and how Israel must not reject the opportunity to share in the promise. The plan argues that Jesus is Lord of all, so the gospel can go to all. Israel will miss blessing if she refuses to share in the call Jesus makes to all humanity.

---

fulfillment are distinct and should not be combined or overlapped is simply wrong. For all that is valuable in Litwak's narrative treatment of Scripture in Luke and for his excellent job of focusing on this key rhetorical device, the building of a chasm between discursive framing and the prophetic appeal to Scripture simply ignores the force of the summary texts we cited to open this chapter. Discursive framing works and has appeal because the belief is that Scripture has revealed

what God promised and what God will do or has done. That Jesus fits into this frame is a rhetorical claim *and* an appeal to prophetic realization. Here is where narrative reading without historical roots produces lopsided results cut off from history for the sake of rhetorical analysis. Once again what we have is a both-and, not an either-or.

9. See chs. 7–8 above.

10. See note 7 above and the bibliography for this chapter.

21.4 AXIOM 3: SCRIPTURE AS AN INTERPRETER OF DIVINE EVENT AND CURRENT CRITICAL DISCUSSION: A DEFENSE OF PROMISE-FULFILLMENT IN LUKE-ACTS

These axioms suggest key elements in Luke's perspective about the relationship between Scripture and event. God and his plan stand behind the events. Such expectations also existed in Judaism because of God's promises in Scripture. Central to both Christian and Jewish hope was the declaration of the various covenants and the deliverance they anticipated. Most importantly, history was read by both groups in a way that looked for divine patterns of activity that signaled the reemergence of divine design in salvific events.[11]

This feature of pattern is why prophecy is not limited to directly prophetic prediction. Prophecy also includes the noting of a divine pattern or the typological-prophetic reading of the Bible. Promise for the early church included prophetic texts and pattern texts, along with appeal to covenant hope now freshly realized. The premise behind reading history as involving promise and pattern is divine design and the constancy of God's character as he saves in similar ways at different times. Jewish imagery reused exodus motifs or new creation language; this is how Judaism accepted this cyclical and patterned view of history. Reading history this way also fuelled Luke's perspective in seeing divine design in the events tied to Jesus. Understanding this "pattern fulfillment" dynamic is crucial to understanding how Luke reads Scripture.

The center of that hope involved a pivotal figure. Luke's claim is that the events of Jesus' life and ministry began the arrival of that promised era. Scripture is an interpreter of those events, explaining them and their design. At the same time, the events themselves, as unusual and unique as they are, draw one to Scripture to seek explanation. It would be wrong to view promise and fulfillment as a unidirectional activity, where a repository of texts was simply lined up with events, though that is what some critiques of reading prophecy and fulfillment in Luke have claimed for such a view.[12] For example, Soards comments:

---

11. Here two studies, deeply rooted in historical study of the Jewish sources, are key: Leonhard Goppelt, *Typos: The Typological Interpretation of the Old Testament in the New* (Grand Rapids: Eerdmans, 1982); and Francis Foulkes, *The Acts of God: A Study of the Basis of Typology in the Old Testament* (London: Tyndale, 1958). Here is where the presence of pattern is described as a historically present way of reading the texts in the ancient period.

12. Those who have critiqued promise-fulfillment or prophecy-fulfillment argue its approach is too unidirectional or too limiting a perspective. Already noted above are the studies of Green and Litwak. See esp. Green, "Problem of a Beginning," p. 66, n. 19. To this can be added Soards, *Speeches in Acts*. The following citation is from this work (p. 201). I have argued from my dissertation that not all fulfillment is unidirectional (going from text to event).

Typological-prophetic fulfillment sometimes requires the fulfillment event to see the pattern and divine design. If Green is talking about a unidirectional prophetic scheme (that excludes the presence of pattern fulfillment), then I agree with his critique that a prophetic model is too limiting. But prophecy in Luke-Acts is not so simple. To continue a story grounded in covenant commitment, as Green correctly argues is present in Luke 1–2, is to continue the story of the realization of promise, so events both reveal and look back. One should not juxtapose as opposites the presence of redemptive story and promise-fulfillment. One can rightly distinguish them, but they often are related to each other. Again in many texts what we have here is a both-and, not an either-or. So also correctly, David Peterson, "The Motif of Fulfillment and the Purpose of Luke-Acts," in *The Book of Acts in Its Ancient Literary Setting*, vol. 1, 83–104. In

When one considers the function of *the past* in the speeches of Acts one finds that a prophecy-fulfilment interpretation of the scripture quotations is too restricted a perspective for understanding the role of the past, especially the scripture quotations, in the speeches. Rather than a mere linear prophecy-fulfilment scheme, one should see that the past, especially the quotations of scripture, is used in the speeches to establish the continuity of the past, the present, and even the future.

This misrepresents the prophecy-fulfillment or promise-pattern fulfillment perspective. The prophecy and fulfillment view affirms the sociological point Soards makes. He states it with reference to time, whereas prophecy and fulfillment have tended to state it with reference to topic. In fact, I argued for this point about continuity by noting that Luke's purpose was "to remove doubt by his justifying of the Gentile mission of God through Jesus the Lord despite the presence of persecution against the church.... Anyone can now see from Luke's account that Jesus' position is proclaimed in the Scriptures as well as being verified by events and his own teaching (Acts 1.1)."[13] I also addressed the relationship of event and text: "We have shown that the relationship between event and text is two-way."[14] I discussed Ps 110, Ps 16, and Isa 55 as three good examples of this phenomenon, where events helped reveal details that emerged in how the pattern fulfillment fits in light of the Christ event.

An important critique of approaches that diminish promise-fulfillment, while emphasizing the role of event, can be made. It is that in most cases, the texts used by Luke were already regarded as either messianic, prophetic, or eschatological within Judaism. The prophecy was not "discovered" by the event. However, there often came with the event a filling out of the text in line with its general theme. Thus the exact significance of the text was revealed with the event. To characterize this relationship between text and event as one way by overemphasizing either the text or event is to fail to appreciate the complexity of the interaction between the two elements.

In some cases, events showed how the texts lined up and how the design worked. The various strands of christological OT use in Luke reveal functions united in one person that Judaism placed in a variety of eschatological figures. Events tied to Jesus' ministry show the unity of function that Luke argues for when he discusses Jesus as the promise bearer. Most of these points are made in Luke's gospel, setting the table for uses of Scripture in Acts.[15] But behind these uses of Scripture stand three

---

making this critique of Litwak and others, I share their views that (1) covenant is key to the use of Scripture; (2) continuity with the past and legitimization of the new movement are a key purpose in Luke's use of Scripture; (3) there is far more to Luke's use of Scripture than what is shown in a specific topic or in merely looking at citations and allusions; and (4) narrative discursive framing is important. What I reject is the idea that these observations somehow preclude the use of prophecy and pattern as a key means of getting there.

13. Bock, *Proclamation from Prophecy and Pattern*, 277. The appeal to Scripture made in this light is inherently an appeal to the past.

14. Ibid., 273.

15. The proof of this point is beyond the scope of this chapter, but *Proclamation from Prophecy and Pattern* showed that in first-century Judaism most of the texts the church claimed addressed Jesus were already read as promise texts. The debate was not whether such texts spoke about salvation or the figures involved in salvation's drama, but whether Jesus was the fulfillment of their contents. In other words, these texts were already placed in a rhetorical prophetic environment.

fundamental Lucan beliefs: (1) the events surrounding Jesus are divinely designed; (2) he is at the center of God's plan and the new era arrival; and (3) Scripture helps to explain what has taken place and is taking place. The events are recent and the era is new, but the plan is not. In this way Luke makes his claim to divine heritage for the new movement.

How does Luke make the case? What topics make the point? Five themes fill out the picture of Luke's use of Scripture.

21.5 FIVE CENTRAL SCRIPTURAL THEMES IN LUKE-ACTS NAMED

The following list parallels one by Craig Evans.[16] This study will first consider the five topics and then discuss their relationship and function. The list includes: covenant and promise; Christology; community mission, community guidance, and ethical direction; commission to the Gentiles; and challenge with warning to Israel.

21.5.1 Covenant and Promise

The theme of covenant and realized promise is fundamental to Luke-Acts, since it was raised as early as Luke 1:54–55 (Abrahamic) and 1:68–70 (Davidic). This emphasis continues in Acts, where all the covenants of expectation, or allusions to them, appear in speeches.

The hope of the Spirit is clearly expressed in the OT in new covenant teaching (Jer 31:31–34; Ezek 36:22–32). In Acts 2:16–19, Peter uses another OT text that raises this promise, Joel 2:28–32 (=3:1–5 LXX). He declares the realization of this promise, but also indicates that "in the last days" this pouring out of the Spirit will come. The remark alludes to Luke 24:49 and the awaiting of "the promise of my Father," as well as to the instruction to await the Holy Spirit in Acts 1:8. Luke also makes another link. John the Baptist had indicated that the stronger one to come would baptize "with the Holy Spirit and fire," a baptism of purging within humanity. This is how one could recognize that the Christ, the promised coming one, was present (3:15–17). In Peter's declaring the Spirit's arrival, not only are the last days present, but also the decisive evidence of the promised presence of Christ.

This christological conclusion is the burden of Peter's speech at Pentecost (Acts 2:32–36). The Spirit's coming is how one can know God has made Jesus both Lord and Christ and has vindicated him through resurrection-ascension. Peter's speech ends with a call to respond and to participate in the promise. This hope is for those who are near and those who are far off, as many as the Lord God has called to himself (2:39). Peter's audience consisted of diaspora Jews gathered to celebrate

16. Craig Evans, "Prophecy and Polemic: Jews in Luke's Scriptural Apologetic," in *Luke and Scripture: The Function of Sacred Tradition in Luke-Acts* (ed. C. A. Evans and J. A. Sanders; Minneapolis: Fortress, 1993), 171–211, esp. 209–10. His five categories are: Christological, Soteriological, Apologetic, Minatory, and Critical (of Israel).

Pentecost, so a claim of fulfillment would be a call to share in national hope opened up to all by God's direction.

The scope of the "all" expands and becomes clearer in Acts 10, when Gentiles are included. Acts 11:15–17 continues the link of covenant and Scripture by looking at Gentile inclusion and comparing the Spirit's coming to what took place "in the beginning," that is, at Pentecost in Acts 2 with the 120 gathered in Jerusalem. The call to share in promise is a call to share in a heritage rooted in Scripture.

Also noted is a tie to Davidic promise. This connection is made in the infancy material as Zechariah praises deliverance coming out of the house of David (Luke 1:67–69) and Mary hears about one born who will rule on the throne of David (Luke 1:31–33). Acts 2:30 notes God's promise to David about a descendant to be set on David's throne. The allusion is to Ps 132:11, which is a commentary on the promise of 2 Sam 7:8–16, the Davidic covenant. The Ps 132 citation serves to link Peter's remarks about the fulfillment of Ps 16:8–11b in bodily resurrection with his remarks about fulfillment in ascension in Ps 110:1. All of this is done by the Jewish hermeneutical technique of *gezerah shewa*, where passages that share terms are linked together to make an exposition of the combination of the verses. Peter argues that the ascension is an initial realization of a promise made to David about one who would take up his authority at the very side of God. The realization of Ps 110:1 in ascension also initially fulfills this promise to David.

Because the remark involving Ps 132 is an allusion, it has not received as much discussion as the three other texts cited in Acts 2, but it is an important conceptual link in Peter's speech, as it ties Jesus' resurrection-ascension to messianic promise. The distribution of the Spirit is evidence of the last days and of resurrection-ascension, as well as of messianic presence and authority made available to the dispersed Jews present in Peter's audience. Peter's speech is about Christology and claims of covenant realization. The promise and the covenant belong together as prophetic Scripture shows.

Paul makes similar detailed claims about the Davidic promise to a synagogue audience in Pisidian Antioch in Acts 13:13–41. Here Paul's speech reviews Israel's history up to the time of David. Then he mentions that from this man's (David's) posterity (lit., his "seed"), God has brought a Savior (v. 23). Next, Paul recalls John the Baptist's promise (cf. Luke 3:15–17). In v. 32, Paul declares that the message about Jesus is "the good news" about "what God promised our ancestors." He then cites Ps 2:7; Isa 55:3; and Ps 16:10. Isaiah supplies the key text in this linkage. Paul appeals to this text when he says that God "will give you the holy and sure blessings promised to David" (v. 34). Whereas Ps 2 declares Jesus to be the Son and Ps 16 shows that resurrection was anticipated in the program, Isa 55 shows that the promise was not intended merely as a private commitment to David, but it was made for the benefit of the nation, for "you [all]" (ὑμῖν, *hymin*; note the plural). Thus, Paul's usage parallels that of Peter. Jesus' arrival is part of a divine plan, so the message of the new community is the appropriate extension and expression of Israel's promise.

The same emphasis appears in Acts 3, only here it is the promise to Abraham that is featured, as well as an allusion to Moses. Not only does a note about covenant appear here (vv. 24–26), but also scriptural warning (vv. 22–23). The reference to Moses appeals to the promise of a prophet like Moses, an eschatological leader-prophet who delivers the people (Deut 18:15). This remark was also anticipated in Luke 9:35, where the divine voice tells the three disciples present at the transfiguration to hear Jesus, alluding to this same passage from Deuteronomy. In Acts 3, it is the Torah that also points to Jesus. There can be no greater heritage claim than to take a Jewish audience back to Moses and the Torah.

The covenant promise appealed to in Acts 3 is Abrahamic. But it is tied to a more fundamental claim, namely, that all the prophets after Samuel proclaimed these days (3:24). The days in view are those surrounding the Messiah's activity (vv. 18–20). Again, Scripture points to events, which in turn should drive the audience back to considering scriptural promise. Peter makes his appeal on the basis of Abraham's promise in v. 25: "You are heirs of the prophets and of the covenant God made with your fathers. He said to Abraham, 'Through your offspring [lit., seed] all peoples on earth will be blessed.'"

There is a delightful ambiguity in the term "seed" (σπέρμα, *sperma*). In the original promise, the seed of Abraham was not every physical descendant he was responsible for producing. It was Isaac over Ishmael and Jacob over Esau. This was before the seed came to be seen as all the descendants of the twelve tribes of Israel as descended from Jacob's twelve sons. This, of course, is a key part of the story of Genesis and Exodus, where a nation emerges from the promise to Abraham. In this original telling, "seed" bears both singularity and corporateness. Peter here focuses in on the singular seed, just like Paul in Gal 3:16, since he goes on in v. 26 to mention the one God has raised up, namely, "his servant [Jesus]." He is the source of blessing to those in the nation who turn back to God.

As with the speeches of Acts 2 and 13, the appeal here is to realized promise, grounded in a claim of heritage reaching back to the nation's foundational covenant. Interestingly, whereas Acts 2 tied together Davidic promise and new covenantlike hope, here the speech ties together messianic (Davidic) hope and Abrahamic promise. Thus Acts 2 and 3 together review the three fundamental covenants of promise (Abraham, Moses, and David) and argue they are all fulfilled in Jesus. Jesus' ministry and the new community's message are not an attempt to break away from Israel, but a claim of the realization of her long-awaited promises.

One more text probably belongs here, though it could also be placed in categories about Christology or community mission. It is Amos 9:11–15 in Acts 15:14–18. Here a slight distinction is noted between what the text says and how it functions in Acts. James, in citing this text, is arguing that Gentiles belong in the community of God's people. God has acted "to choose a people for his name from the Gentiles" (v. 14). In terms of function, this text justifies Gentile involvement in the community, which is why it also should be considered a text about ecclesiology. However, the citation itself deals with rebuilding the fallen Davidic house as at the root of this act of inclusion. The idea of a rebuilt Davidic house corresponds to covenant promise as seen from the perspective of Israel's history, where the monarchy had not existed for some time. Jesus is the source of the rebuilding effort, so that Luke's use also has christological overtones.

The Amos citation in its cited form promises that the fallen Davidic house will be rebuilt and that the nations will be included in its restoration. The cited text is but one that could have been mentioned since the introductory formula tied to James's remarks speaks of how the prophets harmonize with what has taken place (v. 15, "the words of the prophets are in agreement with this, as it is written"). Usually when Luke has such a reference, more than one text is in view, even if he does not mention them. Among possible candidates in James's mind might be Isa 2:2–4; 19:23–25; and 49:6, if not Gentile inclusion texts that were in the Christian tradition such as those found in Rom 15:7–13.[17]

So the Christ event represents the rebuilding of that fallen house, and now Gentiles are included in the promise. The placement of this text under covenant and promise is legitimate because James cites the text to describe what the prophets promised would happen when God completed his promises made about the Davidic house, especially given its historical fall. How would God keep that promise? The interesting feature is that, like Acts 3, this text addresses the issue of blessing for the world through the presence of the one who fulfills this text. Here, even more explicitly than in Acts 3, the claim of heritage in terms of the unusual make-up of the newly reformed people of God is made. Indeed, Gentile inclusion is a part of Davidic hope. The roots of the promised multiethnic makeup of the new community are not as surprising as it seemed initially. On reflection over Scripture, Gentile inclusion also is ancient in origin.

21.5.2 Christology

Many of the texts in the covenant and promise category could also be placed here, but to distinguish the two is helpful, since Christology, as the above texts show, often plays a complementary role to additional claims about God's plan. Texts noted here serve primarily a christological function.

Most of the christological texts treat activity associated with Jesus' ministry. For example, there is the use of Isa 61 and 58 in Luke 4. This synagogue citation summarizes the mission of Jesus, as do the hymns of Luke 1–2, which allude to the Scriptures throughout. Psalm 16:10 appears twice: in Acts 13:35 and as part of a larger citation of Ps 16:8–11b in Acts 2:25–28. The passage argues for divine accreditation for Jesus, an accreditation that started in his ministry (vv. 22–24) and culminates in promised resurrection that serves to vindicate Jesus and his claims.

---

17. A difficult issue here is how this text in its LXX form is related to the Hebrew version, where it looks as if Edom is judged, not included. Bruce nicely treats this issue in *Acts of the Apostles*, 341.

Peter's assertion may represent a novel handling of this text, for he goes to great lengths to defend the fact that the text is not about David, who is buried. Peter argues that the immediate, bodily resurrection was predicted of the Christ (Acts 2:30–31). Now resurrection testifies to this promise's accomplishment and thus to Jesus as the Messiah. The use of Ps 16:10 in Acts 13 about Jesus not being abandoned to see corruption parallels the psalm's earlier use in Acts 2:31b. This part of the citation is Luke's real concern in both passages—that Messiah would be raised was a promise of Scripture. Luke 24:43–47 is a summary citation that makes a similar point. The theme of the divine necessity of Jesus' suffering and being raised also fits in here, as does the allusion to Isa 53 at the Last Supper and in Jesus' remarks about being numbered among the criminals later in that same scene (Luke 22:37). The Last Supper also makes allusion to the new covenant that Jesus' death will set in place (22:19–22).

Another key activity is the ascension of Jesus and his sitting at God's side. This emphasis appears in the many references to the Messiah or Jesus being seated at God's right hand from Ps 110:1 (Luke 21:41–44; 22:69; Acts 2:34–35; 5:31; 7:55–56). Luke prepared for this idea when Jesus asked the question of why Messiah is called Lord by David, his ancestor, and his assertion that "from now on, the Son of Man [i.e., Jesus] will be seated at the right hand of the mighty God" (Luke 22:69). There Jesus claims direct access to the authority of God by sharing in his ruling authority. He also affirms a divine vindication regardless of what the leaders may do to him.

In Acts 2, this claim is evidenced by the distribution of promised salvific blessing, namely, Jesus' distribution of the Holy Spirit on the disciples (v. 33). Acts 5 argues that Jesus' exaltation makes him Leader-Savior, as he offers to Israel repentance and forgiveness of sins. In Acts 7, Jesus stands at the right hand of the Father as Stephen dies. Though the meaning of his standing to receive Stephen is debated, it is likely that he rises to welcome Stephen with heavenly vindication.[18] Regardless of its exact force, this passage does picture Jesus' current authority at God's side in heaven. Thus, in this imagery, a previously foreseen shared rule for Jesus with God is realized, a rule concentrating on the distribution of spiritual benefits to those who respond to Jesus' offer. Here Jesus exercises messianic executive authority, showing his active rule. Christology is present not only to describe who Jesus is, but also to set forth how he functions. Luke's interest in what Jesus does reveals what God has shown him to be.

Isaiah 53:7–8 is another example where how Jesus functions is the point (Acts 8:32–33). Here the Ethiopian eunuch asks if the author of this passage is talking about Isaiah the prophet or someone else. The way the question is raised in 8:34 suggests that perhaps popular opinion centered on Isaiah. What is interesting about

---

18. For the options and a defense of this force, see Luke Timothy Johnson, *The Acts of the Apostles* (SP; Collegeville, MN: Liturgical, 1992), 139.

this Servant citation of Isaiah is that it does not cite the substitutionary verses of Isa 53, but highlights Jesus' unjust suffering. This part of God's designed program was also noted earlier, but without direct citation from the Scripture (Acts 2:23). In Acts 8 a text appears. Jesus suffered silently as an innocent, like a lamb led to slaughter. He was rejected and died unjustly. That summary citation reads very much like the emphasis of Luke's passion story, which highlights Jesus' innocent suffering (Luke 23:4, 14–15, 22). Thus Jesus' unjust death, taking place in the midst of rejection, is set forth in Scripture as the way of Jesus. This text became but the first that Philip would discuss with the eunuch (Acts 8:35) — another example of Luke's summary appeal to Scripture where one text is cited, but others exist on the theme that go uncited (see, again, Luke 24:43–47).

The remaining christological citation in Acts identifies Jesus as Son (Ps 2:7 in Acts 13:33). An allusion to this text appeared in Luke 3:22 and 9:35 (also Heb 1:5). The connection to Ps 2 suggests that it has regal overtones. The promised ruler who conquers in battle is the Son according to this psalm. He has the power and authority to deliver. As already noted in the covenant and promise discussion, the Acts 13 context affirms the realization of Davidic promise, of messianic hope. The scriptural triad of citations in Acts 13 as a whole asserts that the promised Christ is attested to by God through resurrection, as the citation of Ps 16:10 shows. This event demonstrates the presence of the Son (cf. Rom 1:3–4).

A debate about the use of Ps 2:7 in Acts 13 is whether it explains resurrection alone or explains the arrival of Jesus in history. In past debate, that decision turns on the meaning of "raising up" Jesus in Acts 13:32–33 (ἀναστήσας, *anastēsas*), an expression that by itself can refer to resurrection (using ἤγειρεν, *ēgeiren*, 5:30; 10:40; using ἀνέστησεν, *anestēsen*, 2:24, 32) or to arrival on the scene of history (using either ἀναστήσει, *anastēsei* in 3:22 and 7:37, or ἀναστήσας, *anastēsas*, in 3:26; 7:37; using ἤγειρεν, *ēgeiren*, in 13:22). I have argued elsewhere that the introductory formula to this passage in 13:32–33 has three parts and that the passage uses three citations to match portions of the introductory formula (God promised: Ps. 2:7; for us: Isa 55:3; raising Jesus: Ps 16:10).[19] If this is correct, "raising up" refers to resurrection as Ps 110:1 shows, but Ps 2:7 refers only to God's promise about a coming Son.

Regardless of the view taken about "raised up," the passage identifies Jesus as the promised Son. This speech and the other texts that have preceded it make it clear why Luke thinks Jesus is promise realized. The use of Scripture for Christology describes Jesus' career in such a way that his suffering, death, resurrection, and ascension are seen not to be surprising for a Messiah. Luke claims that Scripture points to a suffering but raised Messiah. The idea has old roots. Luke also argues through Ps 110:1 that this Savior is Lord, ruling from God's side. Showing this authority allows Luke to use Christology as a basis for claims in other areas later in Acts, especially Gentile inclusion. Since Jesus is Lord of all, the gospel goes to all.

---

19. Bock, *Proclaimation from Prophecy and Pattern*, 244–45.

21.5.3 Community Mission, Community Guidance, and Ethical Direction

This category includes three diverse texts in Acts: Acts 1:20; 4:24–26; and 13:47. Acts 1:20 appeals to the Psalter to legitimate the selection of a replacement for Judas. Acts 4:24–26 appeals to Ps 2 for understanding why the church is being persecuted. Acts 13:47 explains the mission of Paul and Barnabas as part of the commission of the Servant of God from Isa 49.

Texts pointing to ethics appear in Luke's gospel as the invocation of the call to love God. Luke 10:27 points to a core ethical value from Deut 6:5, which was also introduced in the picture of John the Baptist's work to turn people to God and to each other in Luke 1:16–17. The description of John's calling appeals to Mal 3:1 and 4:5. Turning people to God or loving God results in a difference in how others are treated and how community takes place.

To these texts can be added the already discussed Acts 15:15–18 with its use of Amos 9. Here the inclusion of Gentiles into the community is the point, as well as a christological reminder that the damaged tent of David will be restored to enable this inclusion. So this text really fits in a couple of categories. It shows as well how foundational Christology is for these other categories of use.[20]

Acts 1:20; 4:24–26; and 13:47 help explain community activity and events. They highlight the identity and function of the community's key servants (Acts 1), the call of the new community (Acts 13), and the context of persecution in which that call is likely to be carried out (Acts 4). Acts 1:20 combines two texts (Pss 69:26 [69:25 Eng.] and 109:8) to make two points. First, the Ps 69 text is applied typologically to argue that Judas has suffered the fate of an enemy of God. Second, Ps 109 explains what the community should do after Judas's judgment; namely, they should select a replacement. It also describes the function of the one to be selected as an overseer. In their original setting both psalms treated the theme of how God handles those he rejects and what happens as a result. Seen in that light, their use makes sense. Judas fits in the pattern of those who oppose God. Judas faced divine rejection as a result.

Despite Luke's interest in and emphasis on Paul, everything about the narrative mood of Matthias as one of the Twelve suggests the act to replace Judas with Matthias had Luke's approval. The scene is bathed in prayer, guided by Scripture, directed by Peter, and left in the hands of God. God directs the community before it launches out in mission. It is properly reconstituted, having judged one of its own as unworthy.

In Acts 4:24–26 the community responds in the face of persecution and opposition. They ask for boldness in the midst of opposition, which Scripture shows should not take them by surprise. They cite Ps 2:1 to note the fact that their pres-

---

20. This connection between Christology and other uses is also present in the Ps 2 use in Acts 4, as well as the appeal to the Servant imagery in Acts 13, for Paul and Barnabas share in the calling and ministry that Jesus as Servant had.

ent opposition was anticipated. So the Gentiles rage and the people imagine vain things against the Lord and his anointed. The fulfillment of this is explained in Acts 4:27–28. Herod and Pilate, Gentiles, and the people of Israel were gathered against God's holy servant Jesus to carry out God's predestined plan.[21] Once again, Scripture serves to explain events, revealing the plan about this new community. Their path of suffering is noted; rejection should not surprise them. They are simply repeating the path the anointed one walked. They are following after him.

The third text (Acts 13:46–47) describes the mission of Paul and Barnabas. They warn their synagogue audience not to reject their message, and they cite Isa 49:6.[22] This citation reveals that Jesus alone is not the light, an interesting note in view of the fact that (1) in Acts 8 Jesus had been identified as the Servant from a text in Isa 53; and (2) most likely the Jews understood this text to address the nation as a whole. Koet argues that the text asserts the mission of gathered Israel as opposed to the mission of Paul and Barnabas. To accomplish this, he draws on the LXX reading for the text and then ties its reading to texts about mission in Luke 2:32 and 24:47 (note also Acts 13:47). He goes on to argue that the choice between Jesus, Paul and Barnabas, and gathered Israel as light is a false dilemma. The text's point is to challenge the synagogue audience to be a part of this light and share in the mission.

Koet has a good point, but he overstates its force. This study has already shown that taking texts as they were read by Jews is not an automatic path to understanding Luke's usage (e.g., Ps 16 in Acts 2; Isa 53 in Acts 8; Ps 2 in Acts 4). More important, in our view, is the fact that the text is clearly presented as a command of the Lord given to Paul and Barnabas (Acts 13:47a). They are describing their mission, not attempting to invite others to join them. They are explaining why they are now going to turn to Gentiles. What was true of Jesus, as one preeminently called to be a light to the Gentiles (Luke 2:32), is now true of them.

Though only a slight difference of emphasis, I prefer to read this citation of Isa 49:6 as depicting Paul and Barnabas's mission, which is an extension of the mission of the community that sent them in Acts 13:1–2. As 13:2 shows, the Spirit called them and the community commissioned them with laying on of hands, just as the Spirit enabled the apostles as witnesses in Acts 2. Paul and Barnabas mirror that earlier community enablement as they take up the cause of witnesses to the light. It is that testifying role that probably explains why Luke presents this text. There is no invitation here, though it is indirectly implied that one should turn and embrace the message of Paul and Barnabas. The text presents only a description of

---

21. An interesting hermeneutical move is present here. In the citation of Ps 2 in the past, most readers would have assumed that the enemies gathered against the Lord and his anointed would have been mostly from outside of Israel, being comprised of the Gentile nations. But the hub of the psalm is the identity of the Messiah. So whoever opposes him becomes an enemy. Thus, when the Jewish leadership opposed Messiah and drew the people with them, a psalm of hope became a psalm that challenged and warned them about their opposition to God. It also became a text the church

could look to in order to appreciate the opposition they faced. A psalm of hope for the nation has now become a psalm testifying to the split in God's people, pointing to the opposition of many from within the nation. This theme of the rejection of God's messengers by the people also appears in much greater detail in Stephen's speech in Acts 7.

22. For a careful discussion of this text, see B. J. Koet, *Five Studies of Interpretation of Scripture in Luke-Acts* (Studiorum Novi Testamenti Auxilia XIV; Leuven: Leuven Univ. Press, 1989), 97–118.

the function of the new community's mission as pictured in Paul and Barnabas. Their labor is an extension of the work of Jesus the Servant. The citation justifies a turning to the nations, by explaining that Paul and Barnabas's call as servants of the Lord is to take the message to Gentiles and bring salvation "to the ends of the earth" (Acts 1:8; 26:23).

The Scripture here makes two points. (1) The new community continues the call and ministry of the Lord as Servant. Jesus is not Servant alone; the new community shares in his calling and identity. This use of Servant imagery parallels a more corporate understanding of the Servant, but with a twist, much like we saw in the use of Ps 2 in Acts 4. Blessing is not a matter of heredity but of proper response.

(2) The inclusion of Gentiles in the mission of God's people is the mission of the Servant. This emphasis fits with the use of Amos 9 in Acts 15. Gentiles are among the people of God. The claim of heritage in the promise of God is also not a matter of heredity but of response. These points underscore that a major concern of Luke-Acts is not just the presentation of Christology to elevate Jesus and explain his suffering, but also to justify the commitment of this originally Jewish community to gathering Gentiles. Jesus is Lord of all, so the gospel can go to all. God always designed it to be so. Gentile involvement in God's plan has deep roots in God's promise. His promise is also designed for them.

21.5.4 Commission to the Gentiles

This section can be handled briefly, since the use of Isa 49:6 in Acts 13:47 and of Amos 9:11–12 in Acts 15:15–18 have already been noted and argue for Gentile inclusion. This theme has roots in Luke 2:32; 3:4–6; and 24:47, as well as Acts 1:8.

Luke 2 points to a mission into the world in alluding to Isa 49. Luke 3 cited Isa 40:3–5, while Luke 24:47 made a generic summary appeal to Scripture as the basis for taking a message of repentance into the whole world.

Gentile inclusion was so innovative from a Jewish point of view, not to mention for the disciples, that God had to force its implementation using vision and radical conversion to make the move stick. The amount of time and repetition spent telling the stories of Paul's call to Gentiles and Cornelius's conversion shows just how crucial this sequence is to Luke's overall purpose. Just as God testified to Jesus through resurrection, he testified to Gentile inclusion through the call to Paul and the visions he used to get Cornelius into the fold. Here the promise of the Spirit (Luke 24:49) is reintroduced to make sure the point is not missed (Acts 11:15–18). When Peter refers to the Spirit's coming on the Gentiles as he did in the beginning, he is alluding to the beginning of the realization of promise that came in Acts 2, which in turn echoes the explanation of Joel 2:28–32 and the distribution of the Spirit, as well as the remarks of John the Baptist in Luke 3:16.

This kind of thematic linkage, which indirectly reintroduces scriptural explanation by echo, reveals how much the issue of Gentile involvement is interwoven with Christology and the divine plan is in Luke-Acts. When Paul is introduced in Acts 9 just before the Cornelius incident, a connection is implied. The role of this linkage emerges when Paul summarizes his mission in Acts 26:20 as to the Jew first and then to the Gentile, showing himself going first to those in Damascus, Jerusalem, and throughout Judea, and then to the Gentiles.

The interrelationship between the story of Paul and the conversion of Cornelius becomes evident in the message of Acts. Paul, too, is called to "bring the message of light to his own people and to the Gentiles" (Acts 26:23). The image of Isaiah being a light to the Gentiles speaks not just for Peter's encounter with Cornelius as God's direct leading showed, but for Paul too—even more explicitly as he consistently ministered successfully to them. Such a mission forms the call of the new community (Luke 24:47). To be light means to carry out God's call and to fulfill Scripture in taking a message of forgiveness and repentance to the nations. To be a good Jew is to seek salvation for Gentiles as well. Such an emphasis also shows how false it is to describe Luke as anti-Semitic.[23] He is simply defending what he feels the actual mission of scriptural promise is. In Luke's mind, he is arguing the case for Israel's promise and the hope it extends to people of all nations.

21.5.5 Challenge with Warning to Israel

That the new community is simply carrying out God's long-promised commission puts the nation of Israel in an accountable and vulnerable position where response, not heredity, is imperative. The remaining uses of Scripture in Acts deal with this theme.

The texts addressed to Israel take on various emphases, but the note was already struck in Luke 2:34–35, when Simeon said to Mary that Jesus would be the cause of "the falling and rising of many in Israel," an allusion to Isa 8:14. Some passages explain why Israel is not responding (Ps 2:1–2 in Acts 4:25–26; Isa 6:9–10 in Acts 28:26–27), while others warn the nation of the cost of refusal (Deut 18:19 and Lev 23:29 in Acts 3:22–23; Hab 1:5 in Acts 13:41). Other texts deepen the indictment by chronicling the pattern of the nation's response, treating their current hesitation as part of a history that reflects spiritual disease (Amos 5:25–27 in Acts 7:42–43; Isa 66:1–2 in Acts 7:49–50). Some of these remarks occur in the new community (Acts 4), but most are direct challenges to the nation (Acts 3; 7; 13; and 28).

These texts argue that Israel, in any generation, does not have an inalienable right to promise if she refuses to embrace God's grace. Those in the new community do not rejoice at issuing such a warning. These texts are not words seeking vengeance and vindication. Rather, fellow Jews plead with their neighbors not to miss God's work and so risk a dangerous accountability to God (Acts 3:24–26; 7:60).

The first group of challenge texts seeks to explain what God is doing, even in the midst of national rejection of Jesus. Is God not in control? The Acts 4 citation

---

23. *Pace* Sanders, *Jews in Luke-Acts*, who argues that Luke is anti-Semitic. It must always be remembered that some of the most contentious things said about and to Israel came from her prophets and they were not anti-Semites. The emotion of these texts reflects intense in-house debate over the direction of the people before God.

of Ps 2:1–2 shows that these events do not catch the new community unaware. A look at how God's chosen kings have been treated reveals that the "conspiracy" between Pilate and Herod, as well as between the Gentiles and the people of Israel, is not surprising. As was noted above, the community can expect suffering, but the passage also has a second function. It explains that opposition to God's anointed is to be expected, since it was predicted by the Spirit.[24] The Lord's anointed was not welcomed with open arms. This word to the community, uttered in the midst of prayer, both explains and comforts. God knows what is taking place with this opposition.

The second explanatory text comes from Paul as he addresses Jews in Rome (Acts 28:25–27). The text functions as an implied rebuke that carries an implication: Paul is free to turn to the nations, since Israel has refused to embrace what Paul has shared with her. The Pauline design of "to the Jew first, then to the Gentile" surfaces here (Rom 1:16). Like Isaiah centuries before, Paul's call to divine renewal is falling on hard hearts, dull ears, and darkened eyes. The opportunity for healing is missed. So the message goes to the nations. The interplay between Israel and the nations is always present in these citations in the latter half of Acts, showing concern for both sides of the ethnic question (so also Acts 13:41–47).

This observation about the Israel-nations juxtaposition, along with the attention paid to God-fearers in Acts, likely indicates a false dichotomy when some argue that Acts is written primarily to either Gentiles or Jews. More plausible is an explanation that argues for a broad audience. Luke argues to all that Gentiles belong in the new community and need not be Jews to fit. Perhaps he writes with a special eye to God-fearers who left Judaism for Christianity. These Gentiles originally discovered God through a different route than the new community was arguing for through Jesus. Then they were taught about Jesus and embraced him.

Both the amount of appeal to the Hebrew Scriptures and the racial mix in the various passages suggest such a broad audience with a possible God-fearer concern. Imagine the reshuffling of perspective that such an entry into the new Jesus community initially had required. Theophilus may have been a God-fearer who had come to Jesus from Judaism, but he now finds himself wondering if he should go back to his earlier community.[25] He has a fresh set of questions that events have raised for him and that Luke seeks to address. Does all the Israelite rejection mean the new community is an object of divine judgment? What am I doing as a Gentile in a movement that was originally Jewish and that many Jews reject? Might my earlier community of the synagogue be where I belong with practices that they have long done? Such questions have raised a sense of doubt for Theophilus. Luke

---

24. Although the psalm is only tied to this specific situation, one suspects that a reading of this psalm like that in the midrash on Ps 2 may be at work. In that reading every period of Israel's history has seen such opposition against God's chosen ones. The midrash also expected such opposition in the end times, in the eschaton.

25. For the suggestion that Theophilus may be a God-fearer,

see John Nolland, "Luke's Readers: A Study of Luke 4.22–8; Acts 13.46; 18.6; 28.28 and Luke 21.5–36" (unpublished Ph.D. dissertation; University of Cambridge, 1977); and Jacob Jervell, "Retrospect and Prospect in Luke-Acts Interpretation," in *Society for Biblical Literature 1991 Seminar Papers* (ed. E. H. Lovering Jr.; Chico, CA: Scholars Press, 1991), 383–404, esp. 399.

responds and reassures him that God's heritage and promise, as odd as it sounds, rests in the new community. Even the Jews in the new community understand why Israel refuses to respond. Scripture and Israel's history shows they often have rejected God's way for her.

But the OT also confronts the nation. The second set of texts serves to warn Israel of her culpability. The use of Deut 18:19 along with Lev 23:29 in Acts 3 could hardly take a more confrontational approach. After alluding to Jesus as the prophet like Moses, Peter notes that failure to respond to this prophet leaves one accountable before God. The Lord sends prophets to his people so his message can be heard. In fact, the allusion to Leviticus shows how serious the failure is. There the text speaks of inappropriate worship on the Day of Atonement, leaving one cut off from the people—about as serious a penalty as is possible. Peter reapplies the principle of that text to the one whose atoning offering paved the way for the new people of God. To reject Jesus is to face being cut off from God and the community he always promised he would bring.

Though it might seem inappropriate or even offensive to use a liturgical text this way, the citation may be making another, more subtle point as well. It may see Jesus as the prophetic martyr sacrifice that is representative of a nation, especially in light of some other clearer texts in Luke-Acts on this theme (Luke 20:19–20; Acts 20:28). If so, this becomes the third Lucan text that alludes to the theme of the significance of Jesus' death in terms of sacrifice, representation, and substitution.

Regardless of the possibility of the connection to Luke's view of the cross, Leviticus warns the nation and her citizens that rejection of Jesus leaves one "cut off" (ἐξολεθρευθήσεται, *exolethreuthēsetai*, Acts 3:23) from the people of God. Peter hopes for better things since he ends his speech with an invitation to share in God's covenantal promise. Here again we see how certain texts also combine themes, as covenantal hope and warning take place side by side.

The third set of texts comes from Stephen's speech with its historical overview of Israel's pattern of rejection. The first citation, from Amos 5:25–27, stands close to the LXX version, a point that is not surprising given Stephen is a representative of the new community's Hellenistic wing. The "God gave them over" (παρέδωκεν, *paredōken*, Acts 7:42) theme of this citation is similar to what Paul says (of Gentiles!) in Rom 1:24–32. Yet in Acts, it is Jewish unfaithfulness that Stephen presents through the words of Israel's own prophets. The manner of citation is key, since the nation has a history of missing God's voice, something the book of Deuteronomy warned the nation not to do. Israel often turned to the worship of other gods (Deut 4:19; 17:3; 2 Kgs 21:3–5; 23:4–5; 2 Chr 33:3, 5; Jer 7:18; 8:2; 19:13; Zeph 1:5).[26] Stephen's use of this Amos text argues that from exodus to exile, the nation has responded unfaithfully to God. History shows that God will not stand idle in the face of this response. Stephen's remarks ultimately cause the crowd to react (see Acts 7:54–60).

---

26. Polhill, *Acts*, 201.

The second historical text is similar in force. Isaiah 66:1–2 in Acts 7:49–50 parallels the earlier Amos citation and leads into Stephen's indicting summary in Acts 7:51–53. The point from Isaiah is that one should not make too much of the temple. Though venerated as the house of God, the temple cannot contain him. This idea also has rich roots in the Hebrew Scriptures (1 Kgs 6:11–13; 8:27; 1 Chr 6:8; Isa 57:15; Jer 7:1–34; Mic 3:9–11). Stephen is responding to charges that he has spoken against the temple (Acts 6:13). He is saying nothing other than what prophets have said before him. By not hearing him, the Jews are not hearing Isaiah, nor are they hearing God. They are missing the point yet again, repeating their ignominious history. God is greater than a given locale. The God of heaven and earth is not to be contained in a building, even though he permitted a temple to be built. The heritage of God is not found in a building but in the evidence of the living God's activity.

These historical texts are not only a word to Israel to remember her history of failure and take pause, but they remind the readers that the nation's response to God is not always correct. She has repeatedly failed to respond to God. So Israel's rejection of the community's message reflects error in discerning God's plan and is not as surprising as one might think.[27]

21.6 CONCLUSION

The use of Scripture in Luke-Acts serves a variety of roles.[28] Many texts set forth who Jesus is and explain what he is doing in conjunction with the divine plan and covenants. Many texts in Acts support the new community's claim to the heritage of God revealed in Moses and the prophets. The early church asserted that a faithful response to God would mean: (1) the embracing of Jesus as the promised one, and (2) the inclusion of Gentiles into the community of blessing. Failure to respond has left the nation culpable.

Behind these claims stands the church's understanding of covenant, promise, and Christology. Scripture also allowed the community to appreciate that her current suffering was rooted in the way of Jesus, who had traveled a similar road. History taught the sad lesson that people often reject God's way, even in the nation of promise. Circumstances should not deflect the reader of Acts from seeing that rejection did not evidence God's judgment, but mirrored the path of rejection that Jesus walked. The road they shared was a new road, because of the coming of Christ and the new era, but paradoxically it was an old road as well, since such rejection

---

27. One text in Acts falls outside of these categories. It is the rebuke of Paul citing Exod 22:27–28 in Acts 23:5. This text also is part of the contention over who truly represents God. Here the text is evoked after a Jewish warning to Paul not to violate Scripture. Paul steps back from his challenge as a result. Paul's initial tone in calling the high priest a "whitewashed wall" here is not unlike Jesus' tone and warning in Luke 11:37–52. Who represents Israel's heritage is the question his reaction initially raises, but when confronted with disrespect to the leadership, he steps back and notes the Scripture as he does so, showing respect for the sacred text and the law in the process.

28. This chapter has focused on citations and key allusions. Obviously the use of Scripture and her ideas runs far deeper than these categories alone. But the explicit use of Scripture for these themes shows where major concerns of Luke's theology lie.

was promised by the prophets and practiced earlier by the nation. Thus for Luke, history and the prophetic Scripture show that what was taking place was no surprise.

The new community had every claim of heritage to God's promise in covenant and Christ. They also shared in the suffering that came from those who rejected their message, just as they had earlier rejected the visit of the sent one. To see that connection between promise and suffering was to understand what being in the light meant as one walked in the midst of a dark world. Like Paul, the readers of Acts should understand they were on trial for the hope of God (Acts 26:15–18). Like Paul and the early community before him, the road might not be easy, but what God sought was faithful witness (1:7–8; 4:24–30; 28:30–31).

Luke's use of Scripture underscores that the message being proclaimed is the realization of a promise that God made long ago. Scripture legitimates the claims of the new community to reside in God's promise, plan, and program. There is a line of continuity between what God had revealed to Israel and what took place in Jesus and the new community. Prophetic word and pattern showed this continuity. The claims attached to the new community are in line with Scripture, and even more, with the will of God.

Part Three

LUKE AND THE CANON

Chapter 22

LUKE-ACTS IN THE CANON

BIBLIOGRAPHY

As with chapter 2, for this listing I highlight the key commentaries that also have introductory discussions, as well as key introductions to the New Testament. **Achtemeier, Paul, Joel Green, and Marianne Meye Thompson.** *Introducing the New Testament: Its Literature and Theology.* Grand Rapids: Eerdmans, 2001. **Barrett, C. K.** *A Critical and Exegetical Commentary on the Acts of the Apostles I: Preliminary Introduction and Commentary on Acts I–XIV.* ICC. Edinburgh: T&T Clark, 1994. Idem. *A Critical and Exegetical Commentary on the Acts of the Apostles II: Introduction and Commentary on Acts XV–XXVIII.* ICC. Edinburgh: T&T Clark, 1998. **Bock, Darrell L.** *Acts.* BECNT 5. Grand Rapids: Baker, 2007. Idem. *Luke 1:1–9:50.* BECNT 3a. Grand Rapids: Baker, 1994. Idem. *Luke 9:51–24:53.* BECNT 3b. Grand Rapids: Baker, 1996. **Brown, Raymond.** *An Introduction to the New Testament.* New York: Doubleday, 1997. **Bruce, F. F.** *The Acts of the Apostles: Greek Text with Introduction and Commentary.* 3rd ed. Grand Rapids: Eerdmans, 1990. **Cadbury, H. J.** *The Making of Luke-Acts.* New York: Macmillan, 1927. **Carson, D. A., and Douglas J. Moo.** *An Introduction to the New Testament.* 2nd ed. Grand Rapids: Zondervan, 2005. **Dodd, C. H.** *The Apostolic Preaching and Its Developments.* New York: Harper and Row, 1964. **Fitzmyer, Joseph.** *The Acts of the Apostles.* Anchor Bible. Garden City, NY: Doubleday, 1998. Idem. *The Gospel of Luke I–IX: Introduction, Translation and Notes.* Anchor Bible. Garden City, NY: Doubleday, 1982. **Green, Joel.** *The Gospel of Luke.* NICNT. Grand Rapids: Eerdmans, 1997. **Haenchen, Ernst.** *Acts of the Apostles: A Commentary.* London: Blackwell, 1987. **Hemer, Colin.** *The Book of Acts in the Setting of Hellenistic History.* WUNT. Tübingen: Mohr-Siebeck, 1989. **Hengel, Martin.** *Acts and the History of Earliest Christianity.* London: SCM, 1979. Idem. *The Four Gospels and the One Gospel of Jesus Christ.* Harrisburg, PA: Trinity International, 2000. **Jervell, Jacob.** *Die Apostelgeschichte.* Göttingen: Vandenhoeck & Ruprecht, 1998. **Johnson, Luke Timothy.** *The Gospel of Luke.* SP. Collegeville, MN: Liturgical, 1991. Idem. *The Acts of the Apostles.* SP. Collegeville, MN: Liturgical, 1992. **Köstenberger, Andreas, Scott Kellum, and Charles Quarles.** *The Cradle, The Cross, and the Crown: An Introduction to the New Testament.* Nashville: Broadman and Holman Academic, 2009. **Kümmel, Werner Georg.** *Introduction to the New Testament.* Rev. ed. Nashville: Abingdon, 1975. **Marguerat, Daniel.** *The First Christian Historian: Writing the 'Acts of the Apostles.'* SNTSSup. Cambridge: Cambridge University Press, 2002. **Marshall, I. H.** *The Acts of the Apostles: An Introduction and Commentary.* TNTC. Grand Rapids: Eerdmans, 1980. Idem. *The Gospel of Luke.* NIGTC. Grand Rapids: Eerdmans, 1978. **Nolland, John.** *Luke 1:1–24:53.* WBC.

3 vols. 1989–1993. **Polhill, John.** *Acts.* NAC. Nashville: Broadman, 1992. **Powell, Mark Allen.** *Introducing the New Testament: A Historical, Literary and Theological Survey.* Grand Rapids: Baker, 2009. **Talbert, Charles.** *Literary Patterns, Theological Themes, and the Genre of Luke-Acts.* SBLMS. Missoula, MT: Scholars Press, 1974. **Wenham, David.** *Paul: Follower of Christ or Founder of Christianity?* Grand Rapids: Eerdmans, 1995. **Witherington, Ben.** *The Acts of the Apostles: A Socio-Rhetorical Commentary.* Grand Rapids: Eerdmans, 1997.

This chapter is concerned with two issues: the reception of Luke-Acts into the canon and Luke's contribution to the canon. The second issue looks at both how Luke is like the other books of the NT as well as what is distinctive or emphasized in his presentation of Jesus.

22.1 THE RECEPTION OF LUKE AND ACTS INTO THE CANON

The reception of the four Gospels into the canon was among the first collections of material made for the establishment of the NT.[1] We know by the time Tatian writes his *Diatessaron*, which means "through the four," that the four Gospels were well established, since his unified version could not replace the four versions of the gospel circulating through the church. His work dates from about AD 170. Marcion also used this work, as did Justin Martyr, since he cites parts of Luke's passion unique to his gospel (*Dial.* 103.19). The *Didache* and the *Gospel of Peter* also give evidence of using this gospel, which shows it was well circulated in the second century. More uncertain are whether uses in Clement (*1 Clem.* 13.2; 48.4) go back to Luke or are part of an oral tradition like Luke.[2]

We review authorship notes from our discussion of introduction as they are also relevant. Numerous texts comment on authorship.

Justin Martyr (ca. 160) in *Dial.* 103.19 speaks of Luke's writing an "apostolic memoir" of Jesus. However, Justin only alludes to language about sweating blood, ties it to this expression, but does not name an author.[3] So this association is vague, since Luke is not named.

Later references name an author.

The Muratorian Canon (ca. 170–180) attributes the gospel to Luke, a doctor, who is Paul's companion and did not know of Jesus' ministry directly, but "ascertained" the story of his ministry from sources.

Irenaeus (ca. 175–195) in *Haer.* 3.1.1 and 3.14.1 attributes the gospel to Luke, a follower of Paul, and notes how the "we" sections suggest the connection. It should be noted that Irenaeus probably exaggerates how close Luke was to Paul in describ-

---

1. For a full and careful study of this issue arguing for the Gospels being in place in the second century with titles going back into the turn of the first to second century, see Martin Hengel, *The Four Gospels and the One Gospel of Jesus Christ* (Harrisburg, PA: Trinity International, 2000).

2. The content of the *1 Clement* texts was noted in ch. 2 on introductory matters.

3. The detail about sweating blood is unique to Luke so we know the third gospel is included in this description of being an apostolic memoir.

ing him as a constant or inseparable companion (*Haer.* 3.14.1). It may be that Irenaeus's reference to the inseparable Luke may refer to Luke's loyalty, since it is contrasted to Demas's defection. Regardless, Acts suggests Luke, if he is the "we" figure, was only with Paul here and there.

The so-called Anti-Marcionite Prologue to Luke (ca. 175) describes Luke as a native of Antioch in Syria (Acts 11:19–30; 13:1–3; 15:30–35). It says he lived to be eighty-four, was a doctor, was unmarried, wrote in Achaia, and died in Boeotia.

Tertullian (early third century) in *Against Marcion* 4.2.2 and 4.5.3 calls the gospel a digest of Paul's gospel.

The Monarchian Prologue (date disputed; either third or fourth century) gives Luke's age at death as seventy-four. The difference on Luke's age with the Anti-Marcionite Prologue suggests that not everything in the early tradition about Luke agrees in detail, so such material needs to be sorted out. What they note and its difference do indicate that Luke lived to an old age.

Eusebius (early fourth century) in *Eccl. Hist.* 3.4.2 mentions Luke as a companion to Paul, a native of Antioch, and the author of these two volumes.

We already referred to the important note that closes $\mathfrak{p}^{75}$ from about AD 200 that the gospel was written by Luke. There is a consistency to these references spread across time and regions that is important. A connection to Luke set in fairly early.

The remarks about Acts are similar. Irenaeus speaks of Luke as the author in *Haer.* 3.13.3, calling Acts "the testimony of Luke." Tertullian calls Acts "a commentary by Luke" (*On Fasting* 10). Clement of Alexandria also names Luke as the author (*Strom.* 5.12.82.4). The Muratorian Canon (lines 34–39) names Luke as the author. The key manuscripts of Sinaiticus and Vaticanus name Luke as the author. Longer versions of the title in some later manuscripts of Acts name Luke (33: 9th cent.; 1241: 12th cent.).

So our materials point to authorship of both volumes being consistently tied to Luke starting by the end of the second century. Luke's placement in the fourfold gospel collection is early and consistent, evidencing a reception in the core Jesus collection of the church. Luke also makes a unique contribution to the canon by giving us an important selection of activity of the early community, the only such focused work in the canon.

22.2 LUKE'S CONTRIBUTION TO THE CANON

Luke's contribution to the canon is immense. His writings actually constitute the largest corpus by one author in the canon. His contributions overlap with that of other NT authors, though they also reflect his own unique observations in several places. This survey looks at what Luke says alongside his NT colleagues and what is unique to him.

22.2.1 Contributions Tied to God, Jesus, and the Spirit

The portrait of God and his activity through Jesus and the Spirit is as extensive in Luke-Acts as anywhere in the NT. In part, this is because Luke chronicles the life of the early community in a way other books do not. We see God guiding through dreams, as also occurs in Matt 1–2. Visions are also used, as well as the appearances of Jesus to Paul, something that Gal 1:15–17 also notes, to show an active divine leading of the community. Resurrection appearances to individuals and groups show that Jesus is alive, and Jesus takes meals to show the material nature of that resurrection (Luke 24:30–31, 42–43; Acts 1:1–5). These extraordinary means appear in key events, such as the call of Saul and the expansion of the gospel to the Gentiles. The use of prophets, most prominently in the figure of Agabus, is something 1 Cor 12–14 notes, but Luke gives us detail about events tied to such figures we do not have elsewhere. It shows them addressing events and needs in the community, such as famine relief, that also serve to encourage the community's solidarity.

Most prominent in the book is the program of God as set out in the Hebrew Scriptures. References to Moses, the Prophets, and the Psalms underscore this idea. Other books do this as well, since Matthew makes much of fulfillment, as does much of the book of Hebrews. There are differences in the use. For example, Luke cites Scripture mostly in the language of his characters, while Matthew cites it mostly as narrative notes alongside events.

Beyond this, the eschatology as it relates to the future and restoration of Israel is stronger in these volumes than anywhere else except for perhaps Rom 9–11. Luke suggests that Israel has a future in Acts, with the early question the followers ask in Acts 1:6–7—a question Jesus does not correct but declines to answer. In Acts 3:18–22 Peter declares the future events are noted in the Hebrew Scriptures. Hope is held out for Israel in that her house is desolate until she confesses, "Blessed is he who comes in the name of the Lord" (Luke 13:34–35). In addition, Jerusalem is overrun for a period called "the times of the Gentiles"; this appears to suggest a time when Israel returns in the future (21:21–24). These Lucan texts on Israel are all unique in the canon. The point is important because too many treatments of this theme today look at Jesus' teaching or that of the NT and yet ignore or underdevelop what is Luke's unique contribution to what Jesus taught on this topic.[4]

Divine providence is also a key part of the book. Expansion of the gospel comes through persecution. Protection of Paul takes place through his arrest and placement in Roman custody. Even a deadly storm is not able to stop the gospel from arriving in Rome. There are releases from prison through angels and earthquakes. God uses a variety of means to direct and protect.

The events tied to Jesus and God's work through him receive special additional attention. Half of the parables we have from Jesus occur in Luke. Luke has eighteen

---

4. One of the dangers of Jesus study is that it can harmonize the topics Jesus addresses across the Gospels by surveying one gospel's presentation of a theme and missing the unique contribution of another gospel writer in the process. Today, this is often done in treating the Synoptics by highlighting the gospel of Mark, since many see his gospel as the earliest version of Jesus' ministry. Others focus on Matthew for theological reasons. Those who like issues tied to politics and society often highlight Luke. Another way this is often done is that John, by far the most explicit of the Gospels on many themes, is taken as a lead gospel, causing the teaching of the other gospels to be devalued in the process, often because the Synoptics are less direct than John. It is best to keep an eye on all four Gospels for a theme with attention to both what they share in common and where each makes unique points. Being sensitive to this concern is one of the reasons this chapter is present in a biblical theology on Luke-Acts.

unique parables, most of which appear in the Jerusalem Journey section of his gospel (Luke 9:51 – 19:44). Parables unique to Luke include: the two debtors (7:41 – 43); the good Samaritan (10:25 – 37); the bold neighbor who illustrates prayer (11:5 – 8); the rich fool (12:13 – 21); the parable of the fig tree (13:6 – 9); the parable of seats of honor (14:7 – 14); the parable of the great banquet (whose details differ from Matthew's version in Matt 22:1 – 10; Luke 14:15 – 24); the parable of the tower and warring king (14:28 – 33); the parable of salt (more developed than the other gospels, 14:34 – 35); the lost sheep (15:4 – 7);[5] the prodigal son and forgiving father (15:11 – 31); the shrewd steward (16:1 – 9); the rich man and Lazarus (16:19 – 31); the faithful servant (17:7 – 10); the nagging widow and the judge (18:1 – 8); the parable of the pounds (a similar but distinct story from Matthew's parable of the talents in Matt 25:14 – 30; Luke 19:11 – 27); and the Pharisee and the tax-collector (18:9 – 14).

In addition, much of Jesus' teaching we have in areas beyond parables comes uniquely from Luke. Other unique or emphasized teaching includes the genealogical tie to Adam in Luke 3:37, Jesus as the Spirit-anointed Servant in 4:18 – 19, and the emphasis on Jesus' reaching out to tax collectors and sinners as well as to the poor and blind in 4:18 – 19; 5:30 – 32; 7:21 – 22; 14:12 – 33; 19:1 – 10. Fully 42 percent of Luke is unique in its teaching material (about 485 verses). Here is the list of material unique to Luke in terms of passages (parentheses indicate possible overlap with Matthew or Mark):[6]

1:5 – 2:52	(10:25 – 28)	13:10 – 17	(17:28 – 32)
3:10 – 14	10:29 – 37	13:31 – 33	18:1 – 8
3:23 – 38	10:38 – 42	14:1 – 6	18:9 – 14
(4:16 – 30)	11:5 – 8	14:7 – 14	19:1 – 10
5:1 – 11	11:27 – 28	14:28 – 35 (33?)	19:41 – 44
(5:39)	(12:1)	15:1 – 10	21:34 – 36
7:11 – 17	12:13 – 21	15:11 – 32	22:15 – 18, 27, (31 – 33), 35 – 38
(7:36 – 50)	(12:35 – 38)	16:1 – 15	23:6 – 16
(8:1 – 3)	12:47 – 48	16:19 – 31	23:27 – 31
9:51 – 55	12:49 – 50	17:7 – 10	23:39 – 43
9:61 – 62	12:54 – 56	17:11 – 19	24:13 – 53
10:1, 17 – 20	13:1 – 9	17:20 – 21	

The list, especially the uniquely Lucan material of the parables, shows Luke's pastoral concern. He cares about seeking sinners. He worries about the values held by believers, especially their attachment to money. He wants them to continue to

---

5. Luke's use of the lost sheep parable for finding the lost is distinct from Matthew's image in Matt 18:10 – 14, which is about regaining those in the community. So I treat Luke 15:4 – 7 as unique to Luke.

6. The chart reflects a discussion in Bock, *Luke 1:1 – 9:50*, 12.

look for the Lord's return and be responsible to God in the meantime. Disciples are to be committed, loving, and prayerful. The thrust of the parables is a call to walk with God and to trust him, now and in light of the coming judgment. The impression is that Luke writes to a community under pressure for its faith. They are to hang on and trust God.[7]

Luke also says much more about the dangers of attraction to wealth than the other books of the NT. Here unique parables like the rich fool and the rich man and Lazarus make the point, alongside material shared with Matthew and Mark, such as the discussion with the rich ruler.

The ascension is a specific event told only by Luke (Luke 24:50–53; Acts 1:9–11). This highlights the importance he gives to the vindication of God that the resurrection represents. The entire NT affirms the importance of the resurrection, but Luke underscores it with this event, using it as the link between Luke and Acts.[8]

The eschatological discourse is handled in a distinct way in Luke. There are three locales where eschatology is treated (Luke 12:35–48; 17:20–37; 21:5–38). His emphasis also looks at the imminent destruction of Jerusalem more clearly than the other gospels.

The role of the Holy Spirit is a focal point of Luke. The other Synoptic Gospels share the remark of John that one stronger than he will baptize with the Spirit, but only Luke notes this remark answers the question of whether John is the Christ. In doing this, Luke makes the point that the sign of the new era involves the coming of the Spirit. This is expressed as the theme of Peter's Pentecost speech in Acts 2.

---

7. Ibid., 949.

8. Zwiep, *Christ, the Spirit, and the Community of God*, 38–67, raises an interesting question about the ascension in Luke as to whether it is an exaltation text tied to Jesus' going to the right hand of God or a "rapture" text. He argues that the kerygma usually tied exaltation to the resurrection event. Since Luke has an ascension after forty days, this cannot be making that point. Technically, this is a good point. Jesus says to the leaders at his Jewish trial that "from now on" they will see the Son of Man seated at the right hand of God (Luke 22:69). The resurrection is the moment that makes this all possible. Zwiep correctly notes that all the resurrection appearances are to be understood as "appearances from heaven, manifestations of the *already* exalted Lord" (p. 44). Rapture in this discussion is defined as "bodily translation into the 'beyond'" (p. 46). Exaltation in the ancient world did not have this physical dimension to it as a requirement, and ascensions could be conceived of as heavenly journeys, assumption of the soul, or rapture. He also observes how in a Greco-Roman context, this rapture would be appreciated as testifying to Jesus, even though there is a distinction in that Jesus is not being deified here since we do not have a vision or mere mystical experience. Here he appeals to the background of Enoch and Elijah as precedents within Judaism with the idea that they are taken also to return in the view of Second Temple Judaism (see Mal. 3–4; *1 En.*; and *4 Ezra* 6:26). There is no deification involved here for these two Jewish figures. If this background is in play, and it could well be, then not only does the ascension reflect the exaltation of Jesus by God (not in an initial way, but as a sign for it; Acts 1:2–11) but also anticipates his being received into heaven to return one day with such authority (3:18–22). Our one caveat on this is the distance Zwiep wishes to apply to this rapture and the idea of exaltation that makes many use the link resurrection-ascension for Luke in a way Zwiep is not comfortable using. Jesus' exaltation, whenever it occurred, is unique since it takes him to God's right hand, a locale that does not fit Enoch or Elijah. This means the ascension of Jesus is a reminder and testimony to this exaltation that took place with Jesus' vindicating resurrection. The event as a unit shows who Jesus is because of where Jesus ends up, not just in heaven but at the right hand of God. So we need not choose between associating the exaltation with either the resurrection or the ascension. Rather, the ascension in Luke points to the reality of both the resurrection and the exaltation, while also looking forward to the fact that Jesus can, as a result, return with all the authority his exaltation-ascension indicates. In other words, Luke sees the exaltation-ascension-resurrection as part of one vindication sequence that also points forward to Jesus' right to return. The ascension is a final resurrection story that also evidences exaltation since Jesus has told us where in heaven God is taking him. He was at the right hand of God before this event, but it still testifies to that position. With Zwiep, the ascension is not a scene of deification or apotheosis, but it does have its view on events both past and future. One need not choose between the two temporal links. This is another case of both-and, not either-or.

The miraculous activity of God through Jesus and the apostles is laid out in parallel so that the work of apostles like Peter and Paul shows itself as comparable to what Jesus did.[9] There is one important difference. Apostolic healing is attributed to the name and authority of Jesus and does not indicate personal authority as did Jesus in his miracles. Luke gives us twenty miracle accounts plus three summaries. This compares with Mark's eighteen miracle accounts and four summaries and Matthew's nineteen accounts and four summaries. Together in the Synoptic Gospels there are six accounts of exorcism, seventeen of healing (including three risings from the dead), and eight nature miracles.[10] The gospel of John's seven signs come alongside these with the only clear overlap being the feeding of the five thousand.[11]

Here are the miracles unique to Luke: the miraculous catch of fish at the call of Peter and others (Luke 5:1 – 11); unique details of Jewish cooperation with a Gentile in the healing of the centurion's slave (7:1 – 10); the raising of the widow of Nain's son (7:11 – 17); the Sabbath healing of the crippled woman (13:10 – 17); the healing of the man with dropsy on the Sabbath (14:1 – 6); the cleansing of the ten lepers (17:11 – 19); and the healing of the high priest's servant's ear during Jesus' arrest (22:50 – 51). Seven of Luke's twenty miracles give us significant material when it comes to miraculous activity.

The list of unique divine activity in Acts also presents several types of miracles: healing of the lame (by Peter: Acts 3:1 – 10; 9:33 – 34; by Paul: 14:8 – 10); raising of the dead (by Peter: 9:36 – 42; by Paul: 20:8 – 12); a miracle of judgment against Elymas (by Paul: 13:9 – 11); act of judgment against false exorcists (19:13 – 20); acts of angelic deliverance (12:6 – 11; 15:19 – 20; 16:26); vision of Jesus (9:3 – 9); directive visions for locale of ministry (16:9 – 10; 18:9 – 10; 23:11); visions to Cornelius and Peter for Gentile inclusion (10:3 – 16); movement provided by the Spirit (8:39 – 40); use of Peter's shadow (5:12 – 16); and the touch of Paul's cloths or handkerchiefs (19:11 – 12). This is yet another indicator of how active God is in the book in directing and authenticating those in the church.

Obviously we learn much about an array of ministry in the church that is unique in Acts. In fact, without Acts, we could do little to figure out the chronology of this period, not to mention much of its early key activity.

22.2.2 Contributions Tied to the Activity of the Church

The outreach to the nations is another emphasis in Luke. Only he extends the citation of Isa 40 through 40:5, where all flesh will see the salvation of God (Luke 3:4 – 6). The mention of Adam, already noted, fits here. The details given to Gentile inclusion in the gospel and God's direct hand in making it happen also belong under this theme.

The structure of churches as being in the hands of elders as leaders gets some

---

9. This is nicely traced in Talbert, *Literary Patterns, Theological Themes, and the Genre of Luke-Acts*; and developed by Rothschild, *Luke-Acts and the Rhetoric of History*, 99 – 141.

10. This count comes from Green, *Gospel of Luke*, 16.

11. The tone of the centurion's son's healing in John 4 is so opposite of the Synoptics that this is likely not a parallel.

attention in Acts, especially with the scene involving the leaders at Ephesus in Acts 20:18–38. This charge to the leadership with its call to keep an eye out for false teaching is most like that kind of exhortation we see in Paul's letters to those who lead.

Only Luke notes two missions of disciples in Jesus' ministry, one involving the Twelve and another including a larger group (Luke 9:1–6; 10:1–24). Luke here highlights that ministry is widely distributed and not just in the hands of a few. The distribution of the Spirit on everyone also makes this point.

Luke's treatment of the hub role of certain churches, such as the communities in Jerusalem and Antioch, is part of his unique material in Acts. In Jerusalem, we also see a church still concerned with Jewish practice as a part of their ethos.

Our knowledge of Paul's missionary activity in three journeys would not exist without Acts. This portion of Acts explains the importance of Paul to the early church and for Gentile mission. Some see the point of the two volumes as the defense of Paul, but that does not explain the first three quarters of the work. It is better to see a defense of what Paul represents, a mission to all the nations, as central to Luke's two volumes.

Our understanding of the kerygma of the early church would be impoverished without Acts. Here we get a glimpse at the evangelistic speeches of this early community. There are speeches to Jewish audiences drenched in Scripture, while outreach to Gentiles presents core themes out of a more natural theology, such as God as the Creator to whom all are accountable. The speeches to Jewish audiences have a pattern. There is a call to hear or an explanation of an event that has just taken place, a section of Christology often with scriptural support, and then a call to respond. The short classic study by C. H. Dodd on the apostolic preaching noted this pattern long ago.[12]

Luke emphasizes the value of women and the poor in ways that exceed the other gospels.[13] These categories point to the scope of the gospel reaching those whom normal society either ignored or undervalued.

The emphasis on ethical values in terms of how repentance toward God impacts human relationships is a highlight of Luke's gospel.[14] So Luke alone gives us this emphasis in presenting John the Baptist's call in Luke 1:16–17, as well as in uniquely giving us a sample of John's call to his audience to treat others well in 3:10–14. The parable of the good Samaritan goes in a similar direction (10:25–37); it also is unique to Luke.

Finally, Luke highlights prayer in a way the other gospels do not. Many scenes, including Jesus' baptism by John, are connected to prayer. Alongside this is the presence of hymnic material to set a tone of praise (see the infancy material in Luke 1–2). This tone contrasts with Matthew's notes of conflict and suffering in his infancy material.

---

12. Dodd, *Apostolic Preaching and Its Developments*. See also E. Schweizer, "Concerning the Speeches in Acts," in *Studies in Luke-Acts* (ed. Leander E. Keck and J. Louis Martyn; Nashville: Abing-

don, 1966), 208–16.

13. See ch. 17 for details.

14. This was the concern of ch. 15.

22.3 LUKE'S PARALLELS WITH OTHER PARTS OF THE NEW TESTAMENT

22.3.1 Parallels with the Synoptics

The outstanding overlaps of Luke with Mark and Matthew include his presentation of the authority of Jesus as inseparably linked to the kingdom and plan of God. This emphasis appears especially when one thinks of Jesus' use of the title Son of Man, claims tied to miracles like the healing of the paralytic or remarks about Sabbath authority, or his reception of messianic acclaim during his last week in Jerusalem. So this authority involves forgiveness of sins, the power to exorcize, the right to rule about the Sabbath, as well as power over creation, disease, and death. Whether one considers the controversies of the last week in Jerusalem or the kinds of miracles Jesus performed, these overlaps indicate core ideas these three gospels share in their portait of Jesus.

Jesus' outreach to those in need and on society's fringe also fits here (Luke 5:31–32; 15; cf. Matt 9:12–13; Mark 2:17). His associations with those whom society tended to cast aside are something all the Synoptic Gospels stress, even if Luke makes more of it than the others do.

Another key overlap is the emphasis on the kingdom of God as central to Jesus' message.[15] The call to preach the kingdom in Luke 4:43 is like Mark 1:15. The use of kingdom parables, of which Luke has four in Luke 8 and 13, is also parallel to Mark and Matthew, although Matthew's development is more detailed in using more kingdom parables. The beatitudes also treat the kingdom (Luke 6:20; cf. Matt 5:3). The kingdom mission of the Twelve and Luke's second mission involving a larger group also fit here, paralleling Matthew 10. Mark 1:15 with its note that the time is fulfilled is parallel conceptually to Jesus' declaration that the promise of Isa 61 has met its fulfillment "today" in Luke 4:21 (cf. also John 5:39). Jesus' acts are the evidence for this fulfillment as he appeals to the variety of healing he has done in Luke 7:18–22 and Matt 11:2–5. The victory is not so much about politics with Rome as with the power of Satan, portrayed as a strong man whom Jesus overruns (Matt 12:22–30; Mark 3:22–27; Luke 11:14–23; cf. John 12:31; 18:36). The kingdom as present and future (now, not yet) also shows up in these gospels (now: Matt 12:28; Luke 11:20; 17:20–21; to come: Matt 6:10; 24–25; Mark 13; Luke 11:2; 21). That the new era is something new with new practices is also shared between these gospels (Matt 9:14–17; Mark 2:18–22; Luke 5:33–39).

Themes of discipleship and the suffering it will require also overlap with Matthew and Mark. In places Luke may add an example or two, such as the idea that the one who likes the old wine will not try the new (Luke 5:39) or the picture of the disciple who looks back not being fit for for the kingdom (Luke 9:61–62), but the core teaching is shared.

---

15. This is nicely developed by David Wenham, *Paul: Follower of Christ or Founder of Christianity?* (Grand Rapids: Eerdmans, 1995).

One feature of Luke in comparison to Matthew and Mark is that what they have in a single discourse, Luke tends to distribute across his gospel. So material or themes from Matthew's Sermon on the Mount show up in Luke 6 and 11. Kingdom parables from Mark 4 show up in Luke 8 and 13. The point may reflect the itinerant ministry of Jesus, saying similar things in distinct settings.

Of course, much of the last week and Passion overlap. The appeals to psalms of lament and the emphasis on Jesus' innocence stand out here (though Luke highlights Jesus' innocence more than the other gospels in Luke 23). Luke also uniquely identifies Mark's second cry from the cross as coming from Ps 31:5, while not mentioning the first cry from Ps 22:1. Central to this scene as well is Jesus' death for claiming to sit at God's right hand and to be king of the Jews. Luke lacks a reference to coming on the clouds when he is examined by the Jewish leadership, but the thrust of his reply about being seated at God's right hand is shared. This reply is the technical cause of his being passed on to Pilate to face crucifixion, which the gospels share. In other words, in all the Synoptics Jesus supplies the testimony that leads to his own death. He dies for claiming something that was true in the eyes of the Synoptics, since his claim is vindicated by resurrection in all these gospels.

The importance of dependent faith is shared with other gospels as healings and other exchanges take place (Matt 9:22; Mark 5:34; Luke 8:48; 17:19). The picture of a child as an example of dependence is a central image here. Luke makes more of repentance, but this is another way to highlight the same core response. The example of faith from the centurion who asks for healing for his slave also shows this theme (Luke 7:1 – 10). To them Luke adds the note of the response of a Samaritan leper with gratitude (17:11 – 19), the picture of a sinful woman's anointing Jesus out of a response to God's grace (7:35 – 50), and a parable where the repentant humility of a tax collector justifies him (18:9 – 14). Faith as a trust with humble dependence and as a readiness to follow is something these gospels share.

22.3.2 Parallels with John's Gospel

Luke has a saying in Luke 10:21 – 22 that has been called the "bolt from the Johannine blue." This is because its picture of the Son and Father relationship is stated in terms that sound like many texts in the fourth gospel.

There is also significant conceptual overlap between the Lucan exaltation of Jesus, Jesus' shared authority with God, and John's picture of the Sent One, who acts with authority that inseparably connects to the Father. What Jesus says at the Jewish examination of his position at the right hand of God (Luke 22:68 – 69) is like the link John forges between the Father and the Son (John 5:19 – 27).

Other places where the terminology differs but the concept is parallel are those where Luke speaks of the kingdom of God and John's gospel speaks of eternal life. Central to this overlap is the role given to the Spirit or what John also calls the Paraclete. The key to eternal life for John is tied to the giving of the Spirit of God, whose presence never runs out (John 4; 7; 14 – 16). This is parallel to the gift of the Spirit in Luke that is the sign of the new era and proof that Messiah has come (Luke 3:15–17; 24:49; Acts 2). In fact, the central role Jesus gives to his necessary departure so the Spirit can come (John 14:16–18, 26; 16:7–10) is paralleled by the central way Luke links the departure of Jesus and his ascension so that God can give the Spirit to Jesus to distribute to his people, as Peter declares in Acts 2:30–36.

Many of the points emerging from miracles about Christology we noted in the Synoptics also apply to John's gospel. For both Luke and John these works were signs of the new era denoting who Jesus was. Sabbath authority as seen in Sabbath healings is an especially important overlap, because in Luke and John points are made about Jesus' authority as a result of the controversy that these events raised.

Issues of suffering and tension with the world are parallel. Here one can think of Jesus' teaching on discipleship and what he taught in the upper room in John 14–16. Of course, both Luke and John also share the sense of mission given to Jesus' followers (Luke 24:45–49; Acts 1:8; John 20:21–22). Here not only do the upper room discourses apply for John but Jesus' prayer for his followers in John 17.

Finally, a stress on unity that God provides in bringing his followers together is reflected in distinct language. What Luke presents as the reconciling impact of the kingdom message, John has in stressing the oneness believers are to have as they are one even as the Father and Son are one. The resultant love for one another that John stresses also fits in here by how the community cares for each other as evident in various passages in Acts.

22.3.3 Parallels with Paul

In both Acts and Paul's letters the crucifixion is central to the work of salvation. One need only compare 1 Cor 1–2 with the speeches in Acts 3 and 5, where Jesus is hung on a tree as an act of cultural shame and yet he is able to offer forgiveness of sins. In fact, in Gal 3:13 we see the same allusion as in Acts 5:30 and 10:39.

That the program is summed up in Christ is something both Luke and Paul affirm. One can compare texts such as Luke 1:68–79 or Acts 3:18–22 with Eph 1:3–14 or 1 Cor 15:20–28.

Resurrection as vindication and leading to victory links Luke-Acts with themes we also see especially in 1 Cor 15. What Paul takes as indispensable for the Christian faith, a physical resurrection of Jesus, Luke sees as central to the kerygma, as the role of resurrection in the speeches in Acts shows. Luke also describes the physical nature of the resurrection in the appearances to the Emmaus disciples and then later to the entire group in Luke 24 by showing Jesus taking a meal.

The fulfillment of promise in Jesus showing that the new era is already present is parallel in Rom 1:2–4 with numerous Lucan texts, such as Luke 4:16–23 or 24:43–47. Peter's claim in Acts 2 that the ascension shows that Jesus is the Messiah is like Paul's remark in Rom 1:2–4 that the resurrection "marks out" Jesus as Son of God.

Salvation is already-not yet in Paul as it is in Luke. Thus, cosmic reconciliation is still to come in Rom 8, just as the disciples are still looking forward to Jesus completing his work in Acts 3:18–22.

Sin and need for repentance appear in both authors. Here Rom 3:8–18 is important and parallels the warning of Jesus in Luke 13:1–9. When one looks at how Luke and Paul view the spirtual need of the entire Greco-Roman culture, texts like Acts 17:16–32 and Rom 1:18–32 can be compared. The need to repent, even in Israel, parallels Paul's arguments in Rom 2.

Faith is important to both authors. The most striking overlap is in the use of Joel 2 in Acts 2:16–38 and Rom 10:9–17. For both Luke and Acts, calling on the name of the Lord is key. Luke emphasizes this with his repeated references to the name of Jesus in his second volume (Acts 2:38 and the speech in 3:13–26 are but the first examples of this in Acts).

Of course, the emphasis on Gentile mission and the picture of reconciliation are parallel in both authors. This even includes the "to the Jew first" emphasis we see stated in Rom 1:16 and acted out in numerous locales in Acts 13–28. Reconciliation between Jews and Gentiles as Luke pictures in the healing of the centurion's slave in Luke 7:1–10 parallels what Paul says in Eph 2:11–22 and argues for in Rom 12–15.

Suffering in ministry is something Paul highlights throughout 2 Corinthians, while Luke describes Paul's suffering in numerous places in Acts. Luke even has Paul note how with many tribulations one must enter the kingdom of God (Acts 14:22).

Paul expresses hope for Israel in Rom 9–11 as he looks for all Israel being saved in a context where it is clear he is discussing ethnic Israel and his pain at their lack of response. So also Luke looks to this restoration most clearly in Peter's speech in Acts 3:18–22.

Salvation by faith in the context of grace is what the Jerusalem Council affirms in Acts 15:6–21, even though they also produce a list of actions that are of concern because of the offense they give to Jews. Paul's emphasis is seen most clearly in Eph 2:8–9, as well as in Rom 3–4. But the kind of concern that led the Jerusalem Council to issue a statement of practices for Gentiles to avoid fits Paul's handling of crosscultural tensions. Paul also speaks of being a Jew to the Jew and a Greek to the Greek when it comes to practice in 1 Cor 9:19. This sensitivity to others whose practice is different is also seen in Rom 14–15 and 1 Cor 8–10.

Another parallel between Luke and Paul involves their affirmation that circumcision is not necessary for Gentiles. Acts 10–11 and 15 correspond nicely with Rom 4, where Abraham is justified before he is circumcised, and with Galatians 5:1–12. Also similar is Paul's general relativizing and downgrading of aspects of his Jewish heritage in Philippians 3:2–7.

Luke's many warnings through Jesus about money and possessions in both parables and teaching (Luke 8:1–15; 12:13–21; 16:18–31) are comparable to what Paul teaches in the Pastorals (1 Tim 6:6–10, 17–19). Here we see a parallel set of values and a warning about overattachment to the world.

Community relations and support are important to Luke and Paul. Both speak of the collection made for communities suffering in poverty (Rom 15:25–29; Gal 2:10; 1 Cor 16:1–4; 2 Cor 8–9; cf. Acts 2:42–47; 4:32–37; 6:1–6; 11:27–30).

Paul actually notes the gift to the poor in the community in Jerusalem at Acts 24:17.

22.3.4 Parallels with Key Catholic Epistles

The concept of suffering in ministry so evident in the events of Paul's journeys also appears in 1 Pet 2:18–25 and 3:8–22. First Peter 2 appeals to the example of Jesus' suffering as the model for how believers are to face persecution.

The value of love for another has echoes with much of 1 John, where love for the fellow believer is evidence of genuine faith in God. This link between faith and relationships with others that is impacted by turning to God is a core value of the gospel that we also see so prominent in this letter. This tight connection in terms of faith and action also reflects Jesus' teaching that the one who does God's will is a member of Jesus' family (Luke 8:19–21; 11:27–28). The fact that this teaching is repeated in Luke shows its importance.

The warnings about wealth in Jas 5:1–6 read much like the woes of Luke 6:24–26. Again, it is the values of the disciple that are in view in this parallel. In fact, much of James parallels ideas of Jesus' teaching in Luke, such as not showing favoritism to the rich and faith being reflected in action, not just words (Jas 2:14–26). In Luke, this is presented as Jesus saying his family are those who hear and do God's Word (Luke 8:21; 11:28).

The emphasis on Davidic hope and Ps 110:1 that we see in Hebrews 1 is a mirror of some key christological texts in Luke-Acts. Luke 20:41–44 and 22:66–71 use Ps 110:1, as does Peter's speech in Acts 2:30–36. The image of Jesus found at the right hand also is similar. What Hebrews develops uniquely is the ministry of the Melchizedekian priesthood and the picture of Jesus' ministering as a king-priest in the heavenly temple.

22.3.5 Parallels with Revelation, 2 Peter, and Jude

The victory and vindication to come with Jesus' return, as well as the picture of a harsh judgment in that coming, link Luke and Revelation (see the harsh judgment in Rev 6–19, the victory in Rev 20–22). The eschatological discourse of Luke 17:20–37 points to a sudden judgment that is comprehensive, with the text's ending on the note that where the vultures are, there is where the event occurs. This portrait of a harsh judgment to come also parallels the thrust of judgment imagery in 2 Peter and Jude. The note of both vindication and judgment is prominent in Luke 21:5–38. Vindication also is pictured in the parable of the nagging widow and the judge in 18:1–8.

Also, a similarity exists between Luke's view that delay gives more time for mission and responsible stewardship of the call[16] and Peter's claim that delay allows more to be saved and shows God's patience (2 Pet 3:9).

---

16. See Luke's many eschatological parables, esp. Luke 12:36–50 and 19:12–27, discussed in ch. 20.

22.4 ONE FINAL ISSUE: HOW NORMATIVE IS LUKE-ACTS?

One vexing issue that accompanies these volumes, especially Acts, is how normative the activity in this book is. Between the explicit "supernatural" activity of God and other events like the sharing of possessions, there has been much discussion of what the expectations are for God's people today.[17]

The role of the text as canon certainly means the text describes what God did with an expectation and openness to all it describes as possible from God in the context of his sovereign plan and timing. Nevertheless, distinctions need to be noted. The attestation that came with the apostles and those of the early generation seems to reflect that the church was seen as a unique group of witnesses who launched a special period for the new message. This does not mean that God does not and will not continue to act, even in unusual ways at certain times and places of his own choosing. But it does indicate that what we see described in Acts is part of a special period of attestation, much like the time when miracles in Israel's history concentrated around the time of Moses as a time of initial deliverance and the period of Elijah-Elisha as a time when Israel needed to turn back to God.

It is one thing to say God *can* act in certain ways and quite another to say he *will* do so in a habitual kind of way that is "normative" in the fullest sense of that term.[18] The latter view presumes upon God and the nature of his choice about how he directs, even suggesting he must act in a certain way. God calls us in these volumes to trust him and his timing in the events that surround us. In Acts, some survive persecution; others are martyred. Some have visions, others do not. All of this is in the hands and program of God. All he asks of us is faith, dependence, and faithfulness. God can act in powerful ways and can be appealed to do so, but the timing and nature of his response are in his hands.

This reality makes the question of normativeness of the kinds of things we see in these two volumes at risk of being a misdirection of the walk of faith where the disciples place their spiritual care in the hands of a caring God who responds as he wills. God can act in these ways, but whether he will and wills to do so is his business. The perspective from which we should view the question of normativeness is like what Jesus said about the time of the coming of the end. We may wish for it to come and pray for it to come, but when it actually does come and how are God's business.

As for the sharing of possessions, this is a value the community entered into

---

17. The term *supernatural* is a decidedly modern one. It points to out-of-the-ordinary activities that assume a mostly passive presence for God in his creation. Such events go beyond the normal, natural way of life. Yet there is a sense in which the surprise these kinds of events engendered for those who experienced them in Luke-Acts shows that they were not so common for an ancient society either, even though ancients were far more open to the possibility of the activity of God than many modern people are.

18. *Normative* can mean one of two things. It can mean that which is normal or common, or it can mean the standard by which God *can* act. The first might be considered to be normative in the fullest sense, since it is a standard for God's activity and is also seen as commonly occurring. In the case of Luke-Acts and its events, I would argue Luke-Acts is normative in the second sense, but not necessarily in the first.

voluntarily and not as a matter of command. It showed their solidarity and their commitment to care for one another as a core value. Nothing Luke does or says about this pattern indicates that selling everything was a command (see Zacchaeus) or that it was wrong. In fact, the very way this is told in Acts, and said of Barnabas in particular, sees it as a commendable voluntary act. So this category is an activity that is described and presented with sympathy and commendation for its presence, even though it was never commanded of everyone. That kind of distinction is valuable in thinking about this practice. The church is urged to be sensitive to those who are in need and be ready to reach out to those on the fringe both in the community and outside of it. The command is to love one's neighbor and not be overly attached to possessions. These latter two ideas are what is explicitly commanded in these volumes. How that works itself out takes the Spirit's direction in our communities.

I note these areas in closing because they are part of what gives us pause as we read these two volumes. What Luke calls for from his readers is a genuine pursuit of relationship with God rooted in humility, repentance, and faith, with no sense of entitlement other than to receive what the grace of God gives under his direction. Beyond that we are to reflect values that honor God and show love for our neighbor. To know him is to be impacted to love others better. That is to be especially evident in the community of God's people, which is why the picture of reconciliation between Jews and Gentiles is so central to Luke's theology and story. As we seek to be the reconciled people of God, God will work with us in ways that lead us where we should go as we allow God to direct us as he wills.

22.5 CONCLUSION

Our survey of Luke's reception, its emphases, and its parallels with other NT books shows how integrated his teaching is with the rest of the NT. Sometimes efforts have been made to treat Luke as a late and idealizing text, bringing together in the new faith what really did not belong together. The Baur thesis of the nineteenth century, whose shadow still lurks over some NT studies, tends to pit some of Luke's unique elements against other parts of the NT. It argues that Luke was a second-century synthesis of earlier disparate elements within the earlier Christian movement. Not only is the dating of Luke too late for this view, but the way it argues that Luke glosses over a so-called rift between Paul and James-Peter is much exaggerated.[19] Rather, Luke's emphases and overlaps with the NT often only highlight or develop dimensions of theological belief already present elsewhere. They are not a part of completely distinct forms of early Christian faith. Therefore we can come to appreciate how well Luke fits in with the NT, as well as how significant his contribution to the canon is.

---

19. This is an issue I address in my commentary *Acts* in the BECNT series, especially in the discussion on Acts 15.

Chapter 23

CONCLUSION

BIBLIOGRAPHY

Bock, Darrell L. "A Theology of Luke-Acts." Pp. 87–166 in *A Biblical Theology of the New Testament*. Ed. Roy B. Zuck and Darrell L. Bock. Chicago: Moody Press, 1994. **Bovon, François.** *Luke the Theologian*. 2nd rev. ed. Waco, TX: Baylor University Press, 2006. **Conzelmann, Hans.** *The Theology of St. Luke*. Philadelphia: Fortress, 1982. **Fitzmyer, Joseph.** *Luke the Theologian: Aspects of His Teaching*. New York: Paulist, 1989. **Franklin, E.** *Christ the Lord: A Study of the Purpose and Theology of Luke-Acts*. London: SPCK, 1975. **Green, Joel.** *The Theology of the Gospel of Luke*. New Testament Theology. Cambridge: Cambridge University Press, 1995. **Jervell, Jacob.** *The Theology of the Acts of the Apostles*. Cambridge: Cambridge University Press, 1996. **Maddox, R.** *The Purpose of Luke-Acts*. Edinburgh: T&T Clark, 1982. **Marshall, I. H.** *Luke: Historian and Theologian*. Grand Rapids: Zondervan, 1970. **O'Toole, Robert F.** *The Unity of Luke's Theology: An Analysis of Luke-Acts*. GNS 9. Wilmington, DE: Michael Glazier, 1984.

The biblical theology of Luke-Acts is rich and often underappreciated for what it contributes to canonical theology. These two volumes present the continuity of Israel's story with the new era that Jesus brought and the new community that his ministry generated. What appears to be a new, innovative faith is, in fact, the realization of promises and covenants God had made with Israel long ago. Central to this realization is the figure of Jesus, who came to announce the arrival of the promised kingdom of God, died to provide a means to inaugurate the new covenant, and then with forgiveness in place offered the Spirit to connect people of all nations more directly to God. By doing so, Jesus formed a new enabled community that was called to serve God and engage in mission. That is Luke's message in a nutshell.

The key actor in all of this is God. It is his plan that is described. Jesus is his messenger, and the community reaches out to include the nations on his direct initiative. Luke's goal is to reassure Theophilus, a likely God-fearer, and others like him. Luke's believing readers are precisely where they should be in the plan of God. Their membership in this new community participates in this program of God, despite the persecution the community faces. In this Luke is legitimating the new movement in the face of doubt that others have about it.

23.1 SIX KEY THESES ABOUT LUKE'S THEOLOGY

In the midst of this study of Luke's theology, we have not only walked though the narrative to trace several themes but have summarized those results and set them in the context of discussion among scholars. Although there are many themes, six issues within the scholarly conversation are most important. Where this study falls in relationship to those issues shows where this study fits in that dialogue.

23.1.1 Divine Direction, Salvation History, Continuity of Promise, and Mission

The predominant idea in Luke-Acts is that Jesus' coming represents the inauguration and culmination of a program of promise God introduced to Israel through the covenants to Abraham and David, and the offer of a new covenant. This salvation history did not replace eschatology as Conzelmann claimed, but rather was the eschatology of divine promise outlined in the program of Scripture and event that was a part of the Hebrew tradition.[1] Israel's story was about promise, including the promise to include the nations in blessing. Jesus and the mission of the new community involved announcing the coming of the realization of that promise in Jesus' coming and work. In a sense, Luke-Acts is a *Missionsgeschichte* ("history of mission").[2] It explains why the new faith and its new community exist and what drives it.

23.1.2 Israel's Story Includes the Nations and Is Not Anti-Semitic

This theme makes the point that the conflict one sees in Luke-Acts is not a reflection of anti-Semitism, as J. T. Sanders claimed.[3] Rather, it reflects the kind of in-house debate about legitimacy that one also sees the prophets engage in within the Hebrew Scripture. Israel's story is the key concern of Luke from the infancy material, where the hymns are drenched in the language of Israel's hope, to the final remarks of Paul in Acts 28, where he says that he is in chains for the hope of Israel.

Divine actions have shown that the same blessing as came on those in Israel who believed also fell on Gentiles. In other words, God accepts any who turn to embrace what he has done in Jesus. Gentiles and their inclusion in blessing are a key part of Israel's story of promise and fulfillment. In addition, a divide in Israel has taken place so that persecution and suffering emerged as a result of the rejection of the message by many in Israel. This also is not surprising, as Scripture taught the innocent suffering of God's agent as well as presented Israel's history as full of stories where she has rejected those God sent. So the tension the new community lives under is no great surprise.

---

1. Conzelmann, *Theology of St. Luke.* His position that Luke was concerned about the delay of the return and that his answer to this crisis was to turn to salvation history overestimates the importance of the near return as was traced in our chapter on eschatology in chapter 20.

2. Martin Hengel, "Die Ursprünge der christlichen Mission," *NTS* 18 (1971–72): 25.

3. Sanders, *Jews in Luke-Acts.* Here the work of Jacob Jervell has led the way. See his *Luke and the People of God.*

23.1.3 The Spirit as the Sign of the New Era

Perhaps more than most studies in Luke-Acts, our examination of the themes tied to the Spirit's coming has made a point to show how Jesus' bestowal of the Spirit is a sign of the arrival of the new age. The Spirit is not merely a spirit of prophecy but is an enabler, the arrival of divine power that also purges humanity and enables mission.[4] The Spirit's coming also is evidence that Jesus has been raised, vindicated, and shown to be the Messiah-Lord. The community's reception of the Spirit means that Jesus sits at God's right hand, sharing in the execution of the divine program.

23.1.4 Salvation and Identity Tied to Jesus' Work

Luke spends little time explaining how Jesus saves. Death for sin is mentioned explicitly only twice in these two volumes (Luke 22:18–20; Acts 20:28). Rather, what Luke seeks to achieve is a sense of solidarity and identification with Jesus through what he has done, and Luke highlights Jesus' unique position in the offer of salvation.[5] Salvation is an act of God's grace. It is obtained by seeking God's mercy. It is not an entitlement that comes automatically because of effort or heritage.

Salvation is illustrated powerfully in various ways. Consider the centurion who felt he was not worthy for Jesus to come under his roof, but believed in what Jesus could do from a distance (Luke 7:1–10). Jesus affirmed him. Or consider the sinful woman who, while saying nothing, simply wept at Jesus' feet in appreciation for the forgiveness Jesus offered (7:36–50). Jesus affirmed her act. Or think of the prodigal who returned to his father knowing he was not worthy to be a son—only to have the father receive him back as a son (15:11–32). Jesus illustrates how God receives the lost who come back to him seeking nothing but what he can offer. Or consider the tax collector who simply said while beating his breast, "God, have mercy on me" (Luke 18:13–14). Jesus says this is the attitude God justified.

None of this presumes on God, but turns in trust to him. Jesus' coming was heaven's call and cry to listen to what God has done for us through Jesus. We do not get to God the old-fashioned way—by earning it. We get to God by receiving his forgiveness and the Spirit he offers. The kingdom means that God comes into our lives powerfully present within us to rule and enable us to relate well to him and to others. We come humbly, seeking the mercy and grace God freely gives and believing he will do it by giving us life. We come grateful that God cares enough about us to take us on as a part of his people and program. It is this sense of connection and identity, rooted in gratitude and in Jesus' greatness and uniqueness, that Luke has sought to engender. So the Jesus story is not just another religious account among

---

4. The various works of Max Turner on the Spirit show how comprehensively Luke describes the work of the Spirit. See his "Spirit of Prophecy," 327–48; and *Power from on High: The Spirit in Israel's Restoration and Witness in Luke-Acts* (JPTSup 9; Sheffield: Sheffield Academic Press, 1996).

5. I. Howard Marshall, *Luke: Historian and Theologian* (3rd ed.;

Exeter: Paternoster, 1988) treats salvation as the key theme of Luke-Acts. Our study has tried to specify what about salvation is central to Luke-Acts, including legitimization and the emphases on the continuity of promise as well as Gentile inclusion. Still, the focus on how God saves is a central Lucan concern.

many that can touch our hearts. It is a unique event that seeks to transform our hearts and calls us to sit at God's feet. Luke's account tells this story and wants his readers to appreciate its depth.

23.1.5 A New Era and Structure in a Trinitarian Story

Without using the word, these two volumes tell a trinitarian story. God is the main actor as he sends Jesus as his key representative agent. Jesus in turn gives the Spirit to energize his people and to rule the kingdom from within the hearts and souls of his people. All of this is the result of forgiveness and grace, rooted in divine promise. There is continuity in promise and hope, even as there is discontinuity in structure.

The way Israel functioned in the past has been forever changed. Now it is not a national entity that is the residence for blessing but a messianic multinational community that spreads across the globe. All of this does not mean Israel is cast aside, for she also is to be included as long as she responds. Response leads one into a new structure where Messiah and the Spirit lead and nations are gathered. For the community exists to represent God and to call others to share in the realized promise Jesus brings in a world often hostile to such a message. This explains why following Jesus requires exceptional perseverance and a life of integrity and discipleship that evidences a new way of living.

23.1.6 Realized Promise in Prophecy and Pattern

All that has been done is what was promised in the Hebrew Scriptures. Events tied to Jesus have made these connections clearer, but they are a part of what God had always revealed he would do. The new community is really an old faith. Blessing has come to the world with Jew and Gentile in a reconciled community for which Jesus has cleared the way. In that community resides the Spirit, who not only sanctifies this newly organized social group, but who also calls them to a mission and life that represents God well. The calling is to live in a manner he always had designed people to reflect—to love God and one's neighbor. Both the Messiah's glory and suffering were outlined in the sacred texts of old, as was the hope that one day the promise to Abraham would result in blessing for the nations.

These are the core themes of Luke-Acts. There is much more than the few paragraphs indicate, but these are the most central points around which Luke builds his theology.

23.2 Conclusion: The Mighty God Who Saves and Reconciles

Luke's two volumes are about the mighty God who saves and who does so through Jesus Christ. Mary sang of "the Mighty One" who had done great things (Luke 1:49). In her hymn, she spoke of the hope of salvation, which Luke describes in his two books. Jesus is now seated at the right hand of the mighty God (22:69). This is the God for whom impossible things are possible (1:37; 18:27). He can save individuals and transform hearts. His plan will be accomplished. When God revealed to Peter that salvation was available to all, Peter could not resist serving God's plan even though it took him in directions he had not previously traveled (Acts 11:17). The salvation not only brings individual salvation, but is designed to reconcile the creation and bring people together in faithful service. Luke 1:16–17 and 1:71–79 open the gospel with these notes that never diminish as the story is told. Jew and Gentile together in Christ is the picture of the message in Acts. God's people encompass the nations.

God is also the "Savior," as Mary said (Luke 1:47). His intricate plan "redeemed" his people (v. 68) through a "horn" raised up from the house of David (v. 69). God is calling people (Acts 2:21, 39; 15:14), and in Jesus Christ they see God's salvation (Luke 2:30).

These promises express God's lovingkindness and grace. It is by the divine "tender mercy" that "the rising sun will come to us from heaven to shine on those living in darkness and in the shadow of death, to guide our feet into the path of peace" (Luke 1:78–79). He cares for his own daily (12:24–28), and God desires to reach those who are lost (Luke 15). God visits people in Jesus Christ (1:68; 7:16; Acts 15:4), whether they see it or not (Luke 19:41–42). God's Word reveals that, through Jesus Christ, God is mighty, saving, and compassionate. His arms are open to any who turn to him. Jesus is Lord of all, so the gospel can go to all. The hard times of the church are not signs of God's judgment against her because she has been too generous in offering salvation directly to Gentiles; rather, they are opportunities to stand up boldly for God as the deity spreads his Word through the testimony of those who faithfully witness to the fulfillment of God's promises.

This is the story of reassurance Theophilus needed to hear (Luke 1:4). But Luke's message and theology were not for Theophilus alone. The church still has the responsibility to carry this message to a world that needs such deliverance and reassurance. People need to come to God through Christ to meet, both now and forever, the mighty God who saves. This is the God whom Luke-Acts so powerfully and persuasively describes. People can be reconciled not only to God but also to one another.

BIBLIOGRAPHY

Achtemeier, Paul, Joel Green, and Marianne Meye Thompson. *Introducing the New Testament: Its Literature and Theology.* Grand Rapids: Eerdmans, 2001.

Adams, Dwayne. *The Sinner in Luke.* Evangelical Theological Society Monograph Series. Eugene, OR: Pickwick, 2008.

Aland, Kurt and Barbara. *The Text of the New Testament.* Translated by Erroll R. Rhoads. Grand Rapids: Eerdmans, 1987.

Alexander, Loveday. "Reading Luke-Acts from Back to Front." Pp. 419–46 in *The Unity of Luke-Acts.* Edited by J. Verheyden. Leuven: Peeters, 1999.

Arlandson, James M. *Women, Class, and Society in Early Christianity: Models from Luke-Acts.* Grand Rapids: Baker, 1996.

Arndt, W. F. *The Gospel according to St. Luke.* St. Louis: Concordia, 1956.

Arnold, Clint. *Ephesians—Power and Magic: The Concept of Power in Ephesians in the Light of Its Historical Setting.* Society for New Testament Studies Monograph Series. Cambridge: Cambridge University Press, 1989.

Bachmann, Michael. "Jerusalem and Rome in Luke-Acts." Pp. 60–83 in *Luke-Acts and Empire: Essays in Honor of Robert L. Brawley.* Edited by David Rhoads, David Esterline, and Jae Won Lee. Princeton Theological Monographs. Eugene, OR: Pickwick, 2011.

Banks, R. J. *Jesus and the Law in the Synoptic Tradition.* Society for New Testament Studies Monograph Series 28. Cambridge: Cambridge University Press, 1975.

Barrett, C. K. *A Critical and Exegetical Commentary on the Acts of the Apostles I: Preliminary Introduction and Commentary on Acts I–XIV.* International Critical Commentary. Edinburgh: T&T Clark, 1994.

———. *A Critical and Exegetical Commentary on the Acts of the Apostles II: Introduction and Commentary on Acts XV–XXVIII.* International Critical Commentary. Edinburgh: T&T Clark, 1998.

———. "The First New Testament." *Novum Testamentum* 38 (1996): 94–104.

———. *Luke the Historian in Recent Study.* London: Epworth, 1961.

———. "The Third Gospel as a Preface to Acts? Some Reflections." Pp. 1451–66 in *The Four Gospels 1992.* Edited by F. Van Segbroeck, C. M. Tuckett, G. Van Belle, and J. Verheyden. Leuven: Peeters, 1992.

Bateman, Herb, Darrell L. Bock, and Gordon Johnston. *Jesus the Messiah: Tracing the Promises, Expectations and Coming of Israel's King.* Grand Rapids: Kregel, 2011.

Bauckham, Richard. *Jesus and the Eyewitnesses: The Gospels as Eyewitness Testimony.* Grand Rapids: Eerdmans, 2008.

———. *Gospel Women: Studies of Named Women in the Bible.* Grand Rapids: Eerdmans, 2002.

———. "The Restoration of Israel in Luke-Acts." Pp. 325–70 in *The Jewish World around the New Testament: Collected Essays I.* Tübingen: Mohr-Siebeck, 2008.

Bauernfeind, Otto. *Kommentar und Studien zur Apostelgeschichte.* Wissenschaftliche Untersuchungen zum Neuen Testament 22. Tübingen: Mohr-Siebeck, 1980.

Bellinger, William H. Jr., and William R. Farmer, eds. *Jesus and the Suffering Servant: Isaiah 53 and Christian Origins.* Harrisburg, PA: Trinity International, 1998.

Berding, Kenneth, and Jonathan Lunde, eds. *Three Views on the New Testament Use of the Old.* Grand Rapids: Zondervan, 2008.

Berger, Klaus. "Die königlichen Messiastraditionen des Neuen Testaments." *New Testament Studies* 20 (1973–74): 1–44.

Bird, Michael. "The Unity of Luke-Acts in Recent Discussion." *Journal for the Study of the New Testament* 29 (2007): 425–48.

Blomberg, Craig. "The Authenticity and Significance of Jesus' Fellowship with Sinners." Pp. 215–50 in *Key Events in the Life of the Historical Jesus: A Collaborative Exploration of Context and Coherence*. Edited by Darrell L. Bock and Robert L. Webb. Wissenschaftliche Untersuchungen zum Neuen Testament 247. Tübingen: Mohr-Siebeck, 2009.

———. "The Christian and the Law of Moses." Pp. 397–416 in *Witness to the Gospel: The Theology of Acts*. Edited by I. Howard Marshall and David Peterson. Grand Rapids: Eerdmans, 1998.

———. "The Law in Luke-Acts." *Journal for the Study of the New Testament* 22 (1984): 53–80.

———. *Neither Poverty or Riches: A Biblical Theology of Possessions*. Downers Grove, IL: InterVarsity Press, 2000.

Bock, Darrell L. *Acts*. Baker Exegetical Commentary on the New Testament 5. Grand Rapids: Baker, 2007.

———. *Blasphemy and Exaltation in Judaism and the Final Examination of Jesus*. Wissenschaftliche Untersuchungen zum Neuen Testament. Tübingen: Mohr-Siebeck, 1998.

———. "Blasphemy and the Jewish Examination of Jesus." Pp. 589–667 in *Key Events in the Life of the Historical Jesus: A Collaborative Exploration of Context and Coherence*. Edited by Darrell L. Bock and Robert L. Webb. Wissenschaftliche Untersuchungen zum Neuen Testament 247. Tübingen: Mohr-Siebeck, 2009.

———. "Embracing Jesus in a First Century Context: What Can It Teach Us about Spiritual Commitment?" in *Journal of Spiritual Formation and Soul Care* 3 (2010): 128–39.

———. *Jesus according to Scripture: Restoring the Portrait from the Gospels*. Grand Rapids: Baker, 2002.

———. "Jesus as Lord in Acts and in the Gospel Message." *Bibliotheca Sacra* 143 (1986): 146–54.

———. *Luke 1:1–9:50*. Baker Exegetical Commentary on the New Testament 3a. Grand Rapids: Baker, 1994.

———. *Luke 9:51–24:53*. Baker Exegetical Commentary on the New Testament 3b. Grand Rapids: Baker, 1996.

———. "The Parable of the Rich Man and Lazarus." *Southwestern Journal of Theology* 40 (1997): 63–72.

———. *Proclamation from Prophecy and Pattern: Lucan Old Testament Christology*. Journal for the Study of the New Testament Supplement. Sheffield: Sheffield Academic Press, 1987.

———. *Recovering the Real Lost Gospel: Rediscovering the Gospel as Good News*. Nashville: Broadman and Holman Academic, 2010.

———. "The Reign of the Lord Christ." Pp. 37–67 in *Dispensationalism, Israel and the Church*. Edited by Craig A. Blaising and Darrell L. Bock. Grand Rapids: Zondervan, 1992.

———. "Scripture and the Realisation of God's Promises." Pp. 41–62 in *Witness to the Gospel: The Theology of Acts*. Edited by I. Howard Marshall and David Peterson. Grand Rapids: Eerdmans, 1998.

———. "Single Meaning, Multiple Contexts and Referents: The New Testament's Legitimate, Accurate, and Multifaceted Use of the Old." Pp. 105–51 in *Three Views on the New Testament Use of the Old*. Edited by Kenneth Berding and Jonathan Lunde. Grand Rapids: Zondervan, 2008.

———. *Studying the Historical Jesus: A Guide to Sources and Methods*. Grand Rapids: Baker Academic, 2002.

———. "A Theology of Luke-Acts." Pp. 87–166 in *A Biblical Theology of the New Testament*. Edited by Roy B. Zuck and Darrell L. Bock. Chicago: Moody Press, 1994.

Bock, Darrell L., and James Charlesworth. *Parables of Enoch, Early Judaism, Jesus, and Christian Origins*. London: T&T Clark, forthcoming.

Bock, Darrell L., and Mitch Glaser, eds. *The Gospel according to Isaiah 53: Encountering the Suffering Servant in Jewish and Christian Theology*. Grand Rapids: Kregel, 2011.

Bock, Darrell L., and Robert L. Webb, eds. *Key Events in the Life of the Historical Jesus: A Collaborative Exploration of Context and Coherence*. Wissenschaftliche Untersuchungen zum Neuen Testament 247. Tübingen: Mohr-Siebeck, 2009.

Bockmuehl, Markus. "Why Not Let Acts Be Acts? In Conversation with C. Kavin Rowe." *Journal for the Study of the New Testament* 28 (2005): 163–66.

Bode, Edward L. *First Easter Morning: The Gospel Accounts of the Women's Visit the Tomb of Jesus*. Chicago: Loyola University Press, 1970.

Boff, Leonardo. *Jesus Christ Liberator: A Critical Christology of Our Time*. Maryknoll, NY: Orbis, 1978.

Bolt, Peter. "Mission and Witness." Pp. 191–214 in *Witness to the Gospel: The Theology of Acts*. Edited by I. Howard Marshall and David Peterson. Grand Rapids: Eerdmans, 1998.

Bonz, Marianne P. *The Past as Legacy: Luke-Acts and Ancient Epic*. Minneapolis: Fortress, 2000.

Borgman, Paul. *The Way according to Luke: Hearing the Whole Story of Luke-Acts*. Grand Rapids: Eerdmans, 2006.

Borsch, F. H. *The Son of Man in Myth and History*. New Testament Library. Philadelphia: Westminster, 1967.

Bovon, François. *Luke the Theologian*. 2nd ed. Waco, TX: Baylor University Press, 2006.

———. "Studies in Luke-Acts: Retrospect and Prospect." *Harvard Theological Review* 85 (1992): 175–96.

Bowker, John. "Speeches in Acts: A Study in Proem and Yelammedenu Form." *New Testament Studies* 14 (1967–68): 96–111.

Brawley, Robert. "Ethical Borderlines between Rejection and Hope: Interpreting the Jews in Luke-Acts." *Currents in Theology and Mission* 27 (2000): 415–23.

———. *Luke-Acts and the Jews: Conflict, Apology, Reconciliation*. Society of Biblical Literature Monograph Series. Atlanta: Scholars Press, 1987.

———. "The God of Promises and the Jews of Luke-Acts." Pp. 279–96 in *Literary Studies in Luke-Acts: Essays in Honor of Joseph B. Tyson*. Edited by R. P. Thompson and T. E. Phillips. Macon, GA: Mercer University Press, 1998.

Brooke, G. J. *Exegesis at Qumran: 4QFlorilegium in Its Jewish Context*. Journal for the Study of the Old Testament Supplement 29. Sheffield: JSOT, 1985.

Brown, Raymond. *An Introduction to the New Testament*. New York; Doubleday, 1997.

———. *The Birth of the Messiah: A Commentary on the Infancy Narratives in Matthew and Luke*. Garden City, NY: Doubleday, 1977.

Bruce, F. F. *The Acts of the Apostles: Greek Text with Introduction and Commentary*. 3rd ed. Grand Rapids: Eerdmans, 1990.

———. *The Book of the Acts.* Rev. ed. New International Commentary on the New Testament. Grand Rapids: Eerdmans, 1988.

———. *The Speeches in the Acts of the Apostles.* London: Tyndale, 1942.

Buckwalter, Doug. *The Character and Purpose of Luke's Christology.* Society for New Testament Studies Monograph Series. Cambridge: Cambridge University Press, 1996.

———. "The Divine Savior." Pp. 107–23 in *Witness to the Gospel: The Theology of Acts.* Edited by I. Howard Marshall and David Peterson. Grand Rapids: Eerdmans, 1998.

Bultmann, Rudolf. *The History of the Synoptic Tradition.* Translated by J. Marsh. New York: Harper & Row, 1963.

Burridge, Richard. *What Are the Gospels? A Comparison with Greco-Roman Biography.* 2nd ed. Grand Rapids: Eerdmans, 2004.

Byington, S. "יהוה and אדון." *Journal of Biblical Literature* 76 (1957): 58–59.

Cadbury, H. J. *The Making of Luke-Acts.* New York: Macmillan, 1927.

Carroll, John T. "Luke's Portrait of the Pharisees." *Catholic Biblical Quarterly* 50 (1988): 604–21.

———. *Response to the End of History: Eschatology and Situation in Luke-Acts.* Society of Biblical Literature Dissertation Series. Atlanta: Scholars Press, 1988.

Carson, D. A., and Douglas J. Moo. *An Introduction to the New Testament.* 2nd ed. Grand Rapids: Zondervan, 2005.

Cassidy, Richard J. *Jesus, Politics and Society: A Study of Luke's Gospel.* Maryknoll, NY: Orbis, 1978.

———. "Paul's Proclamation of *Lord* Jesus as a Chained Prisoner in Rome: Luke's Ending Is His Beginning." Pp. 142–53 in *Luke-Acts and Empire: Essays in Honor of Robert L. Brawley.* Edited by David Rhoads, David Esterline, and Jae Won Lee. Eugene, OR: Pickwick, 2011.

———. *Society and Politics in the Acts of the Apostles.* Maryknoll, NY: Orbis, 1987.

Chance, J. Bradley. *Jerusalem, the Temple and the New Age in Luke-Acts.* Macon, GA: Mercer University Press, 1988.

Charlesworth, James H. "Intertextuality: Isaiah 40:3 and the Serek Ha-Yahad." Pp. 197–224 in *The Quest for Context and Meaning: Studies in Biblical Intertextuality in Honor of James A. Sanders.* Edited by Craig A. Evans and Shemaryahu Talmon. Biblical Interpretation Series. Leiden: Brill, 1997.

Cho, Youngmo. "Spirit and Kingdom in Luke-Acts: Proclamation as the Primary Role of the Spirit in Relation to the Kingdom of God in Luke-Acts." *Asian Journal of Pentecostal Studies* 6 (2003): 173–97.

Clark, E. A. *History, Theory, Text: Historians and the Linguistic Turn.* Cambridge, MA: Harvard University Press, 2005.

Clark, Stephen. *Man and Woman in Christ: An Examination of the Roles of Men and Women in Light of Scripture and the Social Sciences.* East Lansing, MI: Tabor, 1980.

Clarke, Andrew C. "The Role of the Apostles." Pp. 169–90 in *Witness to the Gospel: The Theology of Acts.* Edited by I. Howard Marshall and David Peterson. Grand Rapids: Eerdmans, 1998.

Clarke, W. L. "The Use of the Septuagint in Acts." Pp. 66–105 in *The Beginnings of Christianity. Part 1: The Acts of the Apostles,* vol. 2. Edited by F. J. Foakes Jackson and K. Lake. London: Macmillan, 1922.

Conzelmann, Hans. *Acts of the Apostles.* Hermeneia. Translated by James Limburg, A. Thomas Krabel, and Donald H. Juel. Philadelphia: Fortress, 1987.

————. *The Theology of St. Luke.* Philadelphia: Fortress, 1982.

Cook, Donald E. "A Gospel Portrait of the Pharisees." *Review and Expositor* 84/2 (Spring 1987): 221–33.

Corley, Kathleen. *Private Women, Public Meals: Social Conflict in the Synoptic Tradition.* Peabody, MA: Hendrickson, 1993.

Creed, J. M. *The Gospel according to St. Luke.* London: Macmillan, 1930.

Cunningham, Scott. *"Through Many Tribulations": The Theology of Persecution in Luke-Acts.* Journal for the Study of the New Testament Supplement. Sheffield: Sheffield Academic Press, 1997.

Danker, Fred. *Jesus and the New Age: A Commentary on St. Luke's Gospel.* Rev. ed. Philadelphia: Fortress, 1988.

Dibelius, Martin. *Die Reden der Apostelgeschichte und die antike Geschichtsschreibung.* Sitzungsberichte der Heidelberger Akademie der Wissenschaften, philosophisch-historische Klasse. Heidelberg: Winter, 1949.

————. *Studies in the Acts of the Apostles.* London: SCM, 1956.

Dodd, C. H. *The Apostolic Preaching and Its Developments.* London: Hodder & Stoughton, 1936. Reprint: New York: Harper and Row, 1964.

————. "The Fall of Jerusalem and the 'Abomination of Desolation.'" *Journal of Roman Studies* 37 (1947): 47–54.

Downing, F. G. "Common Ground with Paganism in Luke and Josephus." *New Testament Studies* 28 (1982): 546–59.

Duling, David. "Solomon, Exorcism, and the Son of David." *Harvard Theological Review* 68 (1975): 235–52.

Dunn, James D. G. *Baptism in the Holy Spirit: A Re-examination of the New Testament Teaching on the Gift of the Spirit in Relation to Pentecostalism Today.* Studies in Biblical Theology 2/15. London: SCM, 1970.

————. "Matthew 12:28/Luke 11:20—A Word of Jesus?" Pp. 29–49 in *Eschatology and the New Testament: Essays in Honor of George Raymond Beasley-Murray.* Edited by W. H. Gloer. Peabody, MA: Hendrickson, 1988.

Dupont, Jacques. *Nouvelles études sur les Actes des Apôtres.* Paris: Cerf, 1984.

————. *The Salvation of the Gentiles: Essays on the Acts of the Apostles.* Trans. John R. Keating. New York: Paulist, 1979.

Eisler, R. I. *The Messiah Jesus and John the Baptist according to Flavius Josephus' Recently Discovered "Capture of Jerusalem" and the Other Jewish and Christian Sources.* Translated by A. H. Krappe. New York: Dial, 1931.

Ellis, E. Earle. *The Gospel of Luke.* New Century Bible. Grand Rapids: Eerdmans, 1974.

Esler, Philip. *Community and Gospel in Luke-Acts: The Social and Political Motivations of Lucan Theology.* Society for New Testament Studies Monograph Series 57. Cambridge: Cambridge University Press, 1987.

Evans, Craig. "Exorcisms and the Kingdom: Inaugurating the Kingdom of God and Defeating the Kingdom of Satan." Pp. 151–79 in *Key Events in the Life of the Historical Jesus: A Collaborative Exploration of Context and Coherence.* Edited by Darrell L. Bock and Robert L. Webb. Wissenschaftliche Untersuchungen zum Neuen Testament 247. Tübingen: Mohr-Siebeck, 2009.

————. "Prophecy and Polemic: Jews in Luke's Scriptural Apologetic." Pp. 171–211 in *Luke and Scripture: The Function of Sacred Tradition in Luke-Acts.* Edited by C. A. Evans and J. A. Sanders. Minneapolis: Fortress, 1993.

Fitzmyer, Joseph. *The Acts of the Apostles*. Anchor Bible. Garden City, NY: Doubleday, 1998.

———. "The Contribution of Qumran Aramaic to the Study of the New Testament." *New Testament Studies* 20 (1973–74): 382–407.

———. *The Gospel of Luke I–IX: Introduction, Translation and Notes*. Anchor Bible. Garden City, NY: Doubleday, 1982.

———. *The Gospel of Luke X–XXIV: Introduction, Translation and Notes*. Anchor Bible. Garden City, NY: Doubleday, 1985.

———. *Luke the Theologian: Aspects of His Teaching*. New York: Paulist, 1989.

Foh, Susan T. *Women and the Word of God: A Response to Biblical Feminism*. Phillipsburg, NJ: Presbyterian & Reformed, 1978.

Forbes, Greg W. *The God of Old: The Role of the Lukan Parables in the Purpose of Luke's Gospel*. Journal for the Study of the New Testament Supplement. Sheffield: Sheffield Academic Press, 2000.

Fornara, C. W. *The Nature of History in Ancient Greece and Rome*. Berkeley, CA: University of California Press, 1983.

Forsch, F. H. *The Son of Man in Myth and History*. New Testament Library. Philadelphia: Westminster, 1967.

Foulkes, Francis. *The Acts of God: A Study of the Basis of Typology in the Old Testament*. London: Tyndale, 1958.

France, R. T. *Women in the Church's Minstry: A Test Case for Biblical Interpretation*. Grand Rapids: Eerdmans, 1997.

Franklin, E. "The Ascension and the Eschatology of Luke-Acts." *Scottish Journal of Theology* 23 (1970): 191–200.

———. *Christ the Lord: A Study of the Purpose and Theology of Luke-Acts*. London: SPCK, 1975.

Fuller, Michael E. *The Restoration of Israel: Israel's Regathering and the Fate of the Nations in Early Jewish Literature and Luke-Acts*. Beiheft zur Zeitschrift für die neutestamentliche Wissenschaft. Berlin: de Gruyter, 2006.

Gärtner, B. "Paulus und Barnabas in Lystra: Zu Apg. 14,8–15." *Svensk exegetisk årsbok* 27 (1991): 83–88.

Gasque, W. *A History of the Criticism of the Acts of the Apostles*. Tübingen; Mohr-Siebeck, 1975.

Gathercole, Simon. *The Pre-Existent Son: Recovering the Christologies of Matthew, Mark, and Luke*. Grand Rapids: Eerdmans, 2006.

Gaventa, Beverly Roberts. *Acts*. Abingdon New Testament Commentaries. Nashville: Abingdon, 2003.

Giblin, C. H. *The Destruction of Jerusalem according to Luke's Gospel: A Historical-Typological Moral*. Analecta Biblica 107. Rome: Pontifical Biblical Institute Press, 1985.

Gloer, W. H., ed. *Eschatology and the New Testament: Essays in Honor of George Raymond Beasley-Murray*. Peabody, MA: Hendrickson, 1988.

Godet, F. *A Commentary on the Gospel of St. Luke*. 2 vols. Translated by E. W. Shalders and M. D. Cusin. Edinburgh: T&T Clark, 1875.

Goppelt, Leonhard. *Theology of the New Testament*. 2 vols. Translated by John Alsup. Edited by Jürgen Roloff. Grand Rapids: Eerdmans, 1981.

———. *Typos: The Typological Interpretation of the Old Testament in the New*. Grand Rapids: Eerdmans, 1982.

Goulder, M. D. *Luke: A New Paradigm*. 2 vols. Journal for the Study of the New Testament Supplement 20. Sheffield: JSOT, 1989.

Gowler, David. *Host, Guest, Enemy and Friend: Portraits of the Pharisees in Luke and Acts.* New York: Peter Lang, 1991.

———. "The Reception of Luke and Acts and the Unity of Luke-Acts." *Journal for the Study of the New Testament* 29 (2007): 459–72.

Green, Joel. "God as Savior in the Acts of the Apostles." Pp. 83–106 in *Witness to the Gospel: The Theology of Acts.* Edited by I. Howard Marshall and David Peterson. Grand Rapids: Eerdmans, 1998.

———. *The Gospel of Luke.* New International Commentary on the New Testament. Grand Rapids: Eerdmans, 1997.

———. "The Problem of a Beginning: Israel's Scriptures in Luke 1–2." *Bulletin for Biblical Research* 4 (1994): 61–85.

———. *The Theology of the Gospel of Luke.* New Testament Theology. Cambridge: Cambridge University Press, 1995.

Gregory, Andrew. *The Reception of Luke and Acts in the Period before Irenaeus: Looking for Luke in the Second Century.* Wissenschaftliche Untersuchungen zum Neuen Testament. Tübingen: Mohr-Siebeck, 2003.

Grundmann, Walter. *Das Evangelium nach Lukas.* Theologischer Handkommentar zum Neuen Testament 3. Berlin: Evangelische Verlagsanstalt, 1963.

Guelich, Robert. *The Sermon on the Mount.* Waco, TX: Word, 1982.

Gutiérrez, Gustavo. *A Theology of Liberation.* Maryknoll, NY: Orbis, 1973.

Haenchen, Ernst. *Acts of the Apostles: A Commentary.* Translated by B. Noble, G. Shinn, H. Anderson, and R. M. Wilson. Philadelphia: Westminster/Oxford: Blackwell, 1971 (1987 reprint).

Hagner, Donald A. "Jesus and the Synoptic Sabbath Controversies." Pp. 251–92 in *Key Events in the Life of the Historical Jesus: A Collaborative Exploration of Context and Coherence.* Edited by Darrell L. Bock and Robert L. Webb. Wissenschaftliche Untersuchungen zum Neuen Testament 247. Tübingen: Mohr-Siebeck, 2009.

Hahn, Ferdinand. *The Titles of Jesus in Christology: Their History in Early Christianity.* Translated by H. Knight and G. Ogg. London: Lutterworth, 1969.

Hays, Richard. *Echoes of Scripture in the Epistles of Paul.* New Haven, CT: Yale University Press, 1989.

Hemer, Colin. *The Book of Acts in the Setting of Hellenistic History.* Wissenschaftliche Untersuchungen zum Neuen Testament. Tübingen: Mohr-Siebeck/Winona Lake, IN: Eisenbrauns, 1989.

Hendriksen, W. *Exposition of the Gospel according to Luke.* New Testament Commentary. Grand Rapids: Baker, 1978.

Hengel, Martin. *Acts and the History of Earliest Christianity.* London: SCM, 1979.

———. *The Four Gospels and the One Gospel of Jesus Christ.* Harrisburg, PA: Trinity International, 2000.

———. "Die Ursprünge der christlichen Mission." *New Testament Studies* 18 (1971–72): 15–38.

Hengel, Martin, and Anna Maria Schwemer. *Jesus und das Judentum.* Geschichte des frühen Christentums. Tübingen: Mohr-Siebeck, 2007.

Holtz, Traugott. *Untersuchungen über die alttestamentlichen Zitate bei Lukas.* Texte und Untersuchungen zur Geschichte der altchristlichen Literatur 104. Berlin: Akademie, 1968.

Hooker, Morna. *The Son of Man in Mark: A Study of the Background of the Term "Son of Man" and Its Use in St. Mark's Gospel.* London: SPCK, 1967.

Horsley, Richard A. *Jesus and the Powers: Conflict, Covenant and the Hope of the Poor.* Minneapolis: Fortress, 2011.

Hume, Douglas A. *The Early Christian Community: A Narrative Analysis of Acts 2:41–47 and 4:32–35.* Wissenschaftliche Untersuchungen zum Neuen Testament 2/298. Tübingen: Mohr-Siebeck, 2011.

Janowski, Bernd, and Peter Stuhlmacher, eds. *The Suffering Servant: Isaiah 53 in Jewish and Christian Sources.* Grand Rapids: Eerdmans, 2004.

Jeremias, Joachim. *New Testament Theology: The Proclamation of Jesus.* Translated by J. Bowden. New Testament Library. London: SCM/New York: Scribner, 1971.

Jervell, Jacob. *Die Apostelgeschichte.* Göttingen: Vandenhoeck & Ruprecht, 1998.

———. *Luke and the People of God.* Minneapolis: Augsburg, 1972.

———. "Retrospect and Prospect in Luke-Acts Interpretation." Pp. 383–404 in *Society for Biblical Literature 1991 Seminar Papers.* Edited by E. H. Lovering Jr. Chico, CA: Scholars Press, 1991.

———. *The Theology of the Acts of the Apostles.* Cambridge: Cambridge University Press, 1996.

Jewett, Robert. *A Chronology of Paul's Life.* Philadelphia: Fortress, 1979.

Johnson, Luke Timothy. *The Acts of the Apostles.* Sacra Pagina. Collegeville, MN: Liturgical, 1992.

———. *The Gospel of Luke.* Sacra Pagina. Collegeville, MN: Liturgical, 1991.

———. "Literary Criticism of Luke-Acts: Is Reception History Pertinent?" *Journal for the Study of the New Testament* 28 (2005): 159–62.

———. "Luke-Acts, Book of." *Anchor Bible Dictionary,* 4:404–20.

Judge, E. A. *The First Christians in the Roman World: Augustan and New Testament Essays.* Edited by James Harrison. Wissenschaftliche Untersuchungen zum Neuen Testament 229. Tübingen: Mohr-Siebeck, 2008.

Keck, Leander E., and Louis J. Martyn, eds. *Studies in Luke-Acts.* Nashville: Abingdon, 1966.

Kilgallen, J. J. "Your Servant Jesus Whom You Anointed (Acts 4,27)." *Revue biblique* 105 (1998): 185–201.

Kim, Seyoon. *Christ and Caesar: The Gospel and the Roman Empire in the Writings of Paul and Luke.* Grand Rapids: Eerdmans, 2008.

———. *The Origin of Paul's Gospel.* Grand Rapids: Eerdmans, 1981.

Kimball, C. A. *Jesus' Exposition of the Old Testament in Luke's Gospel.* Journal for the Study of the New Testament Supplement 94. Sheffield: Sheffield Academic Press, 1994.

Kinman, Brent. "Jesus' Role Entry into Jerusalem." Pp. 383–427 in *Key Events in the Life of the Historical Jesus: A Collaborative Exploration of Context and Coherence.* Edited by Darrell L. Bock and Robert L. Webb. Wissenschaftliche Untersuchungen zum Neuen Testament 247. Tübingen: Mohr-Siebeck, 2009.

Klauck, Hans Josef. *Magic and Paganism in Early Christianity: The World of the Acts of the Apostles.* Minneapolis: Fortress, 2003.

Klutz, Todd. *The Exorcism Stories in Luke-Acts: A Sociostylistic Reading.* Society for New Testament Studies Monograph Series 129. Cambridge: Cambridge University Press, 2004.

Knox, John. *Marcion and the New Testament: An Essay on the Early History of the Canon.* Chicago: University of Chicago Press, 1942.

Koet, B. J. *Five Studies of Interpretation of Scripture in Luke-Acts.* Studiorum Novi Testamenti Auxilia. Leuven: Leuven University Press, 1989.

Köstenberger, Andreas, L. Scott Kellum, and Charles L. Quarles. *The Cradle, the Cross, and the Crown: An Introduction to the New Testament*. Nashville: Broadman and Holman Academic, 2009.

Kramer, Ross S. *Her Share of Blessings: Women's Religions among Pagans, Jews, and Christians in the Greco-Roman World*. Oxford: Oxford University Press, 1992.

Kümmel, Werner Georg. "Futurische und präsentische Eschatologie im ältesten Urchristentum." *New Testament Studies* 5 (1958–59): 113–26.

———. *Introduction to the New Testament*. Rev. ed. Nashville: Abingdon, 1975.

———. *Promise and Fulfillment*. Translated by Dorothea M. Barton. Studies in Biblical Theology. Naperville, IL: Allenson, 1957.

Kurz, W. S. *Reading Luke-Acts: Dynamics of Biblical Narrative*. Louisville: Westminster John Knox, 1993.

Lampe, G. W. H. *God as Spirit*. The Bampton Lectures. Oxford: Clarendon, 1977.

Larkin, W. J., Jr. *Acts*. IVP New Testament Commentary 5. Downers Grove, IL: InterVarsity Press, 1994.

Liefeld, Walter, and Ruth A. Tucker. *Daughters of the Church*. Grand Rapids: Zondervan, 1987.

Lindars, Barnabas. *Jesus Son of Man: A Fresh Examination of the Son of Man Sayings in the Gospels in the Light of Recent Research*. London: SPCK, 1983.

Litwak, Kenneth Duncan. *Echoes of Scripture in Luke-Acts: Telling the History of God's People Intertextually*. Journal for the Study of the New Testament Supplement Series 282. London: T&T Clark, 2005.

Longenecker, Bruce. "Lukan Aversion to Humps and Hollows: The Case of Acts 11:27–12:25." *New Testament Studies* 50 (2004): 185–204.

Luce, H. K. *The Gospel according to S. Luke*. Cambridge Greek Testament for Schools and Colleges. Cambridge: Cambridge University Press, 1933.

Maddox. R. *The Purpose of Luke-Acts*. Edinburgh: T&T Clark, 1982.

Manson. T. W. *The Sayings of Jesus: As Recorded in the Gospels according to St. Matthew and St. Luke*. London: SCM, 1949.

Marguerat, Daniel. "Voyages et voyageurs dans le livre des Actes et la culture gréco-romaine." *Revue d'histoire et de philosophie religieuses* 78 (1998): 33–59.

———. *The First Christian Historian: Writing the "Acts of the Apostles."* Society for New Testament Studies Monograph Series 121. Cambridge: Cambridge University Press, 2002.

Marshall, I. H. "Acts and the 'Former Treatise.'" Pp. 163–82 in *The Book of Acts in Its First Century Setting*. Vol. I. *Ancient Literary Setting*. Edited by Bruce Winter and Andrew Clarke. Carlisle: Paternoster, 1993.

———. *The Acts of the Apostles: An Introduction and Commentary*. Tyndale New Testament Commentaries. Grand Rapids: Eerdmans 1980.

———. *The Gospel of Luke*. New International Greek Testament Commentary. Grand Rapids: Eerdmans, 1978.

———. "The Last Supper." Pp. 481–588 in *Key Events in the Life of the Historical Jesus: A Collaborative Exploration of Context and Coherence*. Edited by Darrell L. Bock and Robert L. Webb. Wissenschaftliche Untersuchungen zum Neuen Testament 247. Tübingen: Mohr-Siebeck, 2009.

———. *Luke: Historian and Theologian*. Grand Rapids: Zondervan, 1970. 3rd ed. Exeter: Paternoster, 1988.

———. *New Testament Theology*. Downers Grove, IL: InterVarsity Press, 2004.

————. "Son of God or Servant of Yahweh?—A Reconsideration of Mark i.11." *New Testament Studies* 15 (1965): 326–36.

Marshall, I. Howard, and David Peterson, eds. *Witness to the Gospel: The Theology of Acts.* Grand Rapids: Eerdmans, 1998.

Mattill, A. J., Jr. *Luke and the Last Things: A Perspective for the Understanding of Lukan Thought.* Dillsboro, NC: Western North Carolina University Press, 1979.

McDonald, Lee M., and James A. Sanders, eds. *The Canon Debate.* Peabody, MA: Hendrickson, 2002.

McKnight, Scot. "Jesus and the Twelve." Pp. 181–214 in *Key Events in the Life of the Historical Jesus: A Collaborative Exploration of Context and Coherence.* Edited by Darrell L. Bock and Robert L. Webb. Wissenschaftliche Untersuchungen zum Neuen Testament 247. Tübingen: Mohr-Siebeck, 2009.

Meier, John P. *A Marginal Jew: Rethinking the Historical Jesus*, vol. 2: *Mentor, Message, and Miracles.* Anchor Bible Reference Library. New York: Doubleday, 1994.

Menzies, Robert P. *The Development of Early Christian Pneumatology with Special Reference to Luke-Acts.* Journal for the Study of the New Testament Supplement 54. Sheffield: Sheffield Academic Press, 1991.

Metzger, Bruce. *The Canon of the New Testament.* Oxford: Clarendon, 1987.

Mills, W. E., and A. J. Mattill. *A Bibliography of the Periodical Literature on the Acts of the Apostles (1962–1984).* Leiden: Brill, 1986.

Moessner, David. *Jesus and the Heritage of Israel: Luke's Narrative Claim upon Israel's Legacy.* Harrisburg, PA: Trinity International, 1999.

————. *Lord of the Banquet: The Literary and Theological Significance of the Lukan Travel Narrative.* Harrisburg, PA: Trinity International, 1989.

Moore, T. S. "To the End of the Earth: The Geographical and Ethnic Universalism of Acts 1:8 in Light of Isaianic Influence on Luke." *Journal of the Evangelical Theological Society* 40 (1997): 389–99.

Moule, C. F. D. "The Christology of Acts." Pp. 159–86 in *Studies in Luke-Acts: Essays Presented in Honor of Paul Schubert.* Edited by L. E. Keck and J. L. Martyn. London: SPCK, 1966.

Nielsen, Anders E. *Until It Is Fulfilled.* Wissenschaftliche Untersuchungen zum Neuen Testament. Tübingen: Mohr-Siebeck, 2000.

Nobbs, A. "What Do Ancient Historians Make of the New Testament?" *Tyndale Bulletin* 57 (2006): 285–90.

Nolland, John. *Luke 1:1–24:53.* 3 vols. Word Biblical Commentary. Waco, TX: Word, 1989–1993.

————. "Luke's Readers: A Study of Luke 4.22–8; Acts 13.46; 18.6; 28.28 and Luke 21.5–36." Unpublished Ph.D. dissertation, University of Cambridge, 1977.

————. "Salvation History and Eschatology." Pp. 63–81 in *Witness to the Gospel: A Theology of Acts.* Edited by I. Howard Marshall and David Peterson. Grand Rapids: Eerdmans, 1998.

North, C. R. *The Suffering Servant in Deutero-Isaiah: An Historical and Critical Study.* 2nd ed. Oxford: Oxford University Press, 1956.

Omerzu, H. *Der Prozess des Paulus: Eine exegetische und rechtshistorische Untersuchung der Apostelgeschichte.* Beiheft zur Zeitschrift für die neutestamentliche Wissenschaft 115. Berlin: De Gruyter, 2002.

O'Neill, J. C. *The Theology of Acts in Its Historical Setting.* London: SPCK, 1961.

O'Toole, Robert F. "How Does Luke Portray Jesus as Servant of YHWH?" *Biblica* 81 (2000): 328–46.

———. *The Unity of Luke's Theology: An Analysis of Luke-Acts.* Good News Studies 9. Wilmington, DE: Michael Glazier, 1984.

Osborne, Grant. "Jesus' Empty Tomb and His Appearance in Jerusalem." Pp. 775–823 in *Key Events in the Life of the Historical Jesus: A Collaborative Exploration of Context and Coherence.* Edited by Darrell L. Bock and Robert L. Webb. Wissenschaftliche Untersuchungen zum Neuen Testament 247. Tübingen: Mohr-Siebeck, 2009.

Pao, David. *Acts and the Isaianic New Exodus.* Wissenschaftliche Untersuchungen zum Neuen Testament 2/130. Tübingen: Mohr-Siebeck, 2000.

Parsons, Mikeal, and Richard Pervo. *Rethinking the Unity of Luke-Acts.* Minneapolis: Fortress, 1993.

Pervo, Richard. *Acts: A Commentary.* Hermeneia. Minneapolis: Fortress, 2008.

———. "Israel's Heritage and Claims upon the Genre(s) of Luke-Acts: The Problems of a History." Pp. 127–43 in *Jesus and the Heritage of Israel: Luke's Narrative Claim upon Israel's Legacy.* Edited by David Moessner. Harrisburg, PA: Trinity International, 1999.

Pesch, Rudolph. *Die Apostelgeschichte (Apg 1–12).* Evangelisch-Katholischer Kommentar zum Neuen Testament 5/1. Zurich: Benzinger/Neukirchen-Vluyn: Neukirchener, 1986.

———. *Die Apostelgeschichte (Apg 13–28).* Evangelisch-Katholischer Kommentar zum Neuen Testament 5/2. Zurich: Benzinger/Neukirchen-Vluyn: Neukirchener, 1986.

Peterson, David. "The Motif of Fulfillment and the Purpose of Luke-Acts." Pp. 83–10 in *The Book of Acts in Its Ancient Literary Setting*, vol. 1. Edited by B. W. Winter and Andrew Clarke. Carlisle: Paternoster, 1993.

———. "The Worship of the New Community." Pp. 373–95 in *Witness to the Gospel: The Theology of Acts.* Edited by I. Howard Marshall and David Peterson. Grand Rapids: Eerdmans, 1998.

Pickett, Raymond. "Luke and Empire." Pp. 1–22 in *Luke and Empire: Essays in Honor of Robert L. Brawley.* Edited by David Rhoads, David Esterline, and Jae Won Lee. Princeton Monograph Series. Eugene, OR: Pickwick, 2011.

Pilgrim, Walter. *Good News to the Poor: Wealth and Poverty in Luke-Acts.* Minneapolis: Augsburg, 1981.

Plummer, A. *A Critical and Exegetical Commentary on the Gospel according to St. Luke.* International Critical Commentary. Edinburgh: T&T Clark, 1896.

Plymale, Steven F. *The Prayer Texts of Luke-Acts.* American University Studies. New York: Peter Lang, 1991.

Polhill, John. *Acts.* New American Commentary. Nashville: Broadman, 1992.

Powell, Mark Allen. *Introducing the New Testament: A Historical, Literary and Theological Survey.* Grand Rapids: Baker, 2009.

Rapske, Brian. "Opposition to the Plan of God and Persecution." Pp. 235–56 in *Witness to the Gospel: A Theology of Acts.* Edited by I. Howard Marshall and David Peterson. Grand Rapids: Eerdmans, 1998.

Reicke, Bo. *The Roots of the Synoptic Gospels.* Minneapolis: Fortress, 1986.

Rese, Martin. *Alttestamentliche Motive in der Christologie des Lukas.* Gütersloh: Gütersloher, 1969.

———. "The Jews in Luke-Acts: Some Second Thoughts." Pp. 185–201 in *The Unity of Luke-Acts.* Edited by J. Verheyden. Bibliotheca ephemeridum theologicarum lovaniensium. Leuven: Leuven University Press, 1999.

Rhoads, David, David Esterline, and Jae Won Lee, eds. *Luke-Acts and Empire: Essays in Honor of Robert L. Brawley*. Princeton Theological Monographs. Eugene, OR: Pickwick, 2011.

Ricoeur, Paul. "Philosophies critiques de l'historie: recherché, explication, écriture." Pp. 139–201 in *Philosophical Problems Today*, vol. 1. Edited by G. Florstad. Dortrecht: Kluwer, 1994.

Ridderbos, Hermann. *The Speeches of Peter in the Acts of the Apostles*. London: Tyndale, 1962.

Riesenfeld, H. "Ἐμβολεύειν–Ἐντός." *Nuntius* 2 (1949): 11–12.

Robbins, Vernon K. "By Land and by Sea: The We-Passages and Ancient Sea Voyages." Pp. 215–42 in *Perspectives on Luke-Acts*. Edited by C. H. Talbert. Perspectives in Religious Studies, Special Studies Series, No. 5. Macon, GA: Mercer University Press/Edinburgh: T&T Clark, 1978.

———. "The We-Passages in Acts and Ancient Sea Voyages." *Biblical Research* 20 (1975): 5–18.

Roloff, J. *Apostelgeschichte*. 2nd ed. NTD 5. Göttingen: Vandenhoeck & Ruprecht, 1988.

Rosner, Brian. "The Progress of the Word." Pp. 215–33 in *Witness to the Gospel: The Theology of Acts*. Edited by I. Howard Marshall and David Peterson. Grand Rapids: Eerdmans, 1998.

Roth, S. John. *The Blind, the Lame, and the Poor: Character Types in Luke-Acts*. Journal for the Study of the New Testament Supplement 144. Sheffield: Sheffield Academic Press, 1997.

Rothschild, Claire K. *Luke-Acts and the Rhetoric of History: An Investigation of Early Christian Historiography*. Wissenschaftliche Untersuchungen zum Neuen Testament 2/175. Tübingen: Mohr-Siebeck, 2004.

Rowe, C. Kavin. *Early Narrative Christology: The Lord in the Gospel of Luke*. Beiheft zur Zeitschrift für die neutestamentliche Wissenschaft. Berlin: De Gruyter, 2006.

———. "History, Hermeneutics and the Unity of Luke-Acts." *Journal for the Study of the New Testament* 28 (2005): 131–57.

———. "Literary Unity and Reception History: Reading Luke-Acts as Luke and Acts." *Journal for the Study of the New Testament* 29 (2007): 449–57.

———. "Luke and the Trinity: An Essay in Ecclesial Biblical Theology." *Scottish Journal of Theology* 56 (2003): 1–26.

———. "The Reception of Luke and Acts and the Unity of Luke-Acts." *Journal for the Study of the New Testament* 29 (2007): 459–72.

Sanders, J. T. *The Jews in Luke-Acts*. London: SCM, 1987.

Schnabel, Eckhard. *Early Christian Mission*. 2 vols. Downers Grove, IL: InterVarsity Press/London: Apollos, 2004.

Schneider, G. *Die Apostelgeschichte. Vol. 1: Einleitung, Kommentar zu Kap. 1,1–8,40*. Herders theologischer Kommentar zum Neuen Testament 5/1. Freiburg: Herder, 1980.

Scholer, David, ed. *Social Distinctives of the Christians in the First Century: Pivotal Essays by E. A. Judge*. Peabody, MA: Hendrickson, 2008.

Schottroff, Luise, and Wolfgang Stegemann. *Jesus and the Hope of the Poor*. Maryknoll, NY: Orbis, 1986.

Schürmann, Heinz. "Der Abendmahlsbericht Lk 22,19b–20 als ursprüngliche Textüberlieferung." *Biblica* 32 (1951): 364–92, 522–41.

———. *Das Lukasevangelium*. 2 vols. Herders theologischer Kommentar zum Neuen Testament 3. Freiburg: Herder, 1969 (*Kommentar zu Kap. 1.1–9.50*); 1994 (*Kommentar zu Kap. 9.51–11:54*).

Schweizer, E. "Concerning the Speeches in Acts." Pp. 208–16 in *Studies in Luke-Acts*. Edited by Leander E. Keck and J. Louis Martyn. Nashville: Abingdon, 1966.

Scott, James. "Luke's Geographical Horizon." Pp. 483–544 in *The Book of Acts in its Greco-Roman Setting*, vol. 2. Edited by D. W. J. Gill and C. Gempf. Grand Rapids: Eerdmans, 1994.

Seccombe, David Peter. "The New People of God." Pp. 349–72 in *Witness to the Gospel: The Theology of Acts*. Edited by I. Howard Marshall and David Peterson. Grand Rapids: Eerdmans, 1998.

———. *Possessions and the Poor in Luke-Acts*. Studien zum Neuen Testament und seiner Umwelt. Linz: A. Fuchs, 1982.

Segundo, J. L. *The Liberation of Theology*. Maryknoll, NY: Orbis, 1976.

Seim, T. K. *The Double Message: Patterns of Gender in Luke-Acts*. Edinburgh: T&T Clark, 1994.

Shauf, S. *Theology as History, History as Theology: Paul in Ephesus in Acts 19*. Beiheft zur Zeitschrift für die neutestamentliche Wissenschaft 133. Berlin: De Gruyter, 2005.

Sherwin-White, A. N. *Roman Society and Roman Law in the New Testament*. Oxford: Clarendon, 1963.

Snodgrass, Klyne. "Streams of Tradition Emerging from Isaiah 40:1–5 and Their Adaptation in the New Testament." *Journal for the Study of the New Testament* 8 (1980): 24–45.

———. "The Temple Incident." Pp. 429–80 in *Key Events in the Life of the Historical Jesus: A Collaborative Exploration of Context and Coherence*. Edited by Darrell L. Bock and Robert L. Webb. Wissenschaftliche Untersuchungen zum Neuen Testament 247. Tübingen: Mohr-Siebeck, 2009.

Soards, Marion. *The Speeches in Acts: Their Content, Context and Concerns*. Louisville: Westminster John Knox, 1994.

Spencer, F. Scott. *Journeying through Acts: A Literary-Cultural Reading*. Peabody, MA: Hendrickson, 2004.

Spencer, Patrick E. "The Unity of Luke-Acts: A Four-Bolted Hermeneutical Hinge." *Currents in Biblical Research* 5 (2007): 341–66.

Squires, John T. *The Plan of God in Luke-Acts*. Society for New Testament Studies Monograph Series. Cambridge: Cambridge University Press, 1993.

Stein, Robert. *The Synoptic Problem: An Introduction*. Grand Rapids: Baker, 1987.

Stenschke, Christoph. *Luke's Portrait of Gentiles Prior to Their Coming to Faith*. Wissenschaftliche Untersuchungen zum Neuen Testament. Tübingen: Mohr-Siebeck, 1999.

———. "The Need for Salvation." Pp. 125–44 in *Witness to the Gospel: The Theology of Acts*. Edited by I. Howard Marshall and David Peterson. Grand Rapids: Eerdmans, 1998.

Sterling, Gregory. *Historiography and Self-Definition: Josephus, Luke-Acts and Apologetic Historiography*. Leiden: Brill, 1992.

Strauss, Mark L. *The Davidic Messiah in Luke-Acts: The Promise and Its Fulfillment in Lukan Christology*. Journal for the Study of the New Testament Supplement 110. Sheffield: Sheffield Academic Press, 1995.

Talbert, Charles. *Literary Patterns, Theological Themes, and the Genre of Luke-Acts*. Society of Biblical Literature Monograph Series. Missoula, MT: Scholars Press, 1974.

———. *Reading Acts: A Literary and Theological Commentary on the Acts of the Apostles*. New York: Crossroad, 1997.

———. "Shifting Sands: The Recent Study of the Gospel of Luke." Pp. 197–213 in *Interpreting the Gospels*. Edited by J. L. Mays. Philadelphia: Fortress, 1981.

Tannehill, Robert. *The Narrative Unity of Luke-Acts*. 2 vols. Minneapolis: Fortress, 1986, 1990.

Thornton, Claus J. *Der Zeuge des Zeugen: Lukas als Historiker der Paulusreisen*. Wissenschaftliche Untersuchungen zum Neuen Testament. Tübingen: Mohr-Siebeck, 1991.

Tiede, David. *Luke*. Augsburg Commentary on the New Testament. Minneapolis: Augsburg, 1988.

———. *Prophecy and History in Luke-Acts*. Philadelphia: Fortress, 1980.

Townsend, J. T. "The Date of Luke-Acts." Pp. 47–62 in *Luke-Acts: New Perspectives from the Society of Biblical Literature*. Edited by C. Talbert. New York: Crossroad, 1984.

Tuckett, C. M. "The Christology of Luke-Acts." Pp. 133–64 in *The Unity of Luke-Acts*. Edited by Joseph Verheyden. Bibliotheca ephemeridum theologicarum lovaniensium. Leuven: Leuven University Press, 1999.

Turner, Max. *Power from on High: The Spirit in Israel's Restoration and Witness in Luke-Acts*. Journal for Pentecostal Theology Supplement Series. Sheffield: Sheffield Academic Press, 1996.

———. "'Trinitarian' Pneumatology in the New Testament?—Towards an Explanation of the Worship of Jesus." *Asbury Journal of Theology* 57 (2002–2003): 167–86.

———. "The 'Spirit of Prophecy' as the Power of Israel's Restoration and Witness." Pp. 327–48 in *Witness to the Gospel: The Theology of Acts*. Edited by I. Howard Marshall and David Peterson. Grand Rapids: Eerdmans, 1998.

———. "The Work of the Holy Spirit in Luke-Acts." *Word & World* 23 (2003): 146–53.

Twelftree, G. H. *Jesus the Exorcist: A Contribution to the Study of the Historical Jesus*. Wissenschaftliche Untersuchungen zum Neuen Testament 2/54. Tübingen: Mohr-Siebeck, 1993.

Tyson, Joseph. *Images of Judaism in Luke-Acts*. Columbia: University of South Carolina Press, 1992.

Tyson, Joseph, ed. *Luke-Acts and the Jewish People: Eight Critical Perspectives*. Minneapolis: Augsburg, 1988.

van Unnik, W. C. "Luke's Second Book and the Rules of Hellenistic Historiography." Pp. 37–60 in *Les Actes des Apôtres: Traditions, rédaction, théologie*. Edited by J. Kremer. Bibliotheca ephemeridum theologicarum lovaniensium 48. Louvain: Leuven University Press, 1979.

Varghese, P. V. "The Holy Spirit and the Risen Christ in Luke-Acts." *Indian Theological Studies* 44 (2007): 245–74.

Verheyden, J. "The Unity of Luke-Acts." Pp. 3–56 in *The Unity of Luke-Acts*. Edited by J. Verheyden. Leuven: Peeters, 1999.

Vielhauer, Philip. "The Paulinism of the Acts of the Apostles." Pp. 33–50 in *Studies in Luke-Acts: Essays Presented in Honor of Paul Schubert*. Edited by L. E. Keck and J. L. Martyn. London: SPCK, 1966.

von Baer, H. *Der Heilige Geist in den Lukasschriften*. Stuttgart: Kohlhammer, 1926.

Walton, Steve. "Trying Paul or Trying Rome? Judges and Accused in the Roman Trials of Paul in Acts." Pp. 122–41 in *Luke-Acts and Empire: Essays in Honor of Robert L. Brawley*. Edited by David Rhoads, David Esterline, and Jae Won Lee. Princeton Theological Monographs. Eugene, OR: Pickwick, 2011.

Weatherly, J. A. *Jewish Responsibility for the Death of Jesus in Luke-Acts*. London: Sheffield Academic Press, 1994.

Webb, Robert L. "The Historical Enterprise and Historical Jesus Research." Pp. 9–93 in *Key Events in the Life of the Historical Jesus: A Collaborative Exploration of Context and Coherence*. Edited by Darrell L. Bock and Robert L. Webb. Wissenschaftliche Untersuchungen zum Neuen Testament 247. Tübingen: Mohr-Siebeck, 2009.

―――. *John the Baptizer and Prophet: A Socio-Historical Study*. Journal for the Study of the New Testament Supplement 62. Sheffield: Sheffield Academic Press, 1991.

―――. "The Roman Examination and the Crucifixion of Jesus." Pp. 669–773 in *Key Events in the Life of the Historical Jesus: A Collaborative Exploration of Context and Coherence*. Edited by Darrell L. Bock and Robert L. Webb. Wissenschaftliche Untersuchungen zum Neuen Testament 247. Tübingen: Mohr-Siebeck, 2009.

Wehnert, J. *Die Wir-Passagen der Apostelgeschichte: Ein lukanisches Stilmittel aus jüdischer Tradition*. Göttingen: Vandenhoeck & Ruprecht, 1989.

Weiser, A. *Die Apostelgeschichte Kapitel 1–12*. Ökumenischer Taschenbuchkommentar zum Neuen Testament 5/1. Gütersloh: Mohn, 1981.

―――. *Die Apostelgeschichte Kapitel 13–28*. Ökumenischer Taschenbuchkommentar zum Neuen Testament 5/2. Gütersloh: Mohn, 1985.

Wenham, David. *Paul: Follower of Christ or Founder of Christianity?* Grand Rapids: Eerdmans, 1995.

Wikenhauser, A. *Die Apostelgeschichte*. 4th ed. Regensburger Neues Testament 5. Regensburg: Pustet, 1961.

Wikgren, A. "Ἐντός." *Nuntius* 4 (1950): 27–28.

Wilckens, U. *Die Missionsreden der Apostelgeschichte: Form- und traditionsgeschichtliche Untersuchungen*. 3rd ed. Wissenschaftliche Monographien zum Alten und Neuen Testament 5. Neukirchen-Vluyn: Neukirchener, 1974.

Wilkens, Michael J. "Peter's Declaration concerning Jesus' Identity in Caesarea Philippi." Pp. 293–381 in *Key Events in the Life of the Historical Jesus: A Collaborative Exploration of Context and Coherence*. Edited by Darrell L. Bock and Robert L. Webb. Wissenschaftliche Untersuchungen zum Neuen Testament 247. Tübingen: Mohr-Siebeck, 2009.

Wilson, Stephen G. *The Gentiles and the Gentile Mission in Luke-Acts*. Society for New Testament Studies Monograph Series. Cambridge: Cambridge University Press, 1973.

―――. *Luke and the Law*. Society for New Testament Studies Monograph Series. Cambridge: Cambridge University Press, 1983.

Winter, Bruce, and Andrew D. Clarke, eds. *The Book of Acts in Its Ancient Literary Setting*. Vol. 1: *The Book of Acts in Its First Century Setting*. Grand Rapids: Eerdmans, 1993.

Witherington, Ben. *The Acts of the Apostles: A Socio-Rhetorical Commentary*. Grand Rapids: Eerdmans, 1997.

―――. *The Christology of Jesus*. Minneapolis: Fortress, 1990.

―――. "Salvation and Health in Christian Antiquity: The Soteriology of Luke-Acts in Its First Century Setting." Pp. 145–66 in *Witness to the Gospel: The Theology of Acts*. Edited by I. Howard Marshall and David Peterson. Grand Rapids: Eerdmans, 1998.

―――. *Women in the Ministry of Jesus: A Study of Jesus' Attitudes to Women and Their Roles as Reflected in His Earthly Life*. Society for New Testament Studies Monograph Series. Cambridge: Cambridge University Press, 1987.

Yamazaki-Ransom, Kazuhiko. *Roman Empire in Luke's Narrative*. London: T&T Clark, 2010.

Zeigan, H. *Aposteltreffen in Jerusalem: Eine forschungsgeschichtliche Studie zu Galater 2,1–10 und den möglichen lukanischen Parallelen*. Arbeiten zur Bibel und ihrer Geschichte 18. Leipzig: Evangelische Verlagsanstalt, 2005.

Zuck, Roy B., and Darrell L. Bock, eds. *A Biblical Theology of the New Testament*. Chicago: Moody Press, 1994.

Zwiep, Arie W. *Christ, the Spirit and the Community of God: Essays on the Acts of the Apostles*. Wissenschaftliche Untersuchungen zum Neuen Testament 2/293. Tübingen: Mohr-Siebeck, 2010.

SCRIPTURE INDEX

Genesis

6:8 271
8:22 242
9:26 101
12:1–3 228
12:3 . . . . 280, 299, 375
14:18–20 150
14:22 150
15:13–14 192
16:11 345
18:3 271
19:26 320
21:6 344
22 204
22:12 160
22:16 160
22:18 . . . . 193, 276
26:4 276
29:30–31 270
29:31–32 345
29:32 . . . . 101, 345
30:13 345
30:23 344
33:9–10 271
39:21 271
41:51 159
43:14 271
50:4 . . . . 228, 353
50:24–25 . . . . 102, 284

Exodus

3:6 276
3:12 . . . . 192, 260
3:15 276
3:16 . . . . 102, 284
3:20 295
4:22 188
4:31 . . . . 102, 284
7:1 181
8:19 . . . . 141, 206, 339
11:3 150
11:5 181
12:29 181
13:3 295
13:14 295
13:16 295
13:19 . . . . 102, 284
14:20 193
15:6 295
15:20 350
20:11–12 241
21:1 153
22:27 92
22:27–28 426

22:28 118
23:12 392
23:20 305
30:12 . . . . 102, 284
31:13 194
32:32 266
34:5, 6 193
34:22 350

Leviticus

11 276
11:15 107
14:2–31 190
16:29–34 316
17–18 366
23:26–32 316
23:29 . . . . 192, 273, 276, 286,
             379, 423, 425
24:5–9 275
25 355
25:1–12 . . . . 136, 179
25:8–17 . . . . 161, 232

Numbers

6:1–21 367
10:34 193
10:35 353
11:29 221
19:11 319
24:16 150
24:17 . . . . 155, 245
29:7–11 316

Deuteronomy

4:19 425
4:25–46 87
6:4 242
6:5 420
6:14 221
9:10 206
11:13 260
14:14 107
14:28–29 329
14:29 275
15 232
15:1–3 329
15:2–3 . . . . 136, 179
15:7–12 329
17:3 425
18 . . . . 134, 165
18:15–20 276
18:15 . . . . . . 125, 165, 179, 191,
          192, 286, 365, 416
18:18–19 72

18:19 . . . . 192, 423, 425
20:4 156
21:15–17 270
21:23 . . . . 203, 254
22:1–2 329
22:20 293
23:19 329
24:7–15 329
24:19–21 329
25:13–14 329
26:7 . . . . 101, 345
28–32 379
30:2 135
32:5 234
33:17 154

Joshua

22:22 156

Judges

3:9 156
3:15 156
6:17 271
11:6 199
11:11 199
12:3 156
13:7 162
14:16 270
18:6 257
20:26 316

Ruth

1:6 . . . . 102, 284

1 Samuel

1:11 345
1:17 257
1:18 271
2:5 . . . . 328, 354
2:7 . . . . 229, 353, 354
2:10 154
7:6 316
9:16 . . . . 101, 345
12:22 236
13:14 87
14:24 316
16:7 353
16:23 392
21:6 275
25:32 101
31:13 316

2 Samuel

1:12 316

3:35 316
7. . . . . 134, 178, 182, 234
7:6–16. 87
7:8–17. 151
7:8–16. 415
7:14 . . . . 151, 177, 188
7:24 . . . . 123, 136
12:13 193
12:16–20. 316
15:9 257
15:25 271
16:12 . . . . 101, 345
22:3 154
22:14 150
22:17 155
22:18 260

1 Kings
1:17 181
1:48 101
3:6 181
6:11–13. 426
8:25 181
8:27 426
16:13 241
16:25 241
16:26 241
17–18 189
17:9, 12, 16 190
17:18 190
17:24 190
19:19–21 . . . . .319, 320
21:9 316
21:27 316

2 Kings
4:9 162
5:1–14. 190
13:5 156
14:26 . . . . 101, 345
17:15 241
21:3–5. 425
23:4–5 425

1 Chronicles
6:8 426
17:16 181
22:9 151
29:18 353

2 Chronicles
15:4 135
15:14 135
20:3–4 316
33:3, 5 425

Ezra
6:26 436
8:21, 23 316

Nehemiah
1:4 316
9:6 241
9:27 156

Esther
4:3 316
4:16 316
7:9 159
10:3 150

Job
5:11 . . . . 229, 328, 354
9:2 293
12:3 353
12:19 . . . . 229, 328, 354
15:29 354
18:19 159
19:4 293
23:13–17. 397
36:4 293

Psalms
2. . . . . . . .69, 160, 170, 286, 292,
      293, 294, 297, 415, 419,
          420, 421, 422
2:1–2. . . . . 82, 423, 424
2:1 . . . . 170, 307, 420
2:2 156
2:7 . . . . . . 87, 143, 151, 152, 160,
      161, 164, 173, 177, 178, 179,
          188, 189, 235, 415, 419
4:7 242
6:2 338
7:17 150
8:3 206
8:4 . . . . 102, 284
9:11–12. . . . . 228, 353
9:13 . . . . 101, 338, 345
9:17–20. . . . . 228, 353
9:18 247
10:1–4. . . . . 228, 353
10:17–18. . . . . 228, 353
12:1–5. . . . . 228, 353
16. . . . . 413, 421
16:8–11. . 81, 124, 187, 415, 417
16:9 403
16:10 . . . . .87, 173, 415, 417,
          418, 419
16:34 415
18. 260
18:2 154
18:25–29. . . . . 228, 353
22 . . . . .131, 255
22:1 . . . . 255, 440
22:6–7 255
22:18 . . . . 203, 255
22:26 247
24:5–7. 185

24:5 156
25:5 156
25:18 . . . . 101, 345
29:11 240
31. . . . . .131, 255
31:5 . . . . 203, 255, 440
31:7 . . . . 101, 345
34:10 354
35:13 316
37:11 247
39:4 208
41:1 355
41:4 . . . . 10, 338
41:13 101
46:2–3 142
48:1 150
51:1 338
51:9 266
55:20 295
62:4 236
65:7 142
68:1 353
68:18 365
69. 131
69:10 316
69:21–22. 255
69:26 . . . . 80, 220, 420
72:4 355
72:7 240
72:13 355
72:18 101
74:2 204
75:4–5. 154
75:10 154
77:7 236
78:8 234
78:60, 67 236
80:14 . . . . 102, 284
82:1–2. 136
82:3 355
82:6 150
85:8–10. 240
89:3 167
89:10 . . . . 328, 353
89:26–27 188
89:26 . . . . .151, 164
89:52 101
95:3 150
98:2 . . . . 102, 122, 156
100:1 124
103:1 208
103:11 328
103:12 193
103:13, 17 328
104:3 193
106. 71
106:4 . . . . 102, 284
106:10 143
106:14 143

106:16 162
106:48 101
107. 164
107:9 . . . . 328, 354
107:27−29. 317
109:8 . . . . 80, 420
109:14 266
109:22 208
109:24 316
110. . . . . 166, 167, 181, 182,
391, 413
110:1 . . . . . . 77, 78, 81, 124, 142,
166, 168, 169, 180,
181, 182, 187, 415,
418, 419, 443
116:3−4. 203
118. . . . . . . 76, 77, 131, 200, 283,
284, 322
118:22−26. 128
118:22 . . . . 82, 200, 202
118:26 . . . 74, 166, 189, 283, 284
118:32 235
122:4−5 285
123:3 338
132. . . . . .178, 182, 415
132:11 . . . . . . 81, 124, 169, 182,
234, 415
132:17 . . . . 134, 154, 178
140:12 355
145:6 241
145:15−16 242
146:7 354
147:6 . . . . 229, 354
147:8−9 242
148:14 154

Proverbs

3:17 240
4:23 353
24:16 157

Ecclesiastes

9:7 242

Isaiah

1:18 193
2. 304
2:2 . . . . 109, 384
2:2−4 . . . . 229, 417
2:6−22 304
2:9 304
2:11, 12, 17 304
2:20 242
3:1 126
3:14−15 329
3:15−29. 161
4:4−5. 215
4:4 . . . . .159, 218
5:7−8. 329

5:25 161
6. . . . . .57, 181, 300
6:9−10. . . . . 380, 423
6:9 . . . . 94, 225
6:10 265
7:14 153
8. 157
8:14−15 . . . . 124, 157
8:14 . . . . 178, 423
9:1−2. . . . . 143, 178
9:1 155
9:2−7 245
9:7 167
9:13 265
10:1−3. 329
10:33 126
11:1−10 155
11:1−4. . . . . .159, 218
11:1−2. 167
11:1 155
11:4 247
11:20 161
13:10 142
16:11 208
17:14 397
18:7 161
19:1 193
19:23−25. 417
23:17 . . . . 102, 284
24:19 142
24:20 157
25:6 242
25:9 156
26:9 230
26:19 . . . . 164, 249
28 157
28:13−16. . . . . 124, 157
28:25 220
29:6 215
29:18−19. . . . . . 201, 230, 249
29:18 357
29:28 164
32. 215
32:6−7 329
32:15 . . . .110, 159, 214, 221, 266
33:24 244
35:5−7. 249
35:5−6. . . . . 164, 230, 357
35:5 201
37:4 242
37:8 293
37:17 242
40−41 241
40 . . . . 123, 134, 305
40:1−12. 246
40:1−5. . . . . 305, 437
40:1 281
40:3−5 . . . . 134, 216, 229, 245,
259, 422

40:3−4 304
40:3 . . . . 104, 123, 305
40:4−5 104
40:4 305
40:5 . . . . 102, 156, 246, 297, 377
40:9 282
40:10−11. 246
40:24 215
41. 160
41:8−10 123
41:8 160
41:14 191
41:16 215
42 . . . . 69, 160, 172
42:1−7. . . . . 70, 123
42:1−4. . . . . 136, 299
42:1 . . . . 143, 160, 161, 165,
178, 179
42:6−7 122
42:6. . . . . . . 121, 133, 134, 201,
229, 245, 377
42:16 305
42:18 164
43 123
43:3 185
43:7 . . . . 123, 136, 304
43:11 185
43:14 191
43:21 204
43:25 193
44:2 160
44:3 . . . . .110, 159, 214
44:22−24 191
45:14 208
45:15 185
45:20−23. 384
45:21 185
45:22 138
45:23 284
46:13 245
48:18 240
48:20 . . . . .137, 138
49. . . . . 420, 422
49:1−11. . . . . 136, 161
49:3−6. 253
49:3 199
49:6 . . . . .88, 121, 122, 129, 133,
134, 137, 138, 139, 199,
229, 236, 261, 298, 299,
417, 421, 422
49:9 245
49:13 281
49:26 185
51:3 281
51:4−5. 121
51:6 393
52:1−53:12 172
52:7 . . . . 136, 240
52:9 282

52:10 . . . . 102, 122, 156
52:13–53:12 . . . . . 128, 163, 199
52:13–15 254
53 . . . . 70, 84, 131, 172, 199,
253, 254, 418, 419, 421
53:4 244
53:6 198
53:7–8 . . . . . . 198, 299, 383, 418
53:7 171
53:8 171
53:11–12 198
53:12 . . . . 78, 140, 172, 198, 250,
253, 254, 255, 299
54:1 379
54:10 240
54:13 221
55 . . . . 413, 415
55:3 . . . . 87, 173, 187, 235,
386, 415, 419
55:7 265
57:14–17 304
57:15 426
57:18 281
58 162
58:3 329
58:5 316
58:6–7 329
58:6 . . . . . 69, 135, 161, 178, 192,
249, 269
58:8–10 155
58:8 . . . . 143, 178
58:10 329
59:19 178
60:1–3 . . . . 121, 122
60:1–2 . . . . 143, 178
60:2–3 155
61 . . . . 57, 58, 136, 161,
162, 417
61:1–2 . . . . . . 69, 135, 136, 161,
178, 189, 249
61:1 . . . . 161, 164, 192, 201, 212,
230, 247, 249, 269, 338
61:2 . . . . 281, 355
62:10–11 138
62:10 304
63:4 282
63:11–14 305
65–66 393
66:1–2 . . . . 423, 426
66:1 . . . . 84, 383
66:15 215

Jeremiah

1:1–4 103
2:5 241
3:7 135
3:10, 14 135
4:11–12 215
5:24 242

5:26–28 329
7:1–34 426
7:3–7 258
7:5–6 329
7:12–14 258
7:18 425
8:19 241
8:25 425
10:13 137
12:7 283
12:15–16 384
14:8 . . . . 185, 191
14:12 316
15:8–19 393
16:15 . . . . 129, 393
16:19–31 138
16:38 138
17:11 354
18:8 135
18:23 266
19:9 379
19:13 425
19:41, 43 379
21:8 258
22:5–6 . . . . 283, 379
22:5 . . . . 283, 378
23:5 . . . . 155, 167
23:8 . . . . 129, 393
23:17 236
23:19 215
24:6 393
30:9 167
30:23 215
31:27–34 129
31:31–33 . . . . 215, 221
31:31 414
31:33 225
31:34 . . . . 193, 244
33:15 155
36:6 316
36:9 316
36:20–27 90
38:34 244
44:13 . . . . 102, 284

Ezekiel

1 181
3:19 135
8:10 242
11:5 212
11:19–30 110
13:11–13 215
17:23 393
18:12–18 329
20:9–18 379
20:47 379
28:2, 6, 9 114
29:21 154
32:7 142

33:15 329
34–37 . . . . 129, 221
34 . . . . 196, 233
34:2 196
34:4 196
34:16 196
34:22–23 196
34:25–29 240
36 215
36:22–32 . . . . 221, 414
36:25–27 . . . . 159, 214
36:26–27 . . . . 110, 225
36:26 221
37:14 110
38:22 215
39 403
39:24–29 295

Daniel

2:34 202
2:44 . . . . 202, 295
3:28 179
4:24 . . . . 141, 150
4:28 141
5:23 242
6:17 180
6:21 180
6:27 242
7 179
7:9–14 244
7:9 . . . . 181, 285
7:13–14 . . . . 78, 179, 193, 197
7:13 142
7:18 . . . . 179, 180
7:27 . . . . 179, 180
8:13–14 295
8:15–16 101
9:3 316
9:13 135
9:21 101
9:24 244
9:27 401
10:2–3 316
11:31 401
12:1–3 403
12:2 236
12:3 269
12:5–13 295
12:11 401

Hosea

2:1 242
3:4–5 384
3:5 135
5:4 265
6:1 265
7:10 135
10:8 379
13:4 185

Joel

2 . . . . . 81, 144, 182, 215, 221, 442
2:1–4 . . . . 16–21, 391
2:12–14 265–66
2:12–13 316
2:28–32 . . . . . 80, 109, 132, 143,
159, 214, 223, 373,
414, 422
2:28–29 . . . . 110, 220
2:28 . . . . 212, 221
2:30–31 142
2:31 396
2:32 . . . . 198, 233, 259
3 . . . . 182, 216
3:1–5 . . . . 124, 169

Amos

1:4 215
2:6–8 329
4:6 266
5:2 157
5:11–12 329
5:25–27 . . . . 423, 425
7:4 215
8:4–6 329
8:14 157
9 . . . . 420, 422
9:11–15 . . . . . . .88, 129, 173, 416
9:11–12 . . . . . 115, 235, 298, 384,
393, 422
9:11 187

Micah

2:1–2 329
3:1–3 329
3:9–11 426
5:4 150
6:10–11 329
7:8 157

Nahum

1:15 240

Habakkuk

1:5 423

Zephaniah

1:5 425
1:18 215
2:3 247
3:8 215

Haggai

2:6 142
2:21 142

Zechariah

2:10–11 122
2:11 384

3:8 155
6:12 155
7:9–10 329
8 295
8:22 384
12–14 295
12:3 402
12:4–9 295

Malachi

1:17 280
3–4 436
3:1 . . . . .123, 134, 135, 228, 280,
304, 420
3:2 215
3:5 329
3:7–9 280
4:1 215
4:5–6 . . . . 134, 135
4:5 . . . . .123, 228, 280, 304, 420

Matthew

1–2 434
3:7–14 230
3:7–10 230
3:11 214
4:16 122
5–7 202
5:3 439
5:9 150
5:14 122
5:18 363
5:21–48 202
5:39 236
6:1–8 316
6:2 397
6:5 397
6:10 439
6:16–18 316
6:16 397
7:7–8 258
7:11 219
7:13 258
7:21–23 320
8:12 . . . . 327, 397
8:18–19 318
8:19–22 320
9:12–13 439
9:13 263
9:14–17 439
9:22 440
9:27 . . . . .337, 338
9:30 230
10 439
10:6 196
10:14 380
10:37–39 270
11:2–5 439
12:17–21 299

12:22–30 439
12:22 230
12:23 337
12:28 . . . . 73, 206, 439
12:31–32 249
13 44
13:42 . . . . 327, 397
13:50 . . . . 327, 397
15:22 . . . . .337, 338
15:24 196
15:31 230
17:5 165
17:15 338
18:10–14 435
18:19 384
19:28 393
20:2 . . . . 231, 384
20:33 230
21:9 337
22:1–10 435
22:11–13 320
22:12 258
23:13–29 397
22:13 . . . . 384, 397
24–25 . . . . 44, 439
24:51 . . . . 327, 397
25:10 258
25:14–30 435
25:15 337
25:21 258
25:23 258
25:30 . . . . 327, 397
26:26 109
26:45–46 141
26:45 206
27:46 255
28:18–20 131
28:19 131

Mark

1:8 213
1:15 . . . . 206, 439
2:10 194
2:17 . . . . 263, 439
2:18–22 439
2:27 . . . . 193, 194
2:28 194
3:22–27 439
3:28–30 249
4 . . . . 44, 440
5:7 150
5:19 338
5:34 . . . . 257, 440
6:1–6 201
6:11 380
8:25 230
8:33 158
9:7 165
10:45 172

12:13 334
12:35 337
13. . . . . 44, 439
13:10 . . . . 131, 295
14:22, 26 109
14:62 142
15:34–37 255
16:15 131

Luke

1–4 57
1–2 . . . . . 94, 100, 102, 122, 129,
     136, 177, 184, 361, 362,
     390, 412, 417, 438
1 152
1:1–2:52 . . . . 64, 67
1:1–4 . . . . 56, 64, 67
1:1–2 . . . . 32, 34, 132
1:1 . . . . 39, 129, 409
1:2–4 32
1:2 103
1:3–4 148
1:3 108
1:4 . . . . 29, 156
1:5–2:40 . . . . 64, 67
1:5 334
1:6 . . . . 59, 344, 360
1:10 336
1:11–20 127
1:14–17 . . . . . 122, 134, 135, 410
1:14 328
1:15–17 . . . . 154, 320, 337
1:15 . . . . 144, 212
1:16–17 . . . . . . 68, 136, 154, 241,
     356, 420, 438, 451
1:16 280
1:17 . . . . 123, 135, 228, 265, 304
1:19 . . . . 101, 240
1:20 . . . . 99, 134, 268
1:21 169
1:22 132
1:23 212
1:24–25 344
1:26–38 127
1:26–35 153
1:26 101
1:27 . . . . 187, 337
1:28–29 345
1:30 103
1:30–35 36
1:30–33 154
1:31–35 . . . . 68, 123, 134, 150,
     154, 161, 162, 177, 186,
     218, 228, 294, 394
1:31–33 415
1:31–32 188
1:32–33 . . . . 102, 142
1:32 . . . . . 126, 150, 151, 187, 195
1:33 151

1:34 153
1:35 . . . . 104, 126, 150, 151, 153,
     188, 213, 225, 226
1:37 . . . . 103, 451
1:38 345
1:39–45 331
1:41–45 344
1:41 . . . . 212, 213
1:43 . . . . 154, 155, 197
1:45 . . . . 103, 268, 345, 353
1:46–55 . . . . . 101, 156, 229, 247,
     282, 353
1:46–53 281
1:46–48 171
1:46–47 103
1:47 . . . . . 156, 185, 228, 256, 451
1:48 . . . . 345, 361
1:49–54 202
1:50 . . . . 104, 108, 228, 262,
     328, 353
1:50–55 . . . . 68, 247
1:50–53 328
1:51–55 . . . . 103, 143
1:51 353
1:52–53 . . . . 199, 228, 247
1:52 . . . . 101, 157, 345
1:53 . . . . 202, 242, 329, 355
1:54–55 . . . . . . 68, 123, 199, 228,
     281, 353, 414
1:54 . . . . 199, 262, 354
1:55 . . . . 156, 328
1:57–62 345
1:57 . . . . 99, 212
1:58 262
1:59–64 134
1:64 103
1:66 295
1:67–75 281
1:67–69 415
1:67 . . . . 124, 212, 213,
     219, 226
1:68–79 . . . . . 101, 102, 154, 156,
     191, 207, 261, 276,
     282, 398, 441
1:68–75 . . . . 68, 123, 186
1:68–70 414
1:68–69 . . . . . 76, 173, 284, 305
1:68 . . . . 102, 115, 121, 281,
     298, 451
1:69–79 143
1:69–75 . . . . 229, 394
1:69–74 . . . . 102, 129
1:69 . . . . 102, 143, 152, 154, 178,
     187, 199, 245, 260, 271
1:70–75 185
1:70 393
1:71–79 451
1:71–73 102
1:71 . . . . 155, 260

1:72–73 260
1:72 262
1:73–75 398
1:73–74 147
1:73 260
1:74–75 . . . . 218, 260, 375
1:74 155
1:75 261
1:76–3:4 154
1:76–79 229
1:76–77 . . . . 136, 269
1:76 . . . . 104, 126, 150, 151,
     152, 305
1:77 . . . . 104, 133, 185, 200,
     260, 281
1:78–79 . . . 68, 76, 122, 143, 155,
     173, 178, 245, 281,
     298, 315, 375, 377, 451
1:78 . . . . .102, 103, 115, 262, 305
1:79–80 186
1:79 . . . . 122, 133, 155, 281,
     284, 305, 332
1:80 281
2 422
2:4 . . . . 187, 337
2:6 . . . . 99, 212
2:9–14 127
2:10 . . . . 240, 328
2:11–14 102
2:11 . . . . 102, 135, 154, 156, 178,
     185, 186, 187, 197,
     229, 256
2:13–14 103
2:13 336
2:14 . . . . 126, 257, 271
2:21–24 360
2:21–22 212
2:22 363
2:25–38 . . . . 128, 314
2:25–35 162
2:25–27 213
2:25 . . . . 102, 124, 129, 213,
     281, 282
2:26 . . . . .152, 186, 213
2:27 . . . . 213, 360
2:28–32 . . . . 101, 394
2:28 103
2:29–32 299
2:29–31 152
2:29 . . . . 122, 126, 198
2:30–36 216
2:30–32 . . . . 185, 245, 246, 298
2:30 . . . . .121, 156, 229, 259, 451
2:31–32 156
2:31 282
2:32–36 104
2:32 . . . . 121, 129, 133, 199, 236,
     282, 292, 297, 377, 421, 422
2:34–35 . . . . . 157, 178, 342, 423

2:34 . . . . .123, 134, 157, 282
2:35 157
2:36–38 331
2:36 350
2:37 260
2:38 . . . . 103, 129, 282, 345
2:39 360
2:40 . . . . .159, 271, 272
2:41–52. . . . . 64, 68, 152
2:46 209
2:49 . . . . 101, 140, 158, 178,
                              188, 233
2:52 . . . . .159, 272
3:1–4:13 . . . . 64, 68
3. . . . . 104, 153, 292, 422
3:1–20. . . . . 64, 68
3:1–18. 361
3:1–6. . . . . 136, 361
3:1–2. 57
3:1 297
3:2 103
3:3–14. 263
3:3 . . . . . 133, 200, 243, 262, 269
3:4–5. . . . . 259, 304
3:4–6. . . . . . . 134, 154, 216, 229,
                         394, 422, 437
3:4 305
3:5 305
3:6 . . . . .102, 104, 156, 230, 246,
               292, 297, 299, 305,
                              330, 377
3:7–18. 375
3:7–14. 229
3:7–9. . . . . . . 146, 273, 335, 378
3:7 337
3:8 . . . . 104, 263, 264
3:10–14. . . . . .68, 263, 266, 337,
                              356, 438
3:10 230
3:13 230
3:14 . . . . 230, 297
3:15–20. 361
3:15–18. . . . . 136, 143, 185, 249,
                              373, 391
3:15–17. . . . . .56, 159, 207, 230,
                         342, 440, 441
3:15–16. . . . . 186, 213, 284
3:15 216
3:16–17. . . . . .173, 216
3:16 . . . . . 81, 129, 153, 160, 169,
         173, 174, 184, 213, 214,
      215, 216, 217, 218, 226, 422
3:17 . . . . .214, 215, 216, 218
3:18 . . . . .215, 240, 361
3:21–4:13 . . . . 64, 69
3:21–22. . . . . .159, 160, 179, 218
3:21 325
3:22 . . . . 143, 160, 164, 165, 178,
                         188, 198, 419

3:23–38 161
3:31 337
3:37 435
3:38 . . . . 104, 153, 260, 398
4. . . . . . . .44, 57, 179, 355, 417
4:1–13. . . . . 164, 398
4:1 . . . . 161, 218, 219
4:3 . . . . 152, 188
4:7 33
4:8 . . . . 33, 105, 260
4:9 . . . . 152, 188
4:12 105
4:14–9:50 . . . . 64, 69, 346
4:14–44. . . . . 64, 69
4:14–15. 137
4:14 . . . . 161, 218, 219, 225
4:15 . . . . 201, 244
4:16–30. . . . . 161, 164, 189, 201,
                         244, 261, 283
4:16–23. 441
4:16–20. . . . . .199, 355
4:16–19. 198
4:16–18. 192
4:17–21. 134
4:17–19. 202
4:17–18. 338
4:18–21. 249
4:18–19. . . 136, 178, 218, 243, 435
4:18 . . . . 133, 190, 240, 248, 251,
               262, 269, 328, 356, 357
4:21 . . . . 99, 135, 439
4:23 230
4:24–27 178
4:24 189
4:25–27. . . . . 189, 292, 297, 320
4:25 . . . . 283, 293
4:27 283
4:28–29 158
4:28 212
4:29 157
4:30 244
4:31–37. 251
4:31–32. 201
4:32 244
4:33 169
4:34 . . . . 162, 200, 252
4:36 . . . . .218, 225, 252
4:38–39. . . . . 251, 345, 346
4:40–41. . . . . 246, 251
4:40 230
4:41 . . . . .152, 156, 162, 188, 252
4:42 337
4:43–44 243
4:43 . . . . 105, 140, 240, 439
4:44 . . . . 201, 233
5:1–6:16 . . . . 64, 70
5. 163
5:1–11. . . . . . 163, 250, 251, 268,
                              381, 437

5:1 . . . . 103, 337
5:3 . . . . 244, 338
5:5–37. 286
5:5 200
5:6 336
5:8–9. 252
5:8 . . . . .197, 330
5:10 . . . . .251, 361
5:12–16. . . . . 251, 330
5:12–14. 361
5:12 218
5:14 . . . . 334, 363
5:15–16. 325
5:15 . . . . 230, 252, 337, 338
5:17–26. . . . .136, 164, 230, 259,
                              275, 331
5:17 . . . . 218, 225, 230, 244, 334
5:19 337
5:20 . . . . 267, 286
5:21–24. 193
5:21 . . . . 30, 193, 334
5:23 259
5:24. . .163, 164, 180, 195, 196, 251
5:25–26. 105
5:26 . . . . 135, 212, 252
5:27–32. . . . .164, 202, 248, 275,
                              330, 331
5:28 319
5:29 244
5:30–32. . . . . 248, 263, 264, 435
5:30 . . . . .315, 334
5:31–32. . . . . . 137, 208, 251,
                              327, 439
5:32 . . . . .132, 136, 196, 233,
                              268, 315
5:33–39. . . . . 164, 275, 336, 439
5:33 . . . . 316, 335
5:36 384
5:39 439
6. . . . . 355, 440
6:1–11. . . . . 275, 364
6:1–5. . . . . 164, 362
6:2 105
6:3–4 364
6:4 334
6:5 . . . . .193, 194, 197, 364
6:6–11. 164
6:6–10. 364
6:6 244
6:7 . . . . 230, 334
6:9 . . . . 230, 231, 256
6:11 . . . . 212, 440
6:12–16. . . . . 164, 313
6:12 325
6:13 317
6:17–49. . . . . 64, 70
6:17–19. 201
6:17 . . . . 336, 337
6:18 230

6:19 . . . . .218, 225, 230, 337, 338
6:20–49 . . . . 185, 202, 244, 317
6:20–26 . . . . .157, 202, 329, 354
6:20–23 . . . . 248, 328
6:20–22 202
6:20 . . . . .317, 355, 439
6:21 354
6:23–26 202
6:24–26 . . . . 273, 354, 355, 443
6:24 202
6:25 242
6:27–36 . . . . .146, 202, 254,
               324, 330
6:32–33. 272
6:32 324
6:33 324
6:34 324
6:35 . . . . 126, 150, 324
6:36 . . . . , 262
6:37–42 . . . . .147, 202
6:39 357
6:40 . . . . .317, 318
6:43–46 202
6:43–45. 265
6:47–49. 202
7:1–8:3 . . . . 64, 70
7. 136
7:1–10. . . . . .196, 246, 272, 292,
               437, 440, 442, 449
7:3 230
7:5 292
7:7 230
7:8 246
7:9 . . . . . 246, 267, 283, 338, 377
7:10–17 . . . . 164, 230, 346
7:11–17 437
7:11 . . . . .317, 337
7:12 . . . . 160, 319
7:13–14. 163
7:14 321
7:16 . . . . 102, 105, 115, 173,
               191, 252, 284, 451
7:18–35. . . . . .179, 361, 399
7:18–23. . . . . 164, 249
7:18–22. 439
7:18 317
7:19–35. 136
7:19–20. 390
7:19 284
7:20 201
7:21–22. . . . . .357, 435
7:21 230
7:22–28. 361
7:22–23. . . . . .230, 317, 331
7:22 . . . . 201, 240, 248, 251,
               262, 338, 356, 357
7:24–30. 128
7:24–27. 338
7:24 195

7:26–28. 212
7:26 212
7:27–28. 361
7:27 . . . . .135, 217, 305, 320, 410
7:28–35. 330
7:28 . . . . 105, 141, 248, 305,
               389, 390, 410
7:29 . . . . 105, 248
7:30 . . . . 125, 248
7:34 248
7:35–50. 440
7:36–50. . . . . 164, 191, 248, 331,
               346, 395, 449
7:36–39. 202
7:36 . . . . 244, 335
7:37–50. 324
7:39 . . . . .191, 335
7:40 200
7:41–43. . . . . 231, 435
7:44–46 232
7:50 . . . . 231, 256, 267
7:59 169
8. . . . . 44, 439, 440
8:1–15. 442
8:1–3. . . . . . 329, 331, 346, 349
8:1 . . . . 105, 106, 240, 243
8:2 230
8:4–9:17 . . . . 64, 71
8:4–15. 257
8:4 . . . . .337, 338
8:7 209
8:9 317
8:10 . . . . 105, 106, 257
8:11 . . . . 103, 106
8:12 . . . . 232, 257, 268
8:13–15. 326
8:13 . . . . 328, 439, 440
8:14 . . . . .233, 257, 330
8:15 . . . . 232, 330
8:16 169
8:19–21. . . . . 270, 443
8:19 . . . . .337, 338
8:21 . . . . 106, 443
8:22–56 251
8:22–25 . . . . 164, 251
8:22 317
8:24–25. 324
8:24 200
8:25 . . . . .252, 267, 317
8:26–56 164
8:26–39 . . . . .247, 251
8:28 . . . . .106, 126, 150, 152, 188
8:36 . . . . 230, 256
8:37 . . . . 252, 336
8:39 . . . . 105, 106, 243
8:40–56 . . . . 164, 230
8:40–42 251
8:40 337
8:42 . . . . 160, 337

8:42–48 346
8:43 230
8:45 . . . . 200, 337
8:46 . . . . 218, 225
8:47 230
8:48 . . . . .230, 232, 256, 257,
               267, 440
8:49–56. 251
8:50 . . . . .230, 232, 256, 267
8:56 252
9–14 191
9–19 . . . . .26, 179, 191
9:1–6. . . . . 128, 164, 438
9:1–2. . . . . 250, 252
9:1 . . . . 218, 225, 230
9:2 . . . . . 105, 106, 108, 230, 243
9:5 380
9:6 . . . . 108, 230, 240
9:7–9. . . . . 179, 190
9:10–17 251
9:11 . . . . . . .105, 230, 337, 338
9:12–16. 338
9:15 252
9:16 . . . . 244, 317
9:17 169
9:18–50. . . . . 64, 71
9:18–20. . . . . 164, 251, 382
9:18–19. 252
9:18 . . . . .317, 338
9:19 190
9:20 . . . . .106, 152, 179, 186
9:21–22. . . . . 128, 164, 180, 232
9:22 . . . . 128, 131, 140, 179, 195,
               196, 330, 334, 335
9:23–27 318
9:23–26 . . . . 203, 330
9:23 . . . . .257, 323, 326
9:24 . . . . 232, 257, 270
9:26 . . . . .179, 197
9:27 . . . . 105, 205
9:29 325
9:30 363
9:30–32 320
9:31 99
9:33 . . . . 200, 363
9:35 . . . . 152, 160, 161, 164, 179,
               188, 191, 192, 198, 419
9:37–40 337
9:38 . . . . 160, 200
9:40 318
9:41 . . . . 234, 400
9:43–44 318
9:42 . . . . .230, 251, 252
9:43–45. . . . . 164, 191
9:43 106
9:44–45. . . . . 128, 330
9:44 . . . . 128, 179, 196
9:46–50 324
9:49 . . . . 200, 252

9:51–19:44 . . . 72, 133, 137, 146,
          201, 330, 347, 435
9:51–10:24 . . . . 64, 72
9:51–56. . . . . .247, 297, 318
9:51–55. 324
9:51 . . . . 164, 330
9:54 . . . . 318, 320
9:57–62. . . . . .147, 203, 330
9:57 318
9:58–62. 318
9:58 . . . . .179, 195, 330
9:59–62. 270
9:59–60. 270
9:60 105
9:61–62. . . . . . . 319, 320, 439
9:62 105
10–11 141
10. 363
10:1–24. . . . . 164, 438
10:1–12. 128
10:1–5. 250
10:3 209
10:4 321
10:5–6. 271
10:7 33
10:9 . . . . 105, 106, 141, 205,
          230, 252, 269
10:10–11 380
10:11–15 380
10:11 . . . . 105, 106
10:12–14. 292
10:12 255
10:13–15 273
10:13 264
10:16–19. 379
10:16 . . . . 58, 137, 363
10:17–21. 325
10:17–20. 250
10:17 . . . . 252, 328
10:18–20. . . . . 252, 253
10:18–19. 141
10:18 . . . 201, 205, 206, 250, 269
10:19 218
10:20 252
10:21–22. . . . . . . 105, 248, 440
10:21 219
10:23–24 . . . . 102, 156
10:24–25. 320
10:25–11:13 . . . . 64, 73
10:25–37. . . . 147, 247, 270, 324,
          351, 356, 435, 438
10:25–28. . . . . . . 270, 274, 324
10:25–27. 297
10:25 . . . . . . 200, 236, 269, 335
10:27–28 . . . . . . 106, 203, 420
10:28 269
10:31 334
10:38–42 . . . . 324, 331, 347
10:40 347

11. 325
11:1–13 . . . . .147, 203, 324
11:1–4. 321
11:1 244
11:2 . . . . 255, 439
11:5–8 . . . . 126, 435
11:9–13 126
11:13 . . . . .219, 354
11:14–54. . . . . 64, 73
11:14–23 . . . . 201, 249, 335,
          375, 439
11:14–20. . . . . 251, 338
11:14 252
11:17 169
11:20–23. . . . . .141, 269, 398
11:20 . . . . 73, 105, 106, 108, 165,
          169, 185, 205, 206, 231,
          250, 268, 390, 439
11:21–23. 141
11:21–22. . . . . 206, 249
11:22–23. 398
11:22 249
11:27–28. . . . . . .337, 347, 443
11:27 321
11:28 . . . . 106, 443
11:29–32. . . . . . . 208, 335, 337
11:29–31. 195
11:29 . . . . 234, 337, 400
11:30–32. 292
11:30 179
11:32 . . . . 243, 264
11:37–54. 136
11:37–52. . . . . . .146, 208, 244,
          334, 378, 426
11:37–44. 364
11:37–38. 364
11:37 . . . . 244, 335
11:38 335
11:39–52. . . . . 191, 364
11:39 335
11:40 126
11:41–42. 275
11:42–44. 273
11:42 . . . . .107, 140, 335, 363
11:45 200
11:46–52. 273
11:47–52. 383
11:47–51. 191
11:49–51. 134
11:49 107
11:50–51. 262
11:50 . . . . 268, 292
11:53 . . . . 334, 335
12. . . . . 44, 397
12:1–48. . . . . 64, 73
12:1–12. 326
12:1–10. 330
12:1 . . . . 335, 337
12:3 243

12:4–12. 147
12:4 270
12:6–7 348
12:6 107
12:8 . . . . 102, 179, 383
12:10 . . . . . . 166, 179, 195, 215,
          219, 249
12:11–12. 410
12:11 321
12:12 . . . . 141, 145, 219, 245
12:13–21. . . . 127, 147, 203, 257,
          329, 330, 435, 442
12:13 . . . . 200, 337
12:15 269
12:18 197
12:19–20. 354
12:20 . . . . . . .107, 114, 262, 379
12:21 . . . . .107, 354
12:22–34 . . . . 242, 327, 330
12:22–31. . . . . 126, 321
12:24–28 451
12:24 107
12:28 107
12:30 . . . . 107, 292
12:32 . . . . 106, 107
12:33 . . . . .141, 356
12:35–48. . . . . 75, 165, 180, 203,
          321, 326, 436
12:36–50 . . . . 396, 443
12:37–38. 398
12:37 244
12:40 . . . . .179, 197
12:41 382
12:42–44 395
12:42 396
12:43–44 326
12:45–48. 262
12:45–46. 395
12:45 198
12:46 . . . . 326, 396
12:47–48. 395
12:47 . . . . 326, 397
12:48 . . . . 326, 397
12:49–14:24 . . . . 64, 74
12:49–53. . . . . . .165, 215, 270
12:49–50. . . . . . .159, 164, 214
12:51–52. 271
12:51 . . . . .157, 271
12:52 361
12:57–59. . . . . 127, 262
12:54–56. . . . . 165, 327
12:54–55. 339
13. . . . . 44, 258
13:1–9. . . . . . 127, 262, 339, 442
13:3–5. 273
13:3 . . . . 258, 264
13:5 . . . . 258, 264
13:6–9. . . . . .126, 283, 284,
          378, 435

13:10–17 . . . . 275, 347, 364, 437
13:10–16 364
13:10 244
13:13 106
13:14 . . . . 230, 337, 401
13:15–17 415
13:16 . . . . 140, 231
13:18–21 348
13:18–19 339
13:18 105
13:20 105
13:22–30 . . . . 165, 247
13:22 . . . . 244, 251
13:23 . . . . 232, 257
13:24–30 258
13:25–27 320
13:25 . . . . 258, 395
13:26 244
13:28–29 . . . . 105, 157
13:28 397
13:29 . . . . 106, 244, 258
13:31–35 . . . . 133, 134, 283
13:31–33 379
13:32–33 . . . . 135, 283
13:33–35 157
13:33 . . . . 128, 137, 140, 164,
                              191, 330
13:34–35 . . . . . . 72, 76, 166, 401,
                              402, 434
13:35 . . . . 94, 200, 283, 378,
                              381, 402
14 258
14:1–24 335
14:1–6 . . . . . . 275, 347, 364, 437
14:1 244
14:3 230
14:4 230
14:7–14 . . . . 146, 435
14:8–9 244
14:12–33 435
14:12–24 356
14:13 . . . . 248, 356, 357
14:14 395
14:15–24 . . . . 56, 247, 435
14:15 105
14:16–24 377
14:21–24 . . . . 248, 356, 357
14:23 258
14:25–35 . . . . 64, 74, 147,
                              330, 339
14:25–33 . . . . 203, 257, 323
14:25–27 319
14:25 337
14:26 . . . . 257, 270, 321
14:27 321
14:28–33 435
14:28–30 . . . . 321, 322
14:31–32 . . . . 321, 322
14:33 322

14:34–35 435
15 . . . . 126, 196, 202, 248,
                              339, 439, 451
15:1–32 . . . . 64, 74, 147, 202,
                              244, 330
15:1–31 136
15:1–10 348
15:1–2 248
15:1 . . . . 141, 206
15:2–3 202
15:2 334
15:4–7 435
15:7 . . . . 263, 264, 272,
                              274, 328
15:8–24 274
15:10 . . . . 102, 264, 272,
                              274, 328
15:11 169
15:11–32 . . . . 126, 264, 449
15:11–31 . . . . 272, 435
15:17–21 327
15:26 . . . . 169, 198
15:32 140
16:1–32 147
16:1–31 . . . . 64, 75
16:1–13 . . . . 127, 322, 329
16:1–9 435
16:8, 9 329
16:9–31 273
16:10–12 329
16:12 360
16:13 . . . . 107, 270, 329
16:14–15 146
16:14 335
16:15 107
16:16–17 275
16:16 . . . . . . 105, 106, 240, 275,
                      361, 363, 389, 390,
                              399, 410
16:17 . . . . 259, 274, 275,
                              361, 362
16:18–31 442
16:18 . . . . 335, 362
16:19–31 . . . . 127, 248, 257, 262,
                      275, 329, 331, 354,
                              362, 435
16:19–30 356
16:19–23 329
16:22 348
16:23 329
16:24–29 275
16:24 338
16:25 . . . . 157, 354
16:29 363
16:30–31 140
16:30 264
16:31 . . . . 131, 169, 363
17 . . . . 44, 197, 395, 401
17:1–10 . . . . 64, 75

17:1–2 322
17:3–4 264
17:4 265
17:5–6 . . . . 147, 267
17:7–10 . . . . 147, 395, 435
17:11–18:8 . . . . 64, 75
17:11–19 . . . . 230, 247, 297,
                              437, 440
17:11–17 251
17:11–14 361
17:11 . . . . 137, 330
17:13 . . . . 200, 338
17:14 334
17:15 . . . . 106, 230
17:18 106
17:19 . . . . . . 230, 256, 267, 440
17:20–37 . . . . . . 36, 134, 180,
                      244, 436, 443
17:20–21 . . . . 106, 165, 205, 439
17:20 . . . . 105, 335
17:21 . . . . . . 105, 108, 141, 208,
                      390, 395, 401
17:22–37 . . . . 142, 165, 209,
                              395, 401
17:22 . . . . 179, 322
17:24–25 128
17:24 . . . . 179, 401
17:25 . . . . . . 128, 131, 140, 164,
                      268, 330, 401
17:26–37 262
17:26–29 292
17:26 179
17:27–29 268
17:29–30 215
17:30 179
17:32 . . . . 320, 348
17:37 . . . . 273, 395, 401
18:1–8 . . . . . . 126, 203, 325, 327,
                      348, 435, 443
18:1 140
18:8 . . . . 179, 267, 325, 326,
                              399, 400
18:9–30 . . . . 64, 76
18:9–14 . . . . . 137, 146, 157, 248,
                      272, 325, 335, 353,
                              435, 440
18:11 107
18:13 107
18:14 . . . . 126, 265
18:15–17 322
18:16–17 105
18:18–30 257
18:18–23 329
18:18 . . . . . . 197, 200, 236, 269
18:19 107
18:22 . . . . 356, 382
18:24–30 324
18:24–27 262
18:24–26 196

18:24–25. 105
18:25 258
18:26 . . . . 233, 258
18:27–30. 258
18:27 . . . . .107, 382, 451
18:28–30. . . . . 322, 324
18:28 382
18:29–30. . . . . 269, 270
18:29 105
18:30 . . . . 236, 382
18:31–19:44 . . . . 64, 76
18:31–34. . . . . 164, 330
18:31–33. 128
18:31 . . . . .137, 179, 196
18:32 . . . . 292, 299
18:35–43. . . . . 230, 357
18:36–38. 337
18:36 337
18:38–39. 187
18:40 141
18:42 . . . . .230, 232, 256,
                            267, 338
18:43 . . . . 106, 252
19–24 334
19. . . . . 180, 233
19:1–10. . . . .248, 261, 262, 322,
                      329, 339, 435
19:2–3. 339
19:3 337
19:5 . . . . 135, 169
19:7 248
19:8–10. 261
19:8 356
19:9 . . . . 135, 348
19:10 . . . 132, 137, 148, 179, 195,
           196, 233, 258, 259,
           268, 274, 318
19:11–27 . . . . 127, 180, 203,
                      327, 435
19:11 . . . . 105, 402
19:12–27. . . . . . . 142, 402, 443
19:13 169
19:17–19 395
19:17 169
19:23 167
19:24–26. 395
19:26 327
19:28–40. 166
19:29 322
19:37–38. 322
19:37 . . . . 106, 336
19:38 . . . . .126, 189, 200,
                      283, 284
19:39–44. 146
19:39 . . . . 200, 322, 338
19:40–41. 298
19:41–45. 395
19:41–44. . . . . .39, 72, 166, 173,
                284, 379, 398, 401

19:41–42. . . . . 330, 451
19:42 135
19:43 39
19:44 . . . . .39, 102, 115, 157
19:45–24:53 76
19:45–21:4 . . . . 64, 77
19:45–46. 166
19:47–48. 157
19:47 . . . . 244, 334
20 180
20:1 . . . . 240, 244
20:1–8. . . . . 166, 248
20:1–2. . . . . 19, 334, 335
20:5 268
20:9–19. . . . . .166, 180, 247, 335
20:9–18. . . . . 202, 377
20:14–18. 157
20:17–18. . . . . 124, 157
20:19–20. 425
20:19 334
20:20–26 335
20:21 . . . . 108, 159, 169, 200,
                245, 257, 293, 305
20:24 169
20:25 107
20:27 334
20:28 . . . . 200, 363
20:35 169
20:36 . . . . 104, 108
20:37–38 108
20:37 121
20:39 . . . . 200, 335
20:41–44 . . . 142, 166, 168, 180,
                182, 187, 335, 443
20:41 337
20:44 168
20:45–47. . . . . 322, 335
20:46–47 335
21–22 99
21. . . . . 44, 401, 439
21:1–4. . . . . 248, 322, 329, 331,
                346, 348, 354
21:1 337
21:2–27. 142
21:5–38. . . . . . .64, 77, 134, 142,
                      436, 443
21:5–37. . . . . 75, 322
21:5–36. . . . . .36, 168, 180, 209,
                244, 377, 401
21:5–33. 395
21:5–9. 395
21:7 200
21:8–9. 402
21:9 140
21:10 295
21:12–19. . . . . 56, 395
21:12–17. 330
21:13 169
21:15 226

21:19 326
21:20–24. . . . . 39, 395, 401, 402
21:20 400
21:21–24. 434
21:21 209
21:22 . . . . 99, 212
21:24 . . . . . . .40, 134, 247, 284,
                377, 392, 402
21:24–25. 295
21:25 . . . . 400, 402
21:25–36. 401
21:25–28. . . . . 393, 395
21:27 . . . . .179, 193, 197
21:28–36. 327
21:31 . . . . 105, 106
21:32 400
21:34–36. 402
21:36 197
21:37 244
21:41–44. . . . . . .183, 186, 418
22 . . . . 36, 128, 219
22:1–39. 390
22:1–38. . . . . 65, 78
22:1–23. 168
22:2 . . . . 66, 334, 335, 399
22:4 334
22:6 . . . . .337, 339
22:7–30. 322
22:7 140
22:10 321
22:11 . . . . 200, 322
22:14–38. 244
22:14 244
22:15–16. 285
22:15 131
22:16 . . . . 105, 134, 394
22:17–20. . . . . 36, 174
22:18–20. . . . . 36, 250, 449
22:18 . . . . 105, 361
22:19–22. 418
22:19–20. . . . . 207, 256
22:19 . . . . 133, 199
22:20 . . . . .198, 203, 204,
                      269, 391
22:21 36
22:22 . . . . 125, 128, 196
22:24–27 . . . . .168, 198, 318
22:25 296
22:27 209
22:28–30 168
22:28 402
22:29–30 . . . 250, 313, 376, 394
22:29 36
22:30 . . . . 105, 284
22:31–38. 322
22:31–34. 382
22:31–32. 399
22:31 402
22:32 . . . . 265, 267

22:37 . . . . 128, 140, 172, 198,
         253, 254, 299, 322, 418
22:39 – 23:56 . . . . 65, 78
22:39 – 46 . . . . 325, 328
22:40 325
22:41 – 46 325
22:42 . . . . 36, 128, 255
22:45 322
22:47 . . . . 141, 339
22:48 196
22:50 – 51 437
22:51 230
22:52 334
22:54 – 62 . . . . 323, 382
22:55 209
22:59 293
22:63 – 70 108
22:66 – 71 . . . . 168, 443
22:66 334
22:67 . . . . 186, 268
22:68 – 69 440
22:69 . . . . 81, 142, 167, 181, 182,
         196, 391, 418, 436, 450
22:70 188
22:71 181
23 . . . . 78, 94, 131, 168, 172, 198,
         203, 254, 294, 339, 340,
         385 – 386, 403, 440
23:1 – 25 293
23:1 336
23:2 . . . . 186, 296
23:3 . . . . 189, 285
23:4 . . . . 203, 254, 334, 332, 419
23:5 245
23:6 – 12 294
23:10 . . . . 334, 335
23:13 334
23:14 – 15 . . . . 203, 254, 419
23:15 254
23:18 – 19 171
23:20 203
23:22 . . . . 203, 254, 419
23:27 – 31 . . . . 349, 379
23:27 . . . . 336, 339
23:31 379
23:32 254
23:33 – 38 255
23:34 – 36 203
23:34 . . . . 254, 255, 325
23:35 . . . 186, 233, 255, 258, 339
23:36 255
23:37 . . . . 258, 285, 339
23:38 285
23:39 – 43 254
23:39 . . . . . . 186, 233, 258, 339
23:40 – 43 339
23:40 108
23:42 – 43 . . . 106, 135, 400, 403
23:43 – 47 418
23:43 403

23:44, 45 339
23:46 . . . . 295, 325
23:47 . . . . 174, 200, 203, 254
23:48 . . . . 337, 339
23:49 . . . . 339, 349
23:51 . . . . 105, 125, 282
23:55 – 56 349
24 . . . . . . 32, 56, 57, 58, 99, 130,
         168, 184, 215, 219, 233,
         323, 441
24:1 – 53 . . . . 65, 79
24:1 – 12 331
24:1 – 11 349
24:1 – 7 127
24:3 . . . . 169, 197
24:5 – 7 168
24:7 . . . . 140, 196
24:10 346
24:15 141
24:19 – 21 169
24:19 . . . . 108, 191
24:21 . . . . 191, 282, 285
24:25 – 27 . . . . 169, 244
24:25 268
24:26 . . . . 131, 140, 186. 408
24:27 . . . . 44, 274, 364
24:30 – 31 434
24:30 244
24:32 214
24:34 168
24:36 209
24:41 – 47 233
24:41 328
24:42 – 43 434
24:43 – 49 212
24:43 – 47 . . . 124, 360, 369, 407,
         410, 419, 441
24:44 – 49 . . . 125, 148, 207, 328,
         361, 372
24:44 – 47 . . . . 99, 108, 129, 131,
         249, 254, 262, 362
24:44 . . . . 140, 169, 244,
         274, 363
24:45 – 49 441
24:46 – 47 . . . . 128, 131, 133,
         169, 330
24:46 186
24:47 – 49 130
24:47 . . . 135, 200, 246, 256, 263,
         269, 296, 299, 300,
         373, 378, 422, 423
24:48 . . . . 131, 376
24:49 . . . . 81, 125, 129, 133, 136,
         143, 144, 153, 169, 203,
         207, 213, 216, 218, 219,
         225, 226, 250, 373, 391,
         414, 422, 441
24:50 – 53 436
24:52 328
24:53 106

John

1:7 122
1:21 169
1:29 171
1:35 – 36 171
4 440
4:16 – 18 441
5:19 – 27 440
5:22 243
5:27 – 32 243
5:39 439
6:12 242
6:29 109
7 440
7:28 136
7:42 337
9:10 230
9:25 230
10 196
10:7 258
10:29 255
12:25 . . . . 257, 270
12:31 439
12:35 – 48 122
12:38 172
12:46 122
13:33 128
13:34 202
14 – 16 . . . . . 223, 264, 440, 441
14:25 – 26 225
16:7 – 10 441
16:12 – 15 225
17 441
18:36 439
20:21 – 22 441
21 274

Acts

1 . . . . 32, 56, 58, 170,
         209, 323
1:1 – 11 . . . . 65, 79
1:1 – 5 . . . . 65, 80, 100, 434
1:1 . . . . 48, 59, 245, 410, 413
1:2 – 11 436
1:2 . . . . 212, 220, 226
1:3 – 11 169
1:3 131
1:4 – 5 . . . . 81, 94, 129, 136,
         143, 173, 216
1:4 . . . . 125, 220, 226
1:5 203
1:6 – 11 . . . . 65, 80, 170,
         209, 235
1:6 – 7 . . . . 129, 130, 137,
         170, 392, 434
1:6 . . . . 142, 282, 285
1:7 – 14 325
1:7 – 8 . . . . 207, 427
1:7 108

1:8 . . . . . . .90, 94, 128, 130, 131,
        133, 137, 138, 139, 144,
        212, 220, 225, 226, 236,
        246, 250, 297, 298, 299,
        313, 314, 328, 330, 376,
        399, 414, 422, 441
1:9–11. 436
1:10–11. . . . . 106, 127
1:11 209
1:12–26. . . . . 65, 80
1:12–16. 313
1:12–14. 350
1:15–22. 382
1:15 . . . . 209, 339
1:16–20. 134
1:16 . . . . 140, 145, 220, 226
1:20 . . . . 220, 420
1:21–22. . . . . .313, 314, 376
1:22 . . . . .131, 361
1:23–26. 325
1:30 271
2–5 312
2–4 . . . . 108, 220, 323
2. . . . . . . 108, 110, 124, 125, 133,
        142, 143, 144, 182, 213,
        215, 216, 217, 219, 220,
        225, 233, 234, 271, 273,
        286, 365, 373, 374, 381,
        393, 403, 410, 415, 418,
        421, 436, 441
2:1–41. . . . . 65, 80
2:1–4. . . . . 372, 373
2:3 214
2:4 . . . . . 144, 145, 212, 220, 226
2:5–10. 297
2:6 336
2:7 223
2:8 220
2:9–11. 286
2:11 . . . . 109, 220, 350
2:12 223
2:14–40. 382
2:14–36. 372
2:14–22. 250
2:16–39. . . . . 136, 207
2:16–38. 442
2:16–19. 414
2:16–18. . . . . 225, 389
2:16 373
2:17–33. 143
2:17–21. . . . . 124, 132, 223, 373
2:17–18. . . . . .220, 221, 314, 350
2:17 . . . . 110, 113, 124, 144, 216,
        226, 350, 374
2:18 . . . . 350, 373, 374
2:19 214
2:20–36 29
2:20 234
2:21 . . 110, 125, 169, 170, 182, 183,
        198, 205, 233, 234, 259, 451

2:22–24 417
2:22 . . . . 109, 130, 201, 209,
        231, 249, 314
2:23–24 . . . . 203, 204
2:23 . . . . 109, 125, 128, 293,
        295, 419
2:24 109
2:24 . . . . 32, 419
2:25–31. 187
2:25–28 417
2:26 . . . . 110, 403
2:27–28 271
2:27 110
2:29–32. 337
2:30–39 . . . . 207, 375
2:30–38 233
2:30–36 . . . 106, 130, 142, 169,
        256, 441, 443
2:30–34 204
2:30–33 . . . . 198, 374
2:30–31. . . . . .178, 418
2:30 . . . . 134, 182, 415
2:31 . . . . 110, 187, 418
2:32–36 . .47, 182, 250, 391, 414
2:32–34 218
2:32–33. . . . . 109, 200
2:32 . . . . .131, 314, 376
2:33 . . . . 110, 124, 125, 212,
        216, 221, 374, 418
2:34–38 182
2:34–35. 418
2:34 110
2:36–39 . . . . 170, 198
2:36–38 183
2:36 . . . . 109, 110, 182, 183, 184,
        241, 243, 259, 286,
        391, 403
2:38–40 . . . .124, 134, 143, 216,
        221, 259
2:38–39. . . . . 132, 212, 350, 374
2:38 . . . . 124, 125, 132, 133, 170,
        184, 186, 199, 205, 218,
        221, 233, 242, 256, 264,
        269, 271, 442
2:39 . . . . 110, 122, 125, 221, 223,
        245, 373, 414, 451
2:40 . . . . 110, 234, 259, 268, 273
2:41–47. 387
2:42–47 . . . . . .65, 81, 306, 312,
        372, 442
2:42–46 . . . . 306, 312
2:42 244
2:43 250
2:44–46 306
2:44 . . . . 268, 315
2:45 356
2:47 . . . . 110, 234, 258, 312
3–5 . . . . 380, 441
3–4 . . . . 225, 286, 326

3. . . . . .28, 36, 142, 209, 235, 273,
        284, 285, 286, 357, 360,
        365, 393, 416, 417,
        423, 425
3:1–4:31 . . . . 65, 81
3:1–4:22 170
3:1–4:21 253
3:1–10 . . . . 252, 372, 437
3:1 . . . . 276, 325
3:2 321
3:6 . . . . . 132, 170, 184, 205, 250
3:8–9. 110
3:11–26. . . . . 235, 361, 362
3:12–4:12 382
3:12–26. . . . . 276, 378
3:12 . . . . 130, 218, 250
3:13–26 . . . . 372, 442
3:13–15 . . . . 198, 199
3:13–14 . . . . 243, 365
3:13 . . . . .110, 121, 199, 276, 294
3:14–15 . . . . 200, 203, 204
3:15–17 414
3:15 . . . . 110, 131, 170, 271,
        314, 376
3:16 . . . . 132, 184, 205, 218, 250,
        252, 267
3:17 254
3:18–26. . . . . 28, 209
3:18–22. . . . . .94, 129, 399, 434,
        436, 441, 442
3:18–20. . . . . 125, 416
3:18 . . . . 110, 125, 131, 187,
        293, 295
3:19–25. 106
3:19–24. . . . . 165, 207
3:19–23. 209
3:19–21 . . . . . 110, 235, 256, 374,
        381, 391, 394
3:19 . . . . . . .132, 234, 241, 256,
        264, 265, 266
3:20–21. . . . . 204, 209
3:20 . . . . .137, 187, 392, 393
3:21–22. 226
3:21 . . . . 140, 142, 204, 375, 378
3:22–23 . . . . .134, 191, 408,
        416, 423
3:22–26 . . . . 125, 131
3:22 . . . . .110, 192, 276,
        365, 419
3:23 . . . . . . .134, 192, 273, 276,
        286, 379, 425
3:24–26 . . . . 416, 423
3:24 . . . . .249, 393, 416
3:25–26 . . . . 187, 235, 246,
        256, 292, 365
3:25 . . . . 110, 122, 170, 193,
        276, 373, 416
3:26 . . . . .110, 137, 199, 419
4. . . . . 114, 420, 421, 422

4:1–3. 334
4:1–2. 372
4:1. 334
4:2. 245
4:4. 268
4:5. . . . . 293, 334
4:7–12. 225
4:7. . . . . 130, 132, 184, 218
4:8–12. 252
4:8 . . . . . 144, 212, 221, 226, 293
4:9–12. 235
4:9–10. . . . . 170, 205
4:9. 135
4:10–12. 204
4:10 . . . . . 82, 111, 132, 184, 186,
           198, 203, 250, 286
4:11 . . . . 200, 283
4:12 . . . 132, 140, 170, 184, 205,
       250, 256, 258, 259, 261
4:13–22. 170
4:14 235
4:16–22. 250
4:16–18. 226
4:17–18. 132
4:17. 170
4:18 . . . . .170, 184, 245, 293
4:19 . . . . .111, 380
4:20 111
4:23–30 . . . . 307, 380
4:23. 334
4:23–37 372
4:23–35. 312
4:23–31. . . . . 170, 325, 330, 341
4:24–31. 128
4:24–30 . . . . 198, 427
4:24–29 292
4:24–26 420
4:24 . . . . .111, 126
4:25–31. 260
4:25–30 161
4:25–28 286
4:25–26 . . . . 295, 423
4:25 . . . . 145, 220, 226, 293
4:27–28 . . . . 125, 128, 295, 421
4:27 293
4:28 . . . . 125, 128, 255
4:29. 111
4:30 . . . . 132, 184, 205, 255, 295
4:31 . . . . 212, 221, 226
4:32–5:11 . . . . 65, 82, 268
4:32–37. . . . . 312, 329, 387, 442
4:32–36 356
4:32–35. 306
4:32. . . . . .315, 336
4:33 . . . . 130, 170, 250, 272
4:36–37 383
5. 418
5:1–11. . . . . 253, 313, 330,
                  350, 382

5:3–4. 111
5:3 . . . . 145, 212, 222,
                  226, 313
5:5 145
5:9 . . . . 212, 222, 313, 384
5:11 . . . . 144, 307
5:12–16. . . . . 65, 82, 437
5:12 . . . . 250, 372
5:14 . . . . 171, 198, 244, 259, 268,
              312, 336, 350
5:15–26 253
5:16 . . . . 235, 336
5:17 . . . . 334, 375
5:17–42. . . . . 65, 82
5:17–20. 148
5:19–20. 380
5:19 128
5:20 . . . . 236, 271
5:21 245
5:25 245
5:28 . . . . 132, 244, 245
5:29–32. 382
5:29 . . . . .111, 140, 171
5:30–32. 314
5:30–31. . . . . 171, 200
5:30 . . . . 121, 203, 204,
                  254, 441
5:31 . . . . 125, 132, 133, 185, 199,
       234, 235, 256, 263, 269,
              286, 418
5:32 . . . . 131, 145, 171, 222,
                  226, 376
5:35 335
5:38–39. . . . . .111, 128, 147, 380
5:38 125
5:39 171
5:40–42 171
5:40–41. 184
5:40 . . . . 132, 170
5:41 . . . . 205, 380
5:42 . . . . .187, 240, 245
6–8 330
6–7 . . . . 40, 326, 365
6. . . . . 219, 383, 387
6:1–6. . . . . 41, 65, 83, 312, 314,
                  350, 442
6:1 . . . . .311, 323
6:2–3 323
6:2. . . . . .111, 336
6:3 . . . . . 144, 212, 221, 226, 383
6:5 . . . . . 144, 221, 226, 267, 383
6:7–7:60 171
6:7 . . . . .65, 83, 111, 267, 311,
       312, 323, 334, 339
6:8–9:31 . . . . 65, 83
6:8–8:1 . . . . 65, 83
6:8–7:60 382
6:8 . . . . 130, 250, 272, 383
6:9–12. 383

6:10–11. 41
6:10 . . . . 145, 222, 226
6:11–14. 275
6:11 . . . . .111, 365
6:12 334
6:13 . . . . 365, 426
6:14 365
6:15 41
7. . . . . . . 134, 365, 383, 418, 421
7:2 112
7:4–5. 112
7:4 286
7:6–8. 112
7:7 . . . . 192, 297
7:8 365
7:9 112
7:10 . . . . 235, 271
7:17 . . . . 112, 125, 286
7:20 . . . . 112, 365
7:22 . . . . 192, 365
7:23 286
7:25 . . . . .112, 192, 235, 261, 295
7:27 236
7:29 365
7:30–39. 192
7:31 . . . . 116, 365
7:32 . . . . .112, 121, 365
7:34 . . . . 235, 286
7:35 . . . . 112, 365
7:36 112
7:37 . . . . .112, 191, 286, 365, 419
7:38 . . . . 144, 306
7:39 236
7:40 365
7:42–43. 423
7:42 . . . . 112, 286, 425
7:44 . . . . 112, 365
7:45 . . . . 112, 297
7:46 . . . . .112, 121, 271, 272
7:47–49. 286
7:48–50. 112
7:48 126
7:49–50. . . . . 423, 426
7:50 295
7:51–53. . . . . 134, 379, 426
7:51 . . . . 112, 220, 222, 226
7:52–53. 365
7:52 125
7:54–60. 425
7:55–56. . . . . 111, 112, 127, 144,
              148, 226, 383, 400,
                  403, 418
7:55 . . . . 140, 221, 383
7:56 . . . . 188, 197
7:58–8:3 385
7:60 . . . . 254, 423
8–11 139
8–9 307
8. . . . . 222, 312, 385, 421

8:1–4 . . . . 65, 84
8:1 . . . . 144, 307, 323, 375
8:3 . . . . .144, 307, 351, 375
8:4 240
8:5–40 . . . . 66, 84
8:5–13 383
8:5 . . . . .171, 187
8:6 250
8:7 235
8:8 328
8:9–10 222
8:9 . . . . 223, 297
8:10 . . . . 112, 130
8:11 223
8:12–13 268
8:12 . . . . 106, 108, 112, 132, 171,
184, 205, 240, 244,
245, 351
8:13 . . . . 130, 223, 250, 264
8:14–25 376
8:14 . . . . .111, 112
8:15 222
8:16 . . . . 132, 171, 184, 205,
222, 223
8:17 222
8:18 . . . . 112, 222
8:19 222
8:20 271
8:21 112
8:22 . . . . 132, 264
8:25 240
8:26–29 148
8:26 . . . . 127, 222
8:32–35 . . . . 171, 299, 387
8:32–33 . . . . 198, 254, 418
8:32 171
8:33 171
8:34 . . . . 253, 418
8:35 . . . . 171, 240, 244, 419
8:37 188
8:39–40 437
8:39 . . . . 128, 222
8:40 240
8:60 339
9 . . . . . . .113, 127, 172, 313, 422
9:1–31 148
9:1–30 . . . . 66, 84
9:1–19 385
9:1–2 307
9:1 311
9:2 . . . . .307, 315
9:3–9 437
9:6 140
9:10–16 . . . . .127, 148
9:10 116
9:12–16 148
9:12 116
9:13 315
9:14–16 132

9:14 205
9:15–16 385
9:15 . . . . 113, 172, 184, 236,
247, 298, 321
9:16 . . . . 113, 140, 205
9:17–18 252
9:17 . . . 144, 212, 221, 226, 307
9:20–21 172
9:20 . . . . .113, 156, 188
9:21 . . . . 132, 223
9:22–23 287
9:22 . . . . .156, 172, 187, 188
9:25 323
9:26–27 . . . . 376, 383
9:26 311
9:27–29 385
9:27–28 . . . 132, 172, 184, 205
9:27 . . . . 113, 170, 307
9:31 . . . . . .66, 85, 145, 223, 226,
307, 312, 375
9:32–43 . . . . 66, 85, 351
9:32–35 252
9:32 315
9:33–34 437
9:34 . . . . 172, 186, 235
9:35 . . . . 135, 266
9:36–43 252
9:36–42 437
9:38 311
9:41 315
9:42 . . . . 172, 198, 244, 259, 268
10–15 . . . . 133, 367
10–11 . . . . . 113, 122, 139, 216,
247, 261, 271, 298, 312,
366, 367, 442
10:1–11:18 . . . .66, 85, 148, 196,
373, 382
10:1–23 172
10 . . . . . .52, 133, 144, 364, 372,
378, 385, 415
10:2 113
10:3–16 437
10:3–7 127
10:3–4 113
10:3 . . . . 102, 116
10:9–22 330
10:9–16 . . . . 246, 276
10:9–11 325
10:10–16 127
10:13–16 148
10:15 113
10:17 . . . . .113, 116
10:19 . . . . 116, 223
10:22 298
10:23–48 376
10:26 241
10:28–29 288
10:28 . . . . 113, 373
10:31, 33 113

10:34 . . . . . . .113, 235, 293, 373
10:34–43 240
10:34–35 . . . . 137, 240
10:35–39 137
10:35–36 198
10:35 . . . . 244, 246, 298, 373
10:36–42 184
10:36–38 . . . . .161, 201
10:36 . . . . . . 133, 137, 172, 184,
186, 240, 243, 244, 271,
287, 408
10:37 361
10:38–41 240
10:38 . . . 113, 130, 173, 201, 218,
223, 225, 226, 249, 250,
293, 294
10:39–42 173
10:39 . . . . 131, 203, 254,
376, 441
10:40–42 115
10:40 113
10:41 . . . . .113, 125, 131
10:42–43 . . . 133, 134, 207, 243,
268, 287, 372, 408,
410, 411
10:42 . . .108, 113, 125, 128, 200,
209, 259, 262, 273,
394, 395
10:43 . . . 125, 132, 133, 173, 184,
200, 205, 234, 244, 246,
256, 268, 269, 315
10:44–47 144
10:44 223
10:45–48 173
10:45–47 216
10:45 . . . . 113, 216, 223, 271,
298, 366, 374, 375
10:46 . . . . 113, 223, 226
10:47 . . . . 113, 223, 373
10:48 . . . 132, 170, 184, 186, 205
11–20 385
11 . . . . 86, 373
11:1–8 312
11:1 . . . . .111, 113, 298
11:2 366
11:5 116
11:8 217
11:9 . . . . 113, 223, 226
11:11–18 373
11:12 223
11:14 . . . . 235, 258
11:15–18 . . . . 136, 144, 372, 422
11:15–17 . . . . . . .217, 223, 415
11:15–16 . . . . 144, 250
11:15 . . . . . . 144, 223, 372, 391
11:16 223
11:17–18 223
11:17 . . . . 86, 113, 173, 244, 259,
268, 271, 451

11:18 . . . . 113, 132, 200, 217, 226, 236, 257, 263, 271, 298, 373
11:19–30 . . . . . . 33, 66, 86, 433
11:19–26 37
11:19 288
11:20 240
11:21 . . . 266, 268, 295, 312, 315
11:22–30 383
11:22 . . . . .307, 375, 376
11:23 . . . . .114, 271, 272
11:24 . . . . . . 144, 222, 223, 339
11:26 . . . . . . 245, 308, 311, 315, 339, 375
11:27–30 . . . .128, 314, 357, 442
11:27–28 37
11:28 . . . . 145, 212, 223
11:29 . . . . 128, 312
11:30 . . . . 37, 323
12 . . . . 86, 341
12:1–23 . . . . 66, 86, 148
12:1 . . . . 308, 375
12:5 . . . . .114, 325, 375
12:6–11 . . . . 253, 437
12:7–15 128
12:9 116
12:11 . . . . 235, 288
12:12 331
12:13–17 331
12:13 351
12:14 328
12:16 223
12:22 114
12:23 114
12:24–25 . . . . .66, 87, 111
12:24 . . . . .114, 312
13–20 . . . . 312, 386
13–18 442
13:1–15:35 87
13:1–15:12 383
13:1–14:28 . . . . 66, 87
13 . . . . . . 188, 217, 272, 360, 367, 386, 418, 419, 420
13:1–4 219
13:1–3 . . . 33, 148, 312, 372, 433
13:1–2 . . . . 312, 421
13:1 . . . . 128, 308, 375
13:2–3 325
13:2 . . . . 224, 421
13:4 224
13:5 . . . . .111, 114, 288
13:6–12 299
13:6 288
13:7 111
13:8 . . . . 114, 267
13:9–11 . . . . 145, 437
13:9 . . . . .114, 212, 222, 224, 226
13:10–11 114

13:11 . . . . 295, 357
13:12 . . . . 244, 268
13:13–41 415
13:13 128
13:14–48 372
13:14 276
13:15 367
13:16–41 . . . . 173, 188, 261, 386
13:16–22 217
13:16 114
13:17 . . . . . . .114, 121, 287, 386
13:18–19 287
13:19 . . . . 286, 298
13:21 114
13:22 419
13:22–33 125
13:22–30 394
13:22–23 187
13:23–39 372
13:23–25 . . . . 136, 185
13:23–24 200
13:23 . . . .114, 125, 185, 217, 235, 256, 287, 415
13:24 . . . . . . .132, 217, 263, 287
13:26 . . . . .114, 235, 261
13:27 . . . . 131, 254
13:29 . . . . 203, 254
13:31 . . . . .131, 314, 376
13:32–39 . . . . 37, 207
13:32–37 128
13:32–33 419
13:32 . . . . 125, 131, 240
13:33 . . . . 110, 114, 135, 189, 192, 212, 419
13:34–35 361
13:34 187
13:35 417
13:36 . . . . .114, 125
13:37 114
13:38–39 . . . . 200, 236, 257, 269
13:38–41 256
13:38 . . . . . . 125, 133, 234, 367
13:39 . . . . .111, 268, 315
13:40–41 131
13:41–47 424
13:41–45 380
13:41 423
13:43 . . . . .114, 271, 272
13:44 111
13:45 . . . . 288, 340
13:46–14:1 372
13:46–49 378
13:46–48 289
13:46–47 . . . . 236, 288, 289, 421
13:46 . . . . . . 111, 115, 140, 190, 271, 298, 377
13:47 . . . 121, 122, 133, 134, 138, 199, 236, 246, 261, 298, 313, 315, 328, 387, 420, 421, 422

13:48 . . . . 125, 299
13:49 312
13:50 . . . . 190, 288, 351
13:51 380
13:52 . . . . 224, 226, 311
14 . . . . 243, 314
14:1 . . . . 236, 336
14:2 288
14:3 . . . . .131, 250, 271, 272
14:4 . . . . 37, 47, 299, 313, 314, 336
14:5 299
14:7 240
14:8–20 299
14:8–18 . . . . 250, 252
14:8–10 437
14:8 . . . . 242, 357
14:9 . . . . 235, 258, 267
14:11 339
14:13 . . . . 334, 339
14:14 . . . . 37, 47, 313, 314, 339, 385
14:15–24 394
14:15–17 . . . . 104, 242
14:15 . . . .115, 116, 241, 266, 368
14:16 . . . . 242, 299
14:17 . . . . 126, 242
14:18 339
14:19 . . . . 288, 340
14:21 240
14:22 . . . .108, 115, 140, 267, 442
14:23 . . . . . . 244, 268, 308, 375
14:26 . . . . .115, 272
14:27 . . . . . . 115, 267, 299, 308, 375, 378
14:28 311
15 . . . .37, 56, 122, 235, 274, 298, 312, 360, 362, 366, 367, 378, 384, 385, 422
15:1–35 . . . . 66, 88, 372, 376
15:1–29 373
15:1 . . . . 235, 245, 366
15:3–4 375
15:3 . . . . . . 265, 298, 308, 328
15:4 . . . . .115, 308, 451
15:5 . . . . 268, 335, 366, 375
15:6–21 442
15:7–9 366
15:7 . . . . .115, 239, 298
15:8–9 88
15:8 . . . . .131, 144, 217, 224
15:9–11 239
15:9 . . . . .235, 267, 372
15:10 . . . . .115, 276, 321, 323
15:11 . . . 173, 235, 258, 268, 272
15:12 . . . . 250, 298, 336
15:13–21 384
15:14–21 173
15:14–18 416

15:14–17 . . . . 122, 235
15:14 . . . . . . 102, 115, 132, 205,
                284, 298, 451
15:15–18 . . . . 420, 422
15:15 . . . . 384, 417
15:16 187
15:17 . . . . 184, 205, 298
15:19–20 437
15:19 . . . . 115, 266, 298
15:21 . . . . 244, 366
15:22 375
15:23 . . . . 298, 308
15:23–29 276
15:26 . . . 132, 173, 184, 186, 205
15:28 . . . . 145, 224
15:30 336
15:30–35 . . . . 33, 433
15:35 . . . . 240, 245
15:36–21:16 . . . . . . 66, 88
15:36–18:23 . . . . . . 66, 89
15:36–40 383
15:40 272
15:41 375
16 231
16:1–3 128
16:1 311
16:3 . . . . 276, 366
16:5 . . . . 267, 308, 312, 375
16:6–10 148
16:6–9 173
16:6–7 212
16:6 . . . . 116, 224
16:7 224
16:9–10 . . . . 127, 437
16:9 116
16:10–17 . . . . 32, 33
16:10 . . . . .115, 116, 240
16:11–15 351
16:14–15 331
16:14 116
16:16–24 351
16:16–18 252
16:17 . . . .116, 126, 150, 237, 308
16:18 . . . . 132, 170, 174, 184,
                186, 226
16:19 403
16:21 351
16:22 . . . . 128, 340
16:24–34 253
16:25 116
16:26 . . . . 128, 148, 437
16:30–31 . . . . 198, 259
16:30 . . . . 237, 258
16:31 . . . . . . 174, 244, 259, 268
16:32 . . . . .111, 259
16:34 . . . . 116, 244, 268
17 . . . . 36, 243, 299
17:1–9 53
17:2–3 408

17:3 . . . . .131, 140, 174, 187
17:4 . . . . 336, 352
17:5 288
17:6–7 . . . . .351, 352
17:7 189
17:8 340
17:11 288
17:12 268
17:13 . . . . . . .111, 116, 288, 340
17:16–34 299
17:16–32 442
17:18–21 408
17:18 240
17:19 244
17:20 264
17:22 209
17:22–37 281
17:22–31 386
17:23 116
17:24–29 104
17:24–25 116
17:24 . . . . 116, 126, 241
17:25–26 241
17:25 . . . . 271, 299
17:26–31 134
17:26 . . . . 116, 125, 128, 268
17:27, 28, 29 116
17:30–32 386
17:30–31 . . . . .204, 259, 273,
                395, 410, 411
17:30 . . . . 117, 132, 241, 254
17:31 . . . 108, 117, 125, 128, 174,
        200, 204, 207, 209, 243,
        244, 256, 262, 268
17:34 . . . . 268, 352
18–22 36
18 . . . . 360, 367
18:1–4 352
18:3–11 378
18:4–6 236
18:5–11 380
18:5 . . . . .174, 187
18:6 . . . . .236, 288, 289, 298,
                299, 372, 377, 380
18:7 117
18:8 . . . . 198, 244, 268
18:9–10 . . . . 127, 437
18:9 . . . . .116, 212
18:11 . . . . 111, 117, 245
18:12–17 299
18:13 . . . . 117, 275, 351, 367
18:15 . . . . 341, 367
18:18 . . . . 276, 367
18:19 . . . . 236, 288
18:21 117
18:22 . . . . 309, 375
18:23 311
18:24–21:16 . . . . 66, 90
18:24–28 352
18:25–26 315

18:25 . . . . .145, 245
18:26 . . . . .117, 309, 331
18:27–28 174
18:27 . . . . .268, 272, 311, 315
19 144
19:1–10 214
19:1–7 385
19:1 311
19:2 224
19:4 . . . . 132, 174, 200, 217, 244,
                263, 268
19:5 . . . . 132, 174, 205
19:6 . . . . 144, 224, 226, 374, 385
19:8–9 236
19:8 . . . . 108, 268
19:9 . . . . .309, 311, 315, 336
19:11–12 437
19:11 . . . . .117, 130, 250
19:13–20 253
19:13 . . . . 132, 174, 184, 244
19:17–20 174
19:17 . . . . 132, 184
19:18 315
19:20 312
19:21–40 288
19:21 . . . . 138, 140
19:23–27 299
19:23 309
19:24–26 340
19:28 190
19:32 . . . . 306, 375
19:33 340
19:32 375
19:35 340
19:39–40 . . . . 306, 375
19:41 375
20 394
20:1 311
20:3 . . . . 123, 288
20:5–15 . . . . 32, 34
20:7–12 252
20:8–12 437
20:17–35 . . . . 314, 390
20:17 . . . . 309, 372, 375
20:18–38 438
20:18–35 386
20:18–21 200
20:19 288
20:20 245
20:21 . . . .117, 118, 132, 174, 198,
                263, 267, 288
20:22, 23 224
20:24 . . . . .117, 174, 240, 272
20:25 244
20:27 . . . . .117, 125
20:28 . . . . . .36, 117, 131, 133, 145,
        171, 174, 186, 199, 203,
        204, 212, 224, 250, 256,
        309, 375, 391, 425, 449

20:30 323
20:32 . . . . .117, 272
20:35 . . . . 38, 174
21–28 . . . . 312, 385
21–26 . . . . 94, 326
21–23 40
21 . . . . 286, 309, 360, 368
21:1–18 . . . . 32, 34
21:4 . . . . .145, 224, 311
21:7–14 314
21:9–10 128
21:9 . . . . .314, 331, 352
21:10–11 145
21:11 . . . . 145, 224, 299
21:13–14 328
21:13 . . . . . . 132, 174, 184, 205
21:14 . . . . 145, 224
21:16 311
21:17–28:31 91
21:17–23:35 91
21:17–26 . . . . 66, 372
21:17–24 384
21:17–19 376
21:19 300
21:20–21 367
21:20 . . . . 268, 315, 368
21:21 . . . . 245, 275, 288, 368
21:23–24 276
21:24 368
21:25–36 281
21:25 . . . . 268, 300, 315
21:26 372
21:27–23:35 66
21:27 340
21:28 . . . . 245, 340, 368
21:33 141
21:34–36 340
21:36 336
21:39 . . . . 280, 288
22 . . . . .174, 175, 368
22:1–21 386
22:3 . . . . 118, 280, 288, 368
22:4 . . . . .307, 309, 315, 352, 368
22:6–16 385
22:6–10 127
22:10 125
22:12–13 368
22:12 . . . . 359, 360
22:14–15 393
22:14 . . . . 118, 121, 125, 174, 309
22:15 . . . . .131, 314, 377
22:16 . . . . 132, 184, 256
22:16 394
22:18 236
22:19 315
22:20 . . . . .131, 314, 377, 394
22:21–22 190
22:21 300
22:30 288

23 . . . . . . 224, 334, 335, 341, 368
23:1–10 386
23:1 . . . . 118, 385
23:3 . . . . 118, 368
23:4–8 125
23:4–5 368
23:4 118
23:5 426
23:6 . . . . 273, 275, 335, 372, 385
23:7 . . . . 335, 336
23:8 . . . . 225, 335
23:9 . . . . 225, 335, 385
23:11 . . . . 94, 131, 138, 140, 437
23:12 . . . . 288, 316
23:14 . . . . 316, 334
23:26–30 340
23:27–29 375
23:27 288
23:29 . . . . 92, 340, 385
24:1–26:32 . . . . 66, 92
24 368
24:1 334
24:2 300
24:5 . . . . 288, 375
24:9 288
24:10–21 386
24:10 300
24:12–27 66
24:12–21 385
24:12 340
24:14–21 275
24:14–16 . . . . 273, 372
24:14–15 . . . . 128, 174, 403
24:14 . . . 118, 121, 134, 244, 268,
                276, 288, 315, 360, 368
24:15–16 118
24:15 385
24:17 . . . . 300, 357, 443
24:18 340
24:22 315
24:24 . . . . 174, 187, 267, 352
24:26 341
24:47 421
24:48 314
25 368
25:1–12 66
25:7 . . . . 109, 288
25:8–11 386
25:8 . . . . .273, 276, 280, 288,
                368, 372, 385
25:10–12 94
25:10 . . . . 140, 288
25:13–26:32 66
25:15 . . . . 288, 334
25:18–19 93
25:19 . . . . 174, 332, 340
25:23 352
25:24 . . . . 288, 336
25:25 . . . . 93, 385

26 . . . . . . 38, 174, 175, 368, 369
26:1–32 386
26:2 288
26:3 187
26:4 300
26:5 . . . . 335, 375
26:5–6 273
26:6–8 . . . . 22, 372, 385
26:6–7 282
26:6 . . . . .118, 125, 175, 288, 403
26:7 403
26:8 118
26:9 . . . . 132, 175, 184
26:10–11 307
26:10 315
26:12–18 385
26:13–18 127
26:15–18 . . . . 408, 427
26:16–18 . . . . . 175, 200, 393
26:16 . . . . .131, 314, 377
26:17–18 399
26:17 . . . . 289, 300
26:18–23 199
26:18 . . . . . . 118, 125, 133, 234,
                256, 264, 266,
                267, 269
26:19–20 200
26:20 . . .118, 132, 263, 264, 266,
                300, 423
26:21 288
26:22–23 . . .122, 125, 128, 133,
                134, 175, 273,
                407, 410
26:22 . . . . 118, 276, 368
26:23 . . . . .280, 300, 369,
                422, 423
26:26–28 276
26:27 . . . . 131, 244
26:28 . . . . .309, 315
26:29 118
26:30 352
26:31 93
26:32 385
27–28 35
27:1–28:16 . . . . . 32, 34, 66, 93
27:1–28:10 148
27 . . . . 138, 237, 385
27:20 . . . . 258, 259, 403
27:21 209
27:23–44 253
27:23–25 94
27:23–24 127
27:23 . . . . 102, 119
27:24 . . . . .94, 119, 140
27:25 . . . . 119, 244, 268
27:26 237
27:31 . . . . .237, 258, 259
27:34 . . . . .237, 261
27:35 119

28 . . . . 57, 225, 448
28:1 237
28:3–5 253
28:4 237
28:6 119
28:7–10. 252
28:7 280
28:8–9 237
28:8 289
28:15 119
28:17–31 . . . . 66, 94
28:17 . . . . 94, 276, 288, 372
28:19 300
28:20 . . . . 94, 175, 287, 403
28:23 . . . . . . .94, 106, 108, 134,
175, 360, 369, 408
28:25–29. 378
28:25–28 . . . . 134, 300, 380
28:25–27 . . . . 380, 424
28:25 . . . . . . 122, 145, 225, 226
28:26–27 . . . . 407, 423
28:27 267
28:28 . . . . . . 119, 236, 237, 246,
260, 298, 300,
372, 377
28:30–31. . . . . . . 237, 245, 300,
372, 403, 427
28:31 . . . . . . 106, 108, 169, 175,
187, 244, 245

Romans

1. 36
1–6 424
1:1–4. 188
1:2–4. . . . . 36, 183, 441
1:3–4. 419
1:3 337
1:4–5. 257
1:4 128
1:16 . . . . 379, 442
1:16–17 . . . . 94, 115, 130, 377
1:18–32. 442
1:20 242
1:21 241
1:24–32. 425
1:25 260
1:30 353
2. 442
2:14–16. 242
3–4 442
3:8–18. 442
4. 442
4:4 380
5:1–11. . . . . 125, 234
5:14 380
6:1–11. . . . . 125, 234
6:7 380
8:3 188
8:18–23. 393
8:29–30 . . . . 128, 295

8:32 160
9–11 . . . . 80, 94, 236, 442
9:31 141
9:31–10:13 363
9:33 . . . . 124, 157
10:9–17 442
10:9–12. 132
10:9 259
10:12–13. 133
10:12 . . . . 184, 241
10:13 259
10:16 172
11:11–32. 284
11:11–14. 378
11:11–12. 296
11:12 284
11:14 284
11:15 296
11:25–27. 284
11:25–26. 296
11:30–32. 296
11:31–32. 284
12–15 442
14–15 442
14:9 243
15:7–13. . . . . 384, 417
15:18–19 37
15:24 242
15:25–29. 442
16:13 35
16:21 35

1 Corinthians

1–2 441
1:18 196
1:20–21. 242
1:26–29. 202
2:6–8 295
2:7 128
2:9 . . . . 274, 324
3:10–17. 397
3:17 397
4:9 109
6:2 285
7:32–34. 158
8–10 . . . . 40, 442
8:4–6. 36
9:1–6. 314
9:9 348
9:12 291
9:19–23. . . . . 36, 384
9:19 . . . . 360, 366, 442
9:21 324
10:11 221
12–14 434
13. 146
15. 441
15:2 320
15:20–28. 441
15:24–28. 393

15:25–28. 166
15:54–55. 403
16:1–4. 442
16:15–17 35
16:17 349

2 Corinthians

2:15 196
3. 225
3:16 135
4:3–6 299
4:3 196
4:6 122
4:7 37
8–9 442
8:14 349
9:12 349
11:9 349
11:24 236
12:9 37
13:5–7. 264

Galatians

1:15–17 434
2. 37
2:1 37
2:3 366
2:10 442
3. 299
3:13 . . . . 203, 441
3:16 416
3:26 416
4:4 188
5:1–12. 442
5:2–6:5 324
5:22–23 264
6:8 236

Ephesians

1:3–14. 441
1:5 128
1:7 204
1:9–10. 402
1:11 . . . . 128, 295
1:13–14. 208
1:14 204
1:19–23. 250
2:8–10. 264
2:8–9. 442
2:11–22. 122, 240, 306, 381, 442
2:11–17. 373
2:17 408
3:3–6. 122
3:4–6. 375
4:7–10. . . . . .141, 250

Philippians

1:12–19. 386
2:10–11. 284
2:11 259

2:15 234
2:30 349
3:2–7 442
3:16 141
3:20–21. 171

Colossians

1:7 35
1:12–14. 260
1:15–20. 188
1:21–23. 320
1:24 349
1:24–29. 375
2:14–15 . . . . 141, 250, 266
4:12 35
4:14 35

1 Thessalonians

1:5 37
1:9–10. . . . . 241, 257
1:10 . . . . 188, 241
2:16 141
3:10 349

2 Thessalonians

2:4 109
2:10 196

1 Timothy

1:1 185
2:3 185
4:1 221
4:10 185
4:15 158
5:18 33
6:1–2. 126
6:6–10. . . . . 17–19, 330, 442
6:12 236
6:17–19. 330

2 Timothy

2:8 337
2:21 126
3:1 221
3:2 353

4:1 243
4:11 383

Titus

1:3 185
2:9 126
2:10 185
2:14 264
3:4 185
3:8 264

Philemon

23. 35
24. 35

Hebrews

1. 443
1:1–2. 221
1:5–13. 142
1:5 419
2:5–8. 393
2:10 199
3–4 392
3:10 234
4:7 128
6:17 295
7–10 225
7:1 150
9:12 204
9:26 221
11:17–19 160
12:1–2. 199

James

1:9–10. 171
2:5 . . . . 274, 324
2:8 324
2:14–26. 443
2:19 162
4:6 353
5:1–6. 443

1 Peter

1:2 204
1:11 . . . . 229, 354

1:17–21. 171
1:19 204
1:20 221
2. 443
2:6–8 . . . . 124, 157
2:18–25. 443
2:18 126
2:21–25. 172
2:25 135
3:8–22 443
3:20–21. 250
3:21–22. 205
4:5 243
5:5 353
5:6 255

2 Peter

2:1 126
3:9 . . . . 402, 443

1 John

2:18 221
2:27 225
4:3 109
4:18 324
4:19 274

Jude

4. 126
25. 185

Revelation

1:5 204
3:5 266
5:9–10. 204
6–19 443
6:10 126
7:1–8. 284
7:16–17 266
19–22 393
20–22 443
20 . . . . 296, 374, 390
21:3–4. 266

Subject Index

Acts. *See also* Luke-Acts
    authorship of, 32–37, 42
    in canon, 432–33
    crowds in, 339–40
    date of, 38–42
    genre of, 46–48
    Gentiles in, 297–301
    God in, 108–19
    Israel in, 285–89
    Jewish groups in, 334–36
    law in, 365–69
    Nations in, 297–301
    outline of, 65–66
    philosophy in, 48–51
    poor in, 352–57
    portrait in, 169–75
    Rome and, 340–41
    salvation in, 233–37, 239–77
    setting of, 38–41
    speeches in, 51–53
    Spirit in, 219–25
    "the Way" in, 306–10
    women in, 349–52
Agabus and church, 86–87
Antioch, 86–88
Apostles and church, 376–77
Ascension
    Final Testament and, 80
    of Jesus, 79–80, 204–5,
        253–56
    review of, 80
authentication
    levels of, 248–50
    of message, 248–56
authority, actions of, 159–69
authorship of Acts, 32–37, 42
axioms, 407–14

Barnabas and church, 86–87, 383
biblical theology of Luke-Acts,
    447–51
blindness, 357

Caesarea, 92–93
canon
    Acts in, 432–33
    contributions to, 433–38, 447
    Luke in, 432–33
    Luke-Acts in, 431–45
Catholic epistles, 443
Christ, Jesus. *See also* Jesus
    as Messiah, 149–209
    response to, 333–42
    story of, 27–30
    work of, 177–209

Christians, and the Way, 306–10
christological confession, 71–72
christological questions, 70–71
christological revelation, 71
Christology, 417–19
church
    activities in, 387, 437–38
    Agabus and, 86–87
    at Antioch, 86–87
    Apostles and, 376–77
    Barnabas and, 86–87, 383
    contributions and, 437–38
    distinction of, 372–73
    ecclesiology and, 371–88
    Israel and, 377–81
    James and, 384
    Jesus' rule and, 374–75
    in Luke-Acts, 303–10
    old and new, 371–72
    Paul and, 384–87
    personalities in, 381–87
    Peter and, 381–82
    Philip and, 383
    as Spirit-indwelt community,
        373–74
    Stephen and, 382–83
    structure of, 387
    worship in, 387
community guidance, 420–22
community life
    Hellenistic widows and, 83
    Judas and, 80
    problems of, 82
    summary of, 81, 83
community mission, 420–22
consummation, 75, 394–95
contributions to canon, 433–38,
    447
controversies
    corrections and, 73
    disciples and, 70
    trust and, 73–74
Cornelius and gospel, 85–86
covenant, 414–17
cross, and Jesus, 203–4, 253–56
crowds
    in Acts, 339–40
    in Luke, 336–39
    multitudes of, 336–40

decision, blessing of, 72
delay and imminence, 399–400
disciples
    gathering of, 70

in Luke-Acts, 315–23
    miracles of, 250–53
discipleship
    God and, 73–74
    instruction about, 71–72
    Jesus and, 73
    neighbors and, 73
    in new community, 311–32,
        447–51
    rejection and, 74
divine direction, 448

earthly ministry, 201–3
ecclesiology
    apostles and, 376–77
    church and, 371–88
    in Luke-Acts, 371–88
epistles, parallels with, 443
eschatology
    accountability and, 395–98
    hope and, 403–4
    in Luke, 389–95
    in Luke-Acts, 389–405
    personal eschatology, 404
    tensions in, 399–400
ethics
    ethical directions, 420–22
    in new community, 145–47,
        311–32

faith
    call to, 71
    in kingdom, 75
    motivation to, 395–98
    movements to, 70–71
    salvation and, 267–68
false teachings, 75
Final Testament, 80
forgiveness
    service and, 75
    of sins, 268–69
fulfillment era, 389–94
future, hope for, 389–405

Galilean ministry, 346
generosity, 75
Gentiles
    in Acts, 297–301
    commission to, 422–23
    gospel to, 85–87
    incorporation of, 87–88
    in Luke, 292–97
    in Luke-Acts, 291–301
    promise for, 245–47
    "the Nations" and, 291–301

geographical progression, 137–40
God
  in Acts, 108–19
  character of, 99–119
  contributions and, 433–37
  directing plan, 127–28
  discipleship and, 73–74
  fulfillment and, 129–30
  Holy Spirit of, 143–45
  infancy material on, 100–103,
    149–59
  intervention of, 147–48
  John the Baptist and,
    100–104, 135–36
  kingdom of, 141–43
  ministry of Jesus and, 104–8
  mission of Jesus and, 136–37
  plan of, 99–119, 121–48
  promise of, 121–48
  salvation of, 121–48, 227–37
  as Savior, 450–51
  son of, 188–89
  themes of plan, 134–48
  trusting, 73–76
good news, proclaiming, 239–45
gospel
  genre of, 43–54
  to Gentiles, 85–87
  in Luke, 159–69
  in Luke-Acts, 239–43
  in Rome, 94–95
grace and salvation, 271–72

heaven, examples of, 74
Hebrew Scripture fulfillment,
  130–34
hermeneutical axioms, 407–14
Holy Spirit
  in Acts, 219–25
  of God, 143–45
  in Luke, 212–19
  in Luke-Acts, 211–26
  power and, 225
hope
  eschatology and, 403–4
  for future, 389–405

imminence, 399–400
infancy material
  on God, 149–59
  Israel in, 280–82
  on Jesus, 149–59
  salvation in, 228–29
  Spirit in, 212–13
  women in, 344–46
Israel
  in Acts, 285–89
  church and, 377–81
  in infancy material, 280–82

in Luke, 282–85
in Luke-Acts, 279–89
nations and, 448
turning away, 74
warning to, 423–27
"It is necessary," 140–41

James and church, 384
Jerusalem
  arrests in, 78–79, 91–95
  ascension and, 79–80
  betrayal in, 78
  community life in, 83
  consultation at, 88
  controversy in, 77
  death of Jesus and, 78–79
  destruction in, 77–78
  early church in, 80–83
  end of, 77–78, 400–402
  fall of, 400–402
  innocence and, 76–79
  journey to, 347–48
  persecution in, 83–87
  resurrection of Jesus and, 79
  trials of Jesus and, 78–79
  turning to, 76
Jerusalem journey, 72–76
Jesus
  arrest of, 78–79
  ascension of, 79, 204–5,
    253–56
  as Christ, 185–87
  church and, 374–75
  "coming after," 69
  contributions and, 433–37
  cross and, 203–4, 253–56
  David and, 187
  death of, 78–79
  discipleship and, 73
  earthly ministry of, 201–3
  infancy narrative on, 149–59
  introduction of, 67
  kingdom and, 205–9
  as Lord, 149–76, 197–98
  as Messiah, 149–77
  from Messiah to Lord,
    177–209
  ministry of, 69–72, 104–8
  miracles of, 250–53
  mission of, 79–80, 136–37
  new community and, 312–15
  opponents of, 333–42
  as prophet, 177–209
  reign of, 205–9
  response to, 333–42
  resurrection of, 79, 204–5,
    253–56
  revelation of, 69–72
  salvation and, 449–50

as savior, 185
self-understanding of, 68
as servant, 177–209
as Son of God, 188–89
as Son of Man, 193–97
story of, 27–30
teachings of, 70
titles of, 185–201
trials of, 78–79
work of, 177–209
Jewish groups, 334–36
Jewish reactions, 334–36
Jewish rejection, 72–76
Jews, promise for, 245–47
John
  arrest of, 81–82
  introduction of, 67
  persecution of, 82–83
John the Baptist
  "coming before," 68
  God and, 100–104, 135–36
John's gospel, parallels with,
  440–41
Joppa, 85
Judas, replacing, 80
Jude, parallels with, 443
Judea and persecution, 83–85
judgment in Luke-Acts,
  389–405

kerygma, 169–75
kingdom
  faith in, 75
  of God, 141–43
  Jesus and, 205–9

lameness, 81, 357
law
  in Acts, 365–69
  in Luke, 360–65
  in Luke-Acts, 359–69
  salvation and, 274–76
Luke. *See also* Luke-Acts
  building on precedent, 67
  in canon, 432–33
  crowds in, 336–39
  genre of Gospel, 44–46
  Gentiles in, 292–97
  gospel of, 159–69
  as historian, 43–44
  Israel in, 282–85
  Jewish groups in, 334–36
  key theses about, 448–50
  law in, 360–65
  narrative fulfillment, 67–68
  nations in, 292–97
  outline of, 64–65
  poor in, 352–57
  preface of, 67

salvation in, 229–33, 237, 239–77
Spirit in, 212–19
use of sources, 43–44
"the Way" in, 304–6
women in, 343–49
Luke-Acts. *See also* Acts; Luke
biblical theology of, 447–51
in canon, 431–45
categories for study of, 61
church in, 303–10
context of, 31–54
disciples in, 315–23
ecclesiology in, 371–88
eschatology in, 389–405
events in, 333–42
Gentiles in, 291–301
gospel in, 239–43
hope for future in, 389–405
importance of, 27–30
Israel in, 279–89
judgment in, 389–405
key theses about, 448–450
law in, 359–69
narrative overview of, 66–67
nations in, 291–301
new era and, 149–76, 211–26
normativity of, 444–45
outline of, 63–95
poor in, 343–58
reading as unity, 60–61
salvation in, 227–37, 239–77
scriptures in, 407–27
social dimensions in, 343–358
Spirit in, 211–26
themes in, 414–27
as unified work, 55–61
"the Way" in, 303–10
women in, 343–58
Lydda, 85

message, authentication of, 248–56
Messiah-Lord, 149–76
messianic power, 76
messianic visit, 398–99
Mighty God, 450–51
ministry
Galilean ministry, 69
of Jesus, 69–72
preparation for, 68
miracles, of Jesus, 250–53
miracles, of Peter, 85
mission
continuity of, 448
of Jesus, 79–80, 136–37
privilege of, 72
missionary journeys, 87–91
money and generosity, 75

nations
in Acts, 297–301
Israel and, 448
in Luke, 292–97
in Luke-Acts, 291–301
new community
activities in, 312–13
commitment to, 323–24, 330–31
disciples in, 311–32
discipleship in, 311–32, 447–51
ethics in, 145–47, 311–32
faith in, 327–28
followers of Jesus and, 312–15
functions in, 313–14
love for God and, 324
love for neighbors and, 324
in Luke, 331–32
members of, 315
possessions and, 328–30
praise for, 328
prayer and, 325
suffering and, 326
testimony for, 328
watchfulness and, 326–27
wealth and, 328–30
new era
arrival of, 159–69
bringing of, 149–76, 447–51
paving way for, 201–9
promise of, 211–26, 447–51
of realization, 409–11
sign of, 449
in Trinitarian story, 450
New Testament, parallels with
parallels with, 439–43
normativity of Luke-Acts, 444–45

outcasts, 247–48

parallels
with Catholic Epistles, 443
with John's gospel, 440–41
with Jude, 443
with New Testament, 439–43
with Paul, 441–43
with Peter, 443
with Revelation, 443
with Synoptics, 439–40
Paul
church and, 384–87
parallels with, 441–43
peace and salvation, 271
Pentecost, 80–81
Peter
arrest of, 81–82
church and, 381–82
gospel to Gentiles, 85–86

miracles of, 85
parallels with, 443
persecution of, 82–83
Philip
church and, 383
in Samaria, 84
philosophy of history, 48–51
poor
in Acts, 352–57
in Luke, 352–57
in Luke-Acts, 343–58
outcasts and, 247–48
possessions and generosity, 75
preaching, 243–44
privilege, 72
promise
continuity of, 448
covenant and, 414–17
for disciples, 80
fulfillment of, 412–14
for Jews and Gentiles, 245–47
in prophecy, 450
of salvation, 273–74
promise, of God, 121–48
prophecy, promise in, 450
provenance, 41–42

rejection, and discipleship, 74
rejection, Jewish, 72–76
repentance and salvation, 262–65
resurrection, 204–5, 253–56
Revelation, parallels with, 443
Rome
gospel preached in, 94–95
journey to, 93–94
as observer of events, 333–42
role of, 340–41
visitors in, 94–95

salvation
in Acts, 233–37, 239–77
benefits of, 268–72
dimensions of, 239–77
faith and, 267–68
forgiveness and, 268–69
gift of, 271
of God, 121–48, 227–37
gospel and, 239–43
grace and, 271–72
healings of, 227–37
history of, 448
identity and, 449–50
in infancy material, 228–29
Jesus' work and, 449–50
judgment and, 262
justifying, 272
law and, 274–76
life and, 269–71
in Luke, 229–33, 237, 239–77

mercy and, 262
message of, 273–74
objective aspect of, 256–62
paving way for, 201–9
peace and, 271
preaching, 243–44
proclaiming good news,
    239–45
promise of, 273–74
repentance and, 262–65
scope of, 245–48
soteriology and, 273–76
subjective side of, 262–68
teaching, 244–45
turning, 265–67
words for, 256–61
work of, 253–56
Samaria, 83–85
Satan, battle with, 398–99
Saul
    church and, 86–87
    conversion of, 84–85
Savior, God as, 450–451
Savior, Jesus as, 185
Scriptures in Luke-Acts, 407–27
sea journey, 93–94

setting of Acts, 38–41
signs and wonders, 82
sinners
    outcasts and, 247–48
    pursuit of, 74
sins, forgiveness of, 268–69
social dimensions in Luke-Acts,
    343–58
soteriology, 273–76
Spirit
    in Acts, 219–25
    contributions and, 433–37
    in infancy material, 212–13
    in Luke, 212–19
    in Luke-Acts, 211–26
    power and, 225
    as sign of new era, 449
Stephen
    arrest of, 83–84
    church and, 382–83
    martyrdom of, 83–84
    speech of, 83–84
Synoptics, 439–40

teaching, 244–45
"today" passages, 135

Trinitarian story, 450
trust in God, 73–76

unity, 57–59

Way, the
    in Acts, 306–10
    Christians and, 306–10
    church and, 306–10
    in Luke, 304–6
    in Luke-Acts, 303–10
women
    in Acts, 349–52
    in Galilean ministry, 346
    in infancy narrative, 344–46
    in journey to Jerusalem,
        347–48
    in Luke, 343–49
    in Luke-Acts, 343–58
    in Passion Week, 348–49
wonders and signs, 82
word, spread of, 84

Author Index

Achtemeier, Paul, 431
Adams, Dwayne, 227, 247
Aland, Barbara, 27
Aland, Kurt, 27
Alexander, Loveday, 57
Arlandson, James M., 343
Arndt, W. F., 296, 319, 320, 396
Arnold, Clint, 90

Bachmann, Michael, 99, 140, 279, 287, 359, 360
Banks, R. J., 362
Barrett, C. K., 27, 31, 56, 57, 63, 109, 129, 138, 244, 293, 392, 431
Bateman, Bert, 177
Bauckham, Richard, 67, 289, 343
Bauernfeind, Otto, 249, 393
Behm, 353
Bellinger, William H., Jr., 253
Berding, Kenneth, 255
Berger, Klause, 187
Bertram, 135, 200, 234, 353
Bietenhard, 132
Bird, Michael, 57
Blomberg, Craig, 71, 75, 359, 362
Bock, Darrell L., 31, 44, 45, 48, 63, 70, 71, 76, 77, 78, 79, 80, 84, 88, 93, 100, 118, 121, 122, 123, 132, 134, 135, 141, 149, 151, 153, 155, 158, 159, 160, 165, 167, 168, 177, 179, 180, 181, 182, 184, 190, 192, 195, 196, 208, 209, 216, 230, 246, 250, 252, 254, 257, 258, 261, 262, 270, 271, 281, 282, 284, 285, 295, 296, 305, 321, 327, 338, 348, 349, 350, 355, 356, 363, 367, 368, 371, 381, 397, 407, 409, 413, 418, 431, 447
Bockmuehl, Markus, 55, 60
Bode, Edward L., 343
Boff, Leonardo, 343, 355
Bolt, Peter, 303, 310, 311
Bonz, Marianne P., 47
Borgman, Paul, 56
Bovon, Francois, 27, 447
Bowker, John, 87
Brawley, Robert, 279, 289, 359
Brooke, G. J., 151
Brown, Raymond, 153, 158, 228, 254, 284, 353, 431

Bruce, F. F., 31, 37, 38, 52, 53, 63, 189, 241, 293, 294, 392, 393, 417, 431
Buchsel, 190, 265, 282, 321
Buckwalter, Doug, 149, 176
Bultmann, Rudolf, 133, 196, 318
Burridge, Richard, 45
Byington, S., 183

Cadbury, H. J., 31, 32, 56, 431
Carroll, John T., 280, 285, 333, 335, 389, 390
Carson, D. A., 431
Cassidy, Richard J., 343, 371, 386
Chance, J. Bradley, 389, 399, 401
Charlesworth, James, 179, 305
Cho, Youngmo, 223
Clark, Stephen, 343
Clarke, Andrew C., 92, 311, 313, 371, 376
Clarke, E. Andrew, 48, 49
Clarke, W. L., 407, 408
Conzelmann, Hans, 33, 52, 137, 165, 271, 389, 393, 399, 447, 448
Cook, Donald E., 333, 335
Corley, Kathleen, 343
Cunningham, Scott, 311, 326, 333

Danker, Fred, 194, 208, 257, 258, 282, 316, 321, 354
Dibelius, Martin, 43, 52
Dodd, C. H., 39, 52, 431, 438
Downing, F. G., 241
Duling, D. C., 187, 338
Dunn, James D. G., 73, 214, 215, 223
Dupont, Jacques, 56, 227, 291, 303

Eisler, R. I., 215
Ellis, E. Earle, 36, 38, 63, 213, 214, 249, 257, 295, 319, 320, 349
Esler, Philip, 39
Esterline, David, 279, 311, 333, 343, 386
Eusebius, Of Caesarea, 28
Evans, Craig, 71, 279, 305, 407, 414

Farmer, William R., 253
Fitzer, 206

Fitzmyer, Joseph A., 27, 31, 34, 36, 38, 41, 42, 63, 92, 107, 110, 121, 123, 141, 150, 157, 162, 165, 191, 215, 222, 236, 240, 242, 243, 244, 258, 259, 294, 298, 345, 362, 396, 431, 447
Foerstner, 156, 249
Foh, Susan T., 343
Fohrer, 156
Forbes, Greg W., 99, 126
Fornara, C. W., 43, 53
Forsch, F. H., 196
Foulkes, Francis, 412
France, R. T., 343
Franklin, E., 99, 227, 447
Fuller, Michael E., 279, 280, 285, 371, 374, 398, 399

Gartner, B., 241
Gasque, W., 27
Gathercole, Simon, 36
Gaventa, Beverly Roberts, 63, 82
Gempf, C., 140
Giblin, C. H., 296
Gill, D. W. J., 140
Glaser, Mitch, 254
Goder, F., 261
Goppelt, Leonhard, 262, 412
Goulder, M. D., 43
Gowler, David, 333, 336
Green, Joel, 31, 57, 63, 99, 211, 214, 227, 239, 247, 257, 381, 407, 410, 412, 431, 437, 447
Gregory, Andrew F., 27, 55, 58, 60
Grundmann, W., 249, 345, 397
Guelich, Robert, 355
Gutierrez, Gustavo, 343, 355

Haenchen, Ernst, 31, 35, 37, 43, 52, 63, 89, 287, 289, 294, 431
Hagner, Donald A., 70, 364
Hahn, Ferdinand, 338
Hauck, 354
Hays, Richard, 409
Hemer, Colin, 31, 34, 35, 40, 41, 43, 47, 431
Hendricksen, W., 284, 354
Hengel, Martin, 27, 31, 34, 35, 43, 47, 48, 53, 303, 305, 318, 431, 432, 448
Holtz, Traugott, 407, 408

Hooker, Morna, 163, 194
Horsley, Richard A., 343
Hume, Douglas A., 303, 306, 356

Janowski, Bernd, 253
Jeremias, Joachim, 70, 172, 196, 230, 253, 258
Jerome, 254
Jervel, Jacob, 31, 63, 99, 121, 130, 183, 185, 211, 217, 220, 242, 279, 280, 359, 361, 371, 393, 424, 431, 447
Jewett, Robert, 34
Johnson, Luke Timothy, 27, 31, 55, 58, 63, 241, 266, 293, 392, 418, 431
Johnston, Gordon, 177
Josephus, 232
Judge, Edwin A., 296, 308, 332
Juel, Donald, H., 33

Keck, L. E., 34, 438
Kellum, Scott, 431
Kilgallen, J. J., 294
Kim, Seyoon, 84, 343
Kimball, C. A., 407, 409
Kinman, Brent, 76
Kittel, 240
Klauck, Hans Josef, 242, 309
Klutz, Todd, 231
Knox, John, 38
Koet, B. J., 421
Kostenberger, Andreas, 431
Krabel, A. Thomas, 33
Kramer, Ross S., 343
Kuhn, K., 206
Kummel, Werner Georg, 99, 141, 389, 390, 431
Kurz, W. S., 27

Lampe, G. W. H., 211, 212
Lang, 215
Larkin, W. J., 139, 184, 192, 216, 221, 234, 266
Lee, Jae Won, 279, 311, 333, 343, 386
Liefeld, Walter, 343
Lindars, Barnabas, 194
Litwak, Kenneth Duncan, 407, 409, 410, 413
Longnecker, Bruce, 86
Luce, H. K., 133, 362
Lunde, Jonathan, 255

Maddox, R., 227, 291, 447
Manson, T. W., 362
Marguerat, Daniel, 31, 46, 47, 48, 99, 124, 431

Marshall, I. Howard, 27, 31, 39, 40, 43, 52, 57, 60, 63, 78, 89, 99, 126, 135, 140, 142, 150, 151, 155, 160, 176, 190, 193, 194, 208, 215, 227, 244, 251, 254, 255, 257, 262, 270, 271, 284, 285, 293, 299, 303, 318, 320, 327, 347, 354, 361, 362, 389, 393, 396, 409, 431, 447, 449
Martyr, Justin L., 33, 34, 67, 155, 432, 438
Mattill, A. J., 27, 209
McDonald, Lee M., 130
McKnight, Scot, 70
Meier, John P., 208
Menzies, Robert P., 211
Metzger, Bruce, 33
Mills, W. E., 27
Moessner, David, 40, 57, 58, 279, 359
Montefiore, C. G., 347
Moo, Douglas J., 431
Moore, T. S., 138
Moule, C. F. D., 36
Muller, 393

Nielsen, Anders E., 389, 390, 394
Nobbs, A., 48
Nolland, John, 31, 63, 101, 155, 195, 196, 231, 232, 345, 389, 390, 399, 424, 431
North, C. R., 253

Omerzu, H., 48
O'Neill, J. C., 38
Osborne, Grant, 79
O'Toole, Robert F., 149, 198, 447

Pao, David, 138
Parsons, Mikeal, 32, 55, 57, 60
Pervo, Richard, 32, 55, 57, 58, 60
Pesch, R., 392
Peterson, David, 140, 176, 299, 311, 312, 359, 360, 412
Philips, T. E., 289
Pickett, Raymond, 311, 331
Pilgrim, Walter, 227, 247
Plummer, A., 250, 252, 265, 281, 318, 319, 329, 354, 396
Plymale, Steven F., 311, 325
Polhill, John, 31, 51, 52, 117, 192, 242, 264, 383, 425, 432
Powell, Mark Allen, 432
Procksch, 162

Quarles, Charles, 431

Rapske, Brian, 303, 326
Reicke, Bo, 39
Rengstorf, 158, 320
Rese, Martin, 279, 287, 289, 407, 409
Rhoads, David, 279, 311, 333, 343, 386
Rhoads, Erroll R., 27, 279, 331
Ricoeur, P., 48
Ridderbos, Hermann, 52
Riesenfeld, H., 208
Robbins, Vernon K., 33, 34, 35
Roloff, J., 47, 48, 91
Rosner, Brian, 140, 297, 311, 312
Roth, S. John, 247, 303
Rothschild, Clair K., 34, 43, 45, 437
Rowe, C. Kavin, 27, 55, 58, 60, 126, 149, 154, 184, 197

Sanders, J. T., 287, 423, 448
Sanders, James A., 130
Schlier, 155, 206
Schmidt, K, 206, 320
Schmitz, 281
Schnabel, Eckhard, 37, 138
Schneider, G., 47, 193, 229, 354
Scholer, David M., 296
Schottroff, Luise, 343
Schrage, 230
Schrenk, 206, 252
Schurmann, Heinz, 36, 102, 103, 121, 162, 218, 251, 257
Schweizer, E., 125, 150, 160, 234, 305, 392, 438
Seccombe, David Peter, 247, 279, 289, 303, 306, 311, 366
Segundo, J. L., 343, 355
Seim, T. K., 343, 346
Shauf, S., 47, 49
Sherwin-White, A. N., 48, 92
Siculus, Diodorus, 46
Snodgrass, Klyne, 77, 305
Soards, Marion, 52, 412
Spencer, Patrick E., 55, 60
Spencer, Scott F., 63, 91
Squires, John T., 99, 101, 127
Stahlin, 281, 327, 396
Stegemann, Wolfgang, 343
Stein, Robert, 38
Stenschke, Christoph, 227, 268, 291
Sterling, Gregory, 47, 408
Strathmann, 260
Strauss, Mark L., 149, 154, 159, 407
Stuhlmacher, Peter, 253

Talbert, Charles H., 27, 34, 38, 56, 57, 63, 432, 437

Talmon, Shemaryahu, 305
Tannehill, Robert, 56, 100, 279, 291
Thompson, Marianne Meye, 431
Thompson, R. P., 289
Thornton, Claus J., 33
Tiede, David, 57, 279, 282, 283, 379, 389, 402
Townsend, J. T., 38
Tucker, Ruth A., 343
Tuckett, C. M., 149
Turner, Max, 211, 212, 219, 221, 226, 227, 365, 449
Twelftree, G. H., 206
Tyson, Joseph, 279, 333

Van Unnik, W .C., 46
Varghese, P. V., 211, 212
Verheyden, J., 55, 57
Vielhauer, Philip, 34, 36
Von Baer, H., 211
Von Rad, G., 206

Walton, Steve, 333, 341
Weatherly, J. A., 333
Webb, Robert L., 44, 68, 70, 71, 76, 77, 78, 79, 181
Wehnert, J., 33
Weiser, A., 94, 116
Wenham, David, 432, 439
Wikenhauser, A., 46, 116

Wilckens, U., 52
Wilkens, Michael J., 71
Wilson, Stephen G., 139, 291, 359, 362, 366, 371
Winter, Bruce, 48, 92
Witherington, Ben., 31, 37, 52, 63, 81, 89, 90, 92, 137, 192, 227, 239, 319, 343, 383, 432

Yamazaki-Ransom, Kazuhiko, 343

Zuck, Roy B., 121, 177
Zwiep, Arie W., 183, 184, 436